VOLUME 2 NORTH
3RD EDITION

Third Edition 2020
Second Edition 2014
First published in Great Britain 2009 by Pesda Press
Tan y Coed Canol, Ceunant,
Caernarfon, Gwynedd
LL55 4RN
Wales

Copyright © 2009/2014/ 2020 Gary Latter
ISBN 978-1-906095-71-0

The Author asserts the moral right to be identified as the author of this work.

All rights reserved. No part of this publication may be reproduced or transmitted, in any form or by any means, electronic or mechanical, including photocopying, recording or otherwise, without the prior written permission of the Publisher.

Maps by Bute Cartographics.
Printed and bound in Poland, www.hussarbooks.pl

Gary Latter

CONTENTS

INTRODUCTION	**4**
ISLE OF SKYE	**10**
BLA BHEINN	**14**
The Great Prow	14
CLACH GLAS	**16**
CORUISK	**17**
Mad Burn Buttress	17
Coruisk Hut Crag	18
Sgurr Dubh Mor	18
Coir'-Uisg Buttress	19
SUIDHE BIORACH	**20**
SGURR NAN GILLEAN	**24**
AM BASTEIR	**25**
SGURR DEARG	**26**
The Inaccessible Pinnacle	26
SRON NA CICHE	**28**
Western Buttress	29
Cioch Buttress	30
Cioch & Cioch Slab	32
Cioch Upper Buttress	35
Eastern Buttress	37
SGURR SGUMAIN	**41**
COIR' A' GHRUNNDA	**43**
SGURR MHIC CHOINNICH	**46**
Coireachan Ruadha Face	46
Bealach Buttress	48
KILT ROCK AREA	**50**
Kilt Rock	51
South of Tempest Buttress	53
Tempest Buttress	53
Chimney Stack Area	54
Fallen Pillars Area	55
STAFFIN SLIP BUTTRESSES	**56**
Staffin Slip North	57
Staffin Slip South	57
RUBHA HUNISH	**61**
Meall Tuath	61
Meall Deas	62
NEIST POINT	**64**
Upper Crag – South Sector	65
Financial Sector	66
Tower Gully Buttress	71
The Green Lady	71
Poverty Point	72
Destitution Point	74

AN T-AIGEACH	**76**
Bay 1	77
Bay 2	77
Bay 3	78
Headland	79
Bay 4	80
Cumhann Geodha	80
Conductor Cove	81
Lighthouse Wall	82
Foghorn Cove	82
APPLECROSS	**84**
SGURR A' CHAORACHAIN	**86**
A' Chioch	86
South Face	89
TORRIDON	**92**
BEINN EIGHE	**94**
Coire Mhic Fhearchair	94
Far East Wall	95
The Eastern Ramparts	99
The Triple Buttresses	100
SEANA MHEALLAN	**103**
Glach Dhorch	103
Western Sector	107
CREAG NAM LEUMNACH	**111**
DIABAIG	**113**
The Pillar	114
The Little Big Wall	115
The Main Cliff	116
The Con Dome	120
The South Wall	121
DIABAIG PENINSULA CRAGS	**124**
Ugly Crag	124
Crofters Crag	124
Rolling Wall	125
GAIRLOCH	**126**
BEINN A' MHUINIDH	**129**
Waterfall Buttress	129
The Bonaid Dhonn	130
STONE VALLEY CRAGS	**133**
Atlantic Wall	133
Rum Doodle Crag	134
Viking Crag	134
Red Wall Crag	135
Stone Valley Crag	136
Playtime Walls	138

Flowerdale Wall	138
The Left Dome	139
CREAG NAN CADHAG	**140**
RAVEN'S CRAG	**142**
AZTEC TOWER	**144**
GRASS CRAG	**145**
LOCH TOLLAIDH CRAGS	**146**
Raven's Nest	147
The Ewe Walls	148
Gairloch Wall	149
The Curra Wall	150
Dinosaur Wall	151
Fraggle Rock	151
Siren Slab	153
The Cloiche Wall	153
Feoir Buttress	153
Hidden Crag	154
CREAG MHOR THOLLAIDH	**155**
Creag nan Luch	155
Upper Tier	156
Lower Tollie Crag	157
Upper Tollie Crag	161
Loch Maree Crag	162
Super Crag Sport	164
FISHERFIELD	**166**
CREAG NA GAORACH	**166**
BEINN LAIR	**167**
CARN MOR	**168**
CARNAN BAN	**176**
Barndance Slabs	176
Maiden Buttress	177
GRUINARD CRAGS	**179**
Birch Crag	180
Beach Crag	181
Post Crag	182
Bog Meadow Wall	182
Road Crag	183
Gruinard Crag	184
Car Park Crag – Flake Buttress	186
Very Difficult Slabs	187
The Side Wall	187
Triangular Slab	188
Inverianvie Crag	188
Dog Crag	189
Riverside Slabs	191
The Apron	191

Lochan Dubh Crag	192
GRUINARD RIVER CRAGS	**194**
Goat Crag	195
Am Fasgadh	199
CARN GORAIG	**201**
JETTY BUTTRESS	**204**
MUNGASDALE CRAG	**208**
COIGACH & ASSYNT	**210**
ARDMAIR CRAGS	**213**
Laggavoulin Buttress	213
Monster Buttress	214
Dancing Buttress	215
Beast Buttress	216
Edinburgh Rock	217
Airs Rock	218
Big Roof Buttress	218
SGURR AN FHIDLEIR	**222**
STAC POLLAIDH	**223**
West Buttress	223
No. 2 Buttress	227
No. 3 Buttress	229
THE REIFF SEA CLIFFS	**230**
The Stone Pig Cliff	231
ROINN A' MHILL	**234**
Pinnacle Area	234
Bouldering Cliff	238
Black Rocks	240
AN STIUIR	**242**
Seal Song Area	242
The Minch Wall	245
The Bay of Pigs	246
Piglet Wall	248
Pooh Cliff	748
RUBHA COIGEACH	**249**
Golden Walls	249
Black Magic Wall	252
Slab Inlet	252
Platform Walls	253
Rampant Wall	254
SPACED OUT ROCKERS CLIFF	**255**
THE LEANING BLOCK CLIFFS	**257**
AMPHITHEATRE BAY	**261**
Jigsaw Wall Point	262

📷 *Karin Magog on the steep Cross-Eyed up the edge of The Leaning Block, Rubha Coigeach, Reiff, Coigach & Assynt with the Assynt hills presenting a stunning backdrop.*

RUBHA PLOYTACH	262
INBHIRPOLLAIDH ROCK GYM	265
SUPER CRAG TRAD	267
OLD MAN OF STOER	274

SUTHERLAND	**276**
ROADSIDE CRAGS	279
Ridgway View Crag	280
The Balcony	281
Four Lochans View Crag	283
Rhiconich Crag	283
CREAG GHARBH MHOR	285
Red Wall	285
Glaciated Slab	286
Red Slab	286
CREAG AN FHITHICH	287
Grey Wall	287
Ruby Wall	288
Russet Wall	289
Triangular Buttress	290
Back Stage	290
SHEIGRA	291
The First Geo	292
The Second Geo	297
Treasure Island Wall	300
Na Stacain Area	301
AM BUACHAILLE	303
SANDWOOD BAY CRAGS	304
FOINAVEN	307
Cnoc a' Mhadaidh	308
Creag Urbhard	308
First Dionard Buttress	310
Second Dionard Buttress	311
CREAG SHOMHAIRLE	311

CAITHNESS	**314**
LATHERONWHEEL	315
Peninsula Wall	316
Big Flat Wall	318
The Stack Area	319
SARCLET	321
Pudding Stone Buttress	322
Occam's Buttress	322
Big Buttress	323
Djapana Buttress	325
Surfer Buttress	325
Tilted Ledge	326
STACK OF OLD WICK	327

LEWIS & HARRIS	**328**
CRULABHIG CRAG	330
CREAG LIAM	332
BEINN NA BERIE	336
AIRD UIG AREA	337
Geodha Gunna	337
Geodha Ruadh	339
The Boardwalk Walls	340
THE PAINTED WALL AREA	344
The Painted Wall	345
Torasgeo	347
FLANNAN AREA	348
Aurora Geo	348
Magic Geo	351
The Black Wall	353
Mitre Wall	354
ARD MORE MANGERSTA	355
MANGERSTA	355
GEODHA AN TAROIN	362
DALBEG	364
Dalbeg Buttress	364
Cave Slab	365
Black Geo	366
Small West Wall	366
Big West Wall	369
Preacher Geo	369
Storm Geo	370
AIRD MHOR BHRAGAIR	371
Folded Wall	371
CREAG DUBH DIBADALE	374
CREAGAN TEALASDALE	376
GRIOMAVAL	377

Tealasdale Slabs	377
SRON ULLADALE	380

PABBAY & MINGULAY	**386**
PABBAY	388
BIG BLOCK SLOC	389
THE BAY AREA	390
PINK & GREY WALLS	392
The Pink Wall	392
The Grey Wall	395
Grey Wall Recess	396
BANDED WALL	398
The Shield	401
South Face	403
RUBHA GREOTACH	405
The Galley	405
The Poop Deck	406
THE GREAT ARCH	410
ALLANISH PENINSULA	413
Hoofer's Geo	413
MINGULAY	416
CREAG DHEARG	417
GUARSAY BEAG	419
Shag's Point	419
GUARSAY MOR	420
The Boulevard	420
The North Pillar	423
The Great Arch	424
The Arena	424
The South Pillar	426
The Undercut Wall	427
Cobweb Wall	430
DUN MINGULAY	432
Sron an Duin	432
RUBHA LIATH	441
Seal Song Geo	441
The Point	446
THE GEIRUM WALLS	447
Hidden Wall	447
The Platform Wall	447
The Main Walls	448

ORKNEY	**452**
HOY	454
THE NEEDLE	454
THE BERRY	454
RORA HEAD	455
Lang (Number 1) Geo	456
Geo 3	457
Mucklehouse Wall	457
OLD MAN OF HOY	459
ST. JOHN'S HEAD	461
YESNABY	464
Point Wall	465
Tower Face	466
Arch Wall	467
Gardyloo Wall	469
The False Stack	470
Castle of Yesnaby Area	471
Spectators Geo	472
The Loose Headland	473

ACKNOWLEDGEMENTS	**474**
ROUTE INDEX	**475**

SCOTTISH ROCK

The area covered by this book, the Highlands and Islands, lies entirely to the north of the Highland Boundary Fault. With its mountain landscapes, deep glens, lochs, rivers and hundreds of islands, it represents one of the most extensive and least populated semi-natural areas remaining in Western Europe. Scotland can also lay claim to the only true areas of 'wilderness' remaining in Britain, with vast tracts of uninhabited areas in the far North West, and the similarly wild and unspoilt high arctic plateaux of the Cairngorm massif. Often, by choosing your venue carefully, it is possible not just to avoid queues but to have whole mountains to yourself.

Within this incredibly varied setting can be found stunning examples of every sub-sport that rock climbing has evolved. In UK terms, we have the longest mountain routes (such as *The Long Climb* on Ben Nevis); the biggest sea cliffs (St John's Head, Hoy), which also harbour the only multi-day big wall route in the country – the 23 pitch *Longhope Route*; the steepest cliff (Sron Ulladale, Harris). But size isn't everything. In contrast, a myriad of miniature sport routes have appeared in recent years, together with a resurgence of interest in outcrop climbing in general. There has also been the opening up of some wonderfully situated bouldering venues, together with exquisite deep-water soloing on a few esoteric locations.

This book is intended as a celebration of the wealth and variety of great climbing that Scotland has to offer. The selection of routes should have something for everyone, from the athlete to the aesthete. Climbing in Scotland is about more than the rock alone; there is the magnificent and awe-inspiring scenery, the sense of history, the wide open spaces, the clean fresh air and the possibility of solitude.

USING THE GUIDE

All the areas covered are described as approaching from the south, where the majority of visitors originate. Similarly, the routes are also laid out in the order they are encountered from the approach. Each area has an introduction outlining the style of climbing, together with detailed up-to-date information on **Accommodation** and **Amenities** – in short everything the visitor requires to familiarise themselves with an area. Each cliff or crag is described in summary, together with specific **Access**, **Approach** and **Descent** details clearly laid out. In addition, maps and photo-diagrams illustrate further. Routes are given an overall technical grade alongside the adjectival grade, with the individual pitch grades incorporated within the description. The abbreviations **FA** and **FFA** refer to the first ascent and first free ascent respectively. **PA** refers to the number of points of aid used on the first ascent. There are very few routes containing aid in this book, though in some instances the use of a couple of points of aid may give a more consistent route, and an alternative grade is offered. On a few harder routes, usually unrepeated, rest points were used and this is mentioned in the hope of encouraging subsequent free ascents. **PR** and **PB** refer to peg runner and belay respectively; **F** and **R** to friends and rocks; **BB** and **LO** refer to bolt belays and lower-offs on the sport crags. **TIC** stands for Tourist Information Centre; **ATM** for Automated Teller Machine.

You should have the relevant Ordnance Survey 1:50,000 map and, particularly for the remoter mountain crags, knowledge of how to use a map and compass is assumed. The middle of the Cairngorms or the top of Ben Nevis is not the place to attempt to learn to navigate. The Grid Reference and Altitude refers to the base of the cliff or crag. The approach times quoted are intended as a general guide (racing greyhounds and ramblers/tortoises can make their own adaptations accordingly), along the lines of Naismith's Rule (4.5km per hour and one minute for every 10m of ascent).

I have attempted to consult as many active climbers in Scotland as possible to get a broad range of opinions and a consensus on grades and quality, but the final selection of routes is a personal one. For instance, not all the routes are on immaculate rock, with some of the older routes in the traditional character-building mode. Jim Bell's famous adage, *"Any fool can climb good rock. It takes craft and cunning to get up vegetatious schist or granite."* may be worth bearing in mind.

ACCOMMODATION

Information on a range of budget accommodation is included for each area, from camp sites and youth hostels to private bunkhouses. There are also a number of well-situated mountaineering club huts in all the main mountain areas. These are available for booking by members of Mountaineering Scotland, the BMC and affiliated clubs. In addition, Tourist Information Centres (**TICs**) are detailed at the start of each main area. These are a good source of information on bed and breakfast, guest house and hotel accommodation. Visit Scotland publishes regional brochures covering accommodation and visitor information. These are available free of charge from any of the TICs across Scotland or as ebrochures from www.visitscotland.com.

EATING OUT

One important point worth bearing in mind, (especially for those used to continental and transatlantic hospitality) is that the majority of Scotland still lurks in the dark ages when it comes to the service industry. Most pubs only serve food over a short period at lunchtime; often 12–2pm, and more importantly, the majority of pubs and hotels stop serving food at 9pm, some at 8pm even! I've had the misfortune to turn up at a restaurant/pub in Skye (in July, the height of the tourist season) to be informed *"We're not serving food: the chef's on his lunch"* – unbelievable. Establishments that are particularly good and worth seeking out are highlighted within the introductory section of each relevant chapter.

ACCESS

The **Land Reform (Scotland) Act 2003** gives statutory access rights to most land and inland water. These rights exist only if exercised responsibly by respecting the privacy, safety and livelihoods of others and by looking after the environment. The Scottish Outdoor Access Code (www.outdooraccess-scotland.scot) provides detailed guidance on the responsibilities of those exercising access rights and those managing land and water.

- Take responsibility for your own actions and act safely.
- Respect people's privacy.
- Assist land managers to work safely and effectively.
- Care for the environment and take any litter home.
- Keep all dogs under proper control.
- Take extra care if organising an event or running a business.

WILD CAMPING

In the rural areas it is often possible to camp at the side of the road. If in doubt, ask permission locally from farmers and crofters. Remember to remove all your litter, all trace of your tent pitch and not to cause any pollution. It should almost always be possible to camp in the hills, except perhaps in some areas during the stalking season.

CARAVANS

Those wishing to bring caravans please don't – go to the Lakes, the Borders or some other rolling hills well away from the Highlands and Islands. Even better, stay at home and play tiddlywinks or golf, or take up macramé or embroidery or some other suitably sedate pastime. Alternatively, travel under the cover of darkness, preferably at 3am on a Sunday morning.

BIRDS

Some of the sea cliffs are affected by nesting seabirds and should be avoided during the nesting season of April – July inclusive. Almost all birds, their nests and eggs are protected. The proliferation of guano on such cliffs makes it in the climber's interest to choose another venue. In particular, some popular routes, such as the *Old Man of Stoer* and *Hoy*, have the occasional fulmar nest on ledges, and it is definitely in the climber's interest to avoid close encounters, as they have the nasty habit of vomiting semi-digested fish oil onto uninvited visitors. It should still, however, be possible to climb these routes during the nesting season. In the unlikely event of coming across birds of prey (especially peregrine falcons, golden or white tailed sea eagles – all Schedule 1 birds) choose another route or cliff. It is an offence, under the Wildlife and Countryside Act 1981, to disturb any Schedule 1 bird, with an unlimited fine, up to 6 months imprisonment or both. Their continued existence is surely more important than another tick in the guidebook? Information on current restrictions is available from Mountaineering Scotland (01738 493942; www.mountaineering.scot).

SEASONAL RESTRICTIONS

The grouse shooting season is from 12 August (the 'glorious' twelfth) – 10 December and deer from 1 July – 20 October for stags and 21 October – 15 February for hinds. More information at www.outdooraccess-scotland.scot. There are few crags or cliffs included where access problems have been encountered in the past. A caring, responsible attitude towards parking, litter, conservation and a polite approach to landowners should ensure that the present situation continues. If any difficulties are encountered, contact the access officer at access@mountaineering.scot. No commercial stalking takes place on National Trust for Scotland properties (such as Glen Coe and Torridon), ensuring access at all times.

DIRECTIONS

All directions (left and right) are given for climbers facing the crag, except in descent. Any ambiguous descriptions also include a compass point, but if you don't know your left from your right, chances are you won't have a clue where the North Pole lies.

CONSERVATION

Try to adopt a minimum impact approach at all times, leaving the place as you would like to find it. Approaches to some of the cliffs can be greatly aided by the use of bicycles. Their use should be restricted to solid paths such as private and forest roads or rights of way, not soft paths and open hillsides where considerable erosion can occur. Where there is a substantial time-saving advantage, such information is included in the approach information. Where repeated abseils from trees is the norm (such as on Creag Dhubh), slings and karabiners or maillons have been left in place, and their use is encouraged to prevent ringing of the bark, leading to the eventual demise of the trees. Always park with consideration for others, and avoid damage to fences and walls. And of course, as the country code stresses, avoid 'interfering' with animals (Aberdonians and Rick Campbell take note!). Do not leave any litter, including food scraps, finger tape, chalk wrappers and cigarette ends and remove any left by others. Bury or burn toilet paper. Scratching arrows or names at the base of routes can clearly be viewed in a modern light as nothing short of vandalism. Established markings are mentioned to aid identification, and it is hoped no further additions will be thought necessary. Many of the areas covered are within National Scenic Areas (NSA), National Nature Reserves (NNR) and Sites of Special Scientific Interest (SSSI), controlling development and ensuring the retention and preservation of the natural environment.

STYLE, PEGS & IN SITU PROTECTION

"Ethics change the experience for others, style only changes your own personal experience."

The use of chalk is no longer a burning issue. Nevertheless, its use should be kept to a minimum, hopefully only on extremes. Chalk has been spotted on descent routes (I kid you not) and on VDiffs, such as *Agag's Groove*, which must be an ultimate low point. Hold improvement is unacceptable on natural rock. If you can't climb a piece of rock with the holds available, leave it unclimbed rather than resort to the hammer and chisel. The use of hammered nuts should be discouraged, as their rapid deterioration soon blocks the placement possibilities for subsequent ascentionists.

Whilst the style a route is climbed in is a personal one, I feel obliged to make a few comments. The use of 'rest points' (i.e. aid) and prior top-roping should be reserved for routes that are pushing new frontiers. It is true to say that such tactics percolate downwards. Try to give the rock a fighting chance, and approach the route on its own terms, in accordance with local practices. The majority of active pioneers in Scotland have attempted to push standards, and many very audacious leads have been achieved on-sight or ground up.

QUALITY ASSESSMENT

I had originally intended to adopt the Farquhar rating system, with its two extremes of PS and FB, but as hopefully there are no 'pure sh≈@‡' routes herein (unless included for historical interest, or to aid in crag descriptions) and masses of '#µ©k*≈g brilliant' routes, I have decided to opt for the conventional star rating system, with three star routes being of truly outstanding quality. As the climbing in Scotland is clearly superior to anything south of the border, a few exceptional routes have the honour of four stars. These are absolute 'must do's' that would rate amongst the best anywhere on the planet, such is their undeniable brilliance. On a few isolated routes, a wire brush symbol denotes that the route may require prior cleaning in its present state, and the stars assume the route is in a clean state. These are routes which were originally climbed following cleaning on abseil, but at the time of writing have not had much repeat traffic, and may require a quick abseil with a wire brush prior to an ascent.

CLIMATE

"They'll all be doing them when the sun comes out."
– Don Whillans.

The Highlands and Islands are dominated by the prevailing southwesterly winds, bringing moist and usually mild air from the Atlantic. In addition, many of the Atlantic depressions pass close to or over Scotland. *"It always rains up there"* is a commonly held myth. It is easy at first sight to confuse a map of annual rainfall with that of a relief map for the two are closely linked. The wettest belt extends from the Cowal peninsula (south and west of Arrochar) in a broad band as far as the hills just south of Torridon. In the mountains an annual precipitation of between 200–300cm and more is the norm, these dreich figures dropping markedly to 150–200cm on the coastal fringe. Within this broad belt there is much variation. As an example, at Dundonnell at the head of Little Loch Broom the annual rainfall is 195cm; 10km south it is 250cm, and 10km further north in Ullapool the average is 150cm.

The coastal promontories, especially in the north, and the Outer Hebrides receive only 130–170cm. Similarly, low ground around the Cairngorms and the eastern edge of the Central Highlands (such as Craig a Barns and The Pass of Ballater) benefit from the rain shadow effect of the hills further west (80–100cm). The higher ground in the Cairngorms receive around half the precipitation than the hills just in from the main Atlantic seaboard, with an average of 225cm recorded on Cairn Gorm summit. Lying in the centre of the country, their climate is more continental, with warmer summers than on the coasts. Many districts in the north and east have, on average over the four summer months from May–August, a total rainfall of less than 40cm, comparing favourably with the drier parts of England. Throughout the country the driest and sunniest period is from May to the end of June, the next driest from mid-September to mid-October.

In the Outer Hebrides gales are recorded on over 40 days of the year, and in the Northern Isles this figure is even greater, though most of these occur in the winter. Prolonged spells of strong wind are uncommon between May and August. Especially in the Western Isles and along the west coast, May is the sunniest month, closely followed by June. April is sunnier than the popular holiday months of July and August. The temperatures on the west coast and the islands are generally a couple of degrees cooler than inland, with the Northern Isles a couple of degrees cooler again. Finally, in midsummer there is no complete darkness in the north of Scotland, with Shetland receiving about 4 hours more daylight (including twilight) than London.

TIDAL INFORMATION

In general, the tide ebbs and flows twice daily. As a rough guide, the tide takes 6 hours to come in, spends a half an hour 'on the turn', then 6 hours to recede, before repeating the same process. Spring tides occur after a new and full moon, and have the greatest amplitude. Tide tables are published annually for specific areas and are available from yacht chandlers and in many newsagents, or from harbour offices. Tidal predictions up to 7 days in advance also available at www.tidetimes.co.uk.

WEATHER INFORMATION

Radio: BBC Radio Scotland broadcasts an outdoor conditions forecast daily at 18.25 weekdays and 07.00 & 19.00 at weekends, in addition to general forecasts at the end of each news bulletin.

TV: BBC Reporting Scotland broadcasts a good general forecast daily at 18.50 weekdays, 17.25 on Saturdays and 18.25 on Sundays.

Online: www.bbc.co.uk/weather provides a detailed weather forecast including details for the week ahead, coastal forecasts and tide tables. In addition to the above www.metoffice.gov.uk provides daily mountain forecasts, as does www.mwis.org.uk, which issues a detailed 3-day forecast daily at approximately 16.30. Another popular option is the Norwegian website www.yr.no.

WEE BASTARDS

Little biting creatures, which the vast majority of tourist-orientated brochures and guidebooks fail to mention, can make a massive difference to one's stay in the Highlands and Islands. Of the thirty-four species of biting midge found in Scotland, only four or five species bite humans. By far the worst and most prevalent, accounting for more than 90 percent of all bites to humans is the female of the species *Culicoides impunctatus*, or the Highland Midge. This voracious creature first makes its appearance around the end of May and can persist until the end of September in a mild summer, with early June through to August being the worst periods. They are particularly active on still, cloudy or overcast days, especially twilight (which lasts throughout the night in Scotland in summer). Wind

Tick, AKA 'wee bastard!'

speeds above a slight breeze force them to seek shelter. Mosquitoes are less of a problem, though the cleg (or horsefly) feeds mainly during warm bright days. Finally, sheep or deer ticks, small black or brown round-bodied members of the genus *arachnid* rest on vegetation, awaiting a host. The tick sinks its head into the victim's flesh, until it eventually swells up and drops off. Ticks in the UK regularly carry Lyme Disease, a potentially serious infection, so they should be removed as soon as possible. Remove with a tick removal tool or tweezers and apply antiseptic cream. If flu-like symptoms persist after a tick bite, you should see a doctor immediately. Avoid ticks by keeping your arms and legs covered if possible; wear light-coloured fabrics so you can see them easily; spray clothing and shoes with the repellent permethrin, such as Lifesystems EX4, available from outdoor retailers; read about correct tick removal and always carry a tick remover. For more information: www.lymediseaseuk.com; www.nhs.uk; www.mountaineering.scot. There are many insect repellents commercially available. Although most contain varying concentrations of diethyl toluamide (DEET), non-toxic alternatives are available such as Smidge; Mosi Guard Natural and Autan Protection Plus are particularly good against ticks.

MOUNTAIN RESCUE

In the event of a serious accident requiring medical attention, call 999 or 112 and ask for Police and Mountain Rescue/Coast Guard. Give concise information about the nature of the injuries, and the exact location, including a six-figure grid reference or the name of the route if possible. Try to leave someone with the casualty, who should be made as comfortable as possible, if injuries allow. If unconscious, be sure to place in the recovery position, ensuring the airway is clear.

If you need to call assistance but cannot make voice calls due to poor mobile phone reception, you can contact the emergency services using a text from your mobile but only if you have already registered with the emergency SMS text service. To register, text the word 'register' to 999. You will get a reply and should then follow the instructions you are sent. More information at www.emergencysms.org.uk.

In a few instances Mountain Rescue posts (containing a stretcher and basic rescue kit) are located in the hills. More information at www.scottishmountainrescue.org.

GRADES

Routes are graded for on-sight ground up ascents, and the climber is assumed to be fully equipped with a wide range of protection devices. On some of the hardest routes skyhooks may be found useful. It goes without saying that people should make their own judgement regarding any in situ equipment encountered including fixed abseil points, all of which will rapidly deteriorate through exposure to the elements. I have tried to be as consistent as possible, though minor regional variations may occur. Any crucial runner information, especially relating to obscure gadgets or hidden or hard-to-place protection has been included where known. Where a route has only received an ascent after extensive top-rope practice this headpointed ascent has been highlighted within the first ascent details where known, in order to record such prior familiarisation.

Karen Latter climbing The Edge of the Sea, Pinnacle Area, Reiff, Coigach & Assynt (page 235)

DISCLAIMER

The author, publisher and distributors of this book do not recognise any liability for injury or damage caused to, or by, climbers, third parties, or property arising from such persons seeking reliance on this guidebook as an assurance for their own safety.

Martin Boyce nearing the top of the pleasant Cioch Nose, on the iconic The Cioch, Sron na Ciche.

ISLE OF SKYE

*either Norse 'Skuy-o' cloud island or Gaelic 'Eilean Sgiathanach' winged island.

ISLE OF SKYE
(CLOUD ISLAND*)

Shaped like a piece from a jigsaw puzzle, Skye is the second largest Scottish island (after The Long Isle – Lewis and Harris). Possibly named after the Norse word for cloud (skuy-o), and somewhat romantically referred to in tourist brochures and car stickers as Eilean a' Cheo (Isle of the Mist, i.e. rain!), the rough gabbro of the Cuillin boasts the most famous mountain range in Scotland. Geographically the island is composed of five peninsulas radiating from the centre, Strath. The famed Cuillin range lies entirely within the squat Minginish peninsula in the south-west, while the Duirinish and Trotternish peninsulas in the extreme west and north harbour the majority of the sea cliffs.

THE CUILLIN

"Skye appears at some remote period to have been exposed to violent internal convulsions which up-heaved its steep and rugged mountains." – Alexander Cameron, 1871
The Cuillin exerts a mysterious, almost mystical magnetic attraction to both climbers and clouds alike. It is far and away the most popular mountain range in Scotland. More than any other area in Scotland the cliffs call for a range of mountaineering skills, not least of which is route finding and locating the often convoluted and problematic descents. One particular piece of what can only be described as 'creative writing' cannot go without mention and that is the brochure produced by the Dunvegan Estate, who state that *"every year, thousands of tourists come to stay in the wonderfully situated campsite in Glen Brittle"* – I was under the misapprehension that they came to climb in the Cuillin and the unremarkable field and black beach at the end of the road were merely convenient stopping off places.

Accommodation: Campsites: Ashaig Campsite, Breakish, Broadford (☏ 01471 822771; www.ashaig-campsite-skye.co.uk). The two most conveniently situated campsites for the Cuillin are at the road end at Glen Brittle (Apr – Sept; ☏ 01478 640404; www.dunvegancastle.com) and Sligachan (Mar – Oct; ☏ 07786 435 294; www.sligachan.co.uk), the latter a very convenient staggering distance from the bar! Further afield there are caravan and campsites at Torvaig, by Portree (Apr – Oct; ☏ 01478 611849; www.portreecampsite.co.uk) & Loch Greshornish (Apr – Oct; ☏ 01470 582230; www.skyecamp.com) – off A850 between Portree & Dunvegan; both convenient for the Trotternish peninsula. Staffin (Easter – Oct; ☏ 01470 562213; www.staffincampsite.co.uk); Kinloch, Dunvegan (Mar – Oct; ☏ 01470 521210; www.kinloch-campsite.co.uk); and Uig Bay (☏ 01470 542714; www.uig-camping-skye.co.uk). Wild camping anywhere in the hills or possibly near the roadside in the vicinity of the sea cliffs, though fresh running water may not be readily available. If in doubt seek permission locally. **Club Huts:** Glen Brittle Memorial Hut (BMC/Mountaineering Scotland), 0.5 mile/0.8km beyond Youth Hostel, near end of the glen. JMCS hut at Coruisk. Open bothy at Camasunary NG 517 183. **Bunkhouses:** Skye Backpackers (☏ 01599 534510; www.skyebackpackers.com); Saucy Mary's Lodge (☏ 01599 534845; www.saucymarys.com) – both Kyleakin; Skye Basecamp, Broadford (☏ 01471 820044; www.skyebascamp.co.uk); Sligachan (☏ 01478 650458); The Bunkhouse, Carbost (next to old inn: ☏ 01478 640205; www.theoldinnskye.co.uk); Portnalong – Croft Bunkhouse (☏ 07834 827524; www.skyehostels.com) or Skyewalker Hostel (☏ 01478 640250; www.skyewalkerhostel.com); Portree Independent Hostel (☏ 01478 613737; www.hostelskye.co.uk); Dun Flodigarry Hostel (☏ 01470 552212; www.flodigarry-hostel.scot); Flora MacDonald Hostel, by Armadale (☏ 01471 844172; www.hostel-scotland.co.uk). **Youth Hostels:** Glenbrittle (Apr–Sept; ☏ 01478 640278); Broadford (Mar – Oct; ☏ 01471 822442) and Portree (☏ 01478 612231) – all www.hostellingscotland.org.uk.

TIC: Portree (☏ 01478 612992; www.visitscotland.com).
Amenities: Café at Glenbrittle Campsite open 8am – 8pm; take away café, Carbost – opposite Talisker Distillery (Mar – Oct 10am–5pm; www.caoradhubh.com); Café

Cullin – Norse 'Kjollenn' keel-shaped ridges.

It should be noted that the Glen Brittle campsite in particular is also home to MWT (midge warfare training), where a plentiful supply of southern blood maintains the gene pool. Other possible contenders for midge city include the camping sites in Glen Torridon or Glen Rosa on Arran, but the Glen Brittle campsite on a still summer's evening definitely takes the biscuit, though others claim that Sligachan is even worse.

Lephin, Glendale, on way to Neist (www.caféléphin.co.uk). Closest pubs to Glen Brittle are the Old Inn at Carbost (9 miles) also PO/shop opposite, with the Taigh Ailean Hotel in Portnalong 3 miles further. Most popular pub on the island is the Sligachan Hotel (☎ 01478 650204; www.sligachan.co.uk), which Runrig aficionados would appreciate. Serves food 7.30am – 9pm and contender for the second most expensive beer (after The Torridon Inn) in the Highlands and Islands. **Outdoor shops:** Inside Out, Portree (☎ 01478 611663; www.insideoutskye.com) or Cioch, Struan (☎ 01470 572707; www.cioch-direct.co.uk).

"… among its bare and rugged hills there are spots which, for wild romantic grandeur, are unsurpassed in Scotland." – Alexander Cameron, 1871

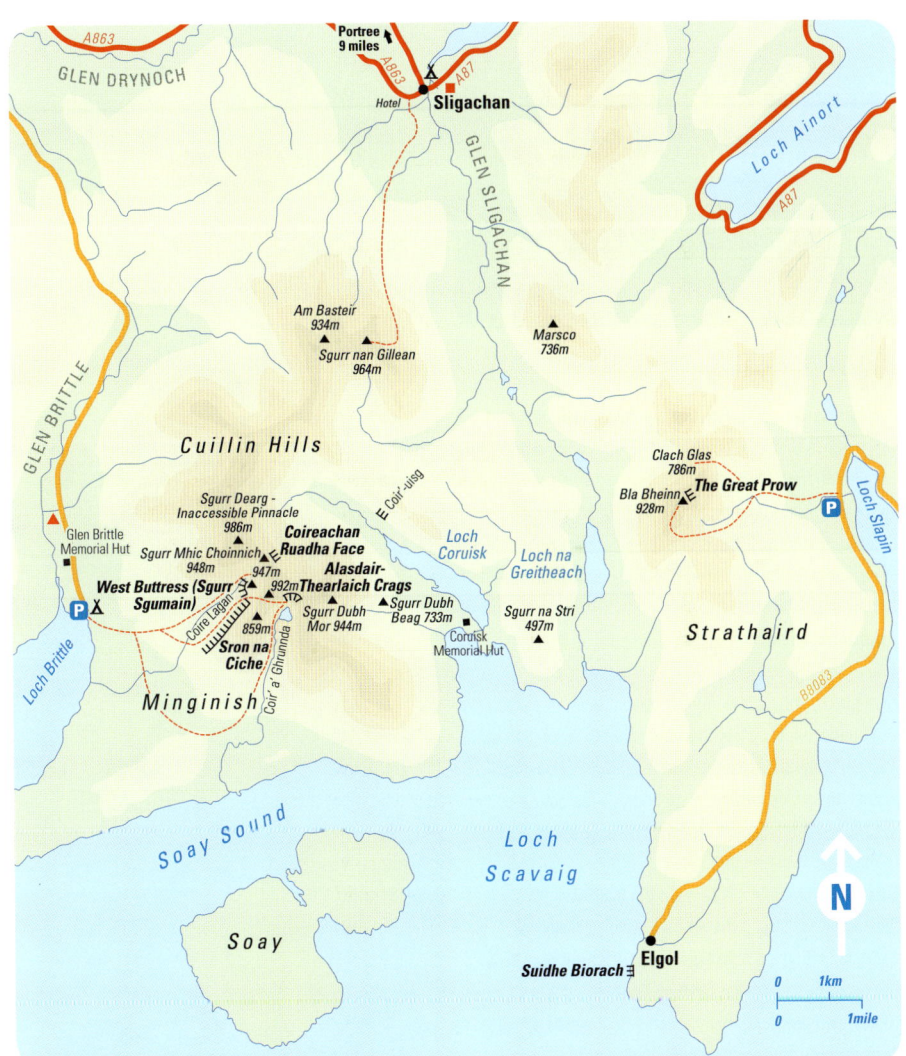

BLA BHEINN
(BLUE MOUNTAIN)

Reckoned by many to be the finest of all the Cuillin mountains, lying outwith the main horseshoe ridge, overlooking the head of Loch Slapin.

NG 534 217 **Alt:** 680m 1¼hr

THE GREAT PROW

An impressive and very distinctive steep projecting fin rising above the huge scree filled bowl that separates Bla Bheinn from Clach Glas.

Access: From Broadford follow the B8083 towards Elgol for 6.2 miles/10km round the head of Loch Slapin to park at a lay-by on the right, 100m beyond the burn of Allt na Dunaiche.

Approach: Follow the well-defined path up the right side of the Allt na Dunaiche burn, crossing it after 1.5km. Continue up the path to cross a smaller burn after 300m and head steeply up the hillside diagonally right then by a vague path up the left edge of the huge scree slope. A pleasanter option may be to continue up the path then by the south-east ridge and descend down **Scupper Gully** to the base of the routes.

Descent: Scramble easily down the back of the prow then down the straightforward scree-filled **Scupper Gully** bounding the right (west) side of **The Great Prow**. The similarly scree-filled **Access Gully** (Moderate) 100m down the slope from the left side involves a short through route and a steep 4m wall at the base.

1 Sidewinder ★   113m Severe 4a

FA Ian Clough, J.Silvers, J.Greenwood & D.Waller 16 Sept 1968

Good climbing up the left edge of the prow. Start beneath a short slabby ramp.

1. **30m 4a** Go up the ramp then the steep groove (often wet at start), taking the right fork to a belay.
2. **15m 4a** The grooves above to a ledge.
3. **43m 4a** Move left and continue directly for 20m in the same line then easily up a trap dyke forming an open chimney to belay on a large ledge just above a chokestone.
4. **25m 4a** Continue up the fault until a grand view of the Great Wall comes into view. Finish easily up the left-slanting ramp.

2 Jib ★★   130m E1 5b

FA Martin Boysen & Dave Alcock; Ian Clough & Hamish MacInnes May 1969

The big corner on the left side of the Great Wall. Start below an overhung gangway 5m right of the true chimney crack.

1. **40m 5b** Follow the left-trending gangway then go up a steep wall to a ledge. Traverse left past the ledge into the main line.
2. **40m 4c** Climb the crack with continuous interest in a fine position.
3. **15m 4c** Climb the chimney above to a stance.
4. **35m 4b** Follow the fine groove on the right to the top.

3 Stairway to Heaven ★★★   125m E5 6a

FA Mick Fowler & Phil Thomas 19 June 1977

An impressive line direct up the centre of the Great Wall. Start 12m to the left of the overhanging basalt dyke of *Jib*.

1. **35m 5b** Climb the groove, move left for 5m then diagonally right to gain the niche below the stance. (This avoids the wide crack which is very dirty and usually wet.)
2. **20m 4c** Follow the crack above to a further niche.
3. **30m 6a** Move up to a fault line, follow this leftwards until it is possible to climb the overhang via a short crack. Traverse right to a narrow ledge above overhangs then go diagonally up right to a short crack leading to a stance and PB.
4. **40m 5b** Follow the crack, climb an overlap and move up to a ledge. Finish up to the right.

4 Finger in the Dyke ★★   130m E5 6a

FA Paul Thorburn, Grant Farquhar & Gary Latter 4 June 1997

Climbs a series of cracks left of the right arête. Start at a slanting dyke 10m right of *Jib* just left of the cave.

1. **25m 6a** Follow the dyke to a small corner (serious) and gain the shelf above. Swing right into an undercut groove and make hard moves up this to better holds. Traverse right across the lip of the roof past a huge pocket into a slabby recess then climb the crack to a hanging belay below a niche.
2. **35m 5c** Continue up the line of the crack then head diagonally right underneath the smooth bulge and round the arête. Traverse an easy gangway back left round the arête to belay in a scoop on the left side of the arête.
3. **50m 5c** Continue directly above the belay crossing a dyke then follow good holds leading rightwards onto the arête. Continue more easily up the wide left-slanting crack and its continuation to belay on broken ground.
4. **20m** Scramble up and leftwards to finish.

5 The Great Prow ★★   85m HVS 5a

FA T.Band, Phil Gribbon, N.Ross & Wilf Tauber 15 June 1968

Fine situations up the big corner bounding the right side of the Great Wall. Start beneath the prominent chimney-corner.

1. **35m 5a** The crack leads with interest to a slab. Climb this to belay at its top.
2. **20m 4h** Continue up the crack to belay on a 'pedestal' ledge.
3. **10m 4b** Return down the crack to level with an orange slab then traverse out left on a thin diagonal fault to the belay on the crest.
4. **20m 4b** Climb the ramp then a crack on the right which leads back right onto the crest and the top.

ISLE OF SKYE CLACH GLAS

6 Ecstasis ★★★ 90m HVS 5a
FA Chris Boulton, Paul Nunn & Bob Toogood 1969

An excellent route up the topmost ramp running left out from *Clough's Cleft*, which is the leftmost of two prominent chimney gullies at the top right end of the wall, up right from **The Great Prow**.

1 **25m 5a** Start up *Clough's Cleft* then follow the slabby ramp pleasantly to a stance.
2 **40m 4c** Continue easily at first to a spike runner. Now climb poorly protected undercut slabs leftwards to a belay in the bay. Quite bold.
3 **25m 4b** Ascend the slab rightwards, finishing up a steep crack.

CLACH GLAS
(GREY STONE)   1¾hr

The magnificent pointed peak north-east of Bla Bheinn is the most difficult of all the Cuillin peaks.
Approach: Follow the well defined path up the right side of the Allt na Dunaiche burn for 1.5km. Head right and slog up the steepening scree chute on the left at the back of Choire a' Caise to gain the bealach (630m) between Sgurr nan Each and Clach Glas.

1 Clach Glas – Bla Bheinn Traverse ★★★   Difficult

A fantastic outing, giving continually interesting scrambling with magnificent situations. From the bealach go up a short steep wall, the slabs, to regain the crest which is followed mainly on its right flank. From the base of a scree gully beneath the final tower climb a straightforward V-chimney on the right past some chokestones then follow a fine exposed line on good holds for about 30m up the excellent slabby headwall to easy ground leading to the broad flat-topped summit platform. At the southern end of the summit is 'The Imposter', a slab with a narrow knife-edge on its wildly exposed right (west) edge. Descend just left of the crest on good holds and cracks with a few steep exposed moves down the rib at the base to gain easy ground. Continue by a path along the ridge, avoiding any difficulties on the left, including the final pinnacles by a rake on the left (east) side to gain a small grassy hollow – the 'Putting Green' forming the bealach between Clach Glas and Bla Bheinn. The complex North-East Face of Bla Bheinn lies up on the right with numerous variations possible. Go along a path on the left of the ridge then easily back right to a small gap. Negotiate a 4m wall above the highest point of the gap on good holds then traverse scree rightwards and up a prominent scree funnel on the left leading into an impressive cul-de-sac. Ascend the chimney at the back of the corner, pulling out right on good holds at the top. Above, descend slightly right round some blocks and finish up a wide scree gully leading to a cairn (795m) on the East Ridge. The broad ridge leads easily to a path leading to the summit. An easier alternative from the 'Putting Green' is to descend the scree slope and gain the East Ridge by an ascent of the straightforward scree of **Scupper Gully** bounding the right side of the distinctive **The Great Prow**.

Clach Glas – Bla Bheinn Traverse with Sgurr nan Gillean in background. Wendy Nieper climbing. Photo Rob Jarvis.

ISLE OF SKYE CORUISK | 17

"… and were surrounded by mountains of naked rock, of the boldest and most precipitous character."
– Sir Walter Scott, 1814

CORUISK
(WATER CORRIE)

Photo Alastair Lee, Posing Productions.

Famed for its rugged and picturesque scenery, this magnificent deep basin cuts into the remote east corner of the Cuillin. The freshwater Loch Coruisk is separated from the sea by the River Scavaig, at only a few hundred metres the shortest river in Britain. It is the particular remoteness that makes the place so special – an 'inner sanctum' deep within the Cuillin. It should be noted that during prolonged wet weather (not unknown in Skye) all the low level terrestrial approaches can become impassable in spate conditions, necessitating crossing the Cuillin ridge by one of the high passes. There is a mountaineering club hut (locked) a little over 100m from the landing stage.

Approach: Either from the west, east or north by the paths from Glen Brittle, Kilmarie via Camasunary or Sligachan or more popularly (particularly by touroids!) by less strenuous means from the south by boat from Elgol. Two boats operate from Mar – Oct, Bella Jane (☎ 01471 866244; www.bellajane.co.uk); Misty Isle (☎ 01471 866288; www.mistyisleboattrips.co.uk)

NG 479 195 **Alt:** 150m 25min

MAD BURN BUTTRESS
A good quick drying diamond-shaped buttress.
Appr: Follow the coast south-west from the hut crossing a couple of small burns then head up the hill to the crag.

① Mayday ★ 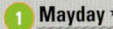 100m Severe 4a
FA Ken Bryan & Malcolm Slesser May 1961
On the left side of the face is a conspicuous left-sloping dièdre starting about 25m up. Start about 15m left of the lowest rocks.
1 25m 4a Gain the dièdre via a line of weakness on smooth wall via a mantelshelf and left-trending crack.
2 30m 4a The delightful dièdre to a small stance.
3 45m 4a Continue left for 3m then up by a crack then walls and ledges to finish more easily.

② Warsle ★ 90m HS 4b
FA Mrs M.Wallace & Malcolm Slesser April 1962
The lowest point of the buttress is formed by a 6m high pulpit with a deep crack above. Gain the pulpit direct then climb the crack above, continuing up the corner to wide grass ledge. Gain the upper of twin left-slanting ledge/crack systems by a vague crack at the right end of grass ledge and follow it until it is possible to move up and right to a good stance. Gain the first terrace immediately above by a delicate slab and difficult thin wall.

CORUISK HUT CRAG

NG 487 198 **Alt:** 20m

The crag immediately behind the hut. The lower wall has 3 main starts from V.Diff. – VS, plus some good bouldering. By linking pitches up to 100m of good climbing can be achieved.

1 The Minke ★   20m E2 5b
FA Grahame & Melanie Nicoll & L.Kass 19 May 1997

The right-slanting basalt dyke starting from behind the hut door.

2 Beached Whale ★   20m E3 5c
FA D.Shepherd & J.Andrew 24 May 1994

A good route protected by small cams. Start 5m right of the hut. Climb directly to the large horizontal break and follow this leftwards with difficulty.

SGURR DUBH MOR
(BIG BLACK CONICAL HILL)

NG 477 208 **Alt:** 40m   20min

Approach: From the stepping stones/hut follow the path along the south shore of Loch Coruisk for just under 1.5km then up slightly to the base.

Descent: Go down the south-west nose to a small dip before a pinnacle then follow grassy rakes leading down leftwards into An Garbh-choire.

1 The Dubhs Ridge ★★★★   900m Moderate
FA William Douglas, William Lamont & James Rennie June 1896

"Apart from the initial trouble in climbing on to the ridge, one may thereafter proceed unroped up broad acres of boiler-plate slabs, whose rock is the roughest gabbro in all the Cuillin. In other words, it is so rough and reliable that only the grossest negligence could bring a man to harm." – W.H.Murray, *Mountaineering in Scotland*, J.M.Dent Ltd, 1947

The finest outing of its grade in the country. A magnificent sweep of rough slabs leads from just above the shore of Loch Coruisk towards the summit of Sgurr Dubh Beag, at 733m the small eastern top of the main peak, Sgurr Dubh Mor. The slabs extend at an average angle of just under 30 degrees for 1.2km to the summit, steepening slightly in their upper section before forming a level plateau leading to just short of the summit. Gain the crest by a grassy gully immediately right of the toe and follow it by immaculate straightforward 'padding', with much variation possible. From the summit make a steep 22m abseil down the west face from a block (slings in situ), and continue more easily along the ridge close to the crest leading to a steep final section. Turn this by a series of ledges on the south flank to gain the main summit.

The Dubhs Ridge. Photo Dan Bailey.

COIR'-UISG BUTTRESS
NG 454 229 **Alt:** 300m
1¼hr

An impressive cliff in a superb location at the head of the loch, characterised by a prominent white scar in the centre.

Approach: From the hut/landing spot, follow the path round the south side of Loch Coruisk past the base of the Dubhs Ridge to the head of the loch, then steeply up the hillside to the cliff.

1 Skye Wall ★★★★   105m E7 6b
FA Dave Birkett & Alan Steele (headpointed) 2 May 2007

A stunning line up the right side of *"the most awesome wall of rock in the UK, a real plum"*. The vertical to just off vertical wall gives thin balancy and pretty scary climbing – protection is difficult to arrange, as many of the cracks flare. Start beneath the obvious compelling thin crack near the right side of the wall.

1 **20m 6b** Follow finger-cracks (small poor wires) to a good ledge (E6 pitch).

2 **35m 6b/c** Move up and right to a small ledge. Thin moves up the wall gain a sloping hold and loose flaky sidepulls. Bold climbing leads to a crack, followed to a ledge.

3 **50m 5b** Move up and left, then go straight up to easy ground.

Photo Alastair Lee, Posing Productions.

Alan Steele and Dave Birkett on first ascent of the top pitch of Skye Wall. Photo Alastair Lee, Posing Productions.

SUIDHE BIORACH
(SHARP-POINTED SEAT)

NG 515 124 20min

This steep Jurassic quartz sandstone crag lies on the west coast of the Strathaird peninsula just south of Elgol with grand views over Rum and the southern Cuillin. The rock is sound with many pockets. Although it is coated in its upper half with a liberal coating of hairy green sea-lichen this doesn't affect the climbing. Most of the routes are very well protected. There are some fulmars nesting, though none on the steeper sections affecting the routes. Most of the routes are clear of the water in settled conditions. There is an excellent sheltered ledge, dubbed **Paradise Ledge**, a couple of metres below the top on the north side of *Jamie Jampot*.

Access: Follow the B8038 south from Broadford for 15 miles/24km to arrive at the village at the road end. Park in the car park down by the jetty.

Approach: Follow the path heading south for about 1.5km to the crag, which is just north of Prince Charles's Cave (another one!)

Descent: Abseil down the main corner line of *Jamie Jampot* (thread and flake belay further back on left). It is also possible to scramble (Moderate) down the gully at the north end of the crag and traverse in at mid-low tide. Routes described from **left to right**, starting from the steep gully at the left (north-west) end of the crag.

Big Edward Nind on the final crack of India.

① Transept ★★   25m E3 5b
FA Dominic Partridge 1993

Midway along the gully wall is a leftwards rising crack. Climb the steep bulging wall to its left using pockets. Turn the capping roof on the left.

② The Pope Must Die ★★   25m E2 5c
FA Colin Moody & Neil Smith 18 September 1993

Climb the left-slanting overhanging corner, pull out right at the top of the corner and continue easily.

③ Hairy Beast ★★   25m E1 5c
FA Neil Smith & Colin Moody 18 September 1993

Start 4m left of the main arête below an overhang split by a crack. Climb up to the overhang, climb the crack through it then follow the corner.

④ Veritas Splendour ★★★   25m E2 5c
FA Steve Hill, Dominic Partridge & Paul Autumn 1993

The lower 11m of the arête has fallen away leaving a steep undercut base. Climb the leftwards rising crack to the left of the triangular overhang to gain thin cracks above (crux) and up these to a break. Swing round on to the right wall of the arête and climb direct to the top.

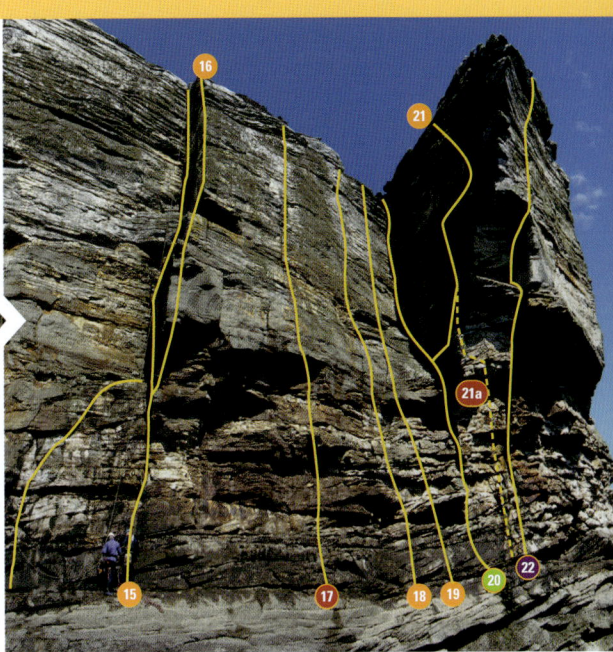

4a Pure Splendour Start ★★★ — 25m E1 5b
FA Mike Lates & Catriona Hayne 1997

Great climbing on perfect rock. Take a rising traverse up and left over the lip of the roof to the arête and finish up this in a superb position.

5 Crack of Zawn ★★ — 30m E1 5b
FA Rob MacDonald 1992

Climb the crack just left of 6 then move left with difficulty to a good flake. Move easily up a ramp to finish up the fine steep crack.

6 Jamie Jampot ★★★ — 30m VS 4c
FA Rob MacDonald & Dominic Partridge 1992

Excellent climbing up the main corner. A fine natural line.

7 Digitalis ★★★ — 30m E3 5c
FA Dominic Partridge & Simon Bally Autumn 1993

Climbs a line up the right wall of the corner. Start up the arôte. Gain and follow a vertical crack then traverse left heading towards some dubious flakes. Climb the wall direct to the right of the flakes, continuing direct to the top.

8 India ★★★ — 30m E3 6a
FA Neil Smith & Dominic Partridge Autumn 1993

The severely undercut arête right of 7.
1 **15m 5c** Climb the crack in the stepped corner to belay directly below the roof at mid-height.
2 **15m 6a** Traverse left on to a hanging slab on the arête and up a crack through an overhang above, to finish up a diagonal crack ('West Coast of India').

9 Altar Ego ★★ — 30m E1 5c
FA Dominic Partridge & Rob MacDonald 1992

1 **15m 5c** Climb the wall to the right of 8 to belay as for that route.
2 **15m 4c** Climb the corner and right wall under the big roof

10 Revenge of an Angry Cosmos ★★★ — 30m E3 6a
FA Edward Nind & Masa Sakano 23 October 2016

A classic line with excellent climbing and good protection. Start up the wall just left of 11. Climb up and right to cross 11 at the large ledge and continue up and right into a huge niche under a wide roof. Traverse right

Karen Latter on one of the many crag classics - Jamie Jampot.

through the roof and move up to a large sloping ledge. Climb the thin crack directly above (crux) then avoid the huge roofs and guano ledges above by moving diagonally up and right (passing a slightly dubious block under a roof) until it is possible to climb steeply up and left breaking through lesser overhangs. From the ledge under the final overhang move left to the arête, climb this on its left side and finish easily. Top of the grade.

11 Ark of the Covenant ★★   30m E3 6a
FA Dominic Partridge & Steve Hill 1994

Start on the wall to the right of the arête.
1. **15m 6a** Climb a crack up to the corner below the overhang then the corner to the overhang. Follow the jam crack through this heading left (crux) to belay as for 8.
2. **15m 5c** Up the leftwards leaning corner to finish in a wild situation just right of 8.

12 Rapid Learning Curve ★★★   30m E6 6b
FA Nick Hancock & M.Smith September 1999

Fantastic climbing through the triple roofs. Crux is attaining a standing position on the lip of the final roof. Exposed moves up the arête lead to a long reach to finish.

13 Tree Route ★★   30m E1 5b
FA Dominic Partridge & Simon Bally 1994

Start to the right of a large roof. Climb a crack up to the small overhang with a small tree above. Take the left-hand crack on jams, passing the tree to top.

14 Busted Flush ★★   30m E2 5b
FA Andrew Holden & S.Marriott 30 September 2006

The left of the three vertical cracks. Climb the lower wall (sometimes wet but on big holds). Continue past a right-facing flake up to the short crack. Climb this and move up to a break (crux). Go up the fine headwall to the top.

15 Fertility Left ★★   30m HS 4b
FA Noel Williams & Willie Jeffrey 11 July 1987

The left V-shaped corner. The start is often wet but on big holds.

16 DIY Arête ★★   30m HVS 5a
FA Mark Hudson & Andrew Holden 31 May 2005;
Direct: Michael Barnard & Doug Bartholomew 13 July 2019

The bottomless arête right of the corner gives straightforward climbing in a spectacular position. Follow the initial wet wall of 15 to the first sloping ledge. Step out right onto the pocketed wall and climb diagonally to the upper arête. Climb the higher arête past a break on the right wall at 4m (good cams) to an easier finish. 16a *Direct* ★★ E1 5c step right at first opportunity and move up (crux) to the ledge.

17 Rum Doodle ★★   30m E3 5c
FA Neil Smith, Mark Philip & Roger Lupton 1995

Climb short corner to an overhang, use a pocket above this to reach right, then finish more easily up cracks.

18 Angel of Sharkness ★★★   25m HVS 5a
FA Mark Philip & Neil Smith 1994

The fine crack up the centre of the wall using pockets in the upper section.

19 Pickpocket ** — 25m HVS 5a
FA Neil Smith & Mark Philip 1995

The pocketed wall to the right of the crack.

20 Fertility Right ** — 25m Severe 4a
FA Noel Williams & Willie Jeffrey 11 July 1987

The right V-shaped corner. Cross the initial bulge easily on the right.

21 Hairy Mary *** — 30m VS 4c
FA Darren McAulay & P.Johnstone 15 May 2002

The exposed wall right of 20. Much better than appearance would suggest. Start as for that route but move right to a platform at 10m then up a wall and crack for 10m to a rightwards traverse along a break to finish by another crack and wall.

21a Mary Hinge ** — 25m E2 5c
FA Gary & Karen Latter 10 April 2018

A spectacular direct start to 21, with good holds and protection. Climb directly up to the roof, cross it (good cam on right over lip), then move leftwards to finish up the upper section of 21.

22 Mother's Pride **** — 30m E4 5c
FA Dominic Partridge & Rob MacDonald 1994

Spectacular climbing up the continuously overhanging crack (large cam useful) on the right side of the crag. Start below the overhang. Through the roof via the large crack and pull into a niche above. Climb out to the arête using the crack under the roof to finish up the wildly overhanging crack. *Left Finish* (5a) swings left round the arête then follows a right trending line up the less steep upper wall, reducing the overall grade to E3.

23 Toast **** — 30m E7 6c
FA Dave MacLeod & Natalie Berry 25 June 2015

A brilliant climb taking on the horizontal roof and steep wall right of 22.

1 **15m 5b** Start about 6m right of 22 and climb the wall on big holds, moving left around a bulge and then traversing slightly right to a belay at the roof.

2 **15m 6c** Arrange a couple of small cams in pockets in the roof and launch outwards using a positive undercut. Reach the next undercut and then gain jugs on the lip with difficulty. Continue directly up the pumpy steep headwall.

24 Hovis ** — 30m E6 6b
FA Dave Turnbull & John Arran (on-sight) 24 May 1998

Start beneath the roof 10m right of 22.

1 **15m 5b** Weave up through the overhanging breaks and ledges to belay under the roof just right of the only line of weakness.

2 **15m 6b** Move left and gain the lip using small flakes. A very difficult heel hooking/mantel manoeuvre gains a precarious standing position on the lip, where bold moves lead first left then right up the blank wall.

Gary Latter on the excellent, steep Mother's Pride. Photo Karen Latter.

NORTHERN CUILLIN

SGURR NAN GILLEAN 2hr
(PEAK OF THE GULLIES/YOUNG MEN)

The most northerly mountain of the Cuillin. Cliffs are described as encountered on the usual approach, first from Sligachan then proceeding south down Glen Brittle.

Access: Park either at the Sligachan Hotel or by the side of the A863 road a couple of hundred metres south-west of the hotel.

Approach: (A) For *Pinnacle Ridge* follow either of two paths for a few hundred metres either south-west or south to cross a footbridge. Continue along a good path for 1.5km then follow it up the right bank of the Allt Dearg Beag for 400m to a bridge. Cross the bridge and follow the path steeply until it forks at a cairn (about an hour from the road). Take the right fork and follow it over the rocky bluffs overlooking the Bhasteir gorge leading to a scree slope on the edge of the corrie beneath *Pinnacle Ridge*. 1¾ hours.

(B) For the *West Ridge*, follow the path from Sligachan as for *Pinnacle Ridge* as far as the footbridge over the Allt Dearg Beag. Continue up the path up the right bank following a line of cairns with occasional easy scrambling over the slabs above the right side of the Bhasteir gorge. Continue into the corrie over the outflow of the tiny Loch a' Bhasteir and head due south and up the boulder field leading to the Bealach a' Bhasteir. 2 hours.

Descent: The only easy route down is via the 'Tourist Route' down the South-East Ridge.

1 Pinnacle Ridge ★★   600m Difficult

FA unknown 1880s

Though fairly benign and indistinctive when viewed from Sligachan the north ridge of Sgurr nan Gillean presents four distinct and impressive pinnacles, clearly seen in profile when viewed further west from Glen Drynoch. The first pinnacle is ascended by its north-west ridge giving about 150m of Moderate scrambling. Thereafter, the second and third pinnacles afford pleasant scrambling, following an obvious well-trodden line close to the crest. The section from the summit of the third pinnacle down to the col constitutes the crux, though can easily be bypassed by abseil, recommended in wet conditions. In the dry, either descend the ridge on the left for a few metres then down a short steep crack with good holds or go down on the right and down a short slippery crack.

Both routes lead to the top of a narrow zigzag 'gully', where a second sling is in situ on large block (23m abseil to col). Alternatively, descend the tight gully first right then diagonally left to the col. The fourth pinnacle, also known as Knight's Peak, is ascended by either of twin diagonal right-slanting ramps, the upper cleaner. From the top a path leads round the right side (west) of the summit to a col. An obvious well-worn path descends right then back left to the col beneath the final summit pyramid. Many options are available, including a chimney on the left, an easy right slanting shelf then easy angled slabs, or directly to the summit.

② West Ridge ★★   150m Moderate
FA Lawrence & Charles Pilkington 1880

"The crest grows steadily more acute until it thins to a hanging tapestry, leaps in fantastic pinnacles, then swirls up and onward to a finely sculptured peak." – W.H.Murray, *Mountaineering in Scotland*, J.M.Dent Ltd, 1947

A pleasant scramble, narrow and exposed in its lower reaches, following the ridge rising from the Bealach a' Bhasteir to the summit. From the bealach contour round on the north side to ascend a steep chimney or the rib to its right, leading to the fine blocky arête. The famous pinnacle known as the 'gendarme' joined its many companions in the corrie floor in the winter of 1987. Continue up the more broken arête, threading a fine window formed by blocks just short of the summit.

AM BASTEIR
(THE EXECUTIONER)

NG 464 252 **Alt:** 880m 2½hr
THE BHASTEIR TOOTH
This very distinctive feature projects out west from the summit of the mountain.

Approach: Follow the approach as for the *West Ridge* on Sgurr nan Gillean to Bealach a' Bhasteir. Am Basteir lies immediately to the west, with the Bhasteir tooth immediately to its west again. **Descent:** Abseil from slings (in situ) down *Naismith's Route*.

① Naismith's Route ★★   35m Very Difficult
FA Willie Naismith & A.Mackay (after top-roping) 1898

Exposed atmospheric climbing, well trodden as part of the classic ridge traverse. From the ridge, make an increasingly exposed traverse right on ledges overlooking Lota Corrie. Continue up from the main ledge to a higher ledge and possible belay. Climb the wall above the right end of the ledge to the cracked chimney or gain the same point by traversing out right and steeply up the diagonal crack. Continue up the easier crack-chimney to beneath a steep crack. Traverse right to another crack and make a difficult move (crux, well protected) to finish.

② Rainbow Warrior ★★   40m E3 6a
FA Steve Hill & Tim Dickinson 12 July 1989

Good spectacularly positioned climbing. Start on the starting ledge of *Naismith's Route*.

1 25m 6a Take a leftwards trending line to reach a crack above a groove. From the top of this traverse left to belay on a ledge on the arête.

2 15m 5c Traverse left until it is possible to surmount the roof. Climb the final roof on the left or right.

③ Captain Planet ★★★   35m E4 6a
FA Es Tresidder & Blair Fyffe 13 September 2000

Excellent climbing taking a direct line up the centre. Gain the crack and groove of 2 direct from below via a steep crack. At the top of the groove, where 2 traverses left, step right and climb the superb headwall direct.

SOUTHERN CUILLIN

SGURR DEARG (RED PEAK) NG 444 216 **Alt:** 950m 2hr

THE INACCESSIBLE PINNACLE

A unique chunk of rock – a free Munro with any route. As the only Munro (Scottish mountain over 3,000 feet/914m) requiring actual climbing to reach the summit it is peculiarly popular, even with non-climbers. In summer expect long queues of 'baggers' on both the ridges. With over a century of heavy traffic the rock is highly polished, particularly in the wet.

Approach: Follow the well worn path (and the hordes if it's a bank holiday!) from opposite the BMC hut in Glen Brittle to just before the Eas Mor (big waterfall) and follow a further path branching east up the boulder-strewn west shoulder.

Descent: Abseil down *West Ridge* from fixed wire around the summit block or climb down the *East Ridge* if not covered in Munro-baggers.

 **East Ridge** ★★★   **60m Moderate**

FA Charles & Lawrence Pilkington 18 August 1880

"A razor-like edge with an overhanging and infinite drop on one side and a drop longer and steeper on the other."
– Lawrence Pilkington, 1880

Graeme Ettle nearing the top of West Ridge. Photo Dave Cuthbertson, Cubby Images.

Move up the flank onto the crest and follow it, soon easing, finishing over huge blocks forming the summit. Can either be split on a ledge at half-height or climbed moving together – take four or five slings.

② West Ridge ★ 20m Very Difficult

FA A.H.Stocker, A.G.Parker & John Mackenzie August 1886

The route up the short end, steep and polished. Start left of the edge on the north face. Trend up left to a sloping ledge and delicately up right, continuing more easily over ledges to gain the final sloping slab.

SOUTH FACE

③ Varicose ★ 30m VS 4b

FA John Harwood 11 August 1964

Start at white marks at the right end of overhangs on the left side of the face. Climb up to and over an overhang on good holds and to a ledge with a perched block. Finish directly up the wall above.

④ South Crack ★★ 30m Hard Very Difficult

FA H.Harland, Ashley Abraham & H.Binns June 1906

The classic alternative to the queues following the prominent crack up the centre of the face with a short deviation at 10m.

NORTH FACE

⑤ The Naked Saltire ★★★ 30m E2 5c

FA Mike Lates & D.McLaughlin 8 August 1999

The perfect gabbro crack up the wall, probably the same fault as *South Crack*. Athletic moves off the ground (crux) lead to a pod. Continue up the crack, sustained, to the crest.

The Gathering, The Cioch. Dave MacLeod on first ascent. Photo Dave Cuthbertson.

COIRE LAGAN (CORRIE OF THE HOLLOW)

SRON NA CICHE (NOSE OF THE PAP OR BREAST)

"From the top of the precipice to the bottom is at least a thousand feet, perpendicular in many places and a narrow knife edge of rock about a hundred feet long runs out from it rather less than halfway down. On each side of the knife edge are steep clean slabs that, at their base, overhang the gullies below. At the end of the knife edge is placed the tower which casts its shadow across the great slab." – Norman Collie.

The biggest and best cliff in the Cuillin and also one of the shortest approaches, therefore very popular. The expansive north-west face overlooking Coire Lagan presents a half-kilometre sweep of cliff, rising to almost 300m with a superb range of routes of every standard. Most of the routes are very quick drying, though any wet streaks may require the afternoon sun to disappear.

Access: From the A850 Kyleakin – Portree road, turn west along the A823 at Sligachan for 5.3 miles/8.2km, turning left (west) onto the B8099 for 1.7 miles/3km, turning left (west again) down the single track road for a further 8 miles/12.8km to the road end at Glen Brittle to a car park just before the campsite (1 hour from bridge).

Approach: Walk through the campsite and follow a well-constructed path from behind the toilet block steeply up the hillside, taking the left fork after 400m. Continue up this until it crosses the Allt Coire Lagan (burn) then break off right across the coire on a smaller path crossing a couple of streams, then by screes up to the base of **West Buttress** 1¼ hours. **Cioch Buttress** lies a further 15 minutes up the hillside, the main bulk of **Eastern Buttress** a similar distance up the boulder field again.

Descent: (A) From the top of the cliff the most convenient descent is **Eastern Gully** with a short slither beneath a huge boulder (or 10m abseil from in situ sling) less than 100m from the top. Continue down and either make a further abseil from in situ slings or make an obvious traverse left (west) onto the shelf which runs directly underneath **Cioch Upper Buttress**. See **Cioch** and **Cioch Slab** section for descents from here.

(B) Scramble east along the cliff top and down the **Sgumain Stone Shoot** NG 448 205, which cuts down to the base of **Eastern Buttress**.

(C) From the top of the **Western Buttress** head south-west down along the top of broken crags, either contouring back right to the base of the cliff or down the Coir a' Ghrunnda path heading back to the campsite.

WESTERN BUTTRESS   1¼hr

NG 443 203 **Alt:** 450m

The large expanse of fairly featureless slabs on the right side of the cliff. The face is split by the two parallel left-slanting diagonal lines of **West Central Gully** and **Central Gully**, the former a rake starting on the right. The routes tend to be long and rambling with interesting route finding thrown in for good measure. Route finding, particularly in the mist, can be a problem as many of the features repeat themselves. Many variations are possible. Be prepared for harder climbing if the line is lost.

1 Median ★★ 350m Very Difficult
FA Ernest Steeple & H.Bowron 1909

One of the best routes of its grade on the island. Start at the base of a long crack-line 40m left of West Central Gully.
- **1+2 90m** Climb the crack and continue to the gully.
- **3 40m** Ascend the gully to the base of a long chimney.
- **4 45m** Climb the chimney leftwards beneath a big overhanging wall to belay on the more open wall above.
- **5 35m** Go up the wall 5m to the right then traverse right and go up to belay at the base of an easy angled slab.
- **6 35m** Go up the slab to belay beneath big fan-shaped corners.
- **7 45m** Go rightwards up a poorly protected depression then left and up a chimney.
- **8+9 60m** Climb either the chimney or the buttress on its left to the final arête. The route is open to much variation, including escape out right from the foot of pitch 6 with 90m of Moderate slabs leading to the final arête.

2 Central Route ★★ 260m HS 4b
FA Derek Leaver & J.Gott July 1957

Another fine long route. Start up *Mallory's Slab and Groove* to Central Gully.
- **1 25m** Go up the gully to just left of the prominent crack then follow steep rock on good holds to a block belay on a sloping platform.
- **2 10m** Climb over the bulge above then move right across a short slab. Cross an overlap at a break to a sloping gangway and move left to a flake belay.
- **3 20m** Ascend the crack, stepping right and up another crack, stepping left at the top. Go up the wall for 5m bearing right to the edge of a gully.
- **4 15m** Go up steeply to a flake belay.
- **5 25m** 4b Step left and go up and right until close to a block by the gully. Move onto a gangway, traverse left and cross a bulge. Continue, bearing right to a sloping ledge with spike belay on the left.
- **6 30m** Cross the bulge and climb easily an easy-angled slab to the base of steeper rocks.
- **7 25m** Climb the dyke above for 10m then an easy slab above to further steep rock.
- **8 25m** Ascend the groove and a short steep slab then easily up the arête to a thread belay under a block.
- **9 25m** Continue easily up the arête, dropping down into a small gully on its right to a triangular grass ledge beneath the final tower.
- **10 40m** Climb steep rock to belay on the edge of the gully at the right side of the tower.
- **11 20m** 4b Make an exposed traverse up and left on small holds to a break in the overhang, cross this (avoiding a loose block) and finish up the left wall of a steep groove.

3 Mallory's Slab and Groove ★★ 300m Very Difficult
FA George Mallory, D.Pye & Leslie Shadbolt 1918

An enjoyable well frequented route. Start on the screes beneath a prominent crack just right of a large overhang, midway between Central Gully and *Cioch Gully*. Follow the crack and the slab above to gain Central Gully. Follow the crack for almost a rope-length to a prominent right slanting crack. Climb this and head towards the overhang on *West Central Arête*. Pass this on the left to gain the gully left of the arête. Move back right and finish up the arête.

ISLE OF SKYE SRON NA CICHE

4 Amphitheatre Arête *   270m Moderate
FA Norman Collie 1907

A pleasant wander. Starting from *Cioch Gully*, climb slabs heading towards the Amphitheatre, crossing Central Gully where it reaches the Amphitheatre. Go right across water-washed slabs to the arête which is followed to the top.

The prominent slanting gully is 5 *Cioch Gully*, Very Difficult followed easily to two pitches leading to the shelf behind the Cioch.

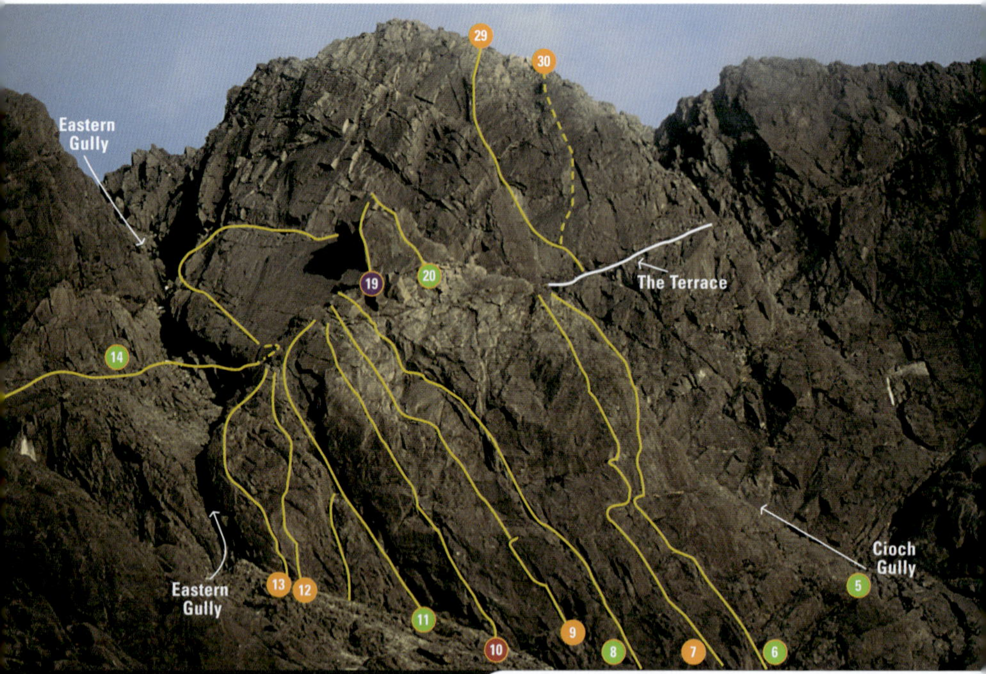

CIOCH BUTTRESS
NG 445 204 **Alt**: 550m 1½hr

The large buttress lying between **Cioch Gully** and **Eastern Gully**, directly beneath the **Cioch**.
Descent: All routes lead to the long diagonal Terrace beneath the **Cioch** and **Cioch Slab**. Walk diagonally left (east) down this, crossing **Eastern Gully** (the lower easy approach section of *Collie's Route*).

6 Cioch West ***   210m Severe 4a
FA Cecil Holland, Herbert Carr & Miss Dorothy Pilley 1919

Excellent climbing with an exposed well protected crux. Start at the first open chimney left of the toe of the buttress, a few metres right of *Crembo Cracks*. (CW scratched at the base).

1. **35m** Climb the open groove and the continuation chimney then the easy-angled groove above to belay on the left.
2. **30m** Continue up the easy-angled groove above to belay in a short steep corner-crack on the left.
3. **20m 4a** Climb up and right across the steep slab

above on good incut holds leading to good flakes and bouldery ledges above. Walk right on a good ledge system to belay beneath and just right of a low flake.

4 **25m** Climb straight up then ascend a prominent right-slanting fault to belay at the base of an open chimney groove.

5 **15m 4a** Go up the open groove to a bulge then traverse out left in a fine position on good holds to belay on a fine exposed ledge.

6 **45m** Traverse the ledge easily round left onto the front face then by easy slabs near the crest to a large boulder belay beneath a short steep wall overlooking *Cioch Gully*.

7 **40m 4a** Climb the improbable-looking wall just right of the arête on huge incut holds to a glacis. Walk diagonally left up this to a pile of jumbled boulders at the right end of the ledge system running beneath the base of the Cioch. *Cioch Nose* provides a logical continuation.

7 Crembo Cracks ★★ 150m HVS 5a
FA Dave Gregory & R.Hutchison (1 PA) 27 July 1958

Good climbing, taking a direct line up the right side of the face. Start at the leftmost of a pair of cracks just left of the toe of the buttress.

1 **40m 4c** Climb the fine crack then step up left and follow a slabby groove past good flakes to a ledge.

2 **40m** Continue more easily up the open chimney-groove to the base of the short steep slab on *Cioch West*. Traverse right and climb the right edge of the flake to jumbled boulders. Traverse right along an easy ledge then climb a shallow flake-groove just left of a grassy ledge to belay left of a prominent rock scar.

3 **30m 5a** Step right and climb the awkward steep groove above then by a series of poorly protected steps slightly leftwards (old PR) to good holds beneath a bulge. Continue up the groove on the left which soon leads to easier ground. Step right to a good belay ledge.

4 **40m** Continue by easy slabs up the crest to the base of the final steep wall on *Cioch West*.

8 Cioch Direct ★★ 180m Severe 4a
FA Henry Harland & Ashley Abraham 1907

An excellent well polished classic and a significant breakthrough for its time. Rated *"exceptionally severe"* by the first ascentionists, the crux chimney still provides a few anxious moments. Start beneath a large open chimney groove, 6m down and right of a little rock shelter built into the base of the cliff.

1 **25m 4a** Ascend the open chimney (easier by the slab on the left, if dry) to a belay.

2 **35m** Continue more pleasantly up the easy-angled groove to the base of the main open chimney.

3 **35m 4a** Climb the chimneys above, negotiating the tight upper chimney with interest (crux). Belay on the left, just above a Y-fork.

4 **50m** Follow a sloping shelf leading up left, passing underneath the prominent 'yardarm' block. Continue the traverse then climb steep parallel cracks to belay on easier slabs above.

5 **35m** Climb slabs and a groove on the right past flakes/boulders to the Terrace.

9 Cioch Grooves ★★ 145m HVS 5b
FA Ian McNaught-Davis & G.Francis (2 PA) 9 September 1951

Very good climbing, following a parallel line just left of *Cioch Direct*. Left of *Cioch Direct* a grass ledge runs rightwards onto the buttress. Start at the right end of this at a crack near a corner.

1 **30m 4c** Follow the crack to a steepening, step left and climb another crack which leads to easier slabs. Climb these then move right to belay below and left of the crux chimney of *Cioch Direct*.

2 **25m 5b** Move back left and climb a steep wall on the left to a block. Make a thin traverse right (crux) and a delicate step up onto a slab above and continue to belay beneath a fine crack.

3 **25m 4a** The crack leads to easier slabs.

4+5 **65m** Continue by the leftmost crack and easier slabs.

ISLE OF SKYE SRON NA CICHE

10 Bastinado ★★ 95m E2 6a
FA John Cunningham, John Allan & Bill Smith 16 July 1956; Variation: Dougie Dinwoodie & Colin McLean 25 July 1983

Fine well protected climbing with a mean strenuous crux. Start 20m left of *Cioch Grooves*, beneath a slightly left-slanting crack.

1. **36m 4c** Climb up to the crack and follow it to a broad grassy ledge.
2. **11m 5c** Climb the corner (very bouldery) then trend left to a sloping ledge.
3. **12m 6a** Traverse left 2m and climb a strenuous groove (crux) to good holds leading right to belay in a triangular corner. A worthy *Variation* (also 5b) climbs the obvious groove and jam crack right of the original route.
4. **36m 4b** Follow the crack immediately behind the corner to the top.

11 Little Gully ★★ 140m Difficult
FA Guy Barlow 1900s

An excellent little route with a fine through route, taking the small gully to the west of Eastern Gully.

1. **50m** Climb easily by either branch to belay at the back of large ledge below the chokestone.
2. **10m** Negotiate the narrow triangular slot at the back of the chokestone by an energetic struggle to gain a large recess above.
3. **30m** Continue directly until the gully steepens. Escape by an easy left-slanting ramp.
4. **50m** Continue and scramble up slabs to finish.

12 Stormy Petrel ★ 65m VS 5a
FA Steve Hill 13 June 1988

Start right of *Petronella* at a thin crack. Climb this until it runs out, traverse left 3m then up to an undercut. A delicate rock-over leads to easier ground trending right. Scramble to finish.

13 Petronella ★ 65m VS 4c
FA G.Francis & Edward Wrangham 29 June 1952

The prominent left-curving crack up the centre of the buttress. Climb the crack, turning the overhangs by a shelf on the left to an airy finish.

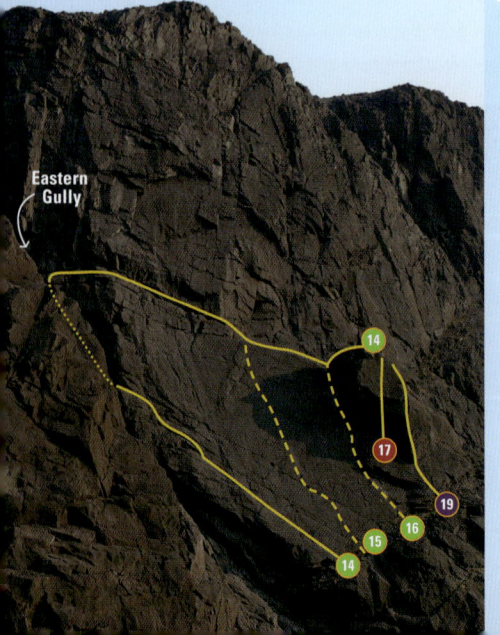

CIOCH & CIOCH SLAB   1¾hr

In the centre of the cliff is a beautiful sheet of low-angled pockmarked gabbro with the unique unmistakable and justly famous landmark of the Cioch block rearing up above its right (west) end. The top of the Cioch is one of the finest picnic spots around. Evidently popular, as it comes complete with its own resident gull, looking for leftovers!

Approach: Usually by a route on the lower tier – **Cioch Buttress**, or easily by **The Terrace** – a right-slanting shelf rising from the base of **Eastern Buttress**, starting about 100m beyond **Eastern Gully** (the lower section of *Collie's Route*).

Descents: By a 40m abseil from thread belay (slings in situ) down *Slab Corner*. Alternatively, a 25m abseil leads to easy scrambling in the lower section. In the dry, competent parties can descend either by *Collie's Route*, or by a diagonal fault (Moderate) spiralling (clockwise) from the neck down the west side of the Cioch, overlooking *Cioch Gully*. A traverse right across the easy glacis at the top of *Cioch West* leads to the west end of **The Terrace** at the base of **Cioch Slab**.

14 Collie's Route ★★★   180m Moderate
FA John Mackenzie & Norman Collie July 1906

"We traversed slabs, we worked up cracks and went right away from the Cioch into the gully on the east side, losing sight of the Cioch altogether. Then we fortunately found a queer traverse that led out of the gully across the perpendicular face of the cliff and back in the direction of the Cioch. But the Cioch itself we could not see, until having got round several corners, suddenly it came into view and we found ourselves on the end of the knife-edge. We sat down on that knife-edge and slowly made our way to the great rock tower at its end, up this we climbed and John and I were mightily pleased." – Norman Collie

From the base of the slab, follow deep twin cracks (lowest and most prominent of several) rising leftwards towards the left edge of the slab and into Eastern Gully. Scramble up this for 18m then traverse back right along a narrow incut shelf. Just beyond some exposed moves past some large blocks the Cioch comes back into view. Continue down the shelf past an easy narrow chimney to a wide grassy platform, where a now somewhat polished narrow ridge leads down to the 'neck'. Step left and up a short wide crack or the ridge directly above to the top. Excellent picnic spot!

15 Arrow Route ★★★   60m Very Difficult
FA Ian Allan 1944

Good climbing up the centre of the slab, sparsely protected in its upper reaches.
  1 20m Climb slightly leftwards up the slab to belay on the most prominent left-slanting diagonal fault.
  2 40m Step left and follow the vague crack above, trending slightly left up the slab above. A bold lead. Much variation possible.

16 Slab Corner ★   50m Difficult
FA unknown 1940s

Good climbing close to the right edge of the slab – not easy in the wet. Follow the obvious line, keeping to the left of the corner to a thread belay (in situ) beneath the neck of the Cioch. By scrambling up the initial 10m to start the route can be finished on the top of the Cioch in one long run out.

16a Slanting Crack ★   60m Severe 4a
FA unknown 1965

A spectacular airy route onto the Cioch, though slow to dry.
  1 44m Follow *Slab Corner* to the base of an obvious right-slanting traverse line leading out right.
  2 16m Climb over flakes and follow the slanting crack beneath a large overhang to an abrupt finish.

Arrow Route, Cioch Slab. Martin Boyce climbing.

17 Overhanging Crack Variation ★★ 45m E2 5b
FA unknown 1965; FFA Murray Hamilton & Geoff Cohen 1978

Scramble up to the base of the prominent hand-crack. Climb the crack, finishing up easy slabs.

18 The Gathering ★★★ 30m E8 6b
FA Dave MacLeod (headpointed) June 2004

"One of the best climbs of its grade in Scotland, but also one of the most serious" – MacLeod

Tremendous climbing up the 'dark underside' of the Cioch. It follows the line of a faint diagonal seam leading to the first protection at a lonely spike in the middle of the wall. Belay on large friends at the base of the seam. Hard technical moves lead to a good crimp. Follow the seam for a few moves then break out right on pock marks with a tenuous sequence leading to good edges and the spike (good rest and sling runner). Continue rightwards past a diagonal crack (F) to gain the easier upper slabs. F7b+ish climbing.

19 The Highlander ★★★ 46m E6 6b
FA Grant Farquhar & Gary Latter 21 April 1989

A stunning pitch up the front arête of the Cioch. Climb easy slabs to the arête. Climb boldly up the right side of the arête to an obvious hole (runners in flake on the right). Continue via a thin diagonal crack to a resting ledge (crucial friends, including F #2.5). Move up to a large flat hold on the arête (RPs) and stand on it with difficulty. A tricky mantelshelf gains the upper slab and easy ground.

20 Cioch Nose ★★ 40m Very Difficult
FA unknown

An excellent exposed finale up the western edge of the Cioch.

1 **15m** From the right end of the Terrace, follow a groove to belay in a short corner.
2 **25m** Traverse left onto a delicate slab and up this to gain the sharp left edge of a steep left-slanting groove. Step into the groove and follow it and the wonderful knife-edge above to the top of the Cioch.

Grant Farquhar on first ascent of The Highlander.

Barry Rose on the superb first pitch of Integrity, Cioch Upper Buttress.

CIOCH UPPER BUTTRESS

1¾hr

The steep buttress immediately above **Cioch Slab**, usually approached by a route on that crag. All the routes end on a glacis just beneath the top, which gives a straightforward scramble to exit at a short step up its left edge.

21 Piety ★★   90m VS 4c
FA Neil Horn & Colin Moody 2 June 1985

Fine climbing up the corner at the left side of the face.
1. **45m 4c** Climb the corner to its top then move left to belay.
2. **45m 4b** Go back right to a hanging arête and climb this to finish up slabs.

22 Atropos Direct ★★   80m E1 5b
FA Hamish MacInnes & Ian Clough (A3) 29 May 1958;
FFA Direct: Mick Fowler & Phil Thomas June 1977

Follows a line of cracks left of and parallel to *Integrity*. Start 6m left of *Integrity*.
1. **20m 5b** Climb the wall to gain a slab then follow a crack to the stance.
2. **30m 4b** Move up left through the overlap to an easy crack leading to the next overhang. Climb this leftwards to a stance on the lip.
3. **30m 5a** Step right and climb the wall to easy ground.

23 Integrity ★★★★   65m HS 4b
FA Derek Haworth & Ian Hughes 11 July 1949

A much climbed classic with an immaculate first pitch. Very well protected. Start beneath a prominent inverted-V.
1. **40m 4b** Climb the steep initial section to pull up onto an immaculate crack splitting the slab. This leads into a right-facing corner. Climb this, crossing an overhang on good holds to belay on a fine ledge beneath a larger roof.
2. **25m 4b** Continue directly by either of the twin cracks.

24 Trophy Crack ★★   70m E1 5b
FA Pat Walsh & Harry McKay 16 July 1956

Well protected climbing, tackling the prominent crack right of *Integrity*. Start by a pinnacle, at the back of the grass patch.
1. **40m 5b** Climb stooply to a groove then up this past a short overhang. Above, laybacking

leads to the crux then step left to the belay.

2 **30m 5a** Continue up the easy crack above then over the large overlap direct, finishing up the widening crack.

25 Kruggerand ** 76m E3 6a
FA Pete Hunter & Cameron Lees 17 May 1980

Another fine well protected route, taking the hanging finger-crack right of *Trophy Crack*. Start 6m right of *Trophy Crack*.

1 **23m 6a** Climb the slab to a large roof. Surmount this on finger-jams then the crack above (crux) to a hanging stance.

2 **23m 5a** Climb up slightly left and pull over the next roof then traverse back right to a crack and follow it to the belay on *Trophy Crack*.

3 **30m** Climb the slab parallel to *Trophy Crack*, crossing the roof by a small ledge. Finish directly up the slab.

26 Wallwork's Route ** 65m Very Difficult
FA W.Wallwork, Harry Kelly & John Wilding 1915

An excellent upper pitch, compensating for the innumerable tottering blocks on the first pitch. Scramble up and right from the right end of the grass ledge then descend a short slab to belay at the base of prominent vertical dyke.

1 **25m** Climb the dyke then move out right beneath a fierce crack. Climb diagonally left up a wide dyke past some tottering blocks then negotiate further blocks steeply to belay just above.

2 **40m** Step out right and over the flake-boulder above then climb a short, tricky corner capped by a small overhang. Continue more easily by a good crack in the slab above, veering diagonally right to avoid a large roof.

27 Archer Thomson's Route ** 70m Very Difficult
FA James Archer Thomson & party September 1911

1 **25m** As for *Wallwork's Route*.

2 **45m** Follow *Wallwork's Route* for 12m then the steep shelf on the right leading to the lower end of the glacis.

The following three routes lie above **The Terrace**.

28 Rib of Doom ** 75m VS 4c
FA C.Smith & A.Cleland June 1949

Fine spectacularly positioned climbing up the rib left of *Crack of Doom*. Start by following *Crack of Doom* to below the crack. Traverse left towards the rib and gain it via a subsidiary groove. Ascend the fine rib to gain the glacis.

29 Crack of Doom Direct ** 165m HS 4b
FA D.Pye & Leslie Shadbolt August 1918; Dt. Approach: Brenda Ritchie & C.Douglas Milner June 1936; Dt. Finish: Alfred Piggott & John Wilding June 1921

An historic route. The prominent curving crack is actually an insecure and usually damp 'thrutch', but the remainder of the route more than compensates. Ascend *Cioch Gully* to the grass terrace which goes out right from a large chokestone in the gully. Start from a point 10m above the grass terrace.

1 **21m** Climb a short square corner to a short slab then diagonally rightwards to an open 'V'. Climb this by the left side to belay beside a detached block.

2 **18m** Descend to the foot of the 'V' and climb rightwards round another slab then by a steep corner to a narrow ledge.

3 Traverse right 2m then climb a steep shallow groove which joins the lower section of *Crack of Doom* about 15m below the terrace.

4 **12m** Climb the crack to a chokestone.

5 **4b** The crack steepens and narrows. Strenuous and often damp, but can be avoided by climbing the wall on the left (4a).

6 **4b** Continue direct up 'very steep rocks' to the top.

30 Crack of Double Doom ** 90m VS 4b
FA Derek Haworth & Ian Hughes 21 May 1947

Fine climbing up the arrow-shaped fault right of *Crack of Doom*. Ascend the fault to the apex of the slab and pull through this to belay beneath a steep corner. Finish up this to gain the lower end of the glacis.

ISLE OF SKYE SRON NA CICHE

1¾hr

EASTERN BUTTRESS

WEST FACE

The face right of *Direct Route*, overlooking **Eastern Gully** and **Cioch Slab**. Although it faces south-west, it is shaded by **Cioch Upper Buttress** until the afternoon.
Approach: Up **The Terrace** or via one of the routes on **Cioch Buttress**.

31 Direct Route ★★　　　　　**180m Very Difficult**
FA Ernest Steeple, Guy Barlow & A.Doughty 1912

Very popular and polished, climbing the edge of the buttress overlooking Eastern Gully.
- **1 20m** Climb the edge on crumbly rock.
- **2 40m** Move left and up a short steep chimney then grooves close to the edge to a good ledge.
- **3 45m** Walk left and climb a narrow chimney then easier up grooves and slab to belay in a niche.
- **4+5 75m** Continue by a crack up the left wall then more easily up broken ground above.

The series of chimneys and corners trending right across the face is 32 *Chimney Route* ★ Difficult. The following four routes are gained by scrambling up from **The Terrace**. All finish up the upper section of *Direct Route*.

33 Trojan Groove ★　　　　　**30m HVS 5a**
FA Ian Heys & K.Roberts July 1965

The leftmost corner.

34 Helen ★★★　　　　　**40m E3 6a**
FA Steve Hill & Colin Moody 31 July 1994

So named as it comes between the Trojans and the Spartans, taking the arête between. Climb the initial bulge of *Spartan Groove* then move up left to a slanting crack which starts from a horizontal crack. Climb the slanting crack then the wall just right of the arête to finish up the arête.

35 Spartan Groove ★★　　　　　**40m E1 5b**
FA Ian Heys & J.Firth July 1965; Variation: Pete Hunter & Sonia Drummond 8 August 1980

The rightmost of the prominent twin corners. Climb the corner to a left-trending overhang, traverse right under this with difficulty then continue more easily. A *Direct Variation* pulls through the overhang by an undercut to a small ledge on the left, finishing more easily up the slab.

The dyke is 36 *The Joker* ★ Very Difficult.

37 Jack o' Diamonds ★★　　　　　**98m HS 4b**
FA Derek Leaver & C.Wilson July 1953
- **1 33m** Climb directly to a grass ledge at the foot of a chimney.
- **2 20m 4b** Climb the steep wall left of the chimney to a ledge at 5m then the steepening groove to a

conspicuous diamond-shaped block. Move right across the top of the block then by a short crack.
3 **33m** Follow a line of blocks and grooves directly above the foot of the final V-chimney.
4 **12m** Climb the chimney to join *Direct Route* below the penultimate (crux) pitch.

38 Shangri-La ★★★   132m VS 4c
FA Ian Clough & A.Nicholls 20 June 1964

Excellent sustained climbing following the continuous line of grooves on the right side of the face. Scramble up to the base.
1 **36m** Climb easy grooves parallel with Eastern Gully to a belay below an overhanging crack.
2 **25m 4b** Climb the crack or more easily by the left wall to a ledge then by an awkward wall and shallow chimney to block belays below an overhang.
3 **33m 4b** Climb the groove for some 15m, crossing the capping overhang direct.
4 **18m 4b** Climb the groove to a large ledge.
5 **20m 4c** Continue strenuously by the leftmost of the twin corners above.

39 Mistral Buttress ★★   105m VS 4c
FA Neil Horn & Colin Moody 16 June 1992

Good climbing up the buttress right of *Shangri-La*. Start approximately 15m right of *Shangri-La*.
1 **40m 4c** Follow a crack in a ramp up right, step right and follow a corner up to an overhang. Move right to belay at a block (the corner can be gained by moving left from the abseil point in Eastern Gully).
2 **50m 4b** Stand on the block and step left on to a slab. Move left to a dyke which is followed left to the buttress crest. Climb this to a ledge.
3 **15m 4b** Left of the right corner are twin cracks. Climb the right crack to an overhang, step left and follow both cracks to the top.

NG 447 204 **Alt:** 700m 1¾hr

An excellent compact buttress extending from **Eastern Gully** up the slope to the lower bouldery reaches of the **Sgumain Stone Shoot**.

Descent: From the top of *Vulcan Wall* area, traverse left (east) across easy angled slabs and down a shelf leading to the boulder field beneath the base of the **Sgumain Stone Shoot**.

MAGIC RECESS

The next three routes are located on an area of recessed rock just before the main steep mass of **Eastern Buttress** is reached on the approach up the boulder field. Quite sheltered and can be slow to dry.

40 Presdigitateur ★★   45m E1 5b
FA Bob Wightman & John Topping 17 June 1987

The rightmost of a trilogy of cracks, starting just right of *The Conjuror*. Climb the rightwards leaning crack to a ledge below a roof. Pull over this then move leftwards out of the groove across the wall to follow the right rib of *The Conjuror* to the top. Finishing direct up the groove reduces the grade to an equally worthy HVS 5a.

41 The Conjuror **   45m E3 5c
FA Murray Hamilton & Rab Anderson 24 May 1983

The steep central crack, 6m right of *Magic*. Climb the corner to a roof and follow the thin crack-line above to the top.

42 Magic ***   45m E4 6a
FA Dave Cuthbertson & Gary Latter 19 June 1982

The leftmost crack. Climb the flake and slab leading to a small overhang in the corner, move right to gain the crack and follow this and corners above to the top.

Continuing up, on the main face:

43 The Snake ***   110m HVS 4c
FA Bill Sproul, Jim Renny & J.Hall 9 August 1965

Fine steady climbing up the blatantly obvious trap fault in the centre of the face. Sparsely protected.

1 **35m 4a** Go up the fault to a small ledge.
2 **35m 4c** Continue up the fault to belay in a groove.
3 **40m 4a** Finish up the fault to the crest of the buttress.

44 Strappado Direct **   95m E2 5c
FA Direct Start George Szuca & Colin Moody 13 June 1988;
Direct Finish Pete Hunter & Cameron Lees 16 May 1980

A better more direct line to the right of the original route.

1 **25m 5a** Climb up to the crack in the slab just left of *The Snake* and climb it (poor protection) to ledge.
2 **35m 5b** Climb the dyke to a slight overhang, traverse right to a lodge, then climb straight up the crack above to a niche.
3 **35m 5c** Climb the arête on the left leading to easy ground.

45 Enigma ***   135m E3 5c
FA Dougie Mullin & Murray Hamilton May 1979

The main pitch follows the fine crack in the steep wall well left of the upper pitches of *The Snake*. Start about 12m right of *Creagh Dhu Grooves* at the right end of a large flat ledge with a deep crevasse at the back.

1 **36m 5a** Climb the wall, first by a left-slanting groove then slightly rightwards by cracks to belay over on the left.
2 **24m 5b** Climb easily right and up, crossing *Strappado* to a thin right-slanting corner-crack; climb this until a large overlap and traverse right to belay on a well situated ledge.
3 **36m 5c** Gain and climb the crack splitting the wall above on the left to belay beyond the final overhang.
4 **39m** Continue easily up the crack.

46 Zephyr *   80m E5 6a
FA Dave Cuthbertson & Duncan McCallum 13 June 1982

The first E5 in the Cuillin. The difficulties are very short lived. Start just right of *Creagh Dhu Grooves*, below a slab leading to a small roof.

1 **40m 5a** Turn the roof on the left then follow flakes and grooves to a large ledge.
2 **20m 6a** Gain a small ledge on arête and up to a horizontal break, then move left round the arête into a slim bottomless groove. Up this and a slab to a small ledge.
3 **20m 4c** Move left and up the wall to the top.

47 Creagh Dhu Grooves ***   90m E3 5c
FA Hamish MacInnes & Ian Clough (some aid) 1957;
FFA Gabriel Regan & Richard McHardy 1977

The striking chimney and hanging grooves in the centre of the face. Pitches 2-4 can readily be run together.

1 **40m 4b** Ascend the obvious chimney behind a huge flake to a chokestone, continuing to a large ledge on the right.
2 **12m 5c** Climb the cracked groove bearing slightly left to a small stance.
3 **25m 5c** Continue up the groove above over two bulges then easier by the right edge to a broad ledge.
4 **13m** Continue more easily to the top.

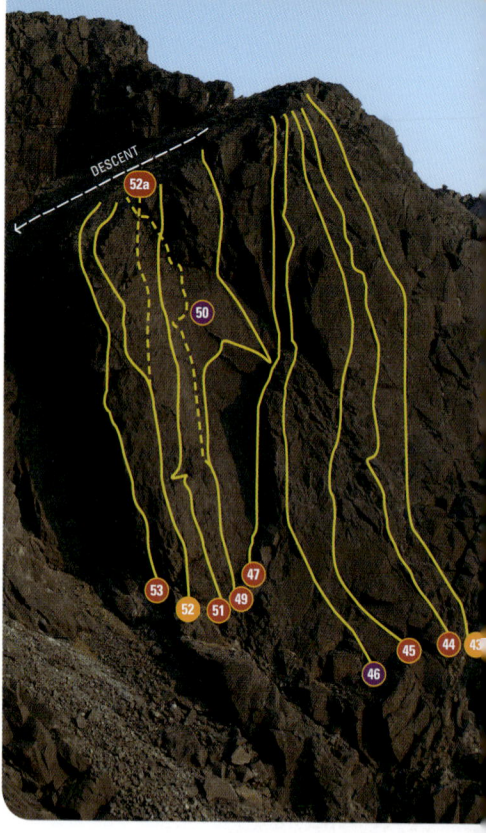

48 Pocks ★★ 85m E3 5c

FA George Szuca & Colin Moody 13 June 1988;
Pitch 2 Neil Smith & Colin Moody 7 June 1992

Fine varied climbing.

1. **35m 5b** Start up *Creagh Dhu Grooves* for 6m then climb a crack on the left to an overlap (*Dilemma* goes over the overlap here). Move right to a ledge, step right then boldly climb the overlap. Move up right to *Creagh Dhu Grooves* belay. A magic pitch.
2. **50m 5c** Climb a steep crack just right of *Creagh Dhu Grooves* to a slab. Follow the slab right to an arête then continue up right to reach a crack leading to the top.

49 Dilemma ★★★ 75m E3 5c

FA Mick Fowler & Phil Thomas 21 June 1977

The original line up the centre of the wall. Start at a thin vertical crack in the centre of the wall.

1. **42m 5c** Climb the crack then move up right to a hanging corner at the left end of the overlap. Go up the corner, then pull out rightwards to gain a descending traverse line down right leading to a small niche just left of the large ledge on *Creagh Dhu Grooves*.
2. **33m 5c** Follow the crack diagonally left up the slab then its continuation steeply through the overhangs to the top.

> An obvious combination of *Dilemma* and *Uhura* gives 49a *Diura* ★★★ E3 5c, 5b.

50 Clinging On ★★★ 65m E4 6a

FA Kev Howett & Scott Muir 12 May 2001

Superb climbing, plugging the final gap on the wall. Start as for *Dilemma*.

1. **55m 6a** A sustained pitch. Climb the initial crack of *Dilemma* to its end then move up to gain the obvious vertical crack just on the left. Follow this to where it fades into tiny cracks and gain an obvious small protruding block above. Step onto the block then left to a foot ledge on *Uhuru*. Step back right and gain a thin crack which leads with difficulty to better holds leading up and right into a final crack under the roofs. Traverse 2m left past the roofs to a vertical crack.
2. **10m 5a** Climb up and left to below a projecting block then hand-traverse out left to finish.

51 Uhura ★★★ 70m E3 6a

FA Kev Howett & Tom Prentice 22 July 1990

Excellent climbing up the fine crack-line in the silver-streaked wall between *Vulcan Wall* and *Dilemma*. Start at cracks just left of the vertical crack of *Dilemma*.

1. **25m 5c** Climb to a small overlap and follow the crack above to a hard move right to gain the ledge on *Vulcan Wall*. Traverse left to flake block belay.
2. **45m 6a** Step right off the block, up cracks and move right over a curving overlap. Move up and right to pull into the main crack which is followed with

difficulty to better holds. Continue up the excellent crack to finish right of the large precarious block.

52 Vulcan Wall ★★★★   70m HVS 5a
FA Hamish MacInnes, John Temple & Ian Clough (some aid) 30 May 1957

Start at the left side of the main wall, just right of the left arête. VW scratched at base.
1 **25m 5a** Climb to a ledge and belay.
2 **45m 5a** Move up to a ledge left of the block then follow cracks to a small ledge on the right. Traverse diagonally left to better holds and continue close to the edge to belay 6m back from the top.

52a The Chambre Finish ★★   45m E2 5c
FA Gary Latter & Dave Cuthbertson 19 June 1982

From the small ledge where the normal route goes left onto easier ground, ascend the thinner and leftmost of two parallel cracks.

53 Spock ★★★   70m E3 5c
FA Pete Hunter & Cameron Lees 18 May 1980

Brilliant climbing up the right edge of the steep left wall. Start 6m left of *Vulcan Wall*.
1 **40m 5c** Follow overhanging cracks on the arête then continue in the same line through a shallow groove to belay above a prominent roof.
2 **30m 5a** Go diagonally right to finish up the steep crack left of *Vulcan Wall*.

SGURR SGUMAIN
(MOUND OR STACK PEAK)

WEST BUTTRESS
1½hr
NG 444 206 **Alt:** 510m

The large slabby crag between upper Coire Lagan and the **Sgumain Stone Shoot**.
Approach: Follow the path from the campsite up into Coire Lagan and cross glaciated rocks on the right side of the loch, dropping down a little to gain a right-slanting rake leading up to the base.
Descent: Go right and down the **Sgumain Stone Shoot**. To return to the base, scramble down the straightforward right-slanting rake.

1 The Slant ★   120m Difficult
FA Tony Greenbank, John Wilkinson & D.Murray 1 Sept 1958

A good natural line crossing diagonally left across the face. Start up slabby rocks to the left of the white blaze (of *Sunset Slab*) and proceed to an open chimney. Climb this, finishing up a fine wall on excellent rough rock.

ISLE OF SKYE SGURR SGUMAIN

Jules Lines on Vulcan Wall.
Photo Dave Cuthbertson, Cubby Images.

Karen Latter on the initial pitch of Sunset Slab and Yellow Groove.

② The Klondyker ★★★   130m E1 5b
FA Andy Tibbs & Derek Bearhop 3 May 1988

"I remember the 4c pitch being space-walking on buckets, one of the most exposed and out there VS pitches I had ever done." – Jules Lines, Skye is the Limit, *Scottish Mountaineering Club Journal*, 2004

A recommended route with some fine climbing. Start about 8m below the white blaze directly below a chimney on *The Slant*.

1 **30m 4b** Climb diagonally leftwards up a slab for 10m to gain a corner left of the initial shallow chimney on *The Slant*. Layback up a corner until it is possible to move rightwards to a cracked slab which leads to a belay at the foot of a steep impressive wall.

2 **30m 5b** Climb by a small corner and cracks to gain the left side of a large sloping ledge about half-way up the steep wall. Gain a weak crack-line above from a perched block on the left, follow this and the wider crack above through an overhang to belay on a large ledge next to an old peg. Joint belay with *Sunset Slab*. An improbable looking pitch for the grade.

3 **15m 4a** Climb the groove above (as for *Sunset Slab*) until an easy left traverse can be made to a ledge at the foot of an obvious groove with a yellow left wall.

4 **30m 4c** Move left round an edge into an exposed position and climb up leftwards past an overhang to a basalt recess. Climb up to a small well positioned ledge and up a short wall to a belay.

5 **25m** Move rightwards and finish up the painfully rough arête.

Both the grooves with yellow left walls have also been climbed at HVS 5a, 4c ★★.

③ Sunset Slab & Yellow Groove ★★   170m VS 4c
FA J.Foster & B.Blake 13 July 1951; Ian Clough, D.Temple, M.Battle & B.Fein (1 PA) 30 June 1964

A fine logical combination, straightening out the original line which traversed out right. Start by scrambling up about 30m to a prominent white blaze at foot crack in slab.

1 **50m 4a** Follow the left-slanting slab (above and parallel to the larger line of *The Slant*) to belay at the base of a steep crack on the right wall.

2 **25m** Ascend the crack for 15m then

traverse right to a belay.
3 **18m** Climb to a corner below an overhanging crack.
4 **12m 4c** Avoid the crack by the wall on the left to a ledge at 6m. Continue up the crack (crux) to large grassy ledge.
5 **15m 4b** Climb an easy slab and move round a corner up a steep groove, moving left to belay on a ledge beneath an overhang.
6 **50m 4a** Climb rightwards to a shallow spike on the arête. Climb the arête, avoiding a steep section near the top by moving out rightwards. Finish by a short steep corner and easy scrambling.

3a Nuggets ★★ 15m HVS 5a
FA Gary & Karen Latter 8 May 2006

About 10m left of the belay at the top of pitch 1 of *Sunset Slab & Yellow Groove* is a striking diagonal crack. Climb it, pulling out right at the top on good holds. Traverse down right to regain the parent route.

COIR' A' GHRUNNDA

THE ALASDAIR /THEARLAICH CLIFFS

Two fine steep very quick drying cliffs immediately beneath the summits of Sgurr Alasdair and Sgurr Thearlaich overlooking the bare rocky upper reaches of Coir' a' Ghrunnda.

Approach: The shortest approach is by Coire Lagan and up the **Sgumain Stone Shoot** (underneath the base of Sron na Ciche) to reach Bealach Coir' a' Ghrunnda. There is a wonderfully situated spring beneath the scree cone beneath the base. To gain this, traverse across scree, skirting beneath a couple of small crags. To gain the base directly, follow the path up the ridge a short way then try

NG 450 207 **Alt:** 850m 2¼ – 2½hr
to follow a vague path, again skirting the base of crags to gain a good path running beneath the base of the cliffs.
Descent: The top of the **Alasdair (Great) Stone Shoot** lies on the ridge just a short way above, leading to a rapid descent into upper Coire Lagan. To return to the base of the cliff traverse Sgurr Alasdair and descend its south-west ridge to gain the Alasdair-Sgumain col, avoiding the Bad Step by the shallow chimney low down on its left. Alternatively, abseil into the TD gap (25m from in situ slings) then descend the mainly scree-filled **Thearlach Dubh Gully** (Moderate) to the base of the cliffs.

Nuggets. Gary Latter on first ascent. Photo Karen Latter.

Commando Crack, Karen Latter climbing.

① Commando Crack ★★★   75m HS 4b
FA Anthony 'Ginger' Cain & B.Dobson July 1950

Excellent exciting climbing up the prominent chimney-crack, the first obvious line from the left. Start 30m left of the prominent large black gully.

1. **10m 4a** Go up a rib right of a crack for 3m then traverse into the chimney on the left and continue up it to belay by a pinnacle on the left.
2. **18m 4b** Climb the wall on the right for a short way then traverse into the chimney, crossing the overhang with difficulty to a block belay on the left.
3. **12m 4a** Return to the crack on the right and climb it to belay in a 'sentry box' beneath an overhanging chokestone.
4. **10m 4a** Thread the chokestone (through route) then get on to the nose on the left and go up to belay.
5. **25m 4b** Layback up the right crack, crossing to left crack which soon leads to easier scrambling. (The top of the Alasdair Stone Shoot lies up to the right).

② The Asp ★★   75m E2 5b
FA John McLean, Bill Smith & Willie Gordon 20 July 1965

Superb well protected climbing up the steep crack 10m right of *Commando Crack*.

1. **40m 5b** Climb an easy open V-groove leading to the base of the main crack. The steep crack widens at 9m to a V-groove. Climb it, mainly by chimneying, crossing an overhang with a difficult move left (crux) to gain the wide upper crack (large Fs). Belay on the ledge above.
2. **35m 5b** Continue up the crack above then easy scrambling to finish.

③ Con's Cleft ★★   60m E1 5b/c
FA John McLean, Bill Smith & Willie Gordon 20 July 1965

Good well protected climbing taking the most prominent corner on the face about 30m left of the **Thearlaich-Dubh Gap**.

1. **15m 5b/c** The corner starts 8m up; the entry overhangs and is the crux. Scramble up right to belay at the base. Climb up to and cross the overhang (crux) on good jams (F #3.5 or #4 useful) and continue up the crack to belay on a good ledge.
2. **10m 4c** Ascend the corner to another ledge.
3. **35m 4c** Continue directly up the fine sustained corner-crack.

Karen Latter and Helen Konkol on the superb main pitch of Grand Dièdre.

Helen Konkol on the initial pitch of Grand Dièdre.

NG 452 207 **Alt:** 850m

THEARLAICH-DUBH BUTTRESS

The section of cliff right of the **Thearlaich-Dubh Gap**.
Descent: Head right (south-east) down the main ridge with a 15m abseil down steep wall (sling in situ on block) towards Bealach Coir' an Lochain, then scramble down right, cutting back right to regain the base.

4 Grand Dièdre ★★★ 60m VS 4c

FA Hamish MacInnes, Ian Clough & Doc Pipes 1 June 1958

Very good well protected climbing up the central dièdre. Start by scrambling up to the base of a prominent right-facing corner.

1 **20m 4c** Climb the fine corner to belay on a good ledge at the base of the upper dièdre.
2 **40m 4c** Climb the dièdre over an overhang (crux) to a small ledge (possible belay). Continue up the dièdre to top.

SGURR MHIC CHOINNICH
(MACKENZIE'S PEAK)

NG 449 213 **Alt:** 780m 2¼hr

COIREACHAN RUADHA FACE

"I stood awestruck at the size of the cliffs and the blatantly obvious unclimbed lines. It was like the cliff that time forgot." – Jules Lines, Skye is the Limit, *Scottish Mountaineering Club Journal*, 2004

Coireachan Ruadha lies on the north-east (Coruisk) side of the ridge between Sgurr Dearg and Sgurr Mhic Choinnich. The face contains some of the best long routes of their grade in the Cuillin in a fine secluded location.

Approach: From upper Coire Lagan scramble up easy rocks to the right of the An Stac screes to the ridge. Descend with care the loose nasty aptly-named **Rotten Gully** for 90m and gain a terrace on the right running beneath the Upper Cliff. Sacks can be left by blocks 20m from the top.

Fluted Buttress ★★　　　　　　　210m VS 4b

FA Bill Brooker & Mike Dixon 1 August 1950

Fine climbing at a reasonable standard. Start on the

terrace to the right of *Cocoa Cracks*. Climb a small rib for 7m then traverse for 15m up under overhangs to a point where the overhang can be climbed to gain a ledge (30m). Follow the ledge to the right then climb an easy-angled chimney to where it steepens beneath the flutes. Traverse out right to a slab beneath a huge overhang. Follow the slab rightwards (right of the overhanging flute on the left) until it steepens then traverse out to the wall on the right. Delicate exposed climbing (crux) leads up and right to an 'easement' above the overhangs. Ascend a broken groove, trending back left to the centre of the buttress then a short groove leading to the terrace of *Crack of Dawn*. Finish up that route.

2 Cocoa Cracks ** 160m E2 5c
FA J.Barraclough & J.Cooper (2 PA) June 1969

The huge right-angled corner in the front of the buttress. Unfortunately, slow to dry. Scramble up a slab to the foot of the corner.

1 **20m** Climb the corner (often wet) to belay on a ledge on the right.
2 **20m** Climb a chimney above to belay below an overhang.
3 **15m 5c** Climb the overhang and continue up a wide chimney to belay in a nook.
4 **15m** Climb the narrowing chimney above via the right arête to reach easy ground. Belay at the next steepening.
5+6 **90m** Easier rocks lead into the *Crack of Dawn*. Finish up this.

3 Crack of Dawn ** 180m VS 5a
FA Bill Brooker & Mike Dixon 6 August 1951

"A terrific crack curved up the wall and soared into the mist, an awe-inspiring sight. A name at once sprang to my mind – "The crack of Dawn" – and I was filled with a desire to climb it." Mike Dixon, The Forgotten Corrie, Scottish Mountaineering Club Journal, 1952

Fine climbing taking the prominent slanting crack up the left side of *Fluted Buttress*.

1+2 **45m 5a, 4c** As for *Dawn Grooves*. Ascend the steep easier chimney to the top of the south-east wall then an easier angled crack slanting across the face until it fades (cairn). Go up a short steep crack immediately left of a small rib of clean rough rock, crossing the rib at the top and passing a large flake. Continue up to the left end of the terrace. Climb the little rib on the left by a crack on the crest to a ledge beneath a 'stupendous overhanging nose' split by a crack. Climb a hard crack in a groove in its right wall. Step left to a ledge then move back right to an easy groove and climb this to a recess. Traverse right to a ledge and go up it, climbing up and right over two small corners to finish on the ridge.

4 Dawn Grooves ** 180m HVS 5a
FA Dick Barclay & Bill Brooker 22 August 1958

Fantastic climbing up the grooves right of the great central cleft. Start beneath a crack which runs into a chimney at 45m.

1 **25m 5a** Ascend the crack to belay in a niche. A superb well protected pitch.
2 **20m 4c** Pull out of the niche and climb the overhanging crack for a few metres then make an exposed traverse across the wall on the right to gain the platform crossing the face.
3 **35m 4b** Climb the groove to belay on a small ledge.
4 **20m 4c** Traverse right 5m to a crack in the right wall. Ascend the crack then the slabby right edge of the buttress to a good ledge. Belay in a short corner.
5 **30m 5a** Climb the wall above then go right along a narrow shelf and climb a good crack to gain a long girdling ledge. Traverse left along this to belay at the base of a chimney which marks the line of grooves.
6 **20m 4c** Climb it to an overhang and exit left to a flake leading to a good ledge above. Move up to a good belay on the next ledge.
7 **30m 4c** Step right and up grooves then easy ground leading to a prominent deep V-groove. Climb this with interest to broken ground above. Scramble a short way to the summit ridge.

⑤ Mongoose Direct ★★★   195m E1 5b

FA Jeff Lamb & Pete Whillance summer 1974;
Direct: Mick Fowler & Phil Thomas 20 June 1977

Grand climbing up the great cleft splitting the centre of the buttress, though a natural drainage line and slow to dry. Start beneath the corner-crack.

1. **25m 5a** Climb the crack to a sloping ledge.
2. **20m 5a** Continue up the crack then a slab to the base of the deep groove.
3. **35m 5b** Climb a crack in the right wall leading to the groove and follow until it splits at a junction with *Dawn Grooves*. Continue up the prominent left branch which forms a clean-cut V-groove (crux) leading to a belay in a niche on the left.
4. **35m 5a** Continue up the chimney-groove leading to a fine spacious ledge.
5+6. **80m** Step up left across the overhang in the chimney, finishing up the fault leading to easy ground.

⑥ King Cobra ★★★   165m E1 5b

FA Chris Bonington & Tom Patey 14 August 1960

Excellent well protected climbing up the buttress immediately right of the left bounding gully. Start by scrambling up the gully for 45m to just beneath where it steepens then traverse right to a large flake at the base of the dièdre.

1. **25m 4c** Ascend the right wall of the dièdre to a large ledge.
2. **25m 5b** Traverse into another dièdre on the right, climb it then easier to a belay.
3. **15m 4b** Continue up the rib on the right easily to a shelf beneath a large overhang overlooking *Dawn Grooves*.
4. **35m 5a** Go up the wall 5m right of the continuation groove to a slab beneath the roof, traverse right then ascend a ramp to a V-groove leading to large overhangs. Move out onto the left wall of the groove, moving across to jammed spikes on the left then more easily up a short chimney.
5. **40m 4c** Traverse left across a slab into a chimney and follow it past a good ledge on the right to belay on a large platform.
6. **25m** Finish up a further chimney in the slender buttress.

⑥a King Cobra Direct ★   145m E3 5c

FA Brian Davison & H.Day 28 June 1992

1. **50m 4c, 5b** The first two pitches of *King Cobra*.
2. **45m 5c** As for pitch 3 up the rib to the shelf at the left end of the big overhang. Go through the left end of the overhang into a groove (crux) and follow this to a ledge with a chokestone in a wide corner-crack.
3. **50m 4c** Climb the corner and chimney to a large ledge then up a corner at the back of the ledge to belay on easy ground a few feet short of the top, gained by scrambling.

  2¼hr

NG 448 214 **Alt:** 700m

BEALACH BUTTRESS

The steep buttress immediately north of the **Coireachan Ruadha Face**, at a lower level.
Approach: As for the **Coireachan Ruadha Face**, descending with care Rotten Gully to a terrace running out left beneath the base of the **Coireachan Ruadha Face**. Sacks can be left by blocks 20m from the top. Alternatively, approach direct up the coire from Coruisk.

① Tinn Lamh Crack ★★   105m E1 5b

FA J.Barraclough & J.Cooper (1 PA) June 1969; FFA John Harwood 1972

The finely situated vertical crack near the centre of the vertical wall. The loose approach to the left-slanting *Thunderbolt Shelf* at mid-height is compensated by excellent climbing higher up. Start directly beneath the crack, level with the base of **Rotten Gully**.

1. **45m 4c** Traverse right along the prominent fault. Surmount a shattered overlap and go up a loose

slab to a grass landing. Go right and through a break to reach *Thunderbolt Shelf* 12m right of the crack.
2 **15m** Follow the shelf to belay left of the crack.
3 **45m 5b** Traverse right into the crack and climb it past a horizontal break (possible belay) at 25m. Continue up the crack, finishing with hard moves up the final steep wall.

2 Lightfoot ★★ 80m E3 6a
FA Murray Hamilton, Rab Anderson & Pete Whillance 24 June 1983

A good steep route amidst impressive surroundings. Start from *Thunderbolt Shelf*, gained by the initial pitch of *Tinn Lamh Crack*.
1 **40m 6a** Climb the obvious leaning corner in the centre of the face over a small roof and continue until moves can be made left to below a roof. Surmount this and move up right above the roof overlooking the corner until hard moves enable a small ledge to be gained.
2 **40m 5c** Follow the obvious crack line to the top.

3 Rainman ★★ 70m E4 5c
FA Pete Benson & Guy Robertson 18 June 2007

A fine route up the smooth right side of the big vertical wall. Start immediately left of a grassy recess below the prominent overlap on the bottom right of the wall (this point can be reached by abseil, or by starting up *Thunderbolt Shelf*).
1 **20m 5b** Climb up left to enter and climb the obvious groove at the left end of the overlap, then continue directly for a few metres to a semi-hanging belay at a small sloping ledge.
2 **30m 5c** Step left, then climb directly up (bold) passing just left of a large niche to gain an obvious sloping ledge. Continue up, then trend right to follow a vague crack line over a small overhang to a good rest. Continue up the crack to below a bigger overhang, pull through this and continue directly to a ledge below a short crack.
3 **20m 5a** Climb the crack, then escape out right to avoid a loose finish.

4 Pinnacle Face ★ 135m HS 4b
FA Mike Dixon & Roger Cra'ster 5 June 1954

Good climbing on solid clean rock, heading for the prominent pinnacle. Follow an easy shallow crack to the lower terrace (30m). Continue up the clean crack above then traverse right across the base of the pinnacle to belay in its right corner. Step back left into the crack from the top of the pinnacle and follow this to a ledge. Continue more easily up the face of the buttress to past a grass patch then a short steep wall, taken right of a basalt fault. Finish up and right above the upper terrace to the summit slopes.

Rainman, Pete Benson seconding the crux second pitch. Photo Guy Robertson.

ISLE OF SKYE KILT ROCK AREA

The coastline extending north from the outflow (waterfall) of Loch Mealt contains an impressive selection of columnar basalt cliffs, including the popular scenic attraction **Kilt Rock**. The views east over Raasay & North Rona and beyond to the hills of Applecross & Torridon are stunning.

Access: Follow the A850 north through Broadford to Portree (31 miles/44km) then turn right through the town onto the A855 and continue north for a further 15 miles/24km to a popular car park and viewpoint at the north-east end of Loch Mealt, just south of the small crofting township of Elishader.

Approach: The cliffs extend northwards for about 2km with **Kilt Rock** about 700m north along the coast (visible from the car park). Cross the stream over a couple of fences and follow the fence line round to the crags.

KILT ROCK 15min

NG 507 662 **Alt:** 50m

DESCENT GULLY AREA – NORTH WALL

1 Sporran ★ 20m E1 5b

FA Willie Jeffrey, Noel Williams & Pete Hunter 10 July 1983

20m down the gully is a J-shaped recess. Gain this and bridge up to holds on the left, reach a projecting block and climb onto it with difficulty. Finish more easily.

2 The Electric Bagpipe ★★ 30m HVS 5a

FA Noel Williams & Pete Hunter 10 July 1983

Start at a short left-facing corner 30m down the gully. Climb the corner and the continuation crack above. Step right and layback up the crack then direct up the wall above to a ledge. Move up and right to finish.

3 Clandestine ★★ 35m VS 5a

FA Noel Williams & Carolyn Hill 28 May 1983

A rising traverse line starting up the same corner as 2. Climb the corner then move right and up to a triangular recess. Step right again and climb a hand-crack to a ledge. Finish up the wide flake-crack above.

4 Brazen ★ 35m E2 5c

FA Pete Hunter & Noel Williams 18 July 1983

Start just down from 3. Gain a small overhung recess from the right with difficulty. Make a hard move up to better holds, join 3 and reach the triangular recess as for that route. Finish up the obvious crack.

5 Joik ★★ 40m E2 5c

FA Gary Latter & Carl Pulley 5 October 2005

Start just left of large flat boulder beneath twin intermittent cracks high in the wall. Climb up onto a small protruding ledge and wee left-facing corner. Continue up the cracks which soon lead to easier climbing up hand-cracks and a flake to a ledge. Finish up a short sporting offwidth forming the left side of a huge flake at the top.

6 Secret Service ★★★ 40m HVS 5a

FA Noel Williams & Pete Hunter 13 July 1983

Near the bottom of the gully a ledge runs horizontally out across the wall. Follow the ledge rightwards then move up to a platform above. Reach a corner and make some awkward moves to gain a leftwards slanting crack, follow this and reach the recess also used by 4. Take the right of the two parallel cracks, finishing up the right side of the pedestal above.

7 Tartan Terror ★★★ 40m E1 5b

FA Pete Hunter & Noel Williams 13 July 1983

Superb sustained climbing above the platform. Climb a broken groove just around the corner from 6 to reach the platform above (probably more pleasant to climb the first part of 6 to this point). Step out right and climb the steep hand-crack. 2 or 3 sets cams 2.5"–3" useful.

8 Skyeman ★★★ 40m E2 5c

FA Pete Hunter & Noel Williams 16 July 1983

Climb the crack in the groove immediately right of 7 to finish in the centre of the slab. Sustained and superb. Cams to 4", doubles particularly of 1"–2.5".

ISLE OF SKYE KILT ROCK AREA

9 Godzilla ★★★ 40m E3 6a
FA Emma Alsford & Paul Donnithorne 1 June 1999

The groove has some tricky moves low down and fine sustained climbing all the way to the top.

10 Wide-Eyed ★★ 40m E2 5b
FA Ed & Cynthia Grindley 22 May 1983

The chimney crack in the corner.

FRONT FACE

Descent: The remaining routes are best approached by abseil. Take 2 spare 50m ropes (one to link stakes). Most have hanging belays at the base.

11 Edge of Beyond ★★★ 45m E2 5c
FA Pete Hunter & Willie Jeffrey 10 July 1983

The next groove right with an excursion onto the left bounding arête at half height. (Climbing the groove throughout is E3 6a.) There is a large boulder at the top of the route.

Unknown climber on the crag classic Grey Panther.

12 Grey Panther ★★★★ 45m 5.10a/E1 5b
FA Ed Grindley, Noel Williams, Willie Jeffrey & Pete Hunter 9 July 1983

Excellent sustained climbing up the groove/recess. Nuts & cams to 4", though >3" not essential.

13 Internationale ★★★★ 45m E3 5c
FA Dick Swinden & Ed Grindley 1 May 1983

The conspicuous jam crack right of 12, moving right to finish. Many large cams to 4".

14 Iron-Crow ★★ 40m E3 5c
FA Dougie Dinwoodie & Brian Lawrie 15 April 1987

The thin crack-line. Good grass stance at bottom. Start up the right crack to a roof. Pull left round the roof and up the crack to the top of a big flake. Climb the crack-line to the top.

> The leftwards slanting lichenous crack is 15 *Footloose* ★ E3 5c.

16 Ruination ★★ 45m E3 5c
FA Pete Hunter 16 July 1983

The fine sustained crack in the shallow groove. Start up 15 for 6m then continue straight up the groove with hard moves to gain the girdle ledge. Finish on slightly broken rock.

17 Road to Ruin ★★★ 45m E2 5b
FA Ed Grindley, Dick Swinden & Noel Williams 31 April 1983

The wide jam crack just left of an obvious chossy chimney. At the top, move right and climb on the left wall of the chimney for the last few moves. Cams up to 5–6" useful.

18 Killer Whale ★★ 35m E4 6a
FA Bill Birkett & Dave Lyle 30 August 1983

The prominent crack up the great open corner right of the chossy gully. Start at a small ledge above the limestone band. Climb the right crack for 25m, move into the left crack for 3m then up and left to finish.

SOUTH OF TEMPEST BUTTRESS
NG 507 663 **Alt:** 50m 15min
Descent: From the base of the **Tempest Buttress** descent gully, head right (south) towards **Kilt Rock** for 100m to a buttress with an obvious block roof on its left side. Stakes 10m back.

❶ Frisky After Whisky ★★   45m E2 5c
FA Luke Steer & Craig Hannah 2 June 1993

A large 'Indian's Nose' shaped block roof can be clearly identified heading north along the cliff top from **Kilt Rock**. The route follows twin cracks up the recess just left of the roof. The right crack is finger-sized, the left a chimney/offwidth. Originally climbed on a wet day – *"Was that wet we visited Talisker Distillery first and sampled a couple of drams."*

❷ Fe Fi Fo Fum ★★★   45m E3 5c
FA Crispin Waddy & Guy Percival 9 June 1987

A brilliant sustained jamming pitch. Start 10m or so right of the block roof below a crack just right of an arête. Climb this finishing right over blocks.

TEMPEST BUTTRESS
NG 507 664 **Alt:** 50m 15min
Lies approximately 200m north of **Kilt Rock**.
Descents: Go down the easy south leading gully 150m north of **Kilt Rock** or abseil to the base from small and medium cams.

❶ The Tempest ★★   45m E3 6a
FA Bob Wightman & Bill Birkett 28 May 1984

Seems unlikely at the grade. This takes a striking line; a distinct crack right of a hanging column. Move up from the ledge and then right via a flake handhold to a thin crack. Up this (crux) to a wider crack, enter a niche and at the top climb directly up an awkward little offwidth.

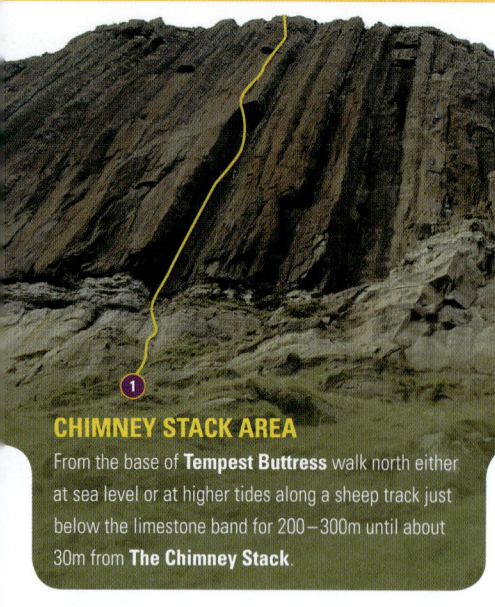

CHIMNEY STACK AREA

NG 507 666 **Alt:** 50m 20min

From the base of **Tempest Buttress** walk north either at sea level or at higher tides along a sheep track just below the limestone band for 200–300m until about 30m from **The Chimney Stack**.

1 Ill Wind ★★★   75m E5 6b
FA Crispin Waddy & Guy Percival 10 June 1987

Three superb pitches. There is a large groove leading to a hexagonal roof with a straight finger-crack rising from its left side and a groove to its right. Start on the grass below the groove.

1 **35m 6a** Zigzag up grass and soft lime/sandstone with care to gain base of the groove (Hex #7 & two #2 RPs). Climb groove, continuously technical and interesting, to belay 3m below the roof. (Some gear in a crack on the right at the start.)

2 **10m 6b** Continue to the roof and *a cheval* into the crack on the left. Climb this strenuously to ledges on the left.

3 **30m 6a** Climb the crack above, passing a small roof with difficulty until a crack leads diagonally left around the arête to the top. Iron fence-post belay.

THE CHIMNEY STACK

NG 507 666 **Alt:** 50m 20min

A remarkable slender free-standing pillar close to the cliff top, split by a crack on three of its four faces.

Descents: From the top of the stack abseil from two bolts (placed 1985) on the summit of the stack. Or from the fence posts back from the edge, make a 30m abseil to the gap between the main cliff and the stack.

2 Sheer Sear ★★★★   30m E5 6b
FA Gary Latter 23 May 1987

Splitting the south face of this very impressive stack is a magnificent shallow searing groove-line capped by a small roof and split by a finger-crack. This provides a brilliant sustained pitch. Follow the crack with a hard move at 10m to a good rest. Continue with interest past a further hard section at a steepening in the groove to gain better holds near the left arête. The easy looking final section is not and the ledges prove awkward to gain. Finish up a short flake-crack to a sharp final pull onto the top to reach a double bolt belay.

3 Over the Rainbow ★★★   40m E5 6b
FA Bill Birkett & Bob Wightman 28 May 1985

The shallow groove on the east face. Serious and difficult to protect – plenty of small nuts/cams required. Move right into crack, bulging at first and climbed on finger ends. Continue, very sustained over two overlaps (second being crux) to reach a PR. Pass this to gain a good resting ledge and further PR. Step left into a little corner then straight to the top.

FALLEN PILLARS AREA

250m north of **The Chimney Stack** are two squat, much less spectacular stacks. The larger southern one is the Bob Bob Stack.
Approach: The fastest approach to the cliff top is to head east through the fields from the campsite

NG 506 668 **Alt:** 50m   20min
at Clachan, midway between **Kilt Rock** and Staffin.
Descent: Descend steeply onto a jammed boulder in the gap between the Bob Bob Stack then go left (north) down grass ledges to a gap behind the northern stack. Scramble under a boulder then down boulders with care

1 Demon Lover ★★★   40m E4 6a
FA Dougie Dinwoodie & Brian Lawrie 17 April 1987

The finger-crack in the groove. Perfect protection but very sustained. Belay near the top.

2 High Noon ★   40m E2 5b
FA Dougie Dinwoodie & Brian Lawrie 16 April 1987

Start beneath twin parallel cracks. Climb these for 12m then move out left up a flake to follow the obvious hand-crack.

3 Toll-Dubh ★   50m HVS 4c
FA Dougie Dinwoodie & Brian Lawrie 17 April 1987

Another fine route for a rainy day! Climbs a remarkable hidden shaft at the back of the leftmost slumped pillars. Enter a cave on the left side of the first pillar or climb a 5b crack on the outside (less rope-drag). Climb the shaft up the back of the pillars emerging in the upper chimney. Continue the through route under a boulder to the top of the pillars. The easiest finish is by a small hanging corner on the right (loose).

Demon Lover, Paul Thorburn climbing.

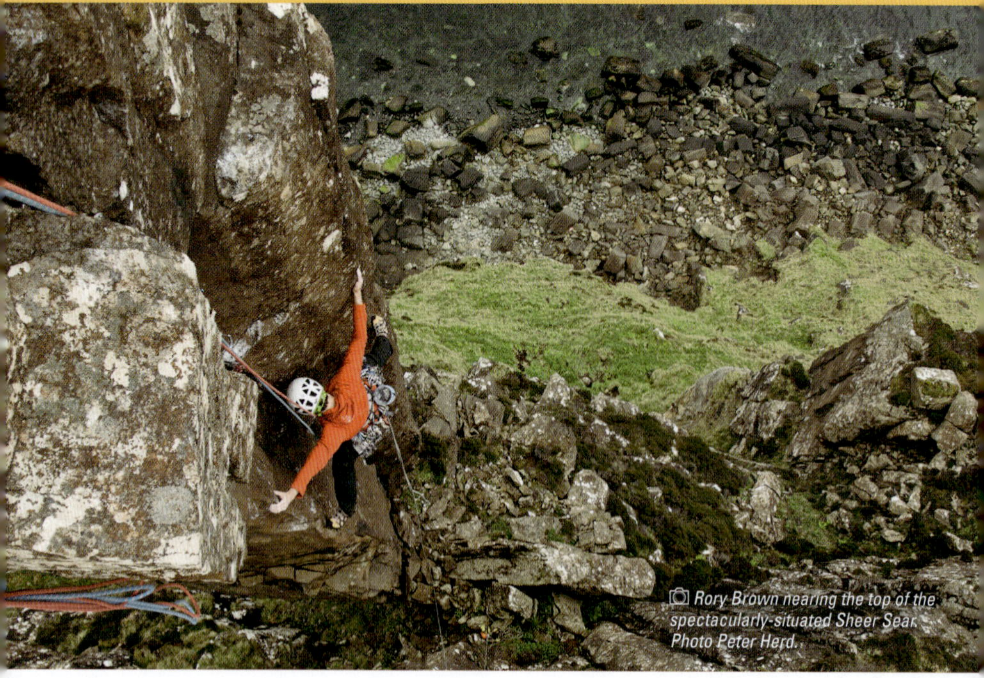

Rory Brown nearing the top of the spectacularly-situated Sheer Sear. Photo Peter Herd.

STAFFIN SLIP BUTTRESSES

A collection of buttresses set well back from the sea with easier approaches and descents than those to the south around **Kilt Rock**. Good venues, often staying dry in showery south-westerlies.

Access: Continue north along the A855 for 1.9 miles/3km beyond **Kilt Rock**, turning right at the bend in the road, 0.25 miles/0.4km beyond Staffin village hall. Follow the single track road down and round the coast for 1 mile/1.6km to park near the slipway at the end.

NG 498 676 **Alt:** 50m
10min
N
NE
Jean and Jim E1 4c, 5b
1
2

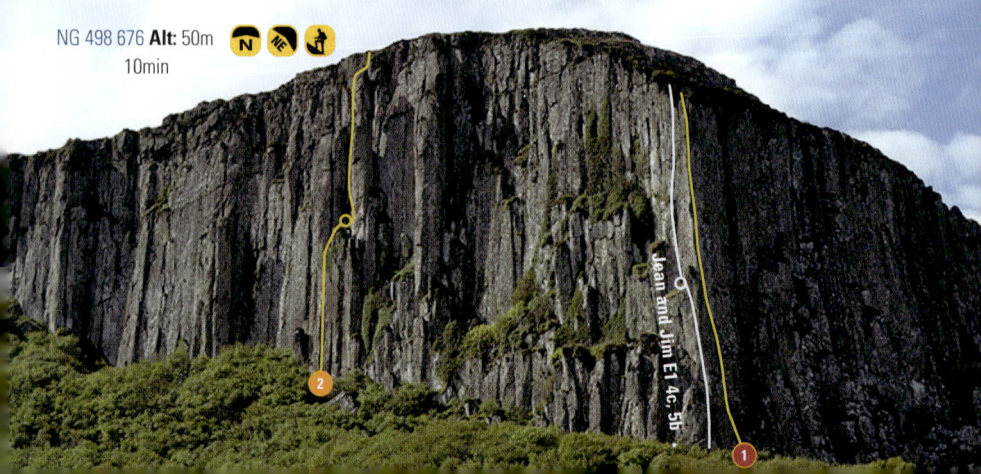

SGEIR BHAN (WHITE ROCK) – STAFFIN SLIP NORTH

The rightmost of the two big crags.
Approach: From behind the boathouse cross boggy ground in the direction of the crag to gain a well constructed path then traverse left from the first bend.
Descent: down the right (west) end of the cliff.

1 Kilt Classic ★★  40m E1 5b
FA Bill Birkett & Ed Grindley 12 August 1987

Memorable climbing up the steep chimney on the right side of the large tapering pillar. Ascend the widening crack *"with considerable interest"*, to belay on top of the pillar. Reasonably protected due to small cracks in the right wall.

2 Return of the Stone ★★ 50m VS 4b
FA Mark Hudson & Roger Holden 30 November 1996

Consistent well protected climbing. Gains and climbs the second column. Start in front of the third column, below a chimney containing an *"ominously-poised"* flake at 5m.
1. **15m 4b** Bridge up the chimney, taking care with the flake, to belay in an ivy dell to the right.
2. **35m 4b** A spectacular pitch. Gain the rear of the second (right) column using some steps to cross the giant flake forming the back wall of the dell. Bridge up behind the column, passing behind a jammed block at 10m. Continue bridging, pausing to pose on top of the column, before transferring back to the cliff face to gain the top. Stake (possibly missing) & R #9 belay 5m further back.

STAFFIN SLIP SOUTH

The bigger leftmost crag above the birches and boulders. One of the premier crack climbing destinations in the UK – if it was rotated 180 degrees (to face south-west), there would be queues at the base of many of the routes! There are 3 separate bolt belays/abseil points at the top of the shorter routes at the right end, and another at the top of *Sasha*; all other routes have boulder or double stake anchors. A single rope is recommended; a triple set of cams for the longer routes.

Approach: Walk south-east along grass just above the shore until beneath the cliff. Weave up sheep tracks then go direct to gain the right end of the cliff. Alternatively, follow the good track to the top of the **Staffin Slip North** then head along the top of that crag and drop down the easy descent gully.

Descents: Down the grassy gully at the right (north-west) end, or by abseil from anchors at the top of many of the routes from *Captain Patience* rightwards – marked on topo.

Pete Herd on the first ascent of the superb long sustained finger crack at Wildwood. Photo James Sutton.

ISLE OF SKYE STAFFIN SLIP BUTTRESSES

1 Lateral Thinking ★★   15m E1 5b
FA Willie Jeffrey 10 May 1990

The rightmost of twin cracks, left of the first wide crack.

2 Hand Jive ★★   17m E1 5b
FA Willie Jeffrey & Noel Williams 14 May 1994

The leftmost crack, finishing just left of a tiny roof.

3 Jugs of Deception ★★   18m E4 6a
FA Michael Tweedley & Colin Moody 10 June 1996

The pillar left of 2 using thin cracks. The final bulge is climbed by a layaway off the edge to reach a hidden hold on the right.

4 Lat up a Drainpipe ★★   17m HVS 5b
FA Gunars Libeks, Ed Grindley & Steve Suthorn 30 May 1988

Strenuous climbing up twin cracks in a corner recess.

5 The Avon Man ★★   18m E2 5c
FA Ed Grindley & Gunars Libeks 3 May 1990

The awkward black crack immediately left of 4.

6 Swillington Common ★★★   20m E2 5c
FA Ian Blakeley, Gunars Libeks & Colin Downer 28 May 1989

The next crack left again with difficulties around mid-height.

7 Dial Card ★★   25m E2 5c
FA Ian Blakeley, Al Pounder, Ed Grindley, Steve Suthorn 30 April 1988

Twin cracks in the right corner of the recess.

Gary Latter on the fine Experimental Learning. Photo: Karen Latter

8 Silly Pollack Two ★★ — 25m E4 6a
FA Bill Birkett & Luke Steer June 1988

The thin crack just left of centre of the recess. Sustained.

9 Captain Patience ★★★ — 30m E3 5c
FA Colin Downer, Gunars Libeks, Ed Grindley, Steve Suthorn, Al Pounder & Ian Blakeley 30 April 1988

Excellent sustained physical jamming up the corner groove on the left.

10 Glorious Five Year Plan ★★ — 40m E2 5c
FA Colin Moody & Michael Tweedley 1996

The corner, starting between a birch tree and an ivy.

11 The Latvian ★★ — 35m E2 5c
FA Colin Downer, Gunars Libeks & Steve Suthorn 30 April 1988

Start above a heather topped pedestal left of three fallen blocks. Twin cracks merging at third height.

12 Lats in Space ★ — 40m E1 5b
FA Ed Grindley & Ian Sykes 24 April 1988

Deep crack in the V-groove immediately left of a sharp prow.

13 Windom Earle ★★★ — 40m E2 5c
FA James & Doug Sutton 14 June 2019

Twin white cracks. Lots of bridging – *"bring some strong calves"*.

14 Sasha ★★★ — 40m E2 5c
FA Ed Grindley & Gunars Libeks 9 June 1990

At the left end of a lichenous wall is a prominent groove with twin cracks leading to stepped black roofs. Climb through a sentry box and up to rest under the roof then through this thuggishly to finish up a short crack.

15 Woman of the Eighties ★★★ — 45m E3 5c
FA Ian Blakeley, Ron Kenyon & Colin Downer 30 May 1988

Strenuous sustained finger-jamming up the second crack in the wall left of the overgrown groove.

16 Gorbachev ★★★ — 45m E2 5b
FA Ed Grindley, Gunars Libeks & Steve Suthorn 29 May 1988

Superb steady climbing up twin ragged cracks and a groove. A good introduction to the crag.

17 The Sheriff's Black Dog ★ — 45m E2 5b
FA Colin Downer, Gunars Libeks & Ed Grindley 29 May 1988

Start left of a prow with a mossy boulder at its base, just right of two 20m high pillars. The thin crack to a roof high up, passed on the right with difficulty.

18 Experimental Learning ★★★ — 45m E4 6a
FA Ian Blakeley & Colin Downer 29 May 1988

Start just left of the two pillars. Climb a finger-crack up a smooth white groove, passing a roof at the top on the right.

19 Fire Walk With Me ★★★ — 45m E3 5c
FA James & Doug Sutton & Matt Barratt 29 June 2019

Perfect sustained finger-crack with great features on the face, finishing at the highest point of the crag.

20 Silly Pollack ★★ — 45m E2 5b
FA Luke Steer & Bill Birkett June 1988

Beyond two poorer routes are twin cracks capped by series of stepped roofs. Move into the leftmost crack to avoid the roofs.

21 Birdman of Bewaldeth ★★★ — 45m E3 6a
FA Colin Downer & Ian Blakeley 27 May 1989

Rightmost crack in a slight recess left of 20. Climb through a small triangular roof at 6m, passing right of a nose high up.

22 The Beast of Bolsover ★★ — 45m E2 5b
FA Colin Downer & Gunars Libeks 29 May 1988

Leftmost crack in the recess, past an undercling left to an easier steep crack. Finish up the crest of a vague prow and left of a nose near the top.

23 Lusting after Glenys Kinnock ★★ — 40m E2 5b
FA Ian Blakeley, Colin Downer, Gunars Libeks & R.Williamson 27 May 1989

The thin crack round to the left, right of a vegetated groove, passing to the left of a long narrow roof at mid-height. An incredible hand crack for lower section.

Dave Kirby on Captain Patience. Photo Dave Fowler.

24 Wildwood ★★★ — 45m E5 6a
FA Peter Herd 23 June 2019

A spectacular hard pitch up the finger crack a few metres right of 25. Recommended rack: triple set cams from BD X4 0.2 to green cam, single set nuts 1-10.

25 Green Vote ★★★ — 45m E3 5c
FA Ed Grindley & Ian Sykes 8 May 1988

One of the best routes on the crag, *"Wider hands, burly, with a traddy feel."* The prominent crack on the white wall just right of 26 *East Chimney Crack* ★★ HVS 5a.

RUBHA HUNISH
(RAVINE OF THE POINT)

The most northerly point on the island with a good range of routes.

Access: Continue north on the A855 from Flodigarry for 3.4 miles/5.5km to park by a telephone box at a bend in the road at Duntulm NG 422 742.

Approach: Head north-west out towards the headland, descending the prominent deep trench separating the impressive lofty cliffs overlooking the east end of Loch Hunish.

NG 412 762
MEALL TUATH   30min
The cliff beneath the northern hill with a former coastguard lookout on the summit.

① Friends in the North ★★ **80m E2 5b**
FA N.Robinson & Bill Birkett 31 May 1996

Good exposed climbing, heading for the central of three leftwards-slanting crack systems just right of centre. Start at a diamond-shaped block.

1 **20m 4a** Move up to a rightwards trending grassy ramp and follow this to belay by a small pinnacle boss at the base of the corner-crack.

2 **35m 5b** Ascend the corner-crack on excellent *"sandpaper rough"* rock, past a wide jam crack at 15m. Step right at the overlap and continue up the corner-crack in dark reddish rock leading to a pinnacle column abutting the headwall. Step up left to gain a ledge then move left to belay on small cams in a short groove.

3 **10m 5a** Climb the short groove then traverse easily left to belay on cams in a steep crack.

4 **15m 5b** Step left and follow thin parallel cracks past a heathery niche to finish by a short groove formed by a large block.

② Northern Lights ★★ 70m E2 5c
FA Bill Birkett & A.Sheehan 9 September 1991

Start beneath the obvious groove system just right of centre.

1. **15m** A loose grassy approach pitch. Move up then diagonally left across a grassy bay. Step left and move up to gain a groove and belay on the left side of a pinnacle.
2. **35m 5a** Move up onto the pinnacle and climb the crack-groove system to the top of a large pinnacle. Continue up and step left awkwardly to leave the groove about 4m below a roof. Move up then step right to climb up to the roof. Gain a handhold on a flat-topped block just below and right of the roof. Pull right into a groove and follow this for 3m until an exit left can be made. Continue up the groove directly above the overhang and pull over blocks to a heathery ledge. Step up and left to a *"perfect eagle's nest"* stance and PB.
3. **20m 5c** A superb pitch, tackling the leaning tapering corner/groove/ramp thingy leading steeply leftwards.

NG 409 761   30min

MEALL DEAS
The big cliff south west (left looking down) of the descent path.

③ The Knowledge/The Scoop ★★ 70m VS 5a
FA pitch 1 Mark Hudson & Andrew Holden 6 June 1997; second pitch 5 October 1996

A good combination. Start directly below a gap in the band of overhangs 10m down and right from the left arête.

1. **40m 5a** Climb a crack then columns and ribs direct to the gap. Chimney through the overhangs (crux) and belay beneath the overhanging cracks above.
2. **30m 4b** Tackle the corner and pull over the lip at 15m. Easier scrambling leads to the stake belay of 4.

The prominent left-facing roof capped corner is 4 *Minch and Tatties* • E1 4b, 4b, 5b.

⑤ Master of Morgana ★ 70m HVS 5b
FA Andrew Holden & Mark Hudson 31 August 1996

A well-protected line following the right side of the face, finishing up the prominent cleft on the skyline. Start 20m right of the start of 2 below the rightmost of two deep chimneys.

1. **30m 4c** Gain the chimney and climb it on improving rock to a ledge on the left. Climb a series of grooves trending left to reach a blocky ledge and nut belays.
2. **40m 5b** Large cams useful. Climb the crack above the stance to reach a higher ledge. Traverse left to gain a leftwards rising ramp leading to a horizontal break. Hand traverse back right to gain the bottom of the final crack. Climb this (crux) to a spectacular grovelling finish.

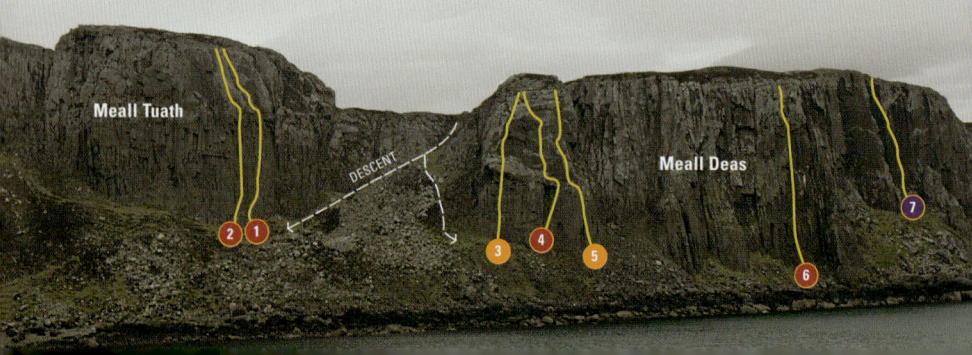

6 Northern Exposure *   90m E2/3 5c
FA Bill Birkett & C.Thorpe 31 May 1993

Tackles the longest and most continuous section of rock on the cliffs. Start about 100m right of 5 by scrambling over boulders and grass to the base of a great crack/groove soaring up through a sizeable double roof.

1. **30m 5a** Ascend a discontinuous crack within a groove to a small overhang and foot-ledge.
2. **50m 5c** A big pitch. Large cams useful. Move into the crack and climb it with hard moves to gain a little roof beneath a deep hanging corner. Cross this and follow the corner to cross the first stepped roof. At the top 3m roof move out left across this to pull out strenuously. Continue to belay atop a great chokestone.
3. **10m 4c** Finish up the wide crack to a stake belay.

7 Passing Out ***   48m E5 6a
FA Nicola Bassnett 10 September 2015

A splendid climb taking a plumbline crack system to join 8 in its upper reaches. The lower section includes a shallow right-facing corner with three spaced overlaps, which present the cruxes. Start atop a steep grassy slope and follow a shallow cracked groove for 8m until a step left brings the corner into line. Above the second overlap make moves to gain the main wall on the left, before stepping back right to reach the final tricky moves and the sustained soaring crack line. Finish up the final section of 8.

8 Whispering Crack ***   55m E3 5c
FA Willie Jeffrey & Noel Williams 6 May 1989

Sustained climbing up the prominent wide left-curving crack splitting the clean wall higher up on the right. Climb up trending right to gain the crack where it becomes better defined. Continue to a small ledge (possible belay). Ascend the crack to gain a pod with difficulty and continue with interest to eventually gain a flake-ledge on the right wall. Move up left and continue to finish. Belay on stakes well back from the edge (leave additional rope beforehand).

Whispering Crack, Grant Farquhar and Paul Thorburn climbing.

NEIST POINT
(HORSE-SHAPED POINT)

This is the most westerly point on Skye with a vast amount of dolerite crags, both on the coast and on the Upper Tier, 70m above the sea. The Upper Crags are described first, from south to north, starting with those nearest the car park. The majority of the crags are within 15–20 minutes walk from the car park, some less than 5 minutes.

Access: From the south turn left along the A863 at Sligachan, heading towards Dunvegan. Turn left down the B884 at Lonmore, following this for 7.5 miles/12km, before turning left down a C-class road to limited parking at the end of the road after a further 2 miles/3.5km.

UPPER CRAG – SOUTH SECTOR

A range of very convenient routes but the rock is not quite as good quality as many of the other crags.
Approach: Go down the path from the car park to just beyond the first set of steps then duck under the railings and head hard left, crossing a stone wall.

1 Juniper Rib ★   15m Severe 4a
FA Colin Moody (solo) 19 July 2003

The rib 12m left (north) of the drystane dyke (drystone wall to you Sassenachs).

2 Prog ★   25m Severe 4a
FA Mark Hudson & Andrew Holden 12 August 2007

Climb the right side of a very thin rib to half height, then direct over small jammed boulders.

3 Jessava ★   25m VS 4c
FA J.Robinson, I.Duxbury & A.McWatt 29 July 1998

Narrow rib with triangular roof at 7m. Climb crack to roof, passed on the right. Finish up the rib and wide crack. 3a *Variation* HVS 5a ascends thin groove left of roof.

4 Baywatch ★★   25m HS 4b
FA Noel Williams & Peter Duggan 12 October 1994

Start 50m beyond the wall beneath a faint rib marked by a triangular roof just left of the crest at one-third height. Climb a groove in the crest of the rib.

5 Curtains ★   25m HS 4b
FA Mark Hudson, Nicola Bassnett & Roger Brown 10 August 2007

Block-choked crack, climbed mainly on the rock on the right.

6 Hummer ★   25m Difficult
FA Nicola Bassnett & Roger Brown 2 February 2008

Ramp in corner of bay, then clean wall leading to final easy slab.

7 Trailer Park - Twin Cracks Finish ★   25m Severe 4a
FA Colin Moody & party 1999; Twin Cracks: Nicola Bassnett & Roger Brown 14 August 2007

Wide crack of stepped blocks in corner, then left up slab to small grass ledge. Move left and up twin cracks. Finishing direct up white rib is VS 4b.

8 Sonamara ★★   25m VS 4c
FA Noel Williams, Stevie Abbott & Linda Taylor 15 April 1995

A short distance further right is a more prominent rib with a recess on its right side. Climb a prominent groove on the left side of the rib.

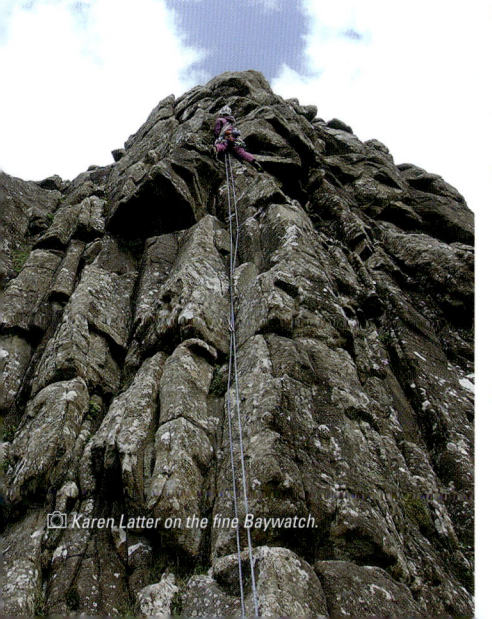

Karen Latter on the fine Baywatch.

9 Pegboy ★ 25m E1 5b
FA Nicola Bassnett & Roger Brown 2 August 2008

Start steeply, then left below roof to gain and follow the distinct open groove.

10 Transitive Nightfall of Diamonds ★ 25m VS 4b
FA J.McCormick, M.Gaddes & I.Smith 16 July 1997

Start at the first rib right of 8 just to the left of the crest. Climb a series of slabs pleasantly to the top, keeping to the left of the crest.

11 Keeping the Bofs Happy ★ 22m Difficult
FA Colin Moody & Louise Gordon-Canning 29 March 1997

The crest of the fourth rib.

12 Don't Leave Your Dad in the Rain★ 20m Severe 4b
FA J.McCormick, M.Gaddes & I.Smith 16 July 1997

Immediately right of 11 is a narrow slab. Pad up the right edge with enjoyable run out moves in its upper reaches.

NG 129 484 **Alt:** 80m

FINANCIAL SECTOR  10min

An excellent area with a high concentration of very good lines.

Approach: From the parking spot walk north along the cliff top for about 10 minutes until 150m north of the ruined coastguard lookout.

Descents: Abseil from a choice of stakes at the top. Alternatively, scramble down **Tower Gully** just to the north (small stream – wet underfoot) then skirt left along a sheep path to the base.

1 Waterfront ★★ 25m E2 5c
FA Chris Cartwright & Stuart Campbell 18 July 1998

The prominent crack curving up to the right is protected by a suspiciously-poised 'Damoclean' block low down. Climb delicately up to the poised block and use this to enter the crack above. Follow this strenuously to the top.

2 Loom of the Land ★★ 25m E1 5b
FA Chris Cartwright & Stuart Campbell 18 July 1998

Shallow right-facing corner to ledge on left, then move right and up into the crack.

3 Bridging Loan ★★ 25m E1 5b
FA Luca Celano & Ali Rose 13 April 2019

The obvious crack splitting the wall. Not as hard as it looks.

4 Earthbound ★★ 35m HVS 5a
FA Colin Moody & Michael Tweedley 13 June 1996

The left groove. Climb an easy slab, two steep cracks then the groove above.

ISLE OF SKYE NEIST POINT

📷 *Karen Latter on the fine introduction to the sector - Shocks and Stares.*

5 Terminal Bonus ★★ 30m HVS 5a
FA Stevie Abbott & Noel Williams 6 May 1996

Move up left to gain the fine right groove, steep to start. Easy for the grade.

6 The Banks of Lochcarron ★ 30m VS 4c
FA Roger Brown & Nicola Bassnett 31 July 2004

The right-facing corner, with a short deviation out right low down, using the large free standing flake.

7 Midas Touch ★★★ 30m VS 4c
FA J.Robinson & A.McWatt 27 July 1998

Climb the left side of alcove, then rightwards into a small recess. Pull over bulge and up onto slabby ramp, then fine flakes and cracks leading to the long curving roof. Step right over the end of the roof to finish on the highest blocks.

8 Insider Dealing ★★ 30m HVS 5a
FA Noel Williams & Stevie Abbott 16 July 1995

Finishes up a prominent groove left of the rib crest. Start by climbing the left side of a small alcove. Continue up and right to a slight recess, pull over a bulge and step left onto a slab ramp. Move hard right a short distance above to gain the main groove-crack line. Follow this past a roof at mid-height to finish more easily. The bold direct start is 8a *Inside Out* ★ E1 5a, the crux protected by RPs.

9 The Price is Right ★★ 30m E1 5b
FA Nicola Bassnett & Roger Brown 28 May 2014

This takes a vertical line to finish up the final crack of 8. Start at a disjointed crack to the immediate right of the corner of the alcove and continue straight up, as it veers left. Step right into the U scoop of 8a and quickly meet the mid-height ledge. The prominent steep crack above is climbed using help from various nubbins on the right wall. This leads to the right side of the 8 overhang and its crack above.

10 Shocks and Stares ★★ 30m VS 4b
FA Noel Williams & Stevie Abbott 1 July 1995

Start on the right side of the rib. Gain and follow the prominent slightly left-slanting hand-crack up the crest of the rib, widening as height is gained.

Sandy Simpson on Piggy Bank.

11 Bridging Interest ★★★ 30m HVS 5a
FA Willie Jeffrey & Noel Williams 16 June 1996

The prominent groove. Make difficult moves to become established on the initial wall then follow the sustained groove with interest. Low in the grade.

12 Grampus ★★ 30m HVS 5b
FA Roger Brown & Nicky Bassnett 9 August 2012

Climb 11 until the corner closes. Step right to a crack left of the arête, which is followed until a capped roof forces a move rightwards to join 13.

13 Security Risk ★★★ 30m E1 5b
FA Willie Jeffrey, Noel Williams & Andrew Holden 16 June 1996

Good climbing up the crest of the buttress. Start up 14 then follow a flake-crack leftwards to the edge. Follow the easiest line with some exciting moves on chicken-heads, finishing easily over ledges.

14 Power-broker ★★ 30m E1 5b
FA Stevie Abbott & Noel Williams 4 May 1996

The groove at the right side of the left buttress. Step left at the mid-height bulge. Finish up a combination of the groove and holds on the left wall. Low in the grade.

15 The Big Money ★★ 30m E4 6b
FA Gary Latter 30 May 2010

Good well protected climbing up the hanging finger-crack just right of the sharp arête. Climb the easier lower wall past ledges to gain thin crack. Go up this with difficult moves to gain good finger-crack leading to a ledge. Finish up a tricky thin curving crack, struggling to avoid stepping into the gully.

16 Venture Capital ★★★ 30m HVS 5a
FA Stevie Abbott & Noel Williams 16 July 1995

Superb climbing up the twin cracks immediately right of the pinnacle. Start up the left crack then step right and climb direct, crossing a bulge at the top.

17 A Fistful of Dollarite ★★ 25m E1 5b
FA Willie Jeffrey & Noel Williams 16 June 1996

The prominent right-facing corner. A Camalot #4 is useful (but not essential) for the entertaining finishing offwidth.

18 Fat Cats ★★ 20m E2 5c
FA Willie Jeffrey & Noel Williams 14 September 1996

The prominent crack in the north-facing wall at the southern end. Start from a belay on top of the pinnacle. Climb a short slab and move left to enter a chimney. Climb this and the crack above with increasing difficulty. Hug a curious column before making committing moves up the crucial headwall.

19 Gammy's Purse ★★ 25m E2 5c
FA Ellis Ash & Tom Bridgeland 23 May 1998

The crack and groove in the left side of the face. Follow 20 to pockets. Move out left to gain the crack. Climb this then move right to the bottom of the groove, which is followed to the top. A left start is less intimidating at the same grade.

📷 *Dave Cowan pulling over the crux roof at the top of Hurricane Hideaway.*

21 Hurricane Hideaway ★★　　　　　30m E1 5c

FA Emma Alsford & Paul Donnithorne 8 June 1997; Direct: Ellis Ash & Tom Bridgeland 23 May 1998

The main corner feature, finishing through the roof left of the corner. Climb the corner until it is possible to traverse left along an obvious break to gain a hanging corner above. Climb this to the roof and undercut rightwards to gain a short finishing corner above, which gives a meaty finish. 21a Direct Finish, *Gampy's Wallet* ★★ E2 5c breaches capping roof to finish up slim groove.

22 Wall Street ★★★　　　　　　　　30m E2 5c

FA Stevie Abbott & Noel Williams 1 July 1995

Just north of the stone wall is a recessed wall capped by a small roof. Climb the cracked wall left of centre until forced to trend rightwards to gain a ledge where the wall steepens. Continue by a crack and some fragile protruding holds on the left to make a hard move to gain a foot ledge. Climb to just under the roof then step left across a slab to a right-facing corner. Swing out left to pass the roof and finish strenuously.

20 Piggy Bank ★★★　　　　　　　　25m E3 5c

FA Tom Bridgeland & Ellis Ash 23 May 1998

A brilliant route, high in the grade. A pinnacle leans against the cliff. Scramble up this to belay on its top. Step down and pull round the arête onto the face. Move up to two good pockets then continue boldly rightwards to the base of a curving ramp. Follow this then move up and right to gain the groove, which provides a fine upper half.

23 A Midsummer Night's Dream ★★　　30m E1 5b

FA Emma Alsford & Paul Donnithorne 21 June 2014

Start just right of 22 by a left-facing blocky corner. Climb blocky cracks up left to a dank niche at the base of a corner. Follow this to a step up right into a steep crack to finish.

ISLE OF SKYE NEIST POINT

24 Charlie Potatoes Direct **   25m E2 5b
FA Roger Brown & Nicky Bassnett 12 April 2007;
Direct: Gary Latter & Alex 'Tam' Thomson 9 June 2012

The shallow right-facing groove. Climb direct up into the groove (bold but straightforward), then direct in the same line.

25 Have a Nice Day **   30m E3 6a
FA Gary Latter & Jon Rabey 8 September 2005

Sustained well protected climbing up the prominent right-facing groove. Climb the groove with increasing difficulty, moving rightwards at the top past a triangular flake to pull over the capping roof spectacularly on good holds at large thread (some loose rock here).

26 Wish You Were Here ****   30m E2 5c
FA George Szuca & George Armstrong September 1990

Excellent sustained climbing up the striking crack forming the right side of the recess, turning the roof at the top on the right.

27 Bit-Coiner **   35m E3 5c
FA Emma Alsford & Paul Donnithorne 22 June 2014

An entertaining pitch starting 2m left of the chimney. Climb a dog-leg crack up and right to a bridged position in the chimney. Pull up left and climb the subsidiary corner until below the large boulder capping the top of the chimney. Follow the steep crack out left, going direct up the exposed rib above to finish through the bulge.

28 Bingo Wings **   35m E3 5c
FA Paul Donnithorne & Emma Alsford 23 June 2014

A characterful climb starting below the low roof right of the chimney.

  1   25m 5c Pull up to the roof, undercut left and pull into the fine crack. Follow this up and right, stepping right to climb a thin crack/groove to join the chimney on the right and thus the belay ledge above.

  2   10m 5c Follow the thin crack up and left to join the exposed rib and finish as for 27.

SOUTH FACE S

29 Slot Machine **   25m E3 5c
FA Paul Donnithorne & Emma Alsford 23 June 2014

A fine exercise in off-width crack climbing, taking the wide crack. Requires a set of cams, up to Camalot 6. A few small wires may also be useful. Finish up pitch 2 of 28.

30 Seven Days ***   30m E4 6a
FA Nicky Bassnett (headpointed) 5 August 2012

"A future classic." An outstanding route, climbing the very obvious thin crack in the south-facing wall. The crack is gained from the right. A sequence of technical and dynamic laybacks provides the crux up the thinnest part of the crack, which is well-protected but pumpy placing gear. The bulging crack at the top provides a fine finish.

31 Daylight Robbery **   30m E3 5c
FA Paul Donnithorne & Emma Alsford 25 June 2014

A superb and energetic route of great character taking the chunky crack just right of 30 and utilising its start. Holds on the right help progress low down and the climb culminates in spectacular jamming through the final bulge.

ISLE OF SKYE NEIST POINT | 71

TOWER GULLY BUTTRESS

A prominent tower 250m north of the old lookout, overlooking the chossy **Tower Gully**, which gives a scrambling descent. Or easier, traverse left from the base of the Financial Sector.

NG 129 485 **Alt:** 70m

 15min

1 Bad Dream ★★   50m E3 5c
FA pitch 1 Colin Moody & Louise Gordon Canning 17 June 1997; pitch 2 Neil Smith, Roger Lupton & Colin Moody 19 July 1997

The big corner at the bottom of Tower Gully. A stunning looking line with considerable exposure – possibly a good route for a rainy day.

1 **25m 5b** Climb the corner to the overhang, move right and climb a crack and move on to the ledge on the right. An excellent pitch.

2 **25m 5c** Step back left and follow the obvious left-slanting fault, finishing by jamming the left side of the summit block.

THE GREEN LADY

An obvious squat pinnacle at the base of the descent gully. **Descent:** Affix a spare rope round a thread at the base of a thin crack on the east (landward) face (no satisfactory abseil anchor on top). Abseil down the overhanging west face.

NG 129 487 **Alt:** 60m

20min

1 The Green Lady ★★   25m HS 4b
FA Tom Patey & R. Harper 26 August 1961

Climb the weakness 2m right of a thin crack near the right end of the east face then traverse diagonally left on a ledge system to the left arête. Finish just right of the edge on good holds.

2 South-East Arête ★★   25m VS 4b
FA Darren McAulay & Tony Wilson 13 September 2001

The best route on the pinnacle, ascending the arête on the south-east wall direct. Better protected and considerably easier than it appears.

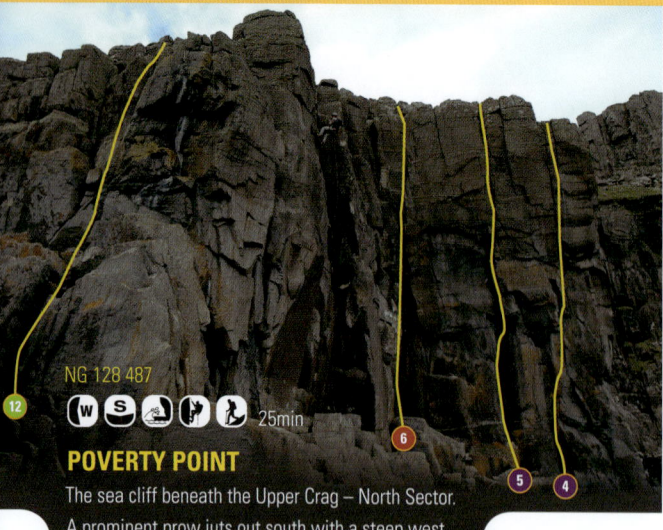

Michelangelo Buonarotti, Gary Latter climbing. Photo Karen Latter.

NG 128 487

25min

POVERTY POINT

The sea cliff beneath the Upper Crag – North Sector. A prominent prow juts out south with a steep west face, finishing at a corner-crack.

Descent: By abseil from blocks at the top, or the stake at the north end.

The landward side of the point forms a large non-tidal bay.

1 Golden Shower ★★★   30m E4 5c
FA Mike Reed & Guy Robertson 23 August 2003

A groovy route with technical climbing all the way, taking the obvious line up the front of the jutting pillar (immediately right of the deep chimney/through cave). Pull directly up onto the pillar then step left and follow the slim groove to a precarious move right onto a sloping ledge. Gain the steep upper groove (bold) by means of a spooky undercut then exit this immediately left to finish up good cracks.

2 The Man from Ankle ★★★   30m E3 6a
FA Guy Robertson & Mike Reed 23 August 2003

This first class route, technical and well protected takes thin cracks and grooves close to the right edge of the prominent pillar right of the chimney recess. Follow the dwindling lower cracks until thin moves lead to a small ledge at the base of the groove. Climb this direct (crux), then easier above.

2a Birdsong ★★★   30m E3 5c
FA Gary & Karen Latter 9 May 2013

Stunning well-protected climbing up the crack and deep V-groove immediately left of 2. Climb the straightforward lower crack, with difficult section to enter the groove. Continue up this, sharing the final easy section with 2, finishing out rightwards.

The stepped corners on the right side of the prow are 3 Michelangelo Buanarotti ★★ E1 5b.

On the steep west face of the obvious promontory lie:

4 American Vampire ★★★   25m E4 6a
FA Pete Benson & Finlay Bennett 15 April 2001

The right crack. Sustained climbing leads up to the overhanging hand-crack with the crux *"as it should be"* – the last move.

5 Fight Club ★★★   25m E4 6a
FA Pete Benson & Finlay Bennett 15 April 2001

A jamming tussle up the left crack, climbed direct.

6 Aqualung ★   30m E2 5c
FA Colin Moody, Neil Smith & Roger Lupton 27 March 1999

The corner.

ISLE OF SKYE NEIST POINT

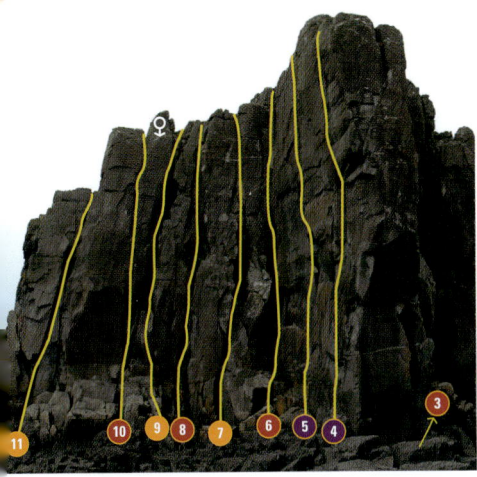

7 At the Whelks ★   30m HVS 5a
FA Colin Moody & Louise Gordon Canning 1 June 1997
The chimney left of the corner-crack which runs into another corner-crack.

8 Recovery Day ★★   25m E1 5b
FA Colin Moody & Louise Gordon Canning 1 June 1997
A corner-crack to the left. The left-slanting crack is also E1 5b.

9 Superlager for Breakfast ★   25m HVS 5a
FA Colin Moody & Louise Gordon Canning 1 June 1997
The chimney to the left with a bulge towards the top.

10 Giro Day ★★   25m E2 5c
FA Colin Moody & Morris MacLeod 20 July 1997
Start next to 9 and climb the crack on the left.

11 Homer ★   20m HVS 5a
FA Colin Moody & Morris MacLeod 20 July 1997
The wide crack.

> The crack round the corner is 12 *Broken Wing* V. Diff. Just north of the main cliffs are:

13 Fool's Gold ★   16m HS 4b
FA Colin Moody & Cynthia Grindley 31 May 2003

Start at the right side of pinnacle at the right end. Climb up left behind it then go up to bulging rock. Move right through the bulge then continue to the top.

14 Chugger's Elbow ★   15m Severe 4a
FA Colin Moody & Pamela Hand 15 November 1998
The wall.

15 Thrift is a Virtue ★   14m Severe 4a
FA Colin Moody & Cynthia Grindley 31 May 2003
The corner right of 16.

16 Any Spare Change? ★★   20m Severe 4a
FA Colin Moody 20 April 2003
The crack between two short corners left (north) of 15.

17 Italian Job ★★   18m E1 5b
FA Roger Brown & Nicky Bassnett 30 October 2004
The smooth wall right of 18, using cracks on its left edge, started from the corner.

> The second corner left of 16 is 18 *Shelter* ★ E1 5b.

19 Keeler ★   25m VS 4b
FA Colin Moody & Cynthia Grindley 7 July 2001
The rib left of the right-slanting recess, using the crack on the rightmost of the way.

SOUTH & EAST

NG 129 489 25min

DESTITUTION POINT

The next prominent headland 100m north of **Poverty Point**. A fine atmospheric crag. The west face has lots of good short routes from Moderate – VS on great rock.

Descent: Routes on the **South** & **West Faces** can be gained by scrambling down an easy (Mod.) groove at the north end, routes 5 onwards on the **East Face** directly by abseil to **tidal** ledges at the base.

SOUTH FACE

1 Flea de Wean ★  14m HVS 5a
FA Mark Hudson & James Sutton 29 October 2004

A series of sharp grooves immediately right of the arête. Reachy climbing with minimal gear placements.

2 Black Groove ★ 15m HS 4b
FA Rob Archbold & Greg Strange 30 May 1998

Pleasant line at left end.

3 Neaster's Crack ★ 15m E1 5b
FA Greg Strange & Rob Archbold 30 May 1998

Crack and hanging ramp at the left side of the promontory.

EAST FACE

4 Squeenius, Right Finish ★ 20m HVS 5a
FA Mark Hudson & James Sutton 29 October 2004;
Right Finish: Gary & Karen Latter 6 May 2019

Start on a dark foot ledge on the left wall of the big chimney. Move up and climb direct up into the tight right-facing groove, finishing with care up the right side of detached pinnacle. The original route swings left to climb a crack up the front face of the pillar - very loose looking, following the huge spring 2009 rockfall.

ISLE OF SKYE NEIST POINT

5 True Colours ★★★   20m E2 5c
FA Neil Smith, Roger Lupton, Morris MacLeod & Louise Gordon Canning 20 April 1999

The leftmost overhanging crack of the inverted V-recess. Belay on a small ledge at the base of the crack. Climb a shallow corner to an overhang. Fist jam right into a corner leading to a further roof and finish through the final roof crack. Excellent rock.

6 Man of Straw ★★   20m VS 4c
FA Steve Kennedy, Morris MacLeod & Colin Moody 14 Nov 1998

The clean slab on the back wall to the right of the corner. Climb cracks in the lower section then move right to the edge of the slab. Continue up the edge then step right below the short headwall into a corner to finish.

7 Come around to my way of thinking ★★ 20m E1 5b
FA Darren McAulay & Murdo MacCuish 28 June 2002

Excellent well protected climbing up the corner-crack immediately right of 6.

WEST FACE
The bay north of the prow, described from north-south.

1 Yellow Crack ★   10m VS 4c
FA Darren McAulay & party 1999

The layback crack.

2 Haggis ★   10m VS 4b
FA Louise & Billy Gordon Canning 1999

Leftmost of three shallow corners.

3 Neeps ★   10m VS 5a
FA Louise & Billy Gordon Canning 1999

Central corner 3m right of 2.

4 Wee Dram ★   10m VS 5a
FA Darren McAulay & P.Johnstone 1999

Wall and thin cracks right of 3, requiring commitment to start before the obvious higher crack is gained more easily.

5 Tatties ★   10m Severe 4a
FA Louise & Billy Gordon Canning 1999

Follow the crack just left of the clean rightmost corner. The corner is unclimbed.

ISLE OF SKYE NEIST POINT

6 Alien Territory ★★   10m E2 5c
FA Roger Brown & J.Holden 25 September 2004

The blunt undercut arête.

7 Steaming Entrails ★   12m Very Difficult
FA Louise & Billy Gordon Canning 1999

The open black chimney to the right in the corner of the bay.

8 Pennywhistle ★   8m Severe 4c
FA Nicola Bassnett & Roger Brown May 2004

The slab 2m right of 7, keeping central for maximum enjoyment.

> The short crack just right again is 5a then continuing right, the short broken corners Severe and V. Diff. The easiest scramble descent here is down the diagonal ramp across the top of 8.
> On southern walls of the bay, 9 *Long Way Home* Severe 4b takes the broken juggy arête; 10 *Black Chimney* Very Difficult the tall black groove just right.

11 Sissy ★★   10m E1 5a
FA James Sutton, Leighton Jones & Mark Hudson 6 June 2005

A bold well positioned line up the front of the blunt rib at the southern side of the bay. Move up to a spike runner, then use pockets above to move right to a scary mantel on good knobbles. Easier than it looks.

NG 128 475   10min

AN T-AIGEACH
(THE STALLION)

The impressive steep 100m high cliff dominating the headland.

Descents: At low tide abseil down the short cliff to the north of the main cliff then scramble and wade round to a large platform above high tide level at the base of the route. Alternatively, an exciting 90m abseil down the lines can be made if the tide is in.

1 Death Pirate ★★★   105m E6 6b
FA Graeme Livingston & Paul Moores June 1987;
pitch 1: Iain Small & Jules Lines 20 April 2015

The stunning left arête of the crag. Excellent climbing with good clean rock, fairly high in the grade. Abseil to good ledges to the left of a recessed wide chimney.

1 **35m 6a** Davy Jones' Locker Start. Follow the snaking crack on good clean rock to an overlap. Pull right into a crack and groove and where it becomes vegetated, step right onto the steep wall and climb into and up a wide groove to the big ledge at the base of the arête.

2 35m 6b Climb thin cracks until it is possible to move onto a 'thank-god hold' on the arête. Gain a standing position on the hold on the arête, then climbing the right side of the arête (crux – run out) to gain a sloping ledge and belay crack below an overhanging corner.

3 20m 6b Climb the corner then the arête to belay on a ledge.

4 15m 5b Finish more easily up rock and grass.

② Supercharger ★★   110m E3 5c
FA Ed & Cynthia Grindley, Willie Jeffrey & Noel Williams 22 August 1981

An impressive line, though with some loose rock on the crux pitch, up the highest central section of the cliff. Start below a crack at the top left end of the platform.

1 25m 5b Climb the crack and short groove above, passing a small roof. A short corner leads to a PB on left.

2 25m 5a Move up left onto a ledge then right into a steep corner. Climb this and an easier groove on the right to traverse right to a large belay ledge.

3 35m 5c Up the steep crack to gain a flake line leading up left to a corner below a big stepped roof. Make a hard move right onto the face then continue right and up to the right end of a large roof. Climb cracks up the overhanging wall. Swing left to pass another small roof strenuously into a leaning groove on the left, leading to an airy stance on the left.

4 25m 5a From the left side of the ledge follow an awkward crack. Easier climbing up a broken arête and then grass leads to the summit.

③ Overcharged ★★   E4 6a
FA Andy Cave & Simon Nadin Easter 1995

1 Climb the A-shaped crack to the right of 2 and belay under a bulge.

2 Move up and right in a superb position on good holds until a right-trending crack can be reached. Follow this to the ledge of 2 and finish up that.

 10min

BAY 1

The tiny bay just south-west from the platform at the base of **An t-Aigeach**.

Descents: Abseil from stakes down the ridge, making a further abseil down the flank to tidal ledges. These can also be gained at very low tide from the north-east.

① Cool Breeze ★★★   35m E4 6a
FA Murray Hamilton & Rab Anderson 23 May 1983

The prominent corner up the left side of the pillar.

② Hot Blast ★★★   30m E3 5c
FA Murray Hamilton & Bob Duncan 2 May 1983

The crack at the right end of the ridge.

④ Golden Mile ★★   30m E3 5c
FA Luke Steer & Bill Birkett 13 June 1988

A fine gold-coloured arête immediately left of the prominent groove, about 15m right of the pillar. Start up a crack just left of the arête. Climb the crack to a ledge then steeply up a groove to gain the arête. Follow the arête and thin cracks on its left to finish.

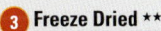 10min

BAY 2

The small bay at the south-west side of the ridge.
Descent: Abseil

③ Freeze Dried ★★   35m E2 5c
FA Murray Hamilton & Rab Anderson 23 May 1983

The obvious crack and flared chimney formed where the pillar abuts the ridge on the opposite side from 2.

BAY 3 15min

The first large bay, a distinctive square-cut bay with boulder beach at back.

5 Two Step * — 35m HS 4b
FA Mick Geddes & Noel Williams 17 December 1977

The prominent leftwards trending ramp furthest round from Bay 3. There are two short steep sections, the first the crux. Finish steeply on good holds. Fulmar in situ.

6 Sunken Howker ** — E2 5c
FA Colin Moody & Mark Shaw 12 June 1995

Start right of 5. Climb to a bulge beneath a crack then the crack and the continuation corner-crack.

7 Agfa * — 30m HVS 5b
FA Colin Moody & Allan Petrie 6 August 1994

Start below the left-facing corner-crack. Climb the corner-crack then step left and climb the right-slanting crack to the top.

NORTH WALL

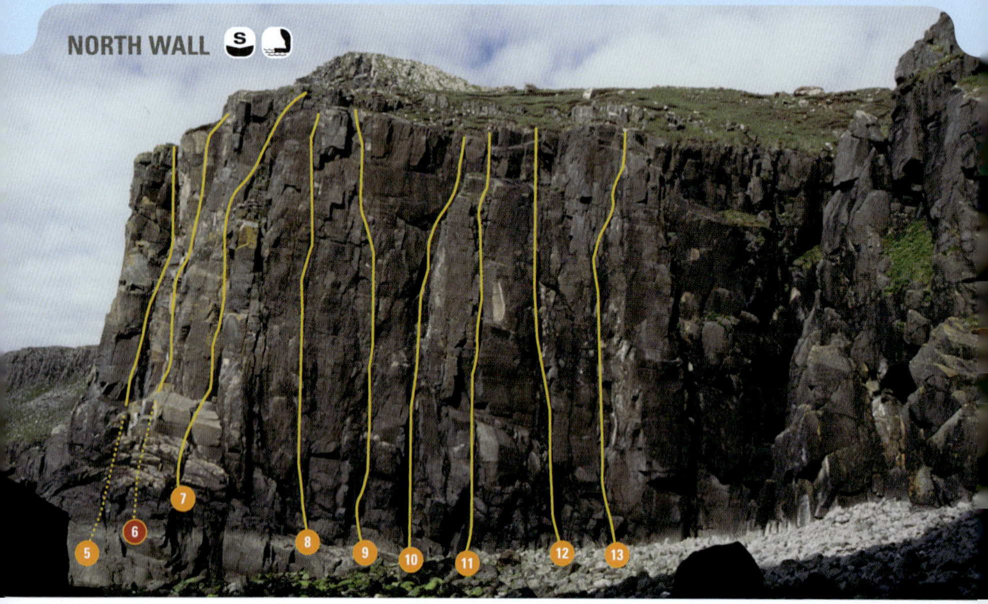

8 Tinderbox ** — 30m HVS 5a
FA Neil Horn & Colin Moody 18 June 1992

Climb the face left of 9 to gain a crack which finishes left of the square nose.

9 Side Step ** — 30m VS 4c
FA Noel Williams & Mick Geddes 17 December 1977

Follow faint grooves trending slightly leftwards to gain the right end of a prominent square nose. Continue up the right side of the nose. The original route on the sea cliffs.

10 Luscious * — 30m HS 4b
FA Colin Moody & Morris MacLeod 20 June 1992

Climb the obvious left-facing corner-crack.

11 Disturbing the Wildlife * — 30m HVS 5a
FA Colin Moody & Morris MacLeod 20 June 1992

The wide crack right of 10. Either start directly up the chimney or move up right from the start of 10. The crack leads to a slab then a short wall.

ISLE OF SKYE NEIST POINT

12 Solar Furnace *   30m VS 4b

FA Colin Moody & Neil Horn 18 June 1992

Start up a shallow corner right of 11, step left and continue up cracks to the slab and short wall.

13 Tourist Attraction ★★   25m HVS 5b

FA Colin Moody & Allan Petrie 6 August 1994

Start just right of 12. Climb the crack on the left side of the clean pillar, trending right to finish at the top of the pillar.

SOUTH WALL — E1 5b

14 Wind and Wuthering ★★   35m HVS 5a

FA Dave Armstrong & Pete Whillance 30 December 1981

The less prominent crack 6m right of the most prominent (often wet) crack on the wall. Start up crack to a large wedged block on a ledge on the right. Follow the groove and crack above leading to an easier finishing crack.

15 Cold Turkey ★★   35m HVS 5a

FA Pete Whillance & Dave Armstrong 30 December 1981

Start 6m right of 14 from a platform at a slightly higher level. Up the chimney crack to a ledge. Continue up jamming cracks to finish up an open, left-facing corner.

HEADLAND

The following 3 routes are on the headland between **Bay 3** and **Bay 4**. **Descent:** Abseil from blocks at the tip of the buttress to a ledge.

16 The Murray Mint ★★   30m E3 6a

FA Murray Hamilton 1 May 1983

On the left side of the headland is an initially thin crack. Follow a thin crack to ledges. Move up to gain the thin crack above, widening towards the top.

17 Grooveless Bodily Harm ★★★   30m E3 6a

FA Murray Hamilton, Kenny Spence & Bob Duncan 1 May 1983

The leftmost of twin grooves in the centre of the headland. Start right of the arête. Up the groove and through a stepped bulge. Continue in the same line, finishing out rightwards.

18 The Cruiser ★★   30m E1 5b

FA Mark Worsley & Grant Urquhart 1 July 1989

The rightmost crack/groove system. From the initial crack gain a right-slanting groove which leads to a wider crack to top.

BAY 4   15min

A broad bay with small white building above the highest point at the back. There is a prominent pillar in the back wall with a through route at its base, best seen from the south side of the bay.

19 Inanimate Objects Fight Back ★★★　30m E4 6a
FA George Smith & Adam Wainwright May 1995

Magnificent sustained climbing up the obvious rightwards curving groove with a jammed block at the top, at the back left of the bay. Gained by abseil to good ledges.

20 Fat Man's Folly ★　35m HVS 5a
FA Rab Anderson & Murray Hamilton 21 May 1983

An atmospheric route up the chimney crack formed by the southern side of the pillar. Up the chimney until further progress is barred. Squeeze out to regain the outside world and continue up the corner-crack to the top.

21 Sealy Dan ★　30m HVS 5a
FA Rab Anderson & Murray Hamilton 22 May 1983

The wall just left of the corner. Start on a ledge on the left side of a rock fin. Pull round right into a groove which leads to the top of the fin. Move up the thin crack above and then rightwards to finish.

22 Starfish Enterprise ★★★　30m E4 6b
FA Murray Hamilton & Rab Anderson 22 May 1983

The prominent V-groove right of the corner. Gain and climb the groove to finish over a small roof and thin crack above.

23 Jellyfish Roll ★★　25m E2 5c
FA Murray Hamilton & Rab Anderson 22 May 1983

The left-hand of the obvious cracks, starting from a ledge 3m up, just right of 22.

24 Sea Enemy ★　25m E1 5b
FA Murray Hamilton & Bob Duncan 2 May 1983

The crack just right of 23, starting from the same ledge.

25 Prawn Broker ★★　30m E3 5b
FA Murray Hamilton & Rab Anderson 23 May 1983

The rightmost of the three cracks.

NG 126 473  15min

CUMHANN GEODHA

Between **Bay 4** and **Conductor Cove** is a long narrow inlet with an extensive series of groove lines on the south-west facing wall. The following routes are all situated above the large ledge at the left (north-west) end.
Descent: Abseil from a block well back from the edge down the wall just left of 2.

1 Curry Island ★　15m E1 5a
FA Colin Moody & Cynthia Grindley 23 October 2005

The left rib. Step down onto sloping foot ledge. Climb rib and wall just right, finishing on the rib.

ISLE OF SKYE NEIST POINT

2. The Old Warden *   15m HVS 5a
FA Gary Latter & Jon Rabey 4 April 1998

The left-facing corner-crack at the left side of the pillar. After some ledges, step right and finish up a hand-crack in the arête, or direct at the same grade.

3. The Old Hex *   15m HVS 5a
FA Colin Moody & Cynthia Grindley 23 October 2005

The crack. Climb the crack and pull left onto a ledge. Continue easily (next to 2), then step right and follow continuation crack.

NG 126 473   15min

CONDUCTOR COVE

Good sheltered mainly non-tidal location with good rock and friction.

Descent: Follow the well concealed conductor, which leads down a short chimney to the base.

> The 'new' corner at the left end is *Desmond the Slapper* • E1 5b.

1. Ruby Groove *   8m VS 4b
FA Andrew & R.Holden 24 September 1990

The first steep chimney groove level with the descent chimney. Start from the lightning conductor.

2. Dulux Corner *   12m HS 4b
FA Mark Hudson & Peter Brown 26 September 1990

Corner with a choice of three finishes, hardest on the right.

3. Gannet Crack *   12m VS 5a
FA Andrew & Roger Holden 25 September 1990

The first crack in the smooth south facing wall.

> The wall and blocky crack 5m further right is route 4 *Natural Look* Severe 4a; the corner is route 5 *Lottery Winner* E1 5c.

4. Quite Fatigued *   15m HVS 5b
FA Gary Latter, Jon & Dave Rabey & Louise Gordon Canning 8 April 1998

The groove on the right side of the pillar, easing in its upper half.

5. Before the Deluge *   15m HS 4b
FA Gary Latter, Jon & Dave Rabey & Louise Gordon Canning 8 April 1998

The left of two narrow chimney-cracks.

6. Quantum Tunnelling *   15m Hard Very Skinny
FA S.Buchanan 23 May 1998

The inside of the chokestoned chimney on the right edge of the ledge. Squirm upwards from the base of the chimney. *"Remove jacket, extraneous protection and helmet as the chimney narrows, before arriving in daylight and climbing easier ground to the top. Not recommended for those with more than a 30" waist, claustrophobia or new lycra."*

6. The Umpire Strikes Back *   25m VS 4c
FA Colin Moody & Bruce Taylor 18 May 1996

The crack a short way further right then a bulge at twin square overhangs.

7. Lucky Strike *   25m HS 4a
FA unknown 1980s

Start beneath the prominent narrow chimney at the base of the wall. Negotiate the chimney with interest then follow the obvious line directly above the right end of the mid-height ledges.

8. Lightning Corner **   25m HVS 5a
FA Tony Furnis & Bill McRae 28 December 1981

Start at the far right end of the wall, where it turns seawards again. Climb the chimney crack to a platform. Move right and follow a small groove over a small overhang to the top by the corner of Lighthouse Wall.

15min

LIGHTHOUSE WALL

Descent: Abseil from metal fence-posts at the north end of the wall surrounding the lighthouse.

1 All Quiet on the Western Front ★★　　　**HVS 5a**
FA Colin Moody & Bruce Taylor 18 May 1996
The leftmost corner, beneath the abseil.

2 How the West Was Won ★★　　　**25m HVS 5a**
FA Bruce Taylor & Colin Moody 18 May 1996
The central corner. The right corner bending left to join it at mid-height is also HVS 5a.

3 Orca ★　　　**25m E2 5b**
FA Gary Latter & Martin Boyce 1 July 1999
The steep corner at the back of the bay, the base gained by a diagonal abseil westwards from the fence posts. Climb the corner, finishing with care up the final wall.

4 Neisty Beisty ★★★　　　**25m E3 5c**
FA Dougie Dinwoodie & Colin MacLean 13 November 1983
The prominent crack and groove system just left of a prominent chimney crack, characterised by undercut blocks and flakes.

5 Horny Corner ★　　　**20m VS 4c**
FA Colin Moody & Bruce Taylor 7 September 1991
The corner beneath the foghorn that faces the rocky island with a squat sea stack.

 15min

FOGHORN COVE

Further west, beyond the foghorn is a short (c. 12m) immaculate wall with two faces dropping into the sea. Ideal for deep water soloing, as there are no ledges at the base (beware the jellyfish though!).

1 Hypertension ★★　　　**12m F6b S0**
FA James Sutton & Leighton Jones (both solo) August 2004
The first line of cracks on the steep north-west facing wall. Traverse in from the left to below a small roof. Pull over the roof to follow the steep crack on improving holds. The crux is at the start.

2 Saline Solution ★　　　**12m F7a S0**
FA Jules Lines 26 May 2012
Start as for 1 and move right on undercuts before pulling through the bulge on sidepulls to reach a jug rail. Rockover onto the rail and step up left and crimp to a horizontal break. Move up and right more easily.

3 Dead Giveaway ★★　　　**12m F6b+ S0**
FA Simon Westaway 8 June 2013
The beautiful golden wall. Climb direct from under the small roof. Possibly the best route on the wall, but slightly eliminate.

4 Diaper Mention ★★　　　**12m F6a+ S0**
FA Ben Wear August 2005
The crack. Traverse in from the right to gain the crack (a lot harder at high tide). Climb the crack to a brilliant cross through to gain a flat ledge. Take a deep breath, mantel and blast on up to the top. "Celebrate by jumping off the top and try the unclimbed blank face to the right (6b?). Just like being on holiday!"

5 Fluid Dynamics ★★　　　**12m F7a S0**
FA Jules Lines 14 May 2009
The wall right of 4. Climb flakes to a blank section, then using a crafty left heel continue in a sustained manner up the wall.

6 Toxic Chemistry ★　　　**12m F6b+ S0**
FA Jules Lines 14 May 2009
A bit eliminate. The arête. Start up a flake left of the arête, move to the arête then back left to another flake, then back to the arête, finishing delicately via small hidden holds.

*Harry Westaway on Dead Giveaway, Tom Starks on Up.
Photo: Simon Westaway.*

6a Chemistry ★★   12m F7a S0
FA Julian Lines 26 May 2012

A far better and more direct line that climbs on the left side of the arête all the way to the top.

7 Up ★★   12m F4+ S1
FA Gary Latter 1 July 1999

The open groove on the arête between the two faces.

8 Immiscible ★★   12m F6c S0
FA Jules Lines 14 May 2009

The fine arête – not sustained, but one technical rockover.

9 Down ★   12m F3+ S0
FA Gary Latter 1 July 1999

The steep hand-crack at the right end, also useful as an approach.

Tony Whitehouse on the upper section of the classic Sword of Gideon, South Face, Sgurr a' Chaorachain. Photo Dave Simmonite.

APPLECROSS

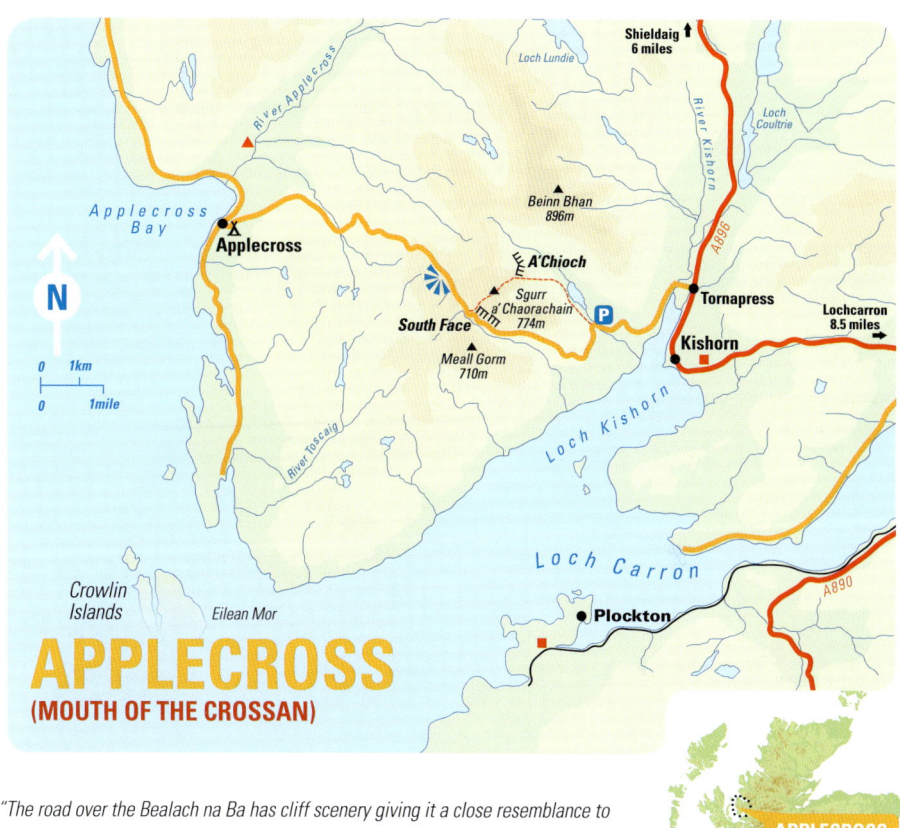

APPLECROSS
(MOUTH OF THE CROSSAN)

"The road over the Bealach na Ba has cliff scenery giving it a close resemblance to an Alpine pass, and a seaward view across the Isle of Skye. The road descends to Applecross through woods of great beauty which, after the moonlike desolation of the stony plateau, make deep imprint on the mind." – W H Murray, *Highland Landscape*, National Trust for Scotland, 1962.

This is the large elevated 'fish-tail' shaped peninsula between Loch Kishorn and Loch Torridon, due east of the north end of Skye and Raasay. It is crossed by a steep winding road over the Bealach na Ba (Pass of the Cattle), the third highest road in Britain, (after Glen Shee and The Lecht) rising from sea level to 625m in less than 6 miles.

Accommodation: Bunkhouses: The Bunkhouse, Plockton (℡ 01599 544235; www.visitplockton.com); Gerry's Hostel, Craig, by Achnashellach (℡ 01520 766232; www.gerryshostel.com); Sanachan Bunkhouse (℡ 01520 733484; www.ourscottishadventure.com); Hartfield House Hostel (℡ 01520 744333; www.hartfieldhouse.org.uk). See also Skye and Torridon. **Campsites:** The Wee Campsite, Lochcarron (Apr–Oct; ℡ 07876 642355; www.facebook.com/oncroftroad); wild camping by the roadside or in corrie beneath A' Chioch; campsite at Applecross village (℡ 01520 744268; www.visitapplecross.com) or campsite adjacent to the Strathcarron Hotel (℡ 01520 722227;

www.strathcarronhotel.com). **Amenities:** Lochcarron has a supermarket, cafés, petrol station and an **ATM**; The Kishorn Seafood Bar is worth a mention (www.kishornseafoodbar.co.uk); The Bealach Café and Gallery at Tornapress is particularly recommended (www.thebealach.co.uk); The Junction café bistro, Applecross; the Potting Shed café and restaurant in the grounds of Applecross House. For good bar food, the Applecross Inn (☎ 01520 744262; www.applecrossinn.co.uk) with splendid outlook comes highly recommended; the Lochcarron Hotel (☎ 01520 722226; www.lochcarronhotel.com) is also reasonable and does good early breakfasts, even for non-residents.

SGURR A' CHAORACHAIN
(PEAK OF THE SHEEP RUN)

The mountain overlooking the north side of the Bealach na Ba, containing a number of fine Torridonian sandstone buttresses, all of quite different character.

1 – 1¼hr

A' CHIOCH (THE BREAST)
NG 797 427 **Alt:** 400 – 550m

Surprisingly, there is no cairn on the top.
Access: Turn west off the A896 Lochcarron – Kinlochewe road at Tornapress at the head of Loch Kishorn. Follow the road steeply up over the Bealach na Ba for 2.2 miles/3.5km to park next to a track on the right, about 200m beyond the stone bridge over the Russel Burn.
Approach: (A) Follow the good track to a small dam at the head of Loch Coire nan Arr then by a boggy path along the west shore before heading steeply north-west up the hillside, crossing the burn and up into the coire. Head out right for the lower tier (1 hour). To gain the **Middle Ledge** head diagonally up left to the right side of the large scree cone 100m left of **South Gully** to pick up a path leading right to the base of the routes. 1¼ hours.

(B) For those wishing to continue to the top of the mountain, drive to the top of the bealach to park on the left opposite a track on the right (6 miles/9.6km). Walk up the track to the radio mast. Descend the open grassy gully 150m east of the mast (NG 787 424) then contour left (east) beneath a number of broken buttresses for about 1km to cut up via a path leading onto **Middle Ledge** (1 hour).
Descent: With care down **South Gully**, which delineates the left side of the buttress, leading back down to the left end of **Middle Ledge**. There are three short steep sections, the first bypassed by a short scramble on the right (facing down), the second by a detour on the left and the third by easy rocks on the right. Perhaps quicker to make short (c. 15m) abseils from in situ slings at all three obstacles.

THE LOWER TIER

① Cioch Corner Superdirect ★★   165m HVS 5a
FA Ted Howard & Clive Rowland May 1970

"…when combined with Cioch Nose Direct this makes one of the longest and finest rock climbs in Britain." – Clive Rowland, *Scottish Mountaineering Club Journal*, 1975
Takes the obvious line of grooves and cracks from the foot of the Cioch to the **Middle Ledge**.

1. **40m 5a** Climb the corner to a blank section, move right then up and back left to a corner and so to the stance.
2. **35m 5a** Continue up the corner.
3. **20m 4c** Climb the right wall to a good ledge.
4+5. **70m 4b** Now follow the obvious chimney crack on the left and the slab above to the Middle Ledge.

THE UPPER TIER

All routes are accessed from **Middle Ledge**, which runs out right across the face from the base of **South Gully**.

② Snothard ★★   110m VS 4b
FA C.Dracup & R.Hobbs May 1969

The line of grooves starting 6m left of the second pitch of *Cioch Nose*.

1. **25m 4a** Start as for the *Cioch Nose* and climb up to the first terrace.
2. **20m 4b** Climb a groove until it is possible to step left onto a slab on the lip of a conspicuous overhang. Climb the slab and crack above to a ledge.
3. **25m 4b** Move left and climb a crack past three overhangs.
4. **40m –** Easy slabs and grooves lead to the top.

③ Cioch Nose ★★★★   135m Very Difficult
FA Tom Patey & Chris Bonington 12 August 1960

"The Diff. to end all Diffs… The party agreed that this route gave the best value for Difficult they have met in Scotland. It had appeared from almost any angle to be of sustained difficulty and great exposure." – Patey, *Scottish Mountaineering Club Journal*, 1961

Excellent exposed climbing, taking the cleanest and quickest drying area of rock on the cliff. An anatomical anomaly. There are two obvious starts, either side of a low overhang about 25m right of a prominent low roof directly above the path. Vandals have scratched CN on the rock at the base of both starts.

1a. **30m Left Start:** Severe 4a Start in a recess just left of a large block. Move out rightwards and up a cracked groove (just right of grass ledges), going up a tricky (very well protected) groove to a terrace. Walk right 6m to belay at the base of a corner.
1b. **30m Right Start:** Start about 10m further right, above a small step in the path and directly beneath the left end of a wide roof at 15m. Move up and climb a wide flake-crack then over ledges, continuing up a further groove on good holds to the terrace. Walk right 5m to belay at the base of the corner.
2. **20m** Climb the corner then break out right and follow easy rocks to a ledge on the very nose of the buttress; block belay and superb situation.
3. **15m** From 3m right of the block climb the steep frontal face on magnificent holds trending diagonally left. A remarkable pitch.
4. **15m** Climb just to the left of the belay, passing to the left of an overhang then back to the right to a thread belay on a terrace.
5. **35m** Walk right 10m to large blocks then climb the obvious line directly above to belay on the next terrace.
6. **20m** Step left and climb grooves in the arête to belay further back.

📷 *Derek Queenan on the third pitch of Cioch Nose on a dreich day.*

tress (or climb direct) then at about Moderate for about 100m to a terrace below the main band of cliff near the top. Climb the open groove in the left arête (35m) to finish more easily (15m) up the final wall. Continue up the east-north-east ridge, over a further five 'Ciochs' with a couple of tricky scrambling descents, to the radio mast.

4 Cioch Corner ★★   97m HVS 5a
FA C.Dracup & R.Hobbs 25 May 1969

The obvious dark corner round the edge from the *Cioch Nose*. Often damp and greasy on the initial pitch.

1. **27m 5a** Climb the corner, stepping out right to a ledge at top. Climb a flaky groove to belay in a grassy recess.
2. **20m 4c** Continue up the groove over a bulge then up the right wall to a ledge.
3. **20m 4a** Above, the groove overhangs at first then leads on to a grassy bay.
4. **30m –** Easier climbing to the top of the Cioch.

3a Cioch Nose Direct Start ★★   50m VS 4c
FA Tom Patey & Hamish MacInnes 9 June 1968

"This direct line excludes the only substandard section on the original 1960 route and further enhances a remarkably fine climb." – Patey, *Scottish Mountaineering Club Journal*, 1970

Start round the corner 30m beyond the original start directly underneath the nose at a huge mossy dièdre.

1. **40m 4c** Climb this for 6m then cross the left wall to reach an awkward 6m slot (crux). This gives access to the bold rib left of the huge dièdre. *"The angle continues vertical but the holds are prolific and the climb henceforward is no more than Difficult."* Belay at first good ledge 20m above.
2. **10m –** Continue straight up fine exposed sandstone to join the original route below the third pitch.

3b Upper Continuation ★   500m Very Difficult

The cliffs above the top of A' Chioch. Follow an obvious worn path round the left side of the first short clean but-

📷 *Karen Latter on the second pitch of The Sword of Gideon.*

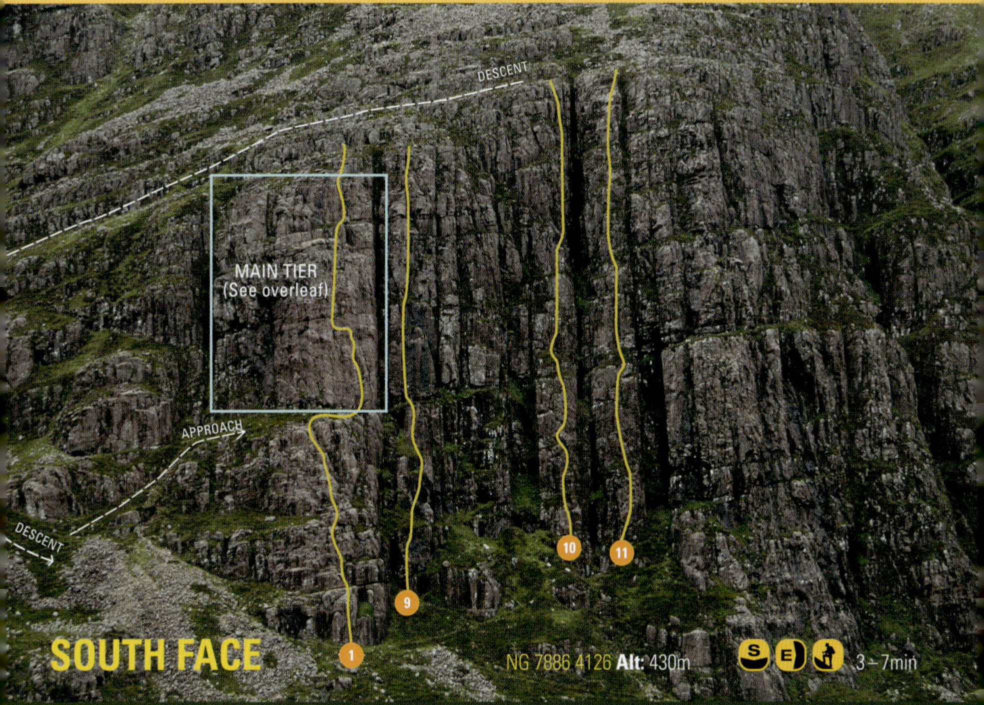

APPLECROSS SGURR A' CHAORACHAIN

SOUTH FACE

NG 7886 4126 **Alt:** 430m   3–7min

A fine sunny face directly above the road in the upper reaches of the bealach with a delightfully short approach for a 'mountain' crag. The face is split by gullies into six fairly distinct buttresses, numbered from left to right.

Access: Continue up the Bealach na Ba past the Russel Burn for a further 2.5 miles/4km to a parking spot on the right (north) side of the road just beyond the leftmost crag.

Approach: Head diagonally right up the hillside. 3 minutes to lower tier; 7 minutes to the main tier.

Descent: From the top, pick up a path heading diagonally left (west) then down to just east of a small outcrop, cutting back round to the base.

1 The Sword of Gideon ★★★   115m VS 4c
FA Tom Patey (solo) 11 October 1961

Start in the centre of the lower tier.

1 **60m 4b** Climb a vague flake on the steep initial wall, stepping left and up. Continue by pleasant scrambling to belay just beneath a terrace. Walk right to the right end of the terrace.

2 **35m 4c** Climb the shallow groove near the right for 15m *"until holds give out"*. Tread delicately across left (crux) to a good ledge in the centre of the face, immediately beneath a prominent discontinuous crack (well seen from below). Climb the crack over a bulge on good holds and continue more easily up the crack to belay on a large ledge (the highest of three). 1a *Original Start* ascends the right arête just right of the normal start, traversing left to join the traverse. This reduces the overall grade to 4b with the traverse becoming the crux.

3 **20m 4b** Continue the logical line up the right side of the face to finish.

4 Gideon's Wrath ★★   35m E1 5b
FA Ken Crocket & Colin Stead 21 August 1971

Good steady climbing with a serious start. Start at a shallow left-slanting groove below an obvious triangular niche.

1. **15m 5b** Climb a thin crack to the niche and traverse left 3m to belay on a ledge beneath an overhang.
2. **20m 5b** Climb the overhang above and follow the obvious line, trending right to finish on good holds just right of the biggest bulge.

4a Direct Finish ★★   35m E1 5b
FA Terry Doe & A.Brooks 19 June 1973

Instead of traversing, continue up a thin crack to a triangular niche then trend right to join 5 at the small roof and PR. Finish as for that route.

4b More Wrath Variation ★★   35m E2 5c
FA Michael Barnard & Alan Hill 29 June 2019

Follow 4a to the triangular niche. Pull straight through this, then move up and left to a 1.5" cam slot. Step back right to reach an easier crack and continue up this.

5 Lost Supper ★★   35m E2 5b
FA Terry Doe & J.Duncan 25 May 1973

Immediately right of 4 is a series of cracks in a grey patch of rock at 5m. Climb up through these and continue up to a small roof. Either pull directly through the roof to easier climbing, or traverse right from immediately beneath the roof to break up a tiny ramp at 5a.

6 Sword Swallower ★★   35m E2 5c
FA John Lyall & Andy Nisbet 15 June 1993

A fine direct line up the centre of the wall. Start 2m left of 1a and climb easily to the right end of a ledge 3m up. Go up cracks (crux) until moves left lead to a small pod. Up this then up and left to clip an old PR beside a small triangular roof (there is another triangular roof below and left). Traverse right and up a crack to an easier finish.

MAIN TIER   NG 7883 4129

Descent: 35m abseil from sling & ring on large block towards left end of terrace/ledges.

2 Old Wounds ★★   40m E3 5c
FA Alex & Martin Moran 19 June 2010

The overhang and enticing crack-line on the left arête gives a good challenge. Scramble up to belay at a crack in the initial wall.

1. **25m 5c** Climb the crack to the halfway ledge, pull boldly through the roof and layback the crack to a finishing bulge.
2. **15m** Climb easy rocks on the right to the top.

3 Wrathchild ★   35m E2 5c
FA Michael Barnard & Alan Hill 27 May 2017

Climbs the next break in the wall left of 4, through a white patch. Continue through the overhang as for that route finishing directly instead of trending right.

1a The Sword of Gideon Direct Start ** 15m E1 5b
FA unknown 1960s?

Good climbing, quite bold. Climb the thin groove leading directly to the prominent crack in the upper part of the normal route. Easier for the tall.

7 The Kings of Midian * 35m E1 5b
FA John Lyall & Andy Nisbet 15 June 1993

Climbs the right edge of the wall. Start just right of 1 at the wall's right arête. Climb a parallel line to 1 to join that route at the start of the crux traverse. Move up and traverse right across a wall with twin cracks to gain a big ledge. Finish easier straight up the scooped wall above.

8 Orcrist ** 60m E1 5b
FA Ross Jones & Andy Nisbet 14 August 2005

The crack in the sidewall gives sustained but well-protected climbing.

1. **30m 5b** Climb the chimney which forms the right side to where a crack leaves the chimney. Follow this to a bulge, move right through this and follow another crack to the arête.
2. **30m 4a** Finish up the arête.

9 Anduril * 98m VS 5a
FA Ben Beattie & J.Napoleoni 7 July 1970

Good climbing following a line of cracks near the left side of **Number 2 Buttress**. Start just right of the gully separating the buttresses.

1. **15m 4a** Follow the left edge of clean slabs to a grass ledge.
2. **20m 5a** Climb a thin groove, going slightly rightwards up the wall on the right then over a short rock step and grass to the base of the next clean wall.
3. **10m 4c** Go up the left edge to a good hold then more easily to a terrace.
4. **18m 4c** Climb the crack leading to a terrace, continuing to a further terrace.
5. **35m 4b** Traverse right to a bay beneath a clean overhanging crack. Climb this then by a prominent deep corner to finish more easily.

10 Bumblytwo * 140m VS 4b
FA Ben Beattie, K.Hiles & E.Gautier June 1970

Good sparsely protected climbing up the slender **Number 3 Buttress**.

1. **25m** – Ascend two walls to a spike on the left.
2. **20m 4b** Step delicately up onto a sloping ledge then traverse right to climb delicate unprotected ground to a ledge.
3. **25m** – Continue straight up, avoiding a steep wall by going left up a ramp to a ledge.
4. **25m 4a** Step up then traverse right to slabby ground and up this to a crack. Climb the crack then move back left to the centre of the face leading to a large block.
5. **45m 4b** The steep wall (avoidable on the left by stepping across the gap to climb a groove – 4a). The best line continues further up and left, trending right across smooth pink rock to finish direct. Unprotected 4b, (possibly HVS).

11 Bumblyone ** HS 4a
FA Tony Cardwell, Ben Beattie & C.Brooker 27 June 1970

Good climbing up the slender **Number 4 Buttress**.

1. **45m 4a** Climb a ramp rightwards to a prominent flake-crack. A better 4b start climbs the steep wall off a block on the right to gain the flake-crack. Continue up the crack to a terrace then easier up the crest to a tree.
2. **30m 4a** Climb the corner to a ledge (possible belay) then the clean wall.
3. **55m** – Finish up the easier crest.

📷 *Karen Latter starting up the first pitch of The Sword of Gideon.*

Matthew Glenn enjoying the evening sun on the immaculate airy classic The Pillar, Diabaig (page 114).

TORRIDON

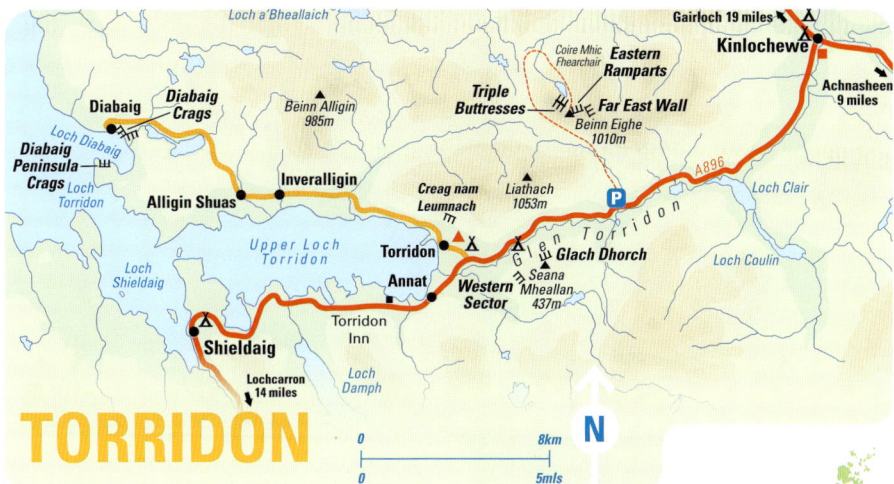

The finest mountain scenery of all the ranges, Torridon is the district name for the area either side of Glen Torridon and Upper Loch Torridon. The mountains give many excellent expeditions and some wonderful winter venues but only one, Beinn Eighe's magnificent Coire Mhic Fhearchair, gives good rock climbing. The recent resurgence of interest in outcrop climbing has led to the development of a number of sandstone outcrops, though the incomparable gneiss crags at Diabaig still prove hard to surpass.

Accommodation: Youth Hostel: Torridon (Mar–Oct; ☎ 01445 791284; www.hostellingscotland.org.uk).

Campsites: Torridon Campsite (tents only) opposite the visitor centre in Torridon village; wild camping in Glen Torridon – most popular spot is in the pine trees on the south side of the road at NG 917 554 about 0.7 mile/1km east of Torridon village, though this can be very midgy. In such conditions a better option (and within staggering distance of the pub!) is on the foreshore at the south-east end of Upper Loch Torridon on the north side of the road opposite Annat (0.5 mile/0.8km east of Torridon Inn). Shieldaig Camping and Cabins (☎ 01520 755224; www.shieldaigcampingandcabins.co.uk). **Club Hut:** SMC Ling Hut at east end of Glen Torridon, opposite car park for Liathach and Beinn Eighe. **Bothy:** Craig (MBA) 2.5 miles/4km walk north along coast from Diabaig.

Amenities: Showers at Loch Torridon community centre (www.lochtorridoncentre.co.uk); Torridon Stores & Café (www.torridonstoresandcafé.co.uk); café & restaurant opposite parking at Diabaig (www.gille-brighde.com); shop in Shieldaig, café (www.nannysshieldaig.com); café & shop at the petrol station, Kinlochewe (www.kinlocheweservices.co.uk). The Torridon Inn (☎ 01445 791242; www.thetorridon.com) is the only decent pub for miles around, though also one of the dearest in the Highlands.

TIC: Nearest is at Ullapool (☎ 01854 612486; www.visitscotland.com). The NT for S Countryside Centre opposite the campsite provides regularly updated weather forecasts (Apr–Sept; ☎ 01445 791221; www.nts.org.uk).

"Glen Torridon, its loch, and the mountains to either side, exhibit more of mountain beauty than any other district of Scotland, including Skye."
– W H Murray, *Highland Landscape*, National Trust for Scotland, 1962

BEINN EIGHE
(FILE MOUNTAIN)

COIRE MHIC FHEARCHAIR
(FARQUHAR'S CORRIE)

The great westerly corrie is the showpiece of the mountain, between the highest top Ruadh-stac Mor (big red stac) NG 951 611 and the most westerly peak Sail Mhor (big heel) NG 938 605. The corrie holds some of the finest situated mountain cliffs anywhere, including the famous and much vaunted **Triple Buttresses** sweeping up to the summit of Coinneach Mhor (the big moss) NG 944 600 at the back of the corrie with exquisite views from the archetypal mountain corrie north over the hills of the Flowerdale Forest. There is a lot of snow-laden hillside above and many of the routes take some time to dry completely.

The cliffs are formed of two distinct rock types. The lower plinth is of Torridonian sandstone but the main upper rocks are composed of a grey Cambrian quartzite, forming square cut features. Many of the routes ascend impressive ground for the grade, the quartzite often offering good holds and protection. The cliffs do not dry quickly, the sandstone tending to be more technical, vegetated and treacherous when wet, though the quartzite is not too slippery away from the cracks. The quartzite sections of the classic **Triple Buttress** routes can readily be climbed in the wet.

Access: Park at the large car park on the north side of Glen Torridon, beneath the east end of Liathach – 5.6 miles/9km from Kinlochewe; 3.6 miles/5.8km from Torridon.

Approach: (A) From the car park follow the good path up the west side of Coire Dubh Mor (the prominent bealach separating Liathach from Beinn Eighe) for 2.5km to cross the stream by a set of stepping stones. Continue for just over a kilometre and take the right fork (just before the path starts to descend) which curves round and eventually leads steeply up by the right side of some waterfalls to the spectacularly-situated loch just beyond the lip of the corrie (2 hours). Follow the path round the right side of the loch then steeply up in the direction of the chosen cliff in a further 50 mins.

(B) Masochists searching for the shortest possible approach can head steeply up the hill due north from the stepping stones (a gruelling slog) over the top, leaving sacs at the top of the chosen cliff. 2¼ hours.

Descent: The best descent back into the corrie is by the prominent scree gully bounding the left (east) side of the **Far East Wall**. From the top of the cliffs the shortest return to the road is to head south-east along the ridge to a col at NG 956 595 then south down a long narrow scree shoot, crossing the Allt Coire Dubh Mor to regain the approach path. Those wishing to climb a second route (or approach from above) on either the **Far East Wall**, **Eastern Ramparts** or **West Buttress, Quartzite Tier** can descend the chosen route by two 50m abseils, retrieving the gear on ascent.

FAR EAST WALL 2¾hr
NG 949 602 Alt: 800m

The long rectangular wall high on the left side of the corrie. The wall starts to catch the sun in June about 3pm and holds it until 10:30pm, consequently drying out faster than much of the **Eastern Ramparts** (which lose the sun at 11am).

1 Sting Direct ** 90m E1 5c
FA Tim Rankin, Guy Robertson & Jason Currie 23 June 2000

A worthwhile direct version taking the prominent crack up the left side of the clean grey wall. Start on a long grassy ledge under the buttress a few metres right of the left end.

  1 45m 5c Follow the obvious crack starting a little way up the lower groove leading all the way to the top of the huge flake.

  2 45m 5b Follow a steep crack then grooves directly to the top (left of the final chimney of original route).

2 Sunscream ** 110m E5 6b
FA Tim Rankin & Guy Robertson 23 June 2000

An excellent varied route taking a direct line based on the wall and slight hanging groove left of *Moonshine*. Not as well protected as other routes hereabouts. Start at the base of the groove of *Sting Direct*.

  1 35m 6a Climb directly up through a bulging nose to a depression in the centre of the wall. Follow the obvious line, trending slightly right on dwindling holds until a scary step up (serious) gains better holds leading directly to the horizontal fault. Pull left through the overhang to belay on small ledges.

  2 25m 6b Climb up left across twin grooves to gain the arête forming the right edge of the deep groove of *Sting*. Move delicately up then make a desperate move back right (crux) to better holds at the base of a slim hanging groove. Climb the strenuous groove until a standing position can be gained on a jug on the right arête. Continue straight up for 10m (common with *Moonshine*) then pull left into a niche under a huge roof. Belay on the left.

  3 50m 5a Step left round the edge into a corner and climb this to swing back right onto the face. Climb straight up past a slight niche and continue up the fine wall to easy ground and the top.

3 Moonshine *** 95m E4 6a
FA Chris Forrest & Andy Nisbet 10 June 1988

The main pitch takes the shallow overhanging groove left of the bulging nose of the buttress. Sustained technical climbing. Start on the long grassy ledge under the buttress, about 10m from the left end by a small rock scar.

  1 25m 5b Go straight up the wall then move right into a flake line and follow this to a belay by the horizontal break.

  2 35m 6a Go diagonally left to gain the base of the

groove (bold). Climb the groove with increasing difficulty to a foothold on the left arête. Climb straight up to an overhang then traverse right and up to a ledge.

3 **35m 5b** Climb the short awkward corner above then move left and up a long easy wall to finish.

4 Angel Face ★★★★　　　　　　　　95m E2 5c
FA Chris Forrest & Andy Nisbet 1 June 1988

Excellent sustained climbing following a sensational and improbable line above the bulging nose of the wall. Protection is excellent apart from bold moves to gain the tiny ramp on pitch 2. Start as for *The Reaper*.

1 **15m 5a** As for *The Reaper*.
2 **35m 5c** Climb *The Reaper* groove to the horizontal fault (technical crux). Traverse left about 5m along the fault to a small pedestal. Climb the wall above then move left to gain a tiny ramp. Go up the ramp to a crack then make a long step left into the base of a thinner crack. Climb the crack to a small roof. Traverse delicately left under the roof to the edge of nowhere then return unexpectedly right to a belay ledge. A crack above the right end of the ledge takes large wires.
3 **45m 5b** Climb the crack, passing the belay nuts.

Rick Campbell and Paul Thorburn on the crux pitch of Moonshine.

When the crack becomes unfriendly move slightly rightwards and up to a large flake-ledge. Go on up the wall above to a smaller flake-ledge. Traverse left to a large block (possible belay). Trend rightwards across slabbier ground to a steep blocky finish.

5 Seeds of Destruction ★★★　　　　　95m E3 5c
FA Andy Nisbet & Willie Todd 9 June 1988

Fine sustained climbing up the wall left of *The Reaper*. Start as for *The Reaper*.

1 **15m 5a** As for *The Reaper*.
2 **20m 5c** Climb *The Reaper* groove to the horizontal fault and traverse left to the pedestal on *Angel Face*. Move rightwards and pull over a bulge into a shallow corner. Belay under a smooth groove on the right.
3 **30m 5c** Climb the groove to a large ledge on the right. Step back down and traverse left until a left-facing corner can be gained. Climb the corner to the right of the large flake-ledge of *Angel Face*. Go up the wall above to the next ledge.
4 **30m 5c** Go up to a small rock scar then steeply up and left to a rest at a horizontal break with a good runner. Traverse right then go up into a curving groove on the right. Above this, go directly up steep blocky ground to finish.

6 The Reaper ★★　　　　　　　　　　95m E2 5c
FA Brian Sprunt & Greg Strange 17 May 1980

The original route on this wall, giving fine bold climbing up the vertical crack-line on the right side of the grey wall. At one point Sprunt, arms flailing and a long way above protection, hooked his chin on a hold for a rest! Start on the long grass terrace at the left end of a long flake embedded against the right side of the lower wall.

1 **15m 5a** Climb a narrow ramp leftwards, move right into a shallow groove and climb it to a grass ledge at the base of a larger groove on the right.
2 **25m 5c** Climb the left-leaning groove to reach the prominent horizontal fault taken by *Angel Face* (technical crux). Traverse right until below the left side of the large recess above. Climb steeply to reach a crack (not visible from the fault) in the left

side of the recess. Climb the crack to belay in a niche.
3 **25m 5b** Continue up the crack to a ledge on the left.
4 **30m 5a** Go up right into a shallow corner, move further right then zigzag to finish up a prominent chimney.

7 Kamikaze *   95m VS 4c
FA Jim Brumfitt & Bill Sproul 30 May 1966

The left edge of the big pillar at the right end of the cliff. Start at a large damp overhung recess.
1 **25m 4c** Climb up the recess until it is possible to traverse right to a shallow groove. Climb this, moving right to belay beneath a chimney in an obvious fault line.
2 **25m 4c** Ascend the chimney to the base of a deeper wider chimney.
3 **25m 4c** Continue up the overhanging chimney leading to a cave beneath a huge projecting 'beak'. Make a spectacular traverse out left and climb a groove to easier ground.
4 **20m** – Finish easily up the groove above.

8 New World Order ***   100m E6 6b
FA Murdoch Jamieson & Guy Robertson 21 July 2014

This follows the obvious corner which leads to roofs to the left of *Fascist Groove Thang*. Strenuous and well protected, at the top end of the grade.
1 **45m 5b** As for *Fascist Groove Thang*.
2 **25m 6b** Climb the corner with increasing difficulty, passing an overlap until it is possible to gain small edges on the left wall. Make moves up right to reach the base of the crack which leads to a roof. Turn the roof on its right to gain another crack. Follow this for a few moves (sting in the tail!) until possible to step right to a small ledge (immediately up left of 'the Fascist Groove').
3 **30m 5b** Traverse left and up into the corner below the roof. Make airy moves out left to gain the arête. Follow this to the top.

9 Fascist Groove Thang ***   105m E7 6c
FA Pitch 1 Ian Taylor, Rick Campbell & Paul Thorburn 24 June 1995;
Complete route Paul Thorburn & Gary Latter 26 June 1995

Climbs a faint weakness up the wall left of *Ling Dynasty* with a very powerful technical crux. Start at the prominent groove 20m left of *Ling Dynasty*.
1 **45m 5b** Follow the groove, loose at first, past two ledges to belay on a slab or small inset ledge.
2 **25m 6c** With a runner in the corner above traverse right under a small overlap to a good hold. Move up left onto a ramp (reasonable rest) then follow a hairline crack to a spike. Move up to the right end of an overlap then make difficult moves up and across the wall right of the 'fascist groove', moving up to belay below a large crack.
3 **35m 5c** Climb the steep crack until the angle eases, follow the left arête then a crack to easy ground.

10 Ling Dynasty ***   100m E5 6a
FA Graeme Livingston & Andy Nisbet July 1987

Superb well protected climbing. Starts up the prominent chimney then continues straight up a magnificent crack and through the big roof above. Start at the wet slit cave at the base of the chimney.

1 **50m 5b** The first pitch of the chimney was wet, so the rib on the right was gained by steep moves out of the cave, returning to the original route above the cave. Continue up the fault then a steep crack and the wall on the right to a ledge.

2 **35m 6a** Step left into the crack-line and climb it to a roof. Pull out rightwards round the roof into the upper continuation of the crack and climb it to the big roof (very sustained). Climb the wide crack in the roof. Go leftwards up the thin ramp above and belay.

3 **15m 4c** Move right and up a corner to the top.

11 Groovin' High ★★★ 100m E1 5b

FA Rob Archbold, John Ingram & Greg Strange 7 July 1973

An excellent well positioned route following a line of grooves near the centre of the steep grey pillar. Start about 6m right of the prominent deep slit cave of *Ling Dynasty*.

1 **30m 5a** Climb short walls and corners to a big ledge.

2 **35m 5a** Climb the steep corner above the left end of the ledge to a belay.

3 **35m 5b** Move out right and continue up steep grooves to the top. A fine pitch.

12 Sumo ★★★★ 85m E3 5c

FA Andy Cunningham & Andy Nisbet 20 June 1987

Brilliant climbing up the vertical crack and wall just right of *Groovin' High*. The superb crux pitch is strenuous, sustained and well protected. Start 2m right of *Groovin' High*.

1 **30m 4c** Climb corners and short walls right of *Groovin' High* arriving on the large ledge 3m to its right. Traverse right along the ledge to belay.

2 **30m 5c** Climb a steep corner then the crack-line to enter a groove below a roof. Move left to good holds and re-enter the groove beside the roof. A strenuous bulge leads to a belay.

3 **25m 5b** Take the shallow groove above to horizontal cracks. Traverse right into a corner, climb the corner and return diagonally left until above the belay at a small roof. Finish rightwards up a small ramp and back left on big holds to the top.

13 Bodyheat ★★★ 80m E5 6a

FA Rick Campbell & Paul Thorburn 25 June 1995

The immaculate cracked wall right of *Sumo*.

1 **30m 4c** Follow *Sumo* to a large ledge, move up right to climb a steep groove to belay right of a large block.

2 **20m 6a** From the block follow ramps up right to a stopping place at large flat holds. Move slightly left onto a steep wall (RPs in thin horizontal crack) then straight up to a flake hold and good nut. A hard move leads to better holds leading to a small belay ledge beneath a flake.

3 **30m 5b** Move up the flake to an overlap, traverse right then follow a shallow groove and wall above to the top.

Dave Cuthbertson cruisin' up Groovin' High. Photo Jo George, Cubby Images.

Bodyheat, Paul Thorburn on first ascent. Photo Rick Campbell.

TORRIDON BEINN EIGHE | 99

NG 947 602 Alt: 800m 2¾hr

THE EASTERN RAMPARTS
The extensive left-flanking wall of the **East Buttress**, split for most of its length by the ledge of the Upper Girdle at a little over one third height.

1 Pale Rider ** 110m E1 5b
FA Andy Nisbet & Brian Lawrie 10 August 1986

The most prominent crack on the wall left of *The Pale Dièdre* – much easier than first impressions would suggest! The crack is characterised by two prominent projecting blocks where the angle eases. Start below and left of *The Pale Dièdre*.

1 **45m 4c** Climb directly up to the base of the corner, avoid the detached block on its left to gain the corner by delicate moves across pale rock. Follow the corner to gain the Upper Girdle. Belay 10m further left, just below and left of the crack (about 20m left of *The Pale Dièdre*).

2 **35m 5b** Climb the crack to a small ledge beside the projecting blocks then easily up right to belay on a large ledge.

3 **20m 4c** Return left to the original line. Avoid a blank section below bulge by going left round an edge then straight up the wall to belay beneath a short chimney on the left.

4 **10m 5a** Finish up the wall on the right.

2 The Pale Dièdre *** 105m E2 5c
FA Brian Sprunt & Greg Strange 18 May 1980

A brilliant route, the highlight being a long 40m pitch up the pale left-facing dièdre in the centre of the face. Start beneath a right-facing groove, directly beneath the prominent upper dièdre.

1 **40m 5b** Climb direct to overhangs, move left then go up and right to below the pale dièdre.

2 **40m 5c** Climb the dièdre.

3 **25m** – Climb the easy groove on the right.

3 Boggle *** 110m E1 5b
FA Robin Smith & Andy Wightman October 1961

A route of similar quality and difficulty as *Groovin' High*. Steep and spectacular climbing for the grade.

1 **45m 5b** Pitch 1 of *The Pale Dièdre*, although the original route started 6m to the right, climbed via a small left-facing corner and joined *The Pale Dièdre* 10m up. Belay 5m right of *The Pale Dièdre* under the left of two corners.

2 **35m 5b** Either climb the left corner or (easier) start up the right and gain the left at mid-height. Move right and climb a wide crack behind a huge flake. Bypass a smaller flake to the right to reach a big left-facing corner. Climb this to half-height, then its right arête to reach a small ledge.

3 **30m 5a** Step left and climb a wide square groove which passes between two roofs and leads to easy ground.

TORRIDON BEINN EIGHE

NG 945 603 **Alt: 700m** 2¾hr

THE TRIPLE BUTTRESSES

The famed buttresses present steep walls on each of the left (north-east facing) flanks of the buttresses. The right-rising **Broad Terrace** separates the sandstone from the quartzite.

EAST BUTTRESS

1 Ordinary Route ★★   200m Difficult

FA George Bennett Gibbs, Edward Backhouse & Wilfred Mounsey

A classic, climbing direct up the crest of the buttress, usually climbed in boots and only marginally harder in the wet. The difficulties on the lower sandstone tier are avoided on the left. Traverse in from the left along Broad Terrace, which marks the top of the sandstone tier. This is straightforward with the exception of a wet exposed section (rope advised). Start about 10m left from the end of the terrace. Climb the steep face on good holds to a large ledge (30m). Continue in the same line (much variation possible), but a line slightly right of the crest is the most travelled. A short vertical corner right of the crest is the crux and the last of the difficulties. A further 50m of easy scrambling leads to the top of the buttress.

CENTRAL BUTTRESS

2 Piggott's Route ★★   270m Severe 4b

FA Fred Piggott & Morley Wood 1922

Start from the highest point of the grass on **Broad Terrace**. The classic original route on the buttress is often referred to as 'Central Buttress'. It follows a fine line up the crest, though the sandstone is quite vegetated and there are many ledges with loose blocks on the quartzite. When damp, the start of *Hamilton's Route* is a better option or miss out the sandstone by starting up **West Central Gully** (on the right between Central & West Buttress), about Moderate and not exposed. The route starts up the sandstone buttress by the obvious left-slanting line (not so obvious from directly below). Start at a pinnacle block lying against the face on the grass terrace just above the lowest rocks about a third of the way in from the right end.

From the block climb to a terrace, move right and reach a black cave clearly visible from below (30m). From the top of the cave follow the grassy rake up left to gain **Broad Terrace**. The next pitch starts from the highest point of the grass in a bay just right of the crest. Move up, trending left to a stance in a corner (20m). Traverse left to the edge and move round it by an exposed chimney on good holds (30m). Continue up easy ground to the base of the final tower (70m).

Alan Clapperton on Hamilton's Route, Central Buttress.

Karen Martin on Ordinary Route, East Buttress.

The route now follows a big groove starting just left of the crest and bending up right to follow the crest. Climb the big open groove over several short steps to a platform. On the right lies a short overhanging chimney crack with a crack to its right. Climb the chimney *"with great difficulty (sac hauling & combined tactics may help!)"* or avoid it, particularly in the wet, by a diversion onto the frontal face on the right, moving up to a prominent crack. Go up right on big blocks across the frontal face then pull up left to a flake on the wall and overlooking the crack. Step left under a bulge to the top of the crack and a bay just above. Either climb a short overhanging wall on the right or easier out left to a big pinnacle and right at the top (70m).

③ Nisbet's Route ★★★   280m VS 4c

FA Central Corner: Andy Nisbet & Neil Spinks September 1976; 1st quartzite tier: J.Colverd, Eddie Gillespie & Andy Nisbet 23 March 1998; top tier unknown

The best climbing on the buttress. The initial pitches (Central Corner) on the sandstone tier are high in the grade, particularly if carrying sacks; the quartzite tiers much more straightforward. Start beneath the very prominent dièdre on the left flank of the buttress.

1 **50m 4a** Climb up to the terrace beneath the corner then take a right-slanting line to the base of the corner.

2 **50m 4c** The corner – a superb sustained pitch, which can also be split. Walk right along Broad Terrace until 40m beyond the crest of *Piggott's Route*, where the highest sandstone forms a platform 10m above the terrace. (Below the right end of two right-facing corners originating at about 20m.)

3 **20m 4a** Climb onto the platform then directly up to the left end of a ledge (as for *Hamilton's Route*).

4 **20m 4b** Follow a fairly direct line up the wall above, slightly right then left to finish up a corner.

5 **40m 4a** Continue up steep blocky ground.

6 **40m** Scramble up to the base of the Upper Tier.

7 **30m 4b** Start between *Piggott's* & *Hamilton's*, just right of the crest and a block resting against the face. Climb a small right-facing corner with jammed flakes then the wider corner-crack above. Move out right and onto the crest.

8 **30m 4a** Finish steeply up the crest on good holds.

④ Hamilton's Route ★★★   270m Severe 4a

FA Hamish Hamilton & W.Kerr 4 June 1936

The other traditional classic line up the buttress gives more sustained climbing. Not as good a line, though the climbing is better, particularly on the Upper Tier. A pleasant easy start up *Slab Route* (Difficult) gains the quartzite tier. Start at the right end of the grass terrace below the sandstone tier, about 10m left of **West Central Gully**. Follow slabby rock parallel to the gully, taking the easiest line on good rock for 70m to a 'barrier slab' beneath Broad Terrace. Trend left up this (spaced protection), to reach the terrace.

Start about 40m right of the crest (*Piggott's Route*), where the highest sandstone forms a platform 10m above the terrace, (below the right end of two right-facing corners originating at about 20m). Climb onto the platform then directly up to the left end of a ledge (20m, 4a). Traverse right along the ledge for about 15m then trend up right to the edge of the buttress overlooking **West Central Gully** (20m). Climb a big left-slanting groove and continue to below a short bulging corner. Either climb the corner (4b) or traverse back right round an edge to climb a short corner, continuing to easier ground leading to the Final Tower. Start about 10m right of the crest below a huge right-curving flange. Climb diagonally right on flakes to gain the right end of a ledge atop large detached flake below the flange. Climb slabs diagonally rightwards (4a) to gain and follow large open chimneys leading to the top, keeping always on the right side of the buttress.

WEST BUTTRESS, SANDSTONE TIER

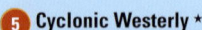 **Cyclonic Westerly** ★★   **90m E3 5c**
FA Andy Nisbet & Gill Ollerhead 29 June 1992

A fine route at the upper limit of its grade with a sustained balancy unprotected section on perfect rock. Start at the base of the straight steep corner.
 1 **10m 4c** Climb to the base of the corner.
 2 **25m 5c** Move out left on juggy rock to the base of a shallow corner in the left arête of the main corner. Step left and climb the arête direct (crux) to a steep line of flakes, which lead to a good ledge.
 3 **40m 5b** Move out left under a roof onto a slabbier face. Trend right then follow a left-slanting groove to a roof. Pull through this then follow two more grooves (not far left of the corner) to a huge ledge.
 4 **15m 4c** Climb easily through the final tier.

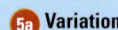 **Variation** ★   **E1 5b**
FA Andy Nisbet & Gill Ollerhead 29 June 1992

On pitch 2, instead of climbing the wall direct, climb diagonally left to a belay near a long groove (5a). Climb a short corner, then make a long deviation rightwards to regain the normal route a few metres below the roof on pitch 3 (5b).

WEST BUTTRESS, QUARTZITE TIER

Gain the **Second Terrace** either by climbing the lower sandstone tier, or up the blocky **Fuselage Gully** to traverse onto the buttress above the sandstone. Climb easily up the buttress until it steepens, move left and climb a short loose V.Diff. pitch leading to the Second Terrace.

 Shoot the Breeze ★★★   **90m E2 5c**
FA Andy Nisbet & Gill Ollerhead 26 May 1992

Excellent climbing with sensational positions, *"one of the wildest at its grade in Scotland"*. The crux is well protected. Start just right of the rock fall scar.
 1 **30m 5b** Climb up to and follow the corner-crack forming the right edge of the scar then direct to a small ledge.
 2 **30m 5a** Continue up the corner, moving leftwards through the capping overhangs at a prominent break. Move up 5m then traverse left and ascend the large arête leading into the corner on the left. Belay where the corner slants right.
 3 **30m 5c** Regain the arête by a foot ledge and climb it into the top of the corner. Return to the arête, follow this to overhangs then pull left into a short corner. Climb this with difficulty to easier, steep blocky ground leading to the top.

SEANA MHEALLAN
(OLD SMALL LUMP) NG 9252 5527 Alt: 290m 40min

GLACH DHORCH (DARK HOLLOW)

An excellent steep Torridonian sandstone crag high on the small hill on the south side of the western reaches of Glen Torridon with grand views over Liathach opposite. Receives the sun after around 2pm.

Access: Park on the A838 running through Glen Torridon, by the cattle grid east of the pines, 1.1 miles/1.8km east of the Torridon village turn-off.

Approach: Walk up the road to passing place overlooking bend in river, head downstream to a larger right bend to cross the River Torridon by some huge stepping stones. Cross initially boggy ground to pick up a fairly well-defined path cutting first rightwards, then leftwards up the hillside.

Descents: Easiest by abseil. For routes at the right end, a 45m abseil can be made down the inset slab of 3 *A Touch Too Much* from sling & maillon on a block on wall at back. For the left end, a 30m abseil from sling and maillon on large block above top of 19 *Mark of A Skyver*; or 27m from slings on blocks above 23 *Sandpiper* or 26 *The Torridonian*. On foot, go down right (east) from a prominent cairn near the top of *The Torridonian* to another cairn then an easier traverse down right to pick up an obvious line. **Care required, particularly in the wet.**

1 Edge of Enlightenment ★★ 30m E3 5c
FA Rab & Chris Anderson May/June 1990

Follow the thin crack up the left side of the arête to a ledge. Step right and climb the steep wall on good holds to a slab, move right and finish up the arête.

2 Path of Righteousness ★★ 30m E2 5c
FA Rab & Chris Anderson May/June 1990

Ascend the thin crack in the centre of the slab left of the arête to a ledge. Step right and follow the steep wall of 1 finishing up the steep corner. A hard move low down, then straightforward.

3 A Touch Too Much ★★★ 30m E3 5c
FA Rab & Chris Anderson May/June 1990

Marvellous climbing up the right-trending crack in the right side of the inset slab. Boldly climb an awkward thin crack to the break then the crack above leading into a shallow groove. Finish up the prominent crack above.

4 Seams Obvious ★★★ 30m E1 5b
FA Rab & Chris Anderson May/June 1990

Steady climbing after a tricky start. The central crack in the slab. Gain a large elongated pocket then a thin crack on the right which leads to a niche. Continue up the right branch of the crack to a ledge, then its continuation.

5 Seems the Same ★★ 30m HVS 5a
FA Rab & Chris Anderson May/June 1990

Take a short crack at the left side of the slab to the break. Step right and climb a thin crack into the niche. Continue up the left branch of the crack to a ledge, then its continuation.

6 Looks Different ★★ — 30m E1 5b
FA Rab & Chris Anderson May/June 1990

Follow 5 to the break then continue directly until moves left lead to a prominent crack. Finish up this.

7 Squeeze 'Em In ★ — 30m E1 5b
FA Rab & Chris Anderson May/June 1990

Follow the wide crack in the corner to ledge. Continue up to a pocket, then out right and up thin crack into a groove. Finish up the left wall.

8 Wide Deceiver ★ — 30m E1 5b
FA Rab & Chris Anderson May/June 1990

Ascend corner, then roof, finishing up crack above.

9 In the Groove ★ — 30m HVS 5a
FA Rab & Chris Anderson May/June 1990

Climb shallow groove to heather ledge, then continue in the same line up corner and crack.

10 Fistfighter ★★ — 30m E4 6a
FA Rab & Chris Anderson May/June 1990

The prominent crack splitting a bulge. Start left of the thin crack leading to the bulge. Gain a ledge, move right a short way to pull into the crack and move up to the break. Finish more easily up crack above.

Unknown climber getting In the Groove.

11 Rock Around the Block ★ — 30m E2 5c
FA Rab & Chris Anderson May/June 1990

Climb 10 to the ledge, then up to the break. Step right and climb left around a huge block into a short corner leading to a swing out right. Continue to heather, finishing up the wall left of the crack.

12 Cook the Shooter ★ — 30m E3 5c
FA Ed Edwards & Martin Moran 2 April 2009

Start up the corner 3m right of 13 and step left under the first roof to join it. Climb this to level with another roof on the left, step left out of the corner and climb a flake in the wall to a small ledge. Climb the wall above direct to a large break. Mantel onto the break and climb the wall above on the right side of the blunt arête to the top.

13 Shoot the Cuckoo ★ — 30m HVS 5a
FA Rab & Chris Anderson May/June 1990

The big open corner. Start up short crack on the left.

14 Hunter Killer ★★ — 30m E5 6b
FA Rab & Chris Anderson May/June 1990

Excellent climbing up the thin crack and arête. Climb up to a standing position on a small undercut shelf (R #1 in rightmost of three hairline cracks). Move up to a peg (very poor – 2019) then up the crack to the arête. Continue up the edge to a small block in a break, move right then direct to finish.

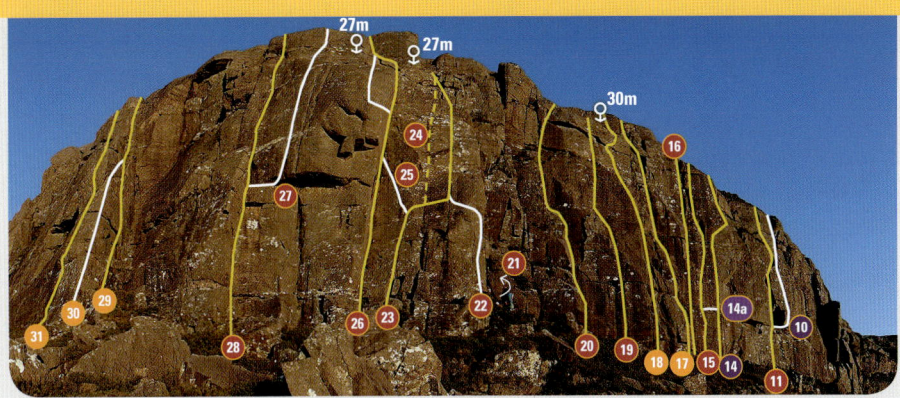

14a Hunter Killer Left Start ★★★   30m E4 6a
FA Ian Taylor & Tess Fryer 12 May 2017

A more balanced route. Start up the crack of 15 to the horizontal break, move right along this into the true line.

15 Exterminator ★★★   30m E3 5c
FA Rab & Chris Anderson May/June 1990

The crack and groove system splitting the centre of the wall.

> The very thin crack just right of 17 is
> 16 *Eliminator* ★ E3 6a.

17 The Deerstalker ★   30m HS 4b
FA Rab & Chris Anderson May/June 1990

The corner, containing a small rowan near the top.

18 Route with a View ★★   30m HVS 5a
FA Rab & Chris Anderson May/June 1990

Follow cracks in the buttress edge left of the corner to gain a blocky ledge, finishing up further cracks, gained from the left. *Direct* is E1 5b.

19 Mark of a Skyver ★★★   30m E2 5c
FA Rab & Chris Anderson May/June 1990

Climb a crack up the right side of the large flake then the thinner crack above.

20 View to a Hill ★   30m E1 5b
FA Rab & Chris Anderson May/June 1990

Follow the corner system to a heathery ledge. Exit right to a slab then by a crack to a niche to finish.

21 Crack of Ages ★★★   30m E2 5b
FA Rab & Chris Anderson May/June 1990

The prominent crack in the left wall of the corner.

22 Sandwich ★★   30m E3 5c
FA Rab & Chris Anderson May/June 1990

Great moves. Climb the arête to a niche, pull left out of this and finish up the final crack of 23.

Karen Latter on Route with a View.

23. Sandpiper ★★ — 30m E1 5b
FA Rab & Chris Anderson May/June 1990

This and the next two routes share a common start up a crack in the wall right of the main corner. Climb the crack a short way then step up right awkwardly to a thin crack. Continue across to the next crack and follow this.

24. Sandstorm ★★ — 30m E3 6b
FA Rab & Chris Anderson May/June 1990

Superb, though eliminate. Climb the thin crack to its end then use a pocket on the left to start the upper wall.

25. Thunderbird ★★ — 30m E3 6a
FA Dave Cuthbertson & Joanna George 25 June 2002

A photogenic, if wandering route. Start as for 23. Climb the crack trending left into the corner of 26 then up this for a few metres. Take the 'flying' hand traverse out to the left arête, step left and finish up a short crack in a fine position to easier ground.

26. The Torridonian ★★★★ — 30m E3 6a
FA Rab & Chris Anderson May/June 1990

The crag classic. The stunning corner, the most prominent feature of the crag. The crux is at the top.

27. Middle of the Road ★★ — 30m E3 5c
FA Rab & Chris Anderson May/June 1990

Around the edge to the left is a short overhanging corner. Climb it to a ledge, move right and follow the central crack.

28. Left in the Lurch ★★ — 30m E1 5b
FA Rab & Chris Anderson May/June 1990

Climb the corner as for 27 to the ledge. Climb the crack on the left to a niche, step right and finish up the wall.

29. Rejection ★ — 25m HVS 5a
FA Allen Fyffe & Anne Salisbury 18 May 1999

The jam crack in the wall, finishing up twin cracks.

30. Reject ★ — 30m VS 4c
FA Colin Moody & Ian Taylor 12 May 1993; Direct: John Lyall, Jonathan Preston & Jimmy Whyte 10 May 2016

The arête right of 31. Follow an obvious shelf right then the corner-crack, or direct up the rib.

31. Rowantree Crack ★★ — 30m VS 5a
FA Rab & Chris Anderson May/June 1990

The hand crack up the far left side of the left retaining rib of the recessed area. Climb the crack, passing a small rowan. A large cam (4 or 5") protects the steep 'one move wonder' crux.

32. Mackintosh Slab ★ — 30m E1 5b
FA Rab & Chris Anderson May/June 1990

The thin crack in the slab immediately left. Climb the crack into a corner beneath the prominent slanting roof. Pull out right, continuing up a crack and its thin continuation.

33. No Brats ★ — 30m E2 5b
FA Ian Taylor & Colin Moody 11 May 1993

Climb the slab rib left of the undercut slanting roof, traverse right above the lip and follow thin cracks to finish up the final crack of 32. The name is an anagram of *"Not Rab's!"*

Thunderbird, Dave Cuthbertson on the first ascent. Photo Jo George.

34 Rare Breed *   10m VS 5a
FA John Lyall & Jonathan Preston 14 May 2009

On the clean slabby wall above the left end of the descent route. The hanging crack, finishing up the steep rippled slab right of the top corner.

35 Neville the Hedgehog *   10m VS 4c
FA Paul & R.Mather 14 May 2006

Climb the left crack to ledge, step right and finish up short corner.

WESTERN SECTOR

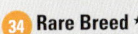 NG 921 547 **Alt:** 290m   SW   1hr

A long broken sill with a number of crags, clearly visible from Torridon village. Although shorter and more spread out than the main crag, they provide good climbing on very clean rock, including many easier routes. With a stunning and very sunny outlook down Loch Torridon, it is a good morning option prior to the sun warming up the main crag which is around 20 minutes away.

Approach: Initially as for **Seana Mheallan**, then branch off right up the prominent grassy trough leading to the terrace running out right at the base of the crags.

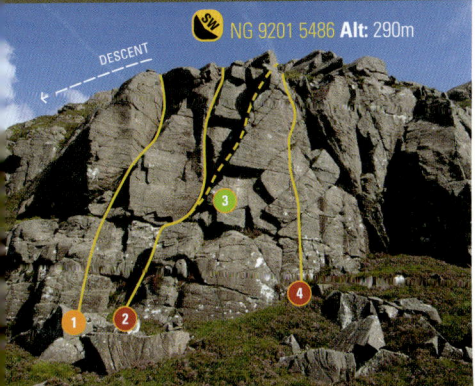

 NG 9201 5486 **Alt:** 290m

THE PROW

The left (east most) crag with three grooves (cairn below) which offers a preliminary change of aspect
Descent: Down an easy slanting shelf at the left (east) side of the crag, leading to the right of the rowan.

1 Cairn Terrier *   15m VS 5a
FA Andy Nisbet & Chris Watkins 13 July 1999

The left groove, with a bulge blocking access to the

well-defined V-groove.

② Terra Incognita ✱✱　　　　　　**15m E2 5c**
FA Gary Latter 14 August 2008

The steep central hanging groove.

③ Cairnaholics Anonymous ✱　　　**15m Severe 4a**
FA Andy & Gill Nisbet & Chris Watkins 13 July 1999

The slabby right groove.

④ Incognito ✱✱　　　　　　　　　**15m E1 5b**
FA John Lyall & Andy Nisbet 2 July 1998

The fine snaking crack-line. Start direct (crux).

PINK WALLS NG 9200 5480

Descents: Easiest by abseil – sling & maillon just left of the top of 3 *Andy had Fish and Chips for Tea*; there is also a large convenient triangular block near the edge towards the left end of **Quartz Slab**. Walking descents are a long way off down the extremities of the sector. Scrambling, the dirty corner and lower flakes above the start of 6 *Outswinger* is Difficult; a broken line right of 15 *Clingfilm* is easier, *"but finishes on some near vertical heather."*

① Fleeced ✱　　　　　　　　　　**20m HS 4c**
FA Steve Kennedy & Cynthia Grindley 16 July 1994

The prominent rib close to the left end. Climb the rib to a crack in a steepening then the crack to finish up a right-slanting corner.

③ Andy had Fish and Chips for Tea ✱✱✱　**15m E1 5b**
FA Colin Moody & Louise Gordon Canning 8 June 1999

The crack rising from the triangular slot, finishing left of a bulging nose.

④ Salt and Vinegar ✱✱　　　　　　**15m E2 5b**
FA Donald King & Nick Carter 7 June 2007

Fine well-protected climbing up the right-slanting groove. Climb the groove mainly by its right arête, then step left and pull over the roof easily.

⑤ Unmasked ✱✱　　　　　　　　　**20m HS 4b**
FA Steve Kennedy & Cynthia Grindley 16 July 1994

The slabby left-slanting corner; start up a wall on the right.

② Skye and Kyle against Trugs ✱　　**15m HVS 5a**
FA Colin Moody & Cynthia Grindley 16 July 2000

The right-slanting crack.

Karen Latter starting up Heather Said Sunshine.

6. Outswinger * — 15m E2 5c
FA Dave McGimpsey & Andy Nisbet 15 July 2000

The corner with twin stepped roofs. Start at the easy dirty corner on the left (high runner). Pull up right into the start of the stepped corner. Climb this, initially bold, leading round the roofs and up.

7. Nasal Abuse ** — 20m E2 5b
FA Colin Moody & Robbie Watson 3 July 1994

Move up and right to a ledge on the left side of the arête. Climb up from the ledge and finish up an easy corner.

8. The Age of Confusion ** — 20m E3 5c
FA Colin Moody & Louise Gordon Canning 17 June 1998

The rib right of 7. Start left of the rib. Move up right to a horizontal break (Camalot #4). Reach up then right to a crack, climb it, stepping left before the final overhang to finish up the rib.

9. Mechanical Sheep *** — 20m E2 5c
FA Colin Moody & Robbie Watson 3 July 1994

The clean-cut corner with an overhang at one-third height and another near the top.

10. Clockwork Rat * — 20m E2 5b
FA Andy Nisbet & Chris Watkins 13 July 1999

Strenuous but well protected. Start up the corner of 9 but move right to gain a crack in its right wall. Follow the crack round the right arête to a roof and rockfall scar. Break through the left side of the roof to finish up the continuation crack.

10a. Oi Big Nose * — 20m E2 5b
FA Gary & Karen Latter 15 April 2018

Climb direct line up the wall to finish over the roof, as for 10.

11. Skate ** — 20m VS 5a
FA Colin Moody & Robbie Watson 3 July 1994

Right of the corner is a short rib. Climb the rib then a crack past the left side of an overhang, finishing up a corner.

12. Hadrian's Wall ** — 20m HVS 5b
FA Colin Moody & Morris MacLeod 11 July 1995

Gain the top of a 2m pinnacle about 2m right of 11. Climb the crack on the right, moving over an overhang to finish up a short steep wall.

13. King Solomon's Marbles * — 15m E1 5b
FA Michael Barnard & John MacLeod 4 October 2015

The obvious thin crack is gained directly (bold). Start on a large block and move up and left to gain the crack.

14. Heather Said Sunshine * — 20m VS 5a
FA Colin Moody & Cynthia Grindley 10 August 2002

Climb a short black corner, pull over the right end of the roof then leftwards up the juggy crack.

15. Clingfilm ** — 15m Very Difficult
FA Colin Moody solo 3 July 1994

Farther right is another grassy corner. Climb the crack in the pillar right of the corner.

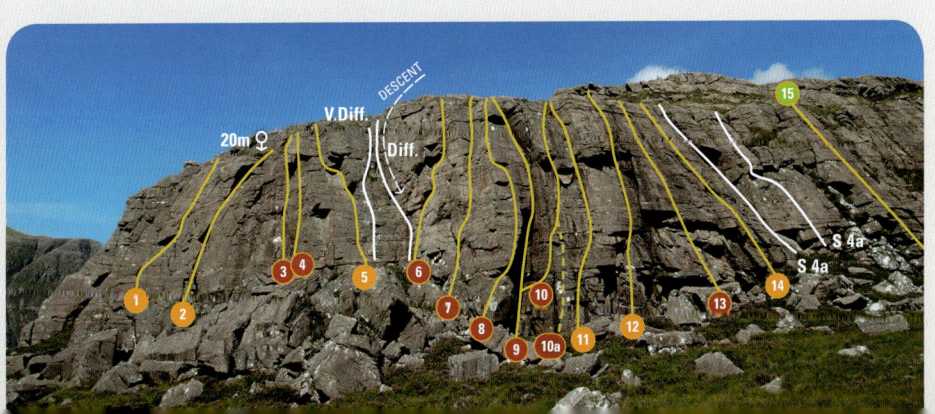

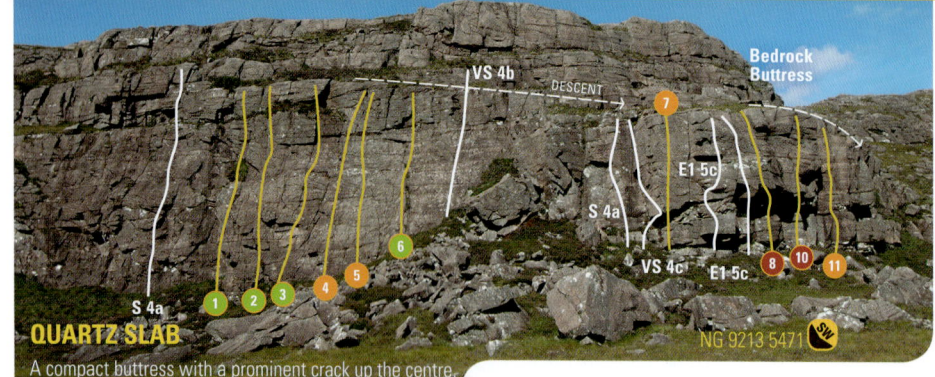

QUARTZ SLAB

A compact buttress with a prominent crack up the centre.
Descent: Traverse right and down the far right end of **Bedrock Buttress**.

1 Trench at Top ★   **18m Very Difficult**
FA Colin Moody (solo) 19 April 2003

Climb past the left end of the first overlap, go past the second overlap by a shallow left-facing corner to a grass ledge then finish up short easy wall.

2 Lap Land ★   **18m Severe 4a**
FA Colin Moody & Cynthia Grindley 10 August 2002

Start 3m right of 1. Follow direct line through overlaps to a heather ledge, finishing up short wall.

BEDROCK BUTTRESS   NG 9216 5469

The small compact rightmost buttress.
Descent: Down the far right end.

7 Archangel ★★   **10m VS 5a**
FA Steve Kennedy & Cynthia Grindley 16 July 1994

The prominent crack with a steep awkward start.

8 Bleached Whale ★★   **10m E2 5c**
FA Colin Moody & Louise Gordon Canning 12 May 1998

A good looking line. Go up a short block, gain an overhanging hand-crack and its continuation.

9 Sky Blue and Black ★   **10m E3 6a**
FA Gary Latter 18 April 2011

Well-protected climbing up the fine arête up the left side of the corner. Start as for 10, pulling left and climb up the arête with difficult moves to good breaks at the top roof. Pull over this on good holds to finish.

3 Quartz Warts ★   **18m Severe 4a**
FA Colin Moody & Cynthia Grindley 16 July 2000

Climb short left-facing corner, passing right end of overlap at 6m. Continue rightwards.

4 Queen of Hearts ★   **15m HS 4b**
FA Andy Nisbet & Jonathan Preston 10 May 2016

A direct line up the slab, passing through quartz to finish up flakes just left of the corner of 5.

5 Off With Her Head ★   **15m VS 4b**
FA Colin Moody & Louise Gordon Canning 12 May 1998

Start left of vertical grassy crack. Climb direct to a shallow right-facing corner and finish up this.

6 The Black Queen ★   **15m Severe 4a**
FA Andy & Gill Nisbet 22 June 1998

The slab just right of the grassy crack, finishing up steep juggy crack.

10 Dolphin Friendly ★★   **10m E1 5b**
FA Colin Moody & Louise Gordon Canning 12 May 1998

The big right-facing corner next right. Sustained.

11 The Knob ★   **10m HVS 5b**
FA John Lyall & Andy Nisbet 2 July 1998

Right of 10 is a short corner leading to a roof. Move round the roof and up cracks to finish up the arête.

CREAG NAM LEUMNACH
NG 8992 5687 **Alt:** 300m 40min
(CLIFF OF THE FROG)

Look directly above Torridon village shop at the top of the open gully. There are two long crags, one above the other. As the village is below, trundling has to be avoided! So named as there used to be a huge plastic frog in the schoolyard at the start of the original path!

Approach: Start at the right side of the second house left (west) of Torridon Stores. Follow a path through the shrubbery and continue up a vague path directly up the open hillside, bearing right then left to avoid the scree slope beneath the crag.

LOWER CRAG

Descents: Either scramble down slanting gully towards left end; down tight gully on right; or 20m abseil from sling & maillon on block at top of 10 *Warmer Cleaner Drier*.

1 Global Warming ★   25m HS 4b
FA Colin Moody 13 February 1994

There is an arête at the left end. Start left of it, step right and climb it.

2 Blind as a Frog ★★   25m E1 5b
FA Colin Moody & Steve Kennedy 14 May 1994

The slanting corner-crack just right of 1
Start from a flake ledge.

3 Squeezin' Yir Heid ★★   30m E5 6a
FA Ian Taylor & Colin Moody 23 May 1994

Climbs the wall just right of 2. A boulder problem start gains the flake ledge. Climb the middle of the wall (gear), trend rightwards to stand on a pinnacle (small Fs). Move up and left and continue to the top. It is possible to go straight to the top of the pinnacle but this would miss out some good climbing.

4 The Vanishing Frog ★   30m E5 6b
FA Ian Taylor (previously top-roped) 8 August 1996

The streaked, rounded nose in the centre of wall right of 3. Bold and not obvious. Start up the second groove right of the wide flake-crack to gain a break. Climb the shattered wall to gain the next break and using hidden holds above, make a hard move rightwards round the nose. Climb the right side of the nose until a move left at the top gains a ledge.

5 Kermit's Crack * 30m E3 6a
FA Paul Thorburn & Ian Taylor August 1999

The thin crack between 4 and the descent gully. Bridge up the gully to a ledge then pull left onto the wall. Climb to a break then pull through a steepening above. Go up the wall then trend right to finish on a heather ledge.

6 Gift Horse ** 30m E2 5b
FA Murdoch Jamieson & Martin Moran 2 June 2008

Start at a layback crack 12m left of 7. Climb the crack, traverse 4m right and pull up to a ledge. Continue up a crack, then move delicately up left to finishing slabs. A varied outing, seemingly ignored by earlier visitors.

7 Torridown Man *** 25m E2 5c
FA Colin Moody & Ian Taylor 25 May 1994

In the centre of the wall right of the descent gully is a steep crack. Climb the crack to a ledge, step left and climb another crack, move left and climb a third crack.

8 The White Streak * 20m E1 5b
FA Neil Smith & Colin Moody 26 March 1994

Halfway up the wall left of 10 is a white streak. Climb the crack left of it. A detour to the left was taken low down. A more direct version is E2 5b.

9 Cross Dressing ** 20m E3 5c
FA Ian Taylor & Tess Fryer 26 May 1996

Bold climbing up the wall left of the crack of 10. Traverse right 5m from the top to finish up that route.

10 Warmer Cleaner Drier *** 20m E2 5b
FA Colin Moody & Ian Taylor 23 May 1994

Climb the steep crack at the right end of the wall. A large (5-6" cam) would be useful to protect the offwidth above the ledge.

UPPER CRAG

The right half of the crag is split by a terrace. At the right end of the terrace is a structure, possibly a burial cairn.
Descent: Down the right side of the crag.

11 Block and Beak * 25m HVS 5b
FA Steve Kennedy & Colin Moody 14 May 1994

At the left side is a block; the cliff above it starts with a small overhang. Start left of the overhang, move right above it and follow the line of weakness above. From a ledge step right (crux) and continue to the top or move left, which reduces the grade to HVS 5a.

12 Completely out to Lunge ** 25m E5 6b
FA Ian Taylor & Paul Thorburn August 1999

A bold route with a bouldery crux climbing the shallow scoop right of 11. Start up that route to a ledge then go right and pull onto a small ramp. Climb the wall above until a long lunge gains a projecting hold. Just above is a good break for large Fs. Finish more easily.

13 The Great Brush Robbery ** 25m E4 6a
FA Ian Taylor & Colin Moody 25 May 1994

High in the grade. Climb the chimney of 14. From the top of the block place runners on the right. Move left to flat holds and climb straight up to a ledge. Finish up the cracked wall. There is a crucial R #3 placement halfway up the left crack.

14 A Million Years BC * 30m E1 5b
FA Colin Moody & Steve Kennedy 14 May 1994

Right of 11 is a bigger block. Climb the chimney formed by its left side, move right and climb the prominent crack in the left-facing corner, passing a large perched block.

15 Toad * 10m HS 4b
FA Michael Barnard & Alan Hill 15 October 2014

A fine vertical flake-crack on the wall at the far right end.

DIABAIG
(DEEP BAY) 10–25min

The tiny hamlet of Lower Diabaig lies at the end of a narrow twisting single track road west of Torridon overlooking the tiny Loch Diabaig. Almost all the crags are on the rocky hillock of Meall Ceanne na Creige, though only a few are visible from the village; **The Main Cliff** itself is hidden on the other side of the hill. They provide an excellent collection of roadside gneiss crags in a wonderful setting and reasonably quick drying.

Access: Continue west along the single track road on the north shore of Upper Loch Torridon for 9.5 miles/15.2km beyond Torridon village to park on the right by the pier.

Approach: Walk past the pier to the last house and follow the signposted footpath (marked 'precipitous path') through the two gates and up through the birches. **The Pillar** and **The Little Big Wall** lie just to the right. Continue steeply up the path, through the gate until it levels out on a wide terrace, just above **The Pillar**. Continue along the path which drops down to the lower left end of the showpiece **The Main Cliff**. Continue round the path for a little over 100m to reach **The Con Dome** and **The South Wall** extending rightwards up the hillside.

Ella Wright nearing the top of the first pitch of Broon's Wall (page 122).

TORRIDON DIABAIG

THE PILLAR 10min

NG 800 597 **Alt:** 50m

The slender pink wall clearly visible from the village with a prominent inset tilted slab in its upper left side.
Descent: Scramble up through the heather to gain the main path and head left down this.

1 Diabaig Corner ★★ 20m E1 5b
FA Roger Lupton & Colin Moody 15 April 1991

The left-bounding corner. An easy shelf leads right from just above the fence into the corner.

2 Dire Wall ★★ 35m E2 5b
FA Andy Nisbet & Rick Allen May 1984

Good climbing up the soaring upper arête, the hardest of the trilogy. Start 3m left of 3. Go up and left into a shallow groove then direct up to the base of the arête. Finish boldly up this.

3 The Pillar ★★★★ 35m E2 5b
FA Murray Hamilton 1983

A superb unrelenting pitch up the centre of the smooth wall, sustaining interest throughout. Start at a rib just left of centre. Up this leftwards and into the base of a flake-crack. Ascend this to pull out right into the centre of the slab. Follow the obvious line of holds and intermittent cracks to a horizontal break. Leave this with interest and continue in the same line to a further break at the top. Step left then easier to a heathery ledge and flake belay.

4 Dire Straights ★★★ 35m E2 5b
FA Joe Brown & Ginger Cain 1986;
Direct Start: Gary Latter & Craig Smith 1 August 1991

Start 5m up right of 3, beneath a thin crack system. Follow the crack then a shallow right-trending ramp. Continue in the same line up thin cracks to finish just left of prominent V-notch The easiest of the trilogy.

4a Diabolic Finish ★★ 35m E3 6a
FA Martin Moran & Robin Thomas 12 May 2015

At the top of thin cracks in the upper wall, move left and make a hard rock-over move to surmount the bulge above. Move left and teeter to the top.

> The following two routes lie above the left end of the terrace above **The Little Big Wall**, gained either by climbing a route on that crag or by scrambling up right from the base of **The Pillar**.

5 Upper Corner ★ 25m HVS 5a
FA Allan Austin, Rodney Valentine & J.Ratcliffe 1976

Up the corner then traverse left to a thin crack in the wall. Up this until it joins the corner proper to finish.

6 The Frieze ★ 25m HVS 5b
FA Martin Moran & Andy Nisbet 8 May 1993

A ramp breaks out right from the corner of 5 into very impressive but surprisingly helpful ground.

THE LITTLE BIG WALL 10min
NG 800 597 **Alt:** 40m

Immediately down and right from **The Pillar** is a shorter overhanging wall, the base hidden from the village, making it look less impressive than it is at close acquaintance.

Descents: Either scramble up and right to gain the path on terrace above or abseil from trees at top of wall.

1. Final Demands * 30m E3 5c
FA Dave Griffiths (with in situ peg and thread) 15 July 1988; (in situ gear removed on lead) Gary Latter & Kev Howett 31 July 1988

Steep strenuous climbing up the fault at the left side of the wall. Follow the crack, passing a juggy block to the overhang. Pull over this and up to good holds then the bulge and crack to finish.

2. Local Hero ** 30m E6 6a
FA Kev Howett & Dave Cuthbertson (both led) 28 May 1987

Superb bold climbing. Start just to the left of the crack. Up to the 'block' in the centre of the wall, turn it on the left then up and right to a good resting place. Using two pockets move up to the bulge with a hard move. Pull left over the lip to good holds and a runner placement. Pull over the bulge rightwards to a good semi-rest below an obvious red streak in headwall. Climb the wall (lots RP #1s required) trending left near the top to pull over on to a slab. Finish up and right around a rib to a tree belay.

3. Rubblesplitskin * 25m E3 5c
FA Kev Howett 27 May 1987

Start below twin cracks just left of the undercut right arête. Up the right crack with a tricky move into jugs at the base of the right groove. Up to the roof and through it on jugs. Pull out right above the roof on to a slab and up this to a tree belay.

4. Edgewood Whymper * 25m E4 5c
FA Kev Howett & Dave Cuthbertson 27 May 1987

Good airy climbing. Start just right of 3 at the undercut right arête. Pull on to the wall then follow the edge rightwards to a groove. Up this to pull out right on to a good ledge. Keep following the edge all the way with a hard move before reaching jugs and a slab.

THE MAIN CLIFF, WEST FACE
NG 8007 5938 Alt: 60m 20min

A pink wall lies just above the boulders on the path at the lower left end of the **Main Cliff**.

1. Dead Mouse Crack * 25m HVS 5a
FA Joe Brown & partner 8 June 1985

Climb the obvious crack in the pink wall wall starting from a small wet slab.

Alex 'Tam' Thomson on the technical crux section of the classic testpiece Northumberland Wall (page 118).

THE MAIN CLIFF NG 802 595 **Alt:** 80m

A fine 60m high slab of perfect rough gneiss, giving a selection of superb routes from HVS to E4.

Descents: There are numerous fixed abseil points: 25m from top of flake at top of 1 *Dead Mouse Crack*; 55m from nuts and maillon left of top of 4 *Route Three*; 55m from anchors on grass ledge 10m right of top of 11 *The Black Streak* (or 30m & 25m from large grass terrace). Alternatively, traverse right from the top of the cliff, crossing the gully to gain a vague ridge. Go down a shallow vegetated V-slot (the upper continuation of the gully right of **The Con Dome**, often muddy) then diagonally rightwards to finish steeply on good holds just south of the start of 16 *Evasion*.

1 Apprentice Bhoys ★   25m Severe 4a
FA Steve Kennedy & Andy MacDonald 31 August 2003

The short steep left-facing corner at the left end of the face. Start at short chimney, then over blocks into corner. Continue in the same line to ledge. Up flake to block belay.

2 The Grunter with Right Finish ★★   65m VS 4c
FA Billy Hood & Laurie Skuodas 26 March 1991; top pitch Gary & Karen Latter 20 November 2018

Good climbing; also the easiest line to the top of the **Main Cliff**. Start at a large flake just right of a heathery recess near the left end.

1 **20m 4c** Climb onto the top of the flake, step left and up cracks, then rightwards on vegetation to belay on a small birch clump.

2 **20m 4c** Climb the fine hand-crack, then slab above to belay up on the right.

3 **25m 4c** Climb shallow corner then traverse right and finish up crack past a steepening.

3 Perfect Days ★★   55m E2 5c
FA Gary & Karen Latter 15 March 2016

1 **15m 4b** Pitch 1 of 4.

2 **40m 5c** Start at large pink patch a few metres left of *Route Three*. Follow twin cracks up slab, then move out rightwards and direct by cracks aiming for thin twin tramline cracks. Follow these which lead to the left-most of the twin

offwidth cracks in the headwall. Finish up this past a small but useful rattly chokestone.

4 Route Three ★★   80m E1 5b
FA Allan Austin & Ed Grindley 4 August 1975

Follows the prominent clean crack-line near the left side of the wall. Start beneath the centre of a heather ledge at 8m.
1. **15m 4b** Climb the blocky right-facing corner to belay at a spike at the left end of the ledge.
2. **30m 5b** Step right then make a hard pull over a steep little wall and up this for 3m then traverse right into a scoop which leads rightwards to the crack. Follow the crack to belay below where it steepens.
3. **35m 5a** Follow the crack over an obvious bulge to the top.

5 Brimstone ★★★   75m E2 5c
FA John Lyall & Andy Nisbet 1 September 1991

A good direct on *Route Three*. Well protected but high in the grade.
1. **15m 4b** Pitch 1 of 7.
2. **20m 5c** Pull out left from the apex of the triangular niche into the left of two thin cracks. Move up then follow the right crack to join *Route Three*. Trend right to the belay.
3. **40m 5c** Follow *Route Two* until it is possible to move left under the overlap. Follow it until it ends then finish up the thin crack above.

5a Gamhnachain's Crack Variation ★★★   40m E2 5c
FA Gamhnachain's Crack: Allan Austin, Charlie Rose & Rodney Valentine 10 August 1976

Instead of joining *Route Three* after the difficulties, head diagonally left up the slab to gain the base of the prominent thin crack containing an obvious dog-leg. Follow this with interest to finish up the wider rightmost of a pair of wide cracks.

5b Afterglow Variation ★★★   30m E3 5c

Even better than the original finish (pitch 3 of *Brimstone*). Climb pitch 2 of *Afterglow* to the keyed-in block, then step back into *Brimstone* and finish up the thin crack.

6 Northern Sky ★★   55m HVS 5a
FA Gary & Karen Latter 15 March 2016

Start up *Route Two* to obvious left-slanting diagonal hand-crack. Take this to small heather clump, then move up to follow obvious left-trending diagonal fault. At its end move up to the cracks above the right edge of the large heather bay. Follow the fine cracks to the top.

7 Route Two ★★★★   70m HVS 5a
FA Allan Austin & Ed Grindley 4 August 1975

A magnificent route up the centre of the cliff. Start at the lowest point of the crag beneath the right end of a heather ledge at 8m.
1. **35m 5a** Climb easily to the right end of the ledge then pull up into the thin crack on the right. Follow it then move up right to a grassy ledge beneath a long crack.
2. **35m 5a** Finish up the superb crack.

Matthew Glenn linking the top pitch of Route Three into Brimstone, one of many superb ways up this section of the crag.

8 Northumberland Wall ★★★★　　　70m E2 5c
FA Andy Nisbet & Richard McHardy May 1984

A brilliant sustained crux pitch with reasonable protection, taking the intermittent crack-line a short way right of *Route Two*. Start a few metres right of *Route Two* beneath a prominent left-facing groove capped by a small roof.

1. **30m 5c** Climb the corner and its capping roof then traverse right to gain the base of the crack-line. Follow the crack-line which deviates right and back left (crux) at a bulge to the middle ledge. Belay on the right.
2. **40m 5c** Climb the faint crack above (as for *The Black Streak*) to the first overlap. Traverse left underneath it then follow the faint crack and its more pronounced continuation to the top.

9 Wall of Flame ★★★　　　70m E4 6a
FA Kev Howett & Cath Thomson (jumared) 10 June 1987

Superb sustained climbing, bold but with no-hands rests between the hard bits. Start just left of *The Black Streak*.

1. **30m 6a** Up the left arête of the corner to a very thin diagonal line running right. Follow it to its end then pull straight over a bulge and through a small overlap above to reach a large flat hold on the right. Straight up for 3m to an impasse. Go up left to reach good small hold in the centre of the slab (crux) then up to a thin crack on the left and up to grass ledge. A more direct line further left is E5.
2. **40m 5c** Move left from the belay and up the wall just left of *The Black Streak* to an overlap. Gain a thin crack on the left and follow the obvious line to easier rocks and top.

10 Afterglow ★★　　　65m E4 6a
FA Gary Latter & Kev Howett 1 August 1988

Good continually interesting climbing following a left-trending line across the centre of the wall.

1. **35m 6a** Start up *The Black Streak* for 5m to a large flake before breaking out left and up to stand on a prominent hold (RPs in horizontal above). Make a hard move through a tiny overlap to another horizontal then continue left through *Northumberland Wall* and follow *Route Two* up and rightwards to a grass ledge.
2. **30m 6a** Move leftwards up a quartz handrail then direct up a slab to a good hold in the base of the smooth thin runnel (RPs just above). Up this to some good slots. Swing left into a scoop at a thin break to reach good undercuts and up past a keyed-in block to reach a thin diagonal crack shooting out left. Cross this with interest (crux) to good holds. The crux is easily avoided (bit eliminate?) by stepping right into *Brimstone* – E3 5c.

11 The Black Streak ★★★　　　70m E1 5c
FA Allan Austin & Rodney Valentine 9 August 1976

Immaculate climbing with a short well protected technical crux.

1. **30m 5c** Climb up to and follow the very thin crack 2m left of the corner. Continue to join *Route One* and up to its stance.
2. **40m 5b** Climb a faint crack just left to the overhang where an excellent hand-rail leads up left to a crack up the right edge of the broad black streak. Follow this to finish.

Verve ★　　　65m E2 5c
FA Gary & Karen Latter 27 February 2019

Start beneath the right-facing corner.

1. **30m 5c** Climb the corner to the roof and move right to block. Cross roof and up to good horizontal break, then up right-slanting crack to grass terrace.
2. **35m 5b** Climb the fine jam crack in the centre of the wall, then slightly rightwards up tricky wall. Continue more easily up the right-slanting crack.

13 Route One ★★　　　70m HVS 5a
FA Allan Austin & Ed Grindley 3 August 1975

Good climbing.

1. **30m 5a** Climb the wall to the right of the corner until it is possible to traverse left to the holly. Step left from the holly onto the face and climb it, trending slightly left to a grassy ledge.
2. **40m 5a** Follow the thin crack on the right,

avoiding a tenuous bulge with a short detour out right. *Direct* is E1/2 5c.

14 Foil ★★ 85m VS 5a
FA Colin Moody & Bob Sharples 24 April 1982

Start right of *Route One*.
1. **35m 5a** Climb direct to the apex of the roof. Pull through this using a right-slanting crack then up to a ledge.
2. **40m 4c** Up the crack at the black streak until 1m short of some grass, then traverse up left to the base of a steep crack and up this to a ledge. The next crack left is 4c.
3. **10m** – Finish up the easy wall and slab.

14a Spirit ★ 35m HVS 5a
FA Gary & Karen Latter 1 March 2019

The central of the three cracks above the large grass terrace. Start up the right of twin cracks in the black streak, then right along shelf. Finish direct up the crack.

15 Bogie ★ 50m E2 5b
FA Sandy Allan & Dave Etherington 29 July 1990; top pitch Gary Latter & Allan Clapperton 15 July 1996

Start right of the base of the gully.

1. **40m 5b** Pull over a rounded nose on the right then pull direct through a red roof and follow cracks parallel to the gully, pulling direct over the small roof near the top.
2. **10m 4c** Climb the short awkward corner above, moving out right to finish easily up the rib.

16 Evasion ★ 40m VS 4c
FA Sandy Allan & Dave Etherington 29 July 1990

Start 8m down from the gully. Follow a series of shallow left trending scoops. Traverse left along the lip of the roof to a crack leading to large ledge (abseil thread).

THE CON DOME, WEST FACE
NG 802 594 **Alt:** 80m 25min

1 Congruent ★ 15m Difficult
FA Karen & Gary Latter 8 April 2019

The leftmost line, finishing up short crack at top.

2 Consensus ★ 15m Difficult
FA Gary Latter (solo) 20 November 2018

Tho thin cracks and ledges about 10m left of the right edge. Either belay on ledge at top, or 10m further back, as for the longer routes on the **South Face**.

3 Condescending ★★ 15m Difficult
FA Gary & Karen Latter 19 November 2018

Fine well-protected climbing up the obvious line of incut holds a few metres right of 2.

THE CON WALL

Adjoining the left side of **The Con Dome** is a short easier-angled wall. There are three belay stakes in the heather 10m back from the top.

4 Confluent *   12m HS 4b
FA Karen & Gary Latter 8 April 2019

5m left of the wide fault is a Y-crack. Take the left line, finishing up fine cracks.

5 Contiguous *   12m VS 5a
FA Karen & Gary Latter 8 April 2019

After the common start, take the right-slanting crack, finishing easily.

6 Contumacy *   12m Very Difficult
FA Karen & Gary Latter 19 November 2018

The fault delineating the left edge of the dome proper, with a prominent sapling at its top.

THE CON DOME   NG 802 594 **Alt:** 70m   25min

Beyond **The Main Cliff** the path turns a corner revealing a large hillside of more broken rock. Between these two is a smooth dome of rock in a slight recess. Very quick drying.

Descent: Traverse left and down the lower section of the blunt ridge, as for **The Main Cliff**.

7 Conflagration **   25m E3 5c
FA Gary Latter 8 April 2019

Start just right of a pedestal a few metres left of 8. Climb the wall on good holds, with protection in the fine cracks on the right. Finish more easily up the sparsely protected blunt rib, on perfect rock.

8 Condome ***   25m E4 6a
FA Dave Cuthbertson & Kev Howett 29 May 1987

The prominent hanging crack. Start below the crack just left of a large boulder at the base of the crag. Gain the crack and follow it with continual interest until it nearly fades out, where it is possible to step left on to the ledges on the edge of the dome. Step up and traverse right to gain the fine slanting crack.

9 Fisherman's Dream **   30m E6 6b
FA Gary Latter 31 March 2016

A direct line up the wall between 8 and 10. Start up 10 for 5m, then move left and follow twin cracks. Where they peter out, continue direct past a peg runner to pull direct into the final crack of 8 and finish up this. Note: The peg has been removed.

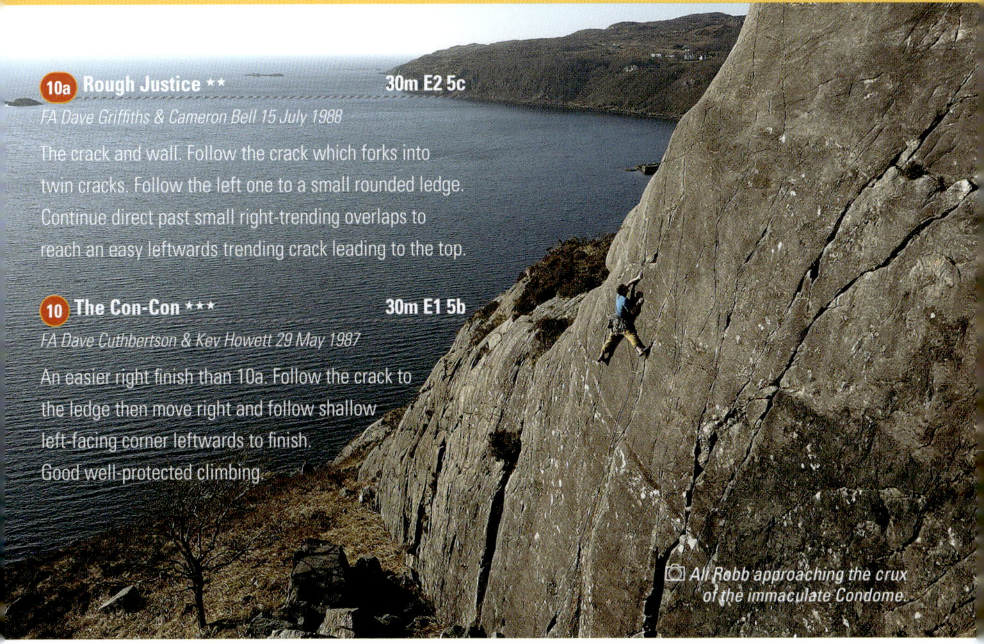

10a Rough Justice ★★　　　　　　　30m E2 5c

FA Dave Griffiths & Cameron Bell 15 July 1988

The crack and wall. Follow the crack which forks into twin cracks. Follow the left one to a small rounded ledge. Continue direct past small right-trending overlaps to reach an easy leftwards trending crack leading to the top.

10 The Con-Con ★★★　　　　　　　30m E1 5b

FA Dave Cuthbertson & Kev Howett 29 May 1987

An easier right finish than 10a. Follow the crack to the ledge then move right and follow shallow left-facing corner leftwards to finish. Good well-protected climbing.

All Robb approaching the crux of the immaculate Condome.

THE SOUTH WALL

NG 803 594 **Alt:** 80m　　25min

The long more broken cliff running up the slope rightwards from **The Con Dome**.

Descents: Traverse left and down the crest of the ridge as for **The Main Cliff**. It is also possible to descend down the right side of the cliff. From sling and abseil ring on a thread in the prominent left-slanting fault 10m below the top of *Charlie's Tower*, a 60m abseil gains the base of the main slab, or 40m abseil heading west down the overhanging wall overlooking **The Con Dome**. This can be gained by easy scrambling leftwards from the top of *Boab's Corner*. There are also slings & maillons on blocks at the base of the right-slanting ramp (22m), and the left end of the terrace beneath the small upper dome (33m).

1 Jeemy ★　　　　　　　　　　　30m VS 4c

FA Karen & Gary Latter 9 April 2019

Start beneath the obvious diagonal fault at left end. Climb up to prominent smooth bulge at 8m. Pull through this via diagonal layback crack then continue more easily to block belay.

2 Wee Eck ★　　　　　　　　70m Very Difficult

FA Gary & Karen Latter 4 December 2018

Start 5m left of *Ma Broon's Variations*.
1 35m Climb direct, up fault, then by good holds slightly rightwards, joining *Ma Broon's Variations* for a short section. Continue direct to block at lower left end of diagonal ramp. Follow this up rightwards to belay as for *Charlie's Tower*.
2 35m Climb up rightwards up obvious stepped grooves, finishing leftwards.

3 Ma Broon's Variations ★　　　　　70m VS 4c

FA Andy Nisbet & party pre 1993;
pitch 2 Ben Sparham & Dave Porter 24 August 2013

The left edge of the fine slab.
1 30m 4c Start by following cracks which form a prominent right-angled arrowhead shape. Continue up the left side of the slab before moving right along small ramp to join *Broons' Wall* at the top of the slab.
2 40m 4c Climb the cracked wall 2m left of the prominent V-groove of *Charlie's Tower*. Continue more easily to the top.

4 Broons' Wall ★★   30m VS 4c
FA Andy Tibbs & partner May 1994

The fine hanging crack. Follow the right-slanting ramp, then up to good holds and protection. Step left into the crack and follow this, finishing up pleasant cracks 2m right of heather slot. Easier to large ledges above.

4a Broons' Wall – top pitch ★   40m HVS 5b
FA Michael Barnard & John MacLeod 30 April 2011

Go up to climb the small steep dome on the left (runners in the crack on the right) to gain and follow easier ground to the top.

5 Charlie's Tower ★★   60m HS 4b
FA Allan Austin, Charlie Rose & Rodney Valentine 10 August 1976

Fine varied climbing on lovely rock. Start by scrambling up right from the base of the slab to the base of a wide heathery crack.

1. **20m 4b** Climb this (good holds on right) and up steeper crack through 'tower', then easily up slab to good ledge.
2. **40m 4b** Climb the prominent V-groove then short steep crack above. Continue up easy slabs, then cracks on right.

6 Soapy Soutar ★★   70m E1 5b
FA Gary & Karen Latter 20 November 2018;
pitch 1 Gary & Karen Latter 26 February 2019

Fine varied climbing. Start just left of *Boab's Corner*.

1. **10m 5b** Step left off of boulder to good flat holds, then the crack on good slots. Step right and finish up wall to terrace and belay at a small spike.
2. **25m 5a** Climb twin diagonal cracks to ledge. Move right and follow easy line up towards small roof. Climb twin cracks through steep wall, then out rightwards to belay beneath large block.
3. **35m 5b** Walk right 5m, then climb curving flange rightwards, briefly joining *Boab's Corner*. Move out left and up into the right-curving quartz flake and follow this to its top. Make tricky moves left to a flared quartz crack and good holds above. Move up to ledge on right (possible belay). Span left past good flake hold, then by easier left-facing corner. Finish up twin cracks in the slab leading to the in situ thread above.

7 Jings *   45m E1 5b

FA Gary & Karen Latter 9 April 2019

Start as for *Boab's Corner*. Climb to the oak, then step left and up past two horizontal breaks to heather terrace. Gain and climb the twin left-slanting tramline cracks, moving up right to follow easy finger-crack leftwards. Climb short steep wall on good holds, then easier ground leftwards to large grass terrace.

8 Crivvens *   80m VS 4c

FA Gary & Karen Latter 26 February 2019

1. **35m 4c** Start as for *Boab's Corner*, but continue to the grass ledge. Climb the shallow groove and crack just left of *Boab's Corner*, then move left and up easier left-slanting finger crack to ledge. Up cracked wall to belay right of perched block.
2. **15m 4b** Climb the crack above the block, then wide crack on right to ledge.
3. **30m 4c** Move up rightwards, then pull up left into the easy groove (*Wee Eck*). Move right along shelf and follow cracks on right, finishing leftwards to the abseil point.

9 Boab's Corner **   80m VS 5a

FA Colin Moody & Boab Sharples 24 April 1982

Start at a tiny stepped vegetated corner with a tiny oak at 3m.

1. **30m 4c** Climb to below the oak, then move right onto the wall and up by cracks to belay at the base of the shallow groove.
2. **30m 5a** Up the groove with one hard move past the roof. The crux moves can be avoided around the corner on the right.
3. **20m 4a** Climb the clean rib on the left by a good crack.

10 Oor Wullie *   90m E2 5c

FA John Lyall & Andy Nisbet 1 April 1998; pitch 2 Tess Fryer & Ian Taylor April 1996

Start 2m right of *Boab's Corner*. A committing first pitch.

1. **30m 5c** Boulder problem start, then climb diagonally right up scoops above the undercut base to a heathery recess. Exit this out of its left corner and make thin moves to heather.
2. **60m 5c** Head up to a black streaked section, and climb this with difficulty to gain a short corner. Ascend this, then a dwindling ramp rightwards to reach easy ground.

11 Help ma Boab **   90m E3 6a

FA Gary & Karen Latter 9 April 2019; pitch 2: 21 June 2019

Good climbing up the thin hanging crack right of *Boab's Corner*. Start 4m right of that route.

1. **30m 6a** Pull left along thin horizontal to good flake hold, then move up rightwards to gain the base of the crack. Climb this with difficult moves where it fades to good finishing hold. Belay at vertical crack at base of short steep wall.
2. **60m 6a** Climb up through short diagonal cracks on left, then the black streak, as for *Oor Wullie*. Follow the lower right-slanting crack to a flake at its end, then the easier continuation flake/ramp up rightwards, continuing up rightwards.

12 Hull Wall **   80m E2 5c

FA Michael Barnard & Mike Rycroft 7 June 2010

Fine sustained climbing after a committing start to exit the initial corner. Start beneath the large roof-capped corner.

1. **35m 5c** Climb the corner to arrange protection beneath the roof. Move left with interest to a prominent large foothold on the arête and good holds and protection on the lip. Move up, then rightwards past heathery recess. Move up from the right end of the overlap. Continue easily to belay at the base of a short steeper wall.
2. **45m 5b** Climb the short diagonal crack to ledge, then up to gain the upper of twin right-slanting cracks. Follow this, and a further right-slanting crack to finish up easier right-slanting corners. A superb sustained pitch.

PENINSULA CRAGS

A collection of smaller crags of immaculate rock on the peninsula across the bay from Diabaig.
Approach: From **The Main Cliff**, follow the Diabaig – Alligin path, dropping down to the shore then across a flat boggy area which leads to the derelict croft. Alternatively, by water-borne means head directly across the bay.

UGLY CRAG
NG 800 588 **Alt:** 100m 50min

The first crag encountered on the approach, 100m above the birch wood.

① Ugly Mug ★★★ **55m E2 5c**
FA Jamie Fisher & Finlay Bennet 4 October 1998

A wild route, steeped in exposure and character, taking a rising right-trending traverse line. Start at a pile of blocks beneath a big block in an open corner.

1 **25m 5c** Climb up and rightwards then pull steeply over a bulge to a good ledge. Traverse strenuously rightwards on good holds to a precarious exit onto a hanging slab. Belay at its right end.
2 **30m 5c** Drop down and continue traversing rightwards on huge holds to the flake on 3. Step up and right to a good slot (F #2) then make a hard move rightwards to another good flake. Pull directly over the bulge above and exit leftwards.

② Handsome Hog ★ **20m E1 5b**
FA Dave McGimpsey & Andy Nisbet 28 July 2000

A strenuous direct line with reasonable protection up the highest and steepest part of the wall. Start at the left side of a black wedge of rock under the lowest overhang, 5m left of 3. Pull through the overhang then move 2m right along a handrail and pull leftwards through the next overhang. Climb up past a knob of rock to a cramped rest. Pull through the next overhang and reach into a small V-niche. Finish direct through more overhangs.

③ Ugly Wall ★ **20m E1 5b**
FA Finlay Bennet & Jamie Fisher 4 October 1998

An exciting outing. Start 5m left of an orange corner. Climb up and left on big holds to a large flake below a roof. Pull over directly and make an awkward exit leftwards.

CROFTER'S CRAG
NG 7933 5876 **Alt:** 50m 1hr

The steep broken crags opposite the ruined croft.
Descent: By 28m abseil from sling and maillon 10m up right from top of 1.

TORRIDON DIABAIG

1. The Applecross Jam ★★★ — 20m E3 5c
FA Ally Coull, Andy Sharpe, Jamie Fisher & Finlay Bennet 3 October 1998

The compelling crack up the centre of the clean wall. A steep start leads to a ledge and a rest. Negotiate the final overhang on spaced holds and jams to a strenuous finish.

2. Diabaig Tiger ★★ — 20m E3 6a
FA Tim Rankin, Jason Currie & Guy Robertson 22 July 2000

Another excellent route up the corner and crack right of 1.

ROLLING WALL
NG 7889 5876 **Alt:** 50m  1hr 10min

The showpiece crag with smooth bulges split by impressive cracks, together with grand views over Applecross and Skye.
Approach: From the bay south of **Crofter's Crag**, head diagonally right up the hill, passing a fenced enclosure.
Descent: By 28m abseil from sling and maillon on huge block back from the centre of the crag.

1. Rolling Home ★★ — 40m E2 5c
FA Jamie Fisher & Finlay Bennet 3 October 1998

Climb cracks up the blunt arête to a junction with 2. Step delicately onto 'the roll' and traverse beneath it. Exit by the far right crack (crux).

2. The Sea, The Sea ★★★ — 25m E2 5c
FA Jamie Fisher & Alice Brockington 5 September 1998

Another gem up cracks right again. Start 2m right of thin initial cracks. Traverse boldly in beneath the first bulge and follow the crack to below the final bulge where the crack fades. Step up and left to an exposed finish up the left edge of the wall.

3a. Brave New World Left Start ★★★ — 25m E2 5c
FA Michael Barnard & Alan Hill 13 October 2014

Equally good. Start as for 2, then take the obvious diagonal crack through the bulge to join the normal route below its second crack.

3. Brave New World ★★★ — 25m E2 5c
FA Jamie Fisher & Alice Brockington (1 PA) 5 September 1998; Direct: Iain Small & partner 2008

An angelic climb up the impressive crack in the centre. Climb the initial crack for a few metres until a delicate traverse leads left to above the first bulge. Follow the crack on good finger jams to a hard finish (crux). 3b *The Direct* is E3 6a.

4. Aquamarine ★★★ — 25m E4 6a
FA Bob Durran 14 May 2000

The right crack. Start easily then swing through the bulge strenuously from the right to gain the crack, which is sustained to easier ground.

5. The Ice Bulge ★★ — 15m E1 5b
FA Jamie Fisher & Alice Brockington 5 September 1998

The prominent quartz bulge, gained direct.

Karen Latter nearing the top of the fine Open Secret, Stone Valley Crag.

GAIRLOCH | 127

GAIRLOCH (SHORT LOCH)

This is the ancient parish between Loch Torridon and Outer Loch Broom. The sea lochs of Gair Loch, Loch Ewe, Little Loch Broom and Gruinard Bay split the coastline into a number of low-lying peninsulas. Sandwiched between Little Loch Broom to the north and Loch Maree to the south, *"the great wilderness"* of the Letterewe and Fisherfield *'Forests'* contains the renowned remote Carn Mor and the contrasting Beinn Lair, which presents the greatest escarpment of Hornblende Schist in the country. At the east end of Loch Maree, the varied quartzite walls of the Bonaid Dhonn on the southern slopes of the more readily accessible Beinn a' Mhuinidh give some atmospheric routes with a fine outlook down the loch. By contrast, around the periphery of the mountains is a fine varied range of easily accessible low lying outcrops, all composed of excellent rough Lewisian gneiss. Recent developments have uncovered a fine range of routes of all grades, many on glaringly obvious venues that must have been driven past on innumerable occasions by countless generations of climbers.

Accommodation: Bunkhouses: Ledgowan Lodge Bunkhouse, Achnasheen (☎ 01445 720252; www.ledgowanlodge.co.uk); Kinlochewe Hotel Bunkhouse (☎ 01445 760253; www.kinlochewehotel.co.uk); The Bunkhouse, Gairloch Campsite (☎ 01445 712373; www.gairlochcampsite.co.uk); Badrallach Bothy & Campsite, by Dundonnell (☎ 07435 123190; www.badrallach.com) on north side of Little Loch Broom, 5.7 miles/9km from Dundonnell. **Youth Hostel:** Gairloch Sands (Apr–Sept; ☎ 01445 712219; www.hostelling.scotland.org.uk) on the north shore of Loch Gairloch, 2.4miles/4km west down the B8021 from Gairloch. **Campsites:** Small basic campsite at Taagan, 1.5 miles north-west of Kinlochewe; Gairloch Holiday Park (Apr–Oct; ☎ 01445 712373; www.gairlochcampsite.co.uk); Sands Caravan & Camping Park with café (☎ 01445 712152; www.sandscaravanandcamping.co.uk); Inverewe Caravan & Camping Club Site, Poolewe (☎ 01445 781249; www.campingandcaravaningclub.co.uk); Gruinard Bay Caravan Park, Laide (☎ 01445 731556; www.gruinardbay.co.uk); Northern Lights Camping & Caravan Park, Badcaul (Apr–Aug; ☎ 01697 371379). Wild camping may be possible by the beach at Redpoint. **Club Huts:** Ronnan Cottage, Aultbea (LSCC); The Smiddy, Dundonnell (Edinburgh JMCS).

Amenities: Petrol stations in Kinlochewe and Laide. Small supermarkets at Kinlochewe, Poolewe, Gairloch & Laide. The Poolewe Hotel is in the village. Tiny swimming pool in Poolewe. There is a sports centre in Gairloch with a small climbing wall. **ATMs**: At Bank of Scotland, supermarket and shop at the pier – all Gairloch. **TIC**: Nearest at Ullapool (☎ 01854 612486; www.visitscotland.com). Local information available at the Gale Centre (☎ 01445 712071; www.galeactionforum.co.uk) which also has a community shop and café.

Mhairi Stewart on Primo, Am Fasgadh (page 200). Photo Ian Taylor.

BEINN A' MHUINIDH
(MOUNTAIN OF THE HEATH/PISSING)

This is the escarpment due north of Kinlochewe, encircled on its western flanks by a band of Cambrian quartzite crags. The outlook over Slioch and down Loch Maree is stunning. The translation from the Gaelic refers to the prominent waterfall.

"We found many attractive possibilities for the making of a delightful and quickly accessible arena for good climbing routes of moderate length on steep, sound rock." – Jim Bell, Some New Climbs in the North-West, *Scottish Mountaineering Club Journal*, 1949

WATERFALL BUTTRESS
NH 024 649 **Alt:** 300m 1¼hr

The cliffs flanking the prominent narrow waterfall, Allt an Still (swift stream), though a bit broken, offer some reasonable routes amidst impressive settings.

Access: Turn north off the A832 towards Incheril 0.3 miles/0.5km east of the Kinlochewe Hotel over a bridge. Turn left after a few hundred metres to park by the farm after a further 400m. If the parking spot is full, there is a larger (signposted) car park to the north-east.

Approach: Follow the track through the farm then the path heading north-west along the north bank of the Kinlochewe River to a fork in the path after just over 2km. Take the right fork which leads to a small ravine after 400m. Slog steeply up the hillside to the base of the cliff. **A much shorter approach**, (saving 20 – 25 minutes) can be made direct from Taagan, the small campsite/farm 1.5 miles/2.4km west of the village. Just beyond the farm, follow the track south-east, then towards the river. Head back downstream for a couple of hundred metres, then wade across the Kinlochewe River (wide and shallow at this point, just upstream of the ravine) to join the path near where it forks.

Descent: Down steep grass down the right (east) side of the waterfall.

1 Blanco ★★ **90m Severe 4a**
FA Andy Nisbet (solo) 26 April 2005

Fine clean rock with very positive holds. Start 25m right of the waterfall at the right end of the low section of wall 10m right of the end of waterwashed rock.
1 15m 4a Climb up left to finish up an exposed arête.
2 30m – Climb up clean walls with bits of heather until right of the second pine.
3 30m 4a Climb a large clean wall until it peters out then move left to climb another clean wall right of the chimney which bounds the rib of *Tuit* on the right.
4 15m 4a Finish up the final wall.

2 Chiaroscuro **   90m Severe 4a

FA Anthony 'Ginger' Cain & P.Davis 25 July 1982

Steep and exposed climbing on good clean rock, though the start may be wet. Start on the black water-washed rock at the right side of the waterfall just left of a prominent corner.

1. **40m 4a** Climb 10m up black rock on the left of the corner then move right into the grey crack in the corner. Follow this on superb holds to its top then move left up the wall to the first pine ledge.
2. **50m 4a** Climb directly behind the pine for a few metres then left towards the base of a rib with a detached block. Step left round the block into the corner and ascend this and the clean wall above, stepping left round a rib at the top.

Karen Latter on the second pitch of Chiaroscuro.

THE BONAID DHONN

NH 023 656   **Alt:** 460m   2hr

(BROWN BONNET)

The large buttress at the corner of Gleann Bianasdail. Its steepest and most compact part is a smooth wall in the centre, defined on its right by an obvious chimney-corner system (*Safari* VS) and on the left by a bulging buttress and corner-crack. At its best the rock is a compact immaculate Cambrian quartzite.

Approach: As for **Waterfall Buttress** to the base of the ravine then head up leftwards to a compact buttress, from where a good goat track leads leftwards along an increasingly exposed dwindling terrace round the corner to beneath the crag. The routes on the flanks (1, 2 & 10) start next to the path. The remaining routes on the main face are all either approached by scrambling up about 60–70m of rock and vegetation from the path, the easiest line leading slightly rightwards, starting from beneath the central chimney-corner system. For the routes away from the flanks a better approach may be to gain the top and abseil in to the chosen route. To locate the abseil point, follow the cliff top north from the top of **Waterfall Buttress** to just below the highest point.

There is a slight bay (NH 022 657; 550m) beneath the last rise, marked by a cairn. Tucked under a small outcrop at the bottom right of the bay is a small exposed platform, from where the big south-facing sidewall of 9 *North by North-West* is visible. The abseil anchor requires large nuts and 8m of slings to reach the cliff edge. The abseil is 53m (60m ropes ideal), but possible with 50m ropes and a short scramble down with care.

Descent: There are no convenient descents – for the routes starting from the path, best to climb with rucksacks. Head north for 300m to a step down in the cliff top, then make a descending traverse south before scrambling down steep broken ground and heather to gain the goat track. Easier descents (with rucksacks) are also possible at the end of the cliff 1km further north, or the grass slope at the east end of **Waterfall Buttress**.

1 Route 1 ★ — 130m Difficult
FA Jim & Pat Bell 9 August 1946

The original route with a delightful airy top pitch. Start from the goat track, right of the main section of the cliff beneath a 'beak' of rock at the corner of the glen just beyond a recess under an overhang.

1. **30m** Climb steep slabs to a recess at 20m then by the edge of a rock rib to a belay.
2. **25m** After a move to the right climb a wall from a huge square block for 10m. Easier climbing leads to a stance.
3. **40m** Climb up a rib then by a short steep wall. Continue up two consecutive steep ribs to easy ground (cairn).
4. **35m** Continue in the same line up the final crux wall, steep and exposed on small, square-cut holds, followed by 10m of final scrambling to the top.

2 Route 2 ★ — 110m Very Difficult
FA Jim & Pat Bell 10 August 1946

Start about 100m left of *Route 1* beyond steep walls and just before the rock becomes vegetated. Rounded ribs leading to a large overhang are visible above. Climb slabby walls for 10m then move left to climb the slabby ribs, passing the left side of the large overhang. Continue up towards the steep wall then traverse right about 20m to a chimney. Climb the wall right of the chimney then the chimney to above the overhang. Finish up the wall on the right leading to scrambling.

3 The Creep ★★ — 70m HVS 5a
FA John Cunningham & Bill March 13 May 1971

Good climbing, poorly protected on pitch 1.

1. **40m 5a** Move diagonally right, first crossing grass ledges then small rock ledges until close to the right arête. Move up to a ledge (PR) then directly up the wall to a roof. Belay on the right.
2. **30m 4c** Continue up the overhanging corner directly above, finishing up a fine steep crack.

4 Dream Ticket ★★★ — 60m E3 5c
FA Tom Prentice & Charles French 17 July 1996

A stunning route up the immaculate wall right of *Vertigo*. "The rock is the finest quartzite around, compact and totally solid; the climbing pleasantly sustained and quite intimidating and the position superb." – Prentice Protection is good but spaced and a double set of cams up to 2" useful. Start at a large block at the base of the wall.

1. **45m 5c** Climb ledges to a prominent pair of thin cracks then move up and right to the left end of a long overlap. Return back left into the centre of the wall and continue to a small overlap level with the top of the *Vertigo* flake. Pull over this, climb the crack above and follow a scoop right to belay on the right edge of the wall.
2. **15m 5b** Move back left and follow the right edge of the wall and easier ground to the top.

5 Vertigo ★★★ — 70m E1 5b
FA John Cunningham & Bill March 13 May 1971

In the centre of the wall is a fine flake-crack with an

overhanging base. Low in the grade.

1 **30m 4c** Climb the flake-crack to small ledge.

2 **20m 5b** Traverse left and step onto a steep grey wall. Move up and slightly left to an obvious spike. Move up the wall above then make an awkward move leftwards into a shallow corner, which is climbed to a ledge.

3 **20m 4b** Climb direct over an overlap then trend rightwards towards an obvious easy corner. Avoid this by climbing the slab on the left.

6 **Balances of Fate** ★★★　　　**65m E2 5c**

FA Charles French & Tom Prentice 17 July 1996

Another excellent route, starting up the wall left of *Vertigo* and finishing up the steep crack directly above. Start as for *Dream Ticket*.

1 **35m 5b** Climb up and left below the flake-crack of *Vertigo*. A small overlap guards access to the wall. Pull over at the narrowest point, continue straight up wall and follow a small slab to belay on top of the flake, as for *Vertigo*.

2 **30m 5c** Traverse right and climb a steep undercut crack to slabbier ground above. Follow the prominent diagonal crack through a steep bulge to an awkward exit. Follow the groove and easier ground to belay right of a large block.

7 **Stoater** ★★　　　**90m HS 4b**

FA John Cunningham & Bill March 13 May 1971

Start at a wide flake-crack left of *Vertigo*.

1 **45m 4b** Climb the flake-crack. When this finishes climb the wall above to belay on a small rock ledge beneath a beak-shaped overhang.

2 **45m 4b** Up to the overhang, over this and up the wall above on excellent holds, moving right through an overlap, to the top of the crag.

8 **Superbug** ★　　　**85m VS 4b**

FA Ross Jones & Andy Nisbet 14 May 2005

A direct line up the clean slabs on the left. Start below and left of a stepped corner.

1 **40m 4a** Climb the slab direct to the large flake.

2 **45m 4b** Move left and climb direct up slabs to break through a steep upper wall by flakes leading left. Step back right and finish at the top of the prominent arête.

9 **North by North-West** ★★★　　　**45m E7 6b**

FA p1 Alastair Robertson, Paul Thorburn & Rick Campbell 19 July 1997; p2 Paul Thorburn & Rick Campbell 20 July 1997

Climbs the steep right wall of the crest taken by *A Walk on the Wild Side*. Start on a grass ledge at the base of a wet corner, below a striking vertical crack.

1 **20m 5c** Climb the crack past a hollow flake until near the huge roof then follow the thin break out left to belay on a small ledge on the arête. (Anchors on the large ledge 4m above.)

2 **25m 6b** From just above the belay, follow a break dipping rightwards to the lower traverse in the roof. Follow this to a spike then climb the sustained right-slanting crack. Continue in the same line to gain a good hold at the top of a faint left-facing groove. Move up left to a break and follow this, pulling over a bulge onto the arête.

9a **Alternative Start** ★★★　　　**40m E7 6b**

FA Dave MacLeod 7 June 2016

A logical single pitch version of the route with an exciting start along the lip of the roof guarding entry to the main wall above. Start up the slab and break left up a short wall to the right edge of the roof. Swing along this on a big break and move steeply up on good holds to gain the parent route at the spike at the base of the crack.

10 **A Walk on the Wild Side** ★　　　**110m Very Difficult**

FA Ian Rowe & Sandy Trees 2 July 1967

Good climbing up the crest of the bulging buttress left of the big left-bounding corner. Start on the path where the angle relents, right of the first overhung bay. Ascend broken walls. Walk up left on heather to gain the base of the buttress. Follow a line of cracks and grooves near the crest, easier to the left, to finish by a fine exposed wall on the crest.

STONE VALLEY CRAGS

30–45min

These crags lie south of the A832 west of Loch Maree on the rocky slopes of the small hill of Meall Lochan a' Chleirich. They dry quickly due to their hummocky nature and this, together with the wonderful outlook over the sea and Baosbheinn makes it a very pleasant place to climb. Extensive planting of indigenous native tree species on the hillside as part of the Millennium Forestry Project is already transforming the open aspect of the lower slopes.

Access: Parking for a half-dozen cars is possible just off the A832 by the side of a green barn at the north side of the road at NG 856 721 just beyond the east end of Loch Bad an Sgalaig. This is 5.5 miles/9km from Gairloch, or 0.6 mile/1km west of where the road leaves the Slattadale Forest if travelling from the east through Kinlochewe.

Approach: Follow the track across the bridge heading south-east into the Flowerdale Forest (a deer forest, hence there are no trees!) towards Poca Buidhe for about 1km where the crags can be seen on the hillside on the left. Leave the track and cross two streams then steeply up the hillside to the crags.

ATLANTIC WALL   30min

NG 866 718 **Alt:** 210m

Well to the left of **Rum Doodle Crag** is a shallow amphitheatre with a short vertical back wall.

1 **Mutineers** * 12m HVS 5a

FA Blyth Wright, Lindsey Cannon & John Mackenzie 25 Aug 1997

Start to the right of the left edge of the crag. Go up a steepening wall direct to a short crack at the top. Turn this by a move on the left or climb it direct at 5c.

Photo Jim Buchanan, Wild West Topos.

2 The Cruel Sea *   12m E2 5c
FA John Mackenzie, Lindsey Cannon & Blyth Wright 25 Aug 1997

By far the best route here. Start near the centre of the crag in a shallow scoop. Climb up to a horizontal crack then finish direct up the overhanging wall.

3 The Ancient Mariner *   12m HVS 5a
FA John Mackenzie, Lindsey Cannon & Blyth Wright 25 Aug 1997

Ascend the wall directly to the left of a flake. Step right to a square perch and continue up and slightly left at the top.

4 Fisherboys *   12m HVS 5a
FA Paul Tattersall 21 September 1999

The thin crack 10m right of 3.

5 The Cat *   12m HS 4b
FA Blyth Wright (solo) 19 August 1997

Go over a bulge and continue up an exposed wall, moving left to gain hidden holds near the top.

RUM DOODLE CRAG

This lies several hundred metres down and left of **Stone Valley Crag**, easily identified by the prominent arête visible from the approach track.

NG 867 717 **Alt:** 220m  35min

Photo Jim Buchanan, Wild West Topos.

1 Rum Doodle Arête *   35m HS 4a
FA Bob Brown & John Mackenzie 14 May 1995

Bold and airy climbing but with good friction. Start below the arête at a little groove to the left. Gain the arête and follow the narrow edge directly, turning the mossy last few metres by a crack just to the left. Either walk off at a ledge above or climb a straight-forward groove on the left. *Variation Finish* VS 4c. A better finish is to climb the steep crack on the back wall.

2 Roman Wall **   35m Severe 4a
FA John Mackenzie & Bob Brown 24 July 1996

Very pleasant climbing on superlative rock up the slabby wall right of 1. Climb the central rib to a small tree. Step left onto the wall and climb up to a rightwards slanting ramp. Follow this to below a vertical wall with thin cracks and step left to take the final few metres of the arête direct (crux) to the ledge. Scramble off right or finish by the central crack (4c).

VIKING CRAG 35min

NG 867 717 **Alt:** 220m

Lies midway between **Rum Doodle Crag** & **Red Wall Crag**, composed of large fallen blocks and short walls.

1 Helga's First Time *   30m Severe 4a
FA Blyth Wright & Asta Parker 14 June 1998

Go up the pleasant rough slab to a boulder-spike. Step left on to a wall then by interesting moves right, finish directly up the rib.

Photo Jim Buchanan, Wild West Topos.

GAIRLOCH STONE VALLEY CRAGS | 135

2 Up-Helly-Aa * — 30m VS 4c
FA Graeme Ettle & Blyth Wright 18 June 1998

Climb the obvious broken groove, step left then up right and follow the twin cracks past a dubious block. Climb a crack on excellent rock, finishing just right of the crest.

3 Little Valhalla * — 12m VS 4c
FA Graeme Ettle & Blyth Wright 18 June 1998

Fine well protected climbing up the prominent groove.

4 Norse Face Route * — 14m E2 5c
FA Graeme Ettle 18 June 1998

Start up 3 to gain a pedestal on the right. Go up the arête and mantelshelf to a pocket (F #3.5). Make hard moves right (wire in slot on right) to a crack then up to finish more easily up right-trending fault.

RED WALL CRAG 35min
NG 868 717 **Alt:** 230m

The steep red wall just down left of **Stone Valley Crag**. The rock here is more fissile, but essentially sound.

1 Bold as Brass ** — 25m E2 5c
FA John Mackenzie & Bob Brown 9 May 1996; Direct Paul Thorburn 18 June 1998

The red-coloured left-bounding pillar of the wall. It gives a sustained and technical climb on perfect rock with the crux near the top. Gain a small ledge just left of 4, step up right to below the flange then climb it, stepping left to below a thin curved crack. The crux section continues up the wall just right of the crack then follows it to the top. The bolder 1a *Direct* climbs direct above the ledge close to the arête.

2 Burnt Offering * — 25m E2 5b
FA Graeme Ettle & Blyth Wright 2 June 1998

Follow 1 to beneath the flange then the wall on the right to a groove with a tiny sapling below an overlap. Pass the overlap on the right with a further deviation on the right avoiding the hardest direct moves.

3 Flaming June ** — 25m VS 5a
FA Bob Brown & John Mackenzie 11 May 1995

The red wall is much steeper than it appears, providing devious but good climbing. Climb onto a small ledge at its right end. Continue to an obvious flange above then traverse right to a ledge with small trees. Climb up the flake-crack and step left into a niche below a small roof then step back right towards heather. Climb up and left into a well-positioned open corner to a ledge, finishing up the short arête above.

Photo Jim Buchanan, Wild West Topos.

4 Lucky Strike ** — 23m VS 5a
FA Bob Brown & John Mackenzie 3 May 1996

Sustained and varied. Climb the pronounced groove on smooth rock to a large spike. Stand on this and climb the *"seemingly blank"* wall up and right on hidden holds to the ledge.

5 Schiltrom * — 25m E1 5b
FA Graeme Ettle & Blyth Wright 18 June 1998

Start at a small spike in the heathery ramp. Make a hard move left to gain the base of a leftwards-trending flake. Follow this to a semi-detached spike then move leftwards to cross an overlap with difficulty. Finish up the clean slab above, moving delicately left to finish.

GAIRLOCH STONE VALLEY CRAGS

STONE VALLEY CRAG
NG 868 717 **Alt:** 250m
35min
The biggest and best crag, easily identified from the track by the silvery arête of *Open Secret*.

1 Cheese-grater Slab * 10m VS 5a
FA John Mackenzie & Bob Brown 10 March 1996

Below 2, forming an excellent approach is a small slab. Climb this centrally for most enjoyment.

2 No Beef * 18m E2 5c
FA Richard McHardy & Bob Brown 24 March 1996

Start on top of the boulder left of 3. Climb the steep wall to a ledge. Climb a shallow groove to a flat ledge, step right and up to an overhang with an undercut hold. Surmount the overhang to a groove then make the crux moves diagonally left to finish by mantelshelves.

3 Touch and Go ** 23m VS 4c
FA John Mackenzie & Bob Brown 11 June 1995

The inset slab left of the crest. Climb the slab's centre (just left of an obvious crack) and step left to a shallow corner at ¾ height, to gain the edge of the main slab at a niche. Step right and finish up the crux of 4.

4 Open Secret *** 35m HS 4b
Andy Brooks, Terry Doe & Dave Jones 18 June 1989

The crag classic, giving excellent climbing up the silvery arête. Climb the crack to where it bends right. Now follow a thin snaking crack which trends left up the steep slabby headwall.

5 Bald Eagle *** 35m HVS 5a
FA Bob Brown & John Mackenzie 11 June 1995

The seemingly bald slab right of 4, giving peerless climbing on immaculate rock. Climb the corner and at its top step left and climb a thin crack to its end. Climb straight up over the two bulges above then the thin crack to its termination. Climb directly up the centre of the pink slab above and straight over the wall at the top.

6 Blood Feud ** 40m E1 5b
FA John Mackenzie & Blyth Wright 30 May 1997

Excellent climbing and a worthy companion to 5.
1 **20m 5b** Climb the short wall right of the tree to a recess. Climb the bald wall behind the tree via a

crack. Reach straight up where the crack veers right, step left and continue up the fine slab.

2 20m 5a Above are a pair of black streaks. Start left of them and traverse right and up into them to holds on their left (or easier but unprotected up the wall right of the black streak). Finish up the crack above, as for 7.

7 Stone Diary * — 40m HVS 5a
FA John Mackenzie & Bob Brown 14 May 1995

A fine route with considerable variety. Start just left of the central chokestoned gully in the lower wall.

1 20m 5a Gain a plinth and climb the steep rib between the gully and a smooth pod. Step left above and friction up a fine slab to a stance and belay.

2 20m 5a Step left from the stance and friction up a steepening scoop to gain holds up right, crux, and exit centrally below a crack that runs up the headwall slab. Climb the crack to the top.

8 Inside Information * — 45m HVS 5a
FA Bob Brown & John Mackenzie 14 May 1995

Good climbing, particularly the upper pitch.

1 20m 5a Climb the steep jam crack on the right of the lower wall to exit by some blocks. Step left and climb the right edge of the gully to some heather. Step left and climb an easy rib to avoid the heather, stepping right at the top to belay below the water worn groove.

2 25m 5a Climb the excellent groove to a ledge. Step left and climb a flake-crack to an awkward exit by a little corner.

On the right above a wide heather terrace is a steep buttress with a shield of *"uncharacteristically smooth"* rock and a series of thin cracks. Gained by scrambling up the central chokestoned gully along the terrace from the right or the lower pitches of 8 or 10.

9 Golden Eagle ** — 25m E3 6a
FA Ian Taylor & Graeme Ettle 14 June 1997

A superb pitch on excellent rock – the best of the cracks on the wall. Climb the excellent left crack on improving holds.

10 Melting Pot * — 45m E3 5c
FA John Mackenzie, Bob Brown & Graham Cullen 24 June 1995

Start at a rib right of a tree.

1 20m 4c Climb the wall and continue to step right to a ledge. Climb the short wall above and scramble up heather to a flake belay.

2 25m 5c Step into a ramp and climb the left crack to a sloping hold, move right and climb the right crack to the shield. Holds now begin and pleasant climbing leads to the top.

11 The Beer Bottle Dilemma * — 30m E3 5c
FA Ian Taylor May 1996

Some good steep climbing. Climb cracks trending slightly rightwards to gain a small ledge. Easier climbing leads pleasantly to the top.

12 The Time Warp * — 30m E3 6a
FA Graeme Ettle & Blyth Wright 21 June 1997

Good sustained climbing up the predictably strenuous crack, finishing up easier ground.

13 Divided Loyalty * — 30m HS 4b
FA Bob Brown & John Mackenzie 10 March 1996

A fine pitch, much easier than it looks. Start beneath a narrow chimney at the back of the bay. Climb into the chimney and up this for 10m to a step left onto the front face. Continue up a slab and then a ramp on the right to the top on excellent rock.

14 Updraught * — 25m VS 4b
FA John Mackenzie & Bob Brown & 10 March 1996

The prominent short corner. Go up the corner until it eases then step right and follow the fine edge on rough rock to the top.

GAIRLOCH STONE VALLEY CRAGS

PLAYTIME WALLS 40min
NG 868 717 **Alt:** 280m

Behind **Red Wall Crag** is a long line of 10m high walls of perfect rock above a grassy ledge.

1 Playtime Wall ★ — 10m E2 6a
FA John Mackenzie & Blyth Wright 30 May 1997

A splendid problem. The obvious and most tempting line is the centrally placed groove above a narrow ledge. The narrow ledge is not reached easily and even then the climbing is not over.

2 School's Out ★★ — 10m E4 6b
FA Rab Anderson 7 May 2000

Move up a thin crack and reach holds out on the left in the brown streak. Climb the cracks to the top.

The cracks just right are 3 *Primary Care* Severe 4b.

FLOWERDALE WALL 40min
NG 868 719 **Alt:** 270m

This pleasant steep crag lies 250m behind **Rum Doodle Crag**.

1 Blyth Spirit ★★ — 25m VS 4c
FA Bob Brown & John Mackenzie 10 June 1997

Stand on top of a rock finger then direct to a small overhang. Pull over this to finish up a thin but helpful crack.

2 Sun Due ★ — 25m VS 4c
FA Jonathon Preston & John Lyall 26 April 2005

The leftmost of twin wide cracks.

3 Lily of the West ★★ — 25m E1 5b
FA Graeme Ettle & Blyth Wright 10 June 1997

Good well protected climbing up the snaking crack. Climb the crack over the crux bulge, finishing directly up the edge.

4 Veinous Fly Trap ★ — 25m HVS 5a
FA Graeme Ettle & Blyth Wright 10 June 1997

The shallow corner bounding the edge of the red slab.

5 Blood Red Roses ★ — 25m HVS 5a
FA Blyth Wright & Graeme Ettle 10 June 1997

Climb the slab on superb dark red rock to runners at 13m. Continue to exit near some heather.

6 White Lining ★ — 25m HVS 5a
FA Paul Tattersall & Jim Buchanan 19 March 2001

Climb the fault right of the arête to a spike, swing left into a groove then gain the flake up the right side leading to easy ground.

The centre of the slim buttress is 7 *Avoid the Paint* ★ VS 4c.

Photo Jim Buchanan, Wild West Topos.

THE LEFT DOME 45min
NG 869 717 **Alt:** 300m

Up and right from **Stone Valley Crag** is the apparent summit buttress — two dome-like crags separated by a gully.

1 Demon Razor ★★   20m E3 5c
FA John Mackenzie & Bob Brown (both led) 24 July 1996

An excellent exercise in positive thinking up the thin flake-crack. Start in the 'cave' and burn to the ledge. Continue up the pleasant arête above.

Further right an overhanging wall is split by a pair of slanting cracks forming a V above a lower wall.

2 The Flashing Blade ★   20m E3 6a
FA Graeme Ettle & Ian Taylor 14 June 1997

The thin left-slanting crack. Climb the blocky groove to the base of the crack. The thin crack gets steadily harder with the crux at the top, well protected by small cams.

3 Cat Burglar ★★★   20m E4 6a
FA Ian Taylor & Graeme Ettle 24 June 1997

The formidable-looking wall between the slanting cracks. Superb sustained climbing, easier and better protected than it looks but high in the grade! From the groove step onto the wall, following a thin overhanging crack all the way.

4 The Thug ★★   20m E2 5b
FA Bob Brown & John Mackenzie 9 May 1996

The superb right-slanting crack. Climb the groove to a small ledge below the crack. The crack yields to a no frills approach and has plenty of gear with the crux at the top. Scramble off left or by steep walking up the straightforward arête.

5 The Lum ★   70m Very Difficult 4a
FA Andy Brooks, Terry Doe & Dave Jones 18 June 1989

Further right the crag turns a right-angle split by a vertical chimney.

1 **25m** Climb the fine chimney to a stance on the right below a shallow red corner.
2 **20m 4a** Left of the corner is an overhung crack. Surmount the bulge (crux, 4a, but short) and follow the crack around to the front face and thence to a terrace.
3 **25m** Continue up easy but pleasant rocks to the summit of the dome or walk off leftwards.

Photo Jim Buchanan, Wild West Topos.

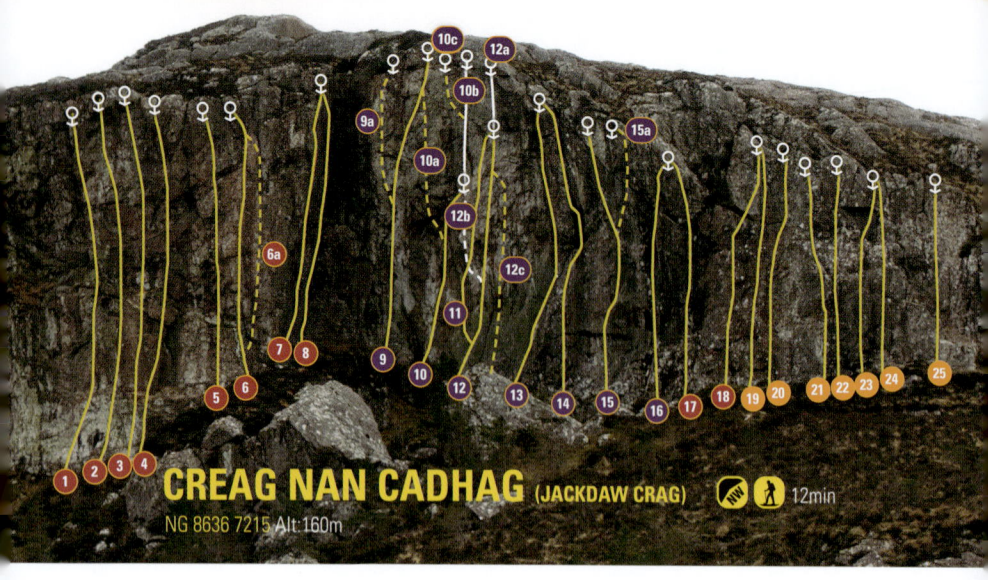

CREAG NAN CADHAG (JACKDAW CRAG)
NG 8636 7215 Alt: 160m 12min

A very accessible sport crag overlooking the A832 road at the top of the Slattadale pass. The climbing is much better than first appearances would suggest.

Approach: From the green barn walk east along the road for 500m, then through a gap in the deer fence and up the boggy hillside to the crag.

1 Fossil Hunters ★ 25m F6b
FA Paul Tattersall 3 June 2015

2 Whispers in the Wind ★ 25m F6a+
FA Paul Tattersall 2016

3 The Craik in Everything ★ 25m F6b
FA Paul Tattersall 2016

4 Entropy ★ 25m F6a
FA Paul Tattersall 2018

5 Old Man's Beard ★ 25m F6a
FA Paul Tattersall 2011

6 Bovnahackit ★★ 25m F6a+
FA Paul Tattersall 2010

6a Bygone Comrades ★ 25m F6b+
FA Paul Tattersall 2015

7 Battle Axe ★★ 15m F6c
FA Paul Tattersall 2007

8 CMB ★ 15m F6b+
FA Paul Tattersall 2019

9 Ronald Raygun ★★★ 20m F7b+
FA Andy Wilby 2012

9a Margaret Thatcher's Funeral ★★ 20m F7c
FA Paul Tattersall 2011

10 Nuclear Litemare ★ 12m F7a
FA Paul Tattersall 2008

10a Fukushima ★ 20m F7c
FA Andy Wilby/Ian Taylor

10b Nuclear Nightmare ★★★ 20m F8a+
FA Alan Cassidy 21 April 2014

GAIRLOCH STONE VALLEY CRAGS | 141

10c Nuclear Cop Out ** — 20m F7c+
FA Andy Wilby June 2015

11 There Goes Gravity * — 15m F7c+
FA Andy Wilby May 2018

12 Game Over ** — 15m F7b
FA Andy Wilby 2011

12a Game Over Extension *** — 20m F8a+
FA Andy Wilby June 2015

12b Thick as Thieves * — 12m F7b
FA Paul Tattersall 2015

12c Coalition Chaos ** — 15m F7b
FA Andy Wilby 2015

13 The Deaf Violinist ** — 15m F7a
FA Paul Tattersall 2007

14 Drip Drip Drip ** — 15m F7a
FA Paul Tattersall 2007

15 Axe Grinder *** — 15m F7a+
FA Martin Moran 2007

15a The Greek Exit * — 15m F7a
FA Paul Tattersall 2007

16 Ball Park Incident * — 15m F6c+
FA Paul Tattersall 2008

17 Pictures of Pluto * — 15m F6c
FA Paul Tattersall 2008

18 Volturi — 14m F6b+
FA Paul Tattersall 2011

19 March of the 56 — 12m F5+
FA Paul Tattersall 2015

20 Flying Scotsman — 12m F5+
FA Paul Tattersall 2011

21 Born to Run ** — 12m F5
FA Paul Tattersall 2011

22 The Lone Triathlete — 12m F5+
FA Paul Tattersall 2015

23 Dunnard — 12m F5
FA Paul Tattersall 2015

24 Referendum Blues — 12m F4+
FA Paul Tattersall 2015

25 Greedy Weeds — 12m F5
FA Paul Tattersall 2015

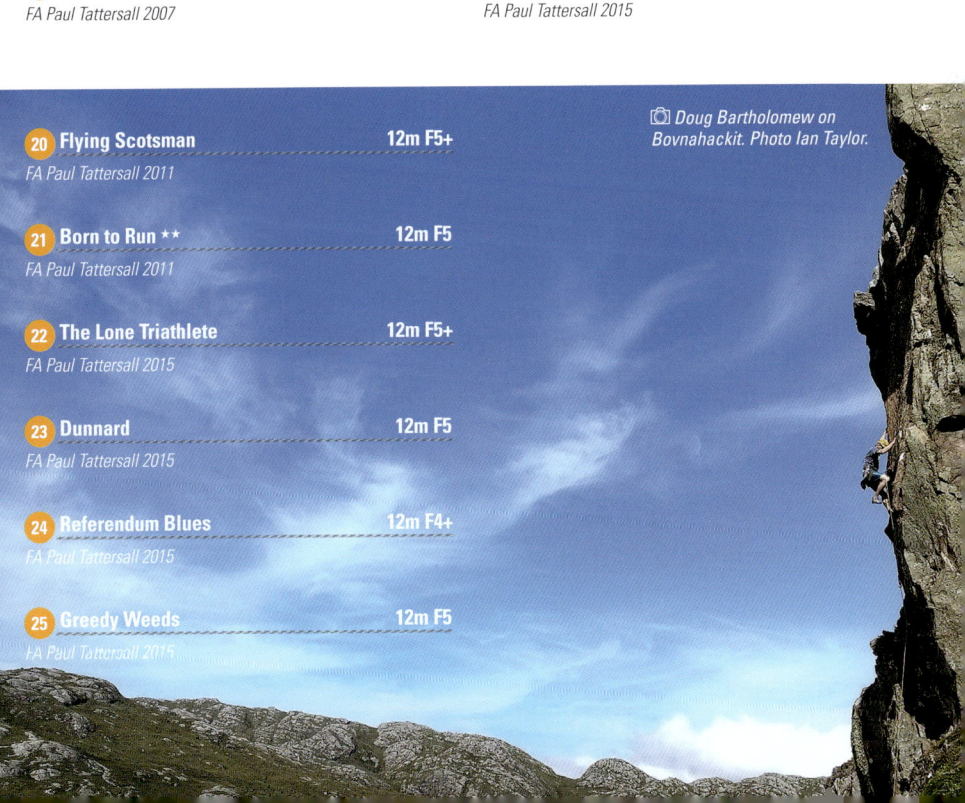

Doug Bartholomew on Bovnahackit. Photo Ian Taylor.

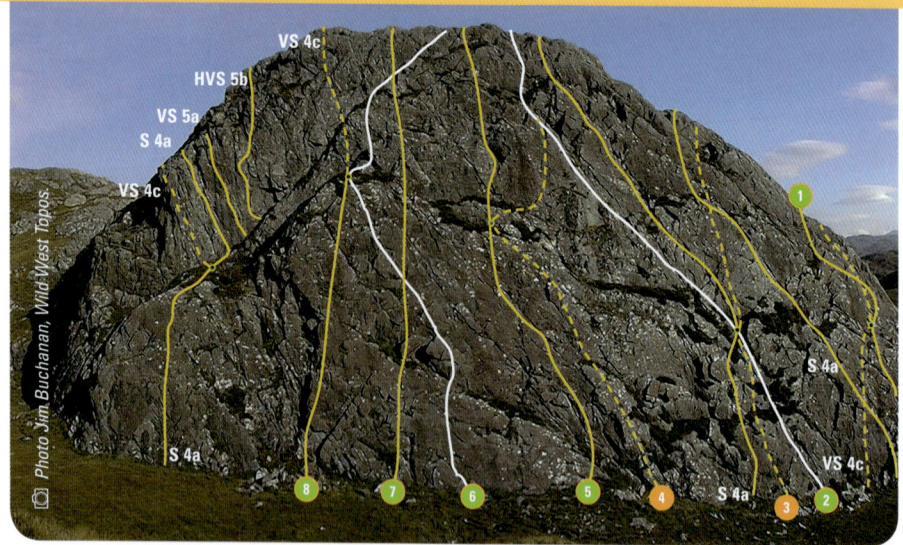

RAVEN'S CRAG

NG 795 714 **Alt:**130m 25min

A pleasant quick drying gneiss crag with a good range of easy routes on generally rough rock. Quite exposed, so often enough of a breeze to keep the midges at bay.

Access: Turn off the A832 2.5 miles/4km south of Gairloch heading west down the B8056 for 1.1 miles/1.8km. Either park on the verge by the farm track on the left just before the Shieldaig Lodge Hotel or in car parking area just beyond the hotel.

Approach: Follow the main farm track south-west for about 0.9 miles/1.5km to reach the small Lochan Fuar on the right. The crag can now be seen in profile on the right. Head directly across the hillside to the base.

Descent: Down either end.

① Hydro Hek ★   44m Severe 4a
FA G.Powell & Steve Chadwick July 1982

Start at the right end of the crag beneath a large clean shield of rock on the upper wall.

1 **20m** – Climb clean brown slabs to the base of the shield.
2 **24m 4a** Step up and right onto diagonal fault then mantelshelf onto the face. Continue up leftwards.

② Lonmore ★★   55m Severe 4a
FA A.Smailes & Steve Chadwick June 1983

Start in the centre of the crag, beneath the diagonal crack in the upper wall.

1 **15m** – Climb directly to tree at right end of heather terrace.
2 **30m 4a** Climb up left and follow the left-slanting fault to further tree and niche. Move out left from the top of the niche to a ledge.
3 **10m** – Finish easily up cracked wall above.

③ The Morning After ★   50m HVS 5a
FA Roger Webb & Simon Richardson 21 May 1995

The upper wall right of 2.

1 **20m** – Climb up to the tree belay of 2 by a short slab and walls to the left.
2 **30m 5a** Climb the wall directly behind the tree.

④ Stage Fright ★★   55m HVS 5a
FA Ian Davidson & Steve Chadwick Spring 1985

The prominent blank-looking wall left of 2.

1 **25m** – Climb vague crest on right side of clean slab to gain right end of the higher left heather terrace.
2 **30m 5a** Climb steeply up the wall to finish up the final section of 2.

5 Charlestone ★★   50m Severe 4a
FA Steve Chadwick & H.Emerson August 1981

A fine direct line up the centre.
1. **25m 4a** Climb slab to the heather gangway. Continue up the prominent weakness to gain the heather terrace beneath cracks.
2. **25m 4a** Continue directly on good holds left of the scoop to finish more easily. The scoop can also be climbed up left to the same finish.

6 Lucy ★★   60m Very Difficult
FA Steve Chadwick & Ian Davidson September 1984

Fine steady climbing just left of centre.
1. **45m** Climb directly up to large blocks at 15m. Pass them on the right, then ascend left-slanting diagonal weakness to the highest heather ledge. Continue up to belay at tree (possible abseil).
2. **15m** Finish easily up rightwards.

7 Mountain Ash ★   60m Very Difficult
FA Doug Lang 1991

Start directly beneath the topmost rowan on the crag. Take a direct line to the top of the crag, passing over huge blocks at 15m. Continue up a shallow depression to finish up the last metre of 6.

8 Entasis ★   60m Very Difficult
FA pitch 1 M.McKay & R.Napier 3 April 1986; Direct Finish D.Conway & R.Napier 6 April 1986

A scoop divides the red slabs beneath the heather terrace. Start from boulders at the base of the scoop.
1. **35m** Climb the right-slanting ramp, then directly up slabs just right of the scoop then directly to heather ledge.
2. **25m** Finish up rightwards, as for 6.

THE DARK SLAB

At the far left end of the crag is a dark slab with prominent jutting blocks on its right side.

1 Jutting Blocks ★   20m Very Difficult
FA Doug Lang (solo) 1991

Climb to and past the blocks on the left and continue to the top.

2 Leac McCac ★   25m VS 4c
FA Dave Neville & Steve Chadwick 1982

After a bouldery start, climb the slab direct on thin edges.

3 Ricicles ★   25m VS 4c
FA Dave Neville & Steve Chadwick 1982

The slab direct, just left of 2.

4 Special K ★   20m Severe 4a
FA Dave Neville & Steve Chadwick 1982

Obvious diagonal right slanting line across the slab; low in the grade.

Photo Jim Buchanan, Wild West Topos.

AZTEC TOWER

A small off-vertical wall of unusual partially metamorphosed sandstone, well endowed with holds. Clearly visible in profile when driving from Gairloch towards Poolewe.

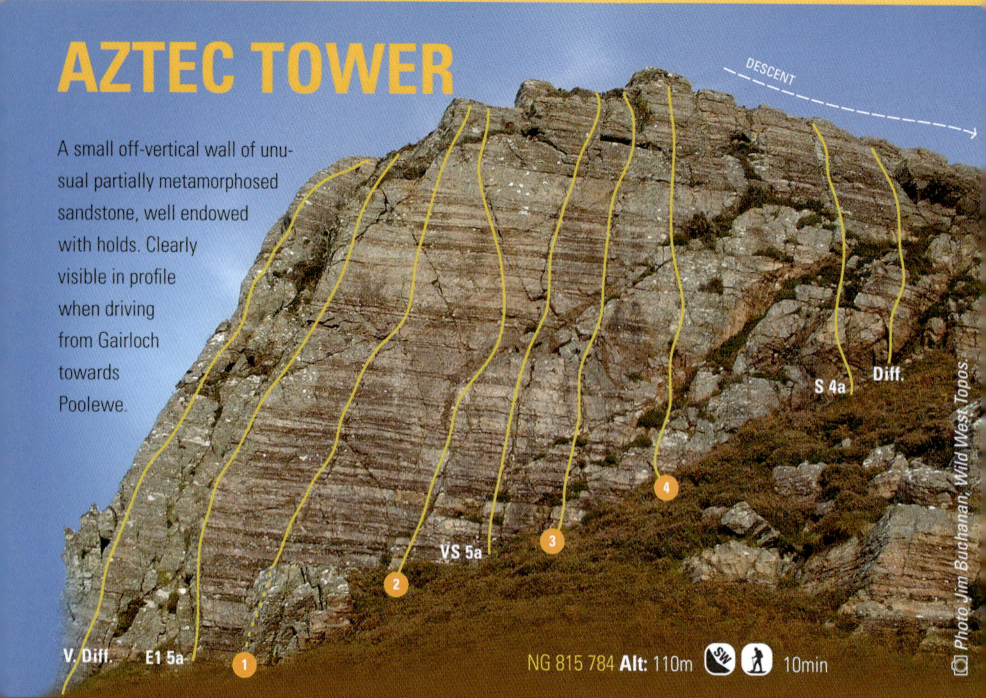
DESCENT
V. Diff.
E1 5a
1
2
VS 5a
3
4
S 4a
Diff.
NG 815 784 Alt: 110m
SW
10min

Photo Jim Buchanan, Wild West Topos.

Access: follow the A832 north from Gairloch for 1.3 miles/2km to park considerately on the east side of the road at the quarry entrance on the right.

Approach: Head directly across rough ground, skirting beneath the base of boulders and smaller crags.

1 Human Sacrifice ** — 15m VS 4c

FA Alan Gorman & Jim Buchanan 19 April 1997

Crack 2m right of arête.

2 Warrior God * — 15m VS 4c

FA Jim Buchanan & Alan Gorman 19 April 1997

Central crack then wall, finishing up a left-slanting crack.

3 Cortes * — 12m HS 4b

FA Jim & Mary Buchanan 11 August 1996

The broken crack-line.

4 Sun God * — 12m VS 4c

FA R.Weld & John Mackenzie 24 August 1998

Pleasant climbing up the right side of the continuous wall.

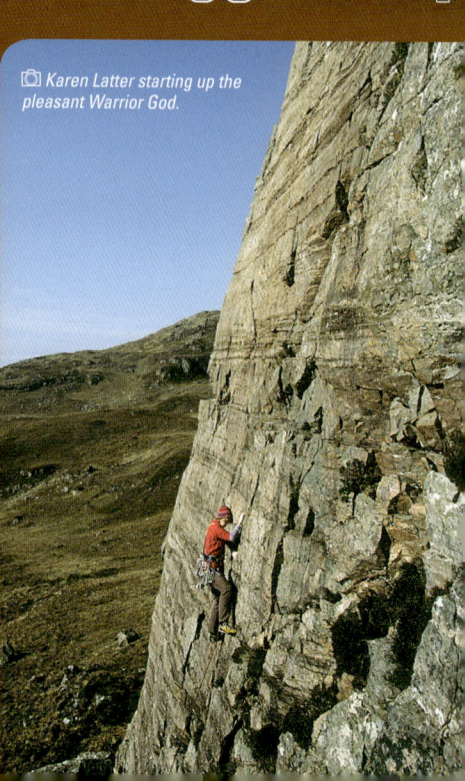

Karen Latter starting up the pleasant Warrior God.

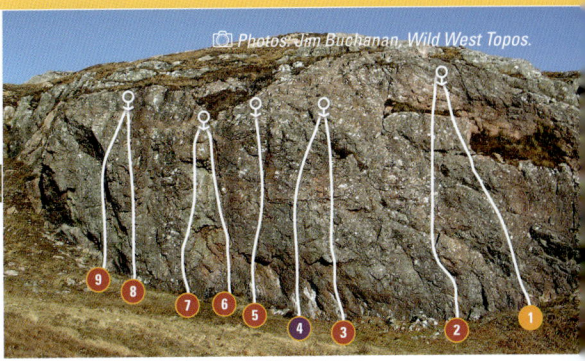

Photos: Jim Buchanan, Wild West Topos.

GRASS CRAG (A' CREAG FHEOIR) NG 817 790 **Alt**: 150m   20min

A small vertical sport crag on the hillside behind and left of **Aztec Tower**. Fairly minor but worth combining with a visit to **Aztec Tower**. Very quick drying.

Access: Follow the A832 north from Gairloch for 1.4 miles /2.2km to obvious parking spot at NG 822 781 a few hundred metres north of the quarry entrance.

Approach: Head fairly directly across rough boggy ground, passing the east side of the loch.

Routes equipped & climbed by Paul Tattersall, Murdoch Jamieson & Andrew Wilby January & February 2006.

#	Route	Length	Grade
1	Third and Final *	10m	F5+
2	Kick Ass Yoga *	10m	F6a+
3	All the Arts	8m	F6c
4	Pants on Fire	8m	F7a
5	The Dump **	8m	F6c
6	Constipated Miser	8m	F6b+
7	The Thinker	8m	F6b
8	Invest Wisely	8m	F6a
9	Joint Account	8m	F6a
10	Sign of the Jug	8m	F5+
11	Side Flake	8m	F5+
12	Waiting for the Man *	12m	F6a+
13	Like it Hot? *	12m	F6c+
14	Boyish Behaviour	10m	F6a+
15	Da Bomb	10m	F6a
16	Superspace	10m	F5+

Jeremy Love enjoying The Dump.

GAIRLOCH LOCH TOLLAIDH CRAGS

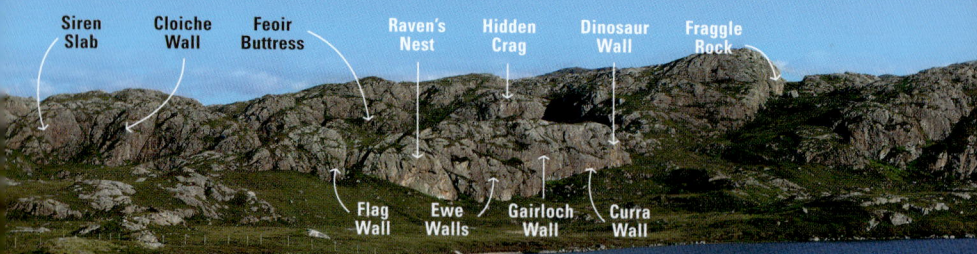

Siren Slab • Cloiche Wall • Feoir Buttress • Raven's Nest • Hidden Crag • Dinosaur Wall • Fraggle Rock

Flag Wall • Ewe Walls • Gairloch Wall • Curra Wall

LOCH TOLLAIDH CRAGS

This is the rocky hillside on the south side of the roadside Loch Tollaidh, overlooking the road between Gairloch and Poolewe. The rock is the usual ubiquitous clean solid Lewisian gneiss.

Approach: Park at the roadside at the east end of Loch Tollaidh. Cross the Tollie Burn by stepping stones at the outflow of the loch and head across boggy ground to reach the first crags in less than 10 minutes. The other crags are all within 5–10 minutes walk from here, either further right or higher up the hillside (see location photo).

Photo Jim Buchanan, Wild West Topos.

LOWER TIER

Closest to the road, this is the main band of crags, running from the first crag, **Raven's Nest** (including **Flag Wall**) away up rightwards to **Fraggle Rock** on the skyline.

Jules Lines starting up Feathering the Nest.

FLAG WALL Alt: 150m   10min

A beautiful overhanging pink wrinkled wall just left of the descent route at the left end. The crack on the right is 2 *Path* • E1 5b.

1 Crossroads ★★   9m E4 6b

FA Paul Tattersall April 1998

Two quartz veins form a fine cross low down in the centre of the wall. Climb the wall through the left half of the cross, making powerful well protected moves leading to the tiny hanging groove and easier ground.

3 Slowed-Down ★   20m E2 5b

FA Rab & Chris Anderson 22 July 1996

Climb the edge and continue before pulling round right and up to a thin crack to finish.

> The base of the main crag also has some good bouldering, including a fine traverse at 6b.

10min

RAVEN'S NEST NG 849 782 **Alt:** 150m

The first crag reached after crossing the outflow from the loch and walking across the flat boggy ground. Unfortunately, there is a large eyrie in the middle of the crag blocking one of the main lines and preventing development of the central section.
Nesting restrictions: The crag should be avoided until June and disturbance kept to a minimum.

4 Boldered Out ★ 20m E3 5c
FA Rab & Chris Anderson 21 July 1996

The thin left-slanting crack. Boulder directly to the crack at 5m then climb this to the top.

5 Blow Out ★★ 20m E5 6b
FA Bill Birkett & Tom Rogers 26 August 1997

Boulder through the overhang to a flake-crack which leads to a right-slanting gangway then easier ground.

6 *Super Sleuth* ★ E2 5b climbs the short left crack and the ramp of 7 to finish up a slim groove on the crest.

7 Semi-Automatic ★★ 30m E4 6b
FA Rab Anderson, Dave Cuthbertson & Chris Anderson 8 Aug 1996

The right crack. Start at the base of the left crack and climb boldly up to the base of the right crack. Follow the crack to a ramp-cum-groove and go up this to near its top. Move left to breach the bulge and continue directly above to reach heathery ground on the crest which leads to the top.

8 MacDonald ★★ 30m E4 6a
FA Paul Tattersall & Angela Katzenmeier June 1999

Start up 7 to the diagonal crack. Pull over a small roof and step right into the groove. At the top of the groove move right to better holds then back left on jugs before climbing up to the slab. Finish up the left edge.

9 Feathering the Nest ★ 30m E4 6a
FA Rab & Chris Anderson 16 August 1996

Good though escapable climbing. Climb to the bulge, pull up onto huge jugs on the right wall. Step left and climb the groove to finish up an easy slab.

The right edge of the crag is formed by a fine pink widening slab with some excellent lines on immaculate rock. Belay stake on top.

Photo Jim Buchanan, Wild West Topos.

GAIRLOCH LOCH TOLLAIDH CRAGS

10 Raven's Edge ★★　　　　　　**35m Very Difficult**
FA Highland Field Craft Training Centre members 1940s

Start at the right edge of the steep wall where it turns round into a big clean slab. Follow the left edge of the slab throughout. The top is less clean.

11 Assault Slab ★★★　　　　　　**35m Very Difficult**
FA Highland Field Craft Training Centre members 1940s

Excellent climbing on clean rough rock with good protection; the start is the crux. Follow the same first 5m of 10 then trend right up the centre of the slab, passing the right side of a curving corner. Many variations of a similar grade are possible.

Karen Latter sauntering up the immaculate Assault Slab.

Photo Jim Buchanan, Wild West Topos

THE EWE WALLS   10min
NG 849 782　**Alt:** 150m

An area of slabs and walls just right of **Raven's Nest**, before the slope rises to **Gairloch Wall**.
Descent: down a heathery ramp leading down rightwards (west) to the base of **Gairloch Wall**.

1 Ewephoria ★★　　　　　　**30m VS 4b**
FA Steve Chadwick & Graham Powell 1982

The fine, dark coloured narrow slab at the left side of the crag is climbed by a central line. *"Protection is scant, but there when required"*.

2 Ewe Tree Slab ★　　　　　　**25m VS 4c**
The slab just left of the moss — better than it appears!

3 Incisor ★　　　　　　**30m E1 5b**
The arête and overhanging corner. Pull strenuously through the overhang into the cracked corner.

4 Peweky ★　　　　　　**20m E1 5b**
FA Mark Garthwaite & Rab Anderson 7 April 2002
The right side of the arête.

5 Ewereka ★　　　　　　**25m E1 5c**
FA Rab & Chris Anderson 8 June 1996
The thin crack which springs from above a small roof at the start, passing just left of the holly.

GAIRLOCH LOCH TOLLAIDH CRAGS | 149

Photo Jim Buchanan, Wild West Topos.

GAIRLOCH WALL   10min
NG 849 782   **Alt:** 150m

Lying to the right, just above a slight rise in the slope above some large boulders. The undercut base is sheltered from the elements.

1 Balding Oldie *   25m E6 6b
FA Rab & Chris Anderson 19 May 1996

The left line. A flake line springs from the slanting break at mid-height. Stopper #1s and small wires essential. Stand on an embedded flake and climb to a good but hollow sounding hold (good RP #1 deep in slot to right). Stand on the hold (sideways RP #3 on left; bombproof Stopper #1 in slot on right) and continue directly to the break. Gain the flake line then make a hard move to reach a crucial nut placement in the base of a small undercut directly above, similar sized placement in horizontal slot just on right. Continue directly up the thin crack, small wires, to pull over onto easier ground leading to a belay just below the top.

2 El Passe **   25m E6 6b
FA Dave Cuthbertson & Rab Anderson 12 May 1996

Bold and committing climbing in the lower half. In the centre of the vertical left wall is a thin hanging crack. Swing right into a calcite weep and up the crack past a poor nut placement, to some small nut slots (F #0.5 in slot up on right). Continue directly above (sustained and technical) to good holds and protection in the horizontal break. Finish up the sustained wall directly above.

3 Old El Pastits ***   25m E6 6b
FA Rab Anderson & Dave Cuthbertson (both led) 11 May 1996

Excellent sustained climbing tackling the vicious hanging finger-crack above the small pointed boulder. Start atop the boulder. Powerful moves up the lower crack lead to a better holds at 4m (good R #6 placement in the upper of 3 prominent slots). Move up until a span up leftwards leads to a good incut hold and nuts just above. Continue directly up the thin cracks in the headwall.

4 Conquistador **   25m E7 7a
FA Dave Cuthbertson September 1996

A contender for the most technical unbolted pitch in Scotland. The route originally sported a PR at 5m (subsequently stolen – F & nut placements also available at this point) pre-clipped on the first ascent. Start atop the boulder. Levitate up to holds in the crack above the protection. Continue slightly easier up the thin and very sustained crack in the headwall. Phew!

5 Ageing Bull *  20m E3 6a
FA Rab & Chris Anderson 26 May 1996

The thin crack which cuts through the bulge above the start of the slanting ramp. Gain the crack after a bouldery start then follow this through the bulge and on up the groove to easy ground.

> 5a *The Ramp* E2 6a finishes more easily rightwards.

6 The Imposter * 20m E3 5c
FA Rab Anderson 26 May 1996

Bouldery moves gain the groove and then the ramp. Move up the ramp a short way, step left onto the wall and climb to easy ground. The thin crack provides some protection but the holds are on the wall to the right.

7 Zig-Zag * 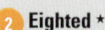 25m HVS 5a
FA Steve Chadwick & Alan Winton 1994

Climb a short corner up left to a niche, move right and surmount the roof then move left onto the edge and climb to the top.

8 Rough Slab ** 25m VS 4c
FA Rab & Chris Anderson 18 September 1995

The slab of fine rough rock via a central (right curving) line. A left finish has also been climbed.

THE CURRA WALL 15min
NG 849 781 Alt: 150m

The extension of **Gairloch Wall** is a low band of steep rock which is useful for bouldering. There is a slabby upper tier.

1 Eight Below *  30m HS 4a
FA Jim & Mary Buchanan 21 November 1992

Start at a big heathery V-groove. Poorly protected. Climb the slab on the right side of the groove (15m). Continue up the cracked rib directly above.

2 Eighted * 30m VS 5a
FA Alan Winton (solo) 1994

Start towards the right side of the low band and climb it by hard moves up via a flake. Go to the upper tier and climb a corner then the left side of the slabby rib of 3.

3 After Eight * 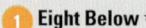 30m Severe 4a
FA Alan Winton (solo) 1994

Climb easily up the right edge of the lower band to the upper tier, where a slabby rib comes down lowest at its right end. Climb the rib.

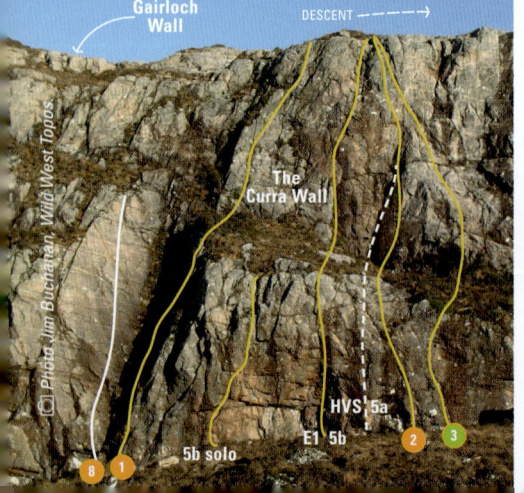

Karen Latter looking smooth in the evening light on Rough Slab.

DINOSAUR WALL   15min

NG 849 781 **Alt:** 150m

Immediately right of **The Curra Wall** is an area of fine reddish rock, beyond which the crag merges into the hillside before rising up towards **Fraggle Rock**. The base of the crag is a bit boggy in places.

1 Reeperbahn *   20m E4 6b
FA Paul Tattersall 19 May 2002

Wall and hanging groove.

2 In the Pink ***   20m HVS 5b
FA Steve Chadwick & Graham Powell 1981

The obvious slim open groove in the middle of the crag. Awkward to start.

3 Red Faced *   20m E1 5b
FA K.Clark & Ian Davidson 1992

The next crack just round the edge to the right leads to a finish, either up the easy wide groove or the arête and slab.

4 Rouged-up *   20m E2 5b
FA Rab & Chris Anderson 17 September 1995

Line up the blunt rib immediately right of the crack.

5 Flushed-out **   20m HVS 5a
FA Jim Buchanan & Dave Neville 18 July 1992

The open groove and slab.

NG 848 779 **Alt:** 170m   20min
FRAGGLE ROCK

This pleasant slabby crag, visible in profile from the road, lies a little over 200m further right along the hillside from **Dinosaur Wall**, higher up at the far right end.

1 Miss Piggy *   25m Difficult
FA Jim & Mary Buchanan 4 July 1992

Gently left-sloping ramp. Climb this then clean rock straight up.

2 Animal *   20m HVS 5a
FA Jim & Mary Buchanan 4 July 1992

Move out right and climb a rib to the big horizontal cave. Traverse left and climb the steep left-slanting groove which springs from the left end of the cave. Starting further right reduces the grade to VS 4c.

3 Kermit Direct **   25m E1 5b
FA Jim Buchanan & Jim Henderson 27 June 1992;
Direct Rab & Chris Anderson 13 August 1995

Climb up the left edge of the slab, close to heathery ledges on the left then up a slim corner. Move out onto the wall to make an awkward finishing move to reach easier finishing ground.

4 Sprocket Direct **   25m E1 5b
FA Jim Buchanan & Jon Robinson June 1992;
Direct Rab & Chris Anderson 13 August 1995

Climb the centre of the slab (poorly protected) to the

GAIRLOCH LOCH TOLLAIDH CRAGS

roof, move right then pull left through the right end of the roof and go up to the next roof. Move out right and climb cracks to the top.

5 Tall in the Saddle ★ — 25m E6 6b
FA Paul Tattersall (headpointed) 2002

The white wall above the split block.

6 Heave-ho ★★ — 25m E4 6a
FA Rab & Chris Anderson 12 August 1995

The thin crack. Pull through the roof and continue up the crack to the top.

7 Fraggle Roll ★ — 25m HVS 5a
FA Terry Doe & Jim Buchanan 8 May 1993

Climb the crack to the right end of a holly bush then a corner left to the pedestal and an overhanging corner above.

> The direct finish through the holly and up the groove and crack is 7a *Roll Up* ★ E3 5c.

8 Joyful Departure ★ — 25m E3 6a
FA Paul Tattersall & Angela Katzenmeier April 1998

Prominent crack-line near the right end of the low roof, to F #4 slot on the lip.

9 Peek Practice ★ — 25m E4 6a
FA Rab & Chris Anderson 13 August 1995

Climb the groove then go right to an alcove and up left with difficulty to easier ground. Go a short way up a slabby groove, climb to a recess under a roof then pull out left through the top of this and continue to the top.

10 Waldorf ★ — 25m VS 5a
FA Jim Buchanan & Jim Henderson 4 July 1992

The reddish coloured intrusion of unusual rock running up the wall. Climb this, finishing directly to easier slabby ground.

11 Cookie Monster ★ — 25m VS 5a
FA Terry Doe & Jim Buchanan 8 May 1993

About 10m from the right end of the wall is this heathery crack with an undercut start.

12 Reddy Ribbed ★ — 25m VS 5a
FA Rab & Chris Anderson 13 August 1995

Just right of 11 is a short V-groove. From the top of the groove pull out left and climb the rib leading to easier ground.

13 Doozer ★ — 20m Very Difficult
FA Jim & Mary Buchanan 4 July 1992

A clean slab. Climb the slab to its top right corner, cross a heather break and finish up a small rib.

SECOND TIER

The second band of crags, higher up the hillside and behind the **Lower Tier**.

SIREN SLAB

1 Strip-teaser ★★　　　　　　　　　　　**35m E4 5c**
FA Rab & Chris Anderson 15 June 1996

The very thin right-slanting crack, right of centre on the slab. Start at the lowest rocks and climb straight up to a heathery ledge below a shallow groove/flake-line. Climb this, stepping right for gear then go up and around the left side of the obvious overlap to reach the thin crack which leads to a bulge just below the top. Pull out and up left to finish more easily.

THE CLOICHE WALL

The wall 50m right of **Siren Slab**.

2 Someone Else's Dream ★★　　　　　**23m E2 5b**
FA Paul Tattersall & Angela Katzenmeier July 1991

Excellent well protected climbing up the right-trending cracked groove at the left side of the crag.

3 White Fright ★　　　　　　　　　　　**20m E2 5c**
FA Rab & Chris Anderson 8 June 1996

Good steady climbing on perfect rock after a bold start. Start in the centre of the wall, 4m right of the cracked groove. Move up rightwards to good holds at 5m. Climb the wall directly above. Low in the grade.

NG 851 782　Alt: 200m　20min

FEOIR BUTTRESS

50m further right, at a slightly lower level a small crag with a pair of cracks almost converging near the top.
Descent: Down either side of the crag.

1 Rock Bottom ★★　　　　　　　　　　**12m E3 6a**
FA Rab & Chris Anderson 17 August 1996

A fine jug haul up the left crack-line.

2 Zeazy Top ★　　　　　　　　　　　　**12m E3 6a**
FA Rab & Chris Anderson 17 August 1996

The zigzag line on the right. Finish easily up the slabby rib.

NG 850 781　Alt: 200m　20min

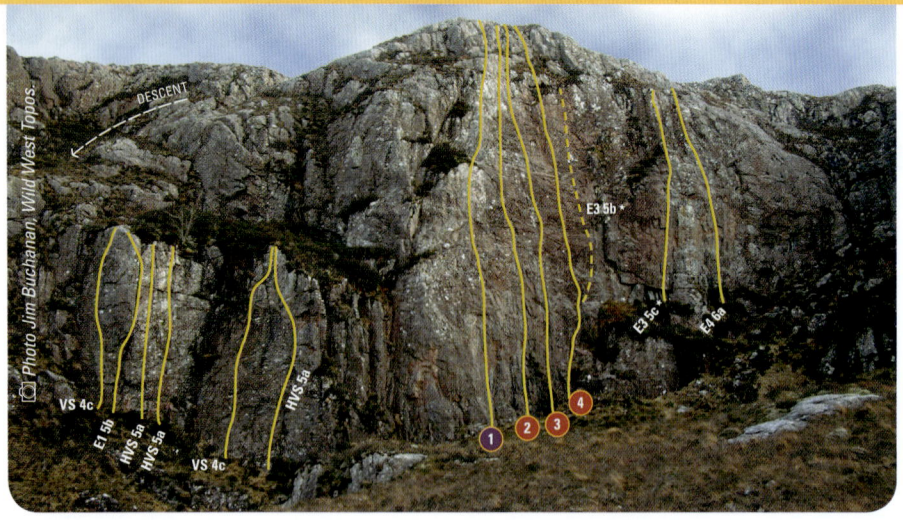

HIDDEN CRAG

A tall reddish coloured wall cut by a number of prominent crack-lines. It lies at the right end of the Second Tier, hidden from the road just behind **Dinosaur Wall**.

NG 851 780 20min

Approach: Cross the slope just beyond **Dinosaur Wall** and cut across The Meadow.

Descent: Down easy slopes at the left end of the crag.

① Flag Iris **   35m E4 5c
FA Paul Thorburn & Jonathon Preston 3 May 2000

Climbs the wall left of 2 with a hard start leading to an easier but sparsely protected finish.

② Water Lily **   35m E1 5b
FA Alan Winton & Alan Gorman August 1994

The well protected left crack-line that runs up and slightly left from a series of soggy sods of turfs. The start is usually wet but on jugs. The finish is thin but try not to escape right to 3.

③ Buena Vista ***   35m E2 5b
FA Alan Winton & Steve Chadwick April 1994

In the centre of the face are two thin intermittent cracks. This climbs the right-most crack. An excellent, continually interesting pitch on perfect rock. Start beneath a very shallow left-facing groove. Near the top, there is a choice of cracks to finish.

④ Malpasso **   35m E2 5b
FA Alan Winton & Jim Buchanan October 1994

The wall right of the crack. Move up onto the ledge just right of 3 and boldly climb the initial short wall to better holds and protection. Climb the vague crack in the wall, step right to another crack and continue to the top.

Peter MacPherson nearing the top of Water Lily. Photo Paul Tattersall.

CREAG MHOR THOLLAIDH

This is the steep craggy hill at the south-west end of Loch Maree with a wide variety of fine gneiss crags.

CREAG NAN LUCH
(CRAG OF THE MOUSE)
NG 8641 7824 **Alt:** 70m   5min

A small relatively quick drying sport crag on the hill overlooking Tollie Farm. Receives the sun until 11am in summer; also sheltered from prevailing westerlies – could save the day when many other crags are wet. Routes equipped by Paul Tattersall, Colin Meek, Murdoch Jamieson, Ray Wilby, Donnie Chisholm, Paul Thorburn, Terry Doe, Jim Buchanan and Alf Chamings.

Access: Turn off south down the tarmaced single track road 0.6 miles/1km south of Poolewe (signed Tollie Farm /No Through Road). Drive down the track for 0.5 miles /0.8km to park on the right, opposite the farm. Please **avoid blocking passing place** in front of the stile.

Approach: Walk down track for 130m to stile on right, over this then leftwards by a well worn path up the hill.

1 Pumpernickel　　　　25m F6a+
FA Paul Tattersall 2008

A hard start, then long easy slab.

2 Old Snapper ★★　　　　15m F6b+
FA Paul Tattersall Spring 2004

Line up groove, starting from the left.

3 Hairdubh ★　　　　18m F6c+
FA Paul Tattersall July 2005

Thin boudery start, then rightwards up steep smooth wall.

4 Pesto Macho ★　　　　15m F7c
FA Andy Wilby 2010

Direct line up the smooth wall.

5 Superblue ★★★　　　　18m F7b
FA Paul Tattersall Spring 2004

The undercut right-curving hanging crack and headwall above.

6 Shottabeena ★★　　　　18m F7b+
FA Paul Tattersall July 2005

Steep line left of 7, crossing that route to finish up the headwall.

7 Astar ★★　　　　20m F6b
FA Paul Tattersall Spring 2004

Start up 8 then trend left up big flakes, crossing 6.

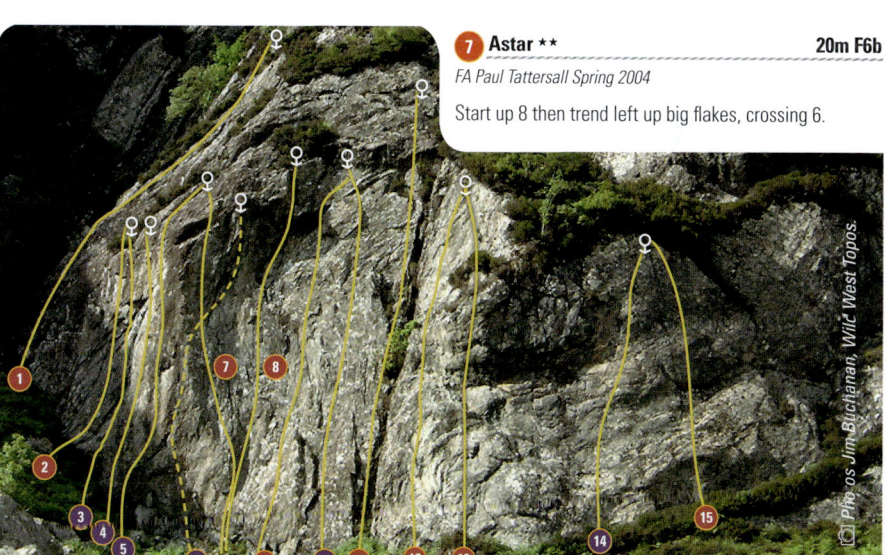
Photos Jim Buchanan, Wild West Topos.

8 Ni Dubh ★★ 20m F6b
FA Paul Tattersall Spring 2004

Left line on slab, crux getting into a short hanging groove at the top.

9 Toss ★★★ 20m F6c
FA Paul Tattersall Spring 2004

Superb climbing taking the central line on the steep slab.

10 Walkaway ★ 20m F7a+
FA Paul Tattersall Spring 2004

The rightmost line on the slab with one particularly desperate thin slabby section.

UPPER TIER

A further 5 minutes up the hill. The crag receives the evening sun and also catches any breeze, therefore may be a midge free option. The **Right Sector** seeps after prolonged rain; the **Left Sector** is permanently dry.

Routes equipped by Paul Tattersall, Murdoch Jamieson & Paul Thorburn.

11 Alice in Wonderland ★ 25m F6a
FA Paul Tattersall 2009

The fault, with or without using the tree!

12 Psychopomp ★★ 20m F6a+
FA Paul Tattersall July 2005

Line to right of vegetated fault in centre of crag.

13 So Phia so Good ★★ 20m F6b+
FA Paul Tattersall 2008

Deceptively tricky climbing up the clean reddish rock.

14 Unfinished Business ★ 12m F7a+
FA Murdoch Jamieson 2005

Reachy climbing with crux at the top on very sharp holds.

15 Mr Smooth ★ 15m F6c
FA Murdoch Jamieson July 2005

Rightmost line, also the last route to dry on the crag.

NG 8636 7823 **Alt:** 120m 10min

Photos Jim Buchanan, Wild West Topos.

LEFT SECTOR

1 Little Leaf ★ — 12m F6c
FA Paul Tattersall February 2006
Shorter line high up on the far left side.

2 This is Jazz ★ — 20m F7b
FA Paul Tattersall 2005
Directly up steep dark wall.

3 King of the Swingers ★★★ — 25m F7a
FA Paul Tattersall July 2005
Fantastically positioned climbing, taking a rising right slanting line above the void.

4 Big Knives ★ — 25m F6c
FA Paul Tattersall 2005
Brutal.

5 Whip and Ride ★★★ — 25m F7c
FA Paul Tattersall 2005

6 Stalks ★★★ — 25m F8a+
FA Alan Cassidy 24 March 2012
A long reach at the roof, then amazing sustained contortions up the hanging groove.

7 Remember to Roll ★★★ — 15m F7a
FA Paul Tattersall 2005
To the first LO.

7a Remember to Rock 'n' Roll ★★★ — 25m F8a+
FA Ali Coull 3 June 2012
Great moves – brilliant and bouldery with a continuous finish.

8 I'm a Tit, I Love Flying ★★★ — 25m F7b+
FA Paul Tattersall 2005

9 Open Project — 25m

RIGHT SECTOR   Alt: 110m

1 Behaving Badly ★★ — 25m F7a
FA Paul Thorburn 2006
Varied and sustained up the left edge of the pink rock.

2 Fighting on all Fronts ★★ — 25m F7a
FA Paul Thorburn 2006
Direct to a tenuous crux around a sentry box.

3 Happily Married ★★ — 25m F7a
FA Paul Tattersall & Paul Thorburn 2006
Graded for grabbing the anchor chain!

4 The Power of Tears ★★ — 25m F7a+
FA Paul Tattersall 2005
Two cruxes – at the start, and latching the finishing jug just past the chain.

5 Swingers ★★ — 25m F7b
FA Paul Tattersall July 2005
'*Superbly slopey*', spoilt only by a no-hands sit rest at halfway.

6 Swallows — 25m F6b+
FA Paul Thorburn 2008
Steep start, followed by sustained slabby climbing. Slow to dry.

LOWER TOLLIE CRAG

NG 8693 7800 **Alt:** 50m   <5min

A finely situated and very accessible vertical 70m high crag overlooking Tollie Bay at the north-west tip of the beautiful Loch Maree. The crag is very sheltered with lots of trees and luxuriant vegetation around the base and can therefore be very midgy later in the summer. Unfortunately the first pitch to many of the routes resembles *"The Hanging Gardens of Babylon"*, but are worth battling with to reach the cleaner upper section. Receives the sun until midday in summer.

Access: Turn off south down the tarmaced single track road 0.6 miles/1km south of Poolewe (signposted Tollie Farm/No Through Road) and follow the track for 0.9 miles/1.5km to a small parking spot on the right at its end.

GAIRLOCH CREAG MHOR THOLLAIDH

Approach: Follow a path from the left end of the car park, crossing a small stream to gain the right end of the crag.

Descents: For routes on the right side of the crag scramble up rightwards through heather and down the open boggy gully bounding the right end of the crag. Alternatively, make a 45m abseil from a block (sling usually in situ) at the top of the right wall of the corner of *Stony Broke*. From the base of this abseil, traverse a large heather ledge rightwards (facing out) to gain the base. There is also a sling & maillon on small birch right of the top of *The Handrail/Decadent Days*.

1 Hamilton's Groove and Arête ★   30m E3 6a
FA Murray Hamilton & Dougie Dinwoodie 1983

Start beneath a prominent crack on the right side of the arête. Climb the shallow groove and crack then the thin finger-crack just left of the arête in the middle section. Finish more easily.

2 Cloud Cuckoo Land ★   25m HVS 5b
FA Grahame Nicoll & Rab Anderson 9 May 1987

Start about 12m left of the right end of the crag, beneath a prominent break in the steep lower wall. Climb a short corner, pull over the steepening and follow a crack stepping up left to finish by a corner-crack.

3 Hostile Witness ★   25m E2 5c
FA Allen Fyffe & Andy Cunningham 26 May 1993

Climbs the wall left of 2, finishing up the fine flake at the top of the wall. Start at the top of the diagonal grass ledge and climb a set of grooves up the left edge of the wall to gain then follow the flake-crack up and right. Move right and finish as for 2.

4 Sailing to Byzantium ★   20m E3 5c
FA R.Conway & Chris Jackson 28 June 1985; Direct Start: Andy Cunningham, Ian Rea & Allen Fyffe 25 May 1993

The obvious steep wide crack in the inset wall at the top of the grassy ramp left of 3. Start up the black corner below the ramp leading into the crack.

5 Second Coast ★   30m E2 5b
FA Grahame Nicoll & Rab Anderson 10 May 1987

Start at a shallow cracked corner groove a short way below and left of 2 where a grassy tree lined ledge slants up leftwards.

1. **10m 5a** Climb the corner /groove to a ledge.
2. **20m 5b** Move up right, climb a crack in the leaning wall and continue above, crossing a small overlap to finish via a short tricky slab.

6 Loctite *   25m E3 6a
FA Rab Anderson & Grahame Nicoll 10 May 1987

Start by scrambling up to a tree lined ledge from the right. Climb a rightwards slanting flake-crack, pull left and follow a thin crack over a bulge to gain a short ramp, step left then up to gain a heathery ledge.

7 North West Orient *   60m E4 6a
FA Rab & Chris Anderson 12 May 1990

A good direct line up the right arête of the headwall. Start to the right of the start of 8 and 9, beneath a short crack springing from a niche between a holly bush on the left and a small tree on the right.

1. **25m 5b** A flake-crack leads to the niche then the short crack is climbed to move up and gain a horizontal handrail. Traverse right for 5m, ascend the wall past a crack to reach a left-slanting ramp then move up to belay as for 8.
2. **35m 6a** Climb the groove above to a flake then step up right to a thin crack, as for 8. Place a high wire then traverse right to a PR and climb the arête and cracks leading to the top.

8 Gudgeon ***   70m E2 5c
FA Chris Jackson & Tom Proctor (2NA) 18 August 1971;
FFA Rab Anderson & Chris Greaves 22 May 1988

A superb relatively popular route, the highlight the main pitch up the headwall. Start 10m up left from the lowest point, beneath the right end of a long roof at 10m.

1. **25m 5b** Climb the corner past a sapling to a pair of saplings, then out right and up to traverse right across the top of the clean slab to belay at the left end of a grassy terrace.
2. **45m 5c** Climb the awkward corner above to a good crack system. Step right and up a thin crack and wider continuation which leads to a flake on the left (possible belay). Move out right and follow easier cracks near the edge of the wall to finish.

9 Decadent Days ***   65m E2 5c
FA Rab Anderson & Murray Hamilton May 1983

A superb long sustained main pitch up the centre of the crag. Start as for 8.

1. **15m 5a** Climb the corner past a sapling to belay just below a pair of saplings.
2. **50m 5c** Climb crack, then move left along break and up main crack-line. Continue up further cracks, then with difficulty up left-slanting crack past old PR (crux). Continue more easily, trending left up slab to small tree on *The Hand Rail*. Move right along this to belay on small birch.

10 Sarah 'n' Dipity and the Forgotten Pill **   55m E3 5c
FA Steve Hill & Sarah Shephard 4 June 1998

An excellent climb in an impressive situation, taking the fine shallow groove in the centre of the wall.

1. **15m 4c** As for 11 to the large oak.
2. **25m 5c** Continue 6m up until it is possible to step right past a perched block. Move up and right to gain good holds at the base of a shallow groove. Follow this over a slight bulge to a junction with *Catastasis*; follow this diagonally left to a niche and old PB.
3. **15m 4a** Pull out of the top of the niche into a slanting crack. Follow this to finish easily.

11 The Trip *   85m E1 5a
FA Chris Jackson & B.Andrews 7 September 1967

The prominent heathery crack up the left side of the main wall. Start at a broken groove beneath the crack.

1. **35m 5a** Go up the groove, pull left over a small overlap then up a left-slanting heathery ramp. At its end move up and right to an oak. Continue up the groove behind the tree and an open chimney to a belay.
2. **25m 5a** Climb over large blocks on the left, step right into a groove and follow this, trending right to the base of a large flake. Move left and up for 4m and traverse right to a small belay stance.
3. **25m 4c** Go over the cracked blocks behind

the belay and step left to avoid a heathery rake. Follow a direct line up zigzag cracks to finish at a heathery shoulder.

12 Gulf Coast Highway ★★   73m E3 6a
FA Rab Anderson & Chris Greaves 3 July 1988

Good climbing up the left side of the main wall. Start about 10m down right of 13.

1. **24m 5b** Move up and traverse right to blocks to gain the obvious right to left-slanting line which is climbed to a tiny sapling. Step right and climb an edge to belay 2m left of a large flake.
2. **24m 5c** Climb a shallow groove to an overlap, pull round left and up to gain a good jug on the right. Move up leftwards to the edge then back right to surmount a roof easily. Continue to a tree belay on 13.
3. **25m 6a** Move diagonally left up a fault to gain a quartz patch. Move up to the base of a thin, right-leaning crack. Climb this with a hard section past a steepening to the top.

13 The Hand Rail ★★   60m Severe 4a
FA Tom Patey & Mike Galbraith 15 May 1966

A fine horticultural ramble crossing some impressive territory for the grade. At the left side of the crag, just right of the right-angled corner of 15 is a prominent vegetated fault. Start at a large birch beneath the fault.

1. **30m** – Tarzan up the fault *"Hey, I've got both my hands and feet on rock"* to a tree belay at the start of the right-slanting ramp.
2. **30m 4a** Climb the ramp to a small holly at its end. Continue round right on the 'handrail' for 6m then step up and finish on good holds.

14 Rain in the Face ★★★   55m E3 6a
FA Dougie Dinwoodie & Alastair Ross 27 August 1987

The prominent arête right of 15. Belay above the initial trees of 13.

1. **20m 5a** Hand traverse a jagged block left to take a hanging belay at the base of the arête.
2. **35m 6a** Make awkward moves out to the arête and up to the base of a slim groove and hidden PR. Ascend the groove to the roof then move right to gain a thin crack springing from the end of the roof. Follow this in a fine position close to the edge to finish more easily.

15 Stony Broke ★   55m HVS 5b
FA John Cunningham & Bill March 9 May 1970

The large open corner at the left end of the crag. Slow to dry. Scramble up left from the base of 13 to a grass terrace.

1. **30m 5b** Go up a short wall to heather then diagonally up right to follow a sloping ramp heading into the corner. Negotiate some shrubbery to gain the corner and follow it to an overhang. Bypass this by the wall on the right leading to a ledge and tree belays.
2. **25m 5a** Climb the corner with occasional deviations on the left wall and some wide bridging to avoid heather.

16 Each Uisge Direct ★★★   50m E4 6a
FA Dougie Dinwoodie & Alastair Ross 27 August 1987; Direct Start: Rab Anderson & Chris Greaves 8 July 1988

'Water horse'. Excellent climbing up the right side of big slab on the left side of the crag. Protection is sketchy in a couple of places and the top crack is sustained. Scramble up left from the start of 13 to start behind a small birch 4m right of large blocks.

1. **25m 6a** Climb the wall to the second horizontal break, step left and up a good crack, stepping left at the top to emerge onto slabs. Follow an obvious flake out right and up to a horizontal break. Step up left and climb quite boldly up right to another break with P and NB.
2. **25m 6a** Climb the slabs up rightwards then straight up to another horizontal break with a PR. Step right and climb a thin crack with sustained interest to a tree at the top.

17 Murray's Arête ★   45m E4 5c
FA Murray Hamilton 1983

Serious sustained climbing up the prominent sharp left arête of the crag. Perhaps only E3 if brushed.

15min

UPPER TOLLIE CRAG
NG 8697 7788 **Alt:** 110m

The fine open crag up and left from the lower crag. Perhaps a better bet if the midges are bad lower down. On a clear day there are grand views towards Fisherfield with the cliffs of Carn Mor visible to the left of the prominent rocky tor of Sgurr an Laocainn. It doesn't even look that far away!

Approach: A steep slog up a small worn path heading diagonally up and left from the left end of the **Lower Crag.**

Descents: Down heathery slopes at the left side, or abseil from sling & maillon on birch right of the top of *The Bug*.

❶ Teddy Bears' Picnic ★★   75m E1 5b

FA Chris Jackson & R.Conway 30 June 1985; p1 Rab Anderson, Stan Pearson & Alastair 'Stuntman' Conkie 18 April 1987

Fine steady climbing, following a line cutting directly through the big diagonal chimney. Start just right of the ramp right of 2.

  1 **25m 5b** Climb the right-slanting corner ramp over a roof towards the chimney. Step up left to gain a horizontal break then pull up to holds and a short crack leading to a tree belay in the chimney.

  2 **20m 5b** Step down to gain and follow a rising crack-line rightwards across the wall and step across to belay beside a perched block.

  3 **30m 5a** Traverse right to climb a crack leading up to the right edge. Step right and continue up easier rock to the top.

❷ The Bug ★★★★   45m E2 5b
FA Pete Botterill & Jeff Lamb (1 tension traverse) 11 June 1974; FFA Colin McLean & Alastair Ross May 1983

An excellent pitch. Start 10m up and left from the rock step just left of the prominent diagonal chimney. Follow the crack which leads to a ramp heading out right. Up this for a short way then continue over the bulge on good holds. Follow the crack leading slightly leftwards to belay where the angle eases. Scramble up then out left. Walk off leftwards.

❸ The Heretic ★★   50m E3 5b
FA Rab Anderson & Grahame Nicoll 10 May 1987

Good sparsely protected climbing up the wall left of 2. Start at the left end of the wall. Climb up right to stand on two blocks. Step right and follow the shallow slabby groove with poor protection to gain a ramp. Make a detour out right to place a runner in the crack on 2 then return to the base of the ramp where there is a good handhold on the wall. Move up then left and gain the start of a diagonal crack which is climbed past a shallow scoop. Stand in the crack where it becomes horizontal and continue first right then left, to gain a diagonal break. Move up to gain another diagonal break and pull over to belay on a slabby ledge. Scramble up right to a ledge then walk off leftwards.

❸ₐ Heresy ★★   45m E4 5c

FA Kev Howett 1992

Bold climbing up the scoop in the centre of the wall left of 2. Start 5m left of 2. Climb the scoop to finish up the upper section of 3.

GAIRLOCH CREAG MHOR THOLLAIDH

  30min   25min

LOCH MAREE CRAG
NG 8786 7686 **Alt:** 60m

An impressive smooth steep wall, rising out of an open gully. It is quite sheltered and can consequently be very midgy for much of the summer. All the routes on the front face are very long and sustained – take plenty of nuts and quick draws.

Approach: Follow a fairly well-defined path close to the shore to beneath the crag, then up worn path to the base. Alternatively, by waterborne means along the lochside.

Descent: Abseil from trees on the grass terrace at the top or from the holly tree.

1 Spirit Air ★★★★　　　　　　　　　**48m E5 6a**
FA Kev Howett June 1987

The soaring arête gives an excellent long sustained outing. Start at the base of the arête. Climb an easy groove then move up left to beneath a hanging crack. Make bold moves up the wall slightly rightwards to better holds at the base of the crack and follow this with continuous interest to a horizontal break where it ends. Traverse left to a shield of grey rock then up its right side past another horizontal break to cracks leading left into the large diagonal fault which leads to a belay on the holly tree at the top.

2 Destitution Man ★★　　　　　　　　**48m E4 5c**
FA Kev Howett June 1987

Ascends the first set of vertical cracks left of the arête to join 1 at the shield. Start 7m up left from the arête at the base of the crack containing some shrubbery at 5m. Climb the crack through bulges and past a block then follow cracks diagonally rightwards onto the wall. Move up then back left to rejoin the crack which leads to the shield on 1. Finish up this.

3 Arial ★★★　　　　　　　　　　　　　**48m E3 5c**
FA Kev Howett, George Ridge & Janet Horrocks 30 May 1992

Excellent sustained well protected climbing up the prominent crack above the start of 2. Follow that route, continuing directly up the crack, which curves to the right, becoming more of a flake. Continue directly up a shallow groove to belay at the holly tree.

4 Pagan Love Song ★　　　　　　　　**55m E4 6a**
FA Kev Howett & George Ridge 6 June 1992

The rightmost of the twin cracks in the wall left of 3, breaking out left with thin climbing, only adequately protected. Start beneath the crack. Lots of ivy in cracks – now quite overgrown.

1 **30m 5c** Pull up into a corner and make tricky moves up right to a small flake leading to a ledge. Climb the bulging crack through a large recess then move up a right-slanting flake until a point above a prominent mossy boss in the fault, 5m below the tree. Traverse left to belay standing on the boss.

2 **25m 6a** Pull out left on the obvious line, move up to a horizontal crack. Follow the flake up and right then traverse left with increasing difficulty to gain the slabby scoop of 5. Go up this for 3m then traverse out right, level with a small slot. Finish diagonally up right and belay 5m up and left.

5 **Blasad Den Iar** ★★ 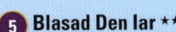 **48m E4 5c**
FA Kev Howett summer 1987

'*A taste of the west*'. A direct line through the centre of the large diagonal fault. Start in the constriction of the gully. Climb a white calcite streak and the crack above to gain the shallow right-slanting ramp and follow it to beneath a short hanging corner. Pull through the left side of the overlap on jugs then up the left side of the corner. The thin hanging crack above leads to the fault. Pull through directly on the left-facing flake and up to a horizontal crack. Thin climbing up the intermittent crack leads to good flat holds then head diagonally right up a slim, right-slanting scoop to just below its top. Climb the wall direct left of a large precarious block to belay on the right.

The huge diagonal fault throughout is taken by 6 *It Wasn't My Fault I Ran Over the Cat* E3 5b, 5b.

7 **Jarldom Reach** ★★★  **50m E6 6a**
FA Kev Howett & Andy Nelson August 1987

Another excellent sustained line, following the wall left of the diagonal fault. Poorly protected with the crux near the top.
Follow 5 to the ramp. Pull immediately left out of this into cracks leading to the base of the fault. Follow this right to a large wedged block. Pull left out of the fault on a flake and climb this to another flake. Make thin moves up and left through a white bulge to a second scoop, traverse right and ascend with increasing difficulty the slim leaning groove to make a hard move right to good holds. Finish left of the large precarious block to belay on the right.

8 **Shadow of the Wind** ★★ **55m E6 6a**
FA Iain Small & Blair Fyffe (on-sight) 27 April 2014

Climbs the black streak at the left end, starting from the base of the messy diagonal fault. Belay/abseil from tree a few metres back from the top.

📷 *Mike Reed on the soaring arête of Spirit Air. Photo Ed Brown.*

GAIRLOCH CREAG MHOR THOLLAIDH

SUPER CRAG SPORT
NG 8786 7686 **Alt**: 60m

1 Waterfall Crack *	25m F7b	
FA Paul Tattersall 2017		
2 Slender Means	25m F6c+	
FA Paul Tattersall 2016		
3 Turtle Pig *	20m F7a+	
FA Paul Tattersall & Tess Fryer 2016		
4 Calamoose **	25m F7b	
FA Paul Tattersall 2016		
5 Boogie Street **	28m F6b	
FA Paul Tattersall 2016		
6 Because I'm Black **	35m F6c	
FA Paul Tattersall October 2017		
7 Big Ballin'	30m F7b	
FA Dave MacLeod & Paul Tattersall 12 May 2018		
8 Bling ***	27m F7a	
FA Ian Taylor March 2017		
9 Sacred Cow **	15m F6c	
FA Paul Tattersall 2016		
10 Sweaty Cow **	20m F7b+	
FA Murdoch Jamieson & Ian Taylor 2016		

GAIRLOCH CREAG MHOR THOLLAIDH | 165

11 Booty Sweat ★★   15m F7c
FA Calum Cunningham 2016

12 Closed Project   20m

13 Wee Muc-Sheilch ★★   15m F7b+
FA Ian Taylor 2015

14 Muc-Sheilch ★★★   30m F7c+
FA Calum Cunningham & Ian Taylor May 2015

15 Talons Out ★★★   30m F8a
FA Calum Cunningham & Ian Taylor October 2015

16 The Big Feckin Project ★★★   50m F8a

17 Hafgufa ★★★   35m F8a+
FA Murdoch Jamieson & Ian Taylor 15 May 2016

18 Rainbow Warrior ★★★   35m F8b
FA Dave MacLeod 2 May 2018

19 Testify ★★★   50m F8b
FA Dave MacLeod 3 October 2017

20 Golgothic ★★★★   35m F7c
FA Ian Taylor 2016

21 The Circus ★★★   15m F7b+
FA Dave MacLeod & Ian Taylor 17 May 2017

22 Hyperlipid ★★★★   50m F8c
FA Dave MacLeod 12 May 2018

23 Spring Voyage ★★★   50m F8b/F8b+
FA Dave MacLeod 24 April 2018

24 Punky Dory ★★   35m F7c/F7c+
FA Murdoch Jamieson & Paul Tattersall October 2017

25 Bunny Ears ★★   30m F7c
FA Paul Tattersall 2017

26 Long Road Heavy Load ★★   30m F7a+
FA Paul Tattersall 2017

Golgothic/Circus ★★★★   50m F7c+
FA Murdoch Jamieson 10 April 2018

Hafgufa/Circus ★★★   50m F8a+
FA Dave MacLeod 17 May 2017

Golgothic/Testify ★★★   50m F8a
FA Murdoch Jamieson 29 April 2018

📷 Ian Taylor on his own mega-classic Golgothic. Photo Tess Fryer.

FISHERFIELD

Sunset from top of Carn Mor.

CREAG NA GAORACH

Three defined buttresses lying immediately south of the south-east end of Fionn Loch. The best route lies on the leftmost east buttress.

NG 974 747 **Alt:** 400m 4hr 2¾hr   1½hr

NANNY GOAT BUTTRESS
The cleanest buttress.
Approach: As for the **Carn Mor** approach to the path junction at the south end of Loch Fada (1km west of the causeway). Head up the right bank of the stream to the cleanest leftmost area of slabs, opposite a prominent large boulder, clearly visible on the approach.

1 Zebra Slabs ★ 135m Severe 4a

FA Mike O'Hara & Miss Marjorie Langmuir 9 April 1957

Start just left of a sapling behind some fallen blocks at the centre of the buttress.

1. **25m 4a** Follow the steep rib, soon easing, leading to a belay beneath a small lip on the left.
2. **25m 4a** Return back right and gain a narrow slabby ramp leading to a crack on the left. Climb this then return to the crest of the rib at the top. Climb the slab above to belay on a ledge left of a shallow chimney on the arête.
3. **35m 4a** Traverse left and follow a blunt rib to belay on large turf ledges.
4. **50m 4a** On the skyline directly above is a block overhang with further overhangs on the right. Climb up to gain a slab rib slanting up left of the block overhang. Finish up the fine rib which leads to a belay on the left edge of the overhang.

Karen Latter on Zebra Slabs.

BEINN LAIR
(MOUNTAIN OF THE MARE)

NG 983 737 **Alt:** 450m
3½–4hr   2¾hr   1½hr

The north-east aspect of Beinn Lair presents the largest outcropping of hornblende schist in the country. The strata dips back into the cliff forming good sharp incut holds. The routes tend to be broken and vegetated, not well protected, and greasy when wet. A good selection of cams will be found useful. Good views of many other fine cliffs.

Approach: As for the **Carn Mor** approach to the path junction at the south end of Loch Fada (1km west of the causeway). Head up the right bank of the stream, passing underneath the three buttresses of Creag na Gaorach on the right. Continue to the head of the col then south-east to the cliffs (15km). A slightly shorter approach is from Kinlochewe, via Gleann Bianasdail, then west along the south shore of Lochan Fada (10km).

WISDOM BUTTRESS

The slender buttress near the right end of the cliff, easily identified by the distinctive deep slot of *Bat's Gash* delineating its left edge.

1 Wisdom Buttress ★   220m Severe 4a
FA J.Smith, Miss Angela Hood & J.Stewart Orr 4 June 1951

Start at the bottom right edge of the buttress.
1. **45m** Climb diagonally left, skirting round the left edge of the broken overhang then trend back rightwards to belay on a grass ledge.
2. **30m** Move out right and climb a wide flake-crack to the left side of an overhang (possible belay on *"two diminutive footholds"*). Move out left and climb the slab to a belay.
3. **30m** Continue directly up slabs on the left, then move right along a ledge to the centre of the buttress.
4. **30m** Climb the nose above by steep sloping holds on the right wall, returning to the crest.
5. **35m** Continue up the crest to a large grass lodge.
6. **25m** Climb the steep initial wall left of the belay, soon easing to grassy slopes leading to a cairn. Scramble up grass (25m) to the summit plateau.

2 Bat's Gash ★   220m Very Difficult
FA B.Smith & Douglas Hutchison 6 June 1951

The deep pronounced gully delineating the left edge of Wisdom Buttress. *"It is a route of maintained interest with impressive cave scenery in the middle section. Near the foot a chimney with a narrow exit leads to a couch of blaeberries. Higher up there is a two-tier followed by a four-tier chimney."* – Jim Bell, New Ways on Beinn Lair, *Scottish Mountaineering Club Journal*, 1952. An overhang in the final chimney is avoided by a detour out left, then regained and followed to finish.

CARN MOR

(BIG CAIRN) NG 980 775 **Alt:** 400m

One of the few big Scottish mountain cliffs that faces south, receiving the sun for most of the day and remarkably quick drying. The rock is a generally solid pale rough Lewisian gneiss at its most accommodating, eroded into a wonderful array of pockets, buckets and curious letter-box slots.

Access: Leave the A832 at Poolewe and follow the road on the east side of the River Ewe to park in a car park on the left about 100m along the road. Cycles may be taken as far as the wood 1 mile beyond Kernsary – a considerable saving. During the stalking season (15th September – 15th November) permission from the Scatwell Estate factor or stalker at Kernsary (01445 781215) to climb in the area outwith weekends should be sought.

Approach: Follow the road for 4.5km to Kernsary Cottage. Continue along the track for about 400m then head right through a large gate into the forest to follow a muddy track by the Allt na Creige, taking the narrower right fork after about 1km. Continue for a further 5km to cross a stream at the base of Strathan Buidhe. Continue east along the path for a further 4km, crossing the causeway at the east end of Fionn Loch to eventually (at long last!) reach Carnmore Lodge, about 0.5km due south of the cliff (20km/13 miles).

Accommodation: The recently renovated barn at Carnmore with its 'climbers welcome' sign is the usual base. Take some midge coils and a large plastic bivi-bag (dirt floor). The estate owners have erected numerous signs throughout the *"wilderness"* attempting to discourage camping and walking outwith the main paths, though in practice these restrictions are not enforced outwith the stalking season. They have requested that between 15th September – 15th November visits are restricted to weekends.

Descent: (A) Follow a prominent grassy rake leading down west from the top of **Fionn Buttress** until underneath a pair of clean 10m walls. Cut down left and head diagonally right (west) to descend some rocky slabs on the left side of the gully. Continue down the right (west) side of the burn then cut back leftwards to gain the deer path contouring round underneath the base of the cliff.

(B) The east descent lies down the grassy slopes of the ravine. From the top of the crag avoid the big gully by moving up over a couple of crests before descending a series of vague paths overlooking the ravine. Near the bottom either cut back west towards the base of the crag or continue down into the lower reaches of the ravine.

FIONN BUTTRESS

The most continuous section of the cliff, bounding the left side of the **Central Bay**. Although slightly vegetated in its lower section there is a marked improvement in the quality higher up.

1 Fionn Buttress ★★★★ 227m VS 4c
FA Mike O'Hara & Bill Blackwood 7 April 1957

Vegetated lower pitches lead to immaculate exposed climbing above. Perhaps the finest route of its grade in the country. Start by scrambling up heather and easy slabby walls to a bay at the highest point of the heather, at the base of a steep clean roof-capped wall.

1. **30m 4c** Climb the right side of the slabby wall for a short way, moving right into the corner (often wet). Climb the right wall of the corner and move round the edge onto a ledge. Up the crack in the right wall then step right onto a slab. Cross the slab to a chokestone belay in the chimney above.
2. **20m 4a** Go up the right wall then trend right on grass to a spike belay at the base of a large left-facing flake in the grey slabs.
3. **20m 4c** Climb the wide flake then slightly right up the slab. Move left and climb past a flange and some pockets to pull direct into a scoop beneath a roof. Step down left to belay. Immaculate improbable-looking climbing.
4. **25m 4c** Traverse left then up left to a recess with large bollards. Climb the wet red corner above (well protected), moving out left at the top to belay in a grass recess.
5. **21m 4c** Continue either up the corner or the pocketed wall just left to the prominent overhang. Cross this spectacularly on good holds by an obvious weakness 3m from its right end. Move up right to belay on a grey shelf.
6. **18m 4b** Traverse the obvious line right across the face, stepping down round the edge to a couple of ledges which lead to an exposed belay on the right edge of the buttress.
7. **18m 4b** Go up the steep groove a short way then step left to gain the flake up on the left. Above the flake, move left a short way then up right to belay in a small recess.
8. **20m 4a** Continue up the slabs on the crest to belay in a niche.
9. **15m 4a** Continue up the crest to perched blocks on a heather ledge.
10. **20m 4b** Move out right over the blocks and up the slab above to a shelf. Climb easily right along this to its top corner.
11. **20m 4a** Move out left over a quartz ledge then up rightwards over ledges to finish.

THE LOWER WALL

A roughly dome-shaped area in the centre of the cliff immediately below the **Central Bay**.

2 Quagga ★★ 140m E1 5b
FA Andy Nisbet & Dougie Dinwoodie 22 May 1988

The prominent groove up the right side of the black streaked wall, angling right in its upper section. Start in a recess just left of the grassy fault running up to the base of the *Red Scar*.

1. **40m 5b** Climb the brown rib on the left then the very shallow groove leading up into the main groove. Continue up this, crossing a bulge into the easier right-slanting groove and up this to a belay.
2. **50m 4c** Follow the rib on the right to belay up and right of a tree (large nest).
3. **50m** – Easy slabs trending rightwards to a large thread belay on the right edge of the *Dragon* slab.

3 Black Mischief ★★ 130m VS 4c
FA Ted Maden & R.Sykes 19 June 1966

Good climbing on excellent rock. A useful approach to *Dragon*. Scramble up heather (past an isolated rowan) to the base of the prominent deep recessed black groove with a prominent square cut overhang at its top.

1. **25m 4c** Follow the recessed groove crossing a couple of bulges to belay on the left.
2. **25m 4b** Climb up to a good spike where the groove steepens at 6m. Move delicately right under a bulge onto a slab. Continue traversing diagonally right, heading towards a conspicuous ledge on the skyline. Climb the crack above to belay on grass ledge (level with and right of the square-cut overhang).
3. **20m 4c** Climb the cracked wall above then more easily to large ledges.
4. **60m -** Easier up to the Central Bay.

④ Balaton ★★★   115m E1 5b
FA Willie Gorman & Con Higgins May 1966

Excellent climbing after a slightly vegetated start. Start beneath a corner at the right side of the large recess near the right end of the Lower Wall left of a prominent black streak.

1. **20m 5a** Up the corner then traverse left under a roof to a stance at the base of corner.
2. **35m 5b** Climb the corner to a roof. Pull over this on superb pockets then trend rightwards across a slab to turn the large roof on the right. Belay just above. An excellent pitch.
3. **60m –** Move up and left of a rib on the skyline then by easy slabs up to the Central Bay.

⑤ Penny Lane ★★   70m HVS 5a
FA Dick Isherwood & Eddie Birch June 1967

Bounding the right edge of the lower wall is a pale overlapping wall immediately above a left-curving grassy rake. Start at the left end of the rake.

1. **30m 5a** Traverse right along a large flake then continue traversing above the lower roof to pull round the corner into the central groove.
2. **25m 4b** Move diagonally left beneath the top overlap then pull over it into a groove.
3. **15m –** Finish right up easy slabs to gain the grassy Gangway.

THE UPPER WALL

The steep and exposed upper band above the **Central Bay** is host to a fine range of routes of considerable character and exposure. The normal approach is via one of the routes on the **Lower Wall**. Alternatively, the left-slanting diagonal **Gangway** running immediately above the pale shield of rock containing *Penny Lane* can be used as a means of access or escape. Other alternative approaches are the broken and vegetated (Moderate) ground to the right of the top slab of *Diagonal Route* (easiest approach into the **Central Bay** from above), or by traversing in from any of the routes on **Fionn Buttress**. Care should be taken in the wet. Alternatively, abseil in from the top of the crag – 50m ropes gain the *Dragon* slab.

GAIRLOCH CARN MÒR | 171

6 Fian Grooves ★★   110m E3 5c
FA Tim Rankin & Guy Robertson 4 June 2000

Fine climbing based around the bulging left arête of the Upper Wall. Start at the base of the obvious *Green Corner*.

1. **45m 5c** A fantastic pitch. Go left into the prominent clean groove and ascend this to an overhang. Swing out left along a handrail and pull round the left end of the overhang into another groove. Move up the wall on the left then back right to a crack which is followed to an awkward mantelshelf. Continue straight up the crest to the base of the corner.
2. **20m 4b** Climb the corner with surprising ease to a terrace and junction with *Green Corner*.
3. **20m 5c** Above is a shallow leaning groove. Gain this from the left with difficulty and follow it with continual interest to step left and belay.
4. **25m 5a** Go directly across the ramp behind to enter and follow a constricted groove leading to easier ground and the top.

7 Death-Wolf ★★   75m E6 6b
FA Graeme Livingston & Dougie Dinwoodie 8 & 9 August 1986

Takes the great roof and wall round to the left of *Abomination*. Traverse left 10m from the foot of *Abomination* to a PB under an obvious overhanging flake gangway in the roof. Alternatively gain this belay by climbing directly up the slabs below.

1. **30m 6b** This pitch is very strenuous with no rests until a ledge 10m above the roof is gained. (The start of the flake is often wet on the inside; this doesn't however affect the difficulty as the flake is climbed on the outside.) Climb the flake gangway out over the lip of the roof and into a little scoop, (hidden sidepull inside crack here). Go straight up the wall to a hidden jug then move right and up onto a small ledge. Climb the arête and groove above to a belay ledge close to the right arête.
2. **30m 6a** From the right end of the ledge move up and across left then up to gain isolated knobbles. Traverse right by a thin horizontal crack to gain better holds and pull out right to easy ground. Move up left to belay at the left end of a heather ledge.
3. **15m 5c** Climb the wall above the belay (unprotected for some distance) veering left under an obvious scooped groove and up the wall to the top.

8 Abomination ★★   100m HVS 5b
FA John McLean, A.Currey & John Cunningham 22 July 1966

Good climbing up the steep crack-groove just left of *Dragon*. Start at the base of the *Dragon* slab.

1. **35m –** Climb the *Dragon* slab rightwards to belay a few metres left of *Dragon's* belay.
2. **35m 5b** Follow the right-hand groove for a few metres, step left and follow the hanging crack to a ledge at 20m. Continue up the crack with increasing difficulty to belay on a sloping ledge.
3. **30m 4c** Continue up the groove to a ledge then the chimney above to a square-cut roof. Move right and up a slab on rattling flakes to finish.

9 Dragon ★★★★   105m E1 5b
FA George Fraser & Mike O'Hara 22 April 1957

An excellent improbable-looking line, climbing some very impressive territory for the grade. A classic not to be missed. Start at the base of the pale grey slab at the left side of the Central Bay.

1. **35m 4b** Climb up to a heather patch in the centre of the slab then slightly rightwards up the slab to belay at the left end of grass ledge at the base of the corner.
2. **35m 4c** Climb the rightmost of three grooves, turning the triangular roof at 8m on the right. Continue up the groove then out left and up an easier groove to belay atop a pedestal on the right.
3. **25m 5b** Climb the wall above the belay into a deep yellow groove. Up this, traversing spectacularly out left on a huge jutting flake at its top to a small perch on the arête. Continue traversing left with interest under the roof to a fine stance in a short corner. An excellent pitch.
4. **10m 4c** Traverse round left and up to the top. Boulder belay.

Luke Arnott enjoying the final airy traverse beneath the capping roofs on the classic Dragon.

Corner-system just left of *Dragon* is 10 *Beastmaster* ∗E4 5b, 6a, 5b. Escape is possible back to *Dragon* in some places but the climbing is very good.

11 Lion Rampant ∗∗   90m E5 6b
FA Graeme Livingston & Dougie Dinwoodie 9 & 10 August 1986

The main pitch climbs the wall right of *Dragon*. A crack in the steep right-bounding wall of *Dragon* slab provides a good introductory pitch. The third pitch takes the obvious break in the roof just right of the *Gob* break.

1. **20m 6b** Climb the obvious crack (strenuous and sustained) and go up to the ledge under the wall.
2. **30m 6a** Climb the original start of *The Sword* past a spike to an expanding block. Pull straight over the bulge and move up right to gain small ledges at the foot of a great shallow scoop in the wall. Go up left then out right and up to an expanding flake. Move out left to another flake and pull up onto the left-slanting ledge above. Continue directly up the unprotected wall above, just beside the arête overlooking the groove of *The Sword*, past a poor peg runner to gain a ledge. Go left along this to belay at the right side of great detached blocks.
3. **25m 6a** Climb the wall right of the belay to gain the *Gob* traverse under the roof. Climb the bulge up into a small corner then pull out right on layaways to reach slabs and belay above.
4. **15m 5c** Climb straight to the roof above. Traverse left and pull over the roof using a jug to swing up and right to gain blocks. Veer left and up the steep wall to an overhanging finish on big flakes.

12 The Sword ∗∗∗   90m E3 5c
FA Dick Isherwood & Eddie Birch (3 PA) June 1967;
FFA Ian Duckworth & Rob Kerr May 1980.

A good direct line up the bottomless groove above the 'cave' in the centre of the wall. Start round on the right side of the *Dragon* slab, beneath a chossy groove (just right of the obvious thin crack of *Lion Rampant*.

1. **10m 4c** Climb the easy chossy groove to a ledge at the top right edge of the *Dragon* slab.
2. **35m 5c** Traverse about 3m right on the lip of the overhang then up and rightwards to enter the main groove. Follow the groove to a small stance at the 'swallow's nest' of *Gob*.
3. **20m 5c** Climb up and right through the steep break in the roof then up the rib to a stance.
4. **25m 4c** Finish up the shallow left-facing corner above.

13 St George ★★★　　　　　　　　80m E1 5b
FA Jeff Cram & Roelof Schipper 28 May 1967

Excellent climbing up the prominent steep crack system in the centre of the wall beneath the roof of *Gob*, finishing up that route. Start directly beneath the crack.

1. **20m 5b** Climb steep heather for 10m to gain the base of the crack. Up the crack and through the roof on good holds then the wide crack up the left side of the huge *"doubtful"* flake to a finely positioned belay at its top.
2. **35m 5a** Up the crack above for 5m to an obvious hand traverse line leading left to a prominent groove. Follow this for 8m then traverse out left round the arête to join *The Sword*, which is followed directly to the 'swallows nest' under the Gob roof. Move left to a good 'pulpit' belay.
3. **25m 4c** Finish up the shallow left-facing corner above.

14 Wild Side ★★★★　　　　　　　　90m E6 6c
FA Iain Small & Guy Robertson 3 June 2018

An outstanding voyage along the big diagonal crack crossing *Carnmore Corner*; brilliant, super-sustained and perfectly protected climbing. Start at the obvious crack between *St George* and *Gob*.

1. **30m 5b** Climb the crack past a block and over a small overhang to a junction with *Gob*, then follow this to where a ledge sneaks right towards the corner. Belay just round the edge at the start of the crack, as for *Wilderness*.
2. **25m 6c** Climb the crack with sustained interest all the way to a good hold in the wall above and knee bar rest a few metres short of the corner. Power on along the crack (crux) to gain the corner and hanging belay.
3. **35m 6b** Continue rightwards out into space on generally good handholds but poor feet to an in situ thread, then plough on through much thinner but less steep terrain to join and finish up *The Orange Bow*.

15 Gob ★★★★　　　　　　　　　　105m HVS 4c
FA Robin Smith & Dougal Haston April 1960

Start at the upper right end of the main face.

1. **30m 4c** Traverse left easily along a ledge past some doubtful blocks to a break in the overhang. Ascend rightwards past a PR and up shallow corner to a belay under the roof.
2. **40m 4c** Traverse left under the roof on good holds past the 'swallows nest' to a good 'pulpit' belay just beyond a large flake.
3. **35m 4c** Climb up to the roof then undercut right to gain the right end of the roof. Finish directly up the line of shallow grooves above.
3a. **40m 4c** The original finish. From the end of the roof traverse easily right for 20m to a shallow left-facing corner. Finish up this.

16 Wilderness ★★★★　　　　　　　80m E4 6a
FA Dougie Mullin & Martin Lawrence (on-sight) May 1980

A stunning route on perfect rock tackling the left side of the smooth left wall of the corner. An impressive on-sight ascent, probably the hardest in the country at the time. Belay on the slab beneath the base of *Carnmore Corner*, a few metres down and right of the prominent diagonal fault.

1. **20m 5b** Follow the diagonal fault leading up to the base of the prominent diagonal crack running across the wall.
2. **30m 6a** Go up the crack for a few metres, hand traverse left on good holds to a crack and up this and the shallow groove above to a small spike at its top. Move out left with a hard move to reach a good flake. Continue out leftwards up the scoop then swing up leftwards to gain better holds on the arête. Pull over and continue more easily up

twin cracks to belay at the base of a short corner.
3 **30m 5c** Climb the corner above, passing a loose-looking block then up a short arête and thin crack to finish.

17 Jivaro Crack ★★ 60m E4 6b
FA Dougie Dinwoodie & Doug Hawthorn 28 April 1987

The thin vertical crack in the left wall of the corner.
1 **20m 5b** Follow the diagonal fault leading up to the base of the prominent diagonal crack running across the wall.
2 **20m 6b** Go up the diagonal crack for a few metres then climb straight up the thin crack to a rest at a bucket. Climb the right fork where the crack splits then up into the prominent slabby groove. Up this to move out right to belay beside a detached block.
3 **20m 5c** Step left from the block and go up a small hanging corner to pull over the bulge to good holds. Continue more easily to the top, as for *Wilderness*.

18a Carnmore Corner Direct ★★★ 50m E3 5c
FA Gary Latter & Luke Arnott 22 July 1997

A brilliant varied pitch, though one of the last routes to dry on the cliff. Belay at some horizontal pockets high on the slab about 8m above the start of *Wilderness*. Climb the corner and hand traverse right on a large block at its top to gain the normal route. Continue up this then direct up an awkward hand-crack (wet) to finish up the easier final corner.

18 Carnmore Corner ★★ 55m E2 5b
FA Rab Carrington & John Jackson (1 PA) 19 June 1968; FFA Rowland Perriment & A.Hodges 1975

A fine line, though a spring at the top ensures it is the last route on the crag to dry. Undercutting the right wall is a curving fault with two recesses. Start below and left of the lower recess.
1 **35m 5b** Climb up and left on the initial slab then up into a niche just up left from the second recess. Continue direct for a short way, then follow a small ramp and continue in the same line leading up left into the corner. Belay beneath the large overhang.
2 **20m 5a** Move left, up then delicately back right to finish more easily up the final corner-crack.

19 The Red Crack ★ 60m E3 6a
FA Dougie Dinwoodie & Andy Nisbet 21 May 1988

The crack-line running up the right wall, parallel to and just right of the corner. Good climbing, more often dry.
1 **20m 5a** As for *Carnmore Corner* to a belay in the niche.
2 **40m 6a** Continue up the crack to a rest at a niche beneath a large bulge. Cross the bulge (crux) to finish up the easier fault.

20 One Hundred Years of Solitude ★★★★ 55m E8 6c
FA Iain Small & Murdoch Jamieson (both led) 7 June 2014

A stunning sustained, technical and run-out route tackling the centre of the impressive orange wall. Belay as for 21a. Move up a slab to the same recess and pull out right onto a pedestal as for that route. From a short rib above follow the arching crack line out left to a small ledge and then gain a larger overhung ledge. From the handrail above move hard right to a hollow flake and climb boldly up and right to a slight crack and better holds. Pull out left to quartzy holds and a good cam in a crozzly crack on the left. Head directly up to the large triangular niche and awkwardly enter it from the right. From this haven arrange plenty of gear in the diagonal crack and further gear out right in a short crack (strenuous to place). Pull directly out of the niche and make big moves up an incipient crack to a rough finger flake then follow crimps out right to a slight horizontal break. Further long moves up a faint crack line and a lunge gain the big horizontal break with a good thread, cams and a shakeout. A further hard move gains the diagonal crack and improving holds to a respite in the angle. Go up to a big diagonal crack with a spike in it and finish directly.

21 The Orange Bow ★★★★ 35m E5 6a
FA Dougie Dinwoodie & Doug Hawthorn 16 June 1985

One of the finest situated pitches anywhere, up the left side of the arête right of *Carnmore Corner*. Start at ledges up on the right, 10m from the top of the last slab of *Diagonal Route*. Traverse out left on a slabby shelf and negotiate a tricky bulge to move up left to big footholds under the bulging arête. Swing out left on flakes and climb a vague intermittent crack-line up the overhanging wall for 10m to a point where the crack gives good protection before petering out. Traverse right and up slightly for 5m to gain the edge and a rest. Climb up the edge to finish up a left-slanting crack on the left side.

 **Left Start** ★★   **25m E5 6b**
FA Dougie Dinwoodie & Andy Nisbet 22 May 1988

Start below and left of the first recess of the curving fault undercutting the right wall of the corner. Move up to the recess and swing up right onto a platform. Go up onto a bulging wall, swing left and up to a resting place (PR on the right). Pull up to a good pocket, move up left to a flake then make a hard move across right to jugs (poor PR). Climb straight up the wall to gain a horizontal fault and a resting place. Traverse right and slightly down to a flake-crack and hanging belay under the *"vague crack"* of the edge pitch.

The prominent crack on the right side of the arête is 22 *Curare* ★ E4 6a.

THE GREY WALL

The wall right of the **Central Bay**, immediately above the **Gangway**. Gain the base by a traverse in from the right, or by scrambling up to the left end from the **Gangway**.

23 Break In ★   **65m HVS 5a**
FA Andy Tibbs & Alan Winton 1 August 1984

Start at the prominent chimney at the right end of the wall.
1 **30m 4c** Climb the chimney for 7m then break out left onto the wall by a short hand traverse. Climb the wall above then trend left to a good stance beneath a leftwards-slanting groove.
2 **35m 5a** Climb the groove breaking out left to finish up the crack above.

24 Trampoline ★   **100m HVS 5a**
FA Bob Jones & Gordon McNair June 1967

Start 12m left of the prominent chimney of *Break In*, beneath a niche.
1 **25m 5a** Climb up to the niche, up this and traverse right steeply to twin vertical cracks where the angle eases. Follow these to belay on a good ledge in a corner.
2 **35m 5a** Follow a crack leftwards up the slab to beneath steep twin cracks. Move right onto the wall right of a short steep corner. Follow the steep crack, finishing by easier slabs leading to block belays.
3 **40m -** Easier up slabs above.

24a The Proprietor ★   **35m E2 5c**
FA Gary Latter & Luke Arnott 22 July 1997

A well protected direct finish to *Trampoline*. Follow that route to beneath the steep twin cracks in the headwall. Climb the left crack, moving into the deeper right crack with difficulty. Up this past a dubious looking block near its top then more easily up slabs above to large block belay at top.

25 Crackers ★★   **70m E3 5c**
FA Doug Hawthorn & Colin MacLean 15 June 1985

The prominent twin parallel cracks up the centre of the wall.
1 **25m 5c** Climb a steep crack.
2 **45m 5a** Continue up cracks, finishing by easier slabs.

26 Firecracker ★   **70m E4 6a**
FA Tim Rankin & Guy Robertson 5 June 2000

Fine strenuous climbing up the obvious crack right of and parallel to *Crackers*. Start at a huge block.
1 **20m 6a** Climb a steep jam crack on the front of the block to the base of the crack proper then forge up this to an evil stretch (crux) to gain the belay.
2 **50m 5c** Continue directly up the groove over a bulge leading to easier ground below a scoop. Pull up left into the scoop then continue steeply, trending rightwards to the top.

CARNAN BAN
(WHITE ROCKY HILL)

This is the prominent rocky ridge on the east side of the Allt Bruthach an Easain, the main watercourse flowing into the north side of the Dubh Loch.

W 4¾hr   3¾hr   2¾hr

BARNDANCE SLABS
NG 998 765 **Alt:** 500m

An extensive outcropping of pale slabby gneiss. Towards the lower left is a prominent clean triangular grey slab coming to a point in an overhanging nose at the bottom right, midway between a pair of diagonal turfy rakes.

Approach: From Carnmore head east steeply up the path towards Shenavall until about 150m beyond a zig-zag in the path. Cross the burn down on the right, opposite a 20m crag and skirt round the right edge and head across boggy ground to the base. 50 mins from Carnmore barn.

Descent: Traverse right and down the side of the boulder cone separating the crag from **Maiden Buttress**, picking up a path leading back to the base.

1 Barndance *   117m Difficult
FA Mike O'Hara & Miss Marjorie Langmuir 28 March 1956

Pleasant climbing. Start at a narrow slab with corner on its right.
1 **12m** Climb either the slab or the corner to belay on the right under an overhang.
2 **15m** Move right to the edge of a large chimney, up 2m, then back left on a ledge beneath an overhang. At its left end, move out and up to grooves running up left.
3+4 **90m** Follow the grooves past a bulge, crossing a right-slanting rake. Continue in the same line *"until interest ceases"*.

2 Strider *   110m Severe 4a
FA D.McLennan & Cam Forrest 17 July 1967

On the mass of slabs left of *Barndance*. Above a great pointed pinnacle in a gully is a leaning rectangular block. Start just left of the block.
1 **25m** Up slabs to a recess, then out right and up to a sloping rock shelf.
2 **27m** Up a gangway on the left, out under an overlap. From the left end go up past a pinnacle to a grass ledge. Belay 5m further left.
3 **40m** Step right and climb a short crack over bulges, then up a reddish slab corner. Move out left when this becomes wet and go up to a shelf and loose flake. Climb direct behind this, then over a bulge by a right-slanting crack leading to a shelf and belay.
4 **18m** Scrambling to the top.

Gary Latter on the initial pitch of Ecstasy. Photo Karen Latter.

MAIDEN BUTTRESS

<5hr <4hr <3hr

NH 001 762 Alt: 510m

Hidden from view in the mini-corrie containing Fuar Loch Beag but visible from the causeway, this compact buttress contains a number of fine routes on immaculate rock. Well worth seeking out and very quick drying. The remotest cliff within this guide.

Approach: Head rightwards from the base of **Barndance Slabs** and up the left bank of the outflow from Fuar Loch Beag then across a boulder field to the base. 1 hour from Carnmore barn. Alternatively, a short traverse right from the top of **Barndance Slabs** leads to the top of the large boulder cone.

Descent: Down the grassy slope at the left side, next to a large boulder cone.

1 Ecstasy ★★★   100m Severe 4b
FA Mike O'Hara & Bob Kendell 20 August 1955

Immaculate climbing with an excellent initial pitch. The most prominent feature of the crag is a striking diagonal finger-crack where the face starts to turn. Start beneath this.
1. **25m 4b** Climb the crack which leads into a steep right-facing corner. Go up this to a ledge then another cracked groove slightly right to a large ledge.
2. **25m** Bypass the steep wall above on the right, continuing direct to a ledge beneath a short cracked wall.
3. **20m** Follow either the crack on the right or twin cracks on the edge (easier) to large ledge.
4. **30m 4a** Move left and climb the fine pocketed wall above, bypassing a blank section. Easier ground leads to the top.

2 Sleeping Beauty ★★   110m VS 4c
FA Andy Nisbet (solo) 8 August 2001

Good climbing up the open corner and continuation crack right of the prominent inverted V.
1. **25m 4b** Climb the corner to a ledge beneath a vertical section with a small overhang.
2. **20m 4c** Continue up the vertical section leading to the top of the V, then the crack-line to a large ledge.
3. **20m 4b** Continue up the initially overhanging crack above.
4. **45m 4a** Finish up the crack past two steep sections.

3 Dishonour ★★   120m Very Difficult
FA Mike O'Hara & Miss Marjorie Langmuir 10 April 1955

A worthy companion to *Ecstasy*, following a line up the left edge of the front face. Start at the base of the slab at the extreme left edge of the front face.
1. **20m** Climb the left edge of the slab to belay on the right below a wall.
2. **20m** Move left round the edge and up past a large loose flake, stepping back right. A harder alternative

climbs the wall direct above the belay. Climb directly up the slab to ledge and large block.

3 **25m** Move right and up an easy chimney, then up leftwards to near the end of the ledge, belaying on the right.

4 **25m** Move right then step left above an overhang, then up a tapering groove to a ledge. The groove on the right leads to a wide terrace.

5 **30m** Climb the wall just right of twin cracks then a second wall by a crack, soon easing.

4 Tweedledum *   115m Severe 4a
FA Bob Kendell & Mike O'Hara 19 August 1955

Start 5m right of *Dishonour*.

1 **20m** Climb the slab midway between two vegetated cracks to belay on the left beneath a steeper wall.

2 **10m** Move right and climb the overhang on the right then up to belay in niche on left.

3 **20m** Climb the rib on the right then the chimney on its right.

4 **20m** Continue up the chimney.

5 **20m** Traverse left on ledges above overhangs, then climb a broad scoop and short V-groove to a terrace.

6 **25m** Climb easily left of the central turfy gully, finishing on good holds up a steep *"boulder problem"* wall.

5 Cakewalk *   80m Difficult
FA Bob Kendell & Mike O'Hara 20 August 1955

Start right of the big overhang at the base of the third narrow slab (red) and immediately below a small overlap.

1 **30m** Climb cracks just right of the overlap, then the outside edge of the slab to belay below steeper rock.

2 **20m** Follow a gangway on the right past loose blocks then up a thin crack to belay on a shelf.

3 **30m** Finish up the prominent crack in the wall on the left (definite crux) to a platform, then easy slabs.

Paul Tattersall on Armburger, Beach Crag, Gruinard (page 181). Photo Jim Buchanan, Wild West Topos.

GRUINARD CRAGS

The numerous crags within the areas bounded by Gruinard Bay (Old Norse *'shallow fjord bay'*) offer some excellent and easily accessible climbing. Though most of the outcrops are short there are longer routes on more impressive crags as well. The rock is perfect Lewisian gneiss. Since the crags are isolated summits there is little drainage and they dry very quickly after rain. The crags are described individually in order of increasing distance from the car park on the south side of the A832 at Gruinard Bay (NG 953 899).

GAIRLOCH GRUINARD CRAGS

Photo Jim Buchanan, Wild West Topos.

Carn na h-Aire · Goat Crag · Am Fasgadh · Post Crag · Bog Meadow Wall · Gruinard Crag · The Apron · Lochan Dubh Crag · Dog Crag · Riverside Slabs · Beach Crag · Birch Crag · Road Crag · Car Park Slabs · Inverianvie Crag

Access: Gruinard Bay and its fine golden sandy beach lies on the northern coast of the Letterewe and Fisherfield deer forests. It can be approached on the A832 from either Garve through Kinlochewe and Gairloch, or by turning off west down the A832 just before the Corrieshalloch Gorge on the main A835 Tore (near Inverness) – Ullapool road 14 miles/22km south of Ullapool (25.5 miles/41km from A835 junction).

Amenities: There is a Spar shop/PO/ Petrol station at Laide, 3.7 miles/6km west of Gruinard Bay. The Aultbea Hotel (01445 731201; www.aultbeahotel.co.uk) 5 miles/8km west of Gruinard Bay, overlooking Loch Ewe, is worth a visit, serving bar food until 9pm.

Accommodation: Discreet camping at numerous fine locations in and around Gruinard Bay, though a sign at the car park says 'No Overnight Parking' – maybe try parking on the verge opposite?

NG 953 904 **Alt:** 5m 10min

BIRCH CRAG

A steep wall behind birches 200m south of the more obvious **Beach Crag**.

1 Hatrick for Patrick ★★   25m HVS 5a
FA Paul & Angela Tattersall 17 March 2002

The groove, finishing up a short hanging groove over a bulge at the top.

Gary Latter on Hatrick for Patrick. Photo Karen Latter.

Photo Jim Buchanan, Wild West Topos.

Photo Jim Buchanan, Wild West Topos.

NG 953 907 **Alt:** 5m 10min

BEACH CRAG

The wall at the far end of the beach to the north of the car park.
Approach: Walk north along the beach. At high tide walk north up the road then through a gate and follow a vague path down to the beach.

1 Sheepless in Seattle ★   10m E2 5b
FA Andy Cunningham & B.Gordon 12 April 2001

Start at the base of a wide crack on the right. Move diagonally left (high runner) to gain the crack.

> The direct start up to the bottomless crack is
> 2 *Saga of Sewage* ★ E5 6a.

3 Capillary Wall ★   20m HVS 5a
FA Andy Cunningham & Lawrence Hughes 19 April 1998

Direct line starting up the pillar at the right end of the crag, passing a niche.

4 Adalat ★   20m VS 4c
FA Andy Cunningham & Dave Neville 30 April 1999

The right-trending crack.

5 Aorta ★   20m E2 5c
FA Andy Cunningham & Dave Neville 30 April 1999

Up an awkward groove to pull through a bulge at a crack. Move slightly left to finish direct.

6 Child's Play ★   20m E2 5b
FA Andy & Jeni Cunningham, Allen Fyffe & Lawrence Hughes 24 April 2005

Leftwards to a tiny sapling in a break below a ledge. Move right and up to the ledge then centre of the smooth headwall.

7 Armburger ★★   20m E2 5b
FA Fraser Fotheringham & Ian Brodie 19 April 1998

Good steep climbing up the disjointed crack in the front face of the tower at the left, pulling through the capping block to finish.

8 Cowrie ★   20m E1 5b
FA Paul Tattersall & Terry Doe 28 March 2005

Climb leftwards up a steep ramp past some jutting blocks then the wall to a ledge. Step left and climb close to the edge to finish.

9 Beach Groove Garden ★   20m VS 4b
FA Andy Cunningham & Lawrence Hughes 19 April 1998

The V-groove, finishing via the left fork.

POST CRAG

A striking small steep wall with a slabbier wall to its right 500m north of the main car park. It has a world-beating outlook over the bay.

Access: There is a convenient small parking place off the road by a gate on the west (seaward) side, about 0.5 mile/0.8km north of the main car park.

Approach: south along road for couple of hundred metres then up the hill, above an electricity pylon.

Photo Jim Buchanan, Wild West Topos.

NG 956 903 **Alt:** 70m 5min

 **Post-it ★**   12m VS 4c

FA Gary & Karen Latter 5 April 2002

The prominent blunt left arête of the smooth wall. Well protected.

 **Scoobie Dubh ★★★**   12m E4 6a

FA Lawrence Hughes & Blyth Wright 31 August 2000

The immaculate steep wall of golden gneiss. Climb boldly up the lower wall to gain the cracks and follow these with a difficult finish. Very well protected at the hard section.

3 Hate-Mail ★   10m E2 6a

FA John Mackenzie & Blyth Wright 25 June 2000

The middle of the darker slabby wall with a difficult mantelshelf into a small letter-box to start. Tenuous climbing leads to a triangular hold on the right then up to better protection and easier climbing.

BOG MEADOW WALL

The obvious steep crag at the northern end of the line of crags overlooking a flat boggy meadow behind **Post Crag**. When the sun comes around onto the crag at around 4pm it is transformed into a wonderful orange colour.

Approach: From the parking spot for **Post Crag** go through the gate on the opposite side of the road and continue up the shallow valley to break out right at the top to higher ground then continue for about 200m. The same line of crags can be reached from the car park by contouring the hillside as for the **Gruinard Crag** approach and before that crag is reached breaking out left to reach the boggy meadow.

Photo Jim Buchanan, Wild West Topos.

NG 958 904 **Alt:** 110m 10min

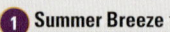 **Summer Breeze ★★**   20m E5 6b

FA Rab Anderson 30 July 2000

Fine climbing up the central bottomless crack which starts just to the right of an obvious slanting overlap. Climb to ledges below the crack and move up to a horizontal break. Climb up to a 'plaque' on the right then move out left from a good horizontal Camalot #0.1 placement and up into the crack. Continue much more easily up the crack to finish.

2 Last Tango *   20m E2 5c
FA Rab Anderson 30 July 2000

The obvious C-shaped crack up the right side of the central part of the wall. Climb to a holly tree, step up left onto a block and make a couple of scruffy moves to the base of the crack. Climb the fine crack to its top, pull out right then step up left onto a ledge and follow slabs up left to a belay.

3 Shivala **   12m E4 6a
FA Andy Cunningham 22 May 2001

The thin crack-line.

ROAD CRAG

The reddish brown wall just above the road, down to the left of **Gruinard Crag**.

Approach: From the car park walk north along the road for few hundred metres then up to the crag.

1 Roadkill *   15m HS 4b
FA Allen Fyffe & Andy Cunningham 10 April 2003

Climb up to the left side of a small roof, pull over then up to the heathery ledge. Finish up cracks on the right.

2 Pockets of Resistance *   15m E1 5b
FA Allen Fyffe & Andy Cunningham 23 March 2003

Follow the diagonal break to the right end of a small roof. Up the short crack and bulge to the horizontal break then right to finish up a crack.

3 Tom Jones **   15m HVS 5a
FA Andy Cunningham & Lawrence Hughes September 2000

The left-curving flake then the wall above to the wide crack.

4 Radical Jewish **   15m E2 5c
FA Paul Tattersall & Terry Doe 6 October 2001

Directly up the brown streak.

5 Raglan Road **   18m E2 5b
FA Andy Cunningham & Paul Holmes 25 March 1999

Up and left into the central scoop. Exit rightwards to the diagonal break. Finish up the crack in the headwall.

6 Mongo *   18m E3 5c
FA Lawrence Hughes & Andy Cunningham September 2000

Follow the diagonal break under a bulge and pull through the capped groove. Swing right and up, then trend leftwards.

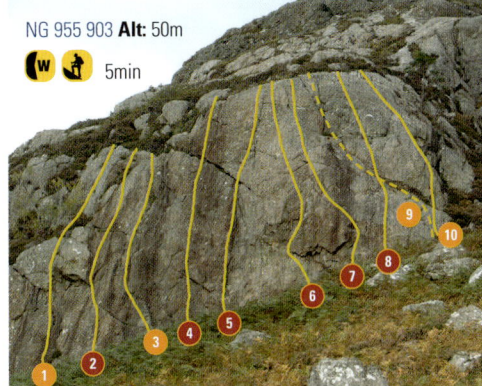

NG 955 903 **Alt:** 50m   5min

Photo Jim Buchanan, Wild West Topos.

7 Trojan **   15m E2 6a
FA Rab & Chris Anderson 4 June 2000

Gain the ledge with difficulty. Climb up to the left end of the roof then the diagonal crack. A fine variation on excellent rough rock moves leftwards from the ledge.

8 Spawn *   15m E2 5b
FA Rab & Chris Anderson 4 June 2000

Boldly up the thin crack just right of the rosebush to the roof. Traverse left beneath the roof then directly above its left end to finish up cracks.

9 Celtic Ray *   15m VS 5a
FA Paul Holmes & Andy Cunningham 25 March 1999

Delicately left under the roof to the deep left-trending crack.

10 Ataka *   15m HS 4b
FA Rab & Chris Anderson 4 June 2000

Gain and climb the short crack in the right arête, continuing up slabby ground to finish.

NG 957 900 **Alt:** 150m 15min

GRUINARD CRAG

A two-tiered crag, better than it appears from the road.
Approach: Walk north along the road for 300 metres then head directly up the hillside to the crags, which are towards the right side of the rocky hillside.

LOWER CRAG

1 Halcyon Days ★★   15m VS 4c
FA Bob Brown & John Mackenzie 14 May 1994

The recessed break on the left has a prominent flake on its right edge. Layback the flake to a large jug. Step right to the blank looking wall which is covered in holds and go left to finish boldly up the steep slab.

2 Who Shot JR? ★   15m HVS 5a
FA Dave Allan & R.Plenderleith 16 May 1999

Start at the same point as 1. Follow a thin crack steeply up right across the pale streak of 3 into a corner. Up the corner and crack above.

3 Ueejit ★   15m E4 6a
FA Neil Morrison & Jon Reed August 1997

Climb just left of the pale streak up the centre of the shield of rock left of 4.

4 Utopia ★   15m HVS 5b
FA John Mackenzie & Bob Brown 14 May 1994

Well protected. The thin vertical crack near the right edge. Climb the wall right of the lower crack and step left below the upper crack. Climb the crack to the top.

5 Simple Perfections ★★   20m Difficult
FA John Mackenzie & Bob Brown 14 May 1994

The right border of the wall is a jug-infested slab. The best line follows the left edge, on perfect rock.

MAIN CRAG

One of the better crags in the area with a good selection of routes.
Descents: Head a long way right and down steep heathery ground. It is also possible to descend down the gully and rib bounding the left side of the crag.

1 Bay-watch ★   45m HVS 5a
FA Andy Nisbet, John Mackenzie & Bob Brown 28 May 1994

Bold airy climbing up the left side of the crag. Start as 2.
1 25m 4c Climb the rib and groove to belay on the large block.
2 20m 5a Climb the blank-looking wall above the smaller top-most block then follow rough rock to the nose which is taken on the right.

2 Paradise Regained ★★   50m E1 5b
FA John Mackenzie & Bob Brown May 1994

Bold varied climbing up the open chimney on the left side of the crag with a holly tree at its base.
1 30m 5b Climb the rib left of the holly and step right into the groove. Up the groove and short chimney onto a ledge on the right. Shuffle along this to its right end (F #0, small nuts above) and climb the bold crozzly wall to an easing. Move slightly left to the blunt rib and up to a hidden right-trending handrail. Follow this, stepping over a bulge above, step left and finish up the rib to a large jammed block.
2 20m 5a Up the blank-looking red wall slightly left of the block, trending back right higher up.

3. Quick on the Draw ★★   35m E5 6a

FA Rab Anderson 25 May 1997

The shallow corner/groove-line immediately right of 2. Start right of the holly, at a left-facing corner. Climb the corner and its shallow continuation to where it blanks out. Move up and right and continue to a heathery ledge. Either belay here (F #2.5) or continue up the crozzly slab on the left.

4. Pistolero ★★   25m E2 5c

FA Rab & Chris Anderson 25 May 1997

The crack-line immediately right of 3. Start up the short corner, swing out right and climb to the left end of the roof. Pull into a recess and continue up the cracks above to belay on a heather ledge (F #2.5). Traverse right to descend.

5. The Big C ★★   30m HVS 5a

FA Bob Brown & John Mackenzie 3 May 1994

The central line taken by the big C-shaped niche (use your imagination!) Start directly below the niche and climb a shallow corner to step left into the niche. Swing right onto the airy wall and follow the right-trending line below the holly. Climb up to the tree and step right. Climb up to a crack above and finish by a sporting mantel to its right.

6. Gunslinger ★★   25m E2 5b

FA Graeme Ettle, Jonathon Preston, Dave McGimpsey & Paul Thorburn 30 April 2000

Climb up to and over the protruding tongue of rock below the right end of the roof. Finish up the wall above to the final moves of 5.

7. Red John of the Battles ★★   25m E2 5b

FA John Mackenzie, Bob Brown & Andy Nisbet 28 May 1994

The straight crack running up an overhanging wall. Climb this on excellent holds to gain a ledge and holly. Continue straight up to finish by the 'sporting mantel' of 5.

8. Coup du Monde ★   25m E3 5c

FA Graeme Ettle & Blyth Wright 16 June 1998

Climb the groove and steep wall then move slightly right up steep flakes to a difficult finish in a small groove.

Photo Jim Buchanan, Wild West Topos.

9 Overlord ★★   25m E1 5b
FA Bob Brown & John Mackenzie 28 May 1994

Very well protected with a short steep crux. Start on the right side of the crag below two tiny corners capped by a roof. Climb these and up the crack-line past blocks to a ledge on the right. Make hard moves leftwards up the daunting wall to a good hidden flake-crack which leads to good holds in the base of a short ramp. Finish direct.

10 How the West Was Won ★★   25m E4 6a
FA Rab & Chris Anderson 27 July 1997; Direct Paul Thorburn & John Lowther 16 June 1998

The thin crack-line. Gain the start of the crack from the groove on the right, pull out left onto a ledge then step right and climb the crack until it stops. Move left, gain a ledge then step right to climb the wall and short slab. The 10a *Direct* ★★ E6 6b climbs directly up the wall above the flake-blocks on spaced holds and protection.

11 Stand and Deliver ★★   25m E4 6a
FA Rab & Chris Anderson 24 May 1997

The thin crack-line. Climb the crack-line to a good ledge. Gain the crack above, either direct or from the right and follow it to better holds to pull awkwardly onto the final slab.

12 Quail   25m Difficult
FA Blyth Wright & Graeme Ettle 16 June 1998

The obvious short fissure leading to a heather ledge, followed by a fine groove round the corner.

CAR PARK SLABS
5min

A number of small buttresses about 5 minutes from the car park.

NG 954 898 **Alt:** 70m   5min

FLAKE BUTTRESS
Short steep buttress down and right of **Very Difficult Slabs**.

1 Black Wall Special ★   12m HS 4b
FA John Mackenzie (solo) 5 August 1999

Ascend the slanting crack on the left and step up to the ramp. Step left and go up the bold wall on sidepulls to a shaky jug.

> 2 *Pothole Slab* and 3 *Flake Chimney* (both V.Diff.) take lines left of the flake; 4 *Bisection Crack* VS 5a the steep thin crack in the centre of the flake

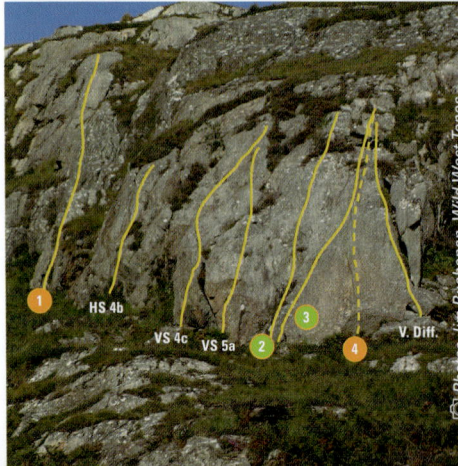

Photos Jim Buchanan, Wild West Tapes

NG 954 898 **Alt:** 50m
VERY DIFFICULT SLABS 5min
The pink slab well seen on the hillside from the car park. The routes are easier than they look.

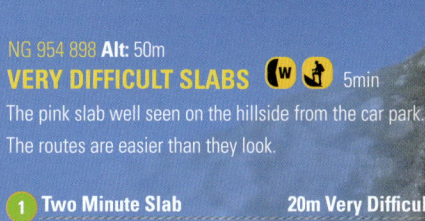

1 Two Minute Slab   20m Very Difficult
FA John Mackenzie (solo) 8 May 1994

Climb the rib left of the vegetated break to blocks and continue straight up.

2 Small but Perfectly Formed *   25m Very Difficult
FA John Mackenzie (solo) 1 May 1994

To the right of the break is a steep, clean rib, giving the best route of the slab. Step off a boulder and climb the rib direct avoiding a heather patch. Step left and climb a steepening to the top.

3 Five Minute Crack   25m Severe 4a
FA Graham Cullen & John Mackenzie 8 May 1994

The thin crack-line just right of the rib.

4 Flaky Wall   15m Very Difficult
FA Graham Cullen & John Mackenzie 8 May 1994

The line of flakes right of the crack.

5 Gneiss Groove *   12m Very Difficult
FA John Mackenzie & Graham Cullen 8 May 1994

The fine groove which cuts up the slab near the right end.

© Photo Jim Buchanan, Wild West Topos.

THE SIDE WALL
The steep west-facing crag below **Triangular Slab** on the right.

1 Atlantic Pillar *   10m HS 4b
FA John Mackenzie (solo) 5 August 1999

The well defined undercut slabby rib, climbed direct on excellent rock.

2 Staircase **   10m Very Difficult
FA John Mackenzie (solo) 5 August 1999

Good climbing up the staircase, first right then left up the black diamond-shaped wall further right.

> 3 *One Scoop or Two* VS 4c ascends the left side of the steep red wall to finish up a crack.

© Photo Jim Buchanan, Wild West Topos.

TRIANGULAR SLAB

Hidden from the car park and steeper than it appears from the road.

 Gneiss *   15m VS 4c
FA John Mackenzie & Graham Cullen 8 May 1994

Left of the central crack is a water-washed streak. Climb the streak towards some parallel cracks and exit (crux) to the right of them.

 **Gneisser ***   15m VS 4c
FA John Mackenzie & Graham Cullen 8 May 1994

The central crack, climbing past a downward pointing flake and exiting right at a notch.

 Gneissest **   15m HS 4b
FA John Mackenzie & Graham Cullen 8 May 1994

Start right of the crack. Climb to an overlap, break through this at a notch and head direct to the top.

NG 954 898 **Alt:** 70m   5min

Not Bad *   18m Very Difficult
FA John Mackenzie (solo) 1 May 1994

Start as for 3 and climb up to where it steepens. Traverse right to a break and climb this to a smooth slab finish.

Photo Jim Buchanan, Wild West Topos.

 hidden from view behind chokestone

INVERIANVIE CRAG

NG 955 896 **Alt:** 70m   10min

THE BAYVIEW WALL

On the first rocky knoll up the glen, seen in profile from the car park.

Approach: A vague rising path from the car park leads up to beneath the lower rocks to the right side of the upper face. Traverse left beneath the upper wall and go along past a huge wedged block to a ledge beneath a wall with a fine crack in it.

Descents: Arrange an abseil from above the crack. The last person can descend the break just right of the huge block passed on the approach. Alternatively, easy scrambling on the west leads to the grassy ledge.

1 The Pleasure Beach *   15m Severe 4b
FA Graeme Ettle & Blyth Wright 21 May 1998

Start at the left end of the ledge. Follow flakes leading to a fine 'whistle-clean' crack.

2 Gneiss and Easy **   15m VS 4c
FA Jon Robinson & party 1990

The crack-line up the wall just left of the heathery break. Start 5m left of the crack. Pleasant climbing with a few awkward moves rightwards into the upper crack.

3 Cask Conditioned *   15m HVS 5a
FA Rab & Chris Anderson 3 August 1995

The line just left of 4, right of a heathery crack sporting a small tree. Climb to the roof and pull rightwards through this (or leftwards at E1 5b) to the edge then up more easily to the top.

4 Root Beer **   15m E2 5b
FA Rab & Chris Anderson 3 August 1995

The prominent fine crack. Low in the grade.

5 Barrel of Fun *   15m E2 5c
FA Rab & Chris Anderson 3 August 1995

The wall just right of the crack leading to much better rock and protection.

6 Chokestone Gully *   15m Difficult

The through route. Care should be taken with blocks - best soloed. Also a useful descent route.

OPTIC WALL

The wall continuing further right.

7 Slippery Nipple *   20m HVS 5a
FA Cath Grindrod, Joy Grindrod & John Mackenzie 28 March 2000

The wall direct with thin protection to an overlap, finishing via a small groove.

8 The Parting Glass *   20m E1 5b
FA Graeme Ettle & Blyth Wright 21 May 1998

Rightward line to cross the roof by a prominent crack.

9 Gill *   20m Severe 4a
FA Graeme Ettle & Blyth Wright 11 May 2000

The short-left facing corner to an edge, finishing up right on good rock.

10 The Saloon of Life **   15m E2 5b
FA Paul Tattersall & Terry Doe 12 May 2002

On the sidewall up right of a tree-filled fault is a fine pillar. Start up the slab below the prow to pull onto it at a flake. Steeply into a crack and continue through bulges.

DOG CRAG 25min

NG 958 893 **Alt:** 90m

This is the long crag near the top of the second rocky dome up Glen Inverianvie from Gruinard Bay.
Approach: From the car park, walk along the road south-west for 100m and through a gate just before the bridge to gain a well-worn track. Follow the track up the east side of the Inverianvie River for about a kilometre (15 minutes) then head diagonally rightwards up the hillside, following a ramp rightwards under a small crag to the base of the crag high on the dome-shaped hill.
Descent: Scramble to near the top of the dome then down either of the easy angled open gullies at either side of the crag.

The undercut corner is 1 *Lassie* HVS 5a; the prominent wide crack 3 *Tess* VS 5a.

GAIRLOCH GRUINARD CRAGS

Photo Jim Buchanan, Wild West Topos.

2 Cailleach ★★   10m E3 5c
FA Andy Cunningham & Jeni Pickering June 1990

The shattered wall and crack to the right of 1.

4 K9 / Easy Tickings ★   30m E1 5b
FA p1 Jon Robinson 1988; p2 Rab & Chris Anderson 1 Aug 1995

1. **20m 5b** The thin crack in the smooth wall. Follow the crack, which is steep and awkward to start then the wall, finishing over a bulge (or easier out left).
2. **10m 5a** Follow the short thin crack up the left side of the dome, which soon forces one out left into an easy-angled groove after a few moves. The groove throughout is 4b.

5 Inverianvie Corner/Spotty Dog ★★   35m E2 5c
FA p1 Jon Robinson & Dave Neville before 1988;
p2 Andy Cunningham & Jeni Pickering June 1990

The shallow open groove forming a more defined corner higher up.

1. **20m 5b** Climb the left side of the groove with a few precarious moves to reach better holds. Continue more easily up and right into the corner and up this to exit by stepping out right at the top.
2. **15m 5c** The prominent crack up the right side of the dome, which soon eases after the initial steep section. Scrambling remains.

6 Pig Monkey Bird ★   20m E2 5b
FA Paul Tattersall & Angela Katzenmeier 21 August 2000

Start up the corner itself until an easing in angle close to 5. Go up a thin flake line on the right then rightwards to finish up a darker flake.

7 Slab Crack ★   25m Severe 4a
FA Jon Robinson 1988

Well right of the corner is a slabby wall. Climb its left edge on excellent holds to gain the terrace. Continue up the crack behind, which widens into a small chimney. Move left to belay at the top.

8 Wanderlust ★★   30m Very Difficult
FA John Mackenzie 1994

The slabs bounding the right edge of the crag can be climbed almost anywhere, on superb rough rock. Go up the centre of the central groove, crossing a quartz vein to a fine continuation slab.

9 Gerda ★★   30m Difficult
FA Karen Martin & Gary Latter 11 May 1996

The right side of the crag is bounded by a fine looking slabby tongue of rock. Up and slightly right of this is a narrow clean slab of rough rock. Climb the slab which leads to a shallow groove just right of the left rib. Finish up this. Fine climbing.

GAIRLOCH GRUINARD CRAGS

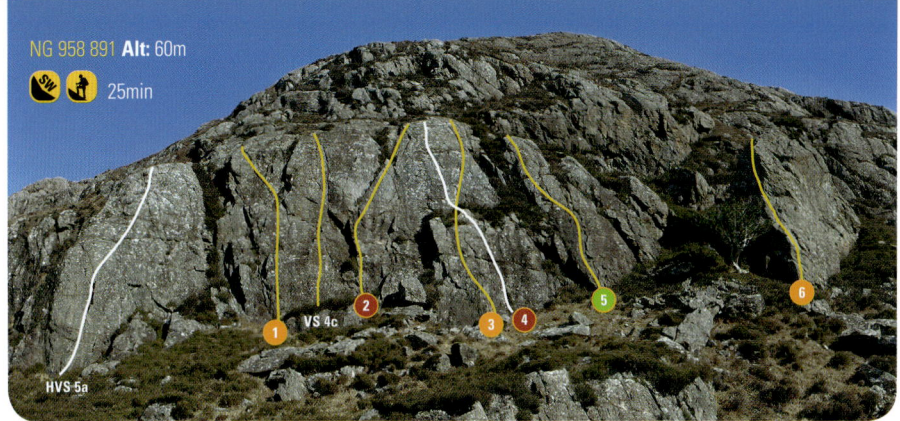

RIVERSIDE SLABS
Immediately above the Inverianvie River path, just beyond **Dog Crag**.

1 Blues Before Sunrise ★ — 15m HVS 5a
FA Allen Fyffe & Andy Cunningham 9 October 2002

Directly up to base of left-facing mossy corner. Finish up the left diagonal crack.

2 Blitzkrieg Bop ★ — 15m E1 5b
FA Andy Cunningham & Allen Fyffe 9 October 2002

The right-trending line through the shallow slot.

3 Sunlight Slab ★ — VS 4c
FA Allen Fyffe & Andy Cunningham 9 October 2002

Cracks to a ledge, then rightwards, finishing up a crack leading back left.

4 Fade to Grey ★★ — 15m E1 5b
FA Allen Fyffe & Andy Cunningham 17 December 2002

Climb diagonally rightwards, pull over a bulge and trend left. Step left to finish directly up the slab.

5 Autumn Rib ★ — 14m Severe 4a
FA Allen Fyffe & Andy Cunningham 9 October 2002

Cracks up the rib, moving left at the top.

6 Echolocation ★★ — 12m VS 4b
FA Allen Fyffe & Andy Cunningham 9 October 2002

The thin crack to the arête. Finish up its left side.

THE APRON
NG 959 895 **Alt:** 150m 25–30min

A pleasant apron of easy-angled slab on the next knoll north of **Lochan Dubh Crag** (on the left side of the open descent gully). The slab reaches the base in two tongues either side of an inverted V of heather and turf.

Descent: Down the easy-angled open gully on the right.

1 Smashy ★ — 50m Very Difficult
FA Rab & Chris Anderson 6 August 1995

The right tongue starts as a short pillar. The skyline block-type feature is climbed by a thin diagonal crack leading to easier angled ground and a belay common with 2.

2 Gneissy ★★ — 50m Difficult
FA Chris & Rab Anderson 6 August 1995

A very pleasant route starting from the base of the left tongue. Climb to a short corner on the skyline and continue up this.

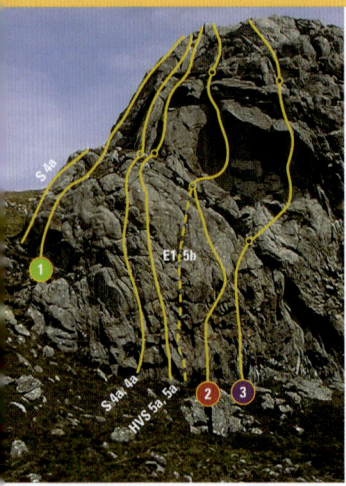 

LOCHAN DUBH CRAG

NG 960 894 **Alt:** 140m 25–30min

By far the best outcrop in the area in an idyllic setting on the north-east shore of Lochan Dubh. The central continuously overhanging 30m high wall offers two of the finest single pitch routes anywhere. With a great outlook to both hills and sea, this is a truly wonderful place to climb. The panorama from the top of the dome is unrivalled by any other outcrop in the country.

Approach: From the car park walk along the road south-west for 100m and through a gate just before the bridge to gain a well-worn track. Follow the track up the east side of the Inverianvie River for about one kilometre (15 minutes) then head diagonally rightwards up the hillside, following a ramp rightwards under a small crag to skirt round the left side of a second slightly higher crag on the dome-shaped hill. Head east over the blunt ridge for 200m to reach the crag.

① Edged Out ★   40m Very Difficult
FA Dundonnell Mountain Rescue Team members 1989

Up the slope from the left edge is a smooth slab with a crack up its right side. Up the crack to a ledge, step left and climb the blunt rib on superb rough holds.

② The Silk Road ★★   50m E2 5c
FA John Mackenzie & Bob Brown 14 April 1994

The short leaning corner left of the overhanging wall. Start on the right rib of the recess.

  1 20m 5b Climb the overhanging wall slightly right to a prominent hold. Pull over the bulge and continue up the break on rough rock to the smooth corner. (A direct line up the lower tier has been climbed).

  2 10m 5c The smooth corner is as difficult as it looks (F #0 useful). Mantel onto the airy slab on the right at the top.

  3 20m – Pull over the bulge on the right and follow rough rock to the top.

③ Flawed by Design ★★   35m E4 6b
FA Paul Thorburn & Rick Campbell 12 May 1996

Spectacular athletic climbing through the disappearing flake-crack breaking through the right side of the leaning roof. Left of the clean rock a left-slanting diagonal crack cuts through a red slightly mossy wall.

  1 20m 5b Gain the crack from the right and follow it to easier ground leading rightwards to belay below a grooved slab at the bottom right end of the heather terrace.

2 **15m 6b** Step right and up a shallow right-facing groove in the slab to the flake. Cross the roof with interest to a rounded finish. Belay on a ledge a short way above.

4 Call of the Wild ★★★   50m E4 6a
FA Martin Moran & Martin Welch 28 April 1995: start as described Paul Thorburn & Gary Latter 11 May 1996

Good climbing up the crack and roof bounding the left side of the central overhanging wall. Start at the same point as 5. Up onto the good ledge, left along this and up to good flakes left of the thin crack. Move out left then back right to a good jug at the top of the crack then more easily up big flakes in the sea-mossy groove to the roof. Head out right to a good flange and layback rounded holds strenuously through the shallow corner/chimney to two huge hollow blocks at the top. Reach out left to a good jam crack and belay on a small ledge a short way above. Scrambling remains.

5 Dead Calm ★★★   50m E6 6b
FA Rab Anderson ('rab'pointed, some gear pre-placed) 6 Aug 1995

The impressive vague hanging crack up the centre of the overhanging wall. Sustained and well protected. Start beneath twin ledges just right of a black water-streak.

1 **30m 6b** Up to the large ledge then easily out right to the vague crack. Direct past an awkward bulge then right to a good hold. Continue direct with a hard move to a good undercut then span up left to a good jug. Continue slightly left then back right to good holds at the top of the smooth 'shield' of rock. Continue up the obvious line slightly left to pull out right to a good flake. Go up a short way and continue into a large niche on the left.

2 **20m 4c** Climb up rightwards and follow the best line to the top.

5a Welcome to the Terror Dome ★★★   50m E7 6c
FA Ally Coull (headpointed) September 2011

The line between 5 and 6. Start mid way between, directly below a small diagonal roof right of the three obvious white streaks. Climb up to the roof and turn it on the right, climb up and right over another overlap to a rest below

the obvious small roof (bold). Pull over this roof and climb diagonally up left passing good gear to a diagonal crack and small overlap. Make hard moves directly up to reach a good flat hold, gear can be arranged to the right (crucial). Use an undercut and poor holds to gain the next break (hard) and continue boldly into a niche. Climb left out of the niche to an easing in angle.

6 Major-domo ★★★★   50m E6 6b
FA Rab Anderson (red-pointed) 3 August 1995

An outrageously brilliant pitch up the niched-crack up the right side of the overhanging wall. Strenuous and sustained right to the very top. Very well protected – carry as many small wires as you can muster.

1 **30m 6b** Follow the crack to good jugs at 10m. A long reach leads to a good rest (knee-lock no-hands rest) under a bulge at just over mid-height. The crack above leads to some powerful moves past an evil sloping hold leading into the shallow groove above. Up this to a large undercut flange. Direct past a further small undercut to good finishing holds. Step left and onto the ledge. Move up past a keyed-in block to belay at the right side of bigger ledge above.

2 **20m 5b** Climb the centre of the buttress right of the awkward leftwards diagonal chimney-groove by a left-trending diagonal line and up to a ledge. Finish up a juggy crack in the final short wall which soon leads to easier ground. Continue in the same line to a belay on the right, just short of the top.

7 The Missing Link ★   50m E2 5b
FA A.Andrew & Martin Moran 26 May 1995; pitch 2 Jon Robinson & Dave Neville 1990; Sunk without Trace Paul Thorburn & Neil Craig 11 May 1996

Follows the right edge of the central wall with a deviation into the recess to the right.

1 **20m 5b** Climb cracked blocks to the roof and pull over to a handrail which leads right into the recess.

2 **30m 5b** Traverse out left onto the steep face and gain a crack line which leads to easier ground. Omitting the escape out right gives 7a *Sunk without Trace* ★ E3 5c.

8 Nick the Niche **   45m E1 5b
FA Jon Robinson & Dave Neville 1989

This fine route follows the first line of weakness right of the overhanging wall. To the right of the overhanging wall is an easy-angled corner topped by a large block. Start up the corner, step right and climb a crack on the right of the block to gain a small ledge. The overhanging wall above is split by a pair of thin cracks. Climb the wall (crux) and gain the large recess. Climb directly up the steep crack above, finishing up easier but pleasant rock to the top.

9 Beat the Beak *   40m VS 4c
FA Dave Neville & Jon Robinson 1989

Takes the best line right of 8. Start on the heather terrace 10m above the loch side directly above a lone tree.

1. **15m 4c** Climb the hanging corner which has a projecting block on the left, to a slab. Left of the little holly tree is a pair of cracks. Climb these trending rightwards to belay at the base of a shallow corner.
2. **25m** – Continue up the easier corner then rightwards up slabbier ground to finish.

> 10 *Ducks with Attitude* • E2 5c, 4c climbs a line in front of the pointed block; 12 *Scrabble* HS –, 4b, – the corner on the far right. Between the top pitches of these, the thin crack with difficult moves into a shallow groove is the worthwhile 11 *Sunset Song* • E1 5b.

GRUINARD RIVER CRAGS

CARN NA H-AIRE
(ROCKY HILL OF THE LORD)
The large rocky hill overlooking the Gruinard River.
Access: Continue along the A832 for 1 mile/1.6km north-east from the parking spot at Gruinard Bay. Park on the east side of the road, just south of the bridge over the Gruinard River.

GOAT CRAG 10min
NG 9642 9110 **Alt:** 90m

Approach: Cross the bridge and drop down the track on the right. Midway between a gate and a house, cross the fence by some logs and follow an initially boggy path steeply rightwards up to the base.

The big crag above the Gruinard River. A lower overhanging wall is capped by an extensive area of easy-angled heathery slabs. The premier sport venue in Scotland, with a superb vista. The crag receives the afternoon sun, and often a breeze to keep the midges at bay. Even in dry weather some routes require the afternoon sun to dry overnight seepage.

LOWER LEFT SECTOR
Down and left of the main crag.

1 Unreliable Virgin ★★　　　　　　　　25m F6b
FA Lawrence Hughes March 2016

Climb the slab left of the turfy corner then up the steep orange headwall.

2 Blacklight Sleaze ★★　　　　　　　　25m F6a
FA Lawrence Hughes March 2016

Line just right of the turfy corner.

3 Jungelknugen ★★　　　　　　　　　25m F5+
FA Lawrence Hughes March 2016

Same start as 2, then follow the right line of bolts.

Lawrence Hughes on Unreliable Virgin and Tess Fryer on Blacklight Sleaze. Photo Ian Taylor.

MAIN CRAG

1 Homosuperior ★★   20m E5 6a
FA Paul Tattersall & Lawrence Hughes October 2000

The first line right of the corner.

2 Twilo Thunder ★★   20m E5 6a
FA Lawrence Hughes & Colin Meek October 2000

Start up 3 but continue to the 'gargoyle' and ledge above. Very well protected.

3 Freakshow ★★★   20m E5 6a
FA Paul Tattersall October 2000

Next line right of 1. Move up to a good flake then pull right and up on good flake holds to move right along a diagonal break (crux) to a crack. Move up to follow an easier prominent curving flake line. Step left into a deep crack and up this to finish with powerful laybacking past the 'gargoyle' fin.

3a Freakshow Direct ★★   20m E5 6a
FA Ian Taylor & Tess Fryer 17 May 2013

Start right of 3 and go direct up the cracked wall until moves diagonally rightwards lead to a loose-looking block (keyed in) on the right. Stand on the block and follow cracks back left to a junction with 3 just below its downward jutting spike. Finish up that route.

4 The Eightsome Reel ★★   25m E5 6c
FA Ian Taylor 8 August 2008

Climbs the thin hanging crack in the upper wall right of 3.

Start right of 3 and follow a couple of stepped corners to gain a sloping shelf below and right of the crack. Swing left and follow the crack past a hard section to good holds then continue via sustained climbing to an easing of angle. Move left to the in-situ belay of 3.

5 Flowsnake — 15m F7b+
FA Ian Taylor 2012

The leftmost sport route up the very steep corner left of the ivy.

5a Poison Ivy (Open Project) — 15m

6 Snowflake *** — 16m F7a+
FA Ian Taylor 2010

First line right of ivy. Climb wall to a giant hanging flake for a rest. Finish steeply up the flake.

6a The Noose * — 15m F7b
FA Ian Taylor 2012

Climb to the right of the ivy. Shares some ground in the middle with 6 then heads left into a niche and finishes at the first chain. The crux is clipping the chain!

6b The Noose Extension * — 15m F7c
FA Calum Cunningham 2015

Continue to the higher lower-off via a bouldery move.

7 Batman and Robin ** — 15m F7b
FA Andy Wilby 2008

7a Open Project — 15m

8 The Joker ** — 15m F7b
FA Andy Wilby 2008

9 The Penguin * — 15m F7b
FA Ian Taylor 2010

Shares some middle ground with 8, but has been climbed direct and independent at 7b+.

10 The Riddler * — 15m F7c
FA Ian Taylor & Andy Wilby 2009

11 Bamboozle * — 10m F6c+
FA Ian Taylor 2010

Up resin bolts, then old style hangers right then back left.

12 The Poodle — 12m F6c+
FA Ian Taylor & Tess Fryer 2019

13 The Noodle — 10m F7b
FA Eadan Cunningham & Lawrence Hughes September 2015

Start up 12 then move right into the roofed groove.

14 Closed Project — 12m

The very steep line left of 15.

15 Broken Silence * — 12m F7c
FA Dave Redpath 24 June 2007

Central line powering through the bulge, with a tricky third clip.

16 Closed Project — 15m

17 St George — 15m F7b
FA Paul Tattersall & Ian Taylor 2014

18 Tom Paines Bones ** — 15m F6b+
FA Paul Tattersall December 2007

The hard start can be missed out by coming in from the right at F6a+.

19 Poster Boy ** — 20m F5+
FA Paul Tattersall 2015

Great varied climbing.

20 Teepee ** — 20m F6a+
FA Murdoch Jamieson, Colin Meek & Paul Tattersall 2007

The corner. Long and sustained.

20a Young Man's Link * — 20m F6c+

Break out right at the 5th bolt to join 21 above its crux.

21 Too Old to be Famous * — 20m F7b
FA Murdoch Jamieson, Colin Meek, Paul Tattersall & Paul Thorburn 2007

Crux breaking through the bulge.

22 The Mighty Atom ** — 20m F7b+
FA Murdoch Jamieson, Colin Meek, Paul Tattersall & Andy Wilby 2007

Crux is steep grey shield near top.

22a Pensioner's Link * — 20m F7a+
Avoid the crux bottom wall of 21 by starting up 22 if you're feeling a bit ancient.

23 Mac Talla **** — 20m F7b
FA Colin Meek & Nic Duboust 18 February 2007

'Echo'. Superb steady climbing, with one harder move up to the top. One of the best routes of its grade in the country.

24 The Prow Direct **** — 20m F7c+
FA Paul Thorburn & Nic Duboust 2007

Another superb route, with a tricky final clip.

24a Gap-Toothed Gypsy * — 20m F7b+
FA Lawrence Hughes 2014

Climb the start of 24 to the sloping ledge, then head straight up, following three new bolts, before pulling left into 23.

24b The Prow Left Finish **** — 20m F7c
FA Paul Thorburn 2007

The stunning prow climbed with the left finish.

25 Plum Prow *** — 20m F8a/8a+
FA Murdoch Jamieson & Ian Taylor June 2019

Climb the arête direct to join the original at the knee-bar. Start on the left and span right to a good finger lock.

26 The Leaning Wall *** — 20m F8a
FA Lawrence Hughes & Paul Thorburn March 2008

Superb, super steep and permanently dry!

26a Fun Prow *** — 20m F8a+
FA Ali Coull 25 March 2012

Link up combining the crux lower section of 26 into crux top of 24, without using the kneebar rest!

27 Hydrotherapy *** — 20m F6c+
FA Tess Fryer 2008

Excellent varied climbing, finishing up the tapering slab.

28 Between the Monsoons ** — 20m F6c+
FA Ian Taylor 2008

A good warm-up, almost always dry. Sustained and pumpy, heading for the obvious groove.

Murdoch Jamieson on the classic testpiece The Prow Left Finish. Photo Ian Taylor

GAIRLOCH GRUINARD RIVER CRAGS

28a Sun Rays *   20m F7a
FA Ian Taylor October 2015

29 Cloudburst *   15m F7a
FA Ian Taylor 2011

Steady up to shield with thin crack, then boulder at top.

30 Caberfeidh **   15m F6b
FA Ian Taylor 2010

Steep and juggy after a tricky start, finishing at the same LO as 29. Good wee warm-up!

30a War Cry *   20m F7b+
FA Ian Taylor 2012

31 Fidgey Muckers **   25m F7a
FA Ian Taylor 2012

Line right of 30 – two steep sections with an easier-angled middle. (Not on topo).

TOP DECK

32 The G.O.A.T. **   55m F6a+
FA Lawrence Hughes 18 March 2016

The leftmost line – *"could be Scotland's longest sport route?"* Start up 19. Just before the normal LO head rightwards and pull over onto the belay ledge.

  2 15m F4 Go up for a few moves, then traverse left to reach another belay ledge (35m abseil from here).

  3 20m F6a+ Follow the cracks and bulges above.

33 Squirticus Maximus **   20m F6a+
FA Lawrence Hughes March 2016

The central line – *"goes up rock so sticky you wont need holds"*.

34 Hashi-Watashi **   20m F5+
FA Lawrence Hughes March 2016

The rightmost line.

📷 *Lawrence Hughes on the first ascent of The G.O.A.T. Photo Ian Taylor.*

AM FASGADH
(THE SHELTER/REFUGE)

NG 9659 9097 **Alt:** 50m   SW 🚶 10min

A steep continuously overhanging wall hidden in a recess at the right end, beneath a prominent left-slanting band of quartz. It is very sheltered and a sun trap, therefore midges/heat can be a problem in summer. Treated by the locals as an *"outdoor climbing wall"*, the majority of the crag stays dry throughout most of the year.
Routes equipped by Paul Tattersall, Colin Meek, Mick Holmes, Lawrence Hughes, Paul Thorburn & Ian Taylor.

Approach: Walk down the track on the north bank of the river for 400m then cut up the hillside to the crag, whose top can just be seen from the track.

1 Bat Day   15m F6a+
FA Tess Fryer & Ian Taylor 2014

Short wall and hanging slab.

2 Toiseach *   12m F7b
FA Colin Meek 2004

'Beginning'.

3) The Brown Streak ★★ — 12m F7b+
FA Paul Tattersall Spring 2005

Not surprising, climbs the brown streak!

3a) Omega Link — 12m F7b+
FA Ian Taylor 2017

4) Warm-Up/Super Warm-Up ★★ — 10m/15m F7b/F7b+
FA Paul Tattersall Spring 2005; Ian Taylor 2013

The original warm-up! From the normal LO gain the undercuts above, move right to a flake and go up steeply to finish.

5) The Pillar ★★ — 10m F8a
FA Alan Cassidy 19 April 2014

'Funky climbing' up the short pillar.

6) Black Sox ★★★ — 12m F7c+
FA Lawrence Hughes Spring 2005

Fine sustained climbing.

6a) Black Sox Left Finish ★★ — 15m F8a+
FA Murdoch Jamieson & Andy Wilby 2011

Up 6 to half-height, then out left with a hard long move out left to a good edge, then span left into crack. Further sustained hard climbing to the LO.

7) Storky's ★★ — 15m F8a+
FA Andy Wilby & Paul Thorburn 2010

Hard and bouldery.

8) Bog Talla ★★★ — 12m F7c
FA Paul Tattersall Spring 2005

'Built wall'. Central line starting off the wall. 8a *Left Finish* is F7c+.

9) Primo ★★★ — 25m F7c
FA Lawrence Hughes & Ian Taylor December 2007

The line left of 11. To the mid-height anchor is 9a *The Curving Crack* F7b+.

10) The Counter Diagonal (Project) — 12m

11) The Crack ★ — 25m F7c
FA Paul Tattersall & Lawrence Hughes April 2000

The steep vague hanging crack at the right end. Boulder out the start and continue up the crack above.

12) B-Movie — 10m F7a
FA Paul Tattersall 2007

Right start, joining 11 at the no-hands rest.

13) The Shield ★★★ — 15m F7b
FA Lawrence Hughes, Paul Tattersall & Ian Taylor November 2007

The hanging shield, gained via a blocky pillar.

14 Scorchio ** — 15m F7a
FA Ian Taylor 2011

A line up the wall right of 13.

15 Teasel * — 15m F6c+
FA Ian Taylor 2011

Surprisingly good climbing.

16 The Groove ** — 15m F6c+
FA Ian Taylor December 2007

Line finishing up a short steep corner.

17 The Hump * — 12m F7a
FA Ian Taylor 2017

CARN GORAIG (ROCKY HILL OF THE SILLY FEMALE)

1½hr / 1hr

NG 994 860 Alt: 100m

An excellent quick drying gneiss crag of immaculate rock with an adventurous approach and remote feel to it. The Upper Tier generally contains all the best pitches and a number of pitches can be conveniently accessed by setting up an abseil to regain the heather terrace.

Approach: Follow the Land Rover track south-east up the west bank of the Gruinard River for about 6km (mountain bikes recommended), whence the crag comes into view. When not in spate, the river can be crossed with care, the best spot being at NG 990 865 where it is wide and straight. Continue across some very boggy ground rightwards to the base of the crag.

Descent: Down either side of the crag, quickest by the steep scrambling rake on the left side that runs beneath a fine-looking vertical wall.

1 Olden Glory ** — 82m VS 4c
FA Blyth Wright & Bob Brown 2 October 1998

A good climb, particularly the fine top pitch taking the easiest line on the upper tier. Start beneath the leftmost of two slabby ribs with some trees to its left.

1. **35m 4b** Climb the crest of the rib using cracks, first right then left, bypassing the obvious split nose on its right to finish up mossy slabs to broken slabs and belay.
2. **12m —** Climb easier rock (Diff.) to belay below an obvious crack with a small tree higher up.
3. **35m 4c** Climb the fine crack to a large block below the tree. Go left at the tree and use flakes to go round the slabby edge. A thin crack leads up leftwards towards an overlap. Climb to the overlap, where a fine hand-traverse leads leftwards to finishing jugs and cracks beside hollow blocks — good stance and belay. An excellent pitch on superb rock.

2 Alba/Return to Mecca ** — 80m E2 5c
FA Return to Mecca: Fraser Fotheringham & Alex Taylor 8 Sept 1988; Alba: John Mackenzie & Blyth Wright 29 Sept 1998

Start beneath a continuous steep rib bottomed by reddish slabs.

1. **45m 4c** Climb the slab direct to the rib which is climbed centrally to exit via a rightwards slanting crack. Scramble up broken ground to below a bowl-shaped scoop on the left side of the top tier.
2. **35m 5c** Return to Mecca Climb the crack to the left of the bowl to a wall. Traverse left 5m across a bulge to a thin crack which is climbed strenuously (crux) to a slab which is climbed up right to a wall. Move back left to a rightwards facing ramp which is taken in a good position to the top. A superb constantly varied and interesting pitch.

3 Wailing Wall *** — 75m E1 5b
FA Fraser Fotheringham & Alex Taylor 11 March 1987

The original and best line on the crag. Start at the left side of the clean section of the lower tier.

1. **20m 5a** Climb up to a small scoop then the thin crack through it to gain a terrace.
2. **25m 5b** From just left of 4, climb steeply up to gain a shelf. Continue up a left-trending fault and rounded

bulge on good holds then easily rightwards to belay on the right at the base of twin parallel cracks (rightmost two of three cracks). High in the grade.

3 30m 5b Climb the splendid cracks, taking the crux bulge direct. Continue to the top, crossing a further bulge more easily.

④ The Highland Cragsman ★★★ 75m E3 5c
FA John Mackenzie & Blyth Wright 7 Oct 1998; Call of the Muwazzin: Andy Cunningham & Fraser Fotheringham 7 Oct 1998

An excellent contrasting route. Start beneath an obvious thin crack system.

1 20m 5c Climb to an arrow shaped slot then the crack strenuously, stepping left then back right (or 6a direct) to the first ledge.

2 25m 5c Directly above is a smooth scoop. Climb the steep flake-crack on the left arête then foot traverse right across small shelf and up to the base of a fine hanging crack. Hand traverse right to a heather patch beneath a steep crack. Climb the crack then leftwards easily to belay at the base of a prominent left-slanting crack.

3 30m 5b *Call of the Muwazzin* A good pitch, following the crack immediately left of the twin cracks of 3 (leftmost of 3 parallel cracks). Where the crack peters out at the half-height bulge, move right into the left crack of 3 (where that route moves right), moving immediately back left into the original line after the bulge.

⑤ Whoopers ★★ 75m E4 6a
FA Gary Latter & Al Siddons 13 October 1998; Cursing Crack: Gary Latter 6 April 2002

A logical combination of pitches, giving the hardest outing. Start beneath a smooth-looking scoop split by some very thin cracks.

1 20m 6a Climb the easy lower slab then by a good crack which soon fades. Continue up the scoop with a hard move to gain a thin horizontal break. Step up right and pull over the final bulge, using a good jug in the crack on the right.

2 25m 5c Directly above is another, smoother scoop. Climb the steep flake-crack on the left arête then traverse right and up to the base of a fine hanging crack. Layback into the crack and pull over onto the slab above. Scramble up leftwards to belay.

3 30m 6a *Cursing Crack* left of the triple cracks of 3 & 4 are a further three parallel left-slanting cracks, the right two similarly close together. Climb the rightmost crack which is viciously sharp with difficulty to better holds in a recess. Continue up the easier crack above then up a wall to finish up a prominent crack at the top, a few metres left of an easier

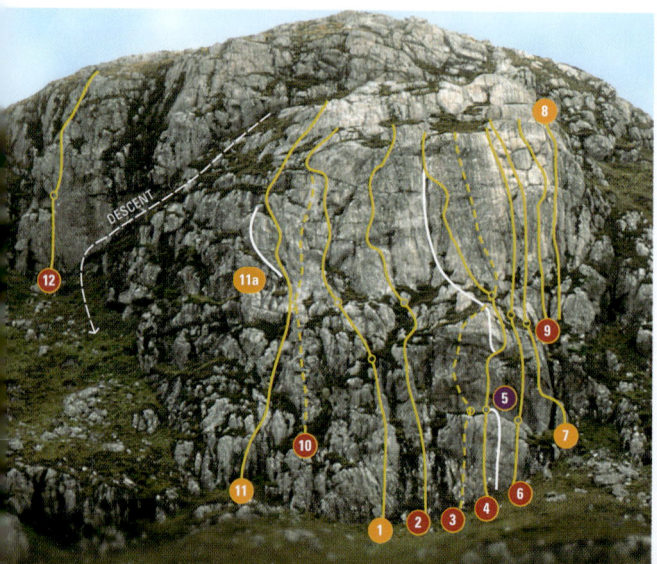

Karen Latter on the introductory pitch of Wailing Wall.

looking slightly lichenous crack. Climbed in error for the final pitch of *Wailing Wall*, hence the name!

6 Ramadan ** 65m E1 5b
FA Andy Cunningham & Fraser Fotheringham July 1995

1. **10m 4a** Climb cracks on the right side of the lower tier to belay by a large overhung recess (or walk round!)
2. **25m 5b** Climb a steep widening crack out of the right side of the recess and up to belay below a wide blocky Y-crack in the upper slabs.
3. **30m 4c** Move up and rightwards via the crack and pull left through the bulge to follow the continuing left crack. A very good pitch.

7 Bootless Crow * 55m VS 5a
FA Andy Cunningham & R.Baines 6 May 2001

Start at a mossy groove at the right side of the middle tier.

1. **25m 5a** Climb clean rock right of the moss then an obvious left-trending line joining the main right crack at an orange hole. Follow cracks above onto slabs, to belay beneath wide blocky Y-crack in top tier.
2. **30m 4c** Move right onto a huge block and climb the rightmost steepening crack and continuation to a heather bay. Finish up vague line of cracks above.

UPPER TIER

Approach: Either by one of the routes on the lower tiers or scramble along the heather terrace from the right.

8 The Fatwah ** 30m HVS 5b
FA Andy Cunningham & Fraser Fotheringham 7 October 1998

The fine crack rising out of the obvious red groove. Follow the crack in the same line after the easing.

9 Dispossessed ** 30m E1 5c
FA Fraser Fotheringham & Andy Cunningham 7 October 1998

Start at the same point as 8. Move left into a scooped line of cracks, small ledges and hidden holds to gain the easing by a small protruding spike. Climb in the same line via cracks and blocks to finish.

MAIN TIER, LEFT SIDE

10 Old Goats *** 65m E3 5c
FA Andy Cunningham & R.Baines 6 May 2001

A very direct and continuous line on clean rock throughout, aiming for the break at the left end of 1's hand traverse. Start up left of the lower tier on a heather rake gained by a short scramble up a crack. The base of a clean rib has a large boulder thread on its left and twin trees on the right.

1. **30m 4b** Climb the rib, turning the small roof on its right and continue on excellent rock to belay in deep cracks at the extreme left end of the Upper Tier.
2. **35m 5c** One of the best pitches on the crags. Go straight up to a cleaned ledge and gain a hold on the left by a long reach. Step right to cracks which lead to another move left (crux) and an easing just left of a rock ledge. Continue directly to a narrow heather ledge then delicately into a smooth scoop leading to the end of the hand traverse.

11 Crusader * 80m HVS 5a
FA John Mackenzie & Blyth Wright 31 May 2000; Saracens: Gary & Karen Latter 6 April 2002

Pleasant climbing. Start at the back of large recess with smooth steep left wall.

1. **35m 4b** Climb steeply up the back left side of the recess and up to bypass a prominent triangular roof on the left then fairly directly to belays as for 10.
2. **45m 5a** Climb up to a left-slanting ramp and flake. Step rightwards into a groove then continue up the fault and a short wall on the right to gain a black groove and crack.

11a *Saracens* ** HVS 5a continues left along the same left-trending line with a long span left to gain a good crack at one point, finishing up a short steep crack to belay at a huge block.

12 The Wicked ** — 35m E2 5c
FA Graeme Ettle, Paul Thorburn & Blyth Wright 9 July 1999

Up and left of the main crag is a prominent steep wall, at the base of the descent ramp.
1 **15m 5b** Follow the prominent crack to a heather ledge.
2 **20m 5c** Climb the finely situated arête on the right on excellent rock.

JETTY BUTTRESS

NG 961 926 **Alt:** 50m

The sprawling crag directly above the road (and, not surprisingly, the jetty!) 1.5 miles/2.5km north of Gruinard Bay. Many of the uncredited routes were climbed by various joint services personnel in the late sixties and early seventies.

Access: Park on the grass verge on the west side of the A832 road directly beneath the left side of the crag.
Approach: Directly up the hillside from the road.
Descents: Down either side of the crag or by careful scrambling (Difficult) down the short open gully above the fence line between the **First South Wall** and **Short West Wall**.

Photo Jim Buchanan, Wild West Topos.

NORTH WALL
The slabbier left-bounding wall, running up the hillside.

base of the wall. Follow the reddish rock up the centre of the depression, finishing up a clean slab.

2 Crack Route ** — 30m Very Difficult
FA Jim & Pat Bell August 1946

The centre of the slim rib just left of a long vertical grass strip with a small Scots pine at the top. Finish up the narrow slab above.

3 Route 6 ** — 25m HS 4b

Start at a small black cave-like recess. Climb wall just right of the cave, then step down left across its top onto the wall. Trend left aiming for a tiny groove in the centre, then a diagonal crack rightwards, returning left to finish.

4 Route Major * — 20m HS 4b
FA Major Ian Leigh & joint services personnel 1970s

Start up left of the deep right-facing corner near the top end of the wall. Ascend small corner, then move right and use an embedded flake to pull over a small pale wall. Continue up the poorly protected grey slab, avoiding the headwall (unprotected 4c) by the slab on the left.

1 Red Slab Route ** — 30m HS 4c
FA Jim & Pat Bell August 1946

"The holds are exceedingly small, but the rock is perfect."
— Bell, Some New Climbs in the North-West, *Scottish Mountaineering Club Journal*, 1949.

Fine open climbing. Start in a depression up left from the

Photos Jim Buchanan, Wild West Topos.

5 Route 2 ★ — 15m Severe 4a
Start at V-groove above a recess near the top of the wall. Climb the groove a short way, step left then immediately right across the top of the groove to slab on right. Finish either close to the left-bounding corner (thin), or the airy groove and slab on the left.

FRONT WEST WALL
The highest section of crag, on the left, nearest the road.

6 North West Arête ★ — 30m HVS 5a
Poorly protected climbing up the left edge of the front face, finishing up much easier ground above.

7 Crab Crack ★ — 30m HVS 5a
Start 5m right of the left arête. Up to a heather ledge then over a bulge and up the thin crack in the slab. Trend leftwards to finish.

8 Route 11 ★ — 30m VS 4c
Start at the same point as 7. From the heather ledge head up right and up the shallow corner past a small hollow-sounding nose, finishing direct.

9 Anthrax Flake ★★★ — 25m VS 5a
Excellent very well protected climbing – the crag classic. Start directly beneath the left side of the huge hanging flake. Up the awkward wall on very smooth rock to a good ledge beneath the flake. Continue steeply up the flake on improving holds, stepping right to a short jam crack leading to easier ground.

10 Justin Time / Prizefighter ★ — 25m E2 5c
FA Graeme Ettle & Justin Findlay November 1992; lower arête John Mackenzie & Bob Brown 26 April 1998

Climb the bold lower arête (5a), step right and climb the shallow overhanging corner and crack on the right. This leads strenuously to a *"fighting finish"* up the overhanging crack.

11 Charlie's Corner ★★ — 25m VS 4c
FA D.C.Forrest & D.M.Jenkins 22 July 1970

Fine airy climbing up the prominent right-facing corner. Up the corner to a ledge on the left then up to the left of the corner and up the left edge of the pale-coloured rock above. Step back right into the main corner above the pale rock.

12 Radio Gnome ★ — 25m E3 5c
FA Paul Tattersall & Angela Katzenmeier 26 June 2000

Start 2m right of 11. Climb the vague weakness up the centre of the wall, stepping right onto the big flake. Finish directly up the wall above.

13 Right Charlie ★★ — 25m E2 5c
FA Fraser Fotheringham & Jon Robinson late 1980s

Steep and sustained, giving fine open climbing. Start just right of the drystane wall, behind two huge larch trees. Climb up to a flake from the left or with difficulty from the short corner on the right. Up the crack to a heathery ledge. Step right and up a shallow corner then left and up a fine crack in the headwall on improving holds.

14 Gaffer's Wall ★★   25m E2 5c
FA John Mackenzie & Richard Biggar 16 May 1999
Excellent steep climbing up the wall right of 13. Start 3m right of that route. Cross the initial overhang and step left onto a shelf. Climb up to and over a slanting flake-crack to gain the ledge just right of 15. Ascend the shallow fault above.

15 South-West Arête ★   15m E1 5b
Poorly protected, steady climbing up the blunt rib above the large pointed boulders, where the face changes direction. Many small nuts required.

FIRST SOUTH WALL
The shorter south-facing wall up the hill beneath the old fence. There is a large prominent Scots pine on a ledge at two-thirds height.

16 Bus Stop ★   15m Severe 4a
The wall and cracks just left of the central groove.

17 Doddle ★   15m Very Difficult
The prominent slabby crack, gained from the left.

SHORT WEST WALL
Right of the broken open gully with a huge larch at its base (possible scrambly descent).

18 Batty ★   20m HVS 5a
Low in the grade. Start just right of the gully. Climb the pale wall then slightly left to a tree. Either finish up the wide corner-crack or climb the front of the block to finish up right of the arête.

19 Starwood ★★   20m HVS 5a
The crack with a small tree near the base. Climb the crack to a ledge then the back wall to a triangular block, trending right onto a large flake on the arête. Go up the edge of the south wall then back onto the arête to finish in a fine position.

SECOND SOUTH WALL

20 Kew ★   20m VS 4b
Ascend the wall up to the detached block on the left arête. Step right onto the wall. After 10m go left onto a large flake, finishing as for 19.

 Karen Latter bridging up Charlie's Corner.

BACK WEST WALL

20a Big Flapper *** 20m E5 6a
FA Ian Taylor & Tess Fryer 24 October 2011

An excellent clean route up the left edge of the wall. Sustained with good protection where it matters. High in the grade.

21 Gogmagog ** 20m E5 6a
FA Paul Tattersall & Angela Katzenmeier 5 May 1998

The *"last great problem"* on the crag. Very bold until past the lower roof, with good but spaced protection above. Scramble up to the big grassy tree-filled ledge. Go up the centre of the wall directly to a small slanting roof and cross this at its lower right end. Move up and right towards a big detached flake, avoiding it by climbing the wall on the left to reach a good ledge. Boldly climb the vague seam/crack on the right on improving holds.

22 Gruinard Corner * 20m HVS 5a
Start beneath a small crack midway along the wall, right of a hanging juniper bush. Climb the crack to a small ledge then the crack left of the ledge, moving left to finish up the corner on the left.

23 After the Storm * 20m HVS 5b
FA Ross Jones & S.McNaught 12 April 2003

Start as for 22 to a shelf at 5m. Continue, stepping right into the base of a corner on the arête above an overhang. Finish up this and the arête above.

24 Trespass ** 20m E2 5c
FA Colin Meek 5 May 2001

The crack just R of the arête, with a move R after the bulge.

25 The Rowan * 20m E1 5b
FA Colin Meek & C.Dryer 20 May 2001

Crack 2m right of 24.

Photos Jim Buchanan, Wild West Topos.

MUNGASDALE CRAG

NG 967 927 **Alt:** 100m

10min

A fine sheltered and very quick drying short crag, with a host of good hard routes. It lies at the south-west end of the rocky whaleback ridge, almost completely hidden from the road.

Access: Continue north beyond **Jetty Buttress** for 0.3 miles/0.5km to car park on the left, overlooking a fine sandy beach.

Approach: Walk east along the road for a few hundred metres and through a gate on the right then diagonally left up the hillside crossing a small stream to the crag.

Descents: From the block containing the first six routes scramble easily off the back and down the left side. For the other routes, leftwards down the lower heather rake left of the centre or down either end of the crag.

1 The Monkey Tribe ★★   8m E3 5c
FA Paul Tattersall & Angela Katzenmeier 17 April 1999
The ragged central crack.

2 Soul Brothers ★   8m E5 6a
FA Paul Tattersall & Angela Katzenmeier 8 July 1999
Thin crack between 1 and 3 using holds on the wall. Very bouldery with gear hard to place.

3 Kneel and Pray ★   8m E1 5b
FA Steve & Jinky Heap O'Neill 1991
Wide banana-shaped offwidth – not as bad as it looks.

4 Bodhisattva ★★   8m E5 6b
FA Paul Tattersall 4 May 1999
Gnarly wall right of the wide crack. Start up the right arête to gain the break. Make hard moves up the wall to finish up a short crack.

5 Habit Forming ★   8m E2 5b
FA Colin Meek & Dave Neville 24 April 1999
Up the right side of the arête to a tiny roof. Place gear in 6 then make a long reach up and left to holds on the arête.

6 Claustrophobia ★   8m VS 4c
FA Colin Meek & Dave Neville 24 April 1999
Negotiate the first chokestone in the wide slot up the right side of the block then climb the widening slot in the left wall past a helpful chokestone.

7 Devil Music ★   15m E2 5b
FA Paul Tattersall & Angela Katzenmeier 4 May 1999
Monkey left through the roof and up a flake-crack.

8 Coughed up from Hell *   15m E5 6b
FA Paul Tattersall 8 May 1999

Place nuts in 9 to protect hard moves to gain the obvious hold in the middle of the wall. Long reaches lead to the horizontal break then slightly left to finish.

9 Genesis *   15m E3 5c
FA Colin Meek, Angela Katzenmeier & Paul Tattersall 5 May 1999

Twin cracks to finish up a slightly dirty easy-angled groove.

10 Rebirth *   15m E2 5b
FA Paul Tattersall & Angela Katzenmeier 5 May 1999

Drooping flake.

11 Officer Jesus **   15m E6 6b
FA Paul Tattersall 5 May 1999

Diagonal fault containing a large quartz patch low down.

12 Thelonius **   15m E5 6a
FA Paul Tattersall & Angela Katzenmeier 30 April 1999

Start 6m right of 11. Gain the vertical crack from the right, finishing by the leftmost crack.

13 Walking on Water **   12m E3 5c
FA Colin Meek, Angela Katzenmeier & Paul Tattersall 30 April 1999

Large left-facing flake-crack.

14 Spioradail **   10m E4 6a
FA Paul Tattersall & Colin Meek 28 March 2000

Climb up and rightwards to a handrail then back leftwards into the crack.

15 The Road to Calvary *   12m E2 5b
FA Fraser Fotheringham & Dave Neville 1991

The deep curving ragged crack just left of the end of the drystane wall.

16 Three Kings *   10m E5 6a
FA Colin Meek & Paul Tattersall 28 March 2000

Direct line through the obvious triangular niche.

17 Trumpet Brains *   10m E5 6a
FA Paul Tattersall & Colin Meek 28 March 2000

Hard blind climbing. Start at the shot hole. Climb the wall, keeping right at the top, past a hidden horizontal jug.

18 Fatmouth *   10m E5 6a
FA Paul Tattersall & Angela Katzenmeier 5 October 1998

Line through slots, finishing up a short crack.

19 Kind of Gentle *   8m E3 5c
FA Paul Tattersall & Angela Katzenmeier 5 October 1998

Thin crack up the wall finishing through a slot at the top.

Photo Jim Buchanan, Wild West Topos

Karin Magog on the spectacular arête of The Gift, The Leaning Block, Rubha Coigeach, Reiff, with Suilven in the background.

COIGACH & ASSYNT

ULLAPOOL

Accommodation: Campsite: Broomfield Holiday Park (Apr – Sept; ☎ 01854 612020; www.broomfieldhp.com) at the west end of town, directly behind harbour and well within staggering distance of lots of pubs. A good selection of hotels and B&Bs. **TIC:** Argyle Street (☎ 01854 612486; www.visitscotland.com). See also www.ullapool.com.
Youth Hostel: Shore Street (Apr-Oct; ☎ 01854 612254; www.hostellingscotland.org.uk).
Bunkhouses: Forest Way, Lael (01854 655330; www.forestway.co.uk); Ceilidh Place (☎ 01854 612103; www.theceilidhplace.com).
Amenities: Well stocked Tesco supermarket at north-west end of town. Numerous eating/drinking establishments. By far the best is the Ceilidh Place (☎ 01854 612103; www.theceilidhplace.com), West Argyle Street, parallel to the shore up behind the campsite which is a café/restaurant/art gallery/bar/bookshop/hotel/bunkhouse combined. Climbing shop and café, Northwest Outdoors (☎ 01854 613383; www.northwestoutdoors.co.uk) just along the road. Fish & chip shop opposite the pier. Loch Broom Leisure Centre (☎ 01854 612884; www.highlifehighland.com) in town has swimming pool and a climbing wall. **ATMs:** Bank of Scotland, Argyle Street and at Tesco. Live music at the Seaforth most evenings in the summer.

COIGACH (PLACE OF THE FIFTHS)

This is the district between Outer Loch Broom and the adjoining Assynt to the north, lying to the west of the A835 Ullapool to Ledmore road. The road also runs along the major fault line of the Moine Thrust. The rocks are composed almost entirely of Torridonian sandstone, standing on a base of Lewisian gneiss, which outcrops on the low coastal fringe in the north-west of the district around Enard Bay. With its distinctive landscape of knobbly ridges and primeval-looking crags rising from the relatively featureless landscape, the sandstone buttresses of Sgurr an Fhidleir and Stac Pollaidh give excellent climbing with some superb vistas. Further west on the coast, the short though very extensive sea cliffs on the Rubha Mor peninsula at Reiff have proved one of the most popular venues in recent years. The range of crags and settings, together with some beautiful beaches and campsites make this area a favourite with many.

Accommodation: Campsites: Ardmair Point (Apr – Oct; ☎ 01854 612054; www.ardmair.com). Port a Bhaigh campsite, below Am Fuaran Bar, Altandhu (☎ 01854 622339; www.portabhaigh.co.uk). Also showers available in Coigach Community Hall, 0.3 miles beyond Summer Isles Hotel in Achiltibuie. For the impecunious, wild camping out on the point on the Rubha Mor peninsula is a possibility, with several enchanting bays and plenty of driftwood around. Roadside camping is not allowed, though a chat with the locals may suggest other possible sites. **Hostel:** Finely situated small hostel at Acheninver (Mar – Nov; ☎ 01854 622283; www.acheninverhostel.com), 2 miles beyond Summer Isles Hotel, 400m walk from road. Numerous chalets and holiday cottages to let – contact Ullapool **TIC** (☎ 01854 612486) for brochure.

Amenities: Village stores in Achiltibuie. Am Fuaran Bar in Altandhu (☎ 01854 622339; www.amfuaran.co.uk) and bar in Summer Isles Hotel (☎ 01854 622282; www.summerisleshotel.com).

ASSYNT (ROCKY PLACE)

Sharing the same geology as the adjoining Coigach in its northern half, the southern end also has numerous outcrops of Lewisian gneiss, undoubtedly harbouring some good cragging. Rearing up from the flat peaty bogs are to be found some of the most spectacular mountains in Scotland, standing in splendid isolation. Although some of the higher mountains such as Quinag and Canisp have prominent quartzite caps, to date there has been no significant quality rock climbing in the mountains, with all the quality climbing thus far on the coast. Assynt is particularly renowned as the setting for much of Norman MacCaig's wonderful poetry. In 1993 the Assynt Crofters' Trust made history with the first ever community buy-out of an estate in Scotland.

Accommodation: Campsites: Achmelvich (May – Oct; ☎ 01571 844393) and Clachtoll (Apr–Sept; ☎ 01571 855377; www.clachtollbeachcampsite.co.uk). Wild camping on the moor around the road end at the Point of Stoer, though no running water. **Youth Hostel:** Achmelvich (Apr–Sept; ☎ 01571 844480 ; www.hostellingscotland.org.uk). **Bunkhouses:** Inchnadamph Lodge (☎ 01571 822218; www.inchnadamph.co.uk) on other side of river opposite Inchnadamph Hotel; An Cala Café & Bunkhouse, Lochinver (☎ 01571 844598; www.ancalacafeandbunkhouse.co.uk). **Club Hut:** Naismith Hut at Elphin (SMC). Innumerable B&Bs throughout the area – more information at the Assynt Visitor Centre, Lochinver (www.discoverassynt.co.uk).

Amenities: Lochinver is the main town, with a small supermarket, petrol station and a couple of bars and cafés. There is also an **ATM**, the last between Ullapool and Durness. Down by the new pier there is also an excellent leisure centre with shower facilities (☎ 01571 844123 ; www.assyntleisure.co.uk). The pie shop, Lochinver Larder (☎ 01571 844356; www.piesbypost.co.uk) comes highly recommended but not for coffee. For rest/rainy days there is also a good bookshop/café, Achins Bookshop (☎ 01571 844262) at Inverkirkaig 4.5 miles/7.2km south of Lochinver.

ARDMAIR CRAGS NH 118 987 10–20min

A series of steep impressive Torridonian sandstone buttresses line the north side of a narrow stream-filled valley that runs at right angles to the road, about 0.4 miles/0.7km east of the campsite at Ardmair Point. With the possible exception of the sea cliffs on Skye they provide some of the best crack climbing in the country and a great place to brush up on your jamming techniques. Take plenty of cams and some tape!

Note: Although there are a number of routes of less than VS, they are generally shorter and the crag really comes into its own from HVS upwards. Most of the routes dry quickly, with the exception of a few drainage lines – with *Moondance*, *Burning Desire* and *Dangerous Dancer* being the last to dry out.

Access: Follow the A835 north out of Ullapool for 3.6 miles/5.5km to a parking spot at the west side of the road by the track leading down to the fish farm.

Approach: Cross the road and walk east 50m then cross fence to follow a well-worn path up the left (north) bank of the burn, which soon cuts up the hillside, running directly underneath most of the buttresses.

LAGGAVOULIN BUTTRESS  10min

The small bulging buttress just above the path, just down and left of the prominent **Monster Buttress**.

1 *Bowmore*, Very Difficult takes cracks up the left side of the slabby wall; 2 *Clyneleish*, Severe 4a takes cracks and heathery breaks near the right side.

3 Laggavoulin * — 10m VS 4c
FA Keith Geddes & Allen Fyffe 1991

Cracks just left of the nose, veering rightwards to finish.

4 Little Red Rooster * — 10m HVS 5a
FA Keith Geddes & Allen Fyffe 1991

Good climbing, starting up the short capped groove then heading right up brown rock.

MONSTER BUTTRESS — 10min
The highest buttress, well seen in profile from the road.

1 The Raven * — 30m Severe 4a
FA Andy Cunningham & George Reid August 1992

The huge left-slanting fault at the left side of the bay. Sometimes occupied by 'a big black bird'.

2 La Petamine ** — 30m HVS 5a
FA Andy Cunningham & Keith Geddes 16 June 1996

The leftmost of the three ramp-lines. Start up 1 to the big bay then climb out rightwards onto the line. Move awkwardly round the big block and finish up the top corner in a gripping position.

3a Ogre *** — 30m E4 6a
FA Andy Cunningham 2007

A superb long route, nicely exposed in its upper reaches. Start a few metres left of 3. Climb up, then left into a scoop which leads to a good ledge. Move up until able to pull left onto a steep pillar, which is followed via cracks and bulges to the top.

3 Shaker Loops * — 30m E1 5b
FA Tom Prentice, Rab Anderson & Chris Greaves 17 June 1989

Further right is a steep crack in the green wall. Ascend the crack to a horizontal break then move left into a short corner and follow this, then the snaking crack above with a difficult move to gain a belay on the rightmost ramp. Scramble over heather terraces to finish.

4 Gravity's Rainbow *** — 25m E1 5b
FA Allen Fyffe & Andy Cunningham July 1989

Good exposed climbing up the right side of the narrow green pillar. Ascend the right-facing corner then climb left under the roof. Climb thin cracks then move right to a ramp. Above, move left to finish up a crack on the crest of the pillar.

5 Big Foot ★★ 20m E4 6a
FA Andy Cunningham & Allen Fyffe July 1989

Steep with a sting in the tail. Follow the crack leading directly to the 'big foot'. Finish up the right-slanting corner above.

6 Summer Isles City ★★ 20m E1 5b
FA Ian Taylor & David Meldrum 2 April 1988

The crack in the right wall of the open corner. Start up shallow cracks, climb up and left onto a glacis then right into a corner. Climb the crack in the right wall.

DANCING BUTTRESS   10min

The buttress immediately right of **Monster Buttress**, forming the right side of a heathery amphitheatre, split by a large flat ledge, 'the **Dance Floor**' at three-quarters height.

Descent: From the **Dance Floor**, walk (or crawl!) rightwards and continue along the grassy gangway to cut back to the base. From the top, scramble down the next break right or continue further to easy ground just before **Big Roof Buttress**.

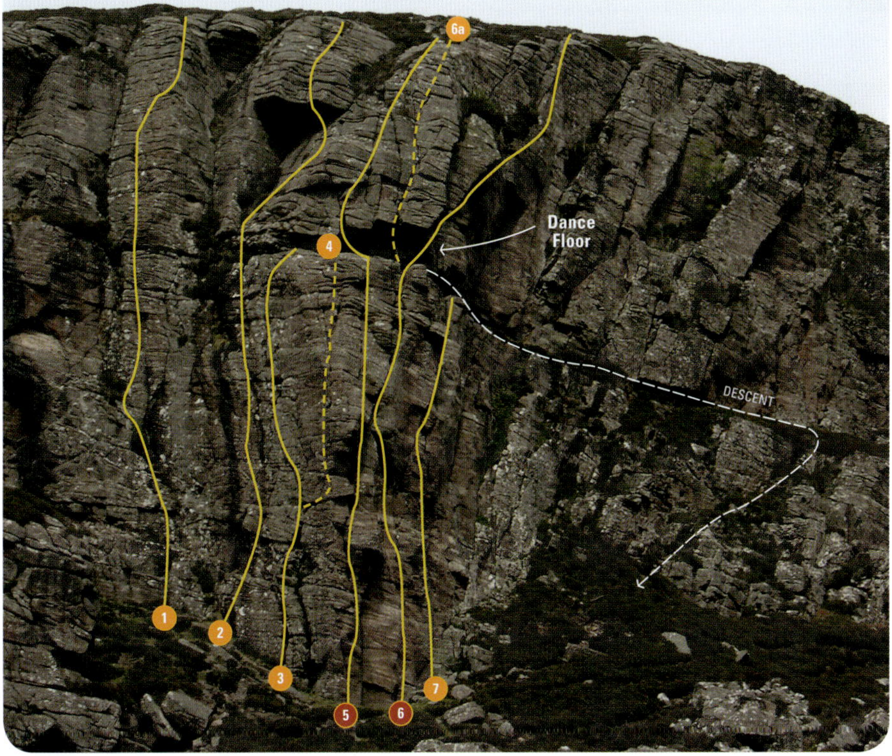

1 Spider Jive ★ 30m HVS 5a
FA Allen Fyffe & Andy Cunningham 9 June 1989

The top left side of the buttress has a prominent blunt rib with a vague crack up its left side. Start up easy rocks at the top right side of the amphitheatre. Climb the dirty corner past a holly and a thread runner to gain a large grass ledge. From the right end of the ledge move up slightly rightwards and up the fine crack and arête above.

2 Carved from Stone * — 35m HVS 5a
FA Richard Mansefield & Libby Healey 20 May 1989

Start 6m up left from the edge of the buttress, below twin cracks just right of a dark brown streak. Move up to a ledge then through a cracked bulge. Follow the leftmost crack, keeping left of a sapling to gain an easy slab. Walk up the slab to the obvious scooped roof and finish athletically through this on big holds.

3 Moondance ** — 20m VS 4c
FA Richard Mansefield & Allen Fyffe 26 May 1989

The deep 'dog-leg' crack in the centre of the wall. Start 2m up left from the right edge. Climb the wide fault and the crack above to its end. Continue up a further thin crack to the Dance Floor.

4 Sculptress *** — 20m HVS 5a
FA Libby Healey & Richard Mansefield 20 May 1989

Fine exposed climbing up the cracks on the right side of the wall. Start up the fault as for 3. Climb the fault, step right and follow the cracks just left of the nose to arrive on the Dance Floor.

5 Totem Pole Crack * — 30m E2 5c
FA Alex Taylor & Fraser Fotheringham Summer 1986

The original route on the crags, now considerably harder since the demise of the Totem Pole! Start on the left edge of the nose.

1. **20m 5c** Move up and step right into the large corner on the front face. Go up this to a ledge then the left crack to gain the Dance Floor.
2. **10m 4c** Cross the block overhang on its left then continue more easily rightwards up slabby cracks to finish.

6 Primitive Dance ** — 30m E2 5c
FA Allen Fyffe & Jas Hepburn 19 May 1989

Good varied climbing. Start at a shallow groove on the front face just right of the arête.

1. **20m 5c** Climb the groove then move up left and up the fault to gain a prominent right-slanting crack. Climb this steeply to belay on the Dance Floor.
2. **10m 5c** Move right to an open corner with an undercut start. Pull over bulges and a small roof with difficulty then up the corner-crack until it fades. Step right to a sloping ledge and finish more easily.

2a. **10m 5a** A cleaner finish climbs the slot through roof and up cracks directly above the belay.

7 Just Add Lib ** — 20m HVS 5a
FA Libby Healey & Richard Mansefield 19 May 1989

The prominent flakes and ramp starting 6m right of the nose. Move up steepening cracks to pull onto a perched block. Trend right up sloping ramps to finish up the prominent V-groove.

BEAST BUTTRESS   15min

Separated from a broken overhanging reddish wall (not described) by a steep tree-filled fault. A compact buttress with a slabbier left wall and an overhanging front face with a prominent left-slanting crack.

"Several impressive, unclimbed cracks exist on the next buttress along to the right." – Ian Taylor, *Scottish Mountaineering Club Journal*, 1989

Descent: Easily down to the right.

COIGACH & ASSYNT ARDMAIR CRAGS | 217

Andy 'Panama' Wren jamming his way up Unleash the Beast.

3 Neart Nan Gaidheal ★★★   20m E5 6a
FA Andy Cunningham August 1989

'Power of the Gael'. The innocuous looking leftmost of the two prominent left-slanting cracks. Start up a short overhanging niche then follow the crack, strenuous and sustained, to finish at the same point as 2.

4 Beastmaster ★   25m E5 6a
FA Martin Burrows-Smith (redpointed) September 1992

Climb the thin crack right of 3 to reach 5. Swing out right and go up the flaky wall to the large break. Move right round a block to finish easily up the crack. Harder than first appearances would suggest.

5 Unleash the Beast ★★★   25m E4 6a
FA Richard Mansfield & Libby Healey 19 May 1989

Sustained well protected climbing up the more pronounced right crack. Bridge up between the pillar and the wall until a hold on the wall allows the crack to be gained. Follow the crack to a large ledge at the top. Either walk off right, or finish up the easier continuation crack.

1 Market Day ★   25m E1 5b
FA Ian Taylor & Steven Ryan 12 April 1988

The scooped corner on the left side of the slabbier left wall. Ascend the corner, passing a small roof to finish by two short walls.

> The corners up left are *Beast in the Undergrowth* Severe 4a.

2 On the Western Skyline ★★   20m E4 6a
FA Andy Cunningham & Allen Fyffe September 1989

Fine sustained climbing up the blunt left arête. Start on the wall on the left. Go up a short awkward corner onto the edge which leads to a ledge. Move right along the ledge to a flake which leads to an in situ thread runner. Move up and left then back right to finish up the final crack of 3.

2a Direct Start ★   6m E5 6b
FA Dave Cuthbertson & Brian Hall May 1994

The thin diagonal crack in the lower wall, protected at half-height by a F #0 inverted in a little niche.

EDINBURGH ROCK   15min

The small buttress up right from **Beast Buttress**, with a large deep groove system up the left side.

1 Small is Possible ★   12m Very Difficult
FA Libby Healey & Jeni Pickering 17 June 1989

The prominent ramps on the left. Move up diagonally right to a ledge then the left-slanting ramp, finishing steeply up a hand-crack.

AIRS ROCK 15min

The next small buttress just beyond **Edinburgh Rock**.

The prominent corner, wall and slab on the left is 1 *Small is Beautiful* ★ HS 4b.

2 Microlight ★★ 16m HS 4b

FA Allen Fyffe & Richard Mansefield 27 May 1989

The fine jamming cracks on the left wall, separated by a heather ledge.

3 The Parapente ★ 20m E1 5b

FA Andy Cunningham & Allen Fyffe 10 June 1989

Ascend the thin flake-crack just left of the edge of the buttress to gain a large ledge. Move right and follow the obvious corner. A harder *Direct Start* (5c) may be made by starting 2m right of the left arête. Climb the inset recess which leads to a right-slanting crack.

4 The Way It Is ★ 15m Difficult

FA Jeni Pickering & Libby Healey 17 June 1989

The right-slanting ramp on the right side of the buttress past a small tree.

The vague edge to the right is *Underpants Arête*, VS 4b

BIG ROOF BUTTRESS
   20min

The best and most extensive crag, typically also the furthest from the road. The main wall contains a very distinctive and impressive beak roof, one of the finest features on any crag in the area.

SIDE WALL

The left side of the crag slanting uphill.

1 Grumpy Groper ★ 45m E1 5b

FA Rab Anderson & Chris Greaves 4 June 1989

The wall and slab just left of the right edge. Follow a vague groove then over a bulge.

2 First Fruits ★ 40m HVS 5b

FA Chris Greaves & Rab Anderson 3 June 1989

The first line in the slab right of the blunt arête. Start on a boulder right of a small corner. Step off the boulder and climb to a crack higher up. Climb this on the right then slabby ground, finishing by heathery scrambling.

Karen Latter on the fine layback crack of Terrace Crack

3 Close to the Bone *   25m HVS 5a
FA Andy Cunningham & Jeni Pickering 1 December 1994

Climb a right-facing groove and short corner onto the slab. Move up and finish via a crack in the wall on the left.

4 Old Dog, New Tricks *   20m E2 5c
FA Allen Fyffe & Jas Hepburn 15 June 1995

Balancy climbing up the blunt arête right of 5. Climb that route to where it goes left round the edge and continue up the edge just right of the arête all the way.

5 Bolshie Ballerina *   20m E2 5c
FA Rab Anderson & Chris Greaves 27 May 1989

The rightmost crack in the wall above the roof of 6. Ascend easier rock and a short corner-crack above the tree then traverse left to follow the crack.

6 Convoluted Contortionist **   20m E3 6b
FA Rab Anderson & Chris Greaves 28 May 1989

The prominent wide crack through the roof near the right side of the wall. Finish up the crack above.

7 Muscle Hustle *   20m E4 6b
FA Rab Anderson & Tom Prentice 17 June 1989

Follow 8 to below the roof. Hand traverse back right to below the edge of the block and surmount the roof using the crack on the right (crux). Continue to a standing position on a small pillar on the headwall, finish by pulling up left.

8 Twitching Twister **   20m E3 6a
FA Rab Anderson & Tom Prentice 17 June 1989

Follow a thin crack to the right of a large block to beneath the roof. Step left and up to the break, cross the roof and finish up the groove above.

9 Acrimonious Acrobat ***   20m E1 5a
FA Rab Anderson & Chris Greaves 27 May 1989

Excellent sustained climbing taking the steep crack and groove. Follow the corner to the roof, moving left to finish up the main crack.

10 A Spot of Deception *   10m E1 5c
FA Ado Liddell & Allen Fyffe 20 May 1989

The crack and short corner just right of 11. Climb the crack to its top. Move right to finish up the short corner and crack above.

11 A Bit on the Side *   10m HVS 5a
FA Allen Fyffe & Andy Cunningham 9 June 1989

Just above some large boulders at the top left end is a crack in shallow left-facing corners. Climb the crack through a bulge to finish up the wider crack above.

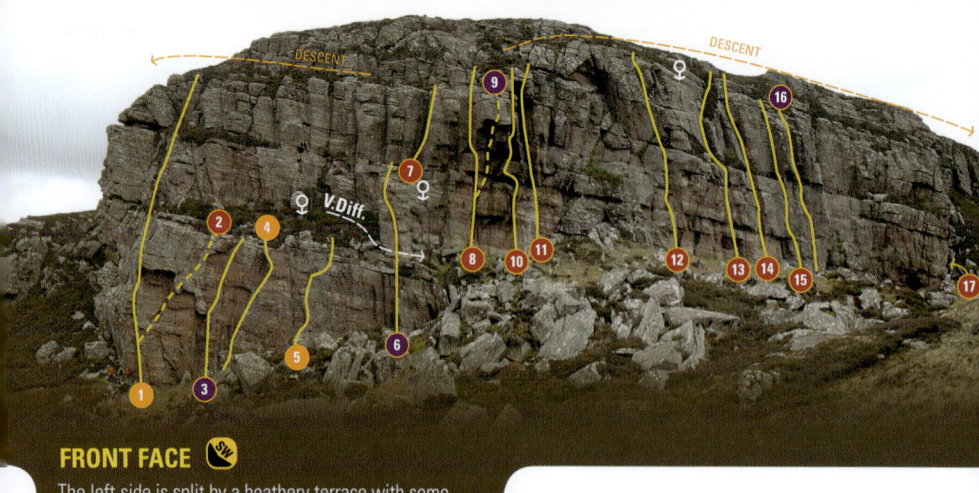

FRONT FACE

The left side is split by a heathery terrace with some small trees and a detached tower at its right end.
Descent: From the terrace: either abseil from the block at right end, or scramble down from the right end, traversing rightwards (about V. Diff.) beneath the tower.
From the top: down either side of the crag, with *Burning Desire* being roughly in the centre, or abseil from sling at top of 13.

1 The Friendly Groove ** 40m HVS 5b
FA Allen Fyffe & Ado Liddell 20 May 1989

Hello there big boy! (No, not that friendly!) Good well protected climbing up the prominent groove in the left edge. Follow the groove and continuation cracks to a horizontal break. Cross the roof at the crack and continue up leftwards.

2 Sunstroke * 20m E1 5b
FA Allen Fyffe & Martin Burrows-Smith August 1989

A diagonal line right of 1. Climb that route for a short way, until moves right lead onto the wall. Climb up to beneath a big roof, move right onto the ramp and finish up this.

3 How Soon Is Now ** 18m E7 6c
FA Tim Rankin (redpointed) May 2006

The fine fading diagonal crack-line up the wall left of 4.

Start up the left-facing corner on the left to gain the crack, follow it (easy at first) to a break. Then move up using a hollow flake and side pulls to a thin break and crucial protection (F #00 very hard to place and two RP #1s). Hard sustained moves lead slightly right up the immaculate orange wall to the top. Belay up and left from the big boulder.

4 Siesta * 15m VS 4c
FA Allen Fyffe & Andy Cunningham 17 June 1989

The prominent ramp in the centre of the brown wall, finishing more steeply onto the terrace.

5 Terrace Crack * 12m VS 4c
FA Allen Fyffe & Richard Mansefield 27 May 1989

Near the right end. Follow the fine right-slanting flake-crack, moving right to finish on the terrace.

6 From Riches to Rags * 15m E4 6a
FA Andy Cunningham & Allen Fyffe 10 June 1989

Sustained and strenuous. Climb the left-facing corner to the break then make some difficult moves up the thin crack in the tower. Finish up a ramp.

7 Relax and Swing * 10m E2 5c
FA Andy Cunningham & Richard Mansefield 3 June 1989

Start at the right end of the terrace above the Tower.

Layback the short slanting corner precariously to finish more easily.

8 Skeletons ★★★ 25m E2 5c
FA Ado Liddell & Allen Fyffe 20 May 1989

The prominent square-cut corner high on the crag just left of the big beak roof. Climb the crack and corners leading directly to the main corner, with hard moves to gain the top of the block. Finish up the superb corner.

9 Burning Desire ★★★★ 25m E5 6b
FA Richard Mansfield & Andy Cunningham 3 June 1989

Stunning climbing through the wildly exposed crack in the huge beak roof that is the crag's finest feature. Start at a crack below and left of the roof, as for 8. Follow the cracks heading right to a ledge beneath an overhanging crack. Climb this with difficulty (crux) to a horizontal rest under the roof. Spectacularly breach the roof crack on an assortment of jams and undercuts to a good jug on the lip. Pull over to finish easily.

10 Space Monkey ★★★ 20m E2 5c
FA Richard Mansfield & Allen Fyffe 27 May 1989

Fine thrutchy climbing up the deep-set groove on the immediate right side of the beak roof. Climb the wide groove just right of the lower roofs then move left into a crack. Follow this past a short diagonal crack to negotiate the groove with interest.

11 Tunnel Vision ★★ 25m E1 5b
FA Chris Greaves & Rab Anderson 4 June 1989

The large V-groove right of the big beak roof. Ascend a thin crack just right of a wide crack to the groove, which leads to a finish through the obvious slot. Salad dodgers can avoid the final slot by traversing out left.

12 Town Without Pity ★★★ 25m E2 5c
FA Jas Hepburn & Allen Fyffe 19 May 1989

The groove and crack in the nose 15m right of the big beak roof. Follow the groove and crack past a tricky bulge to prominent twin cracks at mid-height. Continue mainly by the left crack, finishing up the left-slanting crack.

13 Still Waters ★ 25m E1 5c
FA Allen Fyffe & Andy Cunningham 17 June 1989

Climb the crack in the overhung bay to gain a ledge then by a corner-crack and the crack on its left to a vegetated ledge. Move left and climb a narrow chimney just right of a rowan to finish up a heather ramp.

14 Buried Treasure ★★ 25m E1 5b
FA Allen Fyffe & Richard Mansfield 27 May 1989

The fine left-facing groove running the full height of the crag. Gain the groove via a short wall and climb it past a small heather patch and holly at half-height.

15 Dangerous Dancer ★★★ 25m E3 5c
FA Rab Anderson & Chris Greaves 27 May 1989

The prominent corner in the upper crag. Move up to a large handhold, then step right into the crack which leads to the fine upper corner.

16 Exasperated Escapologist Direct ★★★ 25m E4 6a
FA Rab Anderson & Chris Greaves 28 May 1989; Direct Lawrence Hughes & Andy Cunningham 4 May 1999

Splendid climbing up the thin leaning crack and its wider continuation.

17 Friends Retrieval ★★ 20m E1 5b
FA Alex Taylor & Fraser Fotheringham Summer 1986

The right-facing corner at the right end of the crag. Climb the corner, heading slightly left then a flake-crack and grooves to finish by a jutting nose.

Paul 'Stork' Thorburn on the fine upper corner of Skeletons. Photo Ian Taylor.

SGURR AN FHIDLEIR (PEAK OF THE FIDDLER)

NC 096 057 **Alt:** 500m

Alan Warner enjoying Direct Nose Route, with Stac Pollaidh in the background.

A superbly situated peak with a classic long route and a fine vista north-west over the hills of Coigach and Assynt.

Access: Turn off the A835 at Drumrunie, (10 miles/16km north of Ullapool) and head west down the single track road towards Achiltibuie for 2.2 miles/3.3km to park near the south-east end of Loch Lurgainn.

Approach: Go through the gate in the deer fence, cross the stream flowing into the south-east end of the loch and follow a path up the east bank of the burn (Allt Claonaidh) west to its source, then skirt round the south end of Lochan Tuath, towards the base of the cliff.

Descent: Down a well worn path in the large open scree gully at the left end of the cliff.

1 Direct Nose Route ★★★   260m HVS 5a
FA Neville Drasdo & Mike Dixon May 1962

A well trodden classic, closely following the edge of the two facets. The vegetated lower section gives way to much better climbing in the upper reaches. Start at the toe of the buttress.

1-3 130m 4b Follow a largely vegetated stepped groove system (more defined in its upper section) leading to a cul-de-sac with a good belay under a large roof. Alternatively, climb cleaner rock on either side to the same point. Much variation is possible in the lower section.

4 15m 4a Traverse left along the narrow turf ledge around a rib to a larger ledge. You have now reached good continuous rock.

5 35m 5a Gain the long wide corner above with difficulty from the right, and climb it and its right wall to a spacious ledge and boulder belay on the very crest.

5a 35m E1 5b A fine pitch. Climb the blunt rib on the crest, moving right beneath an overhang on the edge. Climb up a short way to nut belay.

6 25m 4c Climb a short groove left of the crest (or better – the crack in its right wall), to a narrow grass ledge. Move right, pull up onto a slab and climb the left edge of this to belay at some pegs.

7 40m 5a Continue more easily up cracks on the left to a tiny stance (possible belay) on the crest. Steeper climbing in a fantastic position now leads to a thin crack which provides the crux.

8 15m 4b A short corner leads to easy ground. Scramble up (45m) to a large grassy shoulder. Good well-worn paths lead up slightly leftwards (about 100m) to the summit, past a couple of straightforward rock steps near the top.

STAC POLLAIDH
(STACK OF THE BOG/POOLS)
50min – 1hr

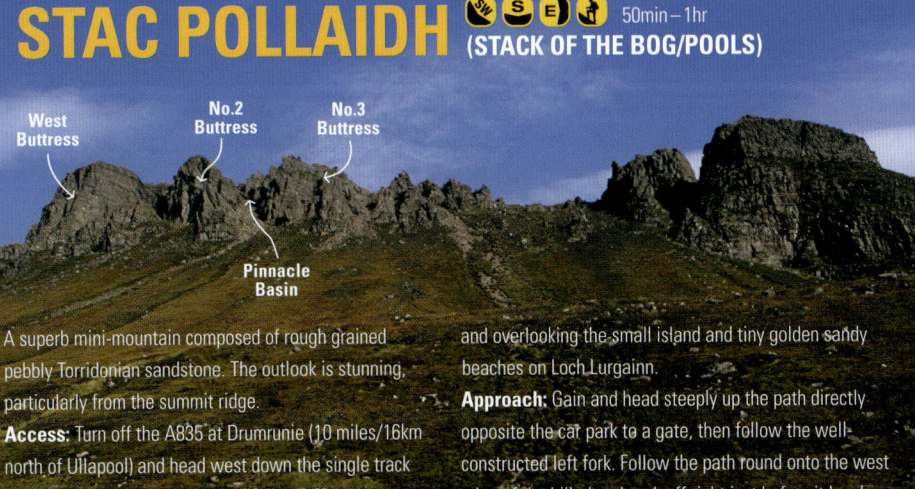

West Buttress | No.2 Buttress | No.3 Buttress
Pinnacle Basin

A superb mini-mountain composed of rough grained pebbly Torridonian sandstone. The outlook is stunning, particularly from the summit ridge.

Access: Turn off the A835 at Drumrunie (10 miles/16km north of Ullapool) and head west down the single track road towards Achiltibuie for 4.25 miles/6.8km to a car park on the left, directly under the very distinctive hill and overlooking the small island and tiny golden sandy beaches on Loch Lurgainn.

Approach: Gain and head steeply up the path directly opposite the car park to a gate, then follow the well-constructed left fork. Follow the path round onto the west edge of the hill, then break off right just before it levels out to traverse rightwards underneath **West Buttress**.

WEST BUTTRESS

NC 107 106 **Alt:** 520m 1hr

The 90m high south (front) face is distinguished near its right edge by two prominent corners and their corresponding arêtes. Round to the right lies an impressive steep smooth clean wall overlooking a wide open scree-filled gully. This is home to a superb range of high standard one and two pitch routes.

Descent: From the summit head east along the ridge and scramble down a short rock step to a col then down an easy slabby shelf and the large scree slope beneath the steep **South-East Face**. There is also a good abseil station in situ above *Expecting to Fly*, gaining the base of *Mid Flight Crisis* in a 50m abseil.

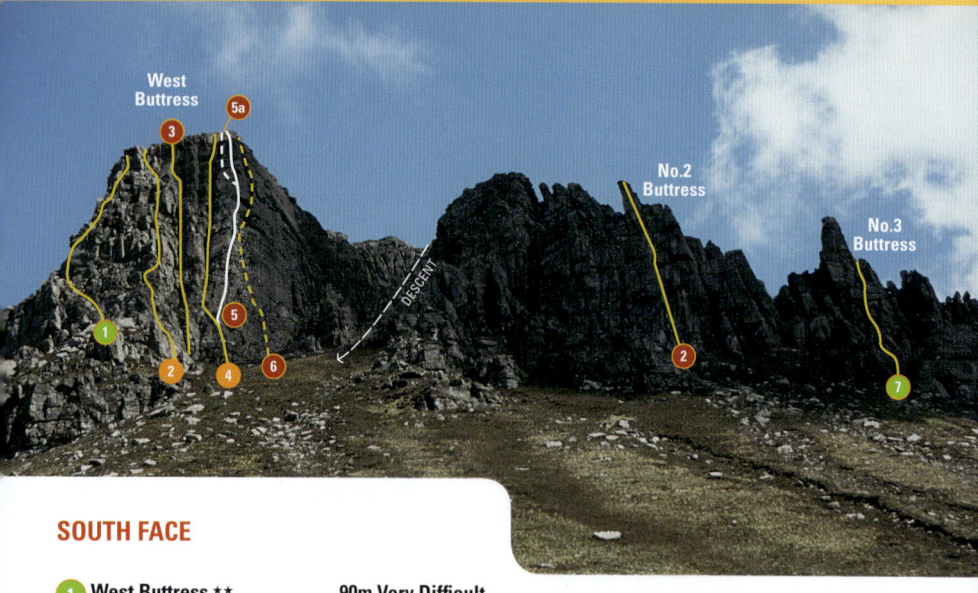

SOUTH FACE

1 West Buttress ★★ 90m Very Difficult
FA Dr William, Mrs Jane & Miss Inglis Clark & Charles Walker 1906

The original route on the mountain and one of the few good easier lines. Start beneath a left-slanting gangway originating 15m right of the prominent large squat pinnacle.
- **1** 30m Climb the easy gangway to a large grass terrace at one-third height.
- **2+3** 60m Continue up the groove directly behind the pinnacle.

2 Party on the Patio ★ 90m VS 5a
FA Andrew Fraser & Ian Dickson (1 PA) 14 May 1985;
FFA Gary Latter & Alan Clapperton 16 July 1996

Follows a line of cracks and corners up the well-defined rib overlooking *Enigma Grooves*. Mostly Very Difficult climbing with one hard move, avoidable on the right (HS 4b). Start at a terrace up and left of *Enigma Grooves*.
- **1** 30m Climb the rib overlooking *Enigma Grooves* for 15m then move up and left to belay beneath a steep corner.
- **2** 10m Traverse right on a ledge and round the corner to belay in a hidden chimney.
- **3** 15m Climb the chimney on the left then continue directly, moving back right near the top to belay on large terrace.
- **4** 15m 5a Immediately right is a steep corner with a crack on its left wall. Climb the corner with a short tricky move over the bulge at the top.
- **5** 20m Move left and climb the chimney with a through route.

2a Party Direct ★ 15m VS 5a
FA Andy Cunningham & party September 1996
- **2** 15m Climb the chokestone chimney above the belay on pitch 1 to belay at the top of pitch 3.

3 Enigma Grooves ★ 70m E1 5b
FA Tom Patey & Dick Barclay (finished up corner on right) August 1965; Direct Finish John Mackenzie & P.Goodwin 18 August 1979

The leftmost of the twin dièdres. Quite vegetated, but worth doing when dry. Start directly beneath the line.
- **1** 25m – Ascend an easy wall left of the wide crack to belay beneath the main corner.
- **2** 25m 5a Climb the crack above (poorly protected and often wet), continuing up the wide chimney to a terrace.
- **3** 20m 5b Continue to a ledge on the left, then the strenuous chimney past a chokestone to finish up the crack.

4 November Groove ★★   100m VS 4c
FA Dan Stewart & G. Cairns 8 November 1953

A fine traditional VS giving a good muscular outing, the best of its grade on the mountain.

1. **35m 4b** Climb wall and bulge up to a fine curving layback crack. Continue up the juggy wall above a short 'pinnacle', then either of two cracks to ledge at foot of the main groove.
2. **25m 4c** Avoid any grass on the right and climb a recessed chimney to the right side of the overhang. Climb this strenuously on good holds to a good stance.
3. **20m 4c** Climb the chimney and the tricky entrance to the groove above, followed by a chokestone groove to a good stance.
4. **20m 4c** Continue up the groove to level with the large ledge below the *Direct Finish* and directly below a wide crack. Move right by a bulge to below another crack and climb this to thread belays. Scramble to finish.

5 Jack the Ripper ★★★   70m E1 5b
FA M.Anderson & G.Mair 26 August 1964; Top pitch John Mackenzie, Graham Cullen & Mark Selwood 14 July 1990

Good climbing with an excellent well positioned top pitch. Start as for *November Groove*.

1. **24m 4b** Climb a wall and bulge, then a fine layback crack to a ledge. Step right and belay behind a detached pinnacle.
2. **21m 5a** Traverse left and climb cracks in the slabby rib until a difficult step up is made on the arête. Blocks and cracks lead to a belay.
3. **25m 5b** Climb the right-slanting crack just above the belay, then move easily up right into the corner. Continue up this with interest to mantel left onto a good ledge at its top. Finish up the short wide crack above.

5a The Fred West Finish ★★   30m E3 6a
FA Guy Robertson & Tim Rankin August 1998

A fine pitch climbing the obvious crack system in the headwall left of the final groove pitch.

6 Felo de Se ★   75m E2 5c
FA Rab Carrington & John McLean (2 PA) July 1969;
FFA Rab Anderson & Tom Prentice 10 September 1989

A tremendous top pitch up the hanging corner on the prow. Start up and right of *Jack the Ripper*.

1. **45m 5a** Climb broken walls leading to a crack which leads to a large ledge.
2. **30m 5c** Follow the awkward chimney on the right to easier ground beneath a block overhang. Continue up the sustained well protected jam crack in the corner to the top.

SOUTH-EAST FACE

1 Shadow on the Wall/Hank Marvin ★★★   65m E4/5 6a
FA Rab Anderson & Tom Prentice 10 September 1989;
Hank Marvin: Ian Taylor & Tess Fryer 5 September 2014

Great climbing taking the prominent groove and crack up the left side of the wall. Start at the left end of a ledge.

1. **35m 6a** Climb the groove, then difficult moves up the crack (crux, 4" cam protects). Continue up the crack and wide flake-crack, then traverse left along the large horizontal break to good belay.
2. **30m 6a** Hand-traverse back right for 2m. Follow the crack above, through an overhang and continue up thin cracks to the large niche. Go up a groove slightly rightwards until below some vegetation, move left and take flared cracks to the top.

2 The Evolution of Wings ★★   30m E5 6a
FA Ian Taylor & Tess Fryer 27 May 2016

A counter diagonal to the first pitch of *Walking on Air*, starting at a block just to its left. Layback up the crack above to good holds. Make a hard move up and left, then a bold section leads to good holds and gear where *Walking on Air* comes in from the right. Move right and go up to a niche, then over a final bulge to the belay

a thin crack with difficulty to the base of the hanging stepped corner. Up this, moving into a wide crack on the left below the top.

④ Mid Flight Crisis ★★★ 65m E4 6a
FA Rab & Chris Anderson 2 September 1989

A very fine route crossing *Walking on Air* from right to left. The highlight is the well situated wide crack on the prow at the top left of the wall. Start beneath twin cracks right of *Walking on Air*.

1 **25m 6a** Climb the right-hand crack for 4m then left and up the other crack. Move back rightwards then more easily up the crack on the left to belay on ledge just left of the large block. (Fs #3 – #4 required for belay.)

2 **40m 6a** Climb the crack directly above the belay to a small niche. Step left to a large hold then traverse diagonally left on good holds into the corner. Step round the edge and traverse left and up into the deep-cut groove. Easily up this to the wide crack and follow this with interest on good jams to an easing near the top.

⑤ₐ Expecting to Fly Direct ★★★ 48m E5 6a
FA Ian Taylor & Tess Fryer 14 July 2014

Start at a crack just left of a short corner. Climb the crack (Camalot 3 and Friend 4 useful) to a ledge, then make a couple of moves up the right of two cracks, to join the original line at a faded thread.

⑤ Expecting to Fly ★★★★ 40m E4 6a
FA Tom Prentice 30 May 1988

Superb sustained climbing following the crack and grey groove above the roof right of the mossy recess. Start above the short gully above the lower wall at a vertical tongue of heather. Up this and move out left on ledges to follow a crack leading up to underneath the roof. Move up left onto a ledge then gain the groove by a flake leading in from the left. Continue past good sidepulls (F #3) to a short difficult section leading to an easier final crack.

③ Walking on Air ★★★★ 60m E5/6 6b
FA Tom Prentice & Rab Anderson (1 PA) 26 August 1989

Exceptional climbing with a very technical crux, following the crack and corner splitting the main overhang. Start from a block on a ledge beneath twin cracks on a very red section of the wall.

1 **30m 6a** Climb the cracks with difficulty until forced leftwards into a groove/crack then up to just below a horizontal fault. Move right and up a scoop and rib to belay on Fs #3 & #3.5 in a horizontal break.

2 **30m 6b** Step up onto a block on the right. Ascend a crack to a triangular niche then up

6 Fear of Flying ★★★   40m E6 6a
FA Gary Latter & Wilson Moir 22 September 1996

A direct line breaking through the apex of the prominent roof at the right side of the wall. Start at the same point as *Expecting to Fly*, at a vertical tongue of heather. Move up to follow a flake and shallow grooves over a bulge to a small ledge beneath the roof. Follow the tiny groove using a good edge on the lip on the right to reach a good hold, then slightly right to a good flake and reasonable rest (PR at foot level in diagonal break on left). Shuffle left and climb direct above the PR past small side-pulls (RP #3 3m above PR) to good rounded holds. Traverse diagonally left on rounded holds to finish up an easy crack.

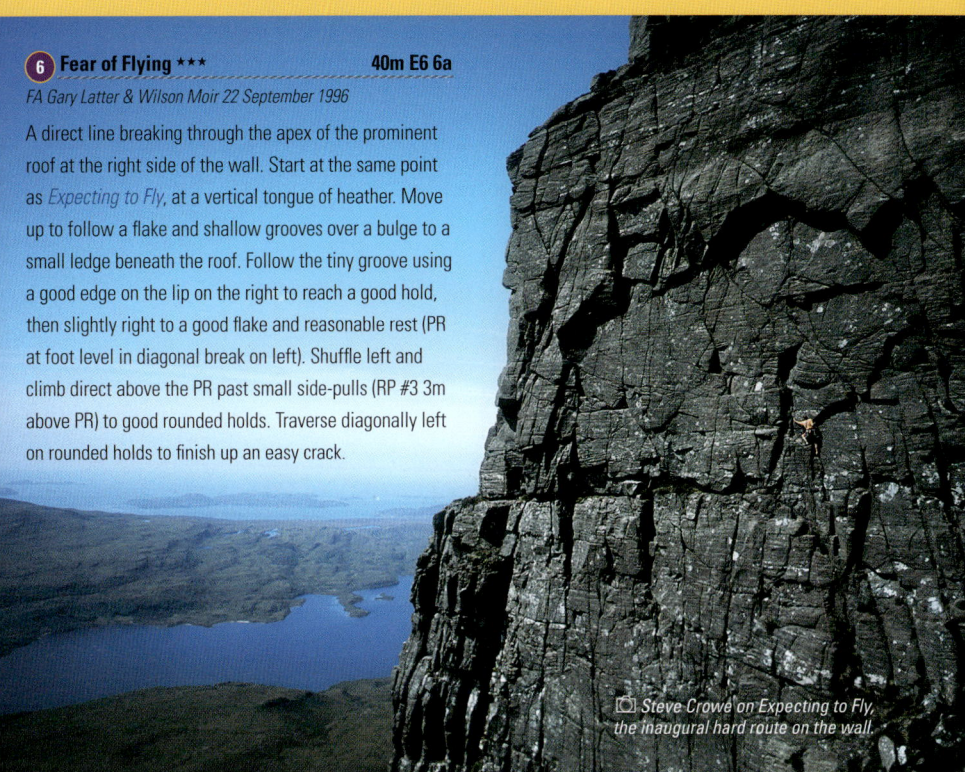

Steve Crowe on Expecting to Fly, the inaugural hard route on the wall.

NC 108 106 **Alt:** 550m   1hr

NO. 2 BUTTRESS

Directly above the path contouring round from the base of **West Buttress**. The front face forms a series of steep crack and groove lines.

1 Release the Bats ★★   115m VS 4b
FA Andrew Fraser & Graham Leslie 5 May 1984

A real magical mystery tour up the full length of the buttress. Start beneath a left-slanting gangway at the left end of the buttress, right of broken rocks.

1. **18m 4b** Climb steep crack for 5m then step left onto gangway, which is followed up left to a ledge. Move right along the ledge to belay in a corner.
2. **12m** Climb the corner to a ledge then up a hidden rightwards sloping chimney to a ledge.
3. **15m 4b** Take the groove above (crux), stepping left where it divides. Step back right round an awkward corner to belay beneath a tower on the arête.
4. **10m** The tower is turned on the left via an easy slab and ledges to belay beneath a second tower.
5. **40m 4b** Climb by a crack on the crest. This leads to the upper, level arête, which after an awkward descent, leads easily to the final headwall. Continue up the crack in the headwall, immediately left of the arête's continuation.
6. **20m 4a** Finish up slabs on the right to belay.

2 Wingless Warlock ★   50m E1 5b
FA Roger Everett & Dai Gaffney 9 September 1989

The prominent groove system. Start 5m left of the right end of a raised terrace.

1. **25m 5b** An awkward steep groove and bulge leads to ledges in the main groove. Move up to the base of a very steep crack then step

right to a crack in the arête. Climb this and the flake-crack continuation, exiting right to a belay.

2 25m 5b Continue up the corner above then by delightful cracks and corners leading to the summit of the pinnacle.

3 The Orifice * 40m E3 6a
FA Adrian Crofton & Guy Robertson August 1999

The offwidth crack round to the left of *Vlad the Impaler*. When combined with pitch two of *Cat on a Hot Tin Roof*, gives two good contrasting pitches to the top of the buttress.

4 Cat on a Hot Tin Roof ** 60m E3 5c
FA Adrian Crofton & Guy Robertson August 1998

Sustained with a bold second pitch.

1 40m 5c Climb the thin cracks left of *Vlad the Impaler*'s first pitch until they join that route after 15m. Continue up *Vlad* to the platform.

2 20m 5c Left of *Vlad*'s second pitch is a prominent hanging finger-crack. Climb this to a step left at the obvious foot hold. Move up using the left arête before stepping back right and pulling through the bulge (crux) to the easier crack above.

5 Vlad the Impaler ** 60m HVS 5a
FA Andrew Fraser & Ian Dickson 29 September 1985

A compelling line tackling the prominent corner and cracked slab on the far right of the buttress. Easy for the grade. Start beneath the slab bounded on the right by an overhanging corner. A great first pitch.

1 30m 5a Climb wide cracks up the centre then the right side of the slab. From the slab's detached summit move up and right to a large ledge.

2 30m 4b At the rear of the large ledge is a twisting crack. Climb this, then move into a left crack after 7m finishing up an easy arête and pinnacle.

6 Nosferatu * 25m HVS 5a
FA Andrew Fraser & Wendy Faulkner 27 September 1987

Climbs the buttress immediately right of *Vlad the Impaler*. Start at the base of the chimney, the eastmost feature of the buttress. Climb the chimney for 7m then move left into the centre of the face. Continue with increasing difficulty up twin cracks in the centre of the buttress to an excellent finish. (The chimney throughout gives a pleasant V.Diff.)

NC 111 105 **Alt:** 480m 1hr
NO. 3 BUTTRESS
The broken buttress forming the right flank of the **Pinnacle Basin**, which separates it from the more defined **No. 2 Buttress**.

Descent: Down the right (east) branch of the scree gully in **Pinnacle Basin**.

7 Summer Isles Arête ★★   120m Very Difficult
FA John & Helen Mackenzie July 1974

Start at a crack right of the lowest rocks and up this to a ledge. Climb a short chimney to level ground and then traverse the arête to avoid a big gendarme. Step down right at its end and climb a deep chimney with a chokestone to a niche. Go right up a groove and quit it for the steep face on the left and climb to a ledge. Climb up a crack and flakes to a small ledge and climb to the base of the 'monolith'. Avoid this on the right easily and climb a steep crack to finish on a level arête.

7a Summer Isles Arête Direct ★★   105m VS 4c
FA Andrew Fraser & Ian Dickson 3 September 1993

A pleasant civilised route with good positions. Just left of the toe of the buttress next to the screes of **Pinnacle Basin** is an obvious corner, the start.

1 **25m 4b** Climb the corner to ledges.
2 **15m 4a** Climb right onto the crest of the ridge beneath a pinnacle then ramble left across a gully and wall to beneath a groove on the left of the buttress.
3 **25m 4c** Climb the groove, exiting right with difficulty to gain and follow an obvious crack-line up the front of the buttress.
4 **25m 4c** On the right side of the tower is a short vicious corner-crack. Climb this, then follow ledges up and right to the final arête. Belay behind the final tower.
5 **15m** Follow the arête directly behind to the summit ridge (this last pitch is optional, as is the *Summer Isles Hotel Direct* – 5 miles).

7b Summer Isles Crack ★   15m E1 5b
FA Andy Cunningham & Colin Downer 20 August 1997

The widening finger-crack in the final tier of *Summer Isles Arête* which is avoided by that route. Access may be made by a traverse in from the **Pinnacle Basin** on the left.

Jack the Ripper, West Buttress (page 225). Photo Dave Cuthbertson Cubby Images.

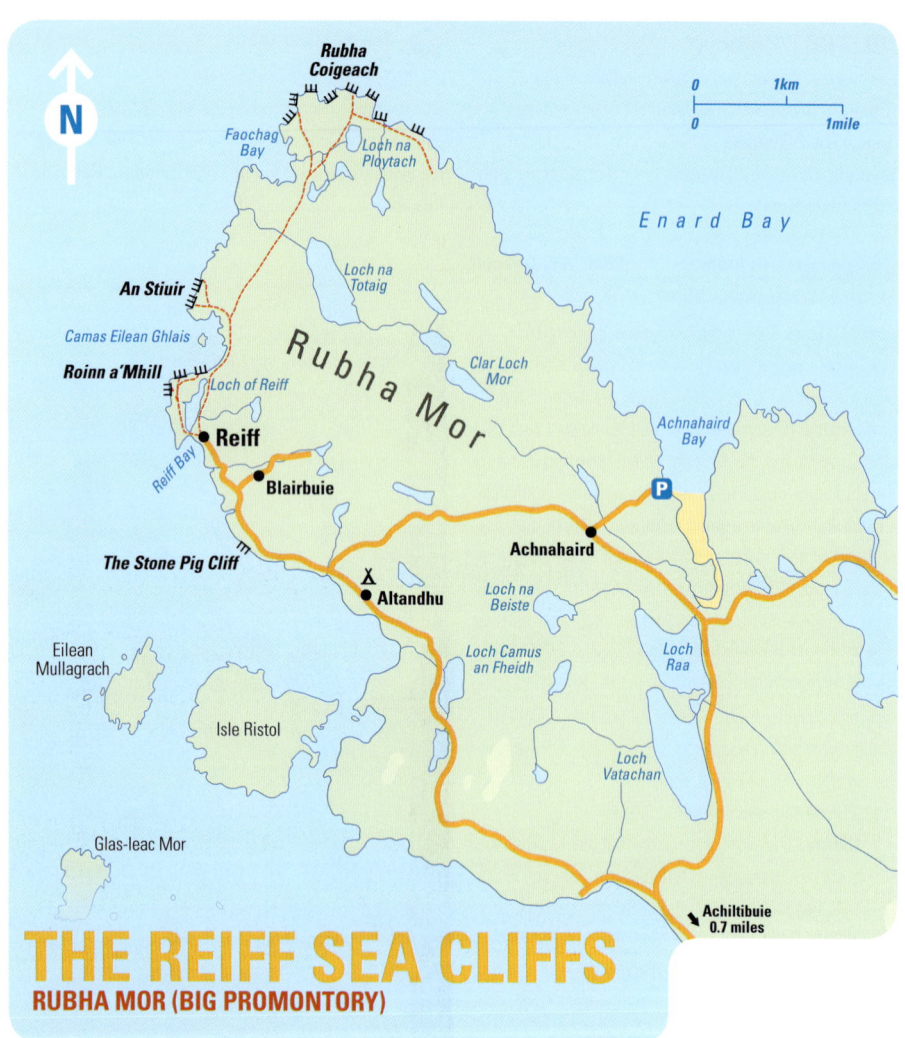

THE REIFF SEA CLIFFS
RUBHA MOR (BIG PROMONTORY)

This is the general name for the extensive crags on the peninsula north of the tiny hamlet of Reiff. The vast majority of routes are generally conveniently located above large non-tidal platforms with only a handful of routes affected by the tide, clearly indicated as so in the text.

General info: Though the majority of crags can be approached by straightforward scrambling, a short length of spare rope is worth taking to arrange abseil descents, saving time if intending to climb a number of routes in the same area. 15–20m of rope is normally adequate for the majority of crags, except for **The Bouldering Cliff** and

Black Rocks (25m), & **Spaced Out Rockers Cliff** (35m). A good selection of cams will also be found useful, particularly the smaller cams on some of the harder routes; often at least two full sets can be put to good use.

Access: From Ullapool follow the A835 north for 10 miles/16km then turn left towards Achiltibuie along single track road, passing underneath Cul Beag and Stac Pollaidh for 11.4 miles/18.2km to a junction at Achnahaird Bay. Turn right, taking a sharp right after 3.1 miles/5km, continuing for a further 1.5 miles/2.4km. Limited parking for 5/6 cars is available overlooking the outflow from the Loch of Reiff, taking care not to cause an obstruction.

THE STONE PIG CLIFF

NB 971 132 1min

A short band of **tidal** crags immediately below the road midway between the turn-off and the road end at Reiff. A prominent boulder overlooking the road does in fact with a bit of imagination, resemble a pig. **Routes described from North to South.**

Access: Continue for 0.7 miles/1.1km from the turn-off to park on the right, immediately beneath the pig.

Approach: Cross the fence and drop down the slope.

1 Slabby Corner Crack   20m Easy
FA Andy Cunningham (solo) May 1989

A useful descent, bounding the left (north) side of the slab.

2 Daunt's Arête ★★★   15m Moderate
FA Andy Cunningham (solo) August 1989

Good climbing up the slabby arête on the left, gained via a curving crack on the right side.

3 Automaton ★   20m HVS 5a
FA Keith Geddes & Andy Cunningham August 1989

Follow the leftmost long stepped corner to the overlap. Pull directly over this, stepping left above to finish up a short hanging groove.

4 Nalaxone ★   15m VS 4c
FA Keith Geddes & C.O'Malley June 1989

The rightmost stepped slab corner.

5 Icarus ★★   15m VS 4c
FA Andy Cunningham & Jeni Pickering May 1989

Good exposed climbing. Follow thin cracks and pockets near the right edge of the rightmost slab.

LEANING WALL

The impressive overhanging wall of the large tidal bay.

Nesting Restrictions: a couple of shags occasionally nest on some ledges on the left side of the cliff. If present (easily seen from the top) do not climb here during the nesting season (April – July).

Descent: The base of the routes can be gained from either side at low tide. Abseil in at other states of tide.

1 Tinsel Town ★   15m E2 5c
FA Andy Cunningham & Jeni Pickering May 1989

At the extreme left end of the wall. Start at the left end of a huge recess. Climb up left to enter a short groove with difficulty. Step up onto a ramp and climb it to bulges at its top. Swing left and finish up 5.

② One for Q ★★   15m E3 6a
FA Karin Magog & Steve Crowe 16 September 2002

Climb into the large cave at the left end then pull out right onto the headwall to a steep finish.

③ Le Cigogne ★★   18m E5 6a
FA Paul Thorburn & Mark Garthwaite 12 May 2002

Ascend the offwidth crack into the cave. Pull left out of the cave heading towards the edge on the left. Move back right along a crack to climb the headwall via thin cracks.

④ 007 ★★   20m E4 5c
FA Steve Crowe & Karin Magog 26 August 2002

So named, as he was always crossing Miss Moneypenny. Start up the wide crack to the ledge. Pull directly over the roof, trend slightly right up thin cracks before going straight up to finish.

⑤ Miss Moneypenny ★★   20m E5 6a
FA Lawrence Hughes & Andy Cunningham 14 June 1998

The central line up the wall. Climb the initial wall to the right of the deep offwidth to a break. Pull over the roof, moving boldly slightly left then back right past a round hole into the line. Finish up a very steep crack.

⑥ If You See Kay ★★   20m E3 5c
FA Andy Cunningham & Lawrence Hughes 14 June 1998

A natural line curving rightwards. Start centrally and climb the initial wall to a large ledge. Pull through the middle of the roof via twin right diagonal cracks and move right into the right-curving line, which is followed steeply to the top.

⑦ Le Pig Penn ★   15m E4 6b
FA Mark Garthwaite & Paul Thorburn 12 May 2002

A direct line left of 8. Start at the crack just left. Pull over the roof and direct to the break on 6. Finish directly up shattered cracks in the headwall.

⑧ Manumission ★★   15m E4 6a/b
FA Lawrence Hughes & Andy Cunningham 18 June 1998

A direct line to the right of 7. Start up a right-slanting diagonal crack above a small pool to the large ledge. Climb the roof above at the widest point and up into the crack-line and shallow right-facing corner to finish.

⑨ Sonique ★★   15m E4 5c
FA Lawrence Hughes & Andy Cunningham 5 May 1998

Near the right side of the wall and before the jaws of the deep slot is a vague crack-line with twin cracks at one third height. Climb to the left of the cracks via horizontal breaks to a small overlap. Move right into the line at a small niche and finish by long reaches on flat holds. A direct start is also possible.

> Just south of the **Leaning Wall** the crag runs south again.

10 Die Another Day ★★   15m E6 6b
FA Karin Magog & Steve Crowe 16 September 2002

The west-facing wall of the pillar. Start up the arête overlooking the wide chimney to reach the horizontal break. Good cams (pre-placed & pre-clipped on only ascent to date). Hand traverse right to the middle of the face (poor cam on right) then a hard sequence leads to a good undercut. Trend up to the right arête and then the top.

11 Headstrong ★★   15m E4 5c
FA Wilson Moir & Paul Allen 22 May 1994

Steep bold climbing up the hanging arête. Climb just left of 12, then move up left to good holds on the arête. Continue up the left side.

11a Headstrong Direct ★★   20m E5 6a
FA Ian Taylor & Tess Fryer 29 August 2015

Start up the steep left side of the arête, pulling round right to join the original line at its crux.

12 Strongbow ★★★   15m E1 5b
FA Keith Geddes & Andy Cunningham June 1989

Good well protected climbing up the prominent overhanging curving crack, originating as a shallow corner.

13 Clatterbridge ★★★   15m E5 6b
FA Paul Tattersall 17 May 1996

The smooth black concave wall right of 12. Start right of the centre of the wall below a ragged crack. Climb easily to a large ledge (can be reached by abseil at high tide). Climb the ragged crack to a horizontal break, move up and left to the next horizontal break. Difficult moves gain the right end of a higher break. Move slightly left (small cams) then direct past two further breaks to gain the top.

Tess Fryer on Sonique.

Unknown climber on Westering Home, Pinnacle Area (page 236).

ROINN A' MHILL
(SHARP POINTED LUMP)

NB 962 150

 <10min

The headland closest to the road end, about 5–10 minutes north-west from the bridge and visible from the parking spot. The crags extend for about 400 metres northwards, before petering out into the boulders and sand of the fine Camas Eilean Ghlas (Blue-green Island Bay).

PINNACLE AREA

A convenient area with a range of mainly micro-routes of all grades.

Approach: Cross the bridge and follow a choice of sheep paths, first along the side of the loch then across the bog to the crags.

SECOND GEO

The deep inlet immediately east of the prominent toblerone-shaped Pinnacle with a distinctive collection of huge jumbled boulders at the back.

Descent: By abseil, or the easy ramp running underneath the right side of the headwall.

1 Tangle o' the Isles ★★  10m HS 4b
FA Brian Lawrie (solo) 1970s
The central clean-cut corner on the east wall, (opposite the pinnacle).

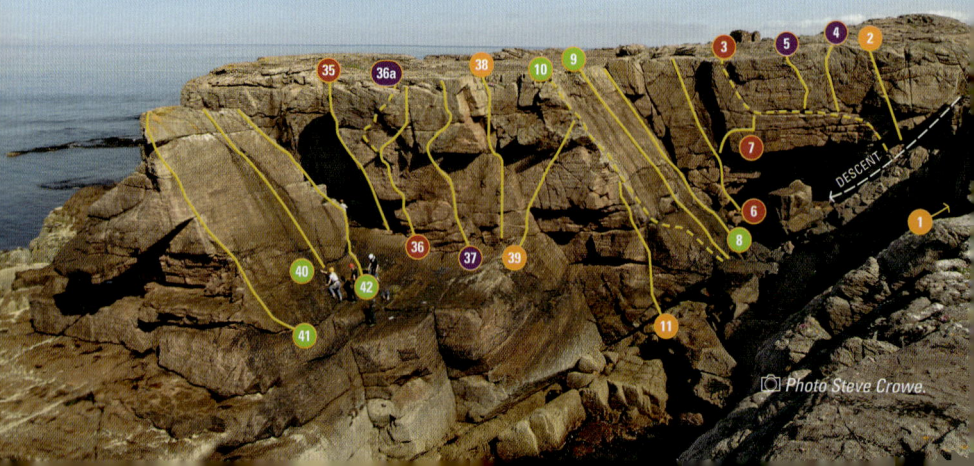
Photo Steve Crowe.

2 Stechie *   8m HVS 5b
FA Andy Cunningham & Stevie Blagbrough October 1988

Climb the wider leftmost of twin crack-lines in the short undercut slab above the descent ramp.

3 A Walk Across the Rooftops ***   20m E3 5c
FA Andy Cunningham & Keith Geddes October 1988

Excellent strenuous climbing, traversing left across the headwall. Start up the crack of 2 then follow the prominent horizontal crack (large cams) to finish up vague cracks.

4 Strangeways **   10m E4 6b
FA Richard Mansefield June 1990; Direct: Gary Latter 31 May 2014

The overhanging cracks above the start of 3, finishing out right where the cracks curve left. The direct start through widest part of roof is *Sanderlings* ** E6 6b.

5 Absent Friends **   15m E5 6b
FA Nick Clement 11 May 1995

Traverse into the middle of the wall, as for 3, to an obvious hole. Move right up off a big undercut past two breaks to finish slightly left.

6 Immaculate Deception **   12m E1 5b
FA Andy Cunningham & Keith Geddes October 1988

Start by a protruding block at the base of the slab on the west side of the geo. Cross the small roof on good holds and finish up the left-slanting crack. The crux roof can be avoided by traversing in from the left – VS 4c.

7 Immaculate Walk **   15m E3 5c
FA Andy Cunningham & Lawrence Hughes 26 March 1999

A good link pitch. Climb the crux of 6 then hand traverse the lower horizontal break right to finish up the final crack of 3.

8 Slab and Corner *   15m Difficult
FA Brian Lawrie (solo) 1970s

The right edge of the slab. Also useful as a descent route.

9 Jellyfish Slab *   15m Difficult
FA Brian Lawrie (solo) 1970s

Fine climbing up the centre of the slab.

10 Edge of the Sea *   18m Very Difficult
FA Brian Lawrie (solo) 1970s

Start near the centre of the slab. Trend diagonally left to finish up the exposed left edge.

11 Underworld *   20m VS 4c
FA Andy Cunningham & Jeni Pickering July 1995

Beneath 10 starting in the tidal boulders. Climb the corner and move right to the edge. Up this via the horizontal breaks.

PINNACLE WALLS
Routes from left to right.
Descent: Down an easy fault at the north end of the crags just before two small promontories.

12 Junior's Groove *   8m Very Difficult
FA Brian Lawrie (solo) 1970s

Deep groove in the right wall of the gully between the two promontories just north of the descent.

13 La Mer *   5m HVS 5b
FA Brian Lawrie (solo) 1970s

Right (south) of the descent is a large block in front of the crag. Climb a crack and pockets on the front face.

14 Diagonal Crack *   8m Very Difficult
FA Brian Lawrie (solo) 1970s

The left-slanting crack, started from the top of the block.

> The steep leaning wall left of the crack gives 15 *Brace Yersel Becky* * E2 6a. 16 *Cave Wall* Severe 4a ascends the centre of the wall above the centre of the block.

17 More of the Same *   10m VS 4c
FA Brian Lawrie (solo) 1970s

Just left of a small pool is a small right-slanting corner. Ascend this, finishing left over a bulge.

18 Salt Pans ★ — 10m E3 6b
FA Ian Taylor July 2004

Climb the wall just left of 19 to a sloping ledge. Step right and finish up right-facing corner.

19 Earth Shaker ★★ — 10m E2 6a
FA Brian Lawrie (solo) 1970s

On the leaning wall above a little pool is a short corner. Boulder to it from either side then slightly left to finish directly.

20 Reiff Case ★ — 8m E3 6b
FA Neil Morrison (solo) 1990s

A boulder problem up the wall just right of 19 via a small vertical layaway in the centre of the wall.

21 Sandstone Shuffle — 10m Very Difficult
FA Brian Lawrie (solo) 1970s

Climb up and left round the left arête, finishing directly above a ledge.

22 Midreiff ★ — 10m Severe 4a
FA Brian Lawrie (solo) 1970s

The shallow corner in the centre of the wall gained by traversing diagonally right from the arête.

23 Velvet Scoter — 10m Severe 4a
FA Brian Lawrie (solo) 1970s

The wall and crack just left of the corner.

24 Descent Corner — 10m Difficult
FA Brian Lawrie (solo) 1970s

The cracked corner at the left side. Also useful as a descent.

25 Westering Home ★★ — 10m E1 5b
FA Brian Lawrie, Neil Morrison & Martin Forsyth July 1985

The short thin crack up the slab left of the arête, difficult at the top.

An eliminate, 26 *A Song in the Air* ★ E2 5c avoids either of the adjacent lines.

27 Hy Brasil ★★ — 10m VS 4c
FA Brian Lawrie (solo) 1970s

Start left of the arête. Follow the first prominent line out right onto the arête to finish direct. Nice airy climbing.

28 Mac's Route ★ — 10m VS 5a
FA Tom Redfern & George McEwan 25 May 1993

Direct line up the wall, starting as for 29. Finish by prominent circular hold in the shallow open groove.

29 Pop-out ★ — 10m HVS 5a
FA Brian Lawrie (solo) 1970s

Start beneath a groove right of the arête. Climb up into then out of the groove with difficulty to finish up the right side of the arête.

30 Puckered Wall ★ — 10m VS 4b
FA Brian Lawrie (solo) 1970s

Climb the steep wall left of 31 on good holds.

31 The Krill — 10m VS 4b
FA Brian Lawrie (solo) 1970s

The recessed overhanging crack, finishing direct.

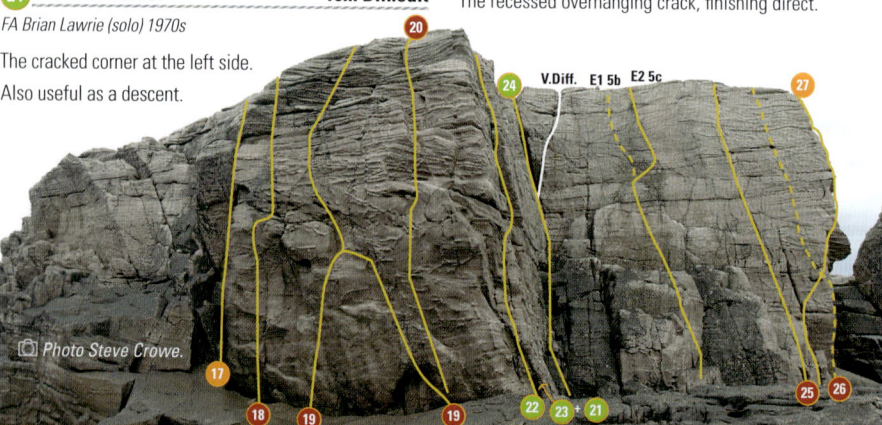
Photo Steve Crowe.

Xyles   10m HS 4b

FA Brian Lawrie (solo) 1970s

The shallow groove and diagonal crack.

 Skel   10m Severe 4a

FA Brian Lawrie (solo) 1970s

The diagonal crack parallel to and left of the corner.

 **Slanting Corner** *   10m Severe 4a

FA Brian Lawrie (solo) 1970s

The corner just left of the overhanging wall.

 **Yellow Dogs** *   10m E3 5c

FA Andy Cunningham & Keith Geddes November 1988

The shallow leaning groove up the left side of the overhung wall. At the top of the groove swing out right round the break on good holds. Stand on this then easily above.

 **Channering Worm** **   9m E3 5c

FA Brian Lawrie, Neil Morrison & Martin Forsyth July 1985

Fine bold climbing. Start in the centre of the undercut buttress. Cross the roof and climb past a good flake hold then up right to protection in the easy left-slanting crack.

36a *Worm on Viagra* * E4 5c moves left at the break to finish steeply via the thin right diagonal crack.

37 Totally Tropical *   9m E4 6b

FA Wilson Moir & Brian Lawrie June 1991

Climb a thin left-slanting crack to underclings at the left end of the halfway roof. Move up right to a shelf and finish up the short wall.

38 Barrier Reiff *   9m HVS 5b

FA Stevie Blagbrough, Andy Cunningham & Jeni Pickering October 1988

Start 2m left of the edge of the platform. Ascend a thin corner-crack, pull left round a small roof and finish direct.

39 Sip from the Wine of Youth Again **   12m HVS 5a

FA Brian Lawrie, Neil Morrison & Martin Forsyth July 1985

Start at the same point as 38. Climb the prominent right-slanting diagonal crack out to the right edge, to finish up the slab.

THE PINNACLE

Descents: Either by abseil, or climb down the stepped right edge (*Special K* Difficult) of the landward (east) side.

The edges are taken by 41 *Pinnacle Slab Left Edge* * Severe 4b and 42 *Right Edge* * Very Difficult respectively.

40 Moon Jelly **   10m Very Difficult

FA Brian Lawrie (solo) 1970s

Fine climbing up the shallow runnel up the centre of the slab.

The 'small but perfectly formed' (eh?) Mike 'No Vat Man' Reed deep water soloing (well almost) the steady Sip from the Wine of Youth Again

Photo Steve Crowe.

BOULDERING CLIFF

A bit of a misnomer with some of the longest routes on Roinn a' Mhill.

Approach: Cross the bridge and follow a choice of sheep paths heading north (parallel to the loch) to the crag.

Descent: Scramble easily down a broken (usually wet) easy-angled fault with short step at base, at the west end of the cliff, immediately north of a large rock pool on the cliff top.

1 The Corner ★ 10m VS 5a
FA Brian Lawrie (solo) 1970s
The short stepped corner.

2 White Horses ★ 10m E2 6a
FA Brian Lawrie (solo) 1970s
A bouldery start leads to easier climbing above.

> The right wall of the corner gives two problems – 3 *Black Zone* ★ HVS 5b up the diagonal ramp to ledge, finishing out right; and 4 *Scallog* ★ HVS 5c just left of the arête.

5 Golden Eyes 10m E1 5c
FA Brian Lawrie early 1980s
The short stepped corner.

6 Scooped Arête ★★ 10m E4 6c
FA Andy Wren (solo) Summer 1996
A powerful problem up the blunt right arête.

7 Romancing the Stone ★★ 10m E4 6b
FA Brian Lawrie Summer 1984
The thin cracks left of the arête, finishing direct. Very bouldery with the crux gaining the break.

8 The Hand Traverse ★★ 15m HVS 5a
FA Brian Lawrie (solo) early 1980s
Start up the ramp and finish up the blunt arête.

9 The Ramp ★★ 15m HS 4b
FA Brian Lawrie (solo) 1970s
The prominent stepped right-slanting fault, just right of the pool.

10 Rampant Groove ★★ 18m E4 5c
FA Steve Crowe & Karin Magog (both led) May 2004
Climb 9 to near its top. Place good cams in the large break then step left and boldly continue up the hanging groove.

11 Toad in the Hole ★★ 20m E5 6a
FA Andy Cunningham (headpointed) July 1990

The tapering wall right of the corner, climbed direct past three obvious large breaks and three good pockets. Large cams (3.5–4") useful in the breaks. Great climbing, only spoiled by being very close to 12 at the top.

> The lower wall to the break is 11a *Hole in the Wall* ★★ E2 6a escaping out right along the break into the ramp.

12 Wyatt Earp ★★★ 20m E3 6a
FA Murray Hamilton & Rab Anderson July 1985

The huge open corner in the centre of the crag. Fine climbing but slow to dry.

13 Undertow ★★★ 20m E7 6c
FA Dave Cuthbertson (1 bucket for aid) July 1995;
FFA Dave Birkett 1998

The once 'futuristic wall' is now reality. Persons shorter than 6' apply to Cubby for loan of bucket for start. Start at a little stepped overlap. Reach the undercuts and gain the podded crack and climb this to the upper and smaller of three breaks (F #4 in middle break). Step right and climb the next podded crack with a long reach to the central break. Move right into the cave, exit this using a horizontal crack on the right and go up to a pocket. Gain the groove of a short right-facing hanging groove which leads strenuously (crux) to the top.

14 Leaning Meanie ★ 20m E3 6a
FA John Cunningham & Brian Lawrie May 1982

The mean leaning hand-crack gives a thuggish problem. Finish up the easier chimney above the big ledge.

15 Wanton Wall ★ 20m E6 6b
FA Steve Crowe & Karin Magog (headpointed) 31 August 2002

Reasonable climbing but the protection is difficult to locate and place. Start up the ramp start to 17. Pull over the overlap and continue up the wall above joining 16 at the final break.

16 Desire Direct ★★★★ 20m E3 6a
FA Andy Cunningham July 1990

Climb the bottom section of 17 as far as the ledge. Pull over the roof and up the crack on perfect slots. Stunning.

17 The Crack of Desire ★★★ 20m E3 6a
FA Dougie Dinwoodie July 1985

Start at the short right-facing corner beneath a prominent rightwards slanting diagonal crack. Climb the easy lower corner and the hand-crack above to a ledge at mid-height. Break out left above the bulge and finish straight up the wall on good holds. The route can also be started by the leftwards slanting ramp on the right wall at E4 6a – poorly protected.

18 Monster Breaker ★ 25m VS 4c
FA Alastair Matthewson & Andy Tibbs 3 May 1987

The pale right-slanting tapering slab at the far left end of the crag. Gain the base by walking round narrow shelf.

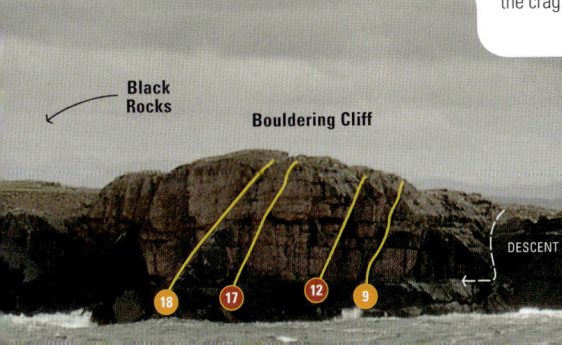

NB 964 152 10min

BLACK ROCKS

Contains some of the best long lower grade routes on the coast.

Approach: As for the **Bouldering Cliff**, continuing 150m further east along the coast.

Descent: Abseil from large block down *The Grooves*. At low tide it is possible to gain routes at the extreme left end by scrambling initially down an easy-angled slab at the east (far left end, facing in).

1 Barrel of Laughs *   25m VS 4c
FA Andy Cunningham & Jeni Pickering April 1989

Climb the slab corner at the base of the descent slab then finish along the ramp.

2 Hourglass Groove **   15m HVS 5a
FA Andy Cunningham & Jeni Pickering April 1989

The first wide groove above blocky ground at the left end of the crag. Follow the steep crack on the right to the narrows, finishing up the crack over a series of ramps.

3 Shifting Sands *   15m HVS 5a
FA Andy Cunningham & Jeni Pickering April 1989

Cuts through 2. Climb a series of large steps on the left to the narrows then directly up the crack on the right to the roof. Undercling out right to finish.

4 The Grooves *   25m Severe 4a
FA Brian Lawrie (solo) 1970s

The wide groove at the left end of the platform.

5 Enlightenment *   20m VS 4c
FA Andy Cunningham & Jeni Pickering October 1994

Climb the broken right wall of 4 then hand traverse along the break on the right and up to finish. A great position.

6 Leg Over *   20m E2 5b
FA R.Baines & G.McShane June 1998

Climb the first 4m of 7 then traverse along break to the pillar on the left. Go up a crack to the large break then direct up the headwall.

7 Auld Nick *   25m Severe 4a
FA Brian Lawrie early 1980s

Start at the base of the flat-faced arête right of 4. Ascend the deep right-slanting crack, finishing up 10.

8 Black Donald *   25m Severe 4a
FA Brian Lawrie (solo) Summer 1985

The corner up the left side of the slab, finishing up 10.

9 Tystie Left Edge *   25m Severe 4a
FA Brian Lawrie (solo) July 1995

Good climbing up the left edge of the slab, overlooking 8.

10 Tystie Slab ***   30m Very Difficult
FA Brian Lawrie & Neil Morrison July 1985

Excellent climbing, low in the grade. Climb the centre of the slab to pockets and breaks then follow an obvious natural line diagonally left to finish.

COIGACH & ASSYNT ROINN A' MHILL | 241

11 Batman *   **25m HVS 5a**

FA Andy Cunningham & Jeni Pickering November 1988

The hanging groove in the headwall above 10, gained easily up the lower slab right of 10 to a good ledge.

12 Dalriada ** **   **20m E1 5b

FA Andy Cunningham & Jeni Pickering October 1994

The blunt arête left of 13. Start up the short black corner at the right end of the slab then cross the leaning wall onto the arête. Climb this to finish on the right.

13 Pot Black *   **20m HVS 5a**

FA Allen Fyffe & Jas Hepburn 2 October 1993

The wall left of 14. Climb the lower easy section of 14 to a ledge then move left on breaks and up to a pocket. Continue up to finish up a corner up the left edge of the wall as for 12.

14 Black Pig ** **   **20m VS 5a

FA Andy Cunningham & Jeni Pickering November 1988

The slabby black corner cutting into the base of the next buttress to the right. Gain the corner from the left, finishing left beneath the final overlap.

15 Black Gold * * *   **20m HS 4b**

FA Brian Lawrie & Neil Morrison July 1985

Excellent climbing up the centre of the black slab. Start at a short corner at the lowest point of the wall. Go up the corner past a ledge then traverse the first break left to the centre of the slab. Climb directly past numerous breaks and pockets.

Further right, the left-curving crack and upper wall is 16 *Route with no Name* * VS 4c. 17 *Black Guillemot* *VS 4c takes the thin right-curving crack in the black wall further right again.

Just north of the scrambling descent to **Black Rocks** lies the 10m **Orange Wall** with, from the right, *Meikle Neuk* * VS 4b/c, *Flying Pig* * E2 6a, *Orange Wall* ** HVS 5b and *Huffin Puffin* * E1 5c starting at the left end of a triangular niche.

Paul 'Stork' Thorburn in glorious evening light on the lower section of Undertow, Bouldering Cliff.

Barry Rose and Liz MacKay on the well protected Black Gold.

AN STIUIR
(THE RUDDER)

North of the bay of Camas Eilean Ghlais the coast turns round to run north with a compact selection of excellent short crags within a few hundred metre stretch.

Approach: From the parking spot, walk through the farmyard and along the east side of the Loch of Reiff then by a good path round the bay to a shieling. Follow a path west out to the west coast, where the projecting top of the **Bay of Pigs** forms the highest section of the cliff top. **The Minch Wall** extends south for 100m from here with the **Seal Song Area** less than 80m further south again. **Piglet Wall** and **Pooh Cliff** lie just north of the **Bay of Pigs**.

SEAL SONG AREA

An excellent area, mainly above a large non-tidal boulder beach.

25min
NB 964 157

1 Street Surfer *   15m HVS 5a
FA Simon Steer & Andrew Fraser 2 May 1987

The undercut corner on the far right, passing a wafer thin horizontal flake with care near the top.

2 Every Which Way But Loose *   15m VS 5b
FA Brian Lawrie (solo) 1970s

The large undercut slab corner with a boulder problem start (either direct or up the groove on the left) leading to easier climbing.

3 Gussetbuster *   15m E1 5c
FA Brian Lawrie, Neil Morrison & Martin Forsyth July 1985

The prominent diagonal crack in the back of the groove, passing a troublesome bulge at mid-height.

4 Razor's Edge *   15m E1 5b
FA Brian Lawrie, Martin Forsyth & Neil Morrison July 1985

Start right of the chimney high up. Up to and round a small sharp-edged undercut flake then by a crack leading to the chimney.

Photo Steve Crowe

5 Elastic Collision ★★★   15m E3 5c
FA Brian Lawrie & Andy Nisbet 9 August 1986

The right crack is less sustained with a big jug in the middle.

6 Seal Song ★★★   15m E3 6a
FA Neil Morrison, Brian Lawrie & Martin Forsyth July 1985

The left of the twin tramline cracks on the steepest left end of the wall.

7 Diamond Back ★★   20m E1 5a
FA Brian Lawrie (solo) early 1980s

The short wall immediately left of 6 to the ledge. Up the ramp line then into the hanging diamond-shaped groove above.

8 Moody Blues ★★   15m VS 4c
FA Brian Lawrie (solo) early 1980s

The obvious slanting finger-crack under 7. Superb and well protected. The initial steep wall can be avoided on the left.

9 Overhanging Crack ★   15m Severe 4a
FA Brian Lawrie (solo) early 1980s

The parallel crack just left of 8.

10 Final Fling ★   15m E1 5b
FA Simon Richardson & J.Wilkinson 22 June 1997

A counter-diagonal to 8. Start just left of 9. Climb up and right crossing 8 to finish up the short hanging right-angled corner in the centre of the wall left of 7.

> The following routes are all situated on the overhanging south-facing wall at the north end of the **Seal Song Area**.

11 The Executioner ★★★   15m E2 5b
FA Brian Lawrie, Neil Morrison & Martin Forsyth July 1985

The leaning corner-crack up the right end of the wall. Perfect protection. A spectacularly juggy direct finish over the bulge is also possible. So named, as one of the first ascent team almost lost a finger!

12 An Fiosaiche ★★   15m E6 6b
FA Nick Clement & Gary Latter (both led) 14 May 1995

'The Seer'. The right line on the wall. As for 13 to the good break then out rightwards to two good jugs (small cams and good skyhook). Make hard moves to stand on the top jug then step left and more easily up centre of wall.

13 An Faidh ★★   15m E6 6c
FA Nick Clement & Gary Latter (both led) 14 May 1995

'The Prophet'. Fine sustained climbing up the wall. Start in the centre of the wall, right of a right-slanting ramp. Up to and climb the thin crack to good break. Move slightly left to the next break, left along this and up with difficulty (RP #3 1m above good sidepull) to better holds. Step right and easier up centre of wall.

14 Second Sight ★   15m E5 6b
FA Nick Clement & Gary Latter 18 May 1995

The thin diagonal crack 3m right of the arête, starting just right of 15. Up just right of the crack with a long reach (crux) to a break level with the ledge on 15. The crack above, on improving holds.

15 Modern Thinking ★★   15m E4 6a
FA Graeme Livingston, Keith Geddes & Andy Cunningham August 1987

A steep blind start leads to easier climbing up the shallow right-slanting groove. Start by a short thin crack at the left end of the ledge. Up to the first break (F #3), left then up to the left end of a small ledge. Hand traverse this right and pull into the groove. More easily up this. The *Direct Start* is ★ E4 6b.

16 The Mystic ★   15m E5 6b
FA Nick Clement & Gary Latter (both led) 18 May 1995

Spectacular climbing up the left arête of the south wall. Easily up the left side of the arête then swing round right at the second roof and up to ledge. Pull out right and up to a good slot then make hard moves up the arête to finish.

WEST FACE

Round the arête on the **West Face**, the following three routes are affected by the tide:

1 Hairsplitter ★　　　　　　　　　　12m HVS 5a

Follows a line close to the right edge.

2 Skullsmasher ★★　　　　　　　　12m HVS 5a
FA Brian Lawrie (solo) 1970s

The steeper area of rock at the right end of the west wall with the crux moving off the high ledge for the top.

3 Brainbiter ★　　　　　　　　　　12m VS 4b
FA Brian Lawrie (solo) 1970s

The vague crack up the left side of the wall, finishing up an easier groove.

📷 *Andy Wren on The Executioner.*

📷 *Nick Clement on the first ascent of The Mystic.*

COIGACH & ASSYNT AN STIUIR | 245

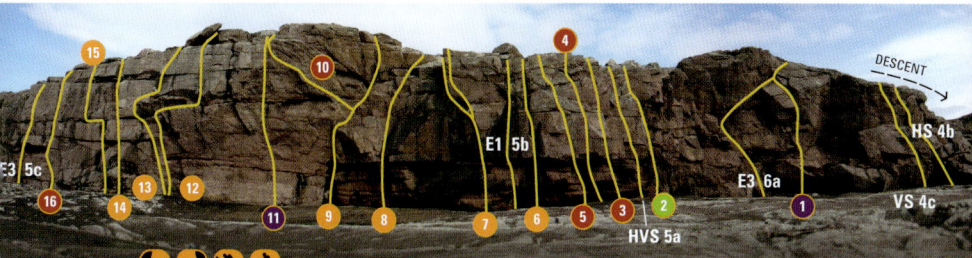

NB 964 159 25min

THE MINCH WALL

A good range of short routes above a wide platform.
Descent: Easily down broken ground at the south end.

1 Impure Thoughts ★   12m E6 6b

FA Wilson Moir (headpointed) 13 June 1993

The prominent hanging corner line just left of an overhanging scooped corner. Start on the right and work up and left to gain the obvious big pinch. Use this to gain an edge on the right and palm up to the base of the corner (serious and committing – R #4 in the corner). Continue up the corner and finish on the right.

2 T Square   8m Very Difficult

FA Keith Geddes (solo) August 1987

Corner-crack 20m north (left) of descent, just beyond a loose blocky area.

Just to the left, 3 *Social Democrat* ★ E1 5b takes the undercut corner, 4 *Scavenger* E1 5c the wall left of the arête and 5 *Parabolic Head* ★ E1 5c the next hanging groove.

6 Judicial Hanging ★   8m HVS 5b

FA Andy Cunningham & Keith Geddes August 1987

The prominent deep undercut crack, 3m left of 5.

The black slab to the left is *In Yer Face* ★ E1 5b.

7 Dunskiing   9m VS 4c

FA Keith Geddes & Andy Cunningham August 1987

Start just left of the crack of the previous route. Move up into a shallow corner, finishing left round the final short prow. The direct finish is 7a *Telemark* VS 5a.

8 Athlete's Foot ★   10m HS 4c

FA Graeme Livingston (solo) August 1987

Boulder problem start to gain triangular niche left of 7 to finish out right.

9 Friends for Life ★   9m HVS 5b

FA Keith Geddes & Andy Cunningham August 1987

The wide bulging right-curving corner-crack.

10 *Bank of Scotland* E3 5c follows the obvious rising traverse line left across the overhanging wall.

11 Beating Heart ★   12m E5/6 6a

FA Steve Crowe & Karin Magog (headpointed) 29 May 1999

The centre of the wall left of 10. Boulder up to the prominent undercut, place small cam (HB #00 or similar, blind and awkward to place correctly) and continue to good break above. Arrange better protection and continue more confidently to finish up the slab.

12 Jim Nastic ★★ — 12m VS 5a

FA Keith Geddes & Andy Cunningham August 1987

Start at the left end of the overhanging wall left of 9. Head up over ledges to a platform at half height. Finish up a thin crack in the slab above the right end of the ledge. The crack at the left end of the platform can also be climbed at the same grade.

13 Domino ★ — 10m HVS 5a

FA Andy Cunningham & Keith Geddes August 1987

Start as for 12. Trend left and up a short hanging corner, finishing rightwards.

14 Slip Jig ★ — 9m HS 4b

FA Andrew Fraser & Ian Dickson July 1987

Awkward climbing up the left-facing stepped corner.

15 Polka ★ — 9m VS 4b

FA Andy Cunningham & Jeni Pickering 4 July 1990

Line up scooped rock left of 14, hand traversing left along break to finish just right of 16.

16 Clam Jam ★ — 9m E1 5b

FA Martin Forsyth, Neil Morrison & Brian Lawrie July 1985

Hanging crack through the right end of the curved roof. Finish more easily directly above.

THE BAY OF PIGS

NB 965 160   25min

The recessed bay just beyond the end of **The Minch Wall**. **Descents:** Abseil in, or scramble down broken ground leading down (Diff.) to the base of *Awesome*; or by climbing down *Chicken Run* (Diff.). Alternatively, a longer approach can be made by walking north beneath the base of **The Minch Wall**.

1 Where the Green Ants Dream ★ — 18m E1 6a

FA Brian Lawrie (solo) 1970s

The grooved arête. A difficult bouldery start leads to much more reasonable (5a) climbing up the stepped groove above.

2 Making Bacon ★ — 18m E5 6a

FA Pete Whillance & Cliff Fanshawe Summer 1990

Start up either of the boulder problem starts to the adjacent routes and hand traverse the first break to some good nut placements. Climb straight up to a good break then direct past another break to finish up an easy open corner.

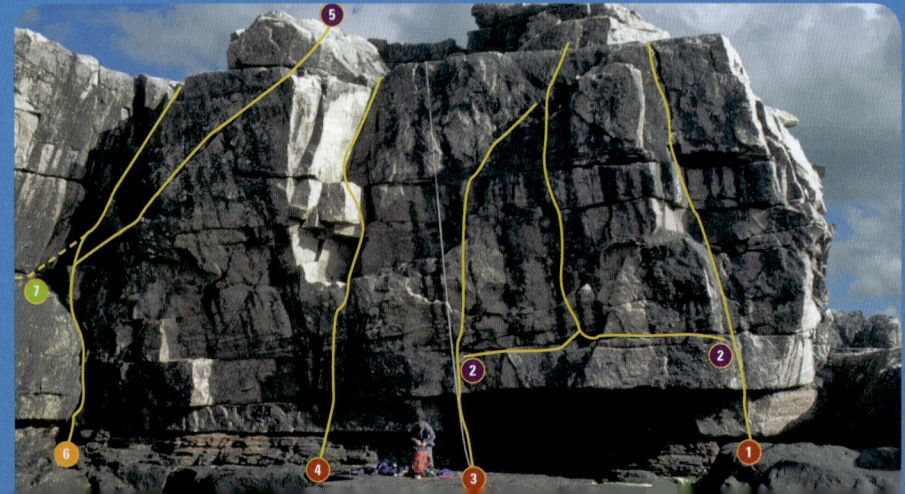

3 Reiff Encounter *   18m E3 6b
FA Pete Whillance & Cliff Fanshawe Summer 1990

The hanging crack above the roof. Boulder to a PR and good nut placements. Climb boldly up leftwards on good incut holds to good ledge then trend more easily rightwards to finish up the final easy corner of 18.

4 Sexcrementalism *   15m E1 5b
FA Brian Lawrie & Ron Kerr July 1985

The prominent short Y-crack 10m left of the edge. Strenuous climbing up the lower crack leads to a ledge then more easily up a corner-crack.

5 Free Base **   15m E5 6a
FA Colin McLean & Wilson Moir July 1989

Superb sustained well protected climbing, tackling the diagonal finger-crack crossing the wall right of 6.

6 Blackadder *   15m VS 5a
FA Keith Geddes & Andy Cunningham August 1987

The open chimney corner in the back right corner. Finish easily up the slabby fault on the right.

7 Chicken Run *   20m Difficult
FA Keith Geddes (solo) August 1987

Start 8m left of the corner. Traverse rightwards along the shelf to finish up the same slabby fault.

8 The Thistle **   12m E4 6a
FA Graeme Livingston, Andy Cunningham & Keith Geddes Aug 1987

The black crack springing from the recess on the overhanging back wall. Well protected with the difficulties very short lived.

9 Walk Like an Egyptian ***   20m E4 6a
FA Andy Cunningham & Keith Geddes August 1987

Excellent character building stuff up the prominent right-facing corner. The crux is the final severely overhung slot (small wires), where the route name will become apparent.

10 Cleopatra's Asp **   20m E5 6a
FA Wilson Moir & Brian Lawrie June 1991

Sustained and strenuous climbing up the right side of the wall left of 9. Start from the second ledge, 5m up the easy ramp. Hand traverse the break rightwards to a rest round the edge. Move up left and climb the wall to a good break (cams). Make a long reach to a good jug then another break, finishing by pulling out right onto ledge. Continue easily leftwards.

11 Awesome **   12m E4 6a
FA Graeme Livingston & Stevie Blagbrough August 1987

Well protected and low in the grade. Start from the second ledge on the ramp, as for 10. Climb slightly right into the prominent crack system which leads to easier ground near the top.

COIGACH & ASSYNT AN STIUIR

NB 965 160 (w) 25min
PIGLET WALL

Nice extended bouldering/micro-routes in sunny location, bounding the left end of **The Bay of Pigs**.

1 Curving Crack ★★   8m HVS 5a
FA Brian Lawrie (solo) 1970s

The shallow left-trending corner-crack on the right.

2 Dreams of Utah ★   8m HVS 5b
FA Keith Geddes & Andy Cunningham August 1987

Start 4m left of 1. Take a thin crack leading to a triangular niche near the top.

3 Vision of Blue ★   8m E1 5b
FA Brian Lawrie (solo) 1970s

The crack just left of a deeper left-slanting crack (*Chokestone Crack* V.Diff.).

4 The Kraken ★   8m E2 6a
FA Brian Lawrie (solo) 1970s

The shallow groove just to the left. Sustained after a bouldery start.

NB 965 161 (w) 25min
POOH CLIFF

About 100m north of the **Bay of Pigs** is a long narrow wall extending north to a boulder beach. Described from the boulder beach southwards **(left-right)**.
Approach: From the boulder beach.

1 Short Sighted ★   8m Severe 4a
FA Andy Cunningham & Jeni Pickering August 1987

The shelfy groove near the left end of the narrow platform tucked under the cliff, starting by a tricky mantelshelf.

2 Tigger ★   8m VS 4b
FA Andy Cunningham & Jeni Pickering August 1987

Start from the left end of the platform. Follow a steep thin crack in the left wall.

3 Pooh Corner ★★★   6m VS 4c
FA Andy Cunningham & Jeni Pickering August 1987

The fine black corner above the centre of the raised platform.

4 The Ramp ★   7m Severe 4a
FA Andy Cunningham & Jeni Pickering August 1987

The prominent left-slanting ramp-line at the right end of the platform.

5 *Honey Pot* HS 4b takes the wide corner-crack further right.

6 Sticky Fingers ★★   7m VS 4c
FA Andy Cunningham & Jeni Pickering August 1987

Start right of 5. Climb a shallow scoop direct over a bulge and finish leftwards.

On the right the platform narrows above the pool into an awkward raised triangular step. The next two routes start from the step.

7 Kanga ★   7m HVS 5b
FA Andy Cunningham & Jeni Pickering August 1987

The short corner above the step.

8 Roo ★   7m VS 5a/b
FA Andy Cunningham & Jeni Pickering August 1987

The shallow corner in the wall at the right end of the step, with a long reach from the horizontal break and pull onto the ledge.

9 Eeyore ★★   7m HVS 5a
FA Andy Cunningham & Jeni Pickering August 1987

Past the triangular step the platform widens once more with a fine concave wall on the right. Steep unobvious climbing up the centre of the concave wall.

10 Jelly Wobbler ★   8m E1 5b
FA Andy Cunningham & Jeni Pickering August 1987

Finger-crack in the black left-curving corner near right end.

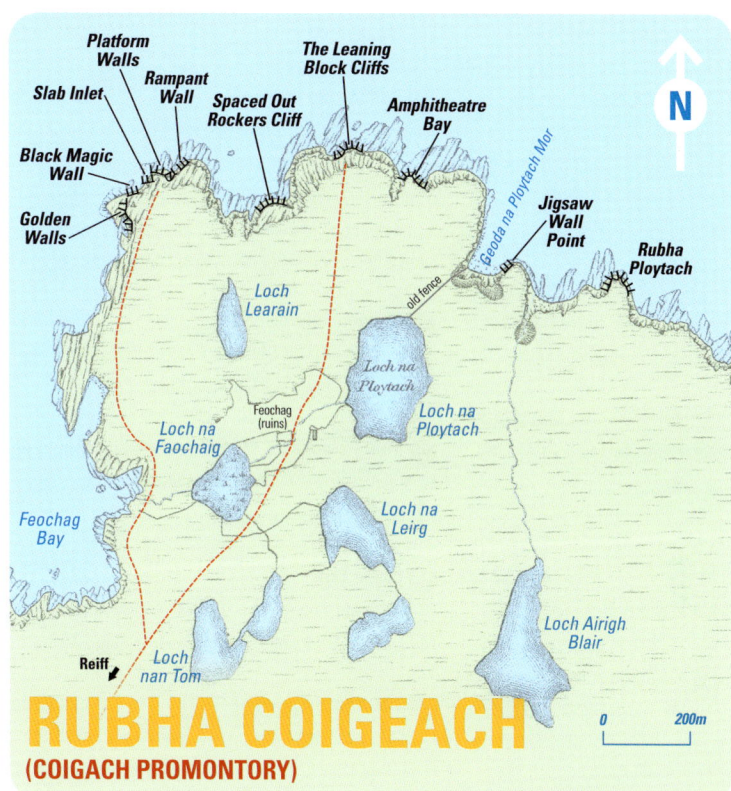

RUBHA COIGEACH
(COIGACH PROMONTORY)

This is the most northerly point of the Rubha Mor peninsula with some of the best climbing on the coastline. The routes are generally longer with a grand outlook over the hills of Coigach and Assynt, making it well worth the approach.

Approach: From the parking spot, walk through the farmyard and along the east side of the Loch of Reiff then by a good path round the bay to a shieling. Follow a line of cairns keeping to the high ground then head north between the coastline and three small lochans to the **Golden Walls**, which can be readily seen in profile on the approach.

GOLDEN WALLS

NB 966 179   1hr

A good range of routes. **Routes from right to left** (from phallic block northwards). Tidal with abseil approach at north end only.

Descent: At the south end of the crag, a peculiar *"phallic"* block marks the start of a narrow raised platform running north under the west-facing walls. This soon narrows into a ledge, before dwindling just beyond 11 *The Rite of Spring*. The remaining routes are tidal, gained by scrambling north along the walls and boulders of the channel separating the cliff from the small rocky island, or more conveniently by abseil.

1. Ruben Tadpole * — 15m E1 5b
FA Wilson Moir, Brian Lawrie & Andy Nisbet June 1987

Beyond a bulging section the ledge widens below two cracks. The right crack.

2. Bubblyjock * — 15m E2 5c
FA Brian Lawrie, Wilson Moir & Andy Nisbet June 1987

The left crack.

3. Murphy's Law ** — 15m HVS 5a
FA Kevin Murphy, Dougie Dinwoodie & Brian Lawrie Easter 1985

The open right-facing corner with a strenuous finish.

4. Halcyon Daze * — 15m HVS 5b
FA Kevin Murphy, Dougie Dinwoodie & Brian Lawrie Easter 1985

The left wall of the corner with a bouldery start. Finish by a prominent 'hole'.

5. Verushka * — 15m E2 5c
FA Martin Burrows Smith, Allen Fyffe & Andy Cunningham November 1990

The rounded pillar. Climb to the undercut and move steeply up to a horizontal break. Move slightly left and back right to finish direct.

6. Carnival of Folly * — 15m E1 5b
FA Dougie Dinwoodie, Brian Lawrie & Kevin Murphy Easter 1985

The bulging wall left of 5. Trend up and right, finishing left of 5.

7. Sniffing the Frog * — 15m E2 5c
FA Richard Mansefield & Dave Etherington Summer 1991

Start just before the Golden Wall. Up the scooped wall to a horizontal break 2m below the roof, large Fs. Move up to the right end of the roof (crux) and pull through this on good holds. Continue up and slightly left to finish.

8. Moronic Inferno ** — 15m E2 5b
FA Brian Lawrie, Dougie Dinwoodie & Kevin Murphy Easter 1985

The rightmost crack, on improving holds.

9. Split Personality *** — 15m E3 5c
FA Andy Nisbet, Niall Ritchie & Stevie Blagbrough August 1987

The thin crack just left.

10. Crann Tara *** — 15m E3 5c
FA Brian Lawrie, Dougie Dinwoodie & Kevin Murphy Easter 1985

The next crack left again, finishing on the right.

11. The Rite of Spring *** — 15m E2 5c
FA Brian Lawrie, Dougie Dinwoodie & Kevin Murphy Easter 1985

The leftmost crack. Gain a round hole 3m up, traverse left into the line and finish up a small corner. Quite bold at the start.

12 Sweet Chastity ★★   18m E1 5b
FA Brian Lawrie, Dougie Dinwoodie & Kevin Murphy Easter 1985

Start lower down on a lower ledge system. Follow the very left edge of the Golden Wall. Up an easy wall then with more difficulty up the edge to the top.

13 The Road to Somewhere ★★   15m E5 6a
FA Wilson Moir & Paul Allan 12 June 1993

The arête right of 14. Step off a big detached flake and climb the crack-line then the arête to the top. Sustained and superb.

14 The Road to Nowhere ★★   15m E4 6a
FA Brian Lawrie, Dougie Dinwoodie & Kevin Murphy Easter 1985

Bold sustained climbing up the shallow groove in the wall right of the corner of 15 *Ordinary Route* Severe 4a. Climb a thin grainy crack to horizontal break then move over the overlap into the groove above. Leave the groove with difficulty and climb boldly past a good flange on improving holds to a thin horizontal break (friend runner). More easily above.

16 Dougie's Ordinary Route ★★   20m E3 5c
FA Dougie Dinwoodie, Brian Lawrie & Mungo Ross June 1989

The slim buttress cut by horizontal breaks midway between the two corners. From the good half-height ledge, move right and ascend flake near the edge to a good break and a PR then left to finish strenuously.

17 Seannachie ★   20m VS 4c
FA Brian Lawrie (solo) 1970s

Gain the corner by a traverse left from 15.

18 Dragons of Eden ★   20m E2 5c
FA Brian Lawrie, Dougie Dinwoodie & Kevin Murphy Easter 1985

Follow thin crack to ledge and finish by a fine flake-crack.

19 Saint Vitus Gets on Down   20m E2 5c
FA Brian Lawrie, Dougie Dinwoodie & Kevin Murphy Easter 1985

Climb the more broken crack just left of 18 to the ledge, finishing steeply up the groove on the left (crux). Finishing up 18 is HVS 5a.

20 Blood of Eden ★   20m E1 5b
FA Paul Allan & Wilson Moir 12 June 1993

The rightmost of two lines left of 19. Scramble up to ledges and belay. Start just right of the crack-line. Gain and climb the crack then take the line of flakes running diagonally rightwards to finish by a short crack.

21 Forbidden Fruit ★   25m E3 5c
FA Wilson Moir & Paul Allan 12 June 1993

Climb corners with a tricky start to a ledge. Move left along this and gain a left-slanting crack in the black and gold-streaked rock. Climb this and the crack above.

22 Shades of Night ★   20m E2 5c
FA Brian Lawrie, Dougie Dinwoodie & Kevin Murphy Easter 1985

Start 10 metres left of 19. Climb out of a large alcove topped by an overhanging crack to gain an easier chimney crack. Follow this to a roof near the top then traverse out right onto the face to finish.

Descent: Abseil from the north end of the west-facing wall. There is occasionally a shags nest at the base.

23 Necronomicon ★★   18m E1 5b
FA Brian Lawrie, Dougie Dinwoodie & Kevin Murphy Easter 1985

The big open corner at the far left (north) end of the walls. The best route of its grade at Reiff with perfect protection. Some wildly turbulent water at the base – don't fall in!

24 The Presence ★★   20m VS 4c
FA Brian Lawrie, Dougie Dinwoodie & Kevin Murphy Easter 1985

Fine exposed climbing up the right-slanting ramp emanating from the start of 23. Climb the corner for the first few metres then move out rightwards and up the ramp. Step right round on ledge to finish up a small groove.

 1hr

BLACK MAGIC WALL

The slabby north-facing wall.

Descent: By abseil onto the platform, or by climbing down *Nothing Special*.

1 Nothing Special ★   15m Difficult
FA unknown 1990

The chimney on the right then a line of steps leading right.

2 Black Magic ★★★   15m VS 4c
FA Brian Lawrie & Neil Morrison Summer 1984

The centre of the wall left of the chimney.

3 Milk Tray ★   15m HVS 5a
FA Gary Latter & Charlie Prowse 30 September 1998

Good climbing up the left side of the black wall with the crux the first 4m to gain a good horizontal break.

4 The Comeback ★★   20m VS 4c
FA Neil Morrison & Andy Nisbet June 1987

Low tide is required for this one. On the slabby wall left of *The Black Chimney* (V.Diff.) in the corner left of 2. Climb the right side of the wall, starting by trending right up a very shallow scoop. Finish up a steep flake.

SLAB INLET

A narrow inlet with a distinctive low-angled slab forming its seaward (north) side.

Approach: Either scramble down the outside (seaward) end (Moderate) of the easy-angled slab or sneak through a tunnel from the east at the back of the **Platform Walls** to emerge at the back of the inlet. Alternatively, abseil to ledges at the base.

1 Turbulent Indigo ★★   12m E2 5c
FA Andy & Jeni Cunningham & Colin Lesenger June 1996

The right diagonal crack up the overhanging west-facing wall above the tunnel entrance. Start off the big block.

2 Break Dance ★   12m E2 5b
FA Brian Lawrie & Andy Nisbet August 1986

The wall to the left of the corner, just right of the arête.

3 The Ali-Shuffle ★★   12m VS 5a
FA Brian Lawrie & Andy Nisbet August 1986

The rightmost and most prominent corner on the landward side. Very well protected. Approach by abseil.

4 Cool Dudes ★   12m E1 5b
FA Simon Richardson & Tim Whitaker 30 May 1999

The blunt edge 3m right of 3. Climb up on good holds just left of the edge to a thin section. Move up then right, finishing on improving holds.

5 Penguin ★   12m VS 5a
FA Gary Latter (solo) 30 September 1998

The stepped groove round the arête right of 3 with the crux pulling through an often wet roof near the top.

6 Polar Bear ★★   23m HVS 5a
FA Gary Latter & Charles Prowse 30 September 1998

A fine line taking the prominent diagonal crack-line up the wall right of 3. Start at the right end of the ledge at the base of 3. Follow the diagonal crack-line to its end then step left and climb the wall above.

7 School's Out ★   20m VS 4c
FA Colin Lesenger & Andy Cunningham June 1996

Climbs the wall right of 3 near the right edge, via amenable horizontal breaks. Access by abseil to a ledge round the corner on the right and start by a swing down on to the wall.

NORTH SIDE 1hr

1 Atlantic Crack ** — 8m E3 5c
FA Andy Nisbet & Brian Lawrie August 1986

A fine short overhanging crack, mostly finger width with the crux at the top.

2 Eag Dubh * — 10m HVS 5a
FA Dougie Dinwoodie (solo) Summer 1985

The *'black notch'* chimney crack left of 1.

PLATFORM WALLS 1hr

East of **Slab Inlet – North Side** an extensive platform tilts westwards into the sea with a long north-facing black wall above the platform. At low tide a subterranean tunnel runs through to the **Slab Inlet** to the west.

Descent: Scramble down a black, usually slimy, slabby area at the back of the geo to the east to gain the platform below the east wall. At low tide a more adventurous approach can be made from the **Slab Inlet** via the tunnel.

Routes from left to right (east to west).

1 Mad Dogs and Englishmen *** — 25m E3 5c
FA Richard Mansefield & Dave Etherington Summer 1991

An exhilarating exposed left-slanting traverse line above the big roofs up the overhanging west-facing wall of the geo. Pull easily onto the prominent traverse line, making an awkward step down at 3m. Move back up to the break and hand traverse to the first groove. Continue round the arête into the next groove. Exit left to a good ledge, finishing easily up the slab above.

2 Autumn Sonata * — 10m E4 6a
FA Brian Lawrie & Andy Nisbet August 1986

Start left of the tunnel entrance, beneath a large roof at 3m. Climb up to below the roof, move right and up to a horizontal break. Gain a good hold high up on the left and move up to a small overlap, finishing up the prominent small corner.

3 The Eaves * — 12m Very Difficult
FA Brian Lawrie (solo) August 1986

Chimney up the outside edge of the tunnel until possible to exit onto the slab. Traverse twin horizontal cracks rightwards then follow the right-slanting crack to the roof, turned on the right. Gaining the end of the traverse direct is VS 4c.

4 Submarine Badlands * — 12m VS 4b
FA Brian Lawrie (solo) August 1986

The shallow groove midway between the slab and the vertical wall further right. Ascend the groove which leads round the corner to a spectacular finish above the steep wall.

5 The Irish Agreement * — 12m E2 5c
FA Andy Cunningham, Ian & M.Rae October 1994

To the right of 4 is a vertical wall. Climb close to the left arête of the wall, moving slightly right with a long reach at mid-height.

6 Spring Sonatina ** — 12m E2 5c
FA Paul Allen & Wilson Moir May 1995

Start to the right of 5. Tackle the fierce crack rising out of the roof of a small recess. Committing.

7 Corner Wall * — 12m Very Difficult
FA Andy Nisbet (solo) August 1986

The leftmost corner. Follow a flake on the left to the ledge then the overhanging corner above.

8 Reap the Wild Wind ** — 12m VS 4b
FA Brian Lawrie (solo) August 1986

Deceptively steep climb up the shallow corner on the right.

9 Under Pressure *   12m E2 5c
FA Colin Lesenger & Jeni Cunningham June 1996

The steep narrow wall to the right of 8. Climb to the roof, move right and pull back left over the overlap to finish up a short right-facing corner.

10 Minch Crack **   12m VS 4b
FA Brian Lawrie (solo) August 1986

Start up the edge to join and follow the crack, or follow it throughout at VS 4c.

11 Mars Crack **   12m Severe 4a
FA Andy Nisbet (solo) August 1986

The fine crack cutting the long juggy wall near its left end.

12 Mickey Mouse *   15m Severe 4a
FA Andy Cunningham & Keith Geddes July 1989

Start beneath the shallow groove line near the right end of the wall containing 11. From the left end of the undercut base, make a long traverse right to gain the groove.

RAMPANT WALL
  1hr

A steep crack-seamed slab, mostly above a convenient platform.

Descent: As for the **Platform Walls** then slither across the boulders diagonally to their end, or scramble down the north end.

1 Micro Crack *   10m HS 4b
FA Brian Lawrie & Andy Nisbet August 1986

The leftmost of the main cracks.

2 Macro Crack *   15m E1 5b
FA Brian Lawrie & Andy Nisbet August 1986

The main crack, opposite the tunnel.

3 The Gods **   20m HS 4b
FA Andy Nisbet & Brian Lawrie August 1986

The rightmost crack starting at sea level. Start easily up a deep flared overhanging chimney and climb up to roofs. Traverse right under the roofs and up onto a finely-situated nose and possible belay (cams). Make a delicate step up into the thin crack above then more easily to finish out left.

1 Spaced Out Rockers on the Road to Oblivion
    **** 65m E4 5c

FA Kevin Murphy & Doug Hawthorn (in 4 pitches) Summer 1985; FA as described Gary Latter & Dave Hollinger 22 August 2000

A stunning right to left diagonal line across the big undercut wall, giving the longest and best route on the peninsula. Start at a big roofed recess just left of the right edge of the wall, gained from the west face by soloing leftwards round ledges.

Karin Magog and Steve Crowe on the long sustained second pitch of Spaced Out Rockers on the Road to Oblivion.

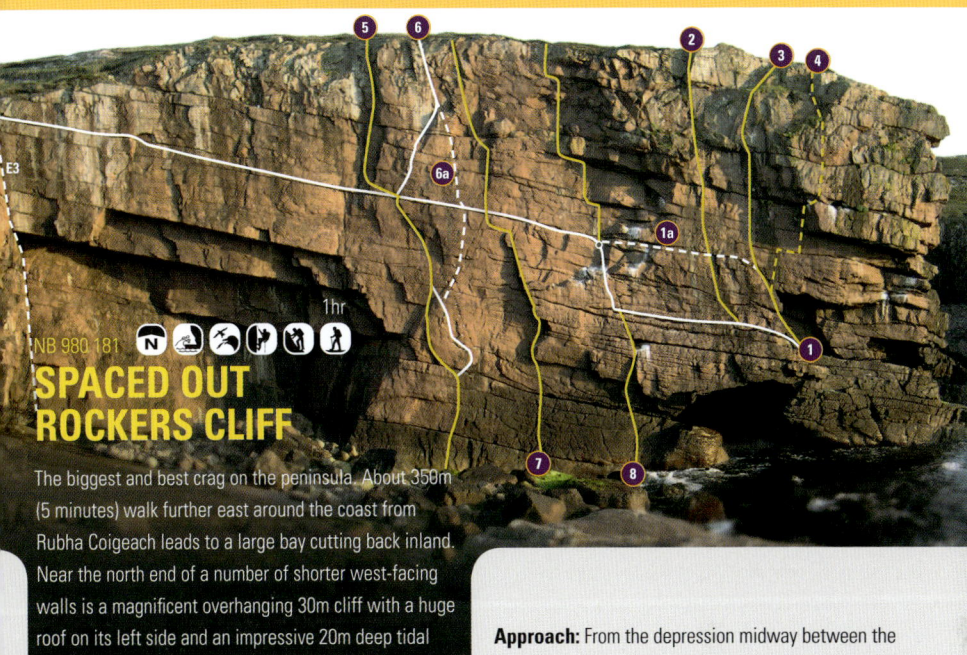

SPACED OUT ROCKERS CLIFF

The biggest and best crag on the peninsula. About 350m (5 minutes) walk further east around the coast from Rubha Coigeach leads to a large bay cutting back inland. Near the north end of a number of shorter west-facing walls is a magnificent overhanging 30m cliff with a huge roof on its left side and an impressive 20m deep tidal cave cutting into its right edge. There are belay stakes (four of them!) above the centre of the cliff.

Nesting Restrictions: a small colony of shags is occasionally in residence on some ledges on the upper right side of the cliff and care should be taken not to disturb them during the nesting season (April – July). The routes are best scoped out from near the huge 'tottering' block atop the wall just to the north (or from the block itself, if you like to live life on the edge!).

Approach: From the depression midway between the two lines of cairns just north of the shieling at the north end of Camas Eilean Ghlais, head north-east, aiming for a depression between the two small knolls, skirting round the side of three small lochans. On arriving at the coast, head right (east).

Descents: Down the steep grassy bank at the back (south-west) of the bay then scramble east. It is also possible at low tide to scramble down to the north of the cliff and cut left along the wide slabby, slanting shelf to the base of the routes. Alternatively, make a 35m abseil from the stakes.

1 **20m 5c** Traverse horizontally left until below the left end of a ledge system. Make hard moves up to gain the ledge and belay at the right end.

2 **45m 5c** Go to the left end of the ledge and up to a prominent handrail and follow this until possible to gain a higher handrail, which cuts through an obvious niche to finish in the corner. Nut belay at top of the corner, or 15m further back. A 'Yosemite big wall' rack of cams from 1 – 4", (mainly 1.5 – 3") will be found more than useful

1a Rockers – The Prequel ★   **25m E4 5c**
FA Ian Taylor & Tess Fryer 26 May 2016

An alternative first pitch. From the same start, follow 3 up the left edge of the cave to a break, then follow this left to join 1 at its belay.

2 Sgeoldair ★★   **25m E5/6 6b**
FA Ian Taylor & Tess Fryer 25 July 2015

Start as for 1 and follow this left for 5m, then go up the left side of a black streak to gain a small hanging corner and a good break. Move left then run it out up the crimpy wall to another good break. Go left up through a break in the overhangs (often wet but on good holds) to a ledge and an easier finish.

3 Aqua Rambling ★★★   20m E5 6a
FA Ian Taylor & Tess Fryer 19 August 2011

Start as for 1. Swing left onto the front face and follow the edge and crack above to gain a good break. Move left, make some thin moves and continue to another break. Go up to a roof and pull over using flat holds, step right and climb up to finish on a ledge just below the cliff-top. Low in the grade with good protection where it matters.

4 Lethe Walk ★★★   20m E3/4 6a
FA Tess Fryer & Ian Taylor 20 July 2012

Start as for 3, taking the black streak above to a break. Go right along the break until under a corner at the left side of the big roof and gain the corner by a hard move. At the top of the corner swing round right onto the front face and go up the wall above.

> The following routes are tidal, accessible from mid-tide onwards.

5 Headlong ★★★   35m E4 5c
FA Gary Latter & Dave Hollinger (on-sight) 21 August 2000

Excellent sustained climbing heading for the prominent hanging groove high up in the centre of the cliff. Climb the wall to a thin diagonal crack then traverse horizontally left along a break, then slightly right up the shallow ramp to an apparent impasse. Climb steeply straight up the wall on hidden holds then traverse left along the excellent break of 1 to a good rest in the base of the final groove. Climb this more easily to finish.

6 Misha ★★★   35m E6 6b
FA Gary Latter & Karin Magog 26 May 2004

The central line up the wall, midway between 5 and 4. Very sustained. Start 6m right of the arête of 2, directly beneath an obvious thin diagonal hanging crack. Weave up first left then rightwards along breaks to pull back left and move up to the vague crack. Climb this leading to undercut flakes and follow these to gain the break on 1. Make hard moves up the wall above (crux) to better holds and a good break. Move out right along this and pull up onto a ledge in the recess. Move out left and continue more easily past large spike to finish. Well protected – three sets of cams required!

6a Misha Direct ★★   35m E7 6b
FA Ian Taylor & Tess Fryer 24 July 2017

Follow 6 to the top of the vague crack where it rejoins 5. Move right and up to a shallow incut break near a round pocket (poor cam 2 and RP in the break). From a good incut above, make a big move to a shallow break, then up to the break on 1. Move slightly left and climb a hard thin seam using a shallow finger pocket. Finish direct. Low in the grade.

7 Culach ★★★   35m E5 6a
FA Gary Latter 1 September 2000

Spectacular climbing up the hanging flake system in the centre of the cliff. Start immediately beneath the flake system. Climb steadily up to protection in the first break at 5m then up and follow the groove/flakes, climbing on good holds steeply up the edge to a good rest beneath the break of 1. Make bold moves straight up to good ledges and continue to large ledge near top. Climbs straight up with a long reach to the final break. Finish slightly left, past a good undercut flake.

8 Shortcut to Oblivion ★★★   35m E4 6a
FA Tess Fryer & Ian Taylor 19 August 2011

Start 5m right of 7 and just left of the sea cave. Climb up and make committing moves to gain a shallow guano splattered groove and follow this to a junction with 1. Continue up 1 to its belay ledge, then carry on more or less directly to a large roof, which is passed on its left via keyed-in blocks to gain a ledge. Steep bulges above lead to another roof. Move left and make a final long reach for the top.

THE LEANING BLOCK CLIFFS NB 982 181   1hr

Lies about 150m east of the **Spaced Out Rockers Cliff**. Perhaps the showpiece crags of the area with plenty of uber-classics throughout a good spread of grades, particularly in the extremes. Coupled with the stunning backdrop of the Assynt and Coigach hills to the east, this really is pretty much as good as it gets.

Descent: Routes on the block itself and the walls to the east are easily approached by a short step at the east end then heading back west.

Routes west of the block: Down the boulder-filled gully on the west side, or by a 15m abseil from large block down the west side of the chimney formed by the block.

1 Pirates of Coigach ★★★ 20m HS 4b
FA Andy Cunningham & Jeni Pickering July 1990

Start from an overhanging ledge on the right (east) side of the descent gully. Swing round onto the front face and climb up to follow a ramp leftwards across the black wall.

Routes 2 to 9 are tidal.

2 Harold ★★ 15m Severe 4a
FA Wilson Moir (solo) July 1989

The black corner left of the descent gully.

2a Sixteen Men on a Dead Man's Chest ★★★ 15m HVS 5b
FA Michael Barnard & Jonnie Williams 31 May 2008

The fine arête. From the smaller ledge at the base of the corner, hand traverse left to gain the edge, which is climbed all the way to the top.

3 Caoraich Mhor ★★★ 15m E2 6a
FA Brian Lawrie & Colin McLean July 1989

Left again are two cracks. The rightmost one with a hard start. Slow to dry.

The wall right of 3 is 3a *Edges and Spaces* ★★ E2 6a; thin hanging crack starting up 3 to first break 3b *Brasso* ★★ E3 6a; wall left of HVS crack is 3c *Skeddadale* ★★ E3 5c and the leaning corner is 3d *Yonipool* ★★ E2/3 5c. The brown corner is 4 *Reiffer Madness* ★ VS 4c – slow to dry.

5 Hydraulic Dogs ★★ 20m E4 6a
FA Andy Cunningham, Rich Biggar & Lawrence Hughes 10 April 2002

Hand traverse break left out of 4 to good hold in the centre. Pull past the first break then directly using breaks, pockets and slots to finish up a shallow scooped corner.

5a Gilt Edge ★★ 20m E4 6a
FA Ian Taylor & Tess Fryer 5 July 2008; Direct Gary Latter 29 May 2014

The arête gives some excellent climbing. Go up the corner for a few metres until able to hand traverse right onto ledge, then follow arête to top. The 5b *Direct Start* is E5 6a ★. The corner is 5c *Mr Bridger* ★ E2 5c.

NORTH & WEST SIDE

6 Goldeneye *   20m HVS 5a
FA Andy Cunningham & Fraser Fotheringham May 1997

The first corner right of the prominent black fault, finishing up the leaning crack on the left.

7 Waigwa **   18m HVS 5a
FA Wilson Moir & Colin MacLean July 1989

The black pocketed cracked wall, left of the wide fault.

7a Veedon Fleece ***   18m E1 5b
FA Michael Barnard & Alex Clarke-Williams 6 June 2008

The continuous crack 2m left of 7, joining 7 at the top.

8 Golden Fleece ***   18m E1 5b
FA Colin McLean & Wilson Moir July 1989

The next left-slanting crack-line a few metres left of 7.

8a Golden Plover **   18m E3 5c
FA Gary Latter 30 May 2014

The left edge. Pull over the roof direct to a good hold in rightmost of twin hairline cracks. Step left and up to a good break, then the pleasant arête above.

> Round the edge east from 8 is an immaculate steep black slab, well endowed with holds. Small cams useful.

9 Sunshine on Reiff **   18m E1 5b
FA Niall Ritchie & Wilson Moir July 1989

Follow a scooped line up the right edge of the wall.

10 Van Hoover's Awa ***   18m E1 5b
FA Niall Ritchie & Richard Mansfield July 1990

Start 3m left of an obvious crack near the right edge. Trend left on good holds up to half-height and finish direct.

11 The Good, the Bad and the Ugly **   18m E1 5b
FA Richard Mansfield, Niall Ritchie & Andy Cunningham Jul 1990

Climb the centre of the slab, starting up a short corner-crack and finishing easily by a short left-facing corner.

12 The Africaan Problem ***   18m E1 5b
FA Andy Cunningham & Jeni Pickering July 1990

Start at the extreme left end of the slab by the entrance to the chimney. Trend right to a big ledge and climb up quite boldly on orange rock via a shallow flake to finish left under a stepped roof.

13 Block Chimney **   18m Very Difficult
FA John Lyall (solo) 1990s

Interesting and fun climbing up the west end of the chimney formed by the Leaning Block.

📷 Andy Nelson on the aptly-named Cyclops.

LEFT END

Approach: Down the huge sloping platform to the east. Routes described from **left to right from looking in from the base (east to west).**

14 Otto ★★★ 12m E7 6c (F7c+)
FA Gary Latter (redpointed) 19 September 2001

Fierce powerful climbing forging directly up the centre of the leaning wall avoided by 15. Climb the good breaks as for 15 then continue directly with difficult moves to gain and leave the prominent flake, stepping left at the top break to finish at a good V-notch. Well protected by small cams.

15 The Quickening ★★★ 18m E4 6a
FA Gary Latter & Andy Wren 6 May 1995

A diagonal line across the grossly overhanging wall bounding the left side of the crag. Start beneath a prominent flake at 3m. Up on good breaks to reach an obvious line of holds and follow these rightwards to underneath the roof on the arête. Swing round and finish up the left edge of the slab. Well protected with cams.

16 Slow Quick Quick Slow ★★ 18m E5 6b
FA Steve Crowe & Karin Magog 25 August 2002

Step off the block and traverse right along the break to the arête. Go up the overhanging left side of the arête, up the stepped groove and swing right at the roof round to finish up 15. Climbing the right side of the arête from the same start to join 15 is E2 5c.

17 Empty on Endorphins ★★ 15m E1 5b
FA Andy Cunningham & Jeni Pickering July 1990

Start on top of a large boulder under the left arête of the face. Up to large horizontal break, move left along this for 3 metres then up, trending slightly leftwards.

18 Brave Heart ★★ 15m E2 5c
FA Richard Mansefield & Niall Ritchie July 1990

Steady climbing up the centre of the wall, crossing the small roof at mid-height.

19 Freedom! ★★ 15m E3 5c
FA Gary Latter & Dave Hollinger 16 September 2001

A direct line up the wall right of 18. Climb directly to bulge at mid-height, cross this to good slots and continue straight up to good holds in a recess. Finish more easily directly above.

20 Olympus ★ 15m E2 5b
FA Andy Cunningham & Jeni Pickering July 1990

A good trip up the prominent wide crack.

21 Coigach Corner ★★ 15m VS 5a
FA Richard Mansefield (solo) July 1990

Start up the ramp.

22 Bow Wave ★　　　　　　　　　　　**15m VS 4c**
FA Andy Cunningham & Jeni Pickering July 1990

Follow a crack right of the ramp to gain the ramp where it tapers. Up the ramp then finish direct. The ramp is 23 *Crossover* V.Diff.

THE LEANING BLOCK

Descent: Step/jump across narrow chimney at the back.

24 Blind Bandit ★　　　　　　　　　　**12m HVS 5a**
FA Niall Ritchie & Andy Cunningham July 1990

On the east-facing wall of the block. Start up a right-facing flake then up past good horizontal breaks to the roof. Pull through the left end of this, trending right to finish.

25 Cross-Eyed ★★★　　　　　　　　　**15m E2 5b**
FA Richard Mansefield & Niall Ritchie July 1990

A stunning diagonal line with good holds and protection. Start just right of the flake. Climb up to gain the wide break and traverse this to a huge thread on the arête. Swing round right and follow a line of improving holds up the alarmingly steep and exposed headwall. Superb.

26 Cyclops ★★　　　　　　　　　　　**18m E2 5b**
FA Andy Cunningham & Jeni Pickering July 1990

Start lower down, on the right side of the arête. Climb a series of breaks to the huge thread then more easily up the shallow groove directly above. The grade is reduced to E1 5b by following the start of 25 to the thread.

27 Losgaidh ★★★　　　　　　　　　　**18m E3 5c**
FA Dougie Dinwoodie, Brian Lawrie & Mungo Ross June 1989

'Burning'. A superb sustained and strenuous pitch, aiming for the hanging groove in the centre of the north face of the block. Climb direct to the ledge then climb the wall past a number of breaks to finish more easily up the final groove.

28a The Bonus ★★　　　　　　　　　　**12m E5 6a**
FA Ian Taylor & Tess Fryer 2008

Climb 28 to the cave, then blast straight up the wall above, with long reaches between breaks.

The following routes are all on the west-facing wall of the block.

Approach: By squeezing through the chimney at the back of the block to gain a convenient raised platform at the base. At low tide it is also possible to gain these from the boulder-filled gully to the west or by walking round the platform underneath the north face.

28 The Gift ★★★　　　　　　　　　　　**18m E5 6a**
FA Richard Mansefield, Andy Cunningham & Niall Ritchie Jul 1990

Another stunning pitch in an incredibly exposed situation. Start up the left edge of the raised platform. Step left onto the seaward face and up into a cave. Move back right and make hard committing moves up right to a jutting block and well earned hands off rest. Another hard move leads to jugs and the top.

29 The Screamer ★★★★　　　　　　　**15m E4 6a**
FA Andy Cunningham & Richard Mansefield July 1990

Immaculate climbing, taking an improbable-looking line up the centre of the face. Start midway between the arête and the crack. Through bulges to the large break. Move diagonally leftwards to a short wide break then trend slightly rightwards to the final wide break (F #3). Move slightly right to finish.

30 Whispers ★　　　　　　　　　　　**15m E5 6b**
FA Gary Latter & Mike Reed 10 May 2001

The thin incipient crack in the wall just right of 29. Climb direct up the wall then the thin crack with hard moves at 2/3rds height. Finish more easily above a good break.

31 Wall of Silence ★★★　　　　　　　**15m E3 5c**
FA Niall Ritchie & Wilson Moir July 1989

Sustained well protected climbing up the fine crack at the right side of the wall. So-named, because the first ascent team didn't speak to each other all the way back to Aberdeen, due to the second suggesting an E1 5b grade! Low in the grade (though not quite E1!).

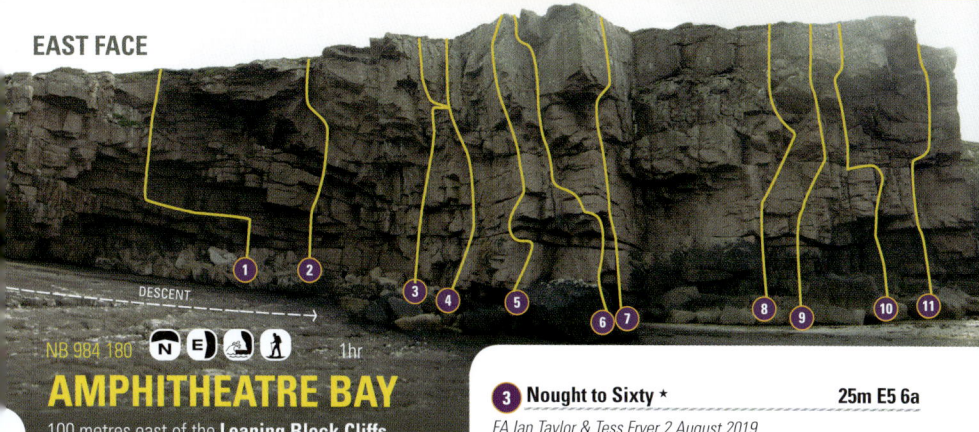

EAST FACE

AMPHITHEATRE BAY

NB 984 180 1hr

100 metres east of the **Leaning Block Cliffs**.
Descent: Down the boulders on the west side for the **North Face**. For the **East Face**, continue further east to scramble down to gain a large dipping shelf leading towards the base.

NORTH FACE

1 An Sulaire ★★ 20m HVS 5a

FA Andy Cunningham & Jeni Pickering July 1990

'The Gannet'. Start directly under the crack in the front of the prow. Follow a shallow hidden black corner to a large ledge, finishing up the fine crack above.

EAST FACE

1 The Convolutionist ★★★ 30m E5 6a

FA Ian Taylor & Tess Fryer 29 June 2014

The route is gained by a cunning traverse line, starting 10m to the right at a corner. Go up the corner to a good break and traverse left, round a nose, to a good ledge. To avoid further rope drag, keep all the gear on the right rope for the first section then drop a loop of the right rope and get re-belayed. Climb up and left and follow the cracks past a pumpy section to a high ledge. Finish up the nose above  via a wide horizontal slot. Save a Camalot 3 for the top bit.

2 Furious Fifties ★ 25m E4 5c

FA Iain Small & Sam Williams May 2014

Groove left of 3

3 Nought to Sixty ★ 25m E5 6a

FA Ian Taylor & Tess Fryer 2 August 2019

Start just left of 4 below a short hanging corner. Climb the corner, step left then follow thin cracks over bulges to a good break at 10m. Move right and make a long move to a big jug on the arête and a junction with 4. Go up the groove of 4 for 5m to good cam 2 placement then down climb and make tricky moves left to gain the bottom of a small hanging groove. Finish up this.

4 The Roaring Forties ★★ 25m E4 5c

FA Steve Clegg & Howard Lancashire 2 June 1994

The leftmost series of overhanging grooves, the first obvious line from the left. An exhilarating pitch, reasonably well protected with Fs #0 – #4 doubled up useful.

5 Warning of gales in Rockall, Malin, Hebrides
★★★ 25m E6 6b

FA Iain Small & Tony Stone 2013

The arête right of 4.

6 Hyperoceanic ★★ 25m E6 6b

FA Iain Small & Gary Latter (on-sight) 4 August 2007

The prominent roof-capped groove, starting directly behind a large black boulder at the base. Start a few metres right of the main groove. Climb the easy wide crack to the right end of the first roof. Make difficult moves out left to large incut hold (crux) then pull over on good breaks. Step left into a groove and protection. Climb leftwards up the wall then make further difficult moves over the next roof to good holds. Continue to a capping block then hand traverse left to good finishing holds.

7 Stonechat ★★   25m E5 6b
FA Simon Westaway June 2008

A line up the left wall of the big square-cut corner. Gain the large raised ledge via a wide crack, then follow the jam crack above until possible to pull out left, moving up to a recess below roofs. Pull steeply up and right to a position below the final headwall, to finish up the thin crack.

8 Lost at Sea ★★   25m E3 5c
FA Iain Small & Gary Latter 4 August 2007

The prominent groove starting just right of the large raised ledge. Climb the groove and the obvious right-trending line leading to the roof. Traverse left then up with difficulty to good holds, finishing more easily up a crack in the headwall.

9 Relatively Free ★★   25m E4 6a
FA Ian Taylor & Tess Fryer 23 July 2011

Start a little to the right of 8 and climb a snaking flake and crack to reach a big break. Go right along the break and pull into a corner, which is followed to the big roof. Move left and go steeply through the roof at a weakness, then finish up a tricky thin crack. Well protected.

10 From Hero to Zero ★★   30m E6 6b
FA Ian Taylor & Tess Fryer 20 July 2012

Start left of 11 at a steep groove with keyed-in blocks. Grunt up the groove to its top and move left to a big ledge. Climb direct to a hanging left leaning crack and follow this to a huge thin hold under the roof. Traverse left with difficulty and pull round to a big jug, then go straight up with a final trying move on small holds. Good pumpy well protected climbing, but loses a star due to flakey rock.

11 Minjeetah ★★   25m E5 6b
FA Mike Reed & Gary Latter 10 May 2001

The corner and cracks through the triple roofs. Cross the initial roof on good holds and climb the corner, moving out left to a large ledge. Traverse right above the second roof and up a crack strenuously to a rest in a depression beneath final roof. Move out left to a good flange, pulling through the final roof on good holds to finish up a short easy corner.

NB 985 978   1¼hr
JIGSAW WALL POINT
The gold-coloured wall about 300m east of **Amphitheatre Bay**.
Descent: Down the wet grassy slope at the right (south) end of the wall.

1 Jigsaw Wall ★★★   15m HVS 5a
FA Allen Fyffe, Andy Cunningham & Jeni Pickering Sept 1990

The prominent vertical crack near the left end of the wall. Start up an easy slab then pull leftwards through the roof to the crack. Go up this then the corner on the right, passing a huge block near the top.

NB 988 178   1¼hr

RUBHA PLOYTACH

A collection of small rocky headlands ringed by non-tidal raised platforms.
Descents: Down the east end, through some large boulders onto the 'Shipshape Block' platform. Alternatively, make a short abseil directly down the wall.

EAST FACE

1 **First and Ten** ★★★　　　　**10m Very Difficult**
FA Allen & Blair Fyffe August 1990

Stepped right-facing corners at the left end of the wall.

2 **Mosaic** ★★　　　　**10m Severe 4a**
FA Allen & Blair Fyffe August 1990

Cracks up the centre of the wall, a few metres right of 1.

3 **Fancy Free** ★　　　　**10m Severe 4a**
FA Jeni Pickering & Andy Cunningham August 1990

Start as for 2. Move up and follow a right-curving line near the right edge of the wall.

4 **Labrador Chimney** ★★　　　　**10m Difficult**
FA Allen & Blair Fyffe August 1990

The chimney bounding the right edge of the wall.

5 **Groovy Mover** ★★★　　　　**10m Severe 4a**
FA Jeni Pickering & Andy Cunningham August 1990

The groove blocked by roofs in the right rib of the chimney.

6 **The Slide** ★★★　　　　**10m Difficult**
FA Allen & Blair Fyffe August 1990

The wide corner just right of the rib of 5, crossing a roof at the base.

7 **The Evil of Spuds** ★　　　　**12m Very Difficult**
FA Colin Angus & Oli Gray 22 July 2004

Pull onto the left side of the slab immediately right of 6. Trend up and right to finish in a prominent notch.

8 **Rodney's Ramble** ★　　　　**12m Severe 4a**
FA Oli Gray & Colin Angus 22 July 2004

Start just left of 9. Climb the steep wall to the overhang. Traverse left on good holds to finish as for route 7.

9 **Touchdown Montana** ★★　　　　**10m Severe 4a**
FA Allen & Blair Fyffe August 1990

The main corner on the wall. Start up a smooth recess.

NORTH FACE

10 **Second and Goal** ★★　　　　**10m Severe 4a**
FA Allen & Blair Fyffe August 1990

A shallow scooped line rising from the left side of a roofed recess low down.

11 **Ace of Diamonds** ★★★　　　　**10m HS 4b**
FA Andy Cunningham & Jeni Pickering August 1990

Start as for 10. Climb into the diamond-shaped recess, then follow the ramp rightwards.

12 **The Joker** ★★　　　　**10m VS 5a**
FA Andy Cunningham & Jeni Pickering August 1990

Start from the right end of the ledge. Climb a direct line up the centre of the wall.

EAST FACE

The next three routes are in a tidal square-cut bay with difficult access. Its east facing wall is gained by descending easily west of 'Shipshape Block' onto a lower platform then walking back under a smooth black seaward wall.

13 **Aquarium Arête** ★★　　　　**8m Severe 4a**
FA Michael Barnard June 2006

Climb beside the left edge of the black seaward wall, left of 14.

14 **Marie Celeste** ★★　　　　**10m VS 5b**
FA Andy Cunningham & Jeni Pickering August 1990

The thin vertical crack in the centre of the wall.

15 **Celtic Horizons** ★★　　　　**10m HS 4b**
FA Andy Cunningham & Jeni Pickering August 1990

Lies at the right end of the bay. Climb steeply up past horizontal breaks to gain a short crack in the upper half.

WEST FACE

16 The Toaster *   6m E2 5c

FA Andy Cunningham & Allen Fyffe September 1990

Weird, strenuous, reachy climbing up a series of widening breaks on the wall just round the edge. There is a short vertical crack at mid-height.

17 Three Step *   8m Very Difficult

FA Allen Fyffe (solo) September 1990

The stepped corner right of 16. 18 *Giant's Steps*, Severe 4a takes its right edge.

19 Pretty in Pink * *   8m Severe 4a

FA Allen & Blair Fyffe September 1990

The first thin crack-line right of the edge.

20 Jug Abuse * *   8m Difficult

FA Allen & Blair Fyffe September 1990

Just right of 19.

21 Trefoil *   8m Very Difficult

FA Allen & Blair Fyffe September 1990

Slightly offset left-facing corners, where the wall changes angle.

22 Ros Bhan *   8m VS 5a

FA Jeni Pickering & Andy Cunningham September 1990

Start 3 metres right of 21. Gain a ledge strenuously at 3m by a wide horizontal break and short corner. Up the crack to a further ledge, finishing up the corner.

23 Lilidh *   8m E1 5c

FA Andy Cunningham & Jeni Pickering September 1990

The crack 4m right of 22. Gain the first break then move right to a short ledge. Trend slightly right then back left to finish up the top section of the crack.

24 An Ros *   8m E2 6a

FA Gary Latter 6 November 2000

Start 2m right of 23. From a good edge, stretch to the sloping break. Gain the ledge above with a long reach, finishing direct past a thin crack.

**25 Omission ** **   8m HVS 5b

FA Allis Ash & Rondy Salter 7 August 1999

The thin right-facing right-angled corner near the right end. Bouldery reachy start.

On the seaward prow of the promontory:

**26 Clansman ** **   8m E2 5c

FA Andy Cunningham & Jeni Pickering September 1990

Start left of centre and climb on small holds up the bulging wall to the big break. Move left then a long reach gains the ledge. Return right and finish up the corner.

**27 Claymore ** **   8m E2 5c

FA Andy Cunningham & Jeni Pickering September 1990

Start under twin diagonal cracks high up. Trend right up the bulging wall and back left to the break. Take the steep crack to the next break and finish by the left of twin cracks.

**28 Sundew ** **   8m VS 4b

FA Allen & Blair Fyffe September 1990

Start at the left edge. Climb to a short right-facing corner, up this and trend left and up to finish.

**29 Nightshade ** **   8m VS 4c

FA Allen & Blair Fyffe September 1990

Start further right, off a jammed boulder. Cross a small roof using a long spike to finish up the crack-line.

**30 Millstone Corner ** **   8m VS 4b

FA Allen & Blair Fyffe September 1990

The tunnel ends at a black shattered corner. Follow the clean open black corner in the right wall.

INBHIRPOLLAIDH ROCK GYM

NC 077 149 **Alt:** 80m 30min

A fine quick drying lenticular shaped gneiss crag near Inverpolly Lodge with a range of good routes. Please use the approach described in order to maintain good relations with the estate owners.

Access: Follow the single track road west towards Achiltibuie from the A835 at Drumrunie for 8.4 miles/13.4km then turn right (north) towards Lochinver for 3.5 miles/5.6km (1.2 miles/2km beyond the fish farm) to park at the north end of a loch to the west of the road.

Approach: Walk round the head of the loch and head west through a wide gap in the hillside to follow the line of the burn draining west past the crag into Lochan Sal.

1 Wall Rox *   25m HVS 5a
FA Andy Cunningham & Barry Chislett 7 May 2000

Start just left of the triangular cave at the right end. Climb cracks to a heather ledge. Move right and up to finish up the fine crack and orange arête on the right of the top wall.

2 Gaia Designs **   30m E3 5c
FA Andy Cunningham & Lawrence Hughes 12 May 2000

Start by boulders. Follow the prominent crack to a niche where the two diagonal breaks converge. Move up and climb the short jam crack through the bulge, moving into the right crack near the high ledge. Either finish up the wider crack and direct above or follow cracked red blocky ground leading to a crack further right.

3 Inertia **   30m E3 5c
FA Andy Cunningham & Barry Chislett 7 May 2000

Start directly beneath the V-Slot. Go steeply up to two holes by the diagonal breaks. Pull into the crack and up to the high ledge. Move right and climb easier cracked smooth rock, then back left above series of steep red grooves and ribs to finish by cracks.

4 Northern Exposure **   30m E5 6a
FA Lawrence Hughes & Andy Cunningham 5 October 2000

A hard eliminate midway between 3 and 5. Start just right of the alcove.

1 **16m 6a** Climb up through the right end of the wide break to the bulge. Pull through this just left of

centre and move right into the centre of the wall. Follow thin vague cracks to the high ledge.

2 **14m 6a** Take the smooth overhanging corner out of the back of the orange alcove. Pass a nose of rock, finishing by easier wide cracks.

5 Original Master ** — 30m E2 5c
FA Andy Cunningham, Stevie Blagbrough & Jeni Pickering August 1987

Go up the right side of the low alcove and through the middle of the wide break to the bulge. Cross the bulge and continue up wide cracks slightly leftwards to the high ledge. Finish by cracks in the rib directly above.

6 Failte Gu Inbhirpollaidh *** — 28m E3 5c
FA Andy Cunningham August 1987

'Welcome to...' Start just left of the alcove. Climb past the left end of the wide break and up a groove leading slightly left to the bulge. Follow the crack through the bulge to the high ledge. Finish in the same line via cracks out of a wide inset recess in the top wall.

7 Tyrantanic *** — 28m E4 6a
FA Lawrence Hughes & Andy Cunningham 12 May 2000

The left crack-line. Start by a head-height niche. Climb by a vague crack to the bulge. Pull over into a scoop then up cracks to the high ledge. Finish by a crack in the left side of the top wall.

8 1–800–Ming ** — 25m E3 5c
FA Lawrence Hughes & Andy Cunningham 12 May 2000

Climb past a triangular niche in the low diagonal break then by thin cracks in the golden rock to the bulge. Pull over the roof and up cracks leading to a smooth slot. Climb rightwards through the slot to the upper ledge, finishing easily by a stepped crack left of a left-facing corner.

9 Inspired Guest * — 18m E2 5b
FA Stevie Blagbrough, Andy Cunningham & Jeni Pickering August 1987

The cracked fault leading slightly leftwards to higher square-cut roofs in the bulge. Climb to the bulge and follow more prominent cracks through it, finishing by a short V-groove.

10 Gneiss Pump ** — 15m E3 5c
FA Colin Lesenger & Andy Cunningham 21 May 1998

Climb past the right side of the holly bush and up to the widest part of the bulge. Pull rightwards through the bulge into a short jam crack then direct up the cracked wall, finishing right of the skyline block.

11 Calum's Rest *** — 15m E1 5b
FA Andy Cunningham & Colin Lesenger 21 May 1998

Climb up just left of the holly bush to a large plaque just under the bulge. Pull over the bulge on good hidden holds, finishing direct up the cracked wall.

12a When I Were a Lad Direct * — 15m HVS 5a
FA Andy Cunningham & Jeni Pickering August 1987

Climb the groove of 12 to the bulge. Pull directly through the bulge and move right into cracks leading through the top bulge.

Andy Cunningham on Gneiss Pump. Photo Ian Taylor.

12 When I Were a Lad *   15m VS 4c
FA Stevie Blagbrough, Andy Cunningham & Jeni Pickering August 1987

Left-slanting groove to the bulge, left through the bulge and follow the same line to finish left of the top overhangs.

13 Return Game **   12m HVS 5a
FA Andy Cunningham & Colin Lesenger 21 May 1998

Start at the right end of the overhung niche at 2m. Climb via scoops into a crack which leads leftwards to the top.

14 Finger Picker *   12m E1 5b
FA Colin Lesenger & Andy Cunningham 21 May 1998

Start just left of an overhung niche at 2m. Climb a vague groove to a triangular niche, move right into thin cracks and finish up the right crack.

15 Future in Computer Hell *   12m HVS 5b
FA Lawrence Hughes & Andy Cunningham 11 June 1998

A direct line up the crack system finishing just right of the heathery groove. Climb to a cluster of jugs at 4m. Pass a downward pointing spike and finish direct.

16 Aspen Croft **   10m E1 5b
FA Andy Cunningham & Lawrence Hughes 12 May 2000

Follow vague cracks past a triangular niche by a jumble of horizontal cracks, finishing directly.

17 Another Rude Awakening *   10m E1 5b
FA Colin Lesenger & Andy Cunningham 21 May 1998

The slim groove leading through a triangular niche, finishing directly up the cracked wall.

18 Droppin' Bombs *   8m E2 6a
FA Lawrence Hughes & Andy Cunningham 12 May 2000

Start 3m right of the fault at a small triangular hole at head height. Climb direct up the cracked wall past a flat topped spike.

SUPER CRAG TRAD   CREAG RODHA MOR

   45min 15min

Far and away one of the best sea cliffs on mainland Scotland, particularly for those operating in the mid-high extremes. The **Main Wall** in particular has many superb long sustained single and two pitch routes, several as good as anything anywhere in the country.

Access: From just north of Lochinver take the B869 road towards Stoer for 1.4 miles/2.2km, then left towards Achmelvich for 0.8miles/1.3km. Follow the very narrow road, signposted 'Footpath to Baddidarrach' for 0.4 miles/0.6km to park at the end of the tarmacked section.

Approach: Continue along track, through a gate for 250m. Look out for a small stream on the right. Follow vague path up past some ruined crofts, continuing in the same direction out onto open ground. Cross a fence and continue following the stream to a narrow lochan, then west over ridges until the ground drops away to the sea. A large heather topped knoll marks the top of the crag, with good views of the **Burnished Walls** gained by dropping down to the left. There is also a handy stream here.

Gary Latter on the first ascent of Gem. Photo Karen Latter

BURNISHED WALLS

UPPER WALL   Alt: 30m

Descent: Scramble rightwards down an easy angled-shelf, with a short step at its base.

1 Falconer Cracks ★   15m VS 4b
FA Tess Fryer & Ian Taylor 1 May 2011

Climb the obvious crack above the big block on Ant Ledge.

2 Bogie Wonderland ★   6m E2 6a
FA Ian Taylor & Tess Fryer 1 June 2011

Above the step in the descent ramp to Ant Ledge is a perched block. Climb the most continuous crack right of the block.

LOWER WALL   Alt: 5m

Shags nest towards the lower right side; avoid this area from April-July.

Descent: Make a 25m abseil from blocks on Ant Ledge, the large grassy ledge above the left end.

3 Captain Beanheart ★   25m E2 5b
FA Michael Barnard & Alan Hill 9 October 2016

Scramble up left from the base of 4 to a raised platform below the right end of the **Main Wall**. Pitch two would make a good upper pitch to 4.

1 **15m 4c** Move left and climb a corner-crack to gain the low angled slab above. Go up and right to belay below an overhanging wall.

2 **10m 5b** Climb the line of weakness up the wall to reach the prominent undercling at the top bulge. Finish up and right.

4 Crystal Shell ★★   20m E3 5c
FA Ian Taylor & Tess Fryer 24 April 2011

Just left of the arête is a flake crack; this climbs the vertical crack to its left. Start by stepping left to the whacky crystalline hollow then follow the surprisingly steep crack to a ledge. Finish up the red corner and short walls above.

5 Champagne Rhubarb ★★   20m E2 6a
FA Ian Taylor & Tess Fryer 22 April 2011

Climb the flake crack just left of the arête until below the roof. Swing rightwards onto the arête and go up a crack at the right end of the roof to a ledge. Finishing leftwards as for 4 makes a nice ★★ E1 5b.

5a Variation Finish ★★ — 20m E2 5c
FA Michael Barnard 11 October 2015

From the ledge above the flake-crack, move up to traverse the headwall on pockets, finishing as for the normal route.

6 Rusty Buckets ★★★ — 20m E3 6a
FA Tess Fryer & Ian Taylor 22 April 2011

The thin crack line, just right of the arête, gives a pumpy little gem. Finish up a brown slab above the break. High in the grade and not a good warm up!

7 The Shiner ★★ — 20m E5 6a
FA Tess Fryer & Ian Taylor 30 April 2012

Start up the left side of the hanging block. Go up, take a diagonal crack leftwards for a couple of metres, then make hard moves up the wall above. Another pumper.

8 Read My Lips ★★ — 20m E4 6a
FA Tess Fryer & Ian Taylor 24 April 2011

Start up the right side of the hanging block to follow a rightwards trending crack to below a nose. Make a mean move to go round the left side of the nose and finish more easily.

9 Small Time Girl ★ — 20m E2 5b/c
FA Tess Fryer & Ian Taylor 29 April 2011

This takes the vague crack line right of 8 until below the very steep headwall. Follow a break rightwards until able to gain the ledge above and finish up the short wall.

10 The Melting ★★ — 20m E2 5c
FA Ian Taylor & Tess Fryer 19 May 2013

Start left of the easy ramp and go more or less directly up the wall to finish up 9. The best route on this section of wall.

11 Vive La Republique ★ — 20m E1 5a
FA Ian Taylor & Tess Fryer 29 April 2011

Start at an easy ramp and go up a crack to a break, move right along the break to a flake and go up this to Ant Ledge.

12 Burnt Umber — 20m E1 5a
FA Ian Taylor & Tess Fryer 7 May 2011

From the easy ramp go up rightwards to the top of a nose, just left of the central crack. Continue using the crack and the wall to its left.

> Watch out for a bit of loose rock at the top of the following three routes.

13 Mega Flake ★★ — 40m E2 5c
FA Tess Fryer & Ian Taylor 22 April 2011

Start at the central crack and climb this for 10m then follow a diagonal line rightwards heading for a big bleached flake in the middle of the right side of the wall. Monkey up the flake and at its top go right and follow a line to the top.

14 Shades of Glory ★ — 30m E2/3 5c
FA Tess Fryer & Ian Taylor 24 April 2011

Start as for 13 but move right and go up a shallow groove and golden crack above to reach easier ground (junction with 13). Go slightly left and climb a steep flake a couple of metres left of the big bleached flake. Belay on the ramp above.

15 Rolling Foam ★★★ — 45m E3 5c
FA Ian Taylor & Tess Fryer 24 April 2011

A well positioned route up the hanging corner round to the right. Traverse right into the corner and follow it steeply until able to pull onto a welcome ledge on the left. Go straight up the wall above then trend right to gain some grey flakes and follow these over a final bulge to the ramp.

16 Foamo ★ — 25m E3 5c
FA Tess Fryer & Ian Taylor 2 June 2013

Go up left-trending ramps easily to gain a right trending crack. Follow this to a grey niche with a steep right wall. Go up rusty rock left of the niche to the top. Worthwhile, but some snappy rock.

17 Midget ★ 25m E2 5c
FA Tess Fryer & Ian Taylor 2 June 2013

The vertical crack above the grass terrace is climbed direct.

18 Gem ★ 25m HVS 5a
FA Gary & Karen Latter 17 April 2019

The vertical crack above the large block in the low roof.

MAIN WALL Alt: 10m

1 Brow Beaten ★★ 55m E4 6a
FA Ian Taylor & Tess Fryer 30 April 2012

Takes a line just right of the left edge of the wall. Below and left of the main cliff is an undercut cave, gained by scrambling down leftwards from the sloping ledge (not at high tide).

1 **20m 5b** A fun little pitch. Start on the right side of the cave at a protruding nose. Move up from the nose to an undercut ledge and shuffle left along this. Surmount the bulge above to gain an open groove, then move left into a hanging corner. Up this to a small ledge below the main cliff.

2 **35m 6a** Climb up to gain a ledge, hand traverse a couple of metres rightwards, then make a committing move up to a diagonal break. Continue up to a flake of lighter coloured rock then hand traverse right and pullover onto an overhung ledge. Go steeply up and left for a few moves then follow a line diagonally rightwards on slabby rock to easier ground.

2 Moonman ★★ 35m E5 6a/b
FA Niall McNair & Iain Small 26 August 2012

Fine sustained climbing up the wall between 1 and 3. Start 5m to the left of 3, where a thin break slants up and to the left on small holds and flakes until some good breaks are gained. From the top juggy break make tricky moves up some small left facing flakes for a few metres until a step right can be made into a black intrusion and cams (common with 3). Move left and continue upwards to a big flat hold, RPs and 0 or 00 BD tricam useful. A further couple of moves leads into the break of 1, finish up this.

Niall McNair on TIFS.

3 The Cullinan ★★★ 35m E6 6b
FA Ian Taylor & Tess Fryer 1 June 2012

Another great route up the centre of the smooth wall left of 6. Start at bowl shaped depression. Climb more or less straight up on positive holds, till a move left at 10m gains a large flake. From a big jug at the top of the flake make a move up, then round to the left to gain a positive hold (good gear down and to the left), then make further hard moves to an easing on a yellow slab. Go up a final crimpy wall to a ledge (possible belay) then finish up and left as for 5.

4 TIFS ★★ 35m E6 6b
FA Ian Taylor & Tess Fryer 2 June 2013

This is the vague hanging groove line on the wall left of 6. Start under a short rightwards curving flake. Gain and follow the flake, then continue direct, with a hard section through brown rock, to a thin break. Continue more easily to another break, move right, then up to the ramp of 5 and a possible belay. Finish up and left as for 5.

COIGACH & ASSYNT SUPER CRAG TRAD | 271

5 Ramp it Up ★★   45m E3 5c
FA Ian Taylor & Tess Fryer 1 May 2011

This route goes up the groove of 6, before escaping off to the left. Climb the groove for 20m to a large lump of black amphibolite, then hand traverse left to gain a yellow ramp and follow this leftwards to gain ledges. Continue left, then pull onto a lichenous slab to finish. Scramble off leftwards.

5a Ramp it up Direct Start ★★   20m E4 5c
FA Tess Fryer & Ian Taylor 3 August 2012

Start left of 6 at a thin crack. Climb the crack which trends rightwards into the big groove and a junction with the original route.

6 Rodha Mor ★★★   40m E5 6a
FA Tess Fryer & Ian Taylor 7 May 2011

A big route with exciting climbing up the large left hand groove line. Start below and to the right of the groove at a 3m flake. From the flake steep moves up and left lead to a small guano ledge at the base of the groove. Follow the groove for 20m, then continue up a thin crack heading for a downward pointing flake. From the flake move up and loft to another flake, then go straight up to a horizontal seam. Go left then finish up a slightly creaky flake.

7 A Man In Assynt ★★   40m E7 6b
FA Iain Small & Blair Fyffe August 2012

A direct line heading straight for the ramp of 8 and boldly tackling the technical headwall. Some hollow flakes on the lower section lose it a star. Start up the 3m flake of 6 to a roof. Pull out and follow a series of flakes until a tricky move out left gains a break and small ledge at the base of the ramp. Awkward moves lead to a break (gear) then a junction with 8 at the top of the ramp. Arrange a nest of smaller wires then make a long reach up to gain sidepulls. From a strenuous position a vital BD micro stopper no. 5 can be placed high in the small left facing corner above. Either reverse for a rest or continue hard left by a series of sidepulls (crux), to gain the hanging flake and some micro cams. Sustained moves lead to a break and holds above allow a foot traverse right along the thin ledge to reach a bigger ledge. Finish up the short wall above.

8 The Ambassadors ★★★★   40m E6 6b
FA Ian Taylor & Tess Fryer 20 May 2012

The central line on the wall, starting up an obvious groove with two downward pointing grey flakes at 15m.

Gary Latter on The Melting. Photo Karen Latter.

Intricate and committing on the crux section. Gain the groove by following a thin flake rightwards to a ledge, then moving left to another ledge. Go up the groove past the downward pointing flakes and make a long move from undercuts to gain a horizontal break in the brown rock. Hard moves up and left lead to a precarious ramp, at the top of which small wires can be fiddled in. Move right, then make more hard moves up to a line of improving holds and follow these rightwards until able to pull awkwardly onto the high guano ledge. Move left 4m, pull onto a sloping ledge and finish easily. Belay well back. Instead of 'following the improving holds rightwards' it is possible to gain the guano ledge more directly. This is *The Embassy Finish* and is slightly harder than the original line.

9 The Heart of Beyond ★★★   40m E7 6b
FA Iain Small & Niall McNair (both led) 23 June 2012

Excellent pumpy climbing followed by an exhilarating crux. Possibly low in the grade. Start 2m left of 10 and climb via big flakes, breaks and blocks for 10m. Go up wall right of corner on pockets and flakes to a good break and good cams. Hand traverse this for 3m then go up on obvious left facing flakes to a second break system (purple camalot on left). Along break (small cam) then up on flakes again to jugs. Move up to flat holds then boldly trend left past a rock scar to a hidden sidepull (crux) and make a long reach for a hand rail on edge of guano ledge. Tackle overhanging wall at right end of ledge to gain a good foot ledge then trend up and right to the top of the crag.

10 The Under Toad ★★★   40m E6 6b
FA Ian Taylor & Tess Fryer 17 June 2011

Start left of 13 at a step in the sloping ledge. Climb up via flakes to gain a ledge below a thin, slightly rightwards trending crack. Follow the crack all the way to the left side of the lower guano ledge. Move left along a flake to a small rock scar and make hard moves up a thin crack to the upper guano ledge. Move right off the ledge to the open brown groove of 13 and finish up this. Bottom of the grade.

11 The Pabbay Express ★★★★ 45m E5 6a
FA Tess Fryer & Ian Taylor 20 May 2012

An alternative first pitch to 13. Slightly harder and slightly better. Start just left of 13 and go straight up past two horizontal breaks to gain a shallow groove line leading to the left end of the lower guano ledge. Continue up the second pitch of 13. Belaying on the guano ledge reduces the grade to E4.

12 The Assyntialist ★★ 35m E6 6b/c
FA Niall McNair & Iain Small (both led) 25 August 2012

Easy pumpy climbing, a powerful crux and a fantastically positioned headwall comprises this route which would be 3★ anywhere else but on this crag is merely a 2★ route. Start as for 13 and where this route goes off leftward along the ramp, forge straight up the grey striated wall boldly to a juggy break (common to *The All Abilities Path*). Useful medium wire on right side of overlap, 2m above juggy break. Make hard moves under the overlap to reach for a small hanging corner on left side of overlap and follow the undercut flake leftwards to a good flake-jug. Continue up the headwall on flakes until a thin break below the top is reached, 0.3 and/or 0.4 camalot on left. Step right and either tackle the orange block directly (powerful) or step right again into a vague corner (awkward) and so to the top.

13 (My Own) Personal Mingulay ★★★★ 45m E4 5c
FA Ian Taylor & Tess Fryer 7 May 2011

An excellent direct route with two great pitches.

1 **20m 5c** Start just left of 14 and go up a line of steep flakes, passing the left of the black 'eyes', to gain the middle of the sloping ramp. A rattling block in the flake line seems to be well keyed-in. Move left and belay as for 14.

2 **25m 5c** Go up the flake crack above to gain the juggy handrail as for 14. Move left, then go up an open brown groove, pulling left onto a sloping ledge at a black band. Continue via a hanging flake, pulling onto a slab to finish.

14 Guanissimo ★★★ 60m E2 5b
FA Tess Fryer & Ian Taylor 1 May 2011

A fine natural line that wanders around to give the easiest route on the wall. A hanging ramp leads up and left to the lower guano ledge and a right facing flake system leads to the right end of the hanging ramp.

1 **20m 5b** From an easy yellow ramp gain and climb the flake passing the right of two black 'eyes'. At its top follow the ramp easily leftwards to belay on the lower guano ledge.

2 **40m 5b** Go up the steep flake crack above, to reach a juggy handrail and follow this leftwards to the higher guano ledge (possible belay - awkward to arrange). Traverse left 4m then make an awkward move onto a sloping ledge. Continue easily to a herbaceous finish.

Niall McNair on the crag classic The Pabbay Express.

15 The All Abilities Path ** 40m E4 6a
FA Tess Fryer & Ian Taylor 19 June 2011

Climbs the steep wall right of 14, followed by an 'escape' up the top section of 13.

1 **20m 6a** Start just right of the yellow ramp and go boldly up the wall to good holds and gear. Make hard moves to gain a flake line and follow this into the left hand groove above. Exit from the groove to belay on a sloping ledge below a dauntingly steep brown wall.

2 **20m 5c** Hand traverse left below the steep wall until below an open brown groove just right of the higher guano ledge. Go up the groove, pulling left onto a sloping ledge at a black band. Continue via a hanging flake, pulling onto a slab to finish.

16 Ruddy Glow Corner ** 30m E4 6b
FA Ian Taylor & Tess Fryer 22 April 2011

The big obvious brown corner at the right end. Start below and right of the corner and go up easily until a diagonal line, over large grey blocks, gains the corner proper. Make some committing moves up the corner then get burly.

17 Le Trip *** 20m E4 6a
FA Tess Fryer & Ian Taylor 7 August 2015

Start as for 16 and where it heads left into the corner, continue up the right side of a grey block to a small ledge. Make committing moves right along a thin break to gain a vertical crack and follow this steeply to good holds and an easier finish with hairy lichen.

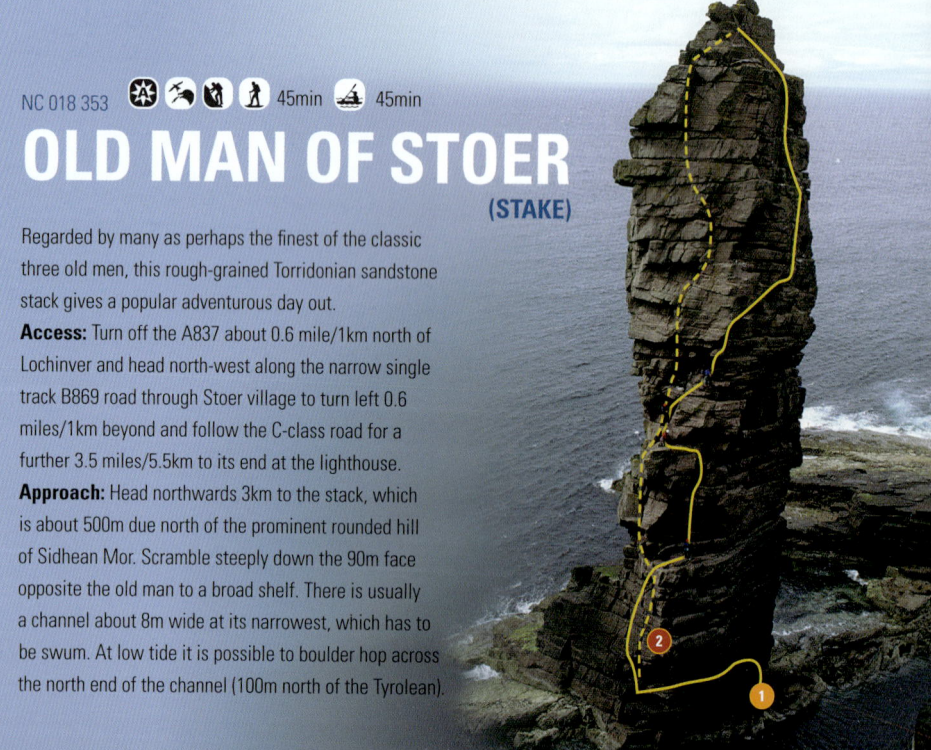

NC 018 353   45min   45min

OLD MAN OF STOER
(STAKE)

Regarded by many as perhaps the finest of the classic three old men, this rough-grained Torridonian sandstone stack gives a popular adventurous day out.

Access: Turn off the A837 about 0.6 mile/1km north of Lochinver and head north-west along the narrow single track B869 road through Stoer village to turn left 0.6 miles/1km beyond and follow the C-class road for a further 3.5 miles/5.5km to its end at the lighthouse.

Approach: Head northwards 3km to the stack, which is about 500m due north of the prominent rounded hill of Sidhean Mor. Scramble steeply down the 90m face opposite the old man to a broad shelf. There is usually a channel about 8m wide at its narrowest, which has to be swum. At low tide it is possible to boulder hop across the north end of the channel (100m north of the Tyrolean).

There is occasionally a rope left in place for a Tyrolean. If not, a Tyrolean can be set up to bring across the rest of the party and to enable retreat (45m of rope required).
Descent: A 40m abseil directly down the landward face leads to a fixed abseil point directly above the first belay ledge. A further 12m abseil leads back to the base. 50m ropes gain the start of the horizontal crack immediately above the belay.

1 Original Route ★★★★   67m VS 5a
FA Tom Patey, Brian Robertson, Brian Henderson & Paul Nunn June 1966

An exhilarating route, with impressive situations. Large cams/hexes useful. Many variations are possible.
1. **15m 5a** From 4m up the landward face follow twin horizontal cracks (often greasy) left onto ledge on the south-west face. (This pitch can be avoided in calm seas by a longer swim, or by walking the long way round the stack at low tide).
2. **12m 4b** Move left and climb by cracks and breaks rightwards to good ledge on the arête.
3. **15m 4b** Climb a steep crack above the ledge to a fringe of overhangs, pass these by a crack on the left (also possible to climb the diagonal crack-line on the left side of the landward face) and step left to reach ledges; continue for 10m to a cave belay above a large chokestone.
4. **10m 4c** Traverse round the edge on the right to the landward face and trend up right, avoiding the first break, to reach a small ledge and belay.
5. **15m** Climb the V-chimney above to easy ground and finish up a slabby left-slanting ramp.

2 Diamond Face Route ★★★   60m E1 5b
FA R.Edwards & B.Gordon 1 June 1987

Start from the belay at the end of the first pitch of 1.
1. **30m 5a** Climb a chimney and crack directly above. In the same line, enter a pod and then a wide continuation crack. Avoid the roof on the left and climb up to belay at the end of pitch 3 of *Original Route*.
2. **30m 5b** Surmount the roof above to gain a groove leading up and right to a large ledge. Stand on top of the block on the left and stretch up to the next break. Trend up left to an obvious corner and up this, traversing a short way right at its top to finish.

3 North-West Corner ★★   60m E4 6a
FA Mick Fowler & Chris Newcombe 29 August 1987

The right arête of the landward face. Take a double rack of cams.
1. **15m 6a** Climb the poorly protected arête on its left side (hard at 6m) to a ledge and friend 3 & 4 for belay.
2. **20m 5b** A layback flake just left of the arête allows holds to be gained leading up right to a resting place on the arête. Move up right round to the right side and follow a left-slanting crack to regain the crest. Move left to a fine belay ledge.
3. **25m 5c** Make long reach to break (crux), then more easily up left-trending ramp to a ledge at its top (junction with *Original Route*). Move out right to a large ledge just left of the arête and follow the arête to the top.

4 Ring of Bright Water ★★   75m E1 5c
FA Stephen Yates & Ian Halliday June 1987

Start at right end of west (seaward) face.
1. **45m 5b** Climb a short wall to a slab under a roof. Traverse left under the roof and round an arête to gain a steep flared crack on the north face. Up this to its top then traverse left along a ledge to PB on the east face.
2. **30m 5c** Make long reach to break (crux), then more easily up left-trending ramp. Follow this up left to gain a deep groove of *Original Route*. Up this and a short corner to the top

Tony Sawbridge on Presumption, Second Geo, Sheigra. Photo Dave Simmonite.

SUTHERLAND

SUTHERLAND
(OLD NORSE – SOUTH LAND)

"Do not be deluded! There is nothing but just a lot of water and rocks. Just a lot of water and rocks – peace and beauty, and the glories of an ancient people." – Hugh MacDiarmid, *The Islands of Scotland*, BT Batsford Ltd (an imprint of Anova Books Company Ltd), 1939

The famous extensive 'flow country', with its miles upon miles of wet moor land is not exactly the first place that springs to mind as a climbing venue. The few cliffs that are here however, are well worth searching out. The Dionard Buttresses on Foinaven give a range of long routes of all grades, made all the more accessible by the relatively recent bulldozing of a track down Strath Dionard. The compact sea-cliffs at Sheigra just south of the wonderful Sandwood Bay, provide a fine selection of routes in a truly idyllic setting.

Accommodation: Campsites: Scourie (Apr – Sept; 01971 502060; www.scouriecampsitesutherland.com), perfectly situated campsite in the field adjacent to the beach at Bagh Sheigra, NC 183 600 – no facilities, donation box. Nearest water available at the toilets at the car park for Sandwood Bay (the stream running through the campsite is not suitable for drinking, being downstream from the houses and given the absence of toilet facilities); Sango Sands, Durness (Apr – Oct; ☎ 07838 381065; www.sangosands.com); Bayview Campsite, Talmine, Kyle of Tongue (Apr – Sept; ☎ 07745 298600); Kyle of Tongue Hostel & Holiday Park (☎ 01847 611789; www.tonguehostelandholidaypark.co.uk). **Bunkhouses:** Inchnadamph Lodge (☎ 01571 822218; www.inchnadamph.co.uk); Lazy Crofter Bunkhouse, Durness (☎ 01971 511202; www.visitdurness.com); Kyle of Tongue Hostel & Holiday Park (☎ 01847 611789; www.tonguehostelandholidaypark.co.uk). **Youth Hostel:** Durness (Apr-Sept; ☎ 01971 511264; www.hostellingscotland.org.uk). **Club Hut:** Naismith Hut at Elphin (SMC). Numerous B&Bs & holiday houses, particularly from Rhiconich-Sheigra. **TIC:** Nearest is at Ullapool (☎ 01854 612486; www.visitscotland.com). **Amenities:** Bervie Stores in Kinlochbervie and London Stores, 2 miles/3km south of Kinlochbervie. Telephone box at Blairmore (0.8 miles/1.2km from Sheigra) in the car park for Sandwood Bay. Remember to bring some cash, as nearest **ATMs** at either Lochinver, Scourie, Durness or Tongue! Petrol stations in Kinlochbervie & Durness. Kinlochbervie Hotel (☎ 01971 521175; www.kinlochberviehotel.com) is nearest pub to Sheigra, though Rhiconich Hotel (☎ 01971 521224; www.rhiconichhotel.co.uk) 4.6 miles/7.5km to east is also an option.

Gary Latter on first ascent of The Swirl, Ruby Wall, Creag an Fhithich Photo Alan Warner.

Rick Campbell on the first ascent of Regeneration, First Dionard Buttress, Foinaven.

SUTHERLAND ROADSIDE CRAGS

RIDGWAY VIEW CRAG

NC 2334 5162 **Alt:** 80m 6min
A compact wall of good clean rock in a fine quiet setting.
Access: Turn west off the A838 0.6 miles/1km north of the second Skerricha turn-off (0.7 miles/1.1km south of Rhiconich) and head west towards Ardmore for 0.9 miles/1.5km to a parking spot at the top of a rise with an electricity pole just to the north (overlooking the middle of the second loch down on the left).
Approach: Walk up the shoulder past the pole to a little lochan, where the crag can be seen on the right.

1 Classic Crack ★★   17m Severe 4a
FA combinations of Bill Birkett, J.Rogers, Tom Rogers & Howard Lancashire 17 August 2003

The fine leftmost crack, unfortunately close to easy (Diff.) ground just to its left.

2 Doddle ★   14m Easy
FA Gary Latter (solo) 25 April 2019

The blocky heathery crack.

3 Michael ★   14m HS 4b
FA Colin Lesenger (solo) 5 August 2011

The cracks immediately right of 2, finishing direct.

4 Row the Boat Ashore ★★   15m VS 4c
FA combinations of Bill Birkett, J.Rogers, Tom Rogers & Howard Lancashire 17 August 2003

The slightly right-slanting diagonal crack up the centre of the slab. Bouldery start.

5 Starry Saxifrage ★★   14m Severe 4a
FA Karen & Gary Latter 10 April 2004

The rightmost crack in the slab just left of a shallow groove.

6 Rodney's Gneiss Route ★   10m Severe 4a
FA Oli Gray & Colin Angus 25 July 2004

Climb a left-facing corner until it is possible to pull on to the arête at half-height. Follow cracks to the top.

6a Groovy ★   10m Severe 4a
FA Colin Lesenger (solo) 5 August 2011

Climb the corner in its entirety.

6b Plonker's Start ★   10m HVS 5a
FA Gary Latter (solo) 25 April 2019

The blunt arête - unprotected.

7 C Weed ★★   8m E1 5b
FA P.Armitage & M.Stubbs 13 July 2004

Start up the slope at the right end below a thin crack running through a break at 4m. Climb up through this on small edges and continue up to ledges. Finish by going left to the top.

8 Orange Flake ★★   10m VS 4c
FA Alan Moore (solo) July 2010

Start up shallow right facing corner for 3m then move left to gain and climb the beautiful orange flake in the headwall.

8a Rowlocks ★   10m HS 4b
FA Ewan Lyons (solo) 1 August 2016

Start up the corner of 8, finishing direct up the wall.

SUTHERLAND ROADSIDE CRAGS | 281

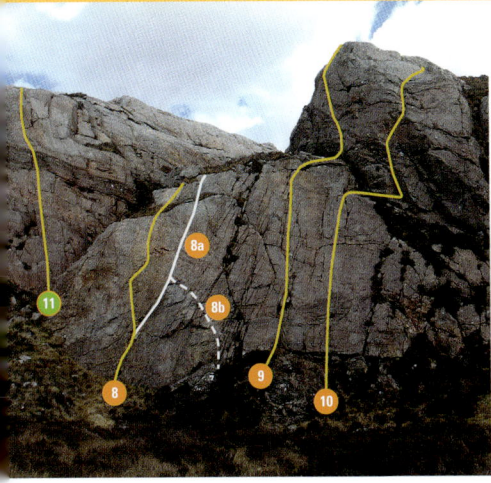

Karen Latter on Row the Boat Ashore.

8b Hornblower *   10m HS 4b
FA Andy Tibbs (solo) 5 June 2010

Climb diagonally left to the top of the corner, then direct up the wall.

9 Oars Aft **   20m VS 4c
FA combinations of Bill Birkett, J.Rogers, Tom Rogers & Howard Lancashire 17 August 2003

Climb either the wall right of the main crack or the crack itself to gain a ledge. Trend leftwards up the pocketed headwall to finish at the highest point.

10 Another Perspective *   20m HVS 4c
FA Ross & Clare Jones 10 April 2011

Climb the slab right of 9 to cracks and a right-facing corner under the headwall. Pull up right and up the overhanging right-slanting niche to the top.

11 Clubmoss **   15m Difficult
FA Karen & Gary Latter 10 April 2004

The fine blunt rib just above the base of the descent gully at the left end of the main crag.

THE BALCONY   10min
NC 229 519 Alt: 80m

Small slabs and walls line the flank of the little knoll north-west of **Ridgway View Crag**. Towards the left is a steep slabby 15m wall with a pleasant heather balcony running along its base. Two waterworn streaks (often wet) with cracks running up them are prominent on the left section. Although the routes are very close together the climbing is excellent.

Access: Continue west along the single track road towards Ardmore 0.2 mile/0.3km beyond **Ridgway View Crag** to park in large bay on right.

Approach: Walk up and around the shoulder to gain the first rocks.

1 Outer Space *   15m E2 5c
FA Rab & Chris Anderson 13 August 2004

Attain a standing position in a horizontal slot, step left and climb a thin crack to a ledge on the edge. Climb the right side of the edge to the top.

2 Moondust **   15m E2/3 5c
FA Rab & Chris Anderson 13 August 2004

Start at a small flange and climb directly to the slanting slot of 3 before moving up and slightly left to the horizontal break. Step left, then climb directly to the top.

6 Little Star ★★   15m E2 5c
FA Rab & Chris Anderson 15 April 2004

The thin crack-line in the centre of the wall. Climb to the left end of the ledge just above the ground. Go up left on to a small ledge at the start of the crack. Climb the crack and the bulge to finish.

7 The Sky's the Limit ★★   15m E3 5b
FA Rab & Chris Anderson 15 April 2004

Climb directly into a shallow scoop, then move right along a horizontal break to step up on to this. A tiny hole is located on the wall above. A skyhook can be placed in this to protect the moves directly past it to reach holds where a step left gains a good horizontal break. Step up right, surmount the bulge and finish leftwards around the nose.

3 Solar Gain ★★   15m E3 5c
FA Rab & Chris Anderson 1 May 2004

A line based around the arched groove toward the left side of the crag. The streak on the left is slow drying and this is a fine alternative. Climb to the base of the groove, then go left to a good slanting slot before going up and slightly right to a horizontal break at the apex of the arch. Climb the thin crack-line above and finish just left of the widening crack at the top.

8 Space and Time ★   15m E2 5b
FA Rab & Chris Anderson 15 April 2004

Climb a mixture of the clean rock to the left of the crack-line and the crack-line itself. The climbing and the rock is better 1m to the left but the gear is in the crack. Move left to the bulge and surmount this rightwards around the nose.

4 Galactica ★★   15m E3 5c
FA Rab & Chris Anderson 1 May 2004

A line based around the thin crack-line up the waterworn orange streak in the centre of the crag. Climb the left side of the crack until it is possible to reach a short diagonal slot and go left to more diagonal slots and a diagonal break. Step left across the arching groove and delicately move up to a small slot, then finish directly.

5 Starstreak Enterprise ★★★   15m E3 5c
FA Rab & Chris Anderson 13 August 2004

The thin crack up the waterworn orange streak in the centre of the crag provides a fine little route. Start to the right of the crack and climb it to the top. A step left just below the upper crack allows good gear to be placed in the diagonal crack of 4.

Neil Foster searching for some Solar Gain.

FOUR LOCHANS VIEW CRAG   10min
NC 2299 5191

The large easy-angled slab 50m down left of **The Balcony**, with lots of pegmatite. Protection is almost exclusively from cams, as many of the cracks are flared.
Descent: easiest down the left end.

1 Do You Expect Me to Talk? * 30m Severe 4a
FA Karen & Gary Latter 29 April 2019

Intermittent cracks up the left side, finishing rightwards.

2 No Mr Tick, I Expect You to Die ** 40m Severe 4a
FA Gary & Karen Latter 29 April 2019

Climb the left-slanting crack, then the central cracks. Continue easily above the terrace to belay further back.

3 Stoneflow * 30m Severe 4a
FA Karen & Gary Latter 29 April 2019

Cracks up the right edge, moving rightwards to ascend slim groove. Finish leftwards to pull through on heather.

RHICONICH CRAG
NC 2581 5195 **Alt:** 90m 15min

A 35m crag of fine crystalline gneiss, hyped (by Englishmen) as *"probably the finest nearest roadside crag in Scotland!"* It's nae bad, but…
Access: Turn off as for Rhiconich Hotel and park on the old road down on the right.
Approach: Follow a good track up the left side of the stream for a few hundred metres, then steeply up the hillside on the left.

1 Short but Beautiful ** 40m HVS 5a
FA Bill Birkett & Howard Lancashire 22 August 2000

1 20m 5a Climb a slabby gangway right of a deep chimney to a shelf on the edge. Move up and right into a steep crack and follow it direct round a small overlap to a ledge.

2 20m 5a Step left and climb the wall direct left of the chimney-groove. Pass a large detached block and continue easily.

The next three routes all share a common start.

② Moral Turpentine ★★   35m E1 5b
FA J.Walker & Neil Wilson Summer 1996

1. **20m 5b** Follow the obvious diagonal crack leftwards to reach the large ledge.
2. **15m 5b** Climb the offwidth crack, passing a holly with interest to easy ground.

③ Black Gold ★★★   35m E2 5c
FA Howard Lancashire & Bill Birkett 22 August 2000

Follow the initial crack of 2 to the first ledge. Make hard moves up the steep initial wall, then more easily up good cracks in the slab to diagonal fault. Follow this into the chimney, then pull rightwards up steep crack on superb holds. Finish steeply on good holds.

④ The Road North ★★   35m E2 5c
FA Bill Birkett & Dave Allan 21 August 2000

Sustained and quite bold – low in the grade. Pull up right by a flake and up to the first overlap. Climb through this and up to a triangular niche in the next little overlap. Stand above this then pull over the next overlap onto the slab above to gain a vague crack. Climb directly up the slab and cracks to a heather ledge.

⑤ Gneiss Too ★   18m HVS 5a
FA Dave Allan & Bill Birkett 21 August 2000

Step up right from a block and move left across the slabby wall to gain a crack and flake. Climb the flake, pull up and move right and up to finish.

⑥ Gneiss Yin ★   18m VS 4b
FA Dave Allan & partner 2000

Climb the wall to a hanging corner. Go up corner and pull out right, finishing up right.

⑦ Gneiss Knowing You ★   18m HVS 5a
FA Brian Davison 27 August 2002

Climb up to a ledge at two-thirds height, move right and follow parallel cracks past horizontal break, finishing slightly leftwards.

CREAG GHARBH MHOR
(BIG ROUGH CRAG)

Just over a mile north of the Rhiconich junction are a number of varied crags on the hillside on the east side of the road.

Access: Drive north 1.1 miles/1.8km beyond Rhiconich junction to park in a small belvedere on the left (west) side of the road.

RED WALL

A long low wall of beautifully coloured deep red gneiss with a reasonable spread of routes. The base is obscured from the road.

Approach: Head leftwards up the hillside.

Many of the routes were climbed by Mark Charlton & A.Cater in 1995 but left unrecorded; routes named & recorded by combinations of Eric Christison, Dave McGimpsey & Andy Nisbet 15 June 2002

1 The Goat of Barten ★★   12m E2 5c
The thin boulidery crack left of the central corner.

The thin crack 1m left of 3 is 2 *Wrycrack* ★ E2 5c.

3 Rhicorner ★★★   15m E2 5b
The well-protected corner.

NC 268 534 **Alt:** 70m
5min

4 Two Colours Red ★★ — 15m E1 5b
Twin tram-line cracks just right of the corner.

The next crack right is 5 *Sweet Compensation* ★ E1 5b.

6 Cramp Crack ★ — 15m HVS 5a
The more pronounced crack system 2m further right.

7 Rikki-Tikki-Tavi ★ — 20m VS 4b
A wandering line up the right end. Start up a left-slanting ramp to gain and follow a traverse ledge rightwards. Move up to follow a narrower ledge back left to finish up a crack over wedged block. Finishing via horizontal breaks further right is 4c. A direct from the same start is E2 5b.

GLACIATED SLAB 10min
NC 268 533 **Alt:** 100m

An anvil-shaped grey slab higher up the hill above the **Red Wall**. A decent length of routes, though slightly more lichenous than most of the other crags in the area.
Approach: Head leftwards up the hillside.

Numerous HVS 5a routes lie either side of here.

1 Jewel in the Crown ★★ — 35m VS 4c
FA D.Wheeler & partner 1994/5

The central line. Start just left of the red 'cave'. Boulder up to a ledge then follow the right trending line up the slab, heading for a faint rib in the headwall. Finish up a crack then out rightwards.

RED SLAB
NC 268 533 **Alt:** 100m 15min

A fine easy-angled slab bounding the right edge of the line of crags right of **Glaciated Slab**. Again, only the less distinct steeper grey left section is visible from the parking spot.

1 Beauty's Edge ★ — 30m VS 4c
FA Karen & Gary Latter 29 September 2002

The hanging groove and cracks up the blunt left edge of the slab.

2 The Crack ★ — 25m Severe 4a
FA Stuart & Kay Charlton 30 August 2001

Start directly below the left end of a curving crack. Gain and follow the crack then the fine slab above.

3 Westering Home ★ — 25m Very Difficult
FA Stuart & Kay Charlton 30 August 2001

Start further up the open gully at a flake. Climb direct, trending left to finish.

CREAG AN FHITHICH (RAVEN CRAG)

NC 258 538 **Alt:** 80m

10min

Triangular Wall • Back Stage • Grey Wall • Ruby Wall • Russet Wall

Three separate good sections of rock on the dome-shaped hill looking down Loch Inchard. Bigger and better than it appears from the road, as the lower section is obscured.
Access: Leave the A838 at Rhiconich and follow the B801 north for 1.1 miles/1.8km to park on the right (east), on the south side of the old bridge at the south end of Achriesgill.
Approach: Head up the hill to the crags. Slightly shorter approaches to **Ruby/Russet Wall** can be made from the large lay-by with picnic tables 300m back up the hill (as for **Back Stage**).

GREY WALL

The narrow pillar of clean rock bounding the left end of the hillside.
Descent: by scrambling off left and down the left side of the crags.

1 The Sound of One Tick Popping ★★ 30m HVS 5a
FA Gary & Karen Latter 28 April 2019

The vertical crack just left of 2. Start a few metres left of that route. Climb the crack to a prominent horizontal, move rightwards along this then direct up the wall. Belay on wall 8m back from top.

2 Gaff ★★ 25m HVS 5a
FA Neil Wilson & Neil Stevenson 17 June 1996

Excellent positive climbing up the prominent diagonal crack. Start at a steep groove right of the crack. Climb the groove then the crack to finish left of the vegetated niche at the top.

RUBY WALL   NC 2570 5387

About 100m further up the hill to the right is a fine steep ruby-coloured wall with a very distinctive band of black striated gneiss in the centre.

Descent: Abseil (sling & maillon in situ) from small shrub above the centre of the crag.

1 The Swirl ★★★   35m E4 6a
FA Gary Latter (on-sight) 4 July 2000

Superb. Climb easily on large pockets just left of the black swirl to better protection beneath a small roof. Step right then left onto a ledge over the roof and finish up the cracked wall on immaculate compact pocketed rock.

2 Ruby Wall ★★★   40m E3 5c
FA Mark Charlton & A.Cater May 1997

The original line. Start as for 1 but trend rightwards to gain an overhung lichen-covered slab. Break through the roof at its highest point, move up and left to a good sidepull on the ledge. Move right and up into an overhung niche. Traverse left via a good crack around the top of a block in a spectacular position. Pull up and left to a steep heathery finish on poor holds.

3 Sapphires ★★   35m E3 5c
FA Gary Latter (on-sight) 30 September 2002

Excellent well-protected climbing, following a direct line cutting through 2. Start a few metres right of 2. Climb easily up leftwards on pockets then by a crack to the base of the prominent fault cutting through the central overhanging section. Go up leftwards on jugs to pull rightwards up onto the overhanging slab (common with 2). After the spectacular traverse, step back right up a narrow ramp to finish up a short crack.

4 A Diamond is Forever ★★   35m E4 6a
FA Howard Lancashire, Tom Rogers & Bill Birkett 20 August 2002

Good climbing up the centre of the crag, though slightly spoilt by a couple of ledges. Start below a small left-facing groove. Make steep moves leftwards then back right to the base of a groove. Make a few moves up the groove and use holds on the right to gain a good small pocket (quite bold). Swing up left past a good blunt spike to easier ground. Continue up the slab to a short corner then out left to two good pockets. Continue up on undercuts and make hard moves left to a ledge. Climb the crack and groove to a good hold, finishing over an overhang leading to an easier slab. Scramble up left on heather to the abseil point.

RUSSET WALL
NC 2567 5382

Continuing further right up the hillside for a little less than 100m is an excellent compact wall, well endowed with letter box slots & pockets. Slow to dry.
Descent: Traverse right across heather and down the right edge of the crags.

1 Dragonfly ★★   25m HVS 5a
FA Gary Latter & Alan Warner 4 July 2000

Climb directly up the wall at the left side to break through the final bulge past a couple of flakes.

2 Apple Pie ★   25m E1 5b
FA Howard Lancashire & Bill Birkett 13 August 2002

Ascend the wall direct to finish through steep ground right of the flakes.

3 Iridescence ★★   35m E3 5c
FA Gary & Karen Latter 28 April 2019

The left-slanting diagonal crack.

  1 20m 5c Climb the crack with increasing difficulty to its end. Pull through the roof with a long reach to gain a superb pegmatite jug and belay just above.

  2 15m 4a Move left 3m and climb the rib left of the gully, crossing the top of the gully rightwards.

4 Horseshit Direct ★   25m HVS 5a
FA Gary Latter & Alan Warner 4 July 2000; Direct: Jonathan & Diane Preston 15 June 2002

Start beneath the hanging crack. Climb up and move left along the diagonal break. Climb directly up the wall on good pockets to finish up a layback crack through the final bulge.

5 Cladonia Dreaming ★★   25m E1 5b
FA Gary & Karen Latter 28 April 2019

A direct line up the wall and hanging crack. Start directly beneath the crack, climb the wall, first leftwards, then rightwards to gain the crack. Climb this, then direct, finishing up the fine pocketed wall left of the niche.

6 Dung Beetle ★   25m VS 4c
FA Jonathan Preston, Dave McGimpsey & Andy Nisbet 5 May 2002

Climb up and right onto glacis. Step back left onto wall and make steep moves, first left, then up edge of wall, finishing through shallow V-slot, then easier above.

7 Red Bull ★   25m HVS 5a
FA Jonathan & Diana Preston 15 June 2002

Start just right of where the crag changes direction. Follow a short steep crack to a sloping ledge. Bypass a small overhang on the right (or direct at 5b) to a corner. Follow this and a further corner on the left then traverse right along the lip of the overhang in a fine position, stepping up to finish.

8 Short Sharp Shock ★   10m E1 5b
FA Jonathan & Diana Preston 15 June 2002

The roof-capped right-slanting corner, moving left at the roof to the continuation corner. Finish out rightwards to a rowan.

TRIANGULAR BUTTRESS

NC 256 537 **Alt:** 170m   15min

About 60m above **Russet Wall** is a triangular buttress and right at roughly the same level a massive gneiss block. **Back Stage** lies directly above and behind the block.

1 Just a Tease ★★   15m HVS 5a

FA Stuart & Kay Charlton August 2004

Climb the hanging arête either direct or from the right then direct to finish.

2 Straight Crack ★   15m VS 4c

FA Stuart & Kay Charlton August 2004

The central crack.

The leftmost crack is 3 *Flaming June Crack* VS 4c.

BACK STAGE  15min

NC 255 536 **Alt:** 190m

A couple of hundred metres up the hillside to the right is a fine short crag directly above a prominent boulder.

1 Back Stage ★★   15m VS 5a

FA Eric Christison, Dave McGimpsey & Andy Nisbet 16 June 2002

Obvious crack, finishing directly up easier slab.

The following 3 routes all start from the slanting shelf, which can either be gained direct via a short steep wall or wide corner crack on left, by 5, or by walking in from the right.

2 Crimson Cruiser ★★   15m HVS 5a

FA Tom Rogers & Bill Birkett 17 August 2002

The thin vertical crack above a slanting shelf, finishing up the blunt rib.

3 Airs ★★   15m E1 5b

FA Gary & Karen Latter (on-sight) 30 September 2002

The pocketed wall directly above a small 'step' in the shelf, a few metres right of 2.

4 Nocturne ★★   14m VS 4c

FA Gary Latter (on-sight solo) 4 July 2000

The pocketed wall further right.

5 Preludes ★★   8m Very Difficult

FA Gary Latter (on-sight solo) 4 July 2000

The hanging flake in the front face of the lower 'boulder', belaying further back.

6 Trident ★★★   9m Severe 4a

FA Gary Latter (on-sight solo – in descent) 4 July 2000

The immaculate hanging finger-crack in the small isolated slab a short way further right.

Neil Craig following on the first ascent of the bold and sustained Something Worth Fighting For, First Geo. Photo Rick Campbell.

The extensive coastline north of the beautiful sandy bay at Sheigra offers two markedly contrasting types of climbing. Perfect Lewisian gneiss extends for the first 800 metres (½ mile) northwards, before dramatically changing to a gnarly, pebble-strewn Torridonian sandstone – an altogether different experience and something of an acquired taste.

Access: From the A838 Lairg – Durness Road, turn off at Rhiconich junction, heading north along the B801 towards Kinlochbervie (4.3 miles/6.9km), where a right turn leads along a single-track road north-west to a small collection of houses at the road end at Sheigra (4.1 miles/6.7km). Just before reaching the houses turn left (west) down towards the beach. Park before the second gate or in the field if camping here.

THE FIRST GEO

NG 180 600

 2min

This narrow sheltered geo is situated immediately north of the bay.

Approach: Couldn't be simpler – follow the fence, which turns north just before the back end of the geo.

Descents: Down a grotty gully in the centre of the north face or easier at mid-tide down the broken area of rocks at the seaward end. More conveniently directly by abseil.

SOUTH WALL – THE INNER WALLS

Opposite the grotty descent gully. Only the last two routes are affected by the tide.

1 Rescue Alcove ★   12m E2 5b
FA Allen Fyffe & Andy Cunningham 28 May 1993

Follow a left to right gangway leading to a bulging finish. Awkward with fiddly protection.

2 Gneiss Won ★★   20m HS 4b
FA Allen Fyffe & Andy Cunningham November 1989

A distinctive black and pink cracked wall towards the back of the geo. Climb this through a slot to finish by a wide flake crack.

Further right are two large steps and an apparent slab, forming a left-facing corner.

3 The Only Way is Up ★   20m HVS 5a
FA Allen Fyffe & Andy Cunningham November 1989

Left of and at the same level as the top slab is a right-slanting overhanging groove. Follow this to finish up a short steep wall.

4 Coopers Crack ★   25m HVS 5a
FA G.Cooper & party Summer 1981

Start at the right side of the top step. Follow a steep blocky crack up left to the base of a corner. Ascend twin cracks in the slab above then traverse right to finish by a steep blocky groove.

5 Tell Tale Signs ★★   25m E3 5c
FA F.Knows & A.N.Other 5 June 1993

Wanders around a thin crack in the steep wall to the left of the overhanging niche of 6. Climb out left past the first crack to gain the second small ledge awkwardly. Move out right on sloping holds to gain a good horizontal break then back left and up the niche onto the large ledge. Finish up the final corner as for 6. Climbing the crack direct is 6a.

6 Road to Reform ★★ 25m E3 5c
FA Andy Cunningham & Allen Fyffe November 1989

Follow the crack line which cuts through the overhanging niche. Finish up the steep corner at the right end of the ledge, left of the big capping roof.

7 Steep for 5 Minutes ★★★ 25m E6 6c
FA Gary Latter 1 July 1995

A direct line attacking the capping roof in the centre. Start directly under the roof. Up a grey ramp and rightwards through a niche to a brilliant incut pocket. Follow the vague crack line on good holds to the roof and make some very powerful moves through this (small nuts) to a superb pocket and large jug in the break above. The short wall above leads to a superb finishing jug.

8 Dying in Vein ★★ 25m E4 5c
FA Grant Farquhar & Clare Carolan 30 June 1995

The funky orange quartz-veined lower wall, as for the above route. Follow the line of the thin crack then pull out rightwards at a prominent pink band to finish up the right side of the capping roof, just left of the pink groove of 9. Stunning.

8a Dying Direct ★★ 25m E4 6a
FA Lawrence Hughes, Andy Cunningham & Alastair Cain 4 Jun 1998

Climb a right-trending crack to the pedestal of 10 (hard). Follow a direct line to a small niche left of the base of the pink groove on 9. Climb the steep crack above to finish through the roof as for 8.

9 Blind Faith Direct ★★ 25m E2 5c
FA F.Knows & A.N.Other 5 June 1993

Follow a direct line heading for the obvious deep pink groove and finish up this.

10 Blind Faith ★★ 25m E2 5b
FA Allen Fyffe & Andy Cunningham November 1989

Gain the rightwards curving crack line from the right and follow its continuation up and left to the base of a deep pink groove. Move out right into a small alcove and finish right up a black crack.

10a Hanuman for a Day ★★ 25m E5 6a
FA Ian Taylor & Tess Fryer 25 May 2008

Start just left of 11. Go up to some hanging flakes, then follow a thin crack slightly left to easier ground (junction with 10). Step right and climb a hard thin crack in the leaning headwall. Low in the grade.

11 Monkey Man ★★★★ 25m E3 5c
FA Andy Cunningham, Allen Fyffe & Jim Kerr 28 May 1993

Superb, sustained and well protected. The left side of the impressive grey wall has twin squiggly cracks heading up towards a flaky groove at the top.

12 Maybe Later ★★★ 25m E7 6c
FA Dave MacLeod 4 May 2006

The thin seam left of 13 gives hard and technical climbing. Start up the diagonal cracks as for 13 but move left and up the wall to good undercuts. Climb the right side of the seam and place crucial runners with difficulty (BD Stopper #3, microstopper #2). Step left and make a hard move to gain the undercut break and good runners. Traverse slightly left and make another hard move to gain good holds leading up the overhang to finish.

Neil Craig aping around on Monkey Man. Photo Rick Campbell.

13 Here and Now ★★★   25m E6 6b
FA Gary Latter & Rick Campbell 29 May 1995

Superb, steep and strenuous climbing with reasonable protection. The right side of the face has a shallow orange hanging groove at the top. Start up a prominent diagonal crack and move right to good undercuts and a flake (also possible to climb direct to here, but runners in the crack are useful higher up) to gain a good hold just above. Move slightly left and up a flared crack with a hard move to gain a good flat hold (good nuts, including Wallnut #10 or #9 on side). Move slightly left and up a further flared crack to good incuts then right and layback sharp flakes to better holds and protection. More easily up the final groove to finish on superb holds.

The next two routes are tidal.

14 Something Worth Fighting For ★★★   25m E6 6b
FA Rick Campbell & Neil Craig June 1995

A very serious lower section above a frightening landing leads to a sustained hard and well-protected upper section. Start on the boulders, directly beneath a small overlap at 8m. Step off boulders onto the grey wall, move up and right to a sidepull in red rock (poor skyhook in a tiny pocket out right). Move up left then back right to better holds and protection in a slim groove above the overlap. Move up and through next overlap to a shake out at flat hold left of a rounded spike. Ascend the most prominent of the thin cracks above with difficulty to top.

15 What the Pool Said, on Midsummer's Day ★★
                                                                      30m E5 6a
FA Gary Latter 4 July 1995

Bold steady climbing up the right edge of the Inner Walls. Start on top of a boulder near the right edge. Up to a pocket (R #5) and move up leftwards past a further pocket to good holds leading to a break level with small roof on left. Step right and up shallow grooves then direct on good holds to pull onto a sloping ledge. Move up an easy slabby groove leftwards and finish up the jug-infested slab.

THE OUTER WALLS

Further right where the geo opens out at a large pool is an extensive overhanging wall with a long ledge system at the base. In the centre is a stunning golden wall with black-streaked cracks up either side.

Approach: either from the back of the geo at mid-tide or by scrambling down into the boulder-choked inlet at the west end then scrambling rightwards back into the geo to gain the ledge system. Easiest directly by abseil.

16 Flotsam ★★   20m E6 6b
FA Ian Taylor & Tess Fryer 18 May 2009

Start just left of 17 and climb more or less directly to a crack at a steepening. Hard but well protected moves lead to better holds and a sloping ledge. Sidle left along the ledge to better holds, then go steeply up via large holds and ledges to the top.

16a Jetsam ★★★   26m E7 6c
FA Steve Crowe & Karin Magog (headpointed with gear pre-placed) 28 June 2014

The direct finish. Crucial gear is hard to place on sight. Continue direct to the top where 16 escapes left. Powerful and long moves on small crimps and undercuts.

17 The Sound of the Surf ★★★   25m E4 6a
FA Gary Latter & Rick Campbell 27 May 1995

The left crack system. Scramble up to the base from the left. Climb the crack with a hard section low down. Higher up, it is possible to bridge into the groove on the left. Pull over the capping roof direct at a good slot and finish on good holds.

18 Looking for Atlantis ★★★ 25m E5 6c

FA Rick Campbell & Gary Latter (both led) 27 May 1995

Superb climbing up the black-streaked crack bounding the right side of the golden wall. From the right end of the ledge move left and up to a large flat ledge then up and left to the base of the crack. Up this to a steep thin crack in the headwall, which leads with difficulty (crux) to a good fingerlock. Stand on the ledge and finish easily.

NORTH WALL

At the back of the geo is a black bulging slab topped by steeper orange rock. The following route lies at the left end of this area, taking two cleaned groove lines. The crag is tidal at the west end.

1 Casey Jones ★ 15m E1 5b

FA Ian Rea & Allen Fyffe 28 May 1993

Trend left on to the slab by an obvious break. Enter the left groove with difficulty and climb to the roof. Move left and follow the rib to the top.

2 Culture of Silence ★ 15m VS 4c

FA Andy Banks & E.Flaherty 16 June 2001

Follow the vertical weakness to ledges below the left edge of the overhung bay. Step left round the edge and ascend the centre of slab to finish up the rib as for 1.

The remaining routes are left (west) from the grotty descent gully.

3 Red Lead ★ 15m Severe 4a

FA Tom Redfern (solo) 13 September 1994

Start at the foot of the black gully and climb the centre of the reddish slab on the left.

4 Rampart ★ 15m VS 4b

FA Tom Redfern & Stuart Younie 13 September 1994

A direct line up the centre of buttress, finishing up 5.

5 Haddie ★ 15m Difficult

FA Catriona Reid & Jeni Pickering 13 June 1993

Above the huge boulders, take a cracked black ramp line rightwards and finish up a black slab.

Next is the main area with a series of black grooves starting by the huge boulders.

6 Credit Zone ★ 15m Difficult

FA Tom Redfern (solo) 13 September 1994

Climb cracks directly up the broken slab near the right side.

7 In the Pink ★ 15m Very Difficult

FA Andy Nisbet & Stevie Blagbrough November 1989

Crack line and groove with a prominent pink vein up the centre of the buttress.

8 Blackballed ★ 15m Severe 4a

FA Andy Nisbet & Stevie Blagbrough November 1989

In the right wall of the roof-capped corner is a wide crack. Climb the crack until it begins to peter out then step right on to the buttress crest and finish up a short groove.

9 R 'n' R ★ 20m HS 4b

FA Andy Nisbet & Stevie Blagbrough November 1989

Just left is another groove with twin cracks leading to a small roof. Climb to the roof, move right round this and continue up and left via a line of blocks. Alternatively, turn the roof on the left at the same grade.

10 Two Step ★ 20m VS 4c

FA Allen Fyffe & Andy Cunningham 28 May 1993

Climb a left-trending crack in the front of a huge quartz-topped pedestal to its top. Continue in the same line up the wall above.

11 Blackjack ★★ 15m Difficult

FA Andy Nisbet November 1989

The last black groove in this area is followed direct on satisfying sound rock.

DIAMOND BUTTRESS

At the seaward end of the **North Wall** and below the high tide mark is a diamond-shaped clean buttress with three left-slanting crack lines. This is the last buttress before this side disappears.

12 Skate ★ 15m HVS 5a
FA Andy Cunningham & Allen Fyffe November 1989

The right crack, going through a roof low down.

13 Cuddane ★ 15m E1 5b
FA George Reid & Andy Cunningham 12 June 1993

The middle crack.

> The left crack is *Flounder* VS 4c.

5min
NG 180 601
BETWEEN THE GEOS

Less than 100 metres north, towards **The Second Geo** is a perfect corner:

1 Crackin' Corner ★★★ 12m VS 4c
FA Gary Latter & Karen Martin 4 July 1995

The short but perfectly formed corner with a parallel crack up the left wall. The crack can be climbed at HVS 5a.

> About 50 metres further on, just south of the start of **The Second Geo** is a long platform about 10m above the sea. Approach from the right (south) and scramble down to reach the right end, then traverse north and back up to large platform at base.

2 Under the Pink ★★ 15m E1 5b
FA Gary Latter 4 July 1995

The shallow right-facing groove at the left end of the ledge leads to the right end of a long sloping ledge. Thin cracks in the arête above.

3 In Between Days ★ 15m HVS 5a
FA Gary Latter & Karen Martin 4 July 1995

The line between, following a blocky crack with a bouldery start.

4 Above the Blue ★★ 15m E1 5c
FA Gary Latter 4 July 1995

The crack near the right arête leads to a good break then easier up the superb shallow groove above.

5 GLOP ★★ 20m E3 5c
FA Paul Thorburn & Paul McNally July 1995

Reputedly stands for *"Gary Latter Over-grading Poof!"* Climb 4 until a traverse can be made above the lip of the leaning arête. At a large pocket move up and gain a slab and belays. Climbing straight up the black streak from halfway along the traverse gives an excellent E1 5c.

Chris Murray making short work of the excellent Crackin' Corner.

THE SECOND GEO

NG 180 602  5min

The climbing on the orange streaked walls surrounding the huge cave is usually on superb pockets. A good selection of large nuts and lots of cams will be found useful. Such is the abundance of pockets, the rock is climbable almost anywhere at 5b or 5c and some of the later routes were climbed in error.

1 Sarah's Route *   **10m Very Difficult**
FA Rick & Sarah Campbell 26 May 1995

Direct line through the black rock at the left end of the wall.

2 Sideslip * **   **18m VS 4b**
FA Rab Anderson & Chris Greaves 22 May 1989

Excellent well-protected climbing. Start at the foot of the left-slanting ramp. Gain a vague curving crack and follow this on superb holds.

3 Sideline * **   **20m VS 4c**
FA Bob Dearman & party mid 1970s

Start as for 2. Move out right and up the wall to a ledge then up the wall left of the upper corner.

4 Juggernaut * ***   **25m E1 5a**
FA Rab Anderson & Chris Greaves 22 May 1989

Start few metres down from the left-slanting ramp of 2. Up a short steep wall on to a small ledge, continue past the left side of the large hole to finish up steep cracks up the right arête of the upper corner.

5 Juglust * ***   **25m HVS 5a**
FA unknown

Exciting climbing taking the easiest line up the overhanging wall. Start up 6 to the hole, join 4 and climb it to just right of the ledge on 3 then finish diagonally rightwards.

6 Bloodlust * **   **25m E1 5b**
FA Paul Nunn & P. Fearnehough May 1978

Start at the point where the slab meets the top of the cave. Gain a small ledge then up a shallow corner and left along a gangway to a huge hole with an old nest. Steep moves on huge pockets lead up right to a small ramp then continue diagonally right to the top.

📷 *Karen Latter on the immaculate rock of Sideslip.*

6a Bloodlust Direct ★★★★   25m E2 5b

From the huge hole go diagonally right then back left to finish direct up the right side of the steep red wall. A more direct version gives an excellent E3 5c.

7 May Tripper ★★★   25m E1 5b
FA Rab Anderson & Chris Greaves 22 May 1989

As for 6 to the first ledge. Follow a zigzag quartz vein diagonally right to gain and follow a small ramp leading to a large hidden pocket right of the first thin black streak. Move up to cross 6 and finish direct.

8 Wanderings ★★★   35m E2 5b
FA Gary Latter 2 July 1995

Start up the same point as 7 to a good break. Traverse this diagonally rightwards to an obvious large pink juggy break. Move up then right and follow the right edge of the orange rock to better holds. More easily up a wide crack past a large spike to finish.

9 Dreams by the Sea ★★   30m E2 5c
FA Gary Latter 1 July 2014

A fine direct line up the centre of the wall. Start from a belay on the shelf, at the start of the roof a few metres down from 7. Pull up rightwards on good slots to good holds (crux) at the small roof in the left-facing groove. Move left and steeply up to good ledge, common with 7. Climb the centre of the orange wall above, between the twin black streaks, finishing direct.

> The following routes are all approached by a 35m abseil from boulders down the right corner line of *Black Night* to the **Black Pedestal**, a large incut ledge at its base. Note: no suitable belay is available here – belay to the abseil rope.

10 The Dark Flush ★★★   45m E2 5b
FA Rick Campbell & Gary Latter 26 May 1995

Start as for 11, but continue traversing the entire lip of the roof to follow a line of huge pockets up the prominent wide black streak.

11 Geriatrics ★★★★   40m E2 5b
FA Rab Carrington & Martin Boysen May 1987

Traverse left from the belay into 14 and continue traversing left on a quartz band across the lip of the cave. From its end move up and continue left in a spectacular position to a ramp at the left end of the cave roof. Finish directly up the wall above.

12 Presumption ★★★★   40m E1 5b
FA Paul Nunn & Bob Toogood May 1983

Follow 14 to just past the first bulge. Traverse horizontally left past the black streaks of 13 and into the stepped left-curving arch. Finish direct just left of the top groove.

13 Exorcist ★★★   40m E1 5b
FA Rab Carrington & Martin Boysen May 1987

Follow 11 to the end of the quartz band and climb via black streaks above to a small ledge below the obvious shallow left-curving arch forming a higher groove. Continue up the black streaks to gain a higher faint groove which leads to the top.

> Further lines include *Muir Wall* ★★ E2 5c between 12 & 13 heading for a hanging groove near the top; *The Cuckoo Conundrum* ★★★E3 5c continues the rising traverse of 10 into 6a, finishing at 4.

14 Dark Angel ★★   30m E1 5b
FA Paul Nunn & Bob Toogood May 1983

Traverse awkwardly left from the belay to climb the fine groove to the large upper shelf. Steep moves up the large upper left-curving corner provide the crux.

15 Black Night ★★   30m HVS 5a
FA Bob Dearman & party mid 1970s

Gain and climb the black groove directly above the belay to the upper shelf. Finish easily on the right.

16 Lucifer's Link ★   35m E2 5b
FA Paul Nunn & Phil Kershaw July 1983

Sustained and quite bold climbing up the left side of the rib above the Black Pedestal in impressive surroundings.

> The following five routes are reached by abseiling from a large block down the large slabby corner round to the right of the **Black Pedestal** (down the line of *Shark Crack*) to a small rectangular ledge about 5m above the water line.

17 Dolphins and Whales ★★★   20m E4 6a
FA Gary Latter & Paul Thorburn 16 June 1996

The pocket-infested wall above the slabby corner of 19. Belay higher up the slabby lower ramp of 19, beneath the centre of the wall. Follow a line of huge pockets diagonally leftwards to a break running across the centre of the wall. Continue up in the same line to a huge pocket just right of the arête. Move up to a good finger pocket then head out rightwards to a good vertical slot. Directly above on better holds to a sloping finish. Many large cams useful. The final short crux wall could be avoided by escaping up the left side of the arête, giving a superb E2 5b.

18 No Porpoise ★★   20m E4 6a
FA Steve Crowe & Karin Magog 17 June 2001

Start as for 17 but continue directly up the right side of the pocketed wall heading for the prominent steep left-facing groove. Power up this to the top.

19 Shark Crack ★★★   30m HS 4b
FA Bob Dearman, K.Bridges, Paul Nunn June 1971

The crack in the main slabby corner right of the pedestal. Excellent climbing on huge holds with a steep unlikely looking finale.

Karen Latter on the spectacularly-situated Presumption.

SUTHERLAND SHEIGRA

20 Fingers ★★   30m E1 5b
FA Bob Toogood 1970s

The thin crack splitting the right wall of the corner, steepening towards the top. Belay on the large slabby ledge below the line.

21 Escape from Reality ★   30m VS 5a
FA Stuart & Kay Charlton 31 May 2003

From the belay as for 20, move right to the arête and follow this to finish up twin cracks.

22 Rhapsody in Blue ★★   35m E3 5c
FA Robert Durran & Jerry Handren 27 July 2015

Abseil to the lower tidal ledge below the start of *Above the Blue*. Hand-traverse a small ramp leftwards onto the steep wall. Go up at its end, then traverse hard left to gain an obvious blunt spike. Climb steeply up the left side of the wall passing a ledge on the left to finish more easily.

📷 *Karen Latter near the top of the finely positioned Tall Pall.*

TREASURE ISLAND WALL
NG 180 603 6min

The northerly continuation of **The Second Geo**, starting below the huge sandstone erratic boulder and running north opposite the low headland of **Na Stacain**, which almost becomes an island at high tide.

Descents: about 50m north of the sandstone boulder is a shallow burn (a trickle really) in a sandstone-boulder-filled depression emanating from a small pool. A steep descent on big holds can be made down the right side (facing out, i.e. north) of the burn at about Difficult. Alternatively, abseil from large blocks just right (north) of the burn.

1 Burn Out ★   30m HVS 5a
FA Andy & Jeni Cunningham 7 April 1996

Start about 20m right (south) of the descent. Ascend a short crack to finish up short corners and steps.

2 Kiska ★   30m VS 4c
FA Andy & Jeni Cunningham 7 April 1996

The two-tiered corner, then easier above.

3 The Devil You Know ★★   30m E1 5b
FA Andy & Jeni Cunningham 7 April 1996

Steep right trending corners starting below and right of 2

4 Sun Spot ★   20m Severe 4a
FA Andy & Jeni Cunningham 7 April 1996

Just left of the descent is an area of orange stepped rock between black rock. Climb cracks up this.

Eclipse V.Diff. takes a wandering line right of this.

5 The Nook ★★★   25m VS 4c
FA Andy Nisbet (solo) November 1989

Sensational climbing, venturing onto some improbable ground for the grade. Up the easy large black V-groove and the black ramp on the right to enter the right groove. Traverse left above the lip of the roof then follow a line of remarkable jugs in a stunning position to the top. The pink upper groove can be followed at about Difficult.

6 Slim Jim ★★   30m VS 4c
FA Andy & Jeni Cunningham 7 April 1996

Climb the V-groove as for 5 to the recess. Traverse 4m left to the first break and move rightwards through a bulge into the base of a wide black stepped groove above the recess. Finish up this.

7 Tall Pall ★★★   35m Severe 4a
FA Paul Nunn June 1975

A brilliant natural line up the right side of the blunt rib. Start at the base of the deep black V-groove of 6. Move up left past two incut black ledges to follow a line of good holds then up the pink-coloured rock by a line of cracks to the top. Excellent holds and protection.

8 Plum McNumb ★★★   30m VS 4b
FA Paul Nunn & Bob Toogood June 1976

A direct line cutting through 7. Start on a small ledge further left, directly under the ill-defined blunt rib. Traverse left then direct up the rib, crossing 7 rightwards to and up a sea of jugs up the 'steep blunt nose' to finish direct.

> The following routes can be approached by traversing a line of flakes (just above the high tide mark) descending leftwards (at about Severe standard) from the second incut ledge on *Tall Pall*, or directly by abseil.

9 Pieces I've Ate ★★   35m E3 5c
FA Gary Latter & Chris Murray 13 June 1996

Start from near the left end of a tapering reddish ledge just above the high tide line, opposite the north end of the long rocky ridge that forms a narrow turbulent inlet along the base of the right side of the crag. (Spike belay, or nut belay 5m up and right if high tide). Climb a line of pockets just right of the prominent thin crack to some sharp pockets on the right. Move hard left to better holds then direct to a small ledge. Continue much easier in a fine position up the rib midway between two shallow grooves above.

10 Billy Bones ★★   55m VS 4c
FA Gary Latter (solo) 13 June 1996

Continuing further left is a large low ledge system which peters out.

1. **30m 4b** Traverse diagonally left then up on huge pockets to a steepening near the top. Step left and up to a ledge. Continue up the shorter rightmost of two black corners to a large ledge above.
2. **25m 4c** There is a choice of lines to finish, the best looking a quartz crack in the slab.

NG 180 604   10min

NA STACAIN AREA

About 120m further on (north) from the shallow burn is a narrow gully running south-west between the main wall and a narrow rib dropping into the geo. Descend the gully dropping underneath some immense wedged blocks to sea level. Turn right under the rib and it is possible to traverse into the geo at mid to low tides. The first 4 routes are above a non-tidal platform.

11 Will o' the Wisp ★   20m Severe 4a
FA Jeni Pickering & Alison Hepburn 18 September 1993

This climbs the actual rib. At the steepening move left on to the front and finish by a steep crack.

12 Tickled Pink ★   15m HS 4b
FA Andy Cunningham November 1989

The first crack at the right end of the wall, curving leftwards.

13 Spare Rib ★★   15m VS 4c
FA Andy Nisbet & Stevie Blagbrough November 1989

Line of left-trending discontinuous cracks up the centre of the wall.

14 Whoomf ★★   15m E1 5b
FA Ian Taylor & Tess Fryer 31 July 2009

Climb the excellent wall left of 13.

15 Fear of the Dark ★   20m E2 5c
FA Tess Fryer & Ian Taylor 31 July 2009

Follow 16 to the move left, then go steeply straight up, keeping right of the black vein.

16 After Dark ★★   25m E1 5a
FA Allen Fyffe & Ian Rea November 1989

Start at the left end of the platform. Gain an awkward ledge and trend left up cracks until a move left can be made on to the black vein above the cave. Climb the weird flake crack above to the top.

> The following routes beyond the platform and on the other side (**Na Stacain**) are approached by scrambling over green seaweedy boulders into the geo at mid to low tides.

17 Flamingo ★★★   25m Severe 4a
FA Allen Fyffe & Andy Cunningham November 1989

The prominent left-trending pink ramp right of a deep cave slit. Follow the perfect crack up the beautiful pink ramp.

18 Flaky Shakes ★   20m E2 5c
FA Allen Fyffe & Andy Cunningham November 1989

Line of deceptively steep flakes immediately right and parallel to the ramp.

19 The Bluff ★   20m HVS 5a
FA Ian Rea, Allen Fyffe & Andy Cunningham 29 May 1993

The corner and continuation flake just right of the chimney, finishing up an easier groove.

> The enticingly-named *Sheep Sheigra* E1 5b ascends the pale wall direct above the start of 18.

20 Squeeze to Please ★★   20m Difficult
FA Andy Nisbet (solo) November 1989

Farther left the geo narrows at a tidal pool, before which is a prominent left-slanting black chimney. Follow this and the narrow rib on its left.

21 Mother Goose ★   15m HVS 5a
FA Andy & Jeni Cunningham 17 March 1996

The crack and flake above the centre of the pool. Gain the ledge at 2m by abseil or a difficult traverse from the right.

22 Rapture ★★★   10m HVS 5a
FA Ian Rea, Andy Cunningham & Allen Fyffe 29 May 1993

A midget gem up the overhanging wall at the far end of the pool, reached by traversing above on the Stacain side. Climb by hidden jugs to a left-trending flake line and finish direct.

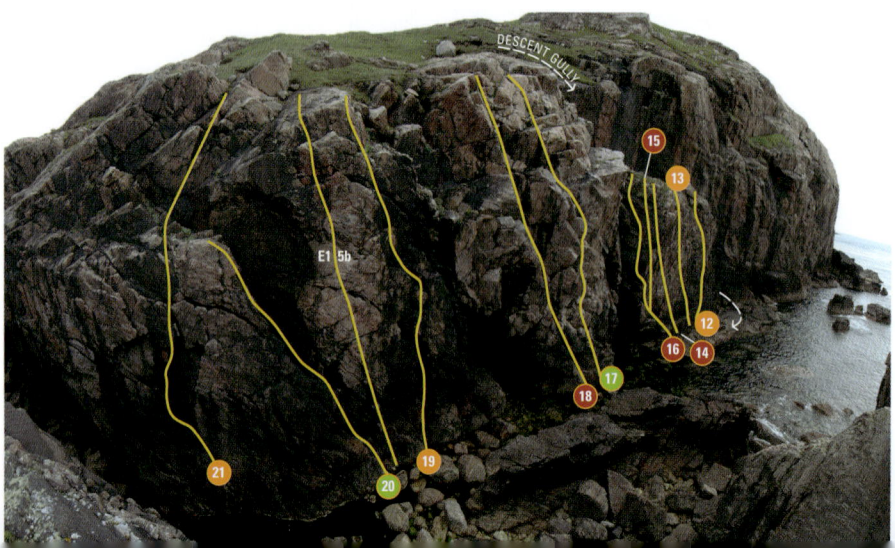

AM BUACHAILLE (THE SHEPHERD)

NC 201 652
  2hr 1½hr 1¼hr

Photo Ian Taylor

This impressive 50m stack of Torridonian sandstone lies 1km south of the beautiful Sandwood Bay, some 6.5 miles/10km north of the quaint wee Highland fishing village (sic) of Kinlochbervie. The fairly remote situation and difficult approach to the base make it far and away the most serious of 'the big three' classic Scottish stacks. It also has its fair share of doubtful rock and it should be noted that it is also host to a flourishing fulmar colony for much of the summer, though there are only one or two birds on the routes.

Access: From Kinlochbervie follow the single-track road towards Sheigra for 3.5 miles/5.4km to a large car park on the left.

Approach: Follow the track north in towards Sandwood Bay. Just under 1km beyond where the path skirts the shore of Loch a' Mhuilinn, leave the path and head north-west over the moor.

Descent to base: Scramble down the open gully bounding the east side of the mainland cliff overlooking the stac. The stac is separated from the mainland by a 60m wide sea-washed platform. At low tide a 15m wide channel has to be crossed, easiest at its right (north-west) end. **It is important to ascertain the time of low tide and make a speedy ascent, otherwise retreat could be very problematic.** It is not practicable to set up a Tyrolean, as there are no high anchors available.

Descent: Abseil down the landward face.

① Original Route ★★   65m HVS 4c
FA Tom Patey, John Cleare & Ian Clough 23 July 1967

Start just left of centre of the landward face.

1 25m 4b Climb overhanging rocks up and onto the prow on the right. Continue straight up until impending rock forces a traverse along a horizontal ledge on the left. Climb the left edge for 4m to belay on a large ledge.

2 **20m 4c** From the inset corner of the ledge make an awkward move up and across the wall to a ledge on the right. Continue up to an inset crack at 10m, which is climbed on dubious rock to another left traverse and belay on the left edge.

3 **20m 4c** Return to the centre below a deep overhanging crack. From its base traverse left below overhangs until a mantelshelf can be made between two large 'soup-plates'. Cross the slab to rejoin the main crack and pull out awkwardly at the top.

2 Landward Face ★★   50m HVS 5a
FA Paul Nunn, D.Peck, Clive Rowland & others July 1967

Climbed shortly after the *Original Route*, it shares some common ground.

1. **15m 4b** as for 1.
2. **35m 5a** Traverse rightwards along break to gain a steep crack. Climb the crack and continue in the same line, then slightly left to a ledge beneath a deep overhanging crack, which leads to a large ledge. Finish more easily.

3 Atlantic Wall ★★   50m E1 5b
FA Simon Richardson & Robin Clothier 15 September 1990; Direct: Dave Turnbull & Chris Rees 29 April 2011

An exposed and intimidating route on the west (seaward) face with good rock and protection. Retreat would be difficult after pitch 1. Start below a left-facing hanging corner on the south face.

1. **15m 5a** Gain and climb the corner to a roof at 5m. Traverse left to the arête and climb this to reach an exposed stance. **3a** *Direct* ★★ E2 5b continues directly from corner to a wide break at 20m, then left and up through stepped corners to a belay ledge on the arête.
2. **15m 4c** Strenuously up the overhanging flake crack on the seaward face directly above the stance and continue more easily to reach a large ledge beneath the steep final wall. Belay up and right beside a huge detached block.
3. **20m 5b** Climb the thin crack above the block to a horizontal break. Traverse left to reach the continuous crack running up the left side of the wall which leads to easier ground and the top. A fine pitch.

SANDWOOD BAY CRAGS

A collection of wonderfully situated crags of immaculate water washed gneiss rising from the beach.

Access: From Kinlochbervie follow the single-track road towards Sheigra for 3.5 miles/5.4km to a large car park on the left.

Approach: Follow the track north into the wonderful extensive mile long Sandwood Bay and continue to the north-east end, crossing the burn at the outflow of Sandwood Loch to the first crag.

 1½hr   <1hr   1½hr

Rick Campbell bouldering on small non-tidal crags above the east end of the bay.

CRAG 1
NC 225 657

An excellent **bouldering** wall with potential for routes up to 15m high. Clear of the water from about mid-tide onwards with the vertical NW facing wall clear a bit longer. There is also a fine ruby-coloured mini geo with excellent 3–4m vertical walls just before the next crag.

CRAG 2
NC 229 656

Continue round the first promontory for 200m. A fine **tidal** crag with a steep 40m slab at the right end, dwindling and steepening leftwards to about 15–20m. The routes at the left end are clear of the water 1 hour either side of low tide, those on the right for about 4 hours.
Descents: Abseil descents from the belays were used to regain the beach, scrambling across broken ground at the top of all the routes. Alternatively, walk a long way right from the top of *Marram* and descend grass and the small rocky promontory.

1 Golden Samphire ★   65m E1 5b
FA Gary Latter, Gary Ellington & Tom Pringle 7 July 2002

  1 **30m 5b** Start beneath a small projecting roof high up at the right end of the crag. Ascend grey rock

1 Sandwood Bay Crack ★★   15m E2 5c
FA Rab & Chris Anderson 16 April 2004

A great little route. Start off the beach at the right side of the crag just left of a steep area of perfect rock. Climb the steep crack past a horizontal break. Scramble down leftwards to descend.

2 Sandwood Bay Craic ★★   12m E1 5b
FA Ewen Russell (on-sight solo) 25 May 2013

20m to the right of 1, vague corner has a rightwards diagonal crack coming out of it. Follow this to the top. Loose block at top out (easily avoidable).

to gain a left curving groove and up this then step right and pull through the roof by a finger crack in the slab. Belay on a ledge above.
  2 **35m 4b** Move up rightwards to climb fine pink slab at top of the crag, finishing up the obvious crack

2 Beach Wall ★   60m VS 4c
FA Rab & Chris Anderson 16 April 2004

A direct line just right of 3. Start on the first rocks at the extreme right side of the beach.

  1 **35m 4c** Climb directly up compact rocks and thin

cracks heading for a shallow corner and thin crack half way up the wall. Move up the corner a short way then out right into the crack and then up right to gain ledges below a small roof. Move up left and around the edge of the steepening to gain large ledges.

2 25m – Scramble to top.

3 Marram ★★★ 60m Severe 4a
FA Gary Latter & Alan Warner 3 July 2000

Start beneath large flakes near the right side of the large slab.

1 35m 4a Climb the flakes and obvious vertical crack and continue steeply directly on good holds to belay on large ledge.

2 25m Scramble directly over short walls and ledges.

4 Sea Campion ★★ 35m HVS 5a
FA Gary Latter & Gary Ellington 7 July 2002

Start just left of the prominent easy flakes on 3. Climb a direct line up the wall, just right of a thin crack low down aiming for an obvious line leading to a step left to finish by the wide layback crack. Abseil off, or finish as for 3.

5 Sea Rocket ★ 40m HVS 5a
FA Bob Hamilton & Steve Kennedy 27 September 2008

Start left of 4 at a stepped crack leading slightly leftwards up the slab (directly below the prominent flake). Climb the crack and slab above to reach the flake, finishing up the edge of the flake, as for 4.

6 Rose Root ★★ 35m VS 5a
FA Gary Latter & Alan Warner 3 July 2000

Climbs a line up the left side of the slab, aiming for the steepest areas of rock. Follow a line heading for a short bulging finger-crack in the upper left edge and climb this to belay on large ledge. Finish as for 3.

> Continuing left the base is guarded by barnacles and green slime for the first 3m. The following two routes both share a common start up a tiny left-facing corner.

7 Wild Wood ★★ 15m E2 5c
FA Gary Latter & Alan Warner 3 July 2000

Negotiate the start and pull up right to good holds. Continue directly on good holds.

8 Sandal Wood ★ 15m VS 5a
FA Gary Latter & Alan Warner 3 July 2000

Prominent left-slanting diagonal crack, after the problematic entry. Can also be gained by starting further left.

9 Mustard Pickle ★★ 15m HS 4b
FA Andy Moles (on-sight solo) 26 May 2009

The obvious rightward-trending crack to the left of 8.

10 Driftwood ★★ 15m E2 5c
FA Gary Latter 3 July 2000

20m further left is a fine looking pink wall with a steep bulge low down. Negotiate the start and make difficult moves over the bulge to finish more easily up the wall.

> The following two routes lie above a large pool. Ledges at 6m were gained by abseil from the rightmost of three large blocks at the top, but could also be gained quite easily by a right slanting line from the broken ridge bounding the left edge of the crag.

11 Thrift ★★ 12m HS 4b
FA Gary Latter & Alan Warner 3 July 2000

The prominent crack up the pink wall, a few metres left of an easy open black corner.

12 Sea Pink ★★ 12m Severe 4a
FA Gary Latter & Alan Warner 3 July 2000

Cracks up the left edge, finishing up the arête to step round the left side of the large boulder.

> Further left, another 9 routes from Difficult – E2 were climbed by *Gary & Karen Latter on 12 September 2015*. All are on great rock, with the exception of the rightmost, longest route (VS 4c) & worth ★ or ★★. Descent was made by abseil from slings and maillons on blocks.

FOINAVEN
(WART MOUNTAIN OR WHITE HILL)

<2¾hr   <1¾hr

The long ridge of Foinaven projects many buttresses on its eastern flanks into the long flat Strath Dionard. At the northern end on Cnoc a' Mhadaidh the rock is Lewisian gneiss, while all the cliffs further south are composed of Cambrian quartzite, the mountain taking its name from the many large pale scree slopes flanking its upper reaches.
Access: Park on the left (west) side of the A838, 4.7 miles/7.5km north of Rhiconich, just over 100m north of Gualin House (plantation).

Approach: Follow the land rover track steeply down the hill for 1.6km then continue along this for 8km to Loch Dionard. 2 hours on foot – mountain bike recommended to reach the loch (<1 hour). Ignore landowners 'no cycling' sign – the track was built and paid for with public money! For **Creag Urbhard** head straight up (15 minutes), for the **First Dionard Buttress** continue round the south (right) side of the loch on deer tracks, cutting up to the cliff (30 minutes).

NC 328 530  1¼hr ¾hr

CNOC A' MHADAIDH
(KNOLL OF THE FOX)

A generally messy crag, despite the impressive overhanging wall dominating the crag. The two described routes follow excellent clean lines.

Approach: Follow the land rover track along Strath Dionard for 45 minutes until the crag comes into view then head diagonally left up the hillside to the base.

1 Wrath ★★   150m E1 5b
FA Paul Nunn, Tim Lewis & Chris Boulton May 1978

An excellent main pitch through the right edge of the leaning wall. Start beneath the right edge.
1. **30m** – From the gully climb easily up the right edge of the slabs, moving in a little to belay beneath the overhanging wall.
2. **35m 5b** Climb a steep groove on the left to a break. Move right and take the flying ramp (PR) to gain slabs above.

3+4 85m – Continue more easily by slabs and grooves.

2 Pilastre ★★   170m HVS 5a
FA Martin Boysen & Paul Nunn June 1973

Good clean climbing following a direct line up a series of corners in the pillar towards the left side of the crag. Scramble across heather from the base of the gully at the bottom left edge.
1. **20m 4c** Climb a crack and bulge on the left to belay on a grass terrace.
2. **30m 5a** Move up and traverse left to a corner and gain it past a jammed flake. At the top move left then step right into the upper continuation corner.
3. **30m 4c** Continue up the corner to an overhang. Traverse left to the crest and climb over cracked blocks then shallow cracks in the red wall to belay on a grass terrace.
4. **15m 5a** Go up the large grassy corner to an overhang. Traverse left and slightly down to its edge then move up and left to a ledge and tree.

5+6 75m Ascend the chimney, scrambling up heather to finish.

NC 352 487 **Alt:** 230m 2¼hr   1¼hr

CREAG URBHARD
(CRAG OF THE DEVIL'S-BIT HERB)

"... ideal for random mountaineering, selecting some general line and then picking one's own way up the innumerable corners, buttresses and open faces."
– Peter Macdonald, Creag Urbhard, *Scottish Mountaineering Club Journal*, 1977

An extensive quartzite cliff, almost Dolomitic in appearance with some excellent atmospheric climbing. Much of the climbing is open to variation.

Descent: Traverse left (east) and down a ribbon of easy-angled slabs to pick up a path running beneath the base of **First Dionard Buttress** then skirt back left beneath the waterfall.

1 Whitewash ★★   165m HVS 5b
FA Arthur Paul & Brian Dunn 11 August 1976

A right-slanting line up the wall to finish up the corner above *Gargantua*. Start at easy-angled slabs right of a left-facing corner and beneath a prominent low overhang.
1. **35m 4a** Climb to the right end of the overhang then through a bulge by a crack which leads to a belay.
2. **35m 4c** Climb vague groove directly for 20m then traverse hard right to belay below a large overhang
3. **30m 4c** Climb the right end of the overhang by a rib to a small blank wall. Turn this on the left by an overhanging groove then go up rightwards to belay at the base of a prominent corner.
4. **45m 4b** Climb the corner to a steepening (possible belay) and continue to belay on a gangway.
5. **20m 5b** Finish up the corner.

2 Gargantua **   175m HS 4b
FA Terry Sullivan & M.Denton 26 April 1959

Follows a long groove up the centre of the left section of the cliff. Start at a short corner below the groove just left of the terrace of *Iolaire*.

1. **10m** Climb the corner.
2+3. **60m** Move left then follow a crack. Move right and climb a vague corner to belay down and left of large overhangs.
4+5. **70m** Ascend the prominent groove passing the overhangs on the left.
6. **35m** Walk up the gangway on the right and finish up a crack in the wall.

3 Iolaire **   155m HVS 5b
FA Dave Broadhead & Des Rubens 13 July 1979

Start at the left end of a rock terrace beneath a big roof.

1. **40m 4b** Climb a crack direct to belay.
2. **25m 4c** Continue up to the roof and trend right under it towards a prominent steep chimney crack, belaying just short of the chimney.
3. **25m 5b** Gain the chimney crack awkwardly and climb it to belay beneath a corner.
4. **25m 4c** Climb the corner to a shelf.
5. **40m** Follow the shelf easily to finish.

4 Fingal **   300m Severe 4a
FA Tom Patey (solo) 12 June 1962

The 'classic' of the crag with all that that implies. Start from a small amphitheatre at the base of the Second Waterfall.

1. **35m** Climb rocks on the left to a terrace.
2+3. **75m** Just before re-entering the watercourse, twin cracks form a shallow fault line splitting the wall on the left. Climb these, following the direct line of cracks to the true first terrace
4+5. **60m** Follow the line of least resistance, ascending leftwards for 15m towards a shallow inconspicuous gully to the second terrace directly below the huge wet V-shaped amphitheatre.
6. **35m** Climb up onto a flake 12m up on the right wall of the amphitheatre and continue to a huge rock fang.
7+8. **95m** Escape rightwards by a traverse round the exposed edge to an inset slab in a corner which leads to easier broken rocks. Follow the prominent chimney on the right for 15m, traversing left to emerge with surprising suddenness at the top of the main face.

FIRST DIONARD BUTTRESS

An impressive buttress with a steep leaning wall in the centre and immaculate clean glaciated slabs above.

Descent: Traverse right and descend either heather or scree to gain the path running beneath the base.

NC 356 485 **Alt:** 280m

2½hr

1¾hr

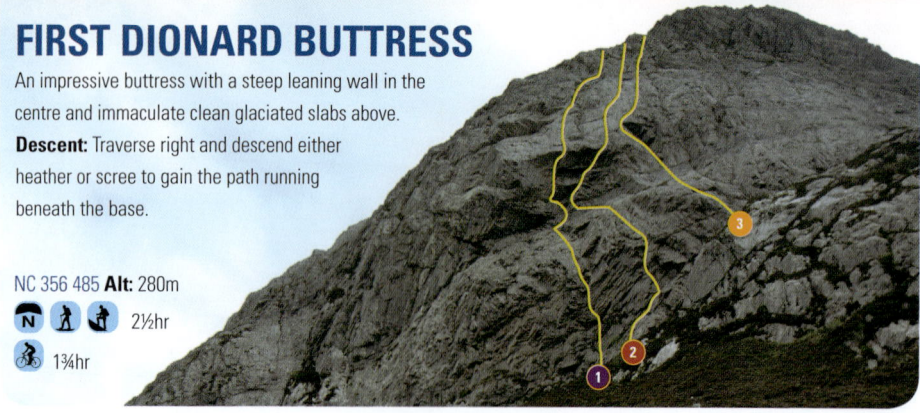

1 Regeneration ★★ 185m E6 6b
FA Rick Campbell & Gary Latter 3 June 2000

Direct line through steep ground up the centre of the cliff. Start directly beneath a prominent roof crack in the right wall of the open groove 10m down left of the fault of 2.

1 **30m 6b** Climb straight up rock and unpleasant heather to gain the base of the crack. Climb this with increasingly difficulty beyond the hanging block (F #3.5) to belay in groove just round the lip.

2 **40m 5c** Continue up the groove, moving out left into another groove. Trend up left beneath a further roof to easier ground and head up rightwards to traverse left along large flakes to belay beneath a crack in the overhanging wall.

3 **25m 6b** Make a long reach off the belay ledge to a good fingerlock then heave into the groove above. Climb more easily to arrange protection in the crack above then swing left into the base of a corner. Climb this mainly on its right wall to belay in a groove just above.

4+5 **90m 5c** – Climb straight up the thin crack and the slab above, trending slightly right to finish up the final fault of *Millennium*. Escape out right along grassy terrace, scrambling down (Difficult) slabs.

2 Millennium ★★ 220m E2 5c
FA Alex Livesey & Paul Nunn 30 – 31 May 1982

A classic, ascending the fault near the right side of the front face then the edge of the central leaning wall by a finely situated ramp. Start up right of the central overhanging groove.

1 **25m 4c** Climb a short wall to a right trending break and follow it to a belay.

2 **45m 5b** Loose and committing. Climb to a wet scoop on the left and up through steep walls to a groove. Go right to an overhang. Climb it, moving right or direct then continue more easily to the slabs.

3 **25m 5c** Go left and up to a steep groove leading right and climb with difficulty to a stance.

4 **25m 5b** Follow the undercut ramp through the roofs and exit onto grey slabs. Spectacular.

5+6 **100m 4b** Finish more easily up shallow grooves and slabs.

3 Cengalo ★★ 210m VS 4b
FA Ted Howard & Clive Rowland June 1969

Excellent climbing on good clean rock, aiming for the prominent inverted L-shaped overhang at mid-height on the right edge of the front face.

1+2 **75m** Climb the lower slabs to a small belay ledge beneath the groove leading up to the overhang.

3 **35m 4a** Climb the left wall for 12m then make a delicate poorly protected leftwards traverse to gain the immaculate smooth slabs on the edge of the frontal face.

4+5 **100m 4b** Continue up the smooth slabs fairly directly, finishing by 70m of easy scrambling to gain the summit ridge.

SECOND DIONARD BUTTRESS

NC 358 484 **Alt:** 280m 1¾hr
2¾hr

The next buttress south, composed of three right-slanting tiers. The middle tier forms a fine long wall.

1 Marble Corner ★★★   75m HVS 5a
FA Paul Nunn & Martin Boysen June 1973

Excellent climbing up the large right-facing corner originating about two-thirds of the way up the wall. Start just right of a pale yellow undercut rock at the base. Dirty to start, but two of the best pitches hereabouts.

1. **35m 4c** Climb the lower groove to a steep section then move right to belay.
2. **40m 5a** Climb the corner, bypassing a bulging section on the left. Finish up slabs.

2 Mr Sheen ★★   70m HVS 5a
FA James Edwards & Dave McGimpsey 15 April 2003

The attractive grey wall near the right end of the crag on excellent rock.

1. **30m 5a** Climb a short pink pedestal then up to a small overlap. Step out right below this and continue right for 5m. Climb straight up to a prominent overlap and belay at its right end.
2. **40m 5a** Step back left and cross the overlap. Climb direct up the wall above to finish up a right-facing corner.

CREAG SHOMHAIRLE (SAMUEL'S CLIFF)

A fine extensive crag with a pleasant outlook. The rock is remarkably diverse with the scree fan below the crag composed of quartzite, the main bulk of the crag Lewisian gneiss and an upper sweep of schist where the influence of the Moine thrust is evident. There is lots of vegetation above the face and many of the routes seep for a few days after rain.

Access: Follow the A838 east from Durness for 11.3 miles /18km to the head of Loch Eriboll. Park at the start of a rough land rover track by a boulder at NC 394 538.

Approach: Follow the track and the vague continuation path, crossing a fence, a stream and through a couple of walls to the fine Strabeg bothy (2km/30 minutes). From here head due south towards a small ruined building for a couple of hundred metres then by a path bordering the edge of the birch woods and the River Beag, which leads round beneath the base of the crags.

Although less than 2km from the bothy, the going is rough (very boggy and lots of boulders to weave around) and takes a further 45 minutes. Cut diagonally up right crossing a scree cone coming down from the right end of the crag. A path runs left along the terrace from here.

Descent: for the majority of routes, traverse across easy slabs to the top of Windy Corner – the broken gully at the left (west) end of the **South Face**. Scramble down 5m to an in situ abseil point and make a 50m abseil.

NC 382 507 **Alt:** 150m   1½hr

Gary Latter on the first pitch of Land of the Dancing Dead. Photo Karen Latter.

SOUTH FACE

1 The Roost ★★   60m VS 4c
FA Caithness Mountaineering Club members 1962

The prominent fine curving crack up the centre of the face. Scramble up from the right to belay at a flake line in the middle of the wall.

1 **30m 4c** Follow the curving left-trending crack to belay on a heather ledge with a holly.
2 **30m 4b** Continue direct to beneath the main overhangs then make an exposed traverse left round into an open corner which leads to slabs above. Traverse left to descend, or scramble for two rope lengths to the top.

2 Hot Pants ★★   55m E4 6b
FA Murray Hamilton & Rab Anderson 29 June 1986

High in the centre of the face is a prominent roof split by two cracks which continue up a short headwall. The route takes the right crack.

1 **30m 4c** As for *The Roost*.
2 **25m 6b** Move right and climb the crack to below the roof. Surmount the roof and continue up a crack in the headwall to the top.

WEST FACE

3 In Woods and Wild Places ★   55m E4 6a
FA Paul Thorburn & Gary Latter 25 August 1995

A line up the pillar on the right side of the crag where the wall turns from west to south-west. Start by a slabby right-sloping ramp.

1 **30m 5b** Easily up past a small rowan and slabby ramp to a left-slanting diagonal crack then by a flaky crack to a small groove. At the capping roof step right round a rib to belay on a ledge.
2 **25m 6a** Traverse left above the lip of the roof to two good pockets. Make committing moves up leftwards to a large rounded hold and continue in the same direction with a further tricky section to good holds. Continue up cracks in the arête to belay on a ledge. An abseil descent down the overhanging wall below (taken by *Tank Top*) was made from a nut and karabiner, left in situ. 50m ropes just reach the ground.

3a Hollow Be Thy Name ★★   55m HVS 5b
FA A.Finch, Graham Harrison & M.McIlraith 27 May 1997

Alternative 2nd pitch to 3, giving a more consistent route.
2 25m 4c Climbing the arête on its left side to the top.

4 Tank Top ★★★★   45m E6 6b
FA Murray Hamilton & Rab Anderson 28 June 1986

The impressive steep crack line at the right end of the face, just right of *Land of the Dancing Dead*.
1. **10m 4c** Climb as for *Land of the Dancing Dead* and move right to a small stance.
2. **35m 6b** Move up and slightly right until moves left can be made to a point underneath the roof. Pull over this and follow the crack to the top.

5 Land of the Dancing Dead ★★★   90m E1 5b
FA Chris Jackson & Tom Proctor 21 August 1971

An excellent route following a thin crack on the right side of the 'Great Slab'. It is characterised by a Damoclean flake at about 20m and an overhanging corner higher up.
1. **35m 5a** Climb the wall to a crack and follow it to a large hanging flake. Move left round the flake and follow its continuation to a small sloping ledge. Traverse back right to a corner and follow this to a small stance.
2. **25m 5b** Climb the corner direct (strenuous but well-protected) to spike belays on a sloping ledge.
3. **30m** Continue up the corner, layback round a roof, climb the groove above and traverse right to belay on slabs.

6 Bardo Thodol ★★★   90m E2 5b
FA Geoff Cohen & Gordon MacNair 1 August 1984

An excellent companion route to *Land of the Dancing Dead*, taking the big slab to the left of that route. Start 8m left of *Land of the Dancing Dead*. The best route here, with three good pitches.
1. **35m 5b** Climb blocks passing an overhang to gain a slab at 7m. Traverse left and go up and left to a small ledge. Go right then directly up to a stance on the 'Great Slab' at the bottom of its right-bounding corner.
2. **25m 5a** Climb the slabby corner and traverse left under a roof till near the left edge. Go up to a steep crack and follow this leftwards to the edge. Go up a short wall to a comfortable stance.
3. **30m 5a** Climb up to a steep crack and follow this leftwards to the edge. Go up a short wall in a fine exposed position to ledges.

7 The Ramp ★★   109m VS 4c
FA R.How & J.Sutcliffe 28 May 1969

The prominent left-trending ramp, starting about 50m left of the right end of the face.
1. **30m** Climb a slab to belay at a large cracked flake beneath an overhang.
2. **20m 4c** Move left and ascend to where a sharp edged flake protrudes from the roof. Continue awkwardly up the fault to a grassy corner beneath the upper slab.
3. **12m** Continue up the left edge of the slab to a good ledge.
4. **35m** Ascend the steepening mossy slab to a crack leading left to a good ledge.
5. **12m** Cross the heathery groove rightwards to finish up easy slabs.

8 Black Gold ★★   85m E1 5a
FA Rab Anderson & Chris Greaves 21 May 1989

A fine route following the prominent black streak in the wall 80m left of *Land of the Dancing Dead*. Walk along under the roofs to reach a buttress which is bounded on its left by a grassy ramp running up about 30m. Start below a crack at the left end of the wall – there is a diagonal crack to the right.
1. **21m 5a** Gain the crack and climb this to a small ramp. Step right and continue to just below a heathery ledge where a move right is made to gain the ledge and a holly bush.
2. **37m 5a** Follow a ramp up left and across a roof to the black streak and move up right into the base of a slim corner. Climb this and continue directly up the black streak to a ledge and tree belay. An excellent pitch on superb rock. Abseil off (recommended), or:
3. **27m 5a** Move right to gain and climb a corner system leading back above the belay to reach a small holly bush. Traverse up right to the arête and climb this in a fine position to the top. Abseil sling left on a rounded spike, single rope doubled reaches the tree below and from here one long abseil reaches the ground.

CAITHNESS

Even more so than the neighbouring Sutherland, the climbing interest here is restricted to the coast with three contrasting venues offering a range of routes on a wide variety of rock types. The low lying coastal fringe benefits from a markedly drier climate than the much more popular west coast sea cliff venues of Reiff and Sheigra.

Accommodation & Amenities: Many hotels & B&Bs in most towns, particularly Wick and Thurso, which also are well provided with supermarkets. **Bunkhouses:** Sleeperzzz Railway Carriages, Rogart (Mar – Sept; ☎ 01408 641343; www.sleeperzzz.com); Helmsdale Hostel (Apr – Oct; ☎ 07971 922 356; www.helmsdalehostel.co.uk); Sandra's Backpackers Hostel, Thurso (☎ 01847 894375; www.sandras-backpackers.co.uk); Corn Mill Bunkhouse, Achumore, on A897, 6 miles south of Melvich (☎ 01641 571219; www.achumore.co.uk). Nearest **TIC** is in Inverness. Local information at www.wicktown.co.uk; www.thursotown.co.uk; www.visitjohnogroats.com.

Campsites: Inver Caravan Park, Dunbeath (☎ 01593 731441; www.inver-caravan-park.co.uk); Wick Caravan & Camping Site (Apr – Sept; ☎ 01955 605420; www.wickcaravansite.co.uk); Loch Watten Caravan Park (Apr – Oct; ☎ 07765 872070; www.centralcaravans.co.uk) midway between Wick and Thurso; Thurso Bay Caravan & Camping Park (☎ Apr – Sept; 01847 892244; www.thursobaycamping.co.uk); Dunnet Bay Caravan Club Site (Mar – Oct; ☎ 01847 821319; www.caravanclub.co.uk); Windhaven Café, Camping & B&B, Brough (☎ 01847 851927; www.windhaven.co.uk); Stroma View, Huna (☎ 01955 611513; www.stromaview.co.uk) just west of John O'Groats; John O'Groats Caravan & Camping Site (Apr – Sept; ☎ 01955 611329; www.johnogroatscampsite.co.uk); North Coast Touring Park, Melvich (☎ 01641 531282; www.thehalladaleinn.co.uk); also discrete wild camping down by beach at Latheronwheel.

LATHERONWHEEL

The pleasant sheltered easily accessible sandstone here gives the friendliest climbing of all the Caithness crags and also the closest for southerners! Its fine picturesque location also affords fine unrestricted views up the Caithness coastline. Due to the horizontal banding cams are very useful, indeed essential on many routes and on some a double set can be put to use.

Access: Turn off the A9 into the village of Latheronwheel and follow the main street for 0.7 miles/1.1km down to the harbour where there is plenty of parking.

Approach: From the harbour walk back up the road to cross the old bridge and follow the coastal path south-west for 400 metres.

PENINSULA WALL

The wall of the peninsula which runs north-eastwards from the **Big Flat Wall**. A tidal cave/arch cuts through the peninsula at the end of the shelf; right of this above the shelf are two arches/caves.
Descent: On foot down the gully on the north side of the peninsula into the dry bay with four stacks then around the end of the peninsula to a shelf.

1 Sticky Fingers *   10m VS 4c
FA Rob Christie 10 July 1992

On the extreme end of the peninsula (directly facing the outermost stack) is a dog-leg crack. Climb to a roof, move left and continue up a crack.

2 Fancy Free *   10m VS 4c
FA John Perry 10 July 1992

Thin crack on the outside corner of the face, 5m south of 1.

3 Reach for the Sky *   12m VS 4b
FA John Sanders & Graham Stein 6 May 1998

Left of 2 lies *Forgotten Corner* Severe 4b. Start immediately south of this beneath a jutting arête. Climb straight up through the overhang on big holds, finishing direct up the arête in a superb position.

4 Positive Mental Attitude **   15m VS 5a
FA John Sanders & Graham Stein 7 May 1998

Fine climbing starting just right of the central arch. Climb directly to a stance beneath the large roof then the overhanging wall above on jugs.

5 Slide *   15m VS 5a
FA Graham Stein & John Sanders 7 May 1998

Fine well protected climbing. Start 2m right of the corner just left of the arch. Climb directly up to the right of the corner to a niche below a bulge. Attack the bulge direct.

6 Pray **   15m HVS 5b
FA Graham Stein & S.Bradbury 29 August 1998

Great strenuous well protected climbing. Start just left of the right arête. Climb an overhanging crack on good holds until forced right around the arête. Make a couple of awkward moves then move back round the arête onto the main face and finish steeply

7 Don't Think Twice **   15m HVS 5a
FA John Sanders & A.Robertson 29 August 1998

Steep bold and pumpy with adequate protection. Start beneath a jutting corner forming an overhang at 8m. Climb the face direct via horizontal breaks (good cams) to

CAITHNESS LATHERONWHEEL

a ledge beneath the corner. Cut loose up the overhanging corner on jugs, pulling through steeply at the top.

8 More Noise ★★ — 15m HVS 5a

FA S.Bradbury & Graham Stein 29 August 1998

The excellent left arête at the end of the platform. Climb it direct, finishing through the roof.

> The following routes lie on the wall left of the tidal through cave and just right of the **Big Flat Wall**. **Descent:** for 9–12 by abseil from the prominent large block, down the crack of 11 to a good ledge. Gain 13 & 14 directly by abseil.

9 Freaker's Crack ★ — 15m HVS 5a
FA K.Wallace 29 September 1991

Start from a prominent narrow alcove. Chimney out of the alcove to an airy position at the base of a crack. Follow the impending crack with difficulty and increasing exposure

10 Imperial Lather ★★★ — 15m E1 5a
FA Rab & Chris Anderson 26 June 2005

Start just right of 11. Climb a thin crack then step right and steeply climb horizontal breaks to the top.

11 Pipit at the Post ★ — 14m Severe 4b
FA Jeni Pickering & Andy Cunningham June 1992

The obvious straight crack close to where the wall changes direction.

12 Heavy Duty ★★ — 14m VS 4b
FA Andy Cunningham & Jeni Pickering June 1992

Fine exposed climbing tackling the pillar where the wall changes aspect. Climb a fading crack left of 11, trending left higher up.

> The next two routes are tidal.

13 Eye of the Storm ★★ — 16m HS 4b
FA K.Wallace 29 September 1991

Fine climbing up the central corner, guarded by an awkward bulge.

14 Primary Corner ★ — 16m Severe 4b

FA K.Wallace 28 September 1991

The left corner (gained directly by abseil). Start from a ledge and finish up a short crack in line with the corner.

CAITHNESS LATHERONWHEEL

ND 188 318
BIG FLAT WALL

The fine continuous long wall, though the routes on the right are marred by a grass ledge near the top (gulls nests in summer), from which weeps emanate.
Descent: Direct by abseil from the rickety fence post, or from either of the adjoining areas at low tide. Routes on the left can be accessed at most states of the tide by descending as for **The Stack Area** and scrambling back north along ledges.

1 Buoy Racers * — 16m VS 4b
FA Raymond Wallace & Gary Latter 8 September 2007

The fine chimney corner bounding the right end. There is an excellent cave belay at the base, just above high tide level.

2 Gle Mha ** — 18m VS 4c
FA Keith Geddes & Andy Cunningham June 1992

The rightmost crack on the wall. Fine sustained well protected climbing.

3 Illuminations ** — 18m E2 5c
FA Simon Clark & R.Macaulay 30 June 1998

Absorbing climbing up the wall left of 2. Start near 4 then move right to cross the roof centrally, finishing direct up a thin crack.

4 Macallan's Choice ** — 18m HVS 5a
FA Andy Cunningham & Keith Geddes June 1992

The prominent crack springing from the cave. Climb the wall right of the cave to holds above the roof then scurry left into the juggy main crack.

5 Cask Strength ** — 18m E1 5b
FA Simon Clark & R.Macaulay 26 August 1998

Follow the left crack and continue direct up the wall above.

6 Cassin's Crack ** — 20m HVS 5a
FA Simon Richardson & Dori Green 9 July 2001

Fine sustained climbing. The right of twin central cracks. Climb the right side of the cave to join the right crack. Follow this to the upper wall where the cracked bulge leads to the top.

7 The Other Landscape ** — 18m HVS 5a
FA Simon Clark 26 September 1991;
Direct Start: Gary Latter 19 August 2018

Steady, finely situated climbing up the left crack. Climb the right edge of the cave as for 6, then move left immediately above it to gain and climb the crack.
7a *Direct Start* is ** E1 5c.

8 Morning Tide ★　　　　　　　　18m E1 5b
FA Gary Latter & Paul Thorburn 24 August 1995

The central wall. From the cave belay, traverse left to a small thread and pull over the bulge. Continue straight up the wall above, moving left at a ledge to finish up a short corner.

9 Gervasutti's Wall ★★　　　　　　15m E1 5b
FA Simon Clark 26 September 1991

The most continuous thin crack to the right of the large niche at the left end. Start from the end of the large ledge (awash at high tide). Move right around an initial bulge to follow the crack and wall direct. 9a A better protected eliminate takes the crack on the left at the same grade.

THE STACK AREA

The area around a partially detached stack (separated by a short jump from the cliff top).

Descents: Either down the chimney (Moderate) at the north end to the little flat wall or a short down climb (Difficult) at the south end, immediately south of the southmost route (18). There are good blocks for direct abseil also.

10 Free Fall ★　　　　　　　　　12m VS 4c
FA Jim Mackintosh Summer 1990

Start in the large alcove near the left end of the wall. Poorly protected. Climb the right corner in the rear of the alcove to exit onto the wall above.

11 Welzenbach ★　　　　　　　　15m HVS 5a
FA Simon Richardson & Dori Green 9 July 2001

Climb the steep crack on the left side of the niche then trend right up the wall above, finishing up a crack.

12 The Grey Coast ★　　　　　　12m VS 4b
FA Simon Clark 26 September 1991

Bridge up the smaller alcove on the far left and pull onto the wall above. Climb this, trending slightly right to finish by a diagonal crack above the ledge.

13 The Beast ★　　　　　　　　　12m VS 4c
FA K.Wallace 13 May 1992

The black offwidth near the left end.

1 Sun Spot ★   14m VS 4c
FA Rob Christie 9 May 1992

Parallel cracks on the wall right of the little flat wall, leading to a notch belay.

2 Two Bit Ram ★   12m Severe 4a
FA Richie Gunn Summer 1990

The corner at the boundary of the right side of the back wall.

3 Underneath the Archers ★   12m HVS 5a
FA Allan & Raymond Wallace 4 September 2003

Climb the right crack (as for 4) to a ledge then a right-trending flake to an arched overlap. Break through the apex of the arch then direct above.

4 Nobody's Crack ★   12m VS 4c
FA N.Obody & Anne Onamus 1990s

Direct up the right crack.

5 Pistachio ★★   12m Severe 4b
FA Rob Christie Summer 1990

The central crack above a triangular notch in the centre of the wall.

Karen Latter stepping out on Stepping Out.

6 Wallnut ★★   12m Very Difficult
FA Rob Christie Summer 1990

Crack 2m left of 5.

7 Stoneware ★   12m Severe 4a
FA Rob Christie Summer 1990

The leftmost crack.

8 The Llama ★★   12m E4 6a
FA Pete 'Oz' Slarke 16 June 1998

"Levitates" up the very steep north face of the stack which forms the left side of the bay. Start a little left of centre and climb straight up past the break then move left to a good flat hold. Trend back to the centre of the face and pass a bulge to gain a ledge.

9 Laphroaig ★★   15m HVS 5b
FA Gordon Milne Summer 1990

Start either up the corner on the lower front of the stack, or the wall to its right to the niche under the roof. "Heart pumping moves" rightwards through the roof gains easier ground.

10 Stepping Out ★★★   Severe 4b
FA Richie Gunn Summer 1990

Varied and exciting; a local classic! Climb the corner on the lower front of the stack and move left to an overhung ledge. Make a committing move back right into the hanging V-groove and climb this and the short wall above.

11 Out of Reach ★   15m VS 4c
FA Roddy Gunn 1996

The wall left of the initial corner of 10 to the ledge then the open groove above the left end of the ledge, finishing up a short wall.

12 Coaster ★★   12m Severe 4b
FA Rob Christie Summer 1990

Beyond a more broken section there is a flat wall with calcite. Climb a juggy line up the right side of the wall then slightly left to pull through the bulge at a shallow niche. Intimidating for the grade.

The bulge left of 12 is 13 *Two Good Friends* *VS 4b.

14 Puffin Attack ** — 12m VS 4c
FA Simon Clark 1992

Climb the centre of the flat calcited wall. Open to variation.

15 Shocket * — 12m Severe 4a
FA Rob Christie Summer 1990

Left of 14 is a blunt arête. Start with balancy moves right of the initial arête, traverse left onto the arête and follow the large flake to the top. The *Direct Start* up the overhanging crack is 5a.

16 The Serpent * — 12m E2 5b
FA Simon Clark 30 May 1992

The narrow face left of 15. Start centrally above a break. Move right to a ragged crack system then back left to join the crack.

17 Guillemot Crack *** — 10m HVS 5a
FA Rob Christie Summer 1990

The large deep crack south of the arête – continuously overhanging with little respite.

18 Fallout * — 8m HVS 5a
FA Richie Gunn Summer 1990

The corner 5m left of 17.

SARCLET

Unlike the usual sandstones along the rest of the Caithness coastline, the rock here is an amazing conglomerate, *"liberally studded"* with boulders, pebbles and pockets. Many of the buttresses drop straight into the sea, giving spectacular steep exposed climbing through improbable-looking ground.

Access: Turn east off the A99, 4 miles/6km south of Wick towards the village of Thrumster. Follow the road for 0.8 miles/1.3km to turn right (south, towards Mains of Ulbster Farm) for a further mile/1.6km to a small car park at the gate of the derelict farm.

Approach: From the farmhouse follow the fence east over the fields, crossing the small Mill Burn and small ruin. **Big Buttress** lies about 300m due east from the ruin. 15–20 minutes. Crags are described from north to south along a 600m section of the coast.

ND 344 424

PUDDING STONE BUTTRESS

Level with the south end of the loch a series of small geos are seen on cresting the brow of the hill from the end of the loch. Lummer's Geo has a large dark sea cave on its north side. North of this a long narrow dog-leg inlet – Oily Geo – cuts behind a peninsula with a 5m boulder at its southern end – 'The Pudding Stone'. West of this (across the inlet) lie the following routes:

Descent: Scramble down from the cliff top to the south.

1 Trevor, I can see your shoes from here ★★   15m VS 4c

FA Rob Christie 7 July 2003

The arête with a vertical crack. Climb this, finishing by bridging to the right of the arête.

2 Sweet Sixteen ★★   15m Severe 4b

FA Alisa King 7 July 2003

Well protected pleasant bridging up the chimney right of the arête.

3 Dynamo Thrum ★★   20m E5 6a

FA Guy Robertson & Trevor Wood 6 July 2003

Superb bold climbing up the obvious smooth square-cut pillar right of the chimney. From the base of the chimney, climb the line of holds up and rightwards to gain a handrail below a blank section (RPs on left). Stand on the handrail and climb blindly up on small pockets to better holds and the top.

4 Grap ★★   25m HVS 5a

FA Allan & Raymond Wallace & Rob Christie 5 September 2003

Enjoyable climbing. Start up the deep cleft behind the pillar of 3 then traverse 2m right along the ledge to a thin crack. Make an awkward move over the small overhang to better holds below the curving flake. Layback to the top of the flake then hand traverse it up and left before pulling over the top.

5 Queen's Mute Termination ★★   28m E2 5c

FA Raymond Wallace & Rob Christie 18 October 2003

Scramble up the left edge of the grey slab to a ledge. Climb a right-facing shallow groove through two small overlaps and continue up a right-trending flake to gain a ledge. Easier moves lead to an open groove and the top.

6 The Censor ★   28m E1 5a

FA Raymond Wallace & Rob Christie 18 October 2003

Scramble up the right edge of the grey slab to a ledge. Climb the shallow right-facing slabby groove through two overlaps then pull into a large scoop. Exit the scoop using the perfect crack in the groove above to finish.

7 Nice One ★★   10m VS 4c

FA Jenny Mackenzie-Ross 20 July 1994

Climb the flat wall on the seaward face of the small headland immediately north of Lummer's Geo.

ND 343 422

OCCAM'S BUTTRESS

On the north side of Lummer's Geo (south-east of the cave) is a prominent prow.

Descent: Gain the base of the routes directly by abseil – good blocks in a recess back from the edge.

1 Thrumster Regatta ★★★   25m E1 5b

FA Iain Small & Susan Jensen 13 May 2006

The left side of the prow. Start from sea-level ledge below the pedestal on 2. Climb the corner to a steep crack and follow to second ledge. Finish up the blank-looking wall out right.

CAITHNESS SARCLET | 323

2 Occam's Razor ★★★ 25m E3 6a
FA Trevor Wood & Guy Robertson 6 July 2003

Impeccable climbing on great rock up the prominent prow. Start on a small pedestal 5m above the sea. Climb directly up to the roof and follow the crack through this to gain a big jug on the right (crux). Gain a standing position on this then continue with interest up the crack to a rest beneath the final headwall. Climb this to an exciting top-out.

3 The Haven ★★ 25m VS 4c
FA Rob Christie 1994

The right-facing corner.

4 Just Visiting ★★ 25m VS 4c
FA Pete 'Oz' Slarke 28 August 1994

The left-facing corner. A finish out right may be necessary to avoid a nesting fulmar at the top.

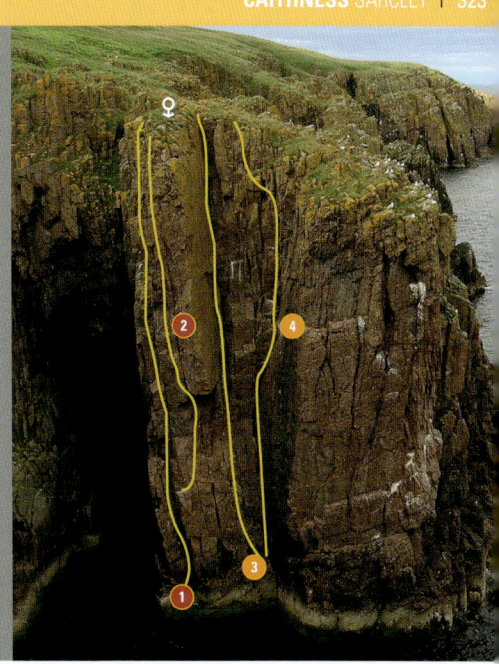

ND 343 421

BIG BUTTRESS

Topping the skyline – a good landmark to aim for on the approach. The best crag here with many superb long pitches.

NORTH-EAST FACE

The face extending leftwards from the back of the bay.
Descent: At low tide the first route can be accessed from the north side of the bay, though easiest by direct abseil (50m rope required) from stakes.

1 *Silver Darlings* ★ E1 5b takes cracks and slim corners, trending right near the top.

2 Skinny Malinky Longlegs ★★   35m HVS 5a
FA Raymond Wallace 19 June 2003

Start on a low square ledge. Climb the right edge of the pillar following a scoop and cracks. Trend left to follow a broken crack to finish.

3 Big Banana Feet ★★   30m E1 5b
FA Raymond Wallace 3 July 2003

Start from a ledge 6m above the sea and immediately right of a big wet chimney. Climb the open groove, trending left at mid-height to easier ground. Finish up steepening broken cracks.

SOUTH-EAST FACE

Descent: Abseil from stakes 15m back from the edge. 50m ropes just reach (worth extending with long slings).

7 The Sarclet Pimpernel ★★★★   35m E1 5a
FA Dave Porter, Guy Robertson & Trevor Wood 28 June 2003

Fantastic steady climbing after a steep committing start. Start from a belay at the base of the groove of 8. Make a rising traverse along a crack to the arête. Climb the arête then step left and follow the superb cracks finishing up an easy groove at the right end of the capping overhang (as for 8).

8 Groove Armada ★★★   35m VS 4c
FA Trevor Wood, Guy Robertson & Dave Porter 28 June 2003

The big groove. Follow the groove with good holds and protection.

4 A Paddler's Tale ★★★   35m E4 6a
FA Guy Robertson, Trevor Wood & Dave Porter 28 June 2003

A superb outing up the slim right (west) pillar. From the base of the chimney climb up and right onto the pillar and follow it, boldly at times, to better holds and an easing in the angle. Continue up cracks then move onto the right arête to finish.

5 Crypt Robber ★★★   35m E2 5c
FA Raymond Wallace 3 July 2003

Fantastic atmospheric climbing up the deep central chimney. Climb from a ledge in the chimney onto the right face. Trend left until directly under a roof. Make strenuous moves over the double roof to a great position bridging onto a massive spike. Follow the chimney above with decreasing difficulty.

6 Walking on Water ★★   35m E2 5c
FA Trevor Wood & Guy Robertson 5 July 2003

A good pitch up the left (east) pillar. From the base of the chimney step down left above the water to gain a crack. Follow this to an easing below a roofed corner. Climb the crack through the roof and continue more easily up fine cracks to finish.

9 Time Bandit ★★   35m E4 6a
FA Trevor Wood & Guy Robertson 5 July 2003

A brilliant sustained pitch snaking past the big overhangs on the left. Start from ledges just up and left of the base of the big groove of 8, below a smooth wall. Climb boldly up the centre of the wall on improving holds and pass a strange protruding blob on its left side. Move up then traverse left under the overhangs to gain blind cracks leading to a prominent flake. Follow the flake to a rest by a wobbly hold below overlaps. Undercut up and slightly left, pull over then step back right to better holds and the top.

10 *The Adventures of Baron Von Midgehousen* ★ E1 5c takes the big flake bounding the left side of the wall.

11 The Orchid Hunter ★★★   35m E3 5c
FA Iain Small & Jason Walker 1 July 2006

The groove and flake line on the left side of the rounded pillar left of 10. From small ledges at the base, tricky moves gain the groove which is followed with interest until it becomes a flake, forming the large top of the pillar. Step off this to finish up the short wall.

ND 343 421
DJAPANA BUTTRESS

The projecting headland south of **Big Buttress** is undercut to form a large natural arch. Access from the top of **Big Buttress** by crossing a precarious rock bridge (or avoid by walking round the end).
Descent: Directly to the base by abseil.

1 Djapana ★★   28m E3 5c
FA Pete 'Oz' Slarke 1994

The demanding crack-line up the centre of the buttress.

2 Northern Alliance ★★★   20m E3 5c
FA Guy Robertson & Trevor Wood 28 June 2003

The striking left (east) arête. Superb – not as hard as it looks! Start on a ledge at the base of the line. Climb the edge using cracks just to its right all the way to a strenuous finish.

ND 342 419
SURFER BUTTRESS

The next landmark south of **Djapana Buttress** is a 100m wide bay with a 40m wide, 35m high buttress at its north end with an overlap running along its left half at mid-height.
Descent: Direct by abseil to ledge at base.

1 Silver Surfer ★★   35m HVS 5a
FA Raymond Wallace & Rob Christie 14 July 2004

In the centre of the cliff is a stunning left-facing overlapping flake/groove system with a generous crack running up its rear. Scramble up an open blocky chimney to reach the base of the flake system. Use the flake to overcome a steep wall then continue up and left until under a roof. Turn this to the left then surmount the hollow sounding blocks to finish up the final square corner.

Further south (NE facing) lie:

2 Lithium Fry-up ★★   35m HVS 5a
FA Raymond Wallace & Rob Christie 29 July 2004

The third black corner from the north end of **Tilted Ledge** has a deep black crack at its rear. From a platform at the base of the corner climb the corner to a steep narrowing. Pull through this to easier ground and continue up the groove to a hanging spike. Move onto the left wall and continue to the top of the corner.

3. Hats off to the Catman ★★ 35m HVS 5a
FA Rob Christie & Raymond Wallace 5 August 2004

Start from the platform at the base of 2. Follow the rising line of right-trending undercut flakes that steepen as they approach a roof. Make awkward moves around right of the roof to move into a narrow corner then climb the slab on the right to reach a stance below two corners. Go up the left corner to easier ground.

📷 Karen Latter on Yawn.

ND 342 419
TILTED LEDGE

250m south from **Djapana Buttress** is a shorter crag with a flat grassy area at the top and a prominent sloping platform at the base.

Descent: scramble down broken ground (Moderate) at the north (right, facing in) end. Routes described from the descent leftwards (southwards).

The black streak finishing directly up the bold conglomerate wall is route 1 *Blackcurrent* ★ HVS 4c; 2 *Conglomerati* ★ VS 4c takes scoop and flake-crack; 3 *Suckin' on Divids* ★ HVS 5a takes broken ramp and faint crack.

4. Wicker Man ★ 12m VS 4c
FA Joanna George & Dave Porter 27 June 2003

Follow the brown streak to join the upper crack of 5.

5. The Ogee ★★ 15m VS 4c
FA Joanna George & Dave Porter 27 June 2003

The prominent overhanging crack splitting the crag – not as steep as it looks.

6. Birthday Boy ★★ 15m E3 5c
FA Dave Porter & Joanna George 27 June 2003

The rightmost of twin parallel cracks. Climb boldly up the initial steep wall on good holds past an obvious hole to join and follow a right-trending crack-line to a stance beneath the overlap. Aiming rightwards to the continuation of the original crack in the upper wall, make a strenuous move over the large overlap on pebbles to gain easier ground.

7 Pullin' on Puddin' ★★   15m E2 5b
FA Joanna George & Dave Porter 27 June 2003

The next diagonal crack 2m left of 6, crossing the overlap near its left end. Climb the wall on good holds, trending right to gain the crack. Follow this through the overlap by a stiff pull to gain a large quartz hold. Keep to the right crack at the top.

The deep wide crack at the left end is 8 *Yawn* ★ VS 4c; wall and flake is 9 *Oblimov* ★ HS 4b; prominent slabby groove 10 *Fishnet Necklace* ★ Very Difficult as is next slabby groove.

STACK OF OLD WICK   ND 369 486
 15min

A superb stack 200m south of the Castle of Old Wick, south-west of the spectacular Brig o' Stack.
Access: On approaching Wick from the south, turn off right (east) about 0.3 miles/0.5km into town, following signs for the 'Castle of Old Wick'. This meanders through a housing estate out onto the headland. Park at the road end car park.
Approach: Follow the coast south-west then south to the remains of Old Man of Wick (castle), continuing a short way beyond the ruined castle to the stack.
Descent: Approach by abseiling from fence posts (additional 50m rigging rope useful) and making a pendulum to ledges at the foot of the landward side of the stack. Traverse right along easy but greasy ledges before moving up to a large ledge on the right arête.

1 Lord Oliphant's Bicycle ★★★   40m VS 4b
FA Mark Robson & Simon Richardson 11 April 2004

Climb a crack and swing left to a large ledge on the arête. Climb up easily until it is possible to move back right to the south-west face. Climb cracks in the middle of the south-west face to the summit. **Descent:** Abseil down the landward face from in situ nuts & slings.

1a On Yer Bike ★★   8m HVS 5a
FA Gary Latter & Lee Fleming 3 September 2008

A useful well protected direct start, with a much more straightforward approach than the tricky pendulum (particularly in the wet). Step across the narrow base and walk to the end of the narrow ledge just above high tide line. Climb the crack, crossing the overhang at the prominent slot to belay on good ledge just above.

Gary Latter & Lee Fleming on the first ascent of On Yer Bike. Photo Karen Latter.

LEWIS & HARRIS

LEWIS & HARRIS

The *'long isle'* of Lewis and Harris comprises the largest of all the Scottish islands and the most northerly of the Western Isles. The bulk of the underlying rock is the eponymous Lewisian gneiss. When weathered this provides some of the finest rock in the country, not to mention by far the oldest at around 2,900 million years. The landscape ranges from bleak moorland in the north, vastly improving to fine hills and mountains in southern Lewis and Harris. The west coast also sports some of the finest golden beaches anywhere. On the Atlantic coast due west of the main town of Stornoway the coastline in the vicinity of the extensive Traighe Uuige (cove sands) has an extensive range of near-roadside sea cliffs for all abilities. Similarly, isolated sections of the coast further north have produced a great range of routes of all standards. In the nearby hills the Tealasdale Slabs on Griomaval and the remote-feeling Creag Dubh Dibadale give excellent long routes. In Harris, the famed Sron Ulladale presents the steepest and most impressive cliff in Britain, hosting some excellent lower grade routes in addition to the highest concentration of long hard extremes in the country.

Access: Caledonian MacBrayne (📞 0800 066 5000; www.calmac.co.uk) operate regular passenger and vehicle ferries from Ullapool – Stornoway (Lewis) and Uig on Skye – Tarbert (Harris). Stornoway airport is also served by flights from Aberdeen, Benbecula, Edinburgh, Glasgow and Inverness. For a trip to Sron Ulladale alone, take a taxi from Tarbert.

Accommodation: Campsites: Idyllic campsite at Uig beach, Ardroil Campsite (📞 01851 672248) close to most of the sea cliffs; stunningly-situated campsite at Traigh na Beirigh, by Cnip (May - Sep; 📞 01851 672332) just south of Valtos; Eilean Fraoich, North Shawbost (Apr – Sep; 📞 01851 710504; www.eileanfraoich.co.uk); Bothag Bhuirgh, Borve (📞 01851 850436; www.bothagbhuirgh.com); Minch View Caravan Park, Drinishader (Apr – Oct; 📞 01859 511207; www.minchview.wordpress.com); Huisinis Gateway Campervan Site (📞 01859 502222; www.north-harris.org); various camping hook-ups between both ferry terminals in Leverburgh and Tarbert (📞 01859 503900; www.westharristrust.org). **Hostels:** Fairhaven (📞 01851 840343; www.hebrideansurf.co.uk); Heb Hostel (📞 01851 709889; www hebhostel.com) - both Stornoway; Gearrannan, Carloway (📞 01851 643416; www.gearrannan.com); Kershader (Mar – Oct; 📞 01851 880236; www.ravenspoint.net); The Backpackers Stop, Tarbert (01859 502742; www.backpackers-stop.co.uk); No5 Drinishader (📞 01859 511255; www.number5.biz); Rhenigidale (www.gatliff.org.uk). **Bunkhouses:** Laxdale, Stornoway (Apr – Oct; 📞 01851 706966; www.laxdaleholidaypark.com); Otter Bunkhouse, Calishader, Uig (📞 07942 349 755; www.otterbunkhouse.com); Galson Farm (📞 01851 850492; www.galsonfarm.co.uk) near Ness; Am Bothan, Leverburgh (Apr – Oct; 📞 01859 520251; www.ambothan.com). **TIC** at Stornoway (📞 01851 703088; www.visitscotland.com).

Amenities: Uig Community Shop also has petrol/laundry/**ATM**; Tearoom at Uig Community Centre Museum nearby at Timsgarry (Apr – Sept). Morven Gallery and café, Barvas (www.morvengallery.com) is worth seeking out. Showers available at the Bayhead Bridge Centre, Stornoway (📞 01851 705808; www.bayheadbridgecentre.co.uk). Further information including locations of showers, public toilets, portable toilet disposal points and recycling points is available at www.visitouterhebrides.co.uk.

CRULABHIG CRAG

A great wee crag 50m from the road, just south of the bridge to Bernera, very useful when the sea is running.

Access: From the A858 at Garrynahine turn south along the B8011 for 3 miles/4.8km then turn right (north) along the B8059 for 4.2 miles/6.7km. At Crulabhig, park 250m up the hill beyond the crag, opposite a gate on the left (west) side of the road (NB 1685 3360).

Approach: Walk back down the road, then through the gate to the crag.

Descent: Down short slot and grassy ramp on left.

1 Lard of the Pies ★★   12m HVS 5a
FA Paul Woodhouse & party 4 June 2002

Steep well-protected climbing up the left-facing hanging corner, gained from the right. Lower from sling & karabiners on tree.

2 All Hail King Silly ★★★   18m E6 6c
FA Mark Garthwaite & Rab Anderson 1 June 2017

Go up and right to climb the obvious line to finish up 5.

3 Chasing Tails ★★   18m E3 6a
FA Rab Anderson 6 July 2006

Start at a short handrail. Climb past two breaks and up to a crack. Move right and up the corner. Pull over the roof to finish up a flange in the headwall.

4 The Cruel Crack ★★★   18m E3 6a
FA Rab & Chris Anderson 13 July 2006

The corner, then the short brutal crack above the roof, finishing direct up the pocketed wall.

5 Mixed Blessing ★★   22m E2 5c
FA Rab Anderson, Neil Morrison, Wilson Moir, Mark Atkins & Paul Allen 9 August 2006

Climb the two corners, then traverse left beneath the roof to its end.

6 Double or Quits ★★   18m E3 6a
FA Rab Anderson & Mark Garthwaite 27 June 2007

The hanging roof-capped corner. Climb the lower crack, then short overhanging wall into the corner. Finish up cracks past small aspens.

7 Crimpology ★★   18m E5 6b
FA Mark Garthwaite & Rab Anderson 27 June 2007

Up wall right of 6, moving left to place gear in that route. Return right to an undercut and make crux moves to holds. Traverse right, then through bulge and wall above.

8 Gneiss to See You, to See You Gneiss ★★★
18m E6 6b

FA Mark Garthwaite & Rab Anderson 3 June 2017

Follow crack up rightwards, stand in the break and power through the bulge. Finish up the final groove of 9.

9 Southern Breeze ★
18m E1 5c

FA Rab & Chris Anderson 4 August 2007

Climb past a plaque to good break. Go right along this, then the crack, finishing leftwards up short groove and wall.

RIGHT SECTOR

50m further right.
Descent: Traverse rightwards down grassy ledges.

10 The Major's Reserve ★
20m E1 5b

FA Rab Anderson & Mark Garthwaite 3 June 2017

Continue direct by ledges to a higher ramp. Move up and right, then swing out right and cross the headwall to finish up the recess.

11 Wild Orchid ★★
20m E1 5b

FA Rab Anderson & Mark Garthwaite 1 June 2017

Gain and climb a short ramp, then up to the roof (micro cams). Ascend the fine crack in the headwall, finishing up a recess.

Gary Latter on the steep juggy start to Lard of the Pies. Photo Karen Latter

12 Letterbox Wall ★
14m HVS 5a

FA Caelan Barnes 20 August 2015

Clean pocketed wall past ledge near top.

13 Burka ★
14m HVS 5a

FA Gary Latter (solo) 15 August 2018

Obvious line a few metres right of 12, above sloping grass ledge.

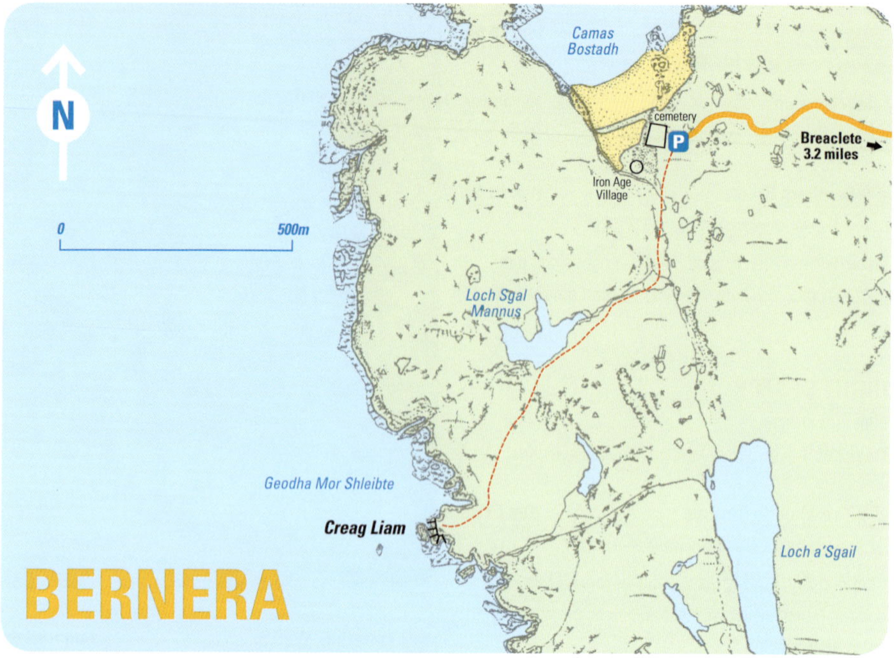

BERNERA

NB 1328 3938   20min

CREAG LIAM

The small headland bounding the south end of the bay.

Access: From the A858 at Garrynahine turn south along the B8011 for 3 miles/4.8km then turn right (north) along the B8059 for 4.7 miles/7.5km to cross the bridge onto **Great Bernera**. Continue north along single track road for a further 4.6 miles/7.4km to car park at the road end at Bostadh.

Approach: Follow the path along the left (south) side of the cemetery, then up the valley for 200m, crossing the stream by a small footbridge. Head south-west up the left bank of a smaller stream, and continue in the same direction, dropping down to the crag.

Descents: Scramble easily left (facing out) then back right under the crag at mid-low tide. Alternatively, abseil direct to the base.

NORTH WEST FACE

1 Focus ★★ 20m E1 5b F6a S3
FA Jules Lines (on-sight solo) 18 June 2007

Take the left crack-line into the left edge of the A, step up and left onto a ledge, then either finish direct via one hard move (NYS 6a) or dangerously traverse left to gain the top (5b). 1a *Right Finish* ★★ E1 5b F6a S1/2 takes the obvious hand traverse right to finish as for 2a.

2 Shock Waves ★★★ 20m E3 5c F6b S2/3
FA Jules Lines (on-sight solo) 14 June 2007

From the right edge of the buttress, climb the crimpy arête (crux) to gain a small ledge, continue to the base of the A-shaped roof. Tackle the right edge of this to gain some flat jugs on the right wall, swing round the ludicrous arête in a mind boggling position to finish. 2a *Right Finish* ★★  is a safer deep water solo F6b S1/2.

3. Mini Tsunami ★★   20m HS 4a F4 S2
FA Jules Lines (on-sight solo) 18 June 2007

The curving stepped arête is a delight, finish slightly right up a groove/slot.

4. Aftershock ★★   20m F7a+ S2
FA Jules Lines (solo) 20 June 2012

Climb the wall just left of the arête to a notch at the overlap. Layback the crack-line to a vague quartz seam. Find a hidden finger slot on the right and cross through for a good flat hold. Slap up the hanging rib to gain a pink boss and continue up on hidden slots and holds in a line which bends slightly left into a blocky finishing groove.

5. Mega Tsunami ★★★★   25m E6 6a/F7a S2
FA Dave Cuthbertson & Joanna George 10 June 2001; FSA Jules Lines 19 June 2007

The superb *"ship's prow"*. Start at the foot of 8. Traverse left along the lower of two breaks to reach a groove beneath an overhang in the arête. Climb up to and over the overhang to the base of a short steep smooth open groove. Climb this to a large hold out on the right, step back left and ascend a groove in the arête to an undercut flake. The next section kicks out to provide a strenuous finale up the thin discontinuous crack just right of the prow.

5a. Mega Tsunami – Prow Finish ★★★★   25m F7b S2
FA Jules Lines 21 June 2012

Absolutely wild – one of the very best DWS in the world. At the big sidepull where the original route follows the pocketed crack up and right, reach left around the prow to a good hold, take a deep breath and slap your way up the underside of the overhanging prow using a series of compression moves to gain good holds at the break. Move to the right side and pull back left to finish on the very prow.

6. Epicentre ★★   25m E5 6a/b F7a S2
FA Jules Lines (solo) 18 June 2007

Great climbing threading its way up the wall to the right of 5. Traverse leftwards to the 'seat' rest at the base of 5. Climb up and rightwards to an impasse, crimp up and snatch leftwards to gain the small ledge (crux S0/1). Make a tricky mantel onto it and make thin moves up the wall to gain better holds leading up right. Take the obvious handrail leftwards and follow the slight groove just right of the arête to the top.

6a. Exact Epicentre ★★★   25m E5 6b F7a+ S2
FA Jules Lines (solo) 20 June 2012

A superb direct on 6, but as a DWS be careful as the reef creeps in on the right – check the tide carefully. Where that route goes left at the impasse, go up and undercut the overlap making hard moves to gain a flat hold in the blank wall. Make a further hard move using a slot on the right to gain a flake hold. Follow flakes more easily up and right to ledges and the final easy groove (S3).

7. Hypercentre ★★   23m F7b S3
FA Jules Lines (solo) 20 June 2012

Traverse in from the right and go up the centre of the wall and climb easily to a large pocket in the pink quartz. A very

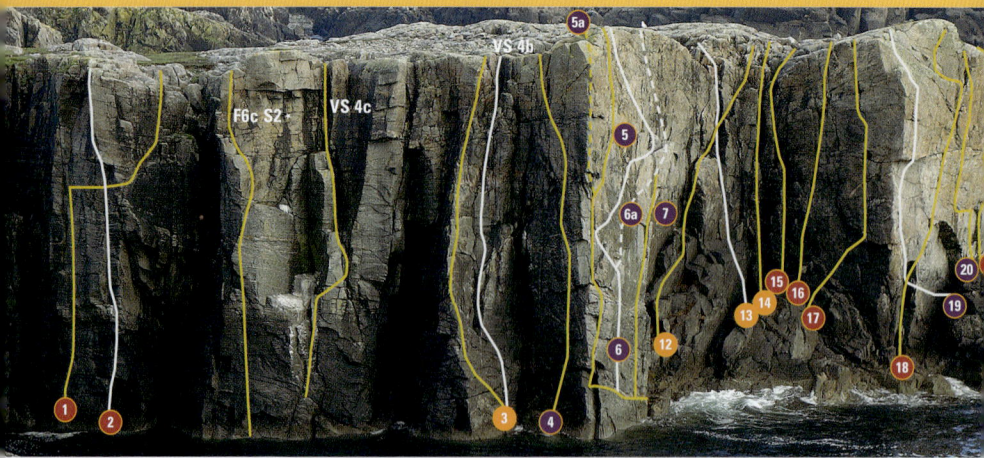

thin seam leads to the overlap where it turns into a tiny vertical corner. Climb just left of the seam and up to the corner. Make a difficult layback move off this to gain flake holds above, which soon get bigger. Finish up the final easy groove, as for 6a. Check the reef and tide carefully.

8 Roag Rage ★★   **20m E3 5b**
FA Rab & Chris Anderson 4 July 2000

The crack up the right side of the smooth wall. Follow the crack to its end, stand up and stretch leftwards for holds and continue to ledges. The thin continuation crack immediately left of the edge provides a fine finish.

9 The Bostadh Strangler ★★   **15m E2 5b**
FA Rab & Chris Anderson 4 July 2000

The overhung stepped corner and wide crack. Finish up the very easy upper corner crack.

10 Great Northern ★   **15m HVS 5a**
FA Andy Cunningham & Finlay MacLeod 7 April 1998

The back left wide corner-crack of the recess.

11 My Wave ★   **15m E5 6a**
FA Ally Fulton & Simon Smith 19 May 2019

The wall between 10 and 12. Climb the crack then move up and left (bold) to a flake. Move back right and finish direct in the centre of the wall.

> The back right corner-crack of the recess is 14 *Na Far Clis* • VS 5a; 12 *Recess Ramp* HS 4b the stepped right diagonal line with same finish.

13 Brigitt's Liberation ★   **15m VS 4c**
FA Brigitt Hogge, Jenny & Andy Cunningham 15 September 1996

The left-trending stepped black dyke, finishing through an awkward slot.

15 Grazing Beast ★   **15m E1 5b**
FA Andy Cunningham & Finlay MacLeod 7 April 1998

Start near the back right of the recess. Ascend the steep black crack to finish up an awkward curving jam crack.

16 Garden of Eadan ★★   **15m E2 5c**
FA Andy Cunningham & Lawrence Hughes 18 May 1999

The fine steep central crack.

17 Ticallion Stallion ★★★   **20m E3 5c**
FA Lawrence Hughes & Andy Cunningham 11 May 1998

Great climbing up the hanging crack at the right end of the wall. Climb up to the left of the undercut crack and make bold moves rightwards to the crack at a small roof (runners). Follow the strenuous crack to the top.

18 The Bernera Prow ★★★★   **20m E2 5b**
FA Andy Cunningham & Lawrence Hughes 11 May 1998

Excellent strenuous climbing up the overhanging crack in

the front of the headland. Start at the left corner of the prow. Climb the groove up to the roof, swing right into the crack and follow this on superb jams to the top.

19 Bridge Builder ★★ 20m E5 6b
FA Dave MacLeod & Tim Emmett 2 June 2010

The left arête is gained by a logical approach from the right, especially in high seas. Start right of the crack. Move leftwards across the wall on big holds and go up to a bulge on the arête. Climb over this, just right of the arête (crux) to better holds above.

20 Mussel Meltdown ★★★ 15m E4 6a
FA Rab Anderson & Mark Garthwaite 29 June 2007

The wall and thin crack. Start at the high point of the ridge, at the base of the arête. Make difficult moves up, then left across the roof to gain the crack and follow this to the top.

21 Interactive ★ 15m E2 5b
FA Andy Cunningham & Lawrence Hughes 11 May 1998

Awkward cracks and shallow corners up the left side of the arête. Start near the top of the ramp below the arête and swing right into the first crack.

Ali Robb on the crag classic The Bernera Prow.

22 Deepest Blue ★ 15m E2 5c
FA Scott Muir & Dave MacLeod June 2005

The right side of the arête.

23 Body and Soul ★★ 18m VS 4c
FA Andy & Jeni Cunningham & Brigitt Hogge 15 Sept 1996

The big corner.

24 Barnacle Butter ★★★ 18m E4 5c
FA Mark Garthwaite & Rab Anderson 29 June 2007

The steep wall between the two corners. Climb up and left to holds, then up right into a scooped area before moving up left. Continue across breaks to finish centrally.

25 Conception Corner ★★ 15m VS 4c
FA Andy & Jeni Cunningham & Brigitt Hogge 15 Sept 1996

The rightmost corner-crack.

BEINN NA BERIE

THE LITTLE BIG WALL

A short smooth near-perfect wall situated just above the machair overlooking the fine golden beach of Traigh na Beirigh. 100m back from the beach, therefore unaffected by the sea.

Access: Turn right off the B8011 at Miavaig (16.3 miles/26.2km) and follow the narrow winding single track road north for 2.4 miles/4km to park at a sharp left bend in the road next to a house.

Approach: Follow the path over a short rise, cross the fence and head slightly leftwards to the crag.

Descent: Down the narrow rock ramp on the right.

The obvious corner at the left end of the wall is 1 *Treighding Places* ★ HVS 5a with an awkward exit.

2 Tunes of Glory ★★   15m E5 6b
FA Rab & Chris Anderson 9 July 1999

A superb route up the staggered crack-line running up the left edge of the wall. Climb the first crack to its top, move right to the upper crack and make a hard move to better holds, finishing much more easily.

The pocketed wall between is 3 *Rogue Traighder* ★★ E5 6b.

4 Barrier Reef ★★★   15m E5 6a
FA Rab Anderson (rabpointed – pre-placed protection) 16 July 1999

Brilliant climbing up the central pocketed wall. Gain the first pocket then make a long reach up left to the next (F #3.5 in pocket above). Move up left to another large pocket. Pull up right to a good pocket (F #4) then a layaway and another hold (small nuts/cams). A stretch gains a good break then easily to finish.

NB 1094 3661 **Alt:** 20m      5min

📷 *Karin Magog enjoying wonderful evening light on Cnip Fit. Photo Dave Macleod*

5 Cnippy Sweetie ★★   15m E7 6b
FA Dave MacLeod & Steve Richardson 12 June 2001

From the first pocket on 4 make a huge dyno straight up to another pocket then continue directly with difficulty up the sparsely protected wall above.

6 Cnip-Fit ★★   12m E4 6a
FA Rab & Chris Anderson 14 July 1999

This and the following two routes start at some embedded blocks just to the right. From a letterbox, swing left into a thin crack then move up this to its top where it is possible to blindly stretch a R #6 up right into a superb placement in a pocket. Gain the break up on the right and follow its diagonal continuation up left to pull onto the ledge and finish more easily.

7 Berie-Berie ★★   12m E4 6a
FA Rab & Chris Anderson 15 July 1998

Climb direct to the prominent horizontal break, step right and go up to another horizontal (gear) then gain a ledge and finish easily.

8 Milk-Traigh ★   12m E3 6a
FA Rab & Chris Anderson July 1997

The obvious crack just right of the blocks to its end. Pull up left to a ledge and finish up right.

AIRD UIG AREA
(PROMONTORY BAY)

A 6km long stretch of coast to the north of the extensive golden sands of Traigh Uig, interspersed with a good variety of superb isolated crags.

CENTRAL SECTION

The next two crags are on the north side of the hill Creag Fiavig, close to a wee lochan Loch Ruadh Guinnerso, which often dries out.

Access: Turn right (north) towards Aird Uig at the west end of the B8011, Glen Valtos, taking the second turn-off on the left towards Crowlista for 0.8 miles/1.2km to park by a land rover track heading north just before the road bends sharply south.

Approach: Head north up the track for 10 minutes then due west to the lochan or alternatively head north-west from the start of the track. **Geodha Gunna** is just west of the lochan; **Geodha Ruadh** 200m further north.

Gary Latter starting up the superb corner of The Legend of Finlay MacIver. Photo Karen Latter

NB 0331 3623 30min

GEODHA GUNNA (GUN CHASM)

A very impressive groove-seamed overhanging wall with a spectacular arch cutting through the face.

Descents: For the **West Face**, by a 35m abseil from blocks; for the **Main Face**, by 45m abseil to small ledges at sea level.

WEST FACE

1 The Legend of Finlay MacIver ★★★   25m E1 5b
FA Mick & Kathy Tighe 29 May 2008

The beautiful stepped right-facing corner-crack at the right end of the impressive overhanging wall.

MAIN FACE

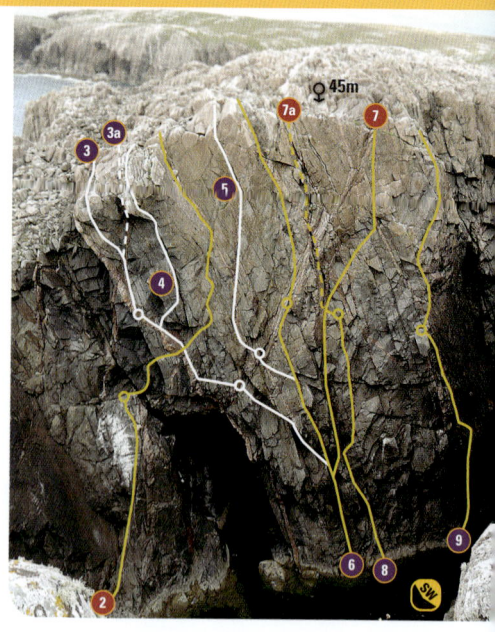

② The Great Flake ★★★   45m E3 5c
FA George Smith & Crispin Waddy alts 14 May 2019

An excellent route (low in the grade) that manages to gain and cross 3 at a surprisingly amenable standard. Start at sea level on the ledges at the bottom of the big slab left of the sea cave.

1. **20m 4a** Climb the easy groove to spikes and ledges.
2. **25m 5c** Pull steeply through the black bulge on the right and into a niche. An exposed swing right on a small stripey ledge gains 3, then move up right under the roof to gain a groove line. Follow this, chimneying to the top.

③ Captain Oates ★★★★   45m E4 6a
FA Donie O'Sullivan & Crispin Waddy alts 23 May 2018

A stunning route of ever increasing wild exposure; probably E5 if the last two pitches are linked.

1. **20m 5b** Where 6 leaves 7, follow a roof-capped left-leaning groove system to belay where a rightwards rising pegmatite vein crosses.
2. **15m 6a** Traverse wildly left along the lip of the roof until it is possible to pull up into a rest in a short groove. Leave this leftwards in a magnificent position, then pull up to belay on spikes in another groove.
3. **10m 6a** Traverse big holds left to the arête, to finish up a short jam crack.
3a. **10m 6b** Climb a thin crack to a desperate short corner, from which slapping the top is the crux.

④ I'm going out now (I may be some time) ★★★
    20m E5 6b/c
FA George Smith & Crispin Waddy 15 May 2019

The mad offwidth roof crack right of the top pitch of 3. Belay as for the last pitch of 3. Pull over the roof via the tough jam crack and follow it to a rest under the obvious roof crack. Somehow climb this. Harder for the short, or for the tall. Size 5 cam useful.

⑤ The Shining One ★★★   40m E3/4 6a
FA George Smith & Crispin Waddy alts 16 May 2019

A brilliant sustained and exposed top pitch.

1. **20m 5c** Follow 6 until a traverse left above the roof of the first pitch of 3 gains a belay at the base of the diagonal rake.
2. **20m 6a** Step left to a well protected crack which leads to the top, with a tricky finish. Take plenty of small wires. In big seas this pitch will probably become an uber classic - accessed from a hanging belay.

⑥ Lucid Visions ★★   45m E4 6a
FA Glenda Huxter & Kath Pyke 14 July 1997

A brilliant *"out there"* route, taking a rising increasingly exposed traverse leftwards through hanging grooves, finishing up the steep headwall. Abseil to ledges at sea level.

1. **25m 6a** Climb the central crack-groove for 3m before weaving up and leftwards into hanging grooves to gain a good exposed stance.
2. **20m 5c** Move left and onto the headwall. Follow a thin crack leftwards on steep ground to finish.

7 *Rabid Wanderings* ★ E3 5c takes the central groove for 20m then heads diagonally right to breach the roof (crux). 7a *Unnecessary Wanderings* E2 5c continues direct up the obvious groove.

8 The False Men ★★★   40m E4/5 6a/b
FA Crispin Waddy & George Smith alts 15 May 2019

Takes the grooves right of 7. Start down and right of that route, in the next obvious corner. Some very good, well protected climbing.
1. **25m 6a/b** Climb the corner until it touches 7; pull back right to the defined slim groove and follow this until hard moves via its left arête gain a belay on the left.
2. **15m 5c** Follow 7 to the top.

9 Prosopagnosia ★★★   45m E4 6a
FA Crispin Waddy & George Smith alts 15 May 2019

Climbs the left arête of the big slab at the right end of the main face. Much easier than it looks - superb in parts but quite an odd line as it avoids the slab on the top pitch for a wild crack just under the left arête, which is better protected and very good climbing, but somewhat harder - hence the name (face blindness).
1. **25m 6a** Start at a small ledge 10m right of the *Rabid Wanderings* belay, at sea level. Move up and right to a block in the overhang. Steeply right through this, then left and back right to an easing at the slabs edge. Traverse left then onto the slab and up it for a few moves before traversing left to a hanging belay under a good crack in the underside of the arête.
2. **20m 5c** Climb the crack until it eases, then with difficulty up the arête trending right to an easier finish.

NB 0345 3643   30min

GEODHA RUADH (RED GEO)
A large open geo distinguished by the beautiful orange slab and 'Separate Reality' type crack through the headwall on the east wall of the geo.

1 Brutal Reality ★★★   30m E6 6b
FA Steve Mayers & Gill Lovick July 1993

The pleasant slab is followed by a brutally overhanging hand crack and with luck the top.

NORTHERN SECTION
This stretch of the coast is more conveniently reached from the settlement at Aird Uig.

Access: Turn north at the west end of Glen Valtos, taking the road north to Aird Uig for 3 miles/4.8km to park on the right.

Approach: Follow the Land Rover track on the left, through a gate for 5 minutes to just before a building then head west downhill skirting the north side of Loch a' Bheannaich to the crags.

Donie O'Sullivan on the first ascent of the crag classic Captain Oates. Photo Crispin Waddy

THE BOARDWALK WALLS

Walls extending south-west above a convenient wide shelf – 'The Boardwalk'. A huge 4m pink block sits at the top of *Chapel Crack*, a useful landmark on the top.
Descents: Either abseil directly down the wall or scramble down to the top (south) end of the shelf.

NB 037 380 25min

BOARDWALK LEFT – THE BLACK WALL

The area extending leftwards from *Chapel Crack* with a couple of storm pools at the base.

1 Colonel Huff ★★ 25m HS 4b
FA Mick Tighe & party 16 September 1986

Climb a prominent short V-shaped cleft about halfway up the crag, gained easily and move onto a ledge, finishing up the short cracked wall.

2 Disco Fever ★ 25m HS 4b
FA Rab & Chris Anderson 16 July 2002

Gain and follow a black shelf up right then direct up into a slim groove leading to a steep finish.

3 Funky Groove ★ 25m HS 4b
FA Rab & Chris Anderson 16 July 2002

The short thin crack in the lower wall immediately left of the storm pool (15m left of *Chapel Crack*). Climb the crack and the continuation into the slabby corner. Climb this leftwards, finishing direct.

4 Diving Board ★ 30m Severe 4a
FA Mick Tighe & party 16 September 1986

Climb diagonally left from the base of 6 along a prominent traverse line leading to a belay at 15m. Climb up 6m to finish up the narrow broken slab on the left.

5 Around the Bend ★ 30m Severe 4a
FA Mick Tighe & party 16 September 1986

Follow the line of 4 but keep 6m higher all the time, finishing up a broader higher gangway to the left.

6 Chapel Crack ★★ 20m VS 4c
FA Mick Tighe & party 16 September 1986

The corner direct with an optional through route to finish.

7 Sally's Dilemma ★ 25m VS 4c
FA Mick Tighe & party 16 September 1986

From halfway up 6 break out right to follow a short curving groove with a mantelshelf at the top. A broad shelf leads off to the right. Walk along this to finish with a short step.

BOARDWALK CENTRAL

The area extending rightwards from *Chapel Crack* to a large boulder-filled bay.

8 Groove Armada ★★   15m E4 6a
FA Rab & Chris Anderson 26 July 2002

Wall and steep V-grooves right of 6, gaining the shelf at the base by easy scrambling.

9 Bloody Hand ★   20m E1 5b
FA Mick Tighe & party 1980s

Start by scrambling easily up left to good ledge from the leftmost boulder beside a pool. Climb a stepped corner into the base of the crack. Climb the crack and its left edge to finish.

10 Divided Fears ★★   25m E2 5c
FA Rab Anderson & Mark Garthwaite 21 July 2002

Obvious crack in the left wall of 11, formed between two distinct types and colour of rock.

11 Coloured Rain ★★   25m E1 5b
FA Mick Tighe & J.Stevenson 7 May 1988

The first corner line round the corner. Climb it direct with hard moves at 10m and 20m. Well protected.

12 Puffing Crack ★★★★   25m E5 6a
FA Mark Garthwaite & Rab Anderson 21 July 2002

Superb and very pumpy. Thin cracks running up the impending right wall of the big corner of 12, climbed directly all the way. Stepping into the right crack near the top is possible, bypassing the final few moves.

13 The River Kwai ★★   25m E4 6a
FA Mark Garthwaite & Rab Anderson 22 July 2002

Just around the edge is another big corner. Climb this to a common finish with 15.

14 Atlantic City ★★★   25m E3 6a
FA Rab Anderson 5 July 2006; Direct Finish: Sam Williams 25 June 2016

An obvious line cutting through 15. Start on a boulder directly below the corner of 13. Move up and right into a corner, then step right around the edge and climb cracks to a ledge. Pull up and around right into a groove, then right again onto a slab, at the junction with 15. Climb the steep groove above with interest and pull out left from the inverted V-shape to finish. 14a *Direct Finish* ★★★ E5 6b spectacularly climbs the thin crack.

15 A Bridge Too Far ★★★   25m E3 6a
FA Mark Garthwaite & Rab Anderson 22 July 2002

Just right is an obvious crack slanting up left into the top of 14. Start from a boulder in the right corner of the bay, beneath an undercut crack. Move off the ground with difficulty (the vertically challenged will have a problem!). Follow the crack up left in a stupendous position to a steep finish.

16 Shadows in the Sun ★★ — 25m E2 5b
FA Mick Tighe, Ian Sutherland & Bill Newton 7 May 1988

The big black chimney/corner with small overhangs at two-thirds height. Avoid the undercut start by traversing into the corner from the right for about 12m. Climb the corner direct, finishing strenuously.

17 Face Off ★★ — 20m E3 5c
FA Rab Anderson 18 April 2003

The groove just right of 16. Climb directly into then up a left-facing groove then the continuation right-facing groove above a ledge leading to easier ground.

BOARDWALK RIGHT

The shorter walls above raised sloping platform, tapering rightwards.
Descent: Scramble down (about Difficult) short line at rightmost end.

18 Jagged Little Thrill ★★ — 12m E1 5a
FA Rab Anderson 17 April 2003

Climb up to the right bounding arête then steeply up its left side via a shallow groove. Step left at the top to pull over the final jutting shelf.

19 Edgy ★★ — 10m E1 5b
FA Rab Anderson 17 April 2003

Climb crack in the arête just left of 20, finishing on its left side.

20 Quartzvein Crack ★★ — 10m VS 4c
FA Rab & Chris Anderson 15 September 2002

The steep quartzy crack just right of the arête.

21 Twostep Crack ★ — 10m VS 4c
FA Rab & Chris Anderson 22 September 2002

Crack up slabby rock, then steeper beyond the diagonal break.

22 Underwhelming Corner ★ — 10m HS 4b
FA Ewan Lyons (solo) 12 August 2018

The left facing corner right of 21.

23 Mind the Gap ★ — 10m HS 4c
FA Ewan Lyons (solo) 12 August 2018

The ramp line just right of 22, starting with a high step.

24 Overjoyed ★ — 10m Severe 4a
FA Karen & Gary Latter & Ewan Lyons 12 August 2018

The obvious large crackline further right, going through two steps.

UNDER THE BOARDWALK

The wall at far right end, just above the sea. Tidal at right end.

① Paranoid ★   20m E2 5c
FA Rab & Chris Anderson 5 September 2002

On the left end of the cliff, passed beneath on the approach is a fine steep grey slabby wall. Climb thin crack through a quartz patch up the centre of the wall.

② Seamed Sane ★   25m HVS 5b
FA Rab & Chris Anderson 15 September 2002

Thin quartz seam just right of the edge, finishing up a short crack.

③ Going Spare ★★   25m HVS 5a
FA Rab & Chris Anderson 15 September 2002

Climb the centre of the stepped rib just right of 2.

④ Utter Nutter ★   25m HVS 5b
FA Rab & Chris Anderson 15 September 2002

The protruding rib just right of the deep chimney. Steep black rock leads to a thin crack.

⑤ Bampot ★★   25m HVS 5b
FA Rab & Chris Anderson 15 September 2002

Corner up left side of the wall.

Ewan Lyons on Black Sabbath.

⑥ Anxiety Nervosa ★★   20m E3 6a
FA Mark Garthwaite & Rab Anderson 21 July 2002

Thin crack up the wall just left of 7.

⑦ Cracking-up ★★   20m VS 5a
FA Rab Anderson & Mark Garthwaite 21 July 2002

The central diagonal crack.

⑧ Black Sabbath ★★★   20m E1 5b
FA Rab & Chris Anderson 15 September 2002

The right crack.

⑨ Spaced Out ★   25m VS 4c
FA Rab & Chris Anderson 19 July 2003

Climb thin cracks immediately right of 8 and just left of a chimney to step across this and gain a ledge. Move up onto ramp and finish up this.

⑩ Losing It ★   25m Severe 4a
FA Gary & Karen Latter April 2005

The obvious line at the right end of the wall, starting a few metres right of the chimney. Continue more easily after a short steep start.

MANGERSTA AREA

The coastline running north from Mangersta Sands presents the highest concentration of developed sea cliffs on the island. Crags are described in three separate areas, firstly the northern section of coast north of the radio mast at the road end, then the Flannan area just south of here, and finally the long mainly multi-pitch routes on the impressively-situated headland of Buaile Chuido 1km further south.

THE PAINTED WALL AREA

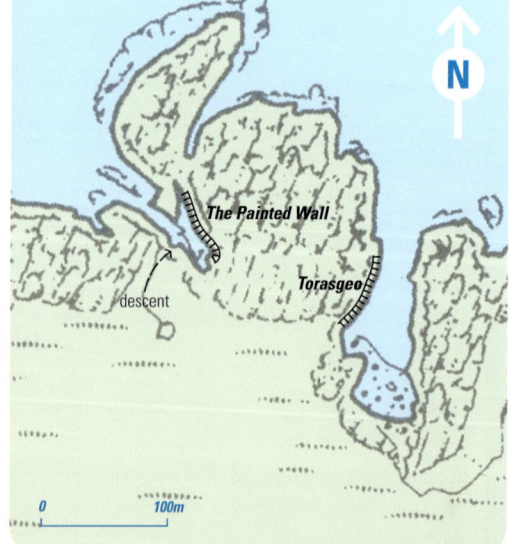

A good range of crags, giving the most accessible climbing on the coast.

Access: From Uig Sands turn right towards Mangersta (Mangurstadh) for 1.2 miles/2km then sharp right just before a fancy barn to follow the road north for 1 mile/1.6km. Park at buildings and radio mast at end of road.

Approach: The geo is about 150m from the buildings, due north-east.

NB 0062 3332 3min

THE PAINTED WALL

An excellent steep, beautifully coloured wall in a very sheltered location, above a fine inviting pool.

Descents: Either scramble down the easy-angled open gully in the centre of the south side of the geo or, more conveniently, abseil directly to the base.

Mick's Corner ★★   25m VS 4c
FA Mick Tighe & Jim Paterson May 1979

The fine open corner at the left end of the face. Belay on the ledge system at the foot of the wall. Trend leftwards across the wall to gain the corner and follow this past a jutting block at the top.

Pink and Black ★★   20m E4 5c
FA Gary Latter 7 June 1985

Ascends the like-coloured wall left of the central corner line. Start on the ledge 6m below the corner proper. From the arête swing leftwards to twin horizontal breaks. Straight up from here following a black seam to gain a good incut ledge. Easier above.

Central corner is the loose 3 *Director's Corner* VS 5a.

❹ Wireless in Wonderland ★★   20m E4 5c
FA Ian Taylor & Tess Fryer 16 July 2012

Start at the base of 3. Traverse hard right to a right-facing corner, and up this to the roof. Make bold moves up and right to gain the right side of a pinnacle flake. From the top of this, finish steeply just left of the arête.

❺ Dauntless ★★   20m E4 6a
FA Gary Latter & Dave Cuthbertson 7 May 1985

Start just right of a pink quartzy wall. Up the wall directly past several breaks, heading for the left side of twin diagonal breaks near the top. Traverse these rightwards a short way then finish direct.

❻ Goodbye Ruby Tuesday ★★★   20m E5 6b
FA Glenda Huxter & Kath Pyke 9 September 1996

A fine strenuous and sustained pitch taking a direct line up the wall. Small cams useful. Start 2m left of 7. Climb directly up the flaky white bands to where the wall steepens. A series of powerful moves between breaks leads to good finishing jugs at the centre of the wall.

Gravity Man ★★   20m E2 5b
FA Mick Tighe & Bill Newton (1 PA) 1980s;
FFA Mick Tighe following day

The fine overhanging crack in the centre of the face.

Ali Robb on the inaugural hard route in the geo – The Painted Wall.

8 The Painted Wall ★★★   20m E4 5c
FA Dave Cuthbertson & Gary Latter 5 May 1985

A diagonal line up the pink wall on the right side of the geo. Start below the left end of the pink vein just right of the previous route. Climb up into a shallow scoop to gain a quartz vein. Follow this and the obvious line to finish.

9 Whisky Galore ★★   25m E5 6a
FA Dave Cuthbertson & Gary Latter 5 May 1985

Takes a direct line through 8. Start at the right side of the ledge system below and right of 8. Up to the right side of the initial overlap and pull over this leftwards. Traverse left above the overlap to gain a vertical dyke. Up this and directly up the bulging wall above.

10 The Dreaded Dram ★★★   25m E4 5c
FA Dave Cuthbertson & Gary Latter 7 May 1985

Start to the right of 9 beneath an obvious short black groove. Up this and wall above to finish as for 8.

11 Tigger ★★★   20m E6 6b
FA Ally Coull & Gordon Lennox (both led) July 2011

Start on the highest ledge to the right of the black groove of 10. Climb the steep short wall onto the slab and move up to the overlap. Pull over this and head directly up to below the bulge. Climb straight up through the steep bulge on positive holds then trend right to the obvious large flake. Launch directly up the striped wall to eventually gain good holds and the top.

12 Gneiss is Nice ★★   25m E4/5 6a
FA Glen Sutcliffe & Dave Cuthbertson June 1994

Start as for 11. Climb a vague crack in the wall to a horizontal break (protection). Pull onto the slab above and go up to the overlap. Traverse right and move up to the base of a prominent overhanging groove. Climb this strenuously to the top.

Trevor Carpenter on Gravity Man.

TORASGEO

A good sheltered wall with some of the longest mid grade routes on the coast.

Approach: Head east from the parking spot at the end of the road.

NB 0074 3325

E 5min

Descent: For routes 1–3 abseil from convenient boulder down a vegetated corner to a large boulder cove (30m north of an obvious decaying stack/fin). For 4, abseil directly to large ledge at right side of wall.

Photo Emma Alsford

1 Argonaut * 55m HVS 5a
FA Paul Donnithorne & Emma Alsford 4 June 2006

Start below the south-facing slab.
1. **35m 5a** Trend up and right across broken grooves then back left up a short groove abutting the main slab. Follow the prominent red quartz seam up right to the right edge of the slab which leads to a slabby ledge.
2. **20m 5a** Follow the tapering ramp up rightwards to its end then steeply up into a groove which leads past a bulge to the top.

2 Triton ** 55m E1 5b
FA Emma Alsford & Paul Donnithorne 7 June 2006

The groove just right of the arête. Start immediately to its right by the largest boulder.
1. **30m 5b** Traverse right just above the high water mark to an obvious shallow slabby groove. Climb this until forced right on big holds to beneath a steep corner. Up this past a bulge to a large sloping ledge.
2. **25m 5b** The corner leads to another slabby ledge. Launch up the orange wall above slightly leftwards to finish up a short groove in the arête.

3 Palace of Colchis *** 80m E1 5b
FA Emma Alsford & Paul Donnithorne 10 June 2006

A spectacular traverse starting up 2.
1. **40m 5b** Follow 2 to below the steep corner. Take the obvious white juggy line up steeply rightwards with good positions, until it is possible to step down right onto brown slabs. Continue traversing horizontally to a small vegetated stance.
2. **30m 5b** Continue in the same line across an orange wall above the large roof to a spike on the arête. Continue traversing, crossing 4 to belay on a ledge in the prominent corner.
3. **10m 5b** Step left and follow the fine thin crack in the streaky wall above.

4 The Black Carrot * 45m E3 5c
FA Paul Donnithorne & Emma Alsford 8 June 2006

Start at the large ledge base of the chimney at the right end. Move left onto a ledge and pull onto a pink slab. Move left along this under small roofs, and up with difficulty to quartz footholds on the arête. A small groove leads to big flakes. Trend up and left more easily to reach the black carrot then climb the crack forming its left side to a small ledge. Climb a short groove leftwards to finish over blocks.

FLANNAN AREA

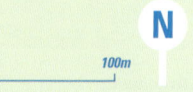

An excellent collection of geos, generally running parallel to the coast with varied routes of all grades. Crags are described from north-south, as encountered on the approach.

Access: As for the **Painted Wall Geo**.

Approach: Walk south from the mast to cross a small burn in a little under 300m. On the right can be seen a long whaleback ridge running parallel to the coast. **Magic** and **Aurora Geos** lie at the south end of this.

NB 002 329

AURORA GEO E S W 10min

The next geo immediately west of **Magic Geo**.

EAST FACE

Abseil down the line of either of the corners.

1 Grand Central ★★ 25m E1 5b
FA Rab & Chris Anderson July 2004

Start from good ledge 5m right of the chimney. Step up left and climb the central stepped groove to a good ledge then a shallow corner to finish up a crack in the centre of the slab.

2 Great Northern ★★ 30m E2 5c
FA Rab & Chris Anderson July 2004

Step up right to climb a shallow groove to the slab then the prominent crack and corner.

3 Wonder Wall ★★ 25m E5 6a
FA Dave Etherington (pre-placed protection) May 1998

Start from the left end of the ledge at the base of 5. Climb directly up to a sloping ledge and move right to the right end of an overhang. Make moves up a thin crack to a small quartz band. Move back left for 3m then make difficult moves up a strenuous thin right-slanting crack.

4 Newton's Law ★★★ 20m E1 5b
FA Bill Newton & Mick Tighe (some aid) June 1974

The prominent two-stepped corner climbed direct with some strenuous moves near the top.

5 Star of the Sea ★★★ 25m E1 5b
FA Mick Tighe & Bill Newton June 1974

Excellent well protected climbing taking the impressive zig-zag corner direct. Sustained.

6 Romancing the Moose ★★★ 30m E5 6a
FA Kath Pyke & Glenda Huxter 7 September 1996

A route of contrast in a committing position directly above the sea cave. The back wall of the geo is characterised by large crossed quartz bands above the sea cave. Teeter gingerly along the lip of the hanging slab to a good rest beneath the roof (RPs only). Jam wildly rightwards through the roof to gain an awkward crack. At its top move right to gain the headwall and climb steeply through the quartz bands to good finishing jugs in the centre.

WEST FACE

A long face with a huge distinctive block near its right (south) end and a large convenient platform extending south from *Presidents Chimney*. Tidal at north end.
Descent: Abseil down the general vicinity of the routes.

7 Presidents Chimney ★★ 20m Very Difficult
FA Mick Tighe & Jim Paterson early 1970'

The deep chimney cutting into the back wall at the left end of the large platform. A Moderate escape route moves out left and up the blocky arête.

8 Immaculate Crack ★★ 20m HS 4b
FA Ian Sykes & Ian Sutherland early 1970s

The prominent sustained crack above the start of the chimney. Often wet.

9 Things are Looking Up ★★ 22m E3 5c
FA Roger Everett & partner 2001

Make a few moves up 8 then step right and climb a crack to a slab. Step left then move up and right through a quartzy section.

10 The Roaring Foam ★★★ 22m E3 5c
FA unknown 1994

Sustained well protected climbing. Start 4m right of the chimney. Ascend the thin crack, trending rightwards in its upper half.

11 Ocean View ★ 23m E3 5c
FA Wilson Moir & Neil Morrison 7 August 2006

Climb a thin crack 2m right of 10 (small RPs) to the top of a pinnacle. Traverse right into 12 and up this a short way. Return left along a small ramp to gain a hidden crack. Finish up flakes to its right.

12 Cioch Crack ★ 20m VS 4c
FA Rab and Chris Anderson 1 July 1997

The prominent wide crack (often slimy), to finish up a thin crack.

LEWIS & HARRIS FLANNAN AREA

Route labels on photo:
- Corner Climb E3 5c *
- Cormorant Corner E1 5b **
- Shag Crack HVS 5a *
- Who Cares! E1 5b *
- A. N. Other VS 5a *
- Who Knows? VS 5a *
- Anonymous E2 5c **
- The Pie Party E2 5b *

13 Poultry in Motion ** — 20m E2 5b
FA M.Dale & M.Bock 30 May 2000

The slim ramp then the thin crack over a bulge.

14 Chicken Run *** — 20m E1 5c
FA Mick Tighe & Jim Paterson May 1979

The fine crack near the right side of the wall.

15 Look Back In Anger * — 20m E3 6a
FA Rick Campbell & Gary Latter (on-sight) June 1993

The thin crack starting from the left edge of the huge block. Bold.

15a Black Affronted * — 20m E2 5c
FA unknown 1994

Climb 15 to a ledge, step right and climb another crack leading to easier ground.

16 Don't Look Now ** — 20m E2 6a
FA Rick Campbell & Gary Latter (on-sight) June 1993

The thin intermittent crack above the right edge of the huge block. The start is gained by falling across the chasm at the base.

17 The Vee ** — 20m VS 4c
FA Mick Tighe & Jim Paterson October 1985

Good climbing up the prominent V-groove behind the step in the huge block.

18 Gannet Crack * — 20m HVS 5b
FA Mick Tighe & Ed Sherstone June 1993

Midway between 17 and 19 is a slabby corner with an overhang giving a well protected layback.

19 The Zed * — 20m HS 4b
FA Mick Tighe & Jim Paterson October 1985

The zig-zag line about 12m right of 18.

MAGIC GEO

A good contrasting geo with a steep slabby east face and overhanging north and west faces.
Descents: Make a 30m abseil down the recessed **Black Wall** directly opposite **The Red Walls** then walk right

NB 002 329 10min
(north) down an easy-angled black ramp to boulders at the back of the geo for all routes starting from the base of the geo. Alternatively, climb down the easy-angled *Solitary Chimneys* (Diff.) at the north end of **The Black Wall**.

THE RED WALLS

The compact area of rock at the left (south) end of the **East Face**. Can be reached by jumping the gap in the geo from the foot of the descent, or directly by abseil from the promontory between **Magic** and **Aurora Geos**. The pair of chimneys at the left side are taken by *Flannan Chimneys* both Severe 4a *.

1 Flannan Crack ★★　　　　　　30m VS 4c
FA Mick Tighe & Jim Paterson May 1979

The prominent rightwards slanting diagonal hand-crack at the left end.

2 Campa Crack ★　　　　　　30m E1 5a
FA Paul Moores & Dave Cuthbertson 7 June 1985

The next crack system to the right.

The right-slanting pink dyke to join 4 at 20m is route 3 *Gas* ★ E3 5b.

4 Limka ★★　　　　　　30m E2 5b
FA Paul Moores & Dave Cuthbertson 7 June 1985

Start a short way right of 2 and break up right to follow the obvious line, finishing up the easy blunt arête.

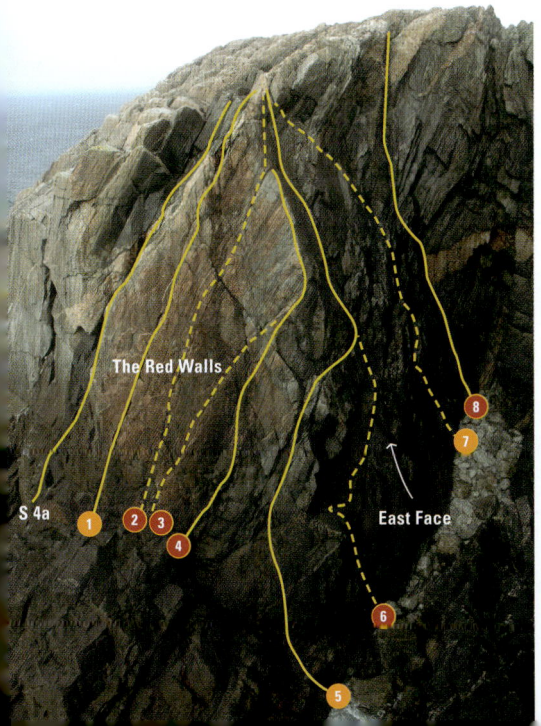
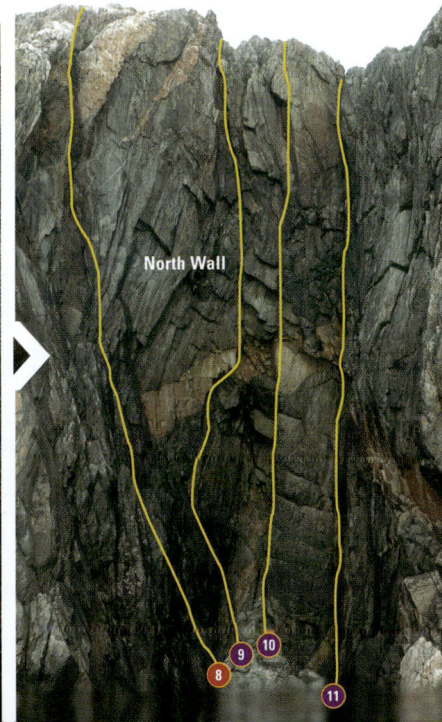

EAST FACE

5 Flannan Slab Left ★★★   45m HVS 5a
FA Mick Tighe & Cameron Davies June 1978

Start beneath the open groove/chimney with an obvious slanting overhang. Climb the groove to a tiny ledge (possible belay). Then up the right-slanting crack to hand traverse a flake system horizontally right for 6m. Step up and gain another flake then follow a line of good holds and left-facing flakes to the top (as for 6).

6 Flannan Slab Direct ★★★   40m E1 5b
FA Mick Tighe & Mick O'Brian around 1980

Excellent climbing. Start near the left end of the wall beneath the mid-point of the large slanting overhang. Climb up a shallow groove with difficulty (crux – often slimy) to better holds in another groove that leads with difficulty to a large ledge on the left arête below the left end of the large slanting overhang. Step back down and traverse right to easier ground then move up to the foot of a series of left-facing flakes and corners. Follow these up and left, finishing up the slab just right of the final arête.

7 Flannan Slab ★★★   45m VS 5a
FA Mick Tighe & Jim Paterson May 1978

Excellent climbing with two contrasting pitches – the first fairly bold, the second steep and airy. Start at the right side of the wall, just right of a left-trending ramp.
 1 **25m 5a** Steep initial bouldery moves lead up and right to a thin crack. Climb the crack to a ledge, go easily left on this then steeply to another ledge and belay.
 2 **20m 4c** Gain a groove above on left. Up this to the obvious handrail which is followed leftwards to finish.

NORTH WALL

The corner bounding the right side of the slabby face is 8 *Kissing the Pink* E2 5b; 11 *Queen's Freebie* • E4 6b tackles the similar feature up the left side of the landward wall.

9 The Crimebusters of the Sea ★★   35m E5 6a
FA Peter Robins & Ben Bransby 11 June 2004

A marvellous outing up the obvious weakness in the back of the geo. Starting at the back, climb the left wall to a flake leading into the pink cave. Shuffle and wriggle on outwards and upwards to an easier finish in the wider chimney.

10 The Eagle Has Landed ★★   35m E6 6b
FA Peter Robins & Ben Bransby 11 June 2004

Another splendid journey up the back of the geo, climbing the obvious lower arête then through the bulge and into the slim finishing groove. The arête is climbed direct and is bold. Going through the bulges is the crux (small cams useful), gaining a block ledge. Step right and go up the pleasant wall and into the finishing groove.

Nick Clement starting up the classic Flannan Slab.

15 The Alchemist *   50m E4 6a
FA Nick Clement & Gary Latter (on-sight) 25 May 1996

The groove and bottomless chimney on the right side of the wall.

1 **20m 5c** Climb the prominent deep black V-groove which soon eases. Above, head diagonally right to belay on the large ledge directly beneath the steep leaning groove.

2 **30m 6a** Strenuously climb the innocuous looking groove with difficulty to better holds on the left wall at 6m. The chimney/groove above provides a pleasant easier finish.

16 Am Burach **   25m E4 6a
FA Rick Campbell & Gary Latter (on-sight) June 1993

The shallow right-facing groove at the right side of the wall, a few metres right of the deep chimney groove of 15. Climb the shallow groove and pull out left onto good holds. Continue up a thin overhanging crack, which leads to a shallow groove and easier climbing to finish.

WEST FACE

12 The Magician ***   40m E5 6a
FA Jim Moran & Dave Pearce 5 May 1985

The impressive vague overhanging crack in the back wall of the geo. Start 6m right of the corner. Gain and climb the crack veering right at the top.

13 The Sorcerer ***   40m E5 6a
FA Jim Moran & Dave Pearce 7 May 1985

Start as for 12. Climb the ramp on the right then back left to a flaky corner. Pull over this and traverse rightwards to finish up the groove above.

14 Gimp Route **   35m E4 5c
FA Ben Bransby & Peter Robins 11 June 2004

Climb the initial corner of 13 to the ledges then move left and pull through the bulge using a flake. Traverse right along a thin seam to gain a ramp which soon becomes a crack (just left of 15?). Go direct to the top.

THE BLACK WALL

The slabby wall above the sea in the open recess opposite **The Red Walls** and just south of the overhanging **West Face**.

1 Island Life **   25m Severe 4a
FA Rab & Chris Anderson 12 July 2000

The corner delineating the left end of the recessed bay, just right of the impressive arête at the right end of the main West Face.

1a Island Fling **   25m VS 5a
FA Barry Rose & Liz Mackay 8 May 2002

A spectacular left finish to 1, taking the obvious incut ledge and slanting crack to finish by pulling round the arête in a fine position.

2 Solitary Chimneys *   25m Difficult
FA Lochaber MC members 1970s

The chimneys at the left side of the slabby bay.

LEWIS & HARRIS FLANNAN AREA

③ Pomarine ★   30m E2 5b
FA Rab & Chris Anderson 10 July 2000

Start below the short exit corner in the centre. Climb up left to the base of the corner on the left, then move up and gain a right-slanting break. Make a few moves along this and stand on it then pull onto a slabby wall to gain a short groove which leads to a short corner finish.

④ Bonxie ★★   30m E3 5c
FA Rab & Chris Anderson 10 July 2000

Start near the right end beneath a thin crack. Climb steeply off undercuts to gain the crack to finish up the corner of the previous route. A *Direct Start* is the same grade.

MITRE WALL

The wall containing three obvious cracks dropping down to the sea from the right side of **The Black Wall**.
Descent: Abseil down open grooves below and left of the wall to ledges just above high tide or scramble easily down rightwards from the base of 2 *Solitary Chimneys*.

The leftmost crack is 5 *Last Orders* ★ HVS 5a, sparsely protected prominent central crack 6 *The Black Crack* ★ E1 5a, 7 *Too Wild for Feral Fyffe* ★ E4 6a the right crack, with lots of small gear.

⑧ The Hooded Claw ★   35m E2 5c
FA Rab & Chris Anderson 11 July 2000

Start from ledges just above the water. Step up right onto the rib and climb to the base of the prominent blind right crack. Traverse hard right into the prominent V-shaped hooded groove/recess on the arête. Climb this, step right to pull up and move back left to climb the arête in a fine position to finish.

Round to the right is 9 *A Night at the Opera* ★★ VS 5a,4a which takes corner and quartz seam up edge of the slab. The big groove right of the arête is a fine looking ★★ HVS 5a.

ARD MORE MANGERSTA

NA 999 325 20min

A prominent *"Cioch-shaped"* block overlooking the rocky island of Eilean Molach.
Approach: Continue south along the cliff top for less than 10 minutes from the **Flannan Area**.

Descent: A prominent ridge, slabby on its west side, connects the neck. Walk down this to the Cioch then down an easy-angled shelf to a jumble of huge boulders. Scramble down these to the base of the routes.

1 Atlantic Crossing ** 100m VS 5a
FA Mick Tighe & Jim Paterson May 1979

This is effectively a rising right to left girdle of the headland block. Start from the boulder choke in the narrows of the geo.

1 **25m 4c** Step off a boulder and pull onto the wall. Up a crack to the right end of the roof, traverse left under this then cross a series of grooves.
2 **15m 4a** Continue left, over a shoulder and belay in a very exposed position on the buttress edge.
3 **15m 5a** Make an awkward step round a corner onto a slab. Now climb the bottomless groove/chimney to a small ledge and belay.
4 **45m 4a** Climb the cracked wall trending left near the top.

2 Waiting for the Crossing ** 45m Very Difficult
FA R.Pettner & J.Ison 2 June 2000

The prominent flake-groove on the left side of the wall about halfway down the descent to 1. Follow the groove and arête above (looks about VS!).

3 Sunset Rib * 70m Difficult
FA Mick Tighe & Jim Paterson May 1978

The quartz wall and prominent slabby arête opposite the start of 1.

1 **20m** Traverse right and up the cracked wall to belay on a blocky ledge.
2 **50m** Step left and climb the crack, finishing up the exposed right edge of the slab.

MANGERSTA
(TRADER'S STEADING)

NB 002 319 10min

BUAILE CHUIDO

This exposed headland contains the longest routes on the sea cliffs with many impressively-situated multi-pitch routes on the walls flanking a huge impressive sea cave. There are also numerous single pitch routes including a number of short non-tidal routes accessed by scrambling down to a large flat platform near the top of the cliff.

Access: Turn off the A858 Stornoway to Barvas road at Garynahine, 13 miles/22km west of Stornoway and follow the B8011 west past Uig sands for 20.9 miles/33.5km. Turn right (signposted Mangersta) for 1.2 miles/2km then turn right just before a modern barn to park 100m on the right, just before the gate.

Approach: Head west following either of the fence lines, skirting round the southern end of the large open inlet Lairegeo. The crags extend on the headland just south of here. On a shoulder left of the highest point sits a distinctive small circular stone. Go straight past this and then slightly left down a ramp on clean rock to a wonderfully situated shelter affording fine views of the main cliff.

THE SCREAMING WALL

An immaculate wall of perfect rock extends north from the arch.

Descent: From the block strewn slope above the south end runs into a 4m light-coloured wall with two large blocks. Abseil directly down from the leftmost (north) block to a good spike above the centre of the platform.

① The Heebie-Jeebies ★★★   50m HVS 5a
FA Gary Latter & Jon Rabey 15 April 1999

A brilliant main pitch on perfect rock. Start by a spike atop a raised 'pinnacle'.

1 **30m 5a** Follow a superb left-slanting pink ramp, continuing up the black ramp above to a spike and NB below a beautiful pink wall.
2 **20m 5a** Climb the wall either side of crack above the belay (or the crack at E1 5b), continuing direct.

② Off the Shelf ★★   45m HVS 5a
FA Rab & Chris Anderson 10 July 2010

Start on top of the 'pinnacle', right of 1.

1 **20m 5a** Ascend the crack up the right side of the edge left of the deep groove to good ledge on 4.
2 **25m 5a** Move up right and climb the prominent corner on great rock, then direct above.

③ Over the Top ★★   45m HVS 5a
FA Rab & Chris Anderson 10 July 2010

Start just right of the deep groove.

1 **20m 4c** Climb thin crack on perfect rock, step left onto a ledge then direct to the ledge at the top of the cleft on 4.
2 **25m 5a** Move up right to the base of the corner on 2. Continue up right around the edge, follow a thin crack to beneath a roof. Finish either side of the roof.

④ Lighthouse Arête ★★   VD to VS 4b
FA Mick Tighe, Bill Newton & party 9 June 1987

The prominent easy-angled stepped blunt ridge, separated by a deep cleft from the steep wall left of the arch. The easiest start is on the right side. The black groove further right is HS 4b; the faint grooves on the left VS 4b. All lead to a ledge at 20m. Continue leftwards up the obvious line, then rightwards towards the abseil blocks, with much variation possible.

> The following 5 routes take the area of rock left of the cave. With the exception of *Necromancer* they have a common start on good ledges reached by a 45m abseil from large blocks above the centre of the wall.

⑤ Necromancer ★★   60m E2 5c
FA Kath Pyke & Glenda Huxter 10 July 1997

Links the prominent black crystalline bands then the crack on the left side of the wall. Gain the start by abseil (60m) to black ledges (non-tidal) 8m diagonally down and left from the start of 6.

1 **30m 5c** Follow black crystalline rock, always trending left steeply at times on a faint prow. For the final 5m move right up a corner to gain an airy square-cut belay perch. Large block and friend belay.
2 **30m 5b** Move left to gain the crack system then jam securely until a step left into an obvious corner line. Finish directly as for 7.

⑥ The Dark Crystal ★★   50m E2 5b
FA Steve Mayers & Gill Lovick June 1993

1 **25m 5b** Trend up leftwards from the stance to eventually reach the base of two grooves. The left groove leads to blocky ledges and a belay.
2 **25m 5b** Continue up and slightly left to finish up an obvious corner.

⑦ Grant's Bad Hair Day ★★   50m E1 5b
FA Howard Jones & Glenda Huxter 29 May 1996

A fine line in impressive surroundings for the grade.

1 **20m 5a** Traverse rightwards until below a shattered corner, move up this and onto the front face of a precarious block then continue to belay on a ledge.
2 **30m 5b** Follow fault-lines easily up and leftwards aiming for the left end of a big overhang. Move left around the arête beneath the overhang in

an exhilarating position and continue easily up leftwards to finish up a cracked corner as for 6.

8 The Crystal Maze ★★★ 45m E6 6b
FA Steve Mayers & Gill Lovick July 1993

1 **20m 5c** Take a line up rightwards to a stance about 5m above the lip of the cave on a small ledge.

2 **25m 6b** Climb the overhanging black wall above the stance (just right of the black corner) to the roof. Cross the roof to the right of the pink quartz, moving slightly right at a horizontal break and then climb the wall above to a small overhang. Pass this on its left to a white quartzy wall which is climbed to an easy rightwards ramp and the top.

9 Distant Voices ★★ 53m E5 6b
FA Mike Tomkins & Steve Mayers June 1993

1 **20m 5c** As for pitch 1 of 8.

2 **18m 6b** Easily up rightwards to a break in the roof and then back across left above the roof to the comfort of some good holds on the rib. The next roof is easier and leads to a good stance above.

3 **15m 5c** Trend leftwards and then up to reach the easy ramp of 8.

10 The Screaming Abdabs ★★★ 75m E6 6b
FA Dave Cuthbertson, Lee Clegg & Callum Henderson
21 & 22 June 1988

A superb route climbing the right side of the big arch before taking a direct line through the overhangs above. Start at the left end of the lower tier, gained by abseil.

1 **20m 5c** Climb an undercut groove then move left to gain an obvious white crack. Climb this to a good ledge and belay.

2 **25m 5b** Traverse left along a horizontal break and up to a ledge on the right. Make a rising leftwards traverse across the orange coloured wall (much easier than its appearance would suggest), to a small ledge and belay at the main girdling break.

3 **30m 6b** Move right and pull over a bulge onto a wall. Now follow a line of black pockets trending leftwards to some large but secure blocks under

the roof. Move right and pull over the roof via an obvious ramp hold (good friend under roof and not so good wire on lip). Go leftwards still with some difficulty (good small flexi-friend) to better holds beneath the next overhang. Climb this by means of a horizontal crack and continue up a corner to the top.

11 The Prozac Link **** 50m E3 5c
FA Howard Jones & Glenda Huxter 29 May 1996

A spectacular exposed diagonal line sweeping above the huge central arch. Climb pitches 1 and 2 of 10.

- **3 30m 5b** Follow pitch 3 of that route as far as the block under the main (crux) roof. Move left round the front of the block onto large holds and continue traversing leftwards to belay beneath a curious downward pointing flake.
- **4 20m 5c** Move left below the flake and continue leftwards and up onto a pink pegmatite wall with difficulty. Climb directly up the wall to meet the rightwards-slanting ramp of 9 and follow this to the top.

Aly Robb on the spectacular but straightforward second pitch of The Prozac Link.

UPPER TIER – WEST ASPECT

The right side of the headwall above & right of the cave.
Descent: By a 20m abseil from just west of the bothy.

12 Shadow Dancer ★★★   40m E7 6b

FA Steve Mayers July 1993

A wild and strenuous route taking a line of sickening exposure up the hanging arête to the right of 10, *"so named because once the leader was on the arête the belayer could only monitor progress by watching his shadow"*. Start as for 13, but on pulling over the overhang make technical moves out left to good holds. Another committing move leftwards brings the line proper, an overhung flake/crack which is climbed ever leftwards to eventually bring a brief respite under a roof. Pull directly over this and then trend rightwards past a peg to the base of a corner which is followed easily to the top. A double set of friends and some long extenders are helpful.

13 Paranoid Slippers ★★   30m E4 6b

FA Grant Farquhar, Rick Campbell & Nick Clement 29 May 1996

A finely situated pitch up the wall between 12 and 14. Start up 14 to pull over the roof. Traverse leftwards on the lip (crux) and move up and left to better holds. Continue up and left to a sentry box. Finish up and leftwards past a horizontal break, left of a wide crack and on the arête overlooking 12.

14 Hughie's Cocktail Mixture ★★★   25m E3 5c

FA Lee Clegg, Callum Henderson & Dave Cuthbertson June 1988

The obvious crack on the left wall of the corner at the left end of the ledge. Best gained by abseil.

> The wall on the right is 15 *Great Gig in the Sky* • E4 6a

UPPER TIER – NORTH WEST ASPECT

The wall directly beneath the bothy.
Descent: Gain the first 2 routes by a 20m abseil from just west of the bothy, the remaining by walking round the terrace past the **West Face**.

The obvious offwidth (cam #5 useful)
is 16  • E2 5b.

17 Whirlwind ★★   20m E8 6c/F8a

FA Dave MacLeod (headpointed) May 2005

The central 'awesomely exposed' crack. The first section up to the break is serious with poor gear and snappy holds. Above the climbing gets steadily harder towards the top but better protected, culminating in a tricky crux right at the top

> 18 *In the Shop – On the Hill* • E2 5c takes prominent steep crack and leftwards scoop; vertical crack is 18a *It's Raining Rocks!* ★★ E3 6a.

© Grant Farquhar pulling over the roof at the start of Hughie's Cocktail Mixture.

WEST FACE

The next two routes are passed just before rounding the arête on the gangway that leads above the **Lower Tier**.
Descents: By an easy scramble down a shelf at the right (south) end, or directly by abseil from a large block 20m south of the bothy.

19 North West Arête ★ 15m E3 6a
FA Steve Crowe & Karin Magog 16 May 1999

The arête, mainly on its right side, escaping right near the top. A hard and bold left finish is about E5/6 6b but could do with a quick brushing.

20 Pinky ★★ 12m HVS 5a
FA Gill Lovick & Steve Mayers July 1993

The left crack just right of the arête.

21 Perky ★ 12m VS 4c
FA Gill Lovick & Steve Mayers July 1993

The corner 2m to the right.

22 Inner Demons ★ 10m HVS 5a
FA Gary Latter (solo) 14 July 2006

Left of 23 is a left-facing groove capped by a block. Climb the crack 2m left of the groove, stepping up right to pull over the block overhang. Finish up the crack above.

23 Screaming Sandhoppers ★ 10m Severe 4a
FA Mike Sullivan & John Garbutt 22 July 1997

Start at a prominent 2m high monolith. Climb the sustained crack direct from the top of the monolith.

24 Screaming Miss Molly ★ 10m VS 4b
FA John Garbutt & Mike Sullivan 22 July 1997

Start 1.5m right of 23. Bridge up between the monolith and the right wall of the cave to reach a crack which is climbed direct.

25 Katrin's Cream ★ 10m Severe 4a
FA Mike Sullivan & John Garbutt 22 July 1997

Start 2m further right again. Climb the left-slanting crack up into a right-facing groove on great holds.

The obvious line further right is about Difficult, a number of lines a few metres right again about Very Difficult.

LOWER TIER – NW ASPECT

Descent: Scramble down to the large terrace at ⅔ height then abseil from a selection of blocks at the north end.

The groove line right of the start of 10 is 26 *Damn Your Eyes!* ★ E4 5c – would make a good starting pitch to 13.

27 Salty Dog ★★★   30m E4 6a
FA Dave Cuthbertson, Lee Clegg & Callum Henderson June 1988

The twin crack system on the left side immediately right of a smooth black slab. Gain the steep undercut groove (the left-most, easier of two) bounding the left side of the overhanging face. Continue up the crack with some deviation to gain the final bottomless groove with difficulty.

28 Rats Don't Eat Sandwiches ★★★   30m E5 6a
FA Leo Houlding & Jason Pickles 9 June 2004

A very good route which pulls out right from 27. Start as for that route but traverse right at about 10m to a ledge. Climb the slim groove above to a roof and pull through this to gain a ledge then on to the top.

29 Killer Fingers ★★★   30m E4 6a
FA Dave Cuthbertson, Lee Clegg & Callum Henderson June 1988

A fantastic pitch. Immediately right of the overhanging face is a prominent hanging slab at about half height. An undercut start and groove system leads to a crack on the right side of the slab. Step down and hand traverse this to gain an obvious layback crack.

30 Suffering Bastard ★★★★   25m E4 6a
FA Dave Cuthbertson, Lee Clegg & Callum Henderson June 1988

Right again is an obvious left-facing corner. This superb jamming pitch climbs the prominent crack to its left. Climb the crack to finish up the bottomless groove.

> The intermittent cracks just right of leftwards-facing corner, moving awkwardly into this at 7m is route 31 *Hullabaloo* ★ E6 6b. 31a *Hullabaloo Left-Foot* ★ E5 6a finishes up hanging ramp/groove leading leftwards.

32 What's the Fuss? ★★   20m E1 5b
FA Rab Anderson, Neil Morrison & Wilson Moir 11 August 2006

Start beneath blunt edge. Go up to the left end of the slab to triangular roofed recess, then move up left into short leaning groove. Pull out right round the blunt edge, finishing steeply up left to easier ground.

33 If All Else Fails ★★   25m Very Difficult
FA Lee Clegg & Calum Henderson June 1988

Gain a ledge above the right end of the raised platform. Trend rightwards and climb a short vague crack up the right side of easy-angled slab to a ledge. Make a very exposed rightwards traverse and finish up a steep wall on good holds. Alternatively, from the ledge move left and up.

> 33a *Direct Finish* ★ up the flake and crack is E1 5b.

LOWER TIER – SW ASPECT

Descent: Scramble down to the large terrace and abseil diagonally leftwards (south) from the south end of the terrace, down the groove of 36 *Claymore* or directly to the base of the routes, as described.

34 I'll Try Up Here Again ★   30m E1 5b
FA D.Ashworth & C.Lofthouse May 1993

Reached by abseil down an obvious VS-looking corner, approx. 15m left of 35. The route takes an improbable line up some steep ground. Climb an easy wall to a steep crack. Pull onto a small slab left of an overhang. Step down to a crucial foothold at the bottom of the slab. Climb around the overhang (runners) and follow the nose to the top.

35 Moscow Mule ★★   30m E1 5b
FA Dave Cuthbertson, Lee Clegg & Callum Henderson June 1988

A good line. Follow the initial corner of 36 for 8m. Traverse left along good handholds to reach a stance. Launch up a cracked slab through crux moves to reach a sloping ledge. Climb the shallow corner above, trending left to finish over ledges.

36 Claymore ★★★   30m HVS 5a
FA Ian Sykes & Ian Sutherland 1970s

Great climbing on great rock, taking the line of slim corners and cracks. Climb the right-facing corner to ledge at 6m, step right into a thin crack and cross an awkward bulge to a ledge on left. Move back right to climb a shallow groove to a small foot ledge (PR). Traverse left (crux) to better holds leading to a small left facing corner to finish.

NB 0020 3003
GEODHA AN TAROIN   6min

A superb wall on the north side of the fine little bay north of the headland of Rubh' an Taroin.

Access: Continue south-west along the single track road towards Islivig for 1.6 miles/2.6km beyond the turn off for Mangersta, to park on east side of road in a rough lay-by at lowest point at .

Approach: Walk south along road for 50m, then head west over the brow of the knoll, then drop down to the headland.

Descents: Abseil from large blocks at the west end, or from stake & boulders at the east end. It is also possible to scramble down the west end.

1 The Dividing Line ★★   30m E3 5c
FA Rab & Chris Anderson 18 July 2013

Climb up (4" cam) and right along obvious line where the black rock and quartz meet. Continue up a steep crack to easy slab.

2 Moac Wall ★★★   30m E1 5b
FA Mick Tighe, Bill Newton, Dave Kirtley & John Pollard 9 June 1974

Superb positive well-protected climbing. Follow cracks and short left-facing groove to good holds in the pegmatite band. Move out left and up, then return rightwards along good break. Continue directly to a steep finish.

3 Twelve Years On ★★★   30m E2 5b
FA Mick Tighe, Ian Donaldson & Ed Nickols June 1986; Direct Start: Gary & Karen Latter & Ewan Lyons 10 August 2018

A fine companion to 2. Start up vertical crack just left of arête, then rightwards to right end of roof. Follow the groove over both roofs on huge holds, then the easier upper groove. 3a the direct start round the cracked roof is *Thirty Two* ★★ E2 5c.

4 Less Awkward than The Principle ★★★   30m E3 6a
FA Dave Etherington & George Reid May 1998

Climb out of the left side of the recess by the steep roof crack, follow it up and leftwards to the edge overlooking 3, then move up and right into prominent sharp edged

V-groove. Follow this *"with great interest"*, finishing up the final section of 3.

5 Achevalier ** · 30m E3 5c
FA Rab & Chris Anderson 4 July 1997

The deep groove system a few metres right of 4. Make bouldery moves up the right side of the recess to a sloping ledge. Continue up the awkward narrow capped groove into the deep V-groove, finishing slightly leftwards.

6 Slotted-in ** · 30m E2 5c
FA Rab & Chris Anderson 23 July 2014

The parallel left-slanting groove just right of 5. From the sloping ledge, move right and up onto another sloping ledge. Follow the groove past an awkward flared slot.

7 Neighbourhood Watch *** · 30m E2 5b
FA Ian Taylor & Tess Fryer 3 July 2011

Start at the right side of wide pink intrusion. Climb the left side of the groove to ledge, then directly up through the bulge, finishing up fine grey ramp.

8 Copper Koala *** · 27m E2 5b
FA Jules Lines (on-sight solo) 16 June 2007

The huge V-groove has great climbing. From a small ledge just above high tide line, follow the groove with increasing difficulty, moving out right around small roof at the top.

9 Frozen Smoke ** · 25m XS 5c S1 S3
FA Jules Lines (on-sight solo) 15 June 2007

Just right of 8 is a tight hanging groove. Follow this awkwardly (crux) to gain the amazing suspended prow above the water. Gain it immediately and climb direct to a large ledge (S1). Continue carefully up the easier slightly loose back wall (S3).

10 Daddy Longlegs ** · 25m E3 5c
FA Mark Garthwaite & Rab Anderson 13 July 2013

The huge leaning stepped corner. Great positions and much technical interest.

Ewan Lyons enjoying the evening sun on the classic Moac Wall.

LEWIS & HARRIS DALBEG

NB 2249 4631 15min

DALBEG (SMALL FIELD)

A compact selection of varied open walls.

Access: follow the A858 north from Gearraidh na h-Aibhne (Garrynahine) past Carloway for 11.5 miles /19km then turn left down single track road for 0.6 miles/1km to park at the road end by the beach.

 15min

DALBEG BUTTRESS

The headland right (north) of Dalbeg beach is split by an obvious deep slot, forming a narrow buttress with an arch through it at the bottom. A large boulder sits prominently at the top of this.

Approach: Follow the path up right through the fields to the top of the headland.

Descents: By abseil from blocks or by scrambling down a gully towards the right (north) before traversing back left on to easy-angled slabs.

1 Limpet Olympics ★★  40m E5 6a

FA Niall McNair, Karin Magog & Steve Crowe 8 July 2003

Start up the ramp until possible to pull onto the wall at a flake and climb to traverse undercut flake right into 2. Break out right to a good jug and gear, then direct up the centre of the headwall.

2 Limpet Crack ★★★★ 30m E3 5c

FA Andy Cunningham & Brian Davison 17 May 1989

The impressive diagonal quartz crack running from the middle of the wall to the left. The crux is at mid-height.

3 Flock Talk ★★  30m E8 6c (F8a)

FA Dave MacLeod (headpointed) June 2005

A serious eliminate up the lovely wall of rippled smooth gneiss between 2 & 4. The crux at 15m is a long way above gear – a sprinting belayer may save you from contact with the platform! Climb the first couple of moves of 2 then break out right across the wall to the huge diagonal flake (good gear in this, the last for a long way). Step left and climb to the rattly undercut (cams in this don't hold bodyweight). Step up and climb leftwards across the wall to a desperate long rockover to reach an overhead undercut. Continue left then up to gain a good jug and gear near 2. Climb the easier wall above direct to finish.

4 Tweetie Pie Slalom ★★★★ 35m E5 6a

FA lower section Brian Davison & Andy Cunningham 24 May 1989; as described Dave MacLeod, Niall MacNair & Steve Richardson (on-sight) 13 June 2001

Start up a blunt rib left of 5 which leads to a small rib after 7m. From here make difficult moves to a small horizontal slot and then left again to a vertical crack before moving up to a large flake/ledge. Continue up the excellent left-trending crack above, stepping left to finish up the final crack on good holds.

5 Neptune ★★★★ — 40m E3 5c
FA Brian Davison & Andy Cunningham 17 May 1989

Superb sustained climbing – low in the grade. Starting at mid-height in the centre of the wall is a groove line running right to left. Start up the wall below this to enter the groove and follow it leftwards to the top.

6 Mercury and Solace ★★ — 35m E5 6a
FA Niall MacNair, Dave MacLeod & Steve Richardson (on-sight) 14 June 2001

Excellent though slightly escapable climbing up the centre of the wall. Start on the arête. Climb up to a ledge, step up into a groove and move left to a large pocket. Climb direct above this into another groove and move left to gain a crack. Follow this (technical) to good holds below the start of a ramp. Follow the ragged diagonal crack on the left to gain the ramp, finishing direct up cracked wall.

CAVE SLAB

From the descent to the **Dalbeg Buttress**, turn right (facing out) at the top of the descent slab to gain access to the following routes. The left edge of the slab is undercut by a large cave whereas the right side runs up to a series of steep grooves below an orange coloured slab with a crack running up its centre. Routes from left to right.

1 The Black Hole ★ — 45m E4 6b
FA Brian Davison & Andy Cunningham 20 May 1989

The crack in the overlap in the far left end, starting by moving into a wide undercut niche and then hard moves onto the next overlap leading into a short steep corner. Swing right and follow the crack in the slab left of the overhang to finish up a short corner.

2 Simple Jim ★ — 35m E3 6a
FA Andy Cunningham & Brian Davison 19 May 1989

Start by hard moves up the crack 3m right of the last route. Follow the red slab up to a roof/overlap. Traverse left and pull over the overlap at a quartz vein. Move up and traverse right to the base of a steep corner. Climb this past a huge block. Finish leftwards.

> The wide crack in the easy red finishing slab is *Beam Me Up Scotty* E1 5b and is loose, as is the smooth-looking groove on the right – *Kling On Corner* E1 5a.

3 Bones ★ — 30m Severe 4a
FA Brian Davison April 1989

Start just right of the previous route and climb up to gain the thinner right crack in the red finishing slab.

> The next routes are at the extreme left end of the slab above the sea but are reached by walking round the headland of **Cave Slab** and abseiling down a short seaward-facing wall to a sloping platform. An overlap at the right side gives access to the extreme left end of **Cave Slab**. Described from the abseil point rightwards.

4 Warp Drive ★★ — 15m HVS 5a
FA Brian Davison 25 May 1989

The abseil wall is pocketed with a crack and a shallow groove running up it 3m left of 5. Climb the wall.

5 Dilithium Crystals ★ — 20m HVS 5a
FA Andy Cunningham & Brian Davison 21 May 1989

Climb the second groove left of the overlap on good cracks and pockets.

6 It's No Good Captain She's Breaking Up ★ — 20m HVS 4c
FA Brian Davison 25 May 1989

The first groove left of the overlap. Start up a ramp, harder than it looks and into the groove.

7 Captain's Log ★ — 30m HVS 5a
FA Andy Cunningham & Brian Davison 21 May 1989

Cross the overlap at its lowest point then move up over two small overlaps on to the top slab and head up towards a groove capped by an overhang. Climb the crack on the left of this to the top.

Gary Latter pulling into the groove on Parting Shot. Photo Carl Pulley.

BLACK GEO NB 2245 4636

The next geo north from **Cave Wall**, marked by two large cairns at top. The geo has an easy slab on its northern side and a steep back wall.

Descent: For 1 scramble down the seaward edge of the easy slab on the north side; for 2 abseil down to the ledge.

1 Parting Shot ★★ 45m E3 6a
FA Glenda Huxter & Kath Pyke 13 September 1996

A direct line up the back wall. Approach down the slab. Start at the rightmost of two grooves.

1. **20m 6a** Gain the pod by awkward moves. Move right at its top round the overhang and up the groove to a fine cave belay.
2. **25m 5b** Move up and left for 3m then straight up via a ledge with a downward 'fang' hold to the quartz break and small ledge. Directly up the final groove above.

2 Old Salt ★ 40m E3 5c
FA Brian Davison & Andy Cunningham 22 May 1989

The left-slanting diagonal quartz crack starting from a ledge halfway up the wall, above the 'cave'. From the left end of the ledge, follow the quartzy crack diagonally left to gain a ledge after about 30m. It would be possible to finish up a groove above here. The crack, however, continues at ledge level, so step down and follow it leftwards to its finish.

NB 2244 4640
SMALL WEST WALL

From the headland north of the **Black Geo**, drop down (moving away from the **Black Geo**) to a black rock platform with a pool in it about 20m above the sea. To the right of the pool is an easy-angled wall with an overhang at the bottom – HS 4b, starting from the right, or with a 5c direct start.

1 Original Route ★ 10m Severe 4b
FA Brian Davison April 1989

The obvious corner right of the slab. It is possible to move out right onto the wall near the top at HS 4b.

2 Solitude ★ 10m VS 4c
FA Brian Davison April 1989

To the right is another corner with an awkward start.

3 Sunday Stroll ★   10m VS 4c
FA Brian Davison April 1989

Start as for 2 then after 4m, swing right onto the nose of the arête and round to a ledge to finish up the wall at the back.

4 Just for the Crack ★   10m VS 4c
FA Eric Pirie & Roy Henderson 26 April 1995

Start right of 5. Pull over the nose and climb the right-trending crack.

> There are a number of short routes left of 1:

5 Zosta Slab ★   Severe 4b
FA Ian Sherrington & Tim Walker 26 April 1995

From the start of 1, traverse left along the base of the undercut slab and up cracks in the left edge.

6 No Choice ★   10m VS 4c
FA Andy Cunningham & Keith Geddes 26 April 1995

The first corner-crack left of the slab. Pull through the initial bulge and turn the next on the right to finish up 5.

7 Quavers ★   12m VS 4c
FA Rab & Chris Anderson 21 July 2017

The corner immediately left of the slab, starting as for 6.

8 Crackers ★   10m VS 4c
FA Rab & Chris Anderson 21 July 2017

The next corner.

9 Pringles ★   10m Severe 4a
FA Keith Geddes & Andy Cunningham 26 April 1995

The third corner-crack left of the slab.

> Below and left of the rock platform is a wall, in the centre of which is a groove capped by an overhang with a hanging plaque of rock to its left. The bottom of the wall can be reached by abseil or scrambling down stepped ledges from the platform. The routes are described from right to left.

10 Tea For Two ★   15m VS 4c
FA Dave McGimpsey & Alison Newey July 1989

The shallow corner right of the overhang, starting up a crack. A variation start up the slab to the left is 5b.

11 Down Under ★   15m E2 6a
FA Brian Davison & Andy MacFarlane 13 May 1989

The groove to the left of the overhang then over it on good finger jams.

12 Gleaning the Bone ★★   15m E2 5c
FA Andy MacFarlane & Dawson Stelfox 28 August 1989

To the left of the groove is a narrow wall/pillar with a hanging plaque of rock. Climb this.

13 Flying Teapot ★   15m HVS 5a
FA Dave McGimpsey & Andy MacFarlane July 1989

Climb the groove left of the narrow pillar.

> Left of 13 past a blunt arête is an easy-angled slab/wall, 14 *Henry's Hard Times* ★ Severe 4a with a Diff. corner on its left.

15 Ian's Easy Times ★   15m Severe 4a
FA Ian Sherrington & Tim Walker 26 April 1995

The right edge of the slab right of 13.

16 Hard to Swallow ★   15m E2 5b
FA Andy Cunningham & Keith Geddes 26 April 1995

Steep, strenuous climbing up the crack-line just right of 17.

17 Endurance ★   15m E4 6b
FA Brian Davison & Andy MacFarlane 21 May 1990

The corner and crack through the right side of the roof. Climb the corner to the bottom of the groove. Awkward moves up the groove lead to the overhang. A foothold on the right helps progress through the overhang to the headwall and a sloping finish.

18 Ruth's Lazy Day ★   20m HS 4b
FA Dave McGimpsey & Chris Allan 21 May 1989

Climbs the groove left of the overhang.

19 Clean Hand Gang * — 20m E3 5b
FA Brian Davison 24 May 1990

Takes the wall to the left as directly as possible. Start at the right side of the wall then make moves up and left to a good hold. A long reach to a flat incut leads to good holds trending right to a ledge. Climb the edge of the groove to the top.

20 Jessie James * — 20m E2 5b
FA Brian Davison 24 May 1990

The arête forming the left side of the wall. Start on the right side of the arête and climb up the left side of the wall to a good hold. Move left to good but spaced holds on the arête leading to a ledge. Finish by moving up and left into 21.

21 Outlaw * — 20m E2 5b
FA Andy MacFarlane, Dave McGimpsey & B.Marshall 23 July 1989

The groove immediately left of the arête, exiting up the corner.

22 Robbery Under Arms * — 20m E1 5b
FA Andy MacFarlane & Dave McGimpsey 1989

The middle of the 3 grooves, starting up the left series of cracks and small ledges. Continue up the hanging nose of rock then step right to finish.

23 Thuggery * — 20m HVS 5b
FA Andy MacFarlane, Dave McGimpsey & B.Marshall 18 June 1989

The left groove, starting up a corner past a flake to continue through the roof.

Scott Muir on one of the best pitches of its grade on the island – the excellent Neptune, Dalbeg Buttress. Photo Dave Cuthbertson, Cubby Images.

Scott Muir starting up the immaculate Limpet Crack, Dalbeg Buttress. Photo Dave Cuthbertson, Cubby Images.

BIG WEST WALL
NB 2244 4646

Immediately after the groove of 23, the wall gains height and is capped by an overhang with a corner running through it at either end. The wall curves round into the next geo where a recess offers a corner climb up either side.

24 New World * — 25m E1 5b
FA Brian Davison 17 May 1990

Left of 22. Start up a steep groove just right of the overhang which runs along the bottom of the wall. At the top of the groove move right to a ledge then climb the wall to a prominent corner at the right end of the top roof.

25 Chew the Route ** — 30m E4 6a
FA Kath Pyke & Glenda Huxter 10 September 1996

The fine hanging arête leading rightwards from 27. Start as for that route and climb the groove to the ledge. Move up and right onto the arête to reach a big basalt (arm) undercling. Gain the crack (crux) and then sustained moves using the arête to a fine belay ledge.

26 Island of No Return * — 35m E2 5b
FA Brian Davison 17 May 1990

About 7m left of where the overhang running along the bottom of the wall ends, a square-cut groove capped by a small roof is to be found. Move up to the top of the groove then hand traverse right 4m to a foothold and ascend the cracks to a basalt intrusion. Move to a ledge on the right then up to another ledge. Traverse left into the bottom of the corner which marks the left end of the top overhang.

About 6m left is the recess which the next 2 climbs take.

27 New Addition * — 40m HVS 4c
FA Brian Davison 17 May 1990

The right corner of the recess, passing a flake/chimney which leads to a ledge. Follow the corner to the top.

28 First Born * — 40m VS 4b
FA Brian Davison 17 May 1990

Climb the left corner of the recess to a ledge then up a wall before stepping left into a shallow chimney and corner leading to the top.

PREACHER GEO
NB 2256 4647

The next geo north has a large block leaning against the wall and a fence ending at its top.

Descent: Abseil into the back of the geo from fencepost.

1 A Prophet's Doom *   20m E3 6a
FA Andy MacFarlane & Dave McGimpsey 16 July 1989

The prominent crack at the top right end of the wall. Sustained.

2 Mr Big Comes Clean   35m E3 5c
FA Andy MacFarlane & Dave McGimpsey 30 July 1989

The rightmost of 3 corners.

> The prominent loose crack near the collapsed block is 3 *Red Hand Gang* E2 5b.

4 Blessed are the Weak ***   45m E5 6a
FA Glenda Huxter 23 May 1996

A brilliant route, taking a direct line up the face left of 3. Climb that route for 6m, make a long step left and climb up and leftwards aiming for the centre of a horizontal overlap. Cross this and go up direct to a good ledge. Climb the hanging flake above then up slightly rightwards on pocketed rock to a crack and finish at the highest point of the cliff. Boulder belay.

STORM GEO   15min
NB 2179 4591

15 minutes west of Dalbeg. This area of cliff in between the sharp inlet of Gob Geodha Sporain and the promontory of Rubha na h-airde. Descend by abseil down easy-angled ground about 100m south of the route at Rubha na h-airde and traverse leftwards (facing in) into the bay. At the left end of the bay is a wave-cut platform below the most compact area of the cliff.

1 The Storm ****   50m E5 6a
FA Glenda Huxter 27 May 1996

Start at the far left end of the wave-cut platform. An overhang ends in a steep crack (the left of two). Climb the crack for 15m to a ledge then straight up for 3m before moving leftwards to follow a vague flake. Move back right and up to the notch in the overhang. Exit rightwards over this into a slabby groove and follow this to broken ground and a ledge on the right with a full 50m of rope out. **Note:** This is an inadequate belay and on the first ascent a backup rope was left some 12m down the cliff and used to abseil off. However, an easy 6m traverse leads to easier finishing cracks.

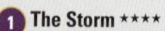

Niall McNair nearing the top of Tweetie Pie Slalom, Dalbeg Buttress. Photo Dave Cuthbertson, Cubby Images.

AIRD MHOR BHRAGAIR

NB 2694 4955 15min

A superb range of routes particularly in the middle grades.
Access: Turn north off the A858 at North Shawbost (Siabost bho Thuath) and follow the single track road towards Fibhig and An Carnan for 0.8 miles/1.3km to park by the peat stack on the left, 50m before the road end.
Approach: Go through a gate by the ruin in front of north-most croft and down to the boulder beach then follow the cliffs north to the crags.

FOLDED WALL

A fabulous sweep of perfect gneiss, climbable almost anywhere at VS – HVS.
Descent: By abseil directly down the wall.

1 Snake Dyke ★★   20m E2 5c
FA Mick & Kathy Tighe 11 July 2000

A superb well protected diagonal fault leads to a ledge at half height. Continue more easily up the immaculate brown groove, or the easy wide crack on the left.

2 Squid ★   25m E1 5b
FA Mick & Kathy Tighe & Howard Clarke 20 July 2000

Start at the same place as 5. Climb the much thinner curving crack below the main one to a ledge at half height. Climb the wall into a shallow chimney to finish by a 3m flake-crack.

3 Octopod ★★   25m HS 4b
FA Mick & Kathy Tighe 11 July 2000

Start at the base of 5. Follow the curving crack for a few metres before heading straight up the gently bulging walls on excellent jugs. Avoid the possible exit right at

Karen Latter wide awake on Sleeping Dogs.

two thirds height by tackling the lovely quartz wall above directly.

4 Extraction ★★   25m E3 5c
FA Rab & Chris Anderson 15 October 2014

Start a few metres up 5, then step onto left wall and up shallow left-facing groove to surmount small roof at widest point. Finish up juggy headwall.

5 Kenny's Cavity ★★   25m VS 4b
FA Mick & Kathy Tighe 11 July 2000

The excellent corner/groove succumbs *'primarily to bridging of various descriptions'*.

6 Edge of Distinction ★★   25m HVS 4c
FA Mick & Kathy Tighe & Jonathon Winter 10 June 2004

The left edge of the main wall before it turns back into 5.

A bold not well protected move low down leads to a more satisfying airy finish.

7 Closer to the Edge ★★   25m E1 5b
FA Rab Anderson & Tom Prentice 6 July 2007

Follow the hairline crack directly.

8 Left Edge ★★★   25m E1 5b
FA Mick & Kathy Tighe 15 July 2000

Start a few metres left from 9 and a similar distance in again from the left edge. Make an intricate series up the lower wall (small wires) to finish up the easier steep upper wall.

9 The Scoop ★   25m E1 5b
FA Mick & Kathy Tighe 10 June 2000

Just left of centre is a concave depression in the upper wall. Start beneath this, 2m left of 10 and climb the fairly bold fingery wall, passing a small triangular niche to a ledge at mid-height. Continue more easily up the scoop.

10 Le Slot ★★★ — 25m E1 5b
FA Mick & Kathy Tighe & Howard Clarke 20 July 2000

Almost in the centre of the wall, low down is a diagonal slot. Step across the trench onto the wall to climb the slot and the immaculate wall above direct. Traversing into the slot from the right is 10a ★★ VS 4c.

11 Fifty Fifty ★★ — 25m E2 5b
FA Rab Anderson & Tom Prentice 6 July 2007

Eliminate starting up thin crack, then direct in same line.

12 Sleeping Dogs ★★★ — 25m VS 4b
FA Mick & Kathy Tighe & Howard Clarke 20 July 2000

Start in the middle of the wall 5m left of 13 below a small triangular groove and overhang at one third height. Climb up into the alcove and pull over the small overhang onto the steep wall above on immaculate holds. Continue to the top, trending left. Trending right is a bit harder but even better.

13 Black Recess ★★ — 25m HS 4b
FA Mick & Kathy Tighe & Howard Clarke 20 July 2000

Slightly higher and a few metres left of 14 is a black recess with quartzy veins in the black rock. Cross the trench and head straight up through the recess.

14 Goodbye Donella ★ — 25m HS 4b
FA Mick & Kathy Tighe & Howard Clarke 20 July 2000

Below and a few metres left of 16 is a small triangular calcified alcove. Get across the trench and follow the curving fault, the crux leaving the alcove.

16 Number 3 ★★★ — 20m Severe 4a
FA Mick & Kathy Tighe & Howard Clarke 20 July 2000

Near the right side at about one third height the rock has folded into a perfect 3 shape. Fall across the trench at the base and climb the wall directly through the 3 or a metre to the right. Similarly graded eliminates either side are 15 *Three Plus* ★★ and 17 *Two By Three* ★★

18 First Fold ★★ — 25m Severe 4b
FA Rab & Chris Anderson 15 October 2014

The right arête.

CREAG DUBH DIBADALE

NB 046 240 **Alt:** 200m

 2¾hr 1¾hr

A large remote and impressive cliff almost 1km long and 200m high in its centre. It lies on the east flank of the small hill of Tamanisdale, overlooking the golden sandy beach at the head of Loch Dibadale. The rock is very compact and the routes are generally not well protected.
Access: From the campsite at the south end of Uig Sands, continue west along the B8011 for 0.9 miles/1.5km to a new track running south for 10km to the sea at Loch Tamanavay (Tamnabhaigh). Follow this to a locked gate where it crosses the Stockgill River after about 1km.
Approach: Mountain bikes recommended. Continue south along the track for 6km to the top of Bealach Raonasgail then head steeply left (east) to a grassy col overlooking the western edge of the coire. Drop down rightwards to the base of the cliff.
Descent: Down either side of the cliff.

1 North Buttress ★★   120m Very Difficult
FA Jack & Mrs H.Ball 1968

A roughly central line up the buttress. Start below a rib on the left edge of the buttress (cairn and arrow) about 3m up from the lowest point.
1 **35m** Ascend the rib then move right along a rake to a belay.
2 **35m** Move slightly left and climb the slab then continue direct to a grass ledge. Move left to another broad ledge.
3 **35m** Move right up the rake, continuing up a right slanting crack leading to a belay on the right.
4 **15m** Move left and finish directly up the wall.

2 Dominis Vobiscus ★★   125m E4 6a
FA Crispin Waddy & Adam Wainwright 4 June 1995

Start at the obvious groove low down and 30m right of *Panting Dog Climb*.
1 **45m 5b** Climb the obvious curving corner into a short chimney and belay at spikes on ledges.
2 **50m 6a** Climb a short corner then move left and back right heading for a prominent right-facing flake in a shallow groove (the right of two flakes). Up the flake to ledges then boldly up and right on slopers to a ledge and on up to belay in niche.
3 **30m 5b** Step right then easily up slabs to the belay ledge. Scramble off.

3 Joplin's Wall ★★   205m E1 5b
FA Rob Archibold & Geoff Cohen 3 July 1974

An obvious slabby tongue of red rock protrudes from the cliff. The route heads for an obvious ramp slanting rightwards across the upper section of the crag. Start on the highest ledge to the right of the tongue.
1 **35m 5b** Step left onto the tongue and climb up to a short black groove. Exit left and zig-zag up the slabby wall above to gain a short groove at 27m. Climb this and step right from its top to an excellent rock niche.
2 **30m 5b** Climb the black corner above and continue up an easy crack for 6m. Move right and climb up under the slanting overhang. Traverse left on underclings to a small perched block, above which a short wall leads to easier climbing into a prominent depression. Continue diagonally right to belay in a chimney/crack system at a point level with a horizontal fault on the right. (Probably in the line of weakness at the start of pitch 3 of *PDC*.)
3 **30m 5a** Make an exposed traverse right along the horizontal fault (with bulging rock above) for about 8m then climb steeply up to gain easier ground.
4–6 **110m 4c** Climb up and right to gain the big ramp which runs diagonally right towards the top.

4 Panting Dog Climb ★★★　　　　　　　180m E3 5c

FA Mick Fowler & Arnis Strapcans 10 July 1980

Shares most of the first two pitches of *Joplin's Wall* then takes a direct line to finish up a series of prominent corners left of that route.

1. **35m 5b** As for pitch 1 of *Joplin's Wall*.
2. **30m 5b** Climb *Joplin's Wall* to the slanting overhang until it is possible to traverse right and gain a prominent grass ledge.
3. **30m 5b** Traverse horizontally right for 6m to a line of weakness in the wall above. Up this for 6m to overhangs, move left onto a slab and pull through the bulges to a good stance at the foot of the obvious corner system.
4. **25m 5a** Climb the corners to belay beneath a rightwards slanting corner with an overhanging left wall.
5. **30m 5c** Ascend the corner avoiding the large rocking block on the right (crux) to good ledges on the left. Step right and undercut and layback an easy angled slab to belay on the next ledge.
6. **30m 4c** Easier to the top.

5 The Big Lick ★★★　　　　　　　　180m E4 5c

FA Mick Fowler & Andy Meyers 1 July 1981

Start on the left side of the obvious red tongue of rock.

1. **30m 5c** A serious pitch. Move onto the front of the tongue and trend diagonally left via shallow grooves. From an excellent hand ledge beneath a bulge move up left with difficulty to a short crack and good ledge.
2. **20m 5c** Climb the groove above the left end of the ledge to its capping overhang. Move round the right side of this to gain a ledge and move up to belay on the next one.
3. **45m 5b** Surmount the overhang directly above the stance to gain the area of slabby rock. Climb this direct to gain a stance at the upper right extremity of the black 'flying saucer' shaped depression on the face.
4. **20m 5c** Gain a pinnacle/flake on the right and step left from its top to climb boldly up the wall on quartz. Continue more or less straight up to a good ledge about 9m below overhangs.
5. **25m 5b** Step down left from the stance and traverse horizontally left on an exposed sloping ledge. Climb a corner for 5m before moving left again for 6m to belay on a ledge beneath a light coloured area of rock.
6. **40m 5c** Above are three groove lines. Gain a sloping ledge in the middle one by coming in from the right groove. Continue with difficulty until it is possible to move into the left groove which gives easier climbing to the top. The leftmost groove line is also possible – cleaner and in a superb situation.

6 Via Valtos ★★★　　　　　　　　150m E1 5b

FA Arthur Ewing & Bill Sproul (4 PA) spring 1970;
FFA Rob Archibold & Geoff Cohen July 1974

The prominent crack in the left side of the face. The crack is ascended more or less directly with occasional excursions onto the flanking walls. Slow to dry.

1. **40m 5a** Climb straight up to a grass patch.
2. **34m 5b** Move out onto the left wall then up to an overhung corner with a sloping slab above.
3. **30m 5a** Move up and right a few feet then go left into a crack and straight up to a ledge.
4. **6m 5a** Go right then left to below an overhung corner, climb this then move left into a crack.
5. **40m** Continue by a chimney and more easily to the top of the crag.

Liz Mackay and Barry Rose on the superb long crack pitch on the upper slabs – the highlight of Islivig Direct, Tealasdale Slabs (page 377).

CREAGAN TEALASDALE

NB 0226 2816 **Alt:** 220m
FAR WEST BUTTRESS  50min

Clearly visible on the lower north-west flank of the biggest hill on Lewis, Mealaisbhal (574m) is a compact collection of buttresses sporting some striking cracks, grooves and chimneys, with potential for many more worthwhile additions. Receives the sun from mid-afternoon.

Access: Follow the single track road south for 2.5 miles/4km beyond the Mangersta turn-off to park on the grass on the left, just beyond a small stream (NA 9990 2860).

Approach: Follow the north side of the shallow burn in the direction of the crag, then cross small valley containing boulder field immediately below the crag.

Descents: Down shallow grassy gully at the right side, or the slanting grassy rake beneath the **Upper Tier**, past a 'bad step' about halfway along. From the top, a 25m abseil from sling and maillon on block 1m down from top of *Grime of the Century*. From the terrace, 60m abseil from sling and maillon on block near the centre.

❶ Ergot Kernel ★★★ 50m E4 6a
FA Malcolm Scott & Pete Graham 4 October 2016

Brilliant climbing up the groove and crack in the pillar.
1 **20m 4b** Follow the easiest line leading to large ledge down and left of the groove.
2 **30m 6a** Follow the striking clean-cut groove with interest to a good rest beneath the roof. Pull round the roof and jam wildly up the continuation crack, then much easier climbing to finish.

❷ Caledonian McBrain Justice ★★★ 75m E2 5c
FA Pete Graham & Malcolm Scott 3 October 2016

Superb well-protected climbing with two contrasting pitches.
1 **20m 5c** Climb direct to left end of ledge, walk right along this and climb the chimney (protection in finger-crack on right), with difficulties easing with height.
2 **25m 5c** Climb fine groove to small ledge, then negotiate tight slot, moving out left onto large ledge just beyond large spike. Pull up steep wall to belay on large terrace.
3 **30m 4c** Take the rightmost of twin wide cracks, then left up ramp, finishing easily rightwards.

❸ Grime of the Century ★★★★ 25m 5.12b/E5 6b
FA Malcolm Scott & Pete Graham 3 October 2016

World class climbing up the twin cracks at the right end of the **Upper Tier**. Gain the base either by one of the previous routes, or the grassy slanting rake. Start up the right crack, then climb mainly by the left crack, culminating in difficult finger-jamming leading to good holds and a sentry box at half-height. Continue more easily up hand cracks above. Double up on grey, purple & yellow cams (1", 1.5" & 3").

GRIOMAVAL (GRIM'S FELL)

NB 0117 2225 **Alt:** 260m 1hr

TEALASDALE SLABS

Excellent slabs leading almost to the summit of the hill.
Access: From Uig follow the single-track road south through Islibhig and Breanais to a small jetty at its end. (6 miles/10km from Mangersta turn-off.)
Approach: Head south-east over the western flanks of Mealasta to drop down into the upper reaches of Glen Tealasdale then up to the base of the slabs.
Descent: From the summit, down either the west or east shoulder, contouring back round to the base.

THE MAIN SLAB

The most continuous section of cliff, defined on its left edge by the right-slanting grassy rake *Golden Gully*, Difficult. Previously described as *"hopeless and manifestly unclimbable slabs"*, in fact much of the rock is climbable at about VS, though protection and belays are generally sparse. All the routes start at a grassy sloping terrace, approached either by scrambling up the left edge of the open grassy gully on the right, or better, by a long Moderate scrambling pitch (70m to a belay) up immaculate easy-angled slabs directly beneath *Islivig Direct*.

1 Islivig Direct ★★★   220m HS 4b
FA Russell Sharp & Bill Sproul 8 June 1969

Excellent sustained climbing, with some long pitches. The highlight is the superb third pitch, where a number of equally stunning options are available. Start about 30m left of the gully, directly beneath a pair of vertical cracks high up.

1. **60m 4b** Climb direct to a prominent left-facing groove, then direct to the cracks leading to the left end of grass ledge.
2. **35m 4b** Continue directly up slabs to belay at the terrace beneath the upper slabs.
3. **60m 4b** From the left end of the terrace, follow a thin crack-line through two small overlaps, then more defined crack (possible belay) leading slightly leftwards, leading to a belay near a small overlap.
3a. **60m HS 4b Right Variations:** Start from the right end of the terrace where it meets the overlap, about 8m right of the belay on the original route. Follow the lovely thin crack, straightforward with good protection, then move left into the original route and follow that. **3b** At **VS 4b**, move right along small ledge at 35m to arrange protection (cams in break – possible belay), then continue directly up the slab past two small overlaps and up the right side of dark streak to belay on a small ledge, just below where the angle eases.
4. **60m 4a** Continue over steepening, then much easier above, avoiding broken ground on the left.
5. **5m** - Move up steeply to a belay.

2 Mistaken Identity ★★   275m HVS 4c
FA Robert Middleton & Helen Fairclough 19 April 2019

Start 10m right of *Comes the Breanish/The Scroll* at a good diagonal cam crack.

Gary Latter on the chimney pitch of the magnificent Caledonian McBrain Justice. Photo Karen Latter.

1 **65m 4c** Climb up and right over bold slabs towards the first of two leftward facing flake features. Small gear can be placed just below the first feature, which is climbed up and left then up more bold slabs to below the second flake. A final tricky step up to the flake feature provides much needed gear, before continuing again up and left over more bold slabs to a crack (gear). From here head diagonally left towards the obvious corner (first belay of *Comes the Breanish*) and belay. A bold pitch on immaculate rock.

2 **60m 4b** Climb up and slightly left up the corner and slabs above to reach a vegetated corner trending right. Follow this, then continue over overlaps and slabs to belay as per *Comes the Breanish* or

above and left at a spike. A well protected if a little vegetated pitch which would go in the wet.

3-5 150m 4b,4b,4a Continuing up the 3rd and 4th pitch of *Comes the Breanish*, then traversing into *Lochlann* to finish makes a lovely consistent route at 4b/c.

3 The Scroll ★★ 295m Severe 4a
FA Jack Ball & Marshall Reeves 13 August 1970

Start beneath the right end of the central overlaps, below and left of a left-slanting line of weakness. The upper section is probably similar to *Islivig Direct*.

1 **35m** Go right for about 9m then follow a weakness trending left above the start to a small grassy ledge.
2 **35m** Continue trending left to reach a good rock ledge.
3 **25m** Go straight up to the end of a long grassy ledge. The grassy gully is just on the left here.
4 **40m** Move 9m right and down the grass to a small groove. Start here and ascend directly until the slab angle eases. Continue by trending right to a small ledge.
5 **40m** Go diagonally right to a grassy ledge.
6 **42m** Climb straight up to a rock ledge.
7 **38m** Climb diagonally right to a crack-line which leads to a small rock ledge.
8 **40m** Climb a crack then more broken slabs to an abrupt finish yards from the summit cairn. Pegs are required for belays.

4 Comes the Breanish ★★★ 275m HVS 5a
FA Rab & Chris Anderson 16 July 1998

A fine direct line making the best use of the rope. Start right of *Lochlan* at the right side of the small overlaps, at the same point as *The Scroll*.

1 **55m 4c** Step right and climb straight up to the left-trending weakness of *The Scroll* then continue straight up onto a quartzy protuberance. Climb a thin crack past a small, narrow wedged block to reach a white slab (*Lochlan* & *The Scroll* belay over to the left) and continue straight up passing a block on its right side to belay higher up beneath an overlap at the top of a short, right-facing corner

(good wires in a horizontal in the overlap). A superb and generally well protected pitch on perfect rock.

2 **55m 5a** This pitch goes up the middle of the main seepage area and although it can be climbed fairly direct when wet, it would be much better if dry. Step left and pull onto the white, quartzy slab above the overlap then climb straight to the left end of an overlap with a pointed bit in its middle. Climb the bulge on the left, just left of a thin crack (possibly easier further right if dry) and continue to a short, overlapped corner. Climb this, or if wet step right and move over a small overlap onto a smooth white slab. A few thin moves gain a small quartz overlap (gear). Step left back into the top of the corner then follow slabs, holds and quartzy seams to a small grass ledge. Gain a grassy, horizontal break and move right to a short, left-facing corner.

3 **55m 4b** Step up right then go up and follow thin cracks in a quartzy line trending up right, passing over a crack-line to reach a more obvious crack-line. Climb the crack for a short way to a small ledge just short of the grassy rake of Golden Gully.

4 **55m 4b** Move right along the ledge a little then climb up and slightly right heading for a twin quartzy crack-line in the left side of the headwall.

Make tricky moves up the cracks and continue to reach a ledge occupied by some blocks.

5 **55m 4a** Move right then climb easily to a wide crack and up to the summit cairn.

5 Lochlann ★★ 240m VS 4c
FA Cam Forrest & J.McEwan 4 June 1970

Midway along the lower area of the cliff the slabs start with a series of black overlaps. Start at the left end of the overlaps and directly below a slab corner starting 9m up. This is some distance left of *Islivig Direct*.

1 **30m** Climb through the overlaps to gain the corner and follow this to the slabs above. Traverse right to a smooth slab and climb this to a small ledge (left of a larger grass ledge), PB.

2 **40m** Climb a groove behind the ledge and move rightwards to gain the end of a ramp running left. Follow this then climb a white scoop. Go leftwards to a crack and climb this through several overlaps to a large grass ledge and belay a few feet to the right.

3 **35m** Climb slabs and corners above, going right to take a belay in a sweep of white water-worn slabs.

4–6 **135m** Go rightwards up slabs crossing *Islivig Direct* and finish up a crack through walls and slabs to the right of that route.

HARRIS CRAGS

CREAG NA TRI PIOSAN (THREE BIT CRAG)

A small 11m *'perfectly formed'* vertical wall of excellent rock above a flat grassy base with superb views to both the west and east coasts. Not visible from the parking – best located when travelling eastwards. All well protected except 5. Stake belays at top.

Access: Follow the A859 south from Tarbert for 5 miles/ 8km to park in any suitable parking place close to the inlet to the east-most of a collection of small lochans on the south side of the road.

NG 122 959 **Alt:** 80m   8min

Approach: Directly up the hill.

The flake-crack is 1 *Two Power Three* ★★ E1 5c, the central corner 2 *One over the Eight* ★★ E1 5c, through the roof via a small square-cut recess is 3 *After Eight* ★★ E1 5b. Cracks and slim right-facing corner 4 *Eight Sisters* ★ VS 4c, 5 *EliminEight* ★ HVS 5a.

CREAG AISNIG

NG 1627 9346 **Alt:** 80m 3min

Another small (15m) immaculate wall, visible from the road.
Access: Follow the A859 south from Tarbert for 3.2 miles/ 5km, then minor road south for 1.4 miles/2.2km, turning left at Greosabhagh for 1 mile/1.6km.

Approach: Directly up the hill.

Left side of quartz wall is 1 *The Shining Path* ** E4 5c, centre 2 *The Golden Road* *** E4 6a, right edge 3 *The Ivory Highway* ** E3/4 6a.

SRON ULLADALE
(NOSE OF OLAF'S DALE)

The steepest and undoubtedly one of the most impressive cliffs in Britain with the highest concentration of long hard sustained routes in the country. It is also worth noting that the cliff also has some very fine shorter easier routes with those on the south extremity of the **West Face** on very fine water-washed Lewisian gneiss.
Access: From the A859 2.5 miles/4km north of Tarbert, turn west and follow the single track B887 for just under 7 miles/11.2km to park on the right just past the outflow from Lochan Beag (0.5 miles/0.8km short of Amhuinnsuidhe Castle).

Approach: It may be possible to obtain a key for the locked gate, making it possible to drive 3km up the track to park at the dam, saving 45 minutes – enquire at the fish farm down right of the gate or the first house on the left beyond the castle. From the dam follow the path north by the east side of Loch Chliostair, descending into Glen Ulladale until the crag comes into view on the right skyline. Leave the path and head steeply up the hillside to the base of the cliff.
Accommodation: There are some good camping spots right of the boulder-field beneath the centre of the **West Face**. There are also some howffs in the boulders, though the midges could prove troublesome.
Descent: Traverse right (south) and down an easy angled grassy gully bounding the south edge of the cliff.

 2hr 1½hr

NB 077 136 **Alt:** 200m

WEST FACE

1 Eureka ★★★ 132m HVS 5a
FA John Grieve & Eric Jones 1 June 1967

A fine route on good clean rock taking a direct line up the front of the South Buttress. The route follows a line of grooves on the lower tier then goes up the bulging nose above the top of The Gangway. Start directly under the nose of the upper tier at a line of thinly-defined cracks 2m right of a brown bulge at the left end of the lower tier.

1. **20m 5a** Go straight up grooves for 18m until a traverse can be made to an overhung slab ledge on the left.
2. **25m 5a** Move right and climb a short wall to a small ledge beneath a steep brown groove. Climb the groove to a heather gangway.
3. **45m 5a** Climb directly up the steep nose above and move left to pull over a bulge to gain a recessed slab, which is climbed to its top right corner.
4. **12m 5a** Climb *"alarmingly overhanging crack"* on magnificent holds.
5. **30m** Finish up easy walls and ledges above.

2 Midgard ★★ 180m Very Difficult
FA Brian Evans, L.A.Howarth & Mrs A.Evans May 1961

A fine route with good situations following the easiest line up the wall. Start at the lowest point of a tongue of rock about 30m left of the right-slanting line of The Gangway on South Buttress.

1. **18m** Go up slabby rock on the left to a band of yellow rock. Move right along a ledge to a belay.
2. **20m** Move up to the right for 6m then left a metre. Traverse right again to belay below an overhang at the obvious traverse line.
3. **30m** Traverse left into a corner then go up a slab and grass patch to a small flake belay.
4–6. **112m** Continue the traverse to the base of a second grass patch. Move down a little and across to an easy gangway which leads to the top.

3 Prelude ★★ 180m HVS 5a
FA Marshall Reeves & John Grieve 28 May 1967

A good route, which starts in the same general weakness as *Midgard*, crossing this and taking a direct route up the wall. Start just left of a light coloured tongue of rock.

1. **40m** Climb the obvious cracked groove left of a pillar then up rightwards to ledges. Move up left along a grassy gangway to belay
2. **30m** Break through bulges by a weakness. Step up and traverse about 9m horizontally right by a smooth sloping ledge to an easy groove. Up this and bear left on slabs.
3–5. **110m** Go straight up with increasing interest, keeping in the centre of a clean ribbon of slabs.

4 Big Luigi ★★★ 75m E4 6a
FA Crispin Waddy & John Biddle 1989

1. **25m 5c** As for Pitch 1 of *Palace of Swords Reversed*.
2. **25m 6a** Step off the right side of the ledge onto an awkward ramp. Continue right along quartzy rock into a groove. Follow this to cracks in a blank wall which lead via a short horizontal traverse to a belay.
3. **25m 5c** Climb grooves and cracks directly above to the top.

NORTH-WEST FACE

5 Palace of Swords Reversed ★★★ 90m E5 6b
FA Crispin Waddy & Rich Rodgers 1989

Start beneath the large corner 15m right of the giant staircase.

1. **25m 5c** Climb the corner to a ledge on the right.
2. **20m 6b** Climb the wall round an overhang above and left of the belay. Continue to a ledge (possible belay). Climb the steep leftmost groove above past a PR to belay on a ledge.
3. **20m 6b** Step left off the ledge and climb boldly up the wall round a roof into a groove. Climb this to belay beneath a large roof.
4. **25m 6a** Traverse horizontally right along a slab then move up left above a roof and continue round an overhanging arête. Finish up easy ground.

NORTH-WEST FACE

6 Flakeway to the Stairs *   120m E2 5c

FA Chris Watts & Sonia Vietoris (6 PA) 1 June 1981;
FFA Andy MacFarlane & Brian Davison July 1990

Climbs the flakes to the left of the obvious inverted staircase.

1. **35m 5c** Climb diagonally left along a fragile ramp to overhanging and detached block flakes. Climb these strenuously to a small belay ledge beneath a roof.
2. **25m 5b** Traverse right beneath the roof. Climb a crack on the right of the flake until it fades. Move left to a second flake and climb the wide crack.
3. **20m 5c** Descend left and round the corner. Move left and up the wall to a ledge.
4. **40m 5a** The corner left of the stance.

7 Beyond the Ranges **   110m E4 5c

FA Dave Cuthbertson & Paul Moores 6 June 1985

The right-facing corners and flakes just right of a pink quartz intrusion. Start near the left end of a terrace, gained after 60m of scrambling.

1. **45m 5c** Up the corner rightwards then back left under an overhang. Move up then back right to a ledge, up through a break then move left and make an awkward move left again to a large flake. Pull up into a quartz crack above with a loose flake hold. Traverse right to a foot ledge, move up then traverse back left across very dubious blocks. Now climb a quartz groove, pull out left in a superb position and continue to a ledge and belay.
2. **35m 5b** Climb the corner above with a tricky move onto a ledge. Up a short brown groove then go rightwards to a belay at the foot of the obvious layback corner.
3. **30m 5a** Climb the corner to a ledge with a block, traverse left to another ledge with a block. Go back right and up to the top.

8 Premonition ***   115m E6 6b

FA Crispin Waddy & George Smith (2 PA) 1994; FFA Ally Coull & Gordon Lennox 27 July 2011

Yet another brilliant route, taking the grooves left of *Stone*.

1. **45m 6a** As for *White Dwarf*.
2. **20m 6b** Climb the cracks in the left wall of the crux corner of *Stone* until a traverse left leads to a rest in a hanging groove. Exit out of the top of this

to a thin ledge then move up to a larger one.
3 **25m 6b** Move up into the left-leaning corner above. Climb this until it is possible to swing right into another corner. Climb this past a PR to its top then step left and up a short crack. Hand traverse wildly right to a belay. Bold in places.
4 **25m 6a** Follow the short crack-groove on the left to a ledge. Continue more easily up cracks and grooves to finish.

9 White Dwarf ★★★   140m E5 6b

FA Crispin Waddy & Rich Rodgers 1989

Follows the next groove right of *Kismet*.
1 **45m 6a** As for *Kismet*, continuing up the ramp to belay as for *Stone*.
2 **15m 5c** Gain the large break and follow this awkwardly left into the base of the large corner (the second corner right of *The Chisel*).
3 **20m 6a** Climb the corner strenuously to belay at its top.
4 **20m 6b** Move up and left then follow a small overhanging groove through a bulge. A steep crack leads to the pew stance on *Kismet*.
5 **15m 6b** Climb straight up (footless initially) then boldly into the acute-angled corner which is followed to a ledge.
6 **25m 5c** Continue directly until a wet mantelshelf leads to the top.

10 Kismet ★★★★   140m E5 6a

FA Crispin Waddy & Rich Rodgers 1989 ; top pitch: Mike Gardiner, Crispin Waddy & Donie O'Sullivan 4 June 2016

The first groove right of the crux pitch of *The Chisel*. Stunning climbing. Start 60m above and right of *Stone*, above the slabs and as far left as is easily possible to go from the giant inverted staircase.
1 **40m 6a** Traverse left along an obvious break then steeply up a diagonal crack to a high niche. Alternatively (5c) climb up a short wall past inverted flakes then continue easily left to the same niche. Step right beneath the bottom right corner of an orange quartzy wall forming the underside of the *Stone* ramp. Continue until a thin crack leads up to the ramp. Belay level with a razor-thin flake running horizontally left.
2 **15m 6a** Follow the flake left until it fades then the groove above to a ledge beneath a large roof formed by the main horizontal break.
3 **10m 6a** Climb flakes across the roof to belay immediately above in a large groove, right of the main groove on *The Chisel*.
4 **25m 6a** Step right and climb a crack in the arête between the two main corners until it joins the right-most corner (*White Dwarf*). Follow this to its belay then traverse right to belay on a ledge.
5 **20m 6a** Follow the shallow groove until it blanks out at 12m then hand traverse left round a blank pillar and pull up to a wonderfully situated belay pew.
6 **15m 6a** Step left into an open groove which leads to cracks and the belay above pitch 6 of *The Chisel*.
7 **15m 6a** A logical finish, if dry. Continue up the corner until it gets hard, then step right into a quartz groove leading to the top. An alternative is to ascend the open corner-groove on the right to traverse right to the arête and finish up the groove of *White Dwarf*.

11 Stone ★★★   200m E5 6a

*FA John Porteous & Kenny Spence 22–23 May 1969;
FFA Mick Fowler & Andy Meyers 3 July 1981*

Start at a large left-facing corner near the right side of the severely overhanging face directly beneath the prominent upper corner.
1 **25m 5a** Corner
2 **35m 4c** Traverse right along a slab and up the wall to belay below an overlap.
3 **25m 6a** Traverse leftwards and turn the overlap on the left then climb the easy slab on the left. Up a quartz groove to exit left in a stunning position. Belay.
4 **25m 4c** Follow a quartz ramp up into the base of the main groove.
5 **45m 6a** The groove. Follow a corner-crack until the

right wall bulges and the crack becomes offwidth. Pull right into the right crack and up this all the way to a grass ledge. A brilliant sustained pitch.

6 **10m –** Up to gain a ledge below the final corner.

7 **35m 5b** Up the corner for 8m then hand traverse rightwards onto the arête. Continue up and right into grooves and finish up easier ground.

12 The Chisel ★★★★ 130m E7 6b

FA Crispin Waddy, Bob Drury & John Biddle (1 PA) 1989;
FFA George Smith & Crispin Waddy 1994

Another very sustained high standard route, heading for the large wide corner at half height, containing a prominent undercut flake on its left wall. Start below and left of orange walls.

1 **20m 5b** Move up and right through overlaps until a wide break leads down and right onto a prominent hanging wall. Continue right to belay in a central crack.

2 **35m 6a** Climb the crack which becomes a groove, curving right. Traverse right at the top of the groove to an arête which leads boldly to ledges. A better protected variation (6a/b) follows a shallow groove to the ledge, starting 3m before the arête.

3 **10m 5c** Climb layback flakes on the left then traverse right to a large ledge.

4 **10m 6a** Move up and right to a break under a roof, which is the most prominent horizontal break on the cliff. Step left and pull steeply into the main groove and up this to a hanging belay.

5 **20m 6b** Well protected but very strenuous and exposed. Climb the groove (*The Chisel*) with difficulty then continue left along the prominent undercut flake until it finally eases near the arête. Above, pull over the roof to a foot-ledge.

6 **20m 6a** Climb a short groove to a lichenous bulge. Move right and go up through this until a very exposed step right leads to a short open groove. Follow this and the crack above to a perfect square ledge.

7 **15m 6a** Climb the corner above until it gets hard. Step right into a quartzy groove which leads to the top.

12a The Gloaming Finish ★★★ 60m E7 6b

FA George Smith & Crispin Waddy (1 PA) 1994

The left finish.

6 **20m 6a** Climb the short groove then traverse left along a break until it eases. Belay in the break.

7 **20m 6a** Step left and climb a roof into a prominent corner. Climb this until a short traverse across a hanging wall leads to a ledge.

8 **20m 6b** Mantel onto the slab above then step right into a crack-groove. Follow this steeply into double narrow grooves. Climb these until a gritstone-like sloping rail leads to the top. Climbed with a rest due to wet conditions.

13 Knuckle Sandwich ★★★ E7 6b

FFA Johnny Dawes & Paul Pritchard 1988

1 **20m 6b** As for *The Scoop* to a perched block belay.

2 **5b** Traverse easily right to a poor belay (old bolt) on a white ledge.

3 **6c** Climb the thin overhanging crack directly above to a tiny ledge. Climb up and right on big loose flakes to old Bs beneath an overhang. Pull desperately round this and move up to a hanging belay below the band of roofs.

4 **5a** Traverse right to beneath the first large corner.

5 **6b** Climb the corner to a difficult traverse right on overhanging quartz. Continue with difficulty to a small ledge.

6 **6a** Climb direct on immaculate rock to the top.

14 The Scoop ★★★★ 210m E7 6b

FA Doug Scott, Jeff Upton, Guy Lee & Mick Terry (A3) May 1969;
FFA Johnny Dawes & Paul Pritchard 1987

Superb climbing, which despite the proliferation of fixed gear still has a serious feel to it. Retreat is possible in one abseil from the top of pitch 3, after which it could be problematic. Scramble up slabs to a PB at the base. Only the first three pitches are common to the original aid line, after which the route follows an inspired line up improbable ground.

1 **25m 6b** Step down then move up to an overhang. Climb this and the wall above past an old bolt to move onto a sloping ramp. Continue up the overhanging wall above, move right and up a short steep crack in a groove to a ledge.
2 **20m 6a** Step right then up the cracked rib leading to a fine corner which is climbed to a good ledge on the left.
3 **25m 6b** Continue up the groove to a roof, move up left and continue to a hanging belay at the base of the huge corner.
4 **25m 6b** The wildly exposed 'flying groove' leads out left above the void. Continue up the groove above, turning the overhang on the left by precarious moves round the arête. A finger-crack and huge flake leads to the welcome relief of a fine 'lie down' ledge. Phew!
5 **40m 6a** Step down onto the huge flake and traverse airily left with increasing difficulty to a corner below the left end of the roof (possible hanging belay on blades). Enter the groove above awkwardly, then take the left arête to a slab. Follow a slim undercut groove out right to a good ledge beneath the impressive capping roof.
6 **25m 6a** A serious pitch. Move right and up over a bulge to PRs. Climb back down and traverse right to a bulge. Committing moves through the bulge lead to a welcome line of jugs and a hanging belay on the lip.
7 **50m** Traverse left on the lip of the roof and up to a ledge, avoiding any difficulties on the left Trend rightwards to the edge and finish up this.

15 Moskill Grooves ★★★ **95m E6 6b**
FA Ben Moon, Johnny Dawes & Paul Pritchard 1989

The prominent ramp groove at the left end of the front face. Start up and left of *The Scoop*.

1 **40m 6b** Pull over the initial bulge into the right-facing corner. Traverse right to a poor PR then move up and follow the huge corner to nut belays at the top.
2 **30m 6a** Continue up the overhanging crack and chimney line directly above to belay on small nuts on a sloping ledge.
3 **25m 5c** Go right across slabs to join and finish up *The Scoop*. Alternatively, abseil off (as on the first ascent).

📷 *Grant Farquhar feeling the exposure on the wildly positioned penultimate pitch of the uber-classic The Scoop. Photo Rick Campbell.*

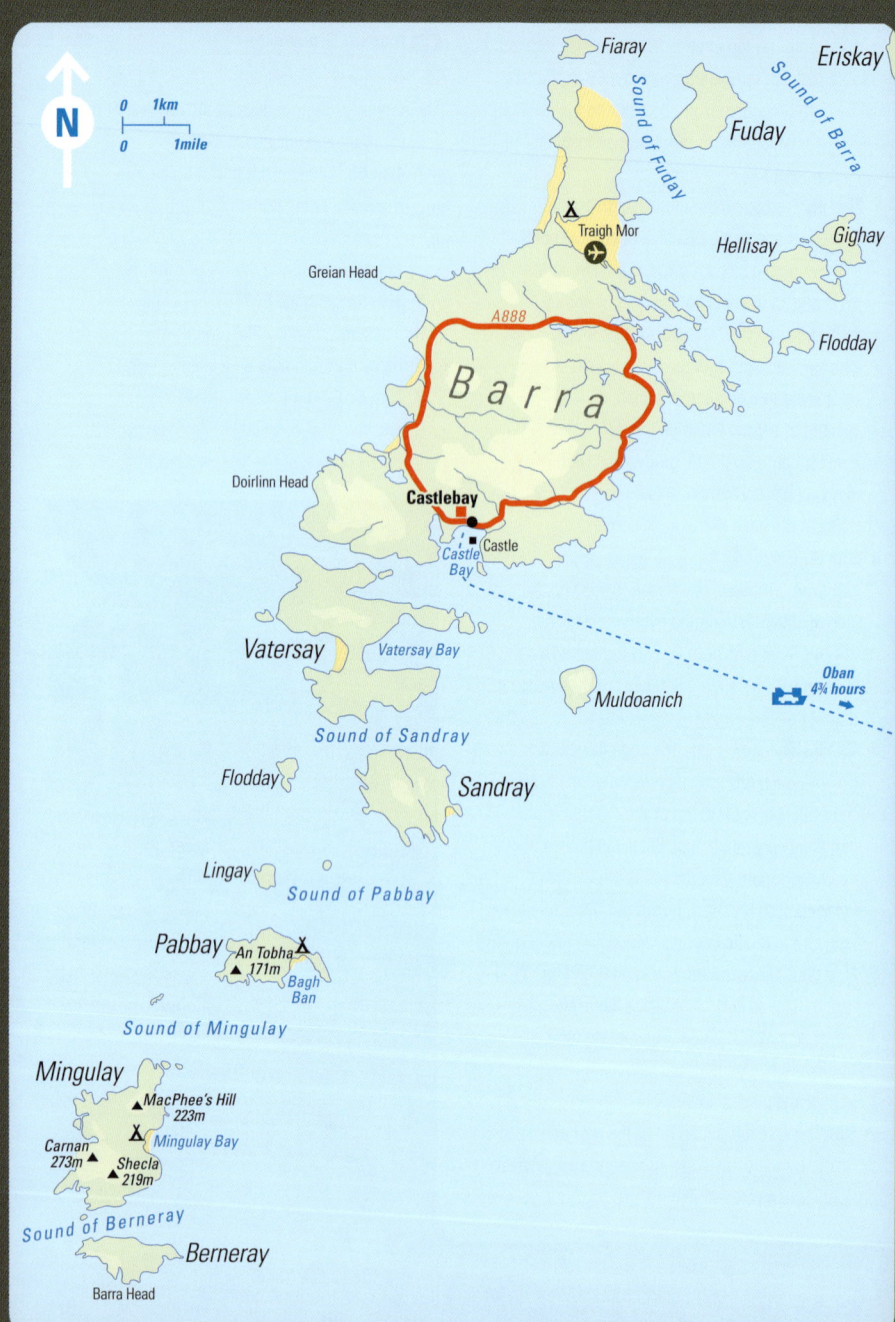

PABBAY & MINGULAY

At the southern extremity of the Western Isles, south of Barra are a collection of small uninhabited islands. Two in particular, Mingulay and Pabbay, rank as some of the finest venues anywhere in the UK. With acres of immaculate weathered Lewisian gneiss, there is still scope for further developments of all grades, if you know where to look. Their remoteness and difficulty of access only adds to their charm. The seriousness of the remote situation should not be underestimated and parties should consider some means of communication (marine band VHF or satellite phone) or at the very least some flares.

Access: Caledonian MacBrayne (☎ 0800 066 5000; www.calmac.co.uk) run a regular daily ferry service (sailing time 4¾ hours) from Oban to Castlebay on Barra. Loganair also operate daily flights from Glasgow to Barra (not Sundays) landing on the beach at Traigh Mhor, 7 miles from Castlebay. Flight time is just over an hour. One of the local fishermen, Francis Gillies transports groups of climbers out to the islands. Costs are arranged at time of booking, capable of carrying 12 plus gear (☎ 01871 810679; www.barrafishingcharters.com).

Accommodation & Amenities: TIC at Buth Bharraigh, a local producer co-operative and community hub (☎ 01871 817948; www.barrashop.co.uk). More information available at www.visitouterhebrides.co.uk or www.isleofbarra.com. Wild camping in Barra is possible on the east side of the bay at Ledaig, though there is no water or facilities, although wild camping in Castlebay is not encouraged. There are a couple of decent-sized supermarkets, a couple of cafés and an **ATM**. **Hostel:** Dunard (☎ 01871 810443; www.dunardhostel.co.uk) lies 300m south of the pier. There are a couple of B&Bs in town, together with pubs in both hotels. The Castlebay Hotel (☎ 01871 810223; www.castlebayhotel.com) serves particularly fine fresh sea food. Do all you can to avoid C&W karaoke in the other one!

Birds: Pabbay, Mingulay and Berneray are all designated as Sites of Special Scientific Interest and Special Protection Areas due to the huge numbers of nesting seabirds. On the cliffs, auks (razorbills, guillemots and puffins), shags, cormorants, kittiwakes and fulmars may all be encountered, breeding between February and mid-July. Disturbance of any birds should be kept to a minimum. The majority of routes described climb clean rock with few nesting birds present, most of which can be avoided. In particular, fulmars have the distinctive trait of vomiting half-digested fish oil when approached on the nest and should be given a wide berth wherever possible. On the hillsides bonxies (great skuas) protect their territory by diving at invaders. On Mingulay the hillsides leading down to Guarsay Mor and Rubha Liath both hold substantial bonxie colonies – be warned! Due to the large number of ground nesting birds, **please do not bring dogs** to the islands.

> *"Not to know the islands is like having a dull sensation at the end of ones fingertips."*
> – Hugh MacDiarmid, *The Islands of Scotland*, BT Batsford Ltd (an imprint of Anova Books Company Ltd), 1939

Abseil ropes: a 100m static is required to access many of the bigger cliffs, along with rope protectors due to some very rough rock/sharp edges. On Mingulay, the **Cobweb Wall** at the southern extremity of Guarsay Mor requires a 130m abseil, but the base can also be gained by traversing in from the adjacent **Undercut Wall** (accessed by 100m abseil).

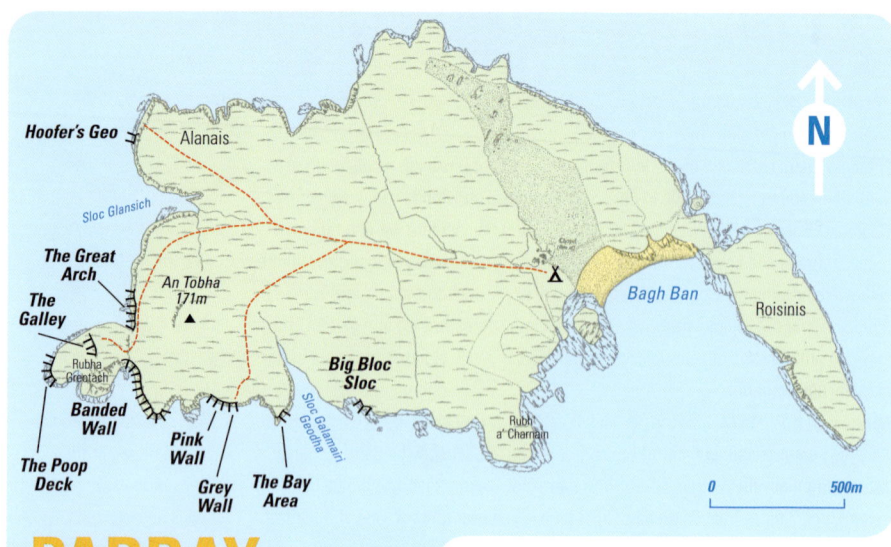

PABBAY

Pabbay lies about 12 kilometres south of Barra, roughly midway between Sandray and Mingulay. Like its southern neighbours, Pabbay slopes up from east to west, presenting a varied selection of cliffs along its southern and western coastlines. With over a dozen different crags and routes of all grades, the island has much to offer a wide range of abilities and aspirations.
The name means hermit's island, or possibly priest's island. The landing place is the sheltered, steeply tilted curve of dazzling white sands of Bagh Ban (white bay) on the east, above which are the ruins of the former settlement. In the 1880s the island held a population of 26, but like the neighbouring Mingulay, the population gradually dwindled in the early years of the century, becoming uninhabited in 1912.

Accommodation & Amenities: The best place to camp is on the area of flat ground at NL 607 873, just over 100m south of the stream.

Crags are described in a clockwise direction from the usual approach from the beach at Bagh Ban.

BIG BLOCK SLOC   NL 600 869

A small open geo east of Sloc Glamarigeo with a very distinctive wedge of clean rock. On the upper seaward side of the wedge a huge block defies gravity.

1 Let Sleeping Storks Lie ★★   25m E4 6a
FA Paul Thorburn & Rick Campbell 27 May 1998

Bold enjoyable climbing up the left arête of the wedge. The crux is protected by micro wires. Belay as for 2 and follow its initial crack as it curves round to the arête. Climb the right wall of the arête then step round to a good hold on the left side under the overlap. Gain the small groove above (crux) then follow it to the break. Climb the right side to the ledge, finishing up the left side of the arête.

2 Lifeline ★★★   25m E3 5c
FA Kev Howett & Graham Little 26 May 1997

Superb climbing up the crack right of 1. Abseil to some footholds at barnacle level just right of the arête. Pull right and climb the crack, step right and follow the continuation crack to a ledge just below the top of the wedge.

3 Immaculate Conception ★★★   25m E2 5c
FA Graham Little & Kev Howett 25 May 1997

Abseil to a small ledge on the outer (southerly) edge of the wedge just above high water line. Move left onto the face to gain a thin ledge. Ascend 3m to a layaway hold in a small hole (protection). Traverse hard left to gain good holds. Climb up into a slim right-facing corner then pull out left just below its capping roof to reach good pockets (common with 2) and thence a break below a roof. Step right and finish up the final corner. Brilliant.

4 Head-Bred-Ian ★★   25m E2 5c
FA Ian Taylor & Tess Fryer May 1999

Climb straight up where 3 traverses left.

At the seaward end is a square-cut bay above tidal ledges. **Descent:** Abseil down the right wall (looking in).

5 Maverick Phenomena ★★   20m HVS 5a
FA Lisa Wright & Paddy Gibson May 2002

Just left of the right arête is a short corner. Climb this and pull right round the overlap then straight up the wall to finish left of the final arête.

THE BAY AREA

The small steep dark alcove (suntrap!) on the tip of the headland that forms the east side of **Shag's Geo**. A wide shelf runs down rightwards beneath the base with only the right (farthest east) routes tidal.

Descent: Go down the headland passing a couple of easy rocky sections then scramble easily down the right (facing out, i.e. west) end of the crag.

The roof and rib is 1 *Baywatch* E3 6a. The crack/black groove on right, or direct up vertical crack is 3 *Honorary Curbar* ★ E1 5c. Starting up this and pulling left into a groove is 2 *Stoney Middleton Lip* ★★ E1 5c. 4 *Irish Rover* ★ E3 6a follows cracks on the left side of the wall left of the next route.

5 Rum, Sodomy and the Lash ★   20m E3 5c
FA Tim Carruthers & Tony Stevenson 26 May 1998

Start 5m further right beneath a left-facing bulging groove. Ascend the groove into a corner and finish up the short corner above.

6 Dogs of Law ★   20m E4 6a
FA Mat Bower & Kev Howett 28 August 1999

The shallow clean-cut corner left of the large corner of 7. Up the steep entry into the shallow corner then its right wall to bulging rock. Undercling right to a ledge on the right arête. Pull up left into a niche below a roof then make tenuous moves left round the arête into a hanging groove and so to a ledge. Finish easily up the wall.

7 The Roaring 40's ★   25m E3 6a
FA Tim Carruthers & Tony Stevenson 28 May 1998

Climb the prominent right-facing corner until 1m below the roof. Pull out left along a sloping break to the arête (crux) in a fine position then *"cruise dreamily"* (?) up the juggy wall.

8 Rebel without a Porpoise Direct ★★★   25m E5 6a
FA Pete & Neil Craig 6 June 2004; Direct Finish: Ali Robb & Niall McNair (on-sight) June 2005; Pegmatite Finish: Paul Thorburn & Rick Campbell June 2005

Start in a black groove just left of the blunt rib left of 9. Climb the groove for a few metres, then right onto the rib. Climb this to the slab under the roof. Make awkward and committing moves leftwards to gain a position above the lip of the lower roof. Continue more easily to the top. **Pegmatite Finish** (8a) takes the scoop on the right;

Original Finish (8b) moves strenuously up and right to a junction with 9.

⑨ The Herbrudean ★★★   20m E5 6a
FA Paul Tanton & Richard Kirby 28 August 1999

Climbs across the impressive steep pegmatite band. Start in the short corner right of 7. Up the corner by difficult bridging to gain a ledge under the roof. Traverse hard right to gain the pink vein and two huge threads under the right end of the roof. Climb the vein (really steep!) then the easier wall above, right of the corner, to the top.

⑩ The Herbaloner ★   20m E6 6b
FA Niall McNair & Ali Robb (on-sight) June 2005

Essentially a dangerous direct start and independent finish to 9. Start 5m to the right of that route and gain the hanging crack on the arête. Climb direct to the pink vein via a very hard and bold move. Gain the huge thread on 9, step right to a hanging corner and right again to finish up a small wall.

⑪ Every Cormorant is a Potential Shag ★★★★   30m E7 6b
FA Dave Birkett (on-sight) 8 June 2008

Superb, sustained well protected climbing. Start at the left side of the big cave beneath the obvious stepped right-facing corner. Make a boulder problem start into the first hanging corner (good R# 7 and F# 1.5). Traverse right to good holds and back left to the V groove. Move up and rightwards into a shallow groove (good holds and gear on the left) to gain the big break under the roof (large cams). Traverse left for 3m using a shattered handrail, then pull through the roof into a shallow corner. Finish up and right.

⑫ B.A.R.T. ★★   20m E5 6a
FA Iain Small & Jonny Clark 5 June 2005

Breaches the main roof where it narrows at the right end of the crag. Start a few metres left of 13. Climb a wall and scoop passing to the left of a roof to gain a large flake-crack. This curves left and leads out left to a rest below a large roof. Follow a handrail out right to make a long reach over the roof for improving holds. Move up and right to a large flat triangular hold then directly to top.

⑬ Jesus Don't Want me as a Shelf Stacker ★★   20m E1 5b
FA Rick Campbell & Malcolm Davies May 1999

Fine climbing up the prominent stepped corner. Pull up through a small roof and bulge to gain a ledge with difficulty. Climb up into the perfect corner above to finish.

⑭ Sea An-enema ★★★   20m E1 5b
FA Roland Strube & Tim Carruthers 28 August 1999

Excellent wild finish. Start as for the corner to the first roof. Climb rightwards across the wall to a downward pointing flake. Up and left into a recess under a capping

Gary Latter starting up the initial corner of The Herbrudean. Photo Paul Thorburn.

roof and pull through direct via a flake-crack leading to the top.

15 Starboard Grooves ★   20m HS 4b
FA Tim Carruthers & Tony Stevenson 26 May 1998

A series of grooves in the arête at the right end of the cove. Scramble rightwards to a ledge above the platform. Move up and step immediately left round the rib. *"Haul joyously"* up grooves to the top.

> The crack/groove in the short steep 10m wall further right is 16 *It's not the size that matters* … VS 4c.

THE PINK WALL NL 596 869

A 120m high wall divided in its central section by a 5m wide terrace at one-third height with the upper section being on much cleaner rock.

Descent: For first 2 routes: At the top are two short rock steps with grass ledges between, the upper one containing a small pool and the lower a large flat block abutting the wall. Make a 70m abseil from this block with the first person down clipping into a few nuts in order to swing into the base. **For remaining routes:** A 70m abseil from a point down and left (facing out, i.e. east) just gains the outer edge of the platform.

> The line of the abseil fault is 1 *Tickled Pink* ★ E2 5a, 5b, 5a.

Pink and Grey Walls
Photo Ian Taylor

Neil Craig on The Ancient Mariners.

PINK & GREY WALLS

2 Where Seagulls Dare ★★   90m E3 5c

FA Leigh McGinley, Mick Pointon & Tom Leppert June 1999

Climbs a line just right of 1. Start as for that route.
1. **10m 5a** Go up the steep cracks to the big ledge.
2. **40m 5c** Pull over the bulge directly above to gain a soaring crack-line which leads to a ledge. *"A truly magnificent experience!"*
3. **40m 5b** Trend up and left over some overlaps to reach the flake-crack of 1. Follow this to the top.

3 Raiders of the Lost Auk ★★   80m E4 5c

FA Paul Thorburn & Rick Campbell 26 May 1998

The central groove and crack-line. Start from a pedestal block at the left end of the large platform.
1. **20m 5c** From the block climb the tricky wall on the left to gain the hanging right-facing groove. Climb it and the cracks above on the right to belay at the left end of a long narrow ledge.
2. **20m 5c** Climb the steepening groove above then make a long traverse left to a vertical crack which leads to a ledge and belay.
3. **40m 5b** From the right end of the ledge follow 5 to the top.

4 Fondue Macpac ★★   70m E6 6b

FA Peter Robins & James McHaffie 2 July 2003

A line up the wall right of 3.
1. **20m 6b** From the small pinnacle at the top of the gully, gain the right side of a small overlap above. Move left and up to a good flake and a steepening. Strenuous moves gain a crack and then a belay on the left side of a small ledge.
2. **50m 6a** Go up a corner and move right to join 5. Pull over the bulge as for that route then move up and right to gain protruding flakes and an undercut break. Continue more easily to the top, first right then left.

5 In Profundum Lacu ★★★★   80m E5 6a

FA Rick Campbell & Paul Thorburn 26 May 1998

'The profound abyss'. The next line right.
1. **40m 6a** Step right off the block to gain cracks and follow them into the hanging V-groove (crux). Climb up and left to a long narrow ledge. Make awkward moves up the crack on the right then gain a left-facing flake. Traverse left and gain a pegmatite flake above the bulge. Continue up left to gain and climb a bottomless groove. Belay on the left.

2 40m 5b Climb a crack on the right and continue to a steep, blocky left-facing groove. Climb this and continue straight up to finish.

6 The Bonxie ★★★★ 75m E6 6b
FA Gary Latter, Rick Campbell & Malcolm Davies (hanging belay) 15 May 2000; as described Paul Thorburn & Rick Campbell June 2005

The long continuous crack system. Sustained and very well protected. Start beneath a short vertical crack.

1 35m 6b Climb the crack and traverse left along a rounded break to the main crack system. Make a long reach past a good undercut to a big jug and continue up the crack, which soon forms twin deep cracks. Continue up these and a third crack higher up to an obvious break beneath the pegmatite band (possible belay). Layback the central of three flared cracks above and pull out left to a jug. Move right up a short diagonal crack tenuously to undercuts. Pull through these to gain good flakes leading up left to a belay.

2 40m 5c Finish as for 8.

7 Huffin' 'n' Puffin ★★★ 75m E6 6b
FA Trevor Wood & Gary Latter 5 June 2005

Another excellent sustained main pitch.

1 30m 6b Start up a short crack between 6 & 8. Climb the crack to a break, stand on this and reach a small flake. Make hard moves up the wall to reach another flake then trend left following flakes. Atop the second flake/plinth, make hard moves up a shield to a break. Traverse left to the original hanging belay on 6.

2 45m 6b Follow 6 until the jugs after the undercuts. Then direct through a black niche and bulges until below an obvious weakness. Pull through this on slopey holds (crux) and continue more easily to the top.

7a Huffin' 'n' Puffin Direct ★★★ 40m E6 6b
FA Sam Williams & Uisdean Hawthorn 15 June 2014

This version follows a more natural obvious line, avoiding the second hard pitch. Follow the original route to the break. Instead of traversing off left to the original hanging belay on *The Bonxie*, make hard moves directly up to reach the crack system on *I Suppose…* Follow this to the huge undercut flake. Instead of going direct over this (crux of *I Suppose…*), hand-jam out right until possible to join the flakes of *The Ancient Mariners* and follow this to its belay. Finish up that route.

8 I Suppose a Cormorant's out of the Question Then? ★★★ 85m E5 6b
FA Rick Campbell & Paul Thorburn 25 May 1998

The most distinct feature on the right side of the wall is a large left-facing hanging corner. The route gains and follows this feature. Start below and right of a series of strange flakes beneath the corner.

1 20m 5c Gain and climb the flakes then follow the diminishing flake-line on the right to a break (crux). Traverse more easily left and go up the easy corner to belay halfway up.

2 25m 6b Climb to the top of the corner, traverse left to some pockets and a crack in the roof and pull through this and up to a huge undercut and good rest. Make difficult moves straight up to pegmatite flakes then undercut left to gain a diagonal line of flakes leading up left to belay in a break.

3 40m 5c Step left then climb a steepening to make an awkward pull left onto a shelf. Continue up a groove to another shelf. Traverse left below a steep wall then step left around a lichenous arête and finish directly.

9 The Ancient Mariners ★★★★ 85m E5 6a
FA Paul Thorburn & Rick Campbell 25 May 1998

Follows cracks right of the hanging corner of 8. Start as for that route. Low in the grade.

1 40m 6a Climb the flakes and make a hard pull right before the break. Climb the cracks above until a flared crack is encountered. Climb the groove to the right then traverse left to gain the pegmatite flakes. Follow these past a pair of spikes to the break. Traverse right and belay under a groove with a short wide crack.

2 45m 5a Ascend the groove to a ledge then continue in the same line, joining 10 to finish.

10 What More Puffin! ★★★   80m E6 6b
FA Steve Crowe and Karin Magog 15 May 2003; as described Steve Crowe and Karin Magog 9 June 2007

The grooved arête on the right edge of the wall.

1 40m 6b The initial arête has a crack on both sides. Start by climbing either crack to gain the ledge, then move up to the Y-shaped crack. Move up then left to fingerlock powerfully through a steep bulge (just right of 9) and gain a good break and awkward kneebar rest. Tip toe rightwards on good crimps to regain the arête and move up steeply to a huge 'thank god' flake. Teeter right to reach easy ground and a good belay in a superbly exposed position on the very edge.

2 40m 5a Move left again to join and finish as for 9.

11 The Guga ★★★★   90m E5 6b
FA Paul Thorburn & Rick Campbell 27 May 1997

The inaugural route on the wall, climbing the large weakness left of the junction between the pink and grey side wall. Start at the base of a black overhanging corner 10m left of the arête. Quite spectacular.

1 20m 6a Climb the corner with a difficult exit left onto a ledge then move up the overhanging wall on the right to belay on a ramp.

2 25m 6b Climb the corner system on the right then make hard moves through the bulge to gain the left-arching pegmatite bulge. Follow this to a crack then move up then rightwards to gain a ledge. Belay on the ledge on the left.

3 45m 4c Climb up left from the belay then follow a direct line to the top.

THE GREY WALL

The wall round the edge from **The Pink Wall**, running into the deep recess.

12 Amber Nectar ★★★   105m E5 6a
FA Rick Campbell & Gary Latter (ground-up) 15 May 2001

A route of considerable character, climbing the right edge of the wall. Start at the base of the left-facing groove at the right side of the wall.

1 15m 5a Climb the groove to belay on the upper of two ledges.

2 30m 6a Move left and up on flakes into a hanging groove. Traverse left and up another flake system to a roof in the pegmatite band. Cross this on good holds and step right to belay at the top of pitch 2 of *Spit in Paradise*.

3 25m 5c Traverse the break leftwards, swing round the corner and climb a groove to the terrace.

4 35m 5a Climb a short corner, pull left at its top and follow a line of stepped corners leftwards to the top.

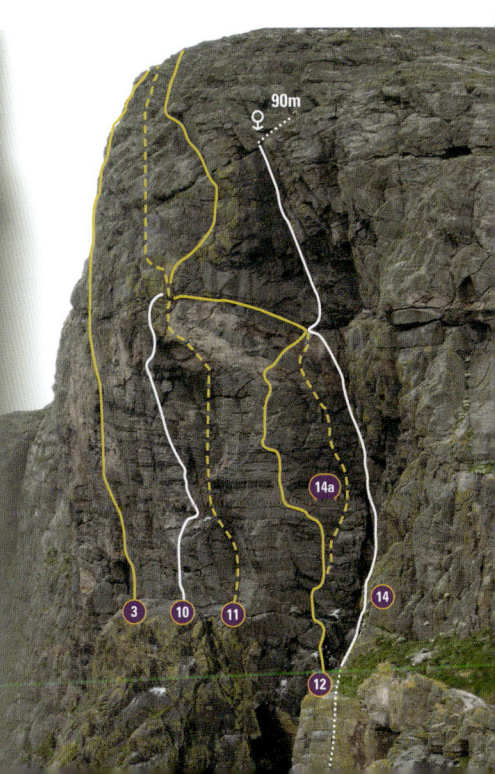

14a Elysium ★★★   35m E4 6a
FA Gary Latter & Rick Campbell (on-sight) 13 May 2001

An excellent pitch up the prominent left-slanting groove bounding the right edge of the wall. Start up the initial groove as for 12 to the second ledge (15m – possible belay). Continue up the orange wall on large flakes leading to a left-facing groove. Climb this, stepping right at the top past a birdy ledge to a thread belay, as for 14. (Climbed this way avoids all the bird shit on pitch 1 of *Spit in Paradise* and the loose chimney at the start of the original way.)

GREY WALL RECESS

Descent: From the high ground above the cliff descend eastwards towards the sea until a grassy terrace with a superb view of **Shag's Geo** is reached. At its west end are jammed boulders above the top of a huge corner. Make a 90m free hanging abseil from the back of the chimney slot formed by a huge boulder (90m rope essential) to the base of the routes – enjoy the ride!

13 Bravura ★★★   100m E7 6b
FA Gary Latter & Rick Campbell (ground-up) p1 15 May 2002; p2 17 May 2002 ; p3 Iain Small & Rick Campbell 15 June 2008

Stunning very sustained climbing up the twin intermittent cracks up the left side of the main wall just right of the arête. Start at the right end of the sea-level platform beneath a short blunt arête.

1. **55m 6a** Arrange a runner/belay in an obvious deep triangular slot up in the right side of the arête. Make hard moves up left side of arête then pull rightwards and up into a groove. Continue up this, passing an overhung jam slot with interest, leading to easier ground. Direct up a crack to belay on a platform directly beneath the arête.
2. **25m 6b** A stunning pitch. Climb a wide gritty crack up the left side of the arête to the top of the pedestal. Hard moves lead past cams in pockets (Camalot # 0.1 crucial) to a good hold in a crack almost on the arête. Move up right and follow the crack system, eventually transferring to a further crack system on the right which eases to a fine finger-crack leading up into an easier short left-facing corner. Belay in this.
3. **20m 6b** Make a long move right from top of groove to hidden flake-crack, bear right and up to flake letterbox (F #0.5) and using a small ear in grey rock above pull with difficulty into huge break on *Amber Nectar*. Trend left along this before awkward moves up and left gain the crack arching in from the left. Follow crack through bulge and follow it right desperately to where it turns vertical and easier. Continue up and right to belay.

14 Spit in Paradise ★★★   105m E4 6a
FA Rolf Witt & Jo Fischer (on-sight) 19 May 1995

Start down and right of an overhanging crack at 15m.

1. **45m 5c** Climb direct over birdy ledges to gain the overhanging crack. Climb this with interest then bear right on easier ground to a good ledge.
2. **35m 6a** Trend left towards a wide overhanging crack and up this to a ledge. Step right to climb the wall right of a prominent corner system to a huge roof. Trend left through overhanging cracks in the pegmatite band (crux) to gain a ledge and good thread belays.
3. **25m 6a** Gain the final corner direct over a couple of roofs and follow this to finish in the abseil slot. An excellent pitch.

15 More Steam McPhail! ★★★   35m E6 6b
FA Paul Thorburn & Rick Campbell 6 June 2005

The undercut flake and wall up the grossly leaning right wall of the final pitch of *Spit in Paradise*. Very well protected. Gain the huge thread belay at the base of the top corner of that route by abseil, placing a few nuts on the way down to maintain contact with the rock!

Undercut out right and climb the strenuous and sustained wall past numerous breaks, with difficult moves above the ledge near the top.

16 U-Ei ★★★ 110m E2 5b

FA Ralf Gantzhorn & Susanne Wacker (on-sight) 19 May 1995

The first pitch ascends the left side of the slabby wall that runs into the sea. Start 5m above the wave washed platform just right of a prominent seepage line.

1 **50m 5b** Climb the wall on good rock for 25m then step left into a short hanging corner. Climb this to the roof and traverse out left to a comfortable ledge.

2 **30m 5a** Follow an easy corner to an overhanging block. Pass this to the right then move left above to gain a commodious belay ledge.

3 **30m 5b** Climb up to an overhang, traverse right underneath it to gain the base of the final fine overhanging corner system. Climb this to finish by a left-slanting ramp.

16a U-th ★★★ 30m E3 5c

FA Tess Fryer & Ian Taylor 12 June 2007

Well protected and low in the grade. Left of pitch 2 of *U-Ei* is a soaring slightly right-trending crack. Gain the crack from the right and follow it through roofs and bulges to join *U-Ei* below its final pitch.

17 The Vital Spark ★★ 70m E6 6a,6b

FA Iain Small & Tony Stone 10 June 2013

Climb the crack right of *U-th*, then the super steep right arête of the *More Steam McPhail* wall.

18 Mixmaster Snipe ★★ 100m E1 5b

FA Malcolm Davies, Paul Newman & Gary Latter (on-sight) 12 May 2002

A direct line up the left side of the right wall of the recess. Start at the base of the prominent crack system right of *U-Ei*.

1 **40m 5b** Climb the crack direct through the prominent roof (or easier on the right) and continue in the same line, trending up right to belay on a good ledge.

2 **30m 5b** Continue up the prominent right-facing corner above then in the same line to traverse left along a shelf to a belay.

3 **30m 5b** Move left and climb a short steep right-slanting groove then continue up a crack system, finishing direct.

Photo Steve Crowe.

㊆ Paradise Regained ★★★   115m E4 6a
FA Ian Taylor & Tess Fryer 12 May 2002

Spectacular climbing through some impressive ground. Finishing up the final pitch of *U-Ei* would give a three star E2.
1. **45m 5a** Start approx. 20m right of *U-Ei*. Climb a crack-line through a small overlap to belay in a niche.
2. **30m 5c** Trend up and leftwards to a hanging corner between two large roofs. Pull left into the corner then follow cracks to a belay on a ledge below the final corner of *U-Ei*.
3. **15m 5b** Traverse left along a break to belay below the final pitch of *Spit in Paradise*. Very exposed.
4. **25m 6a** The final pitch of *Spit in Paradise*.

BANDED WALL

NL 592 871

An excellent long 60m wall crossed by a quartz-feldspar band near the centre.
Descent: At low tide and calm seas routes at the left end (as far as 7) can be gained by traversing rightwards at about 5a. **Abseil points:** for *Ship of Fools* area, abseil slightly northwards from first of three blocks (north of the wall) initially down a grassy hollow, placing some gear in order to maintain contact with the rock.
For *Spring Squill* go straight down from the first block.
For routes in the centre: Abseil down the prominent chimney-corner line of *Corncrake Corner* from the third (farthest south) large boulder set well back with a rope passing at the side of another large boulder just south of the old wall.

Niall McNair flexing on the steep Vomtanion and the Three Punterneers.

① Chockarockaholic **   65m E2 5b
FA Kev Howett & Graham Nicoll May 1998

A spectacular line up the brown walls above the boulders. Belay on the traverse ledges just past the boulders.

1. **40m 5a** Pull steeply up the stepped rib to a horizontal break then up a smaller diagonal crack trending right up the wall to meet the main diagonal crack at its right end. Go up the wall above rightwards to gain a small ledge leading left to a shattered ledge next to luminous green moss/grass. Poor belay on micros.
2. **25m 5b** Pull up the steep groove past flakes and blocks directly above the vegetation to gain a large slabby corner. Trend left across the slab to the arête and climb it to beneath a roof. Finish up a hanging ramp above.

② Geomancer ***   45m E6 6b
FA Niall McNair & Paul Newman May 2003

A stupendous line to the left of 3. Start up a black groove until an obvious traverse can be made out to the roof. Tackle the roof via pockets and a small right-facing flange (crux). Once on the headwall trend slightly left heading for a large pod/flake. Attack the bulge directly above to reach the capping roof/corner. Escape right along this to a belay.

③ Ship of Fools ****   45m E5 6b
FA Paul Thorburn & Rick Campbell 28 May 1998

Stunning super-sustained climbing up the acutely overhanging wall. From the easy ramp below the wall climb boldly up on biotite to gain the slanting roof 4m left of its lowest point. Gain the flake above the lip with difficulty and move up left to cross the bulge by some flakes. Continue straight up until the rock becomes noticeably compact (calcite). Move up and right then back left through a bulge then up right again to pull through another bulge to gain a flake. Step right past a detached flake into a black niche. Step right and climb direct to belay on a slab.

④ Jonny Scuttlebutt ***   45m E5 6a
FA Niall McNair & Ali Robb June 2007

Climbs the wall right of 3. Climb that route to the roof. At the rib at the lowest point of the roof (good Camalot #2 1m right) gain the wall above. Climb slightly left then follow the line of least resistance to an obvious crack in steep brown rock near the top. Finish up this.

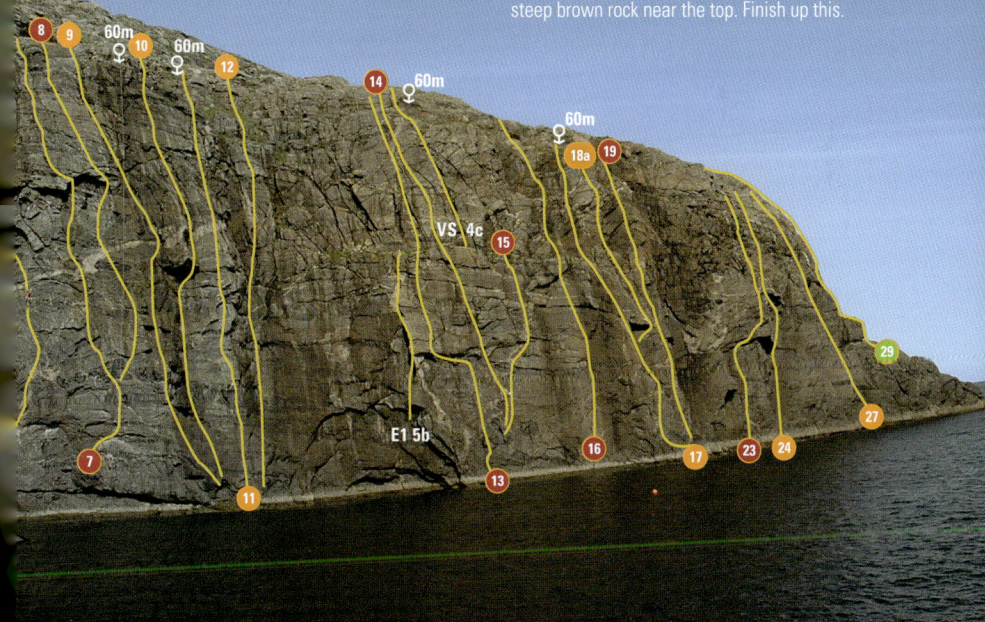

5 Vomtanion and the Three Punterneers ★★
50m E5 6a

FA James McHaffie, Tim Badcock & Pete Robins 4 July 2003

A line up the right side of the wall. Start from the left end of the main ledge. Climb easily up a shallow groove for about 10m to a steepening. Step left beneath the upper of two overlaps; continue awkwardly left for 3m to some large undercuts and a rest. Move up on small holds (crux) to gain a break. A short traverse right gains a flake. Climb more or less directly past some ledges and a vague crack to a final bulge and the top.

6 Endolphin Rush ★★★★
60m E3 5c

FA Kev Howett & Graham Little 27 May 1997

A magnificent and strenuous route on excellent rock. Start by abseiling to the long low ledge below and to the left of the start of 7.

1. **25m 5c** Climb up to and follow the right-trending wide band of pegmatite across the wall until moves can be made up into a crack-line and good rest. Follow this to belay on a small ledge directly underneath big roofs. A pumpy lower half on big holds.
2. **35m 5b** Move up to the big roof then step down and left onto the lip of another roof. Climb a short overhanging wall using a fat black spike to gain a ledge below another worryingly detached roof. Move left to bypass this and finish directly on big holds.

7 Spring Squill ★★★★
55m E1 5b

FA Andy Cunningham & Grahame Nicoll 30 May 1995

Stunning climbing – one of the best pitches of its grade on the islands. Move up and right from the right end of a long ledge to a smaller ledge with a flake and thread belay.

1. **30m 5b** Follow a flake-line rightwards to a ledge then trend steeply back left into the leftmost of two short cracks which leads to easier ground. Move up a vague depression past a huge down-pointing flake then climb a crack through a bulge (crux) and up to belay under a long overhang on the left.
2. **25m 5a** Pull out left through the narrowing in the overhang (thread) and continue directly to the top.

8 Stealing a Seal's Gaze ★★
65m E1 5b

FA Kev Howett & Alistair Todd 15 May 1998

Start as for 7.

1. **30m 5a** Follow 7 up flakes to the steep wall. Move up and right across a black biotite band to under a small isolated overlap. Step right under it and pull over. Climb direct then slightly right into the top of a shallow groove (junction with 9).
2. **35m 5b** Climb out left to a thin crack leading to a quartz band. Move left and up and left into a depression, (above and right of that on 7) below the widest section of the roofs above. Pull out left through the roof and follow a discontinuous crack to the top.

9 Oh No, Norman's in Reverse! ★
65m HVS 5a

FA Grahame Nicoll & Andy Cunningham 30 May 1995

Belay on a tiny ledge at the base of a black slab.

1. **40m 5a** Climb leftwards up the slab to a prominent break in the left arête of the corner. Swing left onto the wall and move up past an awkward little overhang to a ledge on the right.
2. **25m 4a** Move left and follow an orange ramp leading to easy ground.

10 Corncrake Corner ★★
65m HVS 5a

FA Grahame Nicoll & Andy Cunningham 30 May 1995

The prominent chimney-corner.

1. **40m 5a** Climb up into the deep chimney, up this then climb the right wall of the corner to pass an overhang. A quartz-feldspar bulge above leads to easier ground and a ledge in common with the previous route.
2. **25m 4b** Finish directly up the wall above.

11 Spooky Pillar ★★
65m HVS 5a

FA Andy Cunningham & Grahame Nicoll 30 May 1995

The pillar to the right of the prominent chimney-corner of 10.

1. **40m 5a** Climb direct through the bulges slightly left of the edge until a move left round the edge at the top leads into a crack. Climb this to a good ledge and belay.
2. **25m 4a** Climb directly above.

Right of 11 is a flaky corner then two long smooth walls separated by a prominent left-facing corner.

12 Oatcakes for lunch **   50m HVS 5b
FA Ben Darvill & Ian Lovatt June 2004

1. **25m 5a** Start at the base of the easy slab beneath the corner. Climb the slab then direct through bulges, keeping just left of the corner. Finish up a satisfying crack to belay on a 'textbook' stance.
2. **25m 4b** Step right from the stance onto the slabby wall and climb straight up, tackling the juggy overhang to finish.

THE SHIELD

Further south, beyond a more broken section a prominent wide ledge at just over half height divides a fine smooth lower wall, the left section dropping straight into the sea. There are tidal ledges (mid-low tide) at its southern end. Triple cracks towards the left end of the upper section provide pleasant easier finishes.

Descent: The first 4 routes are all accessed by a 50m abseil from a large boulder on the edge of the grass terrace at the top. Hanging belays – calm seas preferred. For rightmost (southern) routes, abseil from good anchors 20m further south.

13 Hyperballad ***   55m E3 5c
FA Lawrence Hughes & Grahame Nicoll 27 May 1997

Tackles a line up the left side of the wall. Start at a foot-ledge 4m right of the base of the corner. Low in the grade.

1. **30m 5c** Climb directly up to an overhang, traverse 6m left and pull spectacularly through at a crack. Continue to the large ledge.
2. **25m 4c** Easy cracks and slabs lead to the top.

14 Mollyhawk **   50m E1 5b
FA Grahame Nicoll & Lawrence Hughes 27 May 1997

1. **25m 5b** Belay at a plaque and small foot-ledge about 5m above barnacle level. Climb a short groove and move up left into a shallow left-trending groove and crack leading to the large ledge.
2. **25m 4c** Easy cracks and slabs lead to the top.

15 The Posture Jedi **   25m E2 5c
FA Gary Latter & Andy Lole 5 June 2006

Start from the same belay as 14. Trend up rightwards and follow superb hidden holds to break through the roof where it dwindles at its right end. Continue easily up left to a large ledge. Low in the grade.

16 A Horizontal Desire *   40m E2 5c
FA Andy Lole & Gary Latter 5 June 2006

Start from a belay in the vertical crack at the base of a right-facing groove right of the main roof system. Climb the groove to below a roof then break out left up a crack. Easier ground leads to the top.

17 Stretch it Out *   60m VS 4c
FA Andy Cunningham & Fraser Fotheringham 23 June 1996

1. **40m 4c** Swing left round the edge from the base of 18 then move up and left into a corner. Follow the corner then continue left onto a large ledge.
2. **20m 4a** Climb straight through the bulge above to finish up easy ground.

18 Warm Up *   40m Severe 4b
FA Ralf Gantzhorn & Rolf Witt 18 May 1995

Start at the right side of the main wall. Climb a crack-line to gain a corner, step left below the prominent roof then up a slab for 7m to gain a ledge. Finish up darker rock.

18a One Foot in the Grave **   45m VS 4c
FA Andy Lole, Fergus Murray & Gary Latter 6 June 2006

Climb the initial corner of 18 but continue to the roof and traverse right underneath it. Finish up a fine easy groove and wall above.

19 Run Daftie Run ★★ 45m E1 5b
FA Andy Lole & Gary Latter 5 June 2006

The right arête of 18. Climb easily up the wall on the left to protection in a black plaque. Step right to good holds on the arête then up the right side and continue more easily directly.

20 Squat Thrust ★ 60m HS 4b
FA Fraser Fotheringham & Andy Cunningham 23 June 1996

1 **40m 4b** Start beneath the open black chimney. Ascend this and the groove above to a ledge. Break rightwards across the wall and go up to a ledge.
2 **20m** — Easy ground leads to the top.

20a Squat Thrust – Right Finish ★★ 40m HVS 5a
FA Gary Latter & Andy Lole 5 June 2006

Climb the initial chimney corner of 20, stepping up right to a shallow groove in the arête and finish directly.

21 Prominent Nasty Looking Off-width Groove ★★ 50m E2 5b
FA Ian Taylor & Glyn Stanworth May 2001

The prominent offwidth groove – not nasty at all as it turns out.

22 Blo' na Gael ★ 50m E3 5c
FA Andy Cunningham & Fraser Fotheringham 23 June 1996

Upgraded since a rock fall has substantially altered the start.

1 **35m 5c** Climb the right edge of the wall right of the groove. Pull through the undercut and move up and left into a curving crack. Move right into a thin crack and up this to a bulge on the edge. Go right through the bulge then move back left and up deep cracks leading to a ledge.
2 **15m 4a** Continue direct through gnarly ground and corners to finish.

23 Wind Against Tide ★★ 50m E1 5b
FA Andy Cunningham & Fraser Fotheringham 23 June 1996

Ascend the right wall of the corner right of 22 to a large horizontal break. Traverse rightwards along the break until level with large roofs. Follow a thin crack then move up and right to a good ledge. Finish more or less directly up easy ground.

23a Wind Against Tide – Right Start ★★ 30m E1 5b
FA Gary Latter & Andy Lole 6 June 2006

Start from the belay at the base of 24. Step left round the arête and follow grooves to gain the wide horizontal fault at the base of the thin crack.

24 Tide Race ★★★ 35m VS 4b
FA Stan Pearson & Alisdair Cain May 1998

The corner system with a small triangular ledge at the base. Climb the corner, turning the first roof on the right. Traverse left beneath the main roof to the edge of the buttress and a junction with 23. Finish straight up.

25 Cup Final ★ 35m VS 5a
FA Stan Pearson & Alisdair Cain May 1998

Climb the wall on flakes to a ledge.

26 Stiff Upper Lip ★ 40m VS 4c
FA Phil Swainson & John Given May 1997

Climb the first crack of 27. Traverse left and turn the overhang on the left to finish up a groove.

27 Steife Breise ★★ 40m VS 4c
FA Jo Fischer & Andreas Seeger 18 May 1995

The corner. Climb direct to a roof, cross this on the right then ascend the corner above on flakes to reach easier ground.

28 At Last ★ 35m VS 4c
FA Stan Pearson & Alisdair Cain May 1998

Climb the easy slab into a prominent left-facing corner. Cross the bulge and finish more easily.

29 Bald Eagle ★ 40m Very Difficult
FA John Given & Phil Swainson May 1997

The spur separating the west and south faces of the wall.

SOUTH FACE

Left looking down (east) of the prominent spur is a large non-tidal shelf along the base.
Descent: Abseil down the spur.

The roof on the prow is 1 *Partial Bastard* • E3 6a.

2 Silver Fox * — 40m HS 4b
FA Phil Swainson & John Given May 1997

Start 5m right (east) of the spur. Ascend the left-facing corner and undercut crack – a gritstone climber's delight.

3 Treasure Island * — 30m VS 4b
FA Jonathan Preston & Graeme Ettle 7 June 2004

Start below a small roof. Climb a black slabby wall to the roof (a ragged crack on the left). Pass the roof on the right and continue up to a superb flake-crack which is followed to the top.

4 Grey Cossack * — 30m VS 4c
FA John Lyall & Malcolm Davies 14 May 2001

The rib just right of 2. Over a roof then up a left facing corner and flakes to the top.

5 The Curious Bulge * — 30m HVS 5a
FA Carl Pulley & Mike Mortimer 5 June 2006

The left-facing corner high on the face. Follow a rib to break through an overlap via a jug. Follow the orange slab to gain the bulging wall. Swing right into the corner and follow it to the top.

6 Yob and Yag Go Climbing – Part 2 ** — 30m E2 5b
FA Alan McSherry & Mike Howard May 1998

The left crack through the triple roofs.

7 Shags and the City * — 30m HVS 5b
FA Mike Mortimer & Carl Pulley 5 June 2006

The right crack through the triple roofs. After the second roof, follow a crack to the right of the final offwidth crack.

8 The Elephant of Surprise ** — 30m HVS 5a
FA Andy Lole & Gary Latter 6 June 2006

The leftmost of the triple cracks, gained by traversing in from either of the adjacent routes.

9 Redundancy Man *** — 30m HVS 5a
FA Stan Pearson & Alisdair Cain May 1998

The central crack.

10 Bye Bye to the Widows *** — 30m HVS 5b
FA Stan Pearson & Alisdair Cain May 1998

Climb through the roof to gain the rightmost crack.

11 Shipping Views ★   35m E1 5b/c
FA Malcolm Davies & John Lyall 14 May 2001

Wall 3m right of 10 to break through the right end of the grey roof. Follow a crack up the right edge then cracks through the roof system.

12 Off Wid Emily's Bikini ★★   35m E2 5b
FA Carl Pulley & Mike Mortimer 5 June 2006

The right-facing corner in the first recess. Follow this into an offwidth/chimney. Cut loose right and go up an overhanging flaky corner to the roof. Swing left to join 11.

13 Cereal Killer ★★   35m HVS 5a/b
FA John Lyall & Malcolm Davies 13 May 2001

First line right of the recess at the right end of the ledge system. Climb a left-facing quartzy corner then cracks through a roof system.

14 Ice Box Prose ★   35m HVS 5a
FA Ross Jones & Mark Gear 6 June 2003

Right-facing corner 4m left of 15, finishing up cracks in the wall.

15 Wine Box Chimney ★   35m E1 5b
FA Alec Erskine & Jez Wardman 6 June 2003

Chimney 2m left of the corner then a short corner (crux), finishing up a steep wall. The last 5m is common with 14.

16 Corn Choked Corner ★★   35m HVS 5a
FA John Lyall & Malcolm Davies 13 May 2001

Right corner with a steep finish through a slot.

17 Refrigerator Poetry ★★   35m HVS 5a
FA Ross Jones & Mark Gear 6 June 2003

Centre of the wall between a corner and crack.

18 Muses from Afar ★   35m VS 4c
FA Ross Jones & Mark Gear 6 June 2003

Traverse right from the corner and climb a crack up the centre of the wall.

Gary Latter on the first ascent of The Posture Jedi (page 401). Photo Andy Lole.

THE CAVE

1 Redemption Ark ★★★   25m E6 6b
FA Niall McNair & Dan McManus June 2007

The first route to breach the impressive 'gothic' cave at the far right end. At the bottom of the geo is a boulder choke with the innermost boulder the size of a small car. Start on top of this. Step hard left for 3m into a wildly overhanging groove/corner system and follow this to a wall and an obvious bow-shaped crack. Take the crack rightwards and up to a step out right under the overhang. Hanging belay from good flakes and quartz spikes on the right. Abseil off (recommended!), or continue (XS 5b, 5c – loose and wet) traversing left to a black corner (30m), finishing up the slimmest of three corner systems.

RUBHA GREOTACH

The most westerly tip of the island contains two immaculate wave-washed walls, **The Galley** and **The Poop Deck**.

NL 589 871

THE GALLEY

The first cliff encountered when heading west out to the headland. Routes described from right to left.

Descent: Scramble down either of two ramp-corner lines near the north side of the headland, the northmost one being easiest.

Note: A large rock fall has left overhanging starts to the following four routes, raising the grade to 5a/b to gain the ledge above the overhung base. The original grades as below are for an abseil approach.

1 Wu-Tang Will Survive ★   30m HVS 5a
FA Lawrence Hughes & Grahame Nicoll 25 May 1997

Start as for 2. Follow a diagonal line rightwards across the wall to finish at the right end of the big roof.

2 Winos in a Barren Land ★★   25m E3 5c
FA Kev Howett & Grahame Little 23 June 1996

Breaks through the roof on the right side of the crag. Traverse the prominent break along the base of the wall (low tide preferable) to belay in the base of a small right-facing corner. Climb the corner to below the roof. Pull left through the roof with difficulty and finish up the wall above.

3 Conch Corner ★   25m VS 4c
FA Grahame Nicoll & Lawrence Hughes 25 May 1997

Left of 2 are two parallel disjointed corners. This route climbs the rightmost of these. Start by climbing rightwards to gain and climb the steep flaky corner. Take care with blocks at the top.

4 Wu-Tang Forever ★   25m E1 5b
FA Lawrence Hughes & Grahame Nicoll 25 May 1997

Follow 3 for a few metres then pull left through a bulge (crux) to gain and climb the leftmost corner-line.

5 Wiggly Wall ★★★   20m HVS 5a
FA Grahame Nicoll, Mel Crowther & Jim Lowther 23 June 1996

The clean wall in the centre of the crag. Traverse in from the left then climb up to a ledge beneath the main wall. Climb first rightwards then direct to finish up a crack that forms the left side of a huge block. An eliminate climbs the wall between 5 and 6 – E2 5b ★★.

6 The Abridged Version ★   20m Severe 4a
FA Graham Little, Jim Lowther & Kev Howett 23 June 1996

The large corner left of 5. Start on the left side of projecting lower buttress. Climb steeply to gain the ledge below the corner and follow this steeply on good holds.

7 Anthology Arête ★★   20m HVS 5a
FA Grahame Nicoll & Bill Wright 14 May 1998

The arête direct to finish at a beak of rock.

8 The Complete Works ★★   20m Severe 4a
FA Grahame Nicoll, Mel Crowther & Jim Lowther 24 June 1996

Start as for 6. Ascend the left corner, finishing up a ramp and an overhang (crux).

9 Jesus Made Me Stumpy ★★   25m VS 4c
FA Tim Carruthers & Paul Trower August 1998

The arête left of 8. Follow the initial corner of that route to a black band. Traverse left round the arête, then ascend a slim groove, passing the roof on its right. Finish up cracks in the slab.

10 Yob and Yag Go Climbing ★   25m HVS 4c
FA Alan McSherry & Mike Howard May 1998

Left of 8 is a severely undercut grey wall with a bottomless corner capped by a large roof left again. Ascend 8 for 5m until an obvious sloping foothold on the left arête can be reached. Traverse left round the arête and climb diagonally up and left across the grey wall into the corner. Climb this, going left past the roof.

11 Absolution ★★   10m E1 5b
FA Ross Jones & Mike Snook 4 June 1999

Climb the right-facing hanging corner to a horizontal crack then the small crack above.

THE POOP DECK

An excellent long steep wall above a convenient wide platform. Only the last few routes at the extreme right (south) end are tidal.

Descent: Abseil from any point along the crag top, a small inset corner at the top of *Bogus Asylum Seekers* in the centre being the most convenient spot.

1 Poop ★   20m Very Difficult
FA Grahame Nicoll (solo) 24 May 1997

The left end of the wall is formed by a curious projecting nose with a razorbill-covered ledge high up on its right side. Climb easily up the crest of the nose, move left and finish up a short V-chimney (crux). The square-cut corner on the left gives a less brutal finish.

NL 588 871

2 One Last Look ★★   25m E4 6b
FA Paul Thorburn & Rick Campbell 29 May 1998

The far left end of the acutely overhanging wall has a shallow recess with a large pegmatite vein up its right wall. Go easily up to a man-size spike then climb cracks up the recess. Hand traverse right through the roof. Make hard moves into a scoop to gain a hole on the right. Step left then direct to the top.

3 101 Damnations ★★★★   25m E7 6b
FA Paul Thorburn, Rick Campbell & Gary Latter (redpointed) 9 June 2004

Stupendous sustained climbing, tackling the twin hanging cracks up the centre of the wall. Start up the first few moves as for 4 then pull up and left onto the incut shelf above (skyhook in pocket). Make a hard move rocking

over to gain the horizontal break above (good runners) and move left and follow the cracks, mainly following the right one to pull into a large break beneath the roof (cams to 5"). Move left to pull rightwards though the roof with very difficult moves to stand on the lip. Continue much more easily directly up the wall above.

4. The Raven ★★★★   25m E5 6a
FA Paul Thorburn & Rick Campbell 25 May 1997

Excellent sustained climbing. Three continuous cracks breach the ludicrously-steep left side of the crag above the pool. Climb the left crack, gained from the left of the pool to the roof. Pull through this at a hairline crack to a large hidden hold then move up to the large break. Step left then direct up the wall past some shallow pockets to the top.

5. Thursday's Setting Sunrise ★★   25m E5 6a
FA Paul Thorburn & Rick Campbell 28 May 1998

The central crack. Start up the rightmost crack then traverse left to a niche or gain the same point by stepping off a boulder in the pool. Difficult and committing moves lead to a jug then climb the crack to the break. Cross the roof by a flange on the left then pull right and finish up parallel cracks on the left.

6. Don't Fool Yourself Girl ★   25m E5 6b
FA Rick Campbell & Gary Latter 13 May 2000

The shorter flared rightmost crack, climbed with increasingly difficult moves to a good ledge. Break left through the roof and finish more easily up the headwall.

7. Bogus Asylum Seekers ★★   25m E3 6a
FA Grahame Nicoll & Lawrence Hughes 23 June 1996

Superb well protected climbing up the short diagonal crack in the headwall. Start 4m left of 9. Climb a left-trending groove-ramp. Above it, step right and attack the overhanging crack in the headwall.

8. Corncrakes for Breakfast ★★★   25m E2 5c
FA Rick Campbell & Paul Thorburn 25 May 1997

Start just left of the corner of 9. Follow a flake to head for a small overlap in the leaning headwall and pass this on the right.

The wall to the right is *Big Al* E2 5c; the diagonal crack out of 7 is 7a *Soggy Cornflakes* • E3 5c.

9 The Stowaway * — 25m Severe 4a
FA Grahame Nicoll & Lawrence Hughes 24 May 1997

The deep corner forming the left side of the projecting buttress. Wide bridging leads to easier ground then a steep finish in another short corner.

9a Walking with Giants *** — 35m E3 5c
FA Ed Nind & Gary Latter 14 June 2014

Superb sustained well-protected climbing. Start from a belay on large ledge just over half way up the easy corner of 9. Move up to the good flake on 8, then hand traverse left on jugs to pull through the roof on 5. Continue left more easily above the roof, stepping down to a steeper juggy traverse, exiting at the extreme left end of the cliff.

10 Incommunicado * — 25m E2 5c
FA Sam Chinnery & Olly Metherell June 1998

Climb the thin crack up the left side of the front face of the projecting buttress, cutting through a small square cut niche to a ledge. Ascend the upper wall to a rightwards rising ramp leading to the centre of the upper wall, finishing at the same point as 12.

11 Pause for Jaws ** — 25m E2 5c
FA Charlie Henderson & Robert Durran 27 July 2000

The slim left-facing groove 5m right of 10 gives surprisingly technical and interesting climbing. Finish direct above the mid-height ledge.

12 Human Cargo ** — 25m HS 4b
FA Grahame Nicoll, Mel Crowther & Lawrence Hughes 23 June 1996

Climb rightwards up steps on the front face of the projecting grey buttress then move left to the highest point. Step left and finish up the steep juggy headwall.

13 Geovannie ** — 25m E1 5b
FA Lawrence Hughes & Scott Muir 24 June 1996

Climb the arête of the slabby corner to the ledge. Finish up the crack-line directly above.

14 Pabbarotti * — 25m E1 5b
FA Neil Morrison & Wilson Moir August 2002

The flaky wall right of 13. Climb the left side of the slab to join 15 just below the ledge. From the ledge step out right to follow flakes and juggy breaks up the wall in a fine position.

15 The Immigrant * — 35m HS 4b
FA Grahame Nicoll & Mel Crowther 23 June 1996

The corner forming the right side of the projecting buttress.
1 15m 4b Ascend the slabby corner-ramp to a ledge at its top.
2 20m 4a Walk left to the end of the ledge and climb steps up and rightwards to the top.

16 The Notorious B.I.G. ** — 30m E3 6a
FA Lawrence Hughes & Grahame Nicoll 24 May 1997

A fierce route tackling the overhang on the left side of this part of the wall. Start just right of the corner of 15. Climb a crack-line to the roof. Make hard moves to surmount this then step right and climb the blunt arête to the top.

17 Wetter than a Day at the Beach *** — 30m E1 5b
FA Lawrence Hughes & Scott Muir 24 June 1996

The hanging corner bounding the left side of the wall. Start beneath isolated roofs near the top of the crag. Follow a crack-line leading into the corner which leads to the top.

18 Who Shot RJ ** — 30m E2 5c
FA Robert Durran & Roger Austin 20 August 2004

The obvious black hanging crack. Gain a spike below and left of the crack with difficulty. Gain and climb the crack, finishing direct.

19 Illegal Alien ★★★   30m HVS 5a
FA Grahame Nicoll & Mel Crowther 23 June 1996

Excellent sustained climbing. Start at the base of a small right-facing corner below the centre of the wall. Ascend the corner to a small ledge on the left then continue up cracks, finishing by twin cracks at the top.

19a Head and Heart ★★   25m E3 5c
FA Gary Latter & Ed Nind 14 June 2014

A direct line up the crack and wall right of 19. Climb the left side of the arête left of that route to the ledge, then the short wide crack. Continue up the wall above, past a good flake/break just before the top.

20 The Craik ★★★   25m E3 6a
FA Kev Howett & Graham Little 23 June 1996

The stunning vertical crack at the right end of the wall. Start as for 19. Step into the corner then climb steeply up and right through a small hanging niche with difficulty to better holds below a deep crack. Go up this to a foot-ledge and finish up the superb thin crack easily.

21 In the Pink ★★   25m E3 5c
FA Graham Little, Kev Howett & Jim Lowther 24 June 1996

The pink quartz corner near the right side of the wall. Start immediately above a fine rock pool under the overhanging base of the wall. Follow a slight groove through an overlap with difficulty to the base of the quartz. Continue up this and the corner above, pulling out left at the top.

22 Castlebay Castaway ★   25m VS 4c
FA Grahame Nicoll & Bill Wright May 1998

The right end of the wall is bounded by a ramp. Start in a chimney at the right side of the ramp. Climb easily up to a pink corner and finish up this by strenuous laybacking.

23 Party Kitchen ★★   20m E2 5c
FA Robert Durran & Rob Adie 18 August 2006

Belay at the bottom of the chimney of 22. Climb the prominent V-shaped slot/chimney on the right (not as bad as it looks!), surmount the overhang to gain a small ledge and finish up the crack above.

Bill Stevenson starting up Wetter than a Day at the Beach.

THE GREAT ARCH

NL 592 873

One of the showpiece cliffs on the island, reaching a height of 100m with a colossal roof spanning the upper right side.

"... traversing a ledge on the face we came to the point where the cliff plunged to the bursting waves below and above us soared the great rock wall crowned by an overhanging arch. We marvelled at its mathematical perfection, its smoothness, too blank of ledges for seabirds. It was a place to savour, all the better for its remoteness and difficulty of access. Nor was there an easy way out. We had to go back the way we had come in order to cross back to the village settlement." – Tom Weir, *Exploring Scotland*, Pelham Books, 1991

Descent: Gain the base by a 100m abseil. For *Prophecy of Drowning* start above the right wall of the corner of *Out of the Womb* (left looking down). This lies down and right (looking out) from the prominent pool on the cliff-top with the top of the corner about 30m from the pool forming an incut vegetated ledge, prominent on the skyline when approaching from the north.

1 Northumbrian Rhapsody ★★   100m E5 6b
FA Karin Magog & Steve Crowe 10 June 2005

Belay on a small ledge on the arête, as for *The Child of the Sea*.

1. **25m 6b** Move leftwards across the wall to cross an overlap to gain easier flakes above. Sweep right to belay below a notch in the right side of the long roof.
2. **25m 6a** Pull through the roof into a groove. Step left out of the top of this to gain the slabby headwall. Continue to a belay ledge.
3. **50m 5b** Continue up solid but lichenous rock above.

2 The Child of the Sea ★★   100m E5 6b
FA Sam Chinnery & Tom Bridgeland (1 PA) June 1998; FFA Paul Thorburn & Rick Campbell 6 June 2005

The impressive left arête of the abseil corner. Start from a hanging belay just above the barnacle level and 3m left of a large chimney pod.

1. **30m 6b** Climb steeply up a groove on the right for 8m until a hard traverse left for 2m gains the base of a hanging flake on the arête (crux). Continue more easily up steep flakes and shallow corners to gain the bottom of an obvious scoop.

2. **35m 6a** Follow the rightwards trending overhanging groove above on large rounded holds, passing spikes to join *Sturm und Drang*. Follow this rightwards through a roof to gain a bottomless corner and continue up this to a belay.
3. **35m 5a** Continue up lichen covered walls and cracks just right of the arête.

③ Hebridean Overtures ★★★ 115m E5 6b
FA Rick Campbell & Malcolm Davies May 1999

Climbs the obvious diagonal crack in its entirety.
1. **35m 5b** From a belay in the black chimney climb to a hanging belay on a flake 3m below roof.
2. **30m 6b** Move up and left and pull spectacularly through the roof and follow the continuation weakness with interest to pull out left onto belay in vegetation.
3. **50m 5c** Climb up cracks in slab then move right to finish up *Sturm und Drang*.

④ Sturm und Drang ★ 115m E5 6b
FA Rick Campbell & Paul Thorburn 25 May 1997

The south face of the pillar to the left of *The Priest*. Abseil to the final foot-hold below the biotite band and belay on nuts and the abseil rope.
1. **25m 6a** With a high side runner, traverse left just above the belay to gain the top of a large slot. Follow cracks up the wall and move left past a loose block to belay on a ramp on the left.
2. **45m 6b** Climb up to a prominent spike then climb the twin grooves above, moving left onto jugs below the roof. Move right into a bottomless corner with care (loose block, crux) and gain the groove above. Follow this to belay on a vegetated ramp.
3. **15m 4b** Traverse right to belay on the left side of a large ledge.
4. **30m 5c** Climb up to a large flake on the right, step left and follow the cleanest crack to the top.

⑤ The Priest ★★★ 110m E1 5b
FA Graham Little & Kev Howett 30 May 1995

Climbs the pillar between the Great Arch and the big open corner (*Out of the Womb* HVS 5a), finishing up the leftmost of the twin roof-capped corners high on the crag. It has great character and atmosphere with big route commitment.
1. **50m 4c** From a tiny ledge some 8m above the sea, climb the slabby right wall of the corner just left of the edge to gain a small ledge and belay on the very edge.
2. **25m 5b** Move up into a groove, step right then enjoy sustained and intricate climbing via cracks and grooves, well right of the edge, leading to a belay on a rusty slab under the roof.
3. **35m 5b** Move up to the roof, step right then climb to the base of the left corner. Climb this fine corner to the big roof then make a short difficult left traverse to finish.

⑥ Prophecy of Drowning ★★★★ 115m E2 5c
FA Kev Howett & Graham Little 24 June 1996

A magnificent route, one of the finest of its grade in the Hebrides, following a line parallel and to the right of *The Priest*. Belay on the lowest small ledge on the right side of the slab.
1. **40m 5b** Climb the right edge of the slab passing to the right of a larger ledge to reach a small block about 10m above. Swing wildly round the overhanging right arête into the base of a hanging groove with a distinctive projecting ledge at its base. Climb the groove and the larger continuation above in an excellent position to exit right onto a shattered rock ledge level with the lip of the great roof of the arch.
2. **20m 5a** From the edge of the roof climb up and right across an immaculate wall to enter a small right-facing groove which becomes a ramp. Belay at its top below the main corner line.
3. **30m 5c** Climb the superb corner with hard moves through its steepest section. Climb the easy corner above to a roof and exit left onto a large ledge below the final corner.
4. **25m 5a** Follow the final corner to the capping roof and exit right in a stunning position, passing large blocks with care.

7 The Breath of Life ★★   105m E3 6a
FA Neil Foster & Clare Reading (on sight) 29 May 2010

A line of slimmer grooves around *Prophecy*. Start as for that route.

1. **40m 6a** Follow *Prophecy* to the hanging groove and climb this to a band of soft grey pillows. Step right and climb the thin crack and continuation groove to the right, before tackling twin parallel cracks to arrive at the *Prophecy* stance from directly below.
2. **45m 5c** Climb the crack left of the *Prophecy* slab, past a triangular overlap, until it curves right. Continue directly up the thin crack, which eases with the angle. Follow the obvious line up and slightly left, passing a short solid corner, before a shattered looking bulge gives access to a fine stance at the base of the arête.
3. **20m 5b** Pull awkwardly into the narrow groove in the arête and where it fades, move left to finish via *The Priest*.

8 The Great Arch ★★★★   95m E8 6c
FA Dave Cuthbertson & Lynn Hill (rest points) June 1997; FFA Dave MacLeod June 2013

A stupendous line through the centre of the arch, though the rock on the upper sections of pitch 3 and on pitch 4 is very poor and unpleasant. Start on huge sea-washed boulders below the centre of the big lower roof.

1. **10m 5a** Climb onto the wall and traverse left under the corner leading up to the roof.
2. **15m 5c** Traverse left across the undercut and overhung wall heading for the arête where the roof above relents. Pull through here and step left and climb up to a good stance beneath a sloping ramp (usually covered in guano).
3. **25m 6b** Climb up and right into an open corner and ascend its right wall onto the right arête which leads to the roof above. Traverse out left on the obvious horizontal break in the roof until a hard pull through the roof rightwards gains a corner. Continue up right up an easy ramp then make a long traverse back left over poor rock to belay below the hanging bomb-bay chimney splitting the big roof.
4. **10m 6a** Climb through the chimney into the huge open corner above the roof.
5. **10m 5a** Climb the easy wall diagonally right into the centre of the wall to belay beneath a shield of grey rock beneath the apex of the arch above.
6. **25m 6c** Climb the shield of rock with difficulty to the apex of the arch. Climb out through this passing some PRs and other pre-placed protection with extreme difficulty and so to the top.

8a *Exit Stage Left* 5c, 5c, 5c continues directly above, instead of traversing out right from the top of pitch 4.

NL 592 873
THE HEADWALL

This 25m high slabby wall lies above the right side of **The Great Arch**, approached by a grassy ledge from the right. 11 routes, mostly one star Severe 4a – VS 5a; from right to left, best are 9 *Es Gibt Reis Baby* ★★ HVS 5b up a black groove & 11 *Leftie* ★★ VS 4c up wall to a roof, passed on the right.

Paul Newman nearing the top of the finely positioned first pitch of Prophecy of Drowning. Photo Dave Cuthbertson, Cubby Images

ALLANISH PENINSULA

The large headland at the north-west end of the island.

NL 592 881

HOOFER'S GEO

The fine open wall (not really a geo!) dividing the westerly wall on the west side of the northern tip of the peninsula. Slow to dry in places.

Descents: An easy scramble down stepped rock just north of the deep square gully cutting into the north end of the face or by descending the right finish to *Right Chimney*, Difficult. Alternatively, by abseil in heavy seas.

1 Boosh ★★   25m E5 6a
FA Peter Robins & James McHaffie (both led) & Neil Dyer 3 July 2003

The striking left-slanting crack on the right side of the deep chimney. Gain the crack and go up to a small overlap. Tricky moves over this lead to better holds as crack nears corner. Climb straight up the wall above to the top.

> The finely situated hanging crack in the arête above the drooping beak-like overhang is 2 *Harry Hoofter* ★ E2 5c.

3 Bint There Dun It ★★   25m E1 5b
FA George Ridge & Kath Pyke 24 June 1996

The first steep wall encountered beneath the beak-like overhang. Belay left of a deep cutting. Follow the blunt rib to a roof right of the beak. Pull over directly and finish up the groove. A better finish moves left across the wall above the roof past a spike to finish up the left arête.

4 Hoofer's Route ★★★　　　　　　25m E1 5b
FA Kath Pyke & George Ridge 23 June 1996

Excellent climbing. Start as for 3. Follow the blunt rib to a roof. Pull over this and trend right to link up with a fine rising crack-line. Jugs lead to the top.

5 The Ramp ★★　　　　　　　　　40m HS 4b
FA Fraser Fotheringham & Andy Cunningham 24 June 1996

To the right of 4 is a wide bay with slabby grooves, cracks and chimneys on either side. This route climbs a shallow groove and crack-line in the centre of the bay. Follow this to its end, to finish on surprising jugs up the headwall.

6 Skuaed ★　　　　　　　　　　　35m HS 4b
FA Harry Salisbury & Val Hennelly 4 June 2003

The crack parallel and right of 5. Move slightly right onto the wall at 5m and up to a ledge. Continue up the crack 2m on the right and climb the chimney above.

7 Cast and Shadow ★　　　　　　35m HVS 5a
FA Dave Carr & Alistair Arnott 4 June 2003

The prominent sharp arête. Climb up to the arête then up this, first on the right then up the arête to a large ledge leading to easier ground.

8 Right Chimney ★　　　　　　35m Very Difficult

The open chimney with a steep finish. A Difficult variation leads out right along a fault, avoiding the steep finish.

9 Hypnotise ★★　　　　　　　　35m HVS 5a
FA Lawrence Hughes & Grahame Nicoll 28 May 1997

Start 4m left of 11. Climb the blunt arête, finishing up easier ground above.

10 Fracture Clinic ★★　　　　　　35m E2 5c
FA Kev Howett & Alistair Todd May 1998

The hanging crack system up the left wall of 11. Climb directly into the cracks by steady climbing up the lower wall. Continue up the cracks which soon ease to a recess and finish more easily.

Gary Latter on the immaculate Sugar Cane Country. Photo Malcolm Davies.

11 Squeeze Job ★   35m HVS 5a
FA Andy Cunningham & Fraser Fotheringham 24 June 1996

In the centre of the cliff a steep corner-crack leads through a bulge. Continue up the chimney which narrows into a leaning offwidth then finish up the left wall.

12 Rite of Passage ★   30m E4 6a
FA Steve Crowe & Karin Magog June 2006

Follow the steep side of the arête just right of 11. Powerful moves at the start lead to more technical climbing up the blunt arête above.

13 Honey Trap ★★   20m E6 6a
FA Niall McNair & Ali Robb June 2005

Superb bold climbing forming a counter-diagonal to 14. Start up the golden wall to the left of that route, up quartz edges, heading for the tri-cam pocket and jugs on 14. Tackle the headwall directly via a black inset flake to gain a hanging crack to finish.

14 More Lads and Molasses ★★   30m E5 6a
FA Rick Campbell & Malcolm Davies May 1999

Serious climbing up the wall left of 16. Start up black flakes, which lead to a break. Move left then up past twin pockets to jugs in the next break. Make tricky moves up left to a black hanging flake and escape up leftwards into a scoop and easy ground above.

15 Fear an Bhata ★★   30m E4 6a
FA Steve Crowe & Karin Magog 5 June 2006

'The Boatman'. Start up the black flakes of 14. After the initial moves, climb boldly up and rightwards to join 16.

16 As Sound as Mr J.A. ★★★   25m E3 5c
FA Kath Pyke & George Ridge 24 June 1996

The prominent hanging groove at the left side of the smooth wall. Belay on a ledge left of the stepped corner. Trend up and left to the base of the groove via steep moves. Follow the straightforward groove, finishing with interest up the offwidth crack directly above.

17 J.A.'s Maelstrom ★   20m E4 5c
FA Niall McNair & Paul Newman May 2003

The flake system right of 16. Start up that route, climbing straight up where that route bends left, finishing on an arête.

18 Sugar Cane Country ★★★★   30m E4 6a
FA Kath Pyke & George Ridge 24 June 1996

Immaculate sustained technical climbing up the thinner right crack up the centre of the smooth wall. Climb on good edges to gain a ledge and the start of the flake-crack. Follow this with difficulty to a ledge. Step left and finish up the steep crack.

19 Brother Ray ★★   30m E5 6b
FA Rick Campbell & Paul Thorburn 11 June 2004

The wall right of 18. Fine climbing though escapable from below the crux. High in the grade and bold. Climb 18 to the start of the crack, traverse right along a break to the centre of the wall before moving up to a pocketed break above (nut runner to the right). Ascend the middle of the wall with difficulty to a good slot (protection) and continue to the juggy flake shake-out on 18. Stroll up the steep headwall above the right end of the flake with surprising ease. *"Named after Ray Charles who died a few hours before and the Razorbills who look just like the cat."* – Rick Campbell

20 Vitrified Cinders ★★   40m HVS 5b
FA Grahame Nicoll & Lawrence Hughes 28 May 1997

Romp up the ramp below 18 then climb the fine corner bounding the right side of the smooth wall.

21 Buckets for Breakfast ★★   40m HVS 4c
FA Paddy Gibson & Lisa Wright 14 May 2000

A good alternative finish to 20. Climb the right side of the ramp to a notch and belay on the large ledge above. Overhead is a large curving roof. Cross this at its widest point on big holds then pull out to finish up a short wall on small holds. Great position.

Right of the right-bounding gully is a fine triangular wall, accessed by scrambling down a shelf from the right. The shorter (15m) wide crack at the right side gives a fine Moderate finishing out left, or Difficult finishing up the short jam crack.

The largest of the Barra Isles (3km x 2km), the name comes from the Norse 'big isle', or possibly 'bird isle'. In the 1880s the island had a population of around 160 but has been uninhabited since 1912. Although there are large areas of vegetated and bird infested cliffs there is also a huge abundance of immaculate clean Lewisian gneiss. Indeed, the 90m high Sron an Duin on Dun Mingulay *"… must lay claim to being one of the finest rock faces in Britain."* – Graham Little, *Skye and the Hebrides, Volume 2, Scottish Mountaineering Club Climbers' Guide*, 1996.

The usual landing place is on the rocks on either side of the wonderful sandy Bagh Mhiughlaigh (Mingulay Bay) in the centre of the east coast or the north end of the beach itself in calm seas. The best camping spot is the large sward of flat ground above the ruins, just north of the burn.

Cliffs are described in an anti-clockwise direction starting from the campsite.

CREAG DHEARG (THE RED CLIFF)

NL 5661 8447 **Alt:** 90–110m

This crag forms the back-wall of Bay Analepp on the north-west side of the island. The top of the crag lies at 150m above sea level. The lower sections are steep but grotty and bird infested. However, the upper 60m wall offers excellent quality gneiss. The wall can be viewed from spurs of land either to the north or south. There are two facets to the wall; a steep and impressive **Left Wall** and the **Upper Right Wall**. The main features of the left side are an almost continuous pink intrusion just right of the left arête and a prominent central yellow streak of lichen.

LEFT WALL

Descent: Abseil 60m down the north edge of the wall down a gully with a brown retaining wall to reach a good ledge below the left arête of the wall (5m above bigger grass ledges below).

1 The Scream ★★ 55m E6/7 6b
FA Steve Crowe & Karin Magog 25 May 2000

The prominent pink intrusion just right of the arête. Start off the ledge. Pull out right from the belay and make a rising traverse to an obvious wide pink slot. Continue to the obvious ledge. Step up and left to arrange good protection. Step back right and make a hard move directly to good undercuts below the hanging groove. Pull into the groove and follow improving flakes to a semi-rest and good protection. A long reach directly up above the flake should lead to a line of holds that lead left and down to the arête. Continue more easily but take great care with hollow blocks to top.

2 K & S Special ★★★★ 58m E6 6a
FA Karin Magog & Steve Crowe (both led) 8 June 2006

Sustained climbing with good protection. Start off the ledge. Follow 1 to the good undercuts below the hanging groove. Follow the right side of the flake then pull leftwards and move up to reach a prominent quartz band. Climb directly through the bulges above to a ledge 6m below the top (possible belay but the hard climbing is not over!). Climb the wall above, stepping right to a testing last move.

3 Dream the Dhearg Goch ★★★★ 60m E6 6b
FA Glenda Huxter & Dave Towse 13 May 1999

Breaches the superb shield of rock via a tenuous line just left of a yellow streak of lichen left of 4.

1 **20m 6a** Pull out right from the belay and climb to an obvious wide pink slot. Traverse right 2m then back up left to the obvious ledge. Traverse this delicately right to a flake and hanging belay.

2 **25m 6b** Climb the pink cracked vein above the belay, trending rightwards as it steepens and pull out onto a wide ledge. Block belay 3m to the left.

3 **15m 6a** Climb the steep wall above just right of the belay towards another pink vein in the roof at the top. Traverse left 2m to an interesting exit.

4 Ocean Voyeur ★★ 65m E5 6a
FA Kev Howett & Hugh Harris 12 May 1999

Climbs a line of least resistance up the centre of the pale sheet at the left side of the wall just right of the yellow streak.

1 **20m 5b** Pull out right from the belay ledge onto the wall and follow the obvious line, traversing rightwards across the lip of the undercut wall and passing a short left-facing corner to climb a flake beyond to a ledge. Awkward belay near the left end of the ledge.

2 **25m 6a** Go up left off the ledge to gain a smaller ledge above bulging rock. Climb excellent flakes direct up the pelt wall to gain a diagonal crack leading right. Follow this into a short black open groove. Struggle all the way up this

with a hard exit onto sloping ledges above.

3 20m 5b Follow the left-facing groove to a small ledge. Pull up left onto another ledge and exit in a wild position out left in space to finish.

(5) Variations on a Dream ★★★ 65m E5 6a

FA Karin Magog & Steve Crowe 24 May 2000

The first pitch follows 3 then makes a rightwards traverse, crossing 4 to continue up the right groove.

1 20m 6a Pull out right from the belay and climb to an obvious wide pink slot. Continue to the obvious ledge and hanging belay.

2 25m 6a Traverse rightwards along the ledge until directly beneath the black groove right of the flakes on 4. Thin moves gain the groove. Follow this with increasing difficulty until it is possible to reach right to a good ledge. Move up to belay above the groove to protect your second, please!

3 20m 5b Trend up and left to the top.

UPPER RIGHT WALL

Descent: Make a 30m abseil directly to the central belay ledge, keeping swinging in order not to miss it.

(6) The Horror Beneath ★★ 35m E1 5b

FA Dave Turnbull & Glenda Huxter 24 May 2000

From the left end of the ledge, climb the perfect right-facing flake, then move right and back left to finish past twin ledges.

(7) Little Miss Sitting Pretty ★★★★ 35m E5 6a

FA Steve Crowe & Karin Magog 21 May 2001

From the centre of the ledge take a leftward rising line to gain the left side of a ledge below the pair of right-facing grooves. Follow the left groove and continue directly with increasing difficulty above the groove until below the left extremity of the final roofs. Ignoring the possibility to escape left, step right and pull over the roof and up the final headwall on jugs.

(8) Big Chief Turning Bull ★★★ 35m E4 6a

FA Dave Turnbull & Glenda Huxter 25 May 2000

Photo Steve Crowe.

Climb from the right edge of the ledge to a wide flake. From this go up and left to a ledge in the centre of the wall. Go up a slim right-facing groove and swing right into a slim left-facing groove at a small ledge (crux). Traverse 5m right and finish direct on jugs.

(9) Fulmar Squaw ★★★★ 35m E3 5c

FA Glenda Huxter & Dave Turnbull 25 May 2000

A superb strenuous route, which follows a curving line up the right side of the upper wall. From the right edge of the ledge climb to the wide flake. Continue up to beneath a hanging right-facing flake. Move up and left then direct to the top. Jugs and overhanging all the way!

(10) The Road to Nowhere ★★ 40m E4 5c

FA Karin Magog & Steve Crowe 21 May 2001

Climb rightwards from the ledge for about 4m to gain a vaguely scooped grey shield of rock. Follow the faint scoop to the ledge. From here climb the black scoop above to a good break. Traverse right slightly to gain a slim right-facing ramp line. Follow this up and left until it reaches 7 and finish up this on increasingly good holds.

GUARSAY BEAG

This is the small headland on the north-west side of the island, due west of the summit of Macphee's Hill.
Approach: From the campsite head west-north-west up the hill towards a prominent boulder and cairn on the flat col, then drop down to the headland.

NL 5514 8445   40min

SHAG'S POINT

A clean wall at the north-west end of the promontory directly beneath a prominent cairn.

1. Condemned to Happiness ** — 45m VS 5a
FA John Sanders & Mike Snook 1 June 1998

From the base of 3, traverse left at sea level for 9m (Difficult) then move around a corner for about 6m to belay beneath a left-facing corner capped by a large black overhang.
1. **25m 4b** Bridge up the right side of the cave until established in the crack.
2. **20m 5a** Move right and pull up strenuously into the rightmost groove (crux) and climb it.

2. The Ultimate Fascinator ** — 40m HS 4b
FA John & Alison Sanders 5 June 2008

Climb the short chimney and the wall above on excellent holds to a corner (poorly protected). From the corner move right, around the overlap, to climb the delicate wall above, and then jugs to the top - superb and sustained throughout.

> The corners bounding either side of the shield are 3 *With a View to a Shag* * VS 4b and 5 *Easy Day for a Shag* * Severe 4b.

4. From the Hole to Heaven *** — 35m VS 4c

FA Graham Little & Kev Howett 1 June 1993

The centre of the shield on excellent holds in an impressive situation. Climb a vertical crack to the base of the hole; bypass it by the wall on the right. Continue up the steepening shield on excellent holds in a great position. Step right under an overlap to finish up a groove.

6. The Wine Box Nomads ** — 35m VS 4c
FA Ian Cooksey & Mark Radtke 29 May 2001

The wall direct on *'perfect clean juggy rock.'* Go through a small roof and bridge up the open book corner to finish.

7. Derek the Shaman ** — 50m HS 4b
FA Mark Radtke & Ian Cooksey 29 May 2001

1. **30m 4b** Climb up and right into a groove, then the intermittent curving groove line diagonally right across the quartz-veined wall, then more direct on perfect juggy rock to enter the yellow grooves immediately right of the corner. Belay overlooking the bird filled niche.
2. **20m 4b** Climb steep juggy rock to finish up the corner.

8. Gobling Grooves ** — 40m VS 4c
FA Paul Donnithorne & Dave Barlow May 2001;
Direct Start: Rory & Kev Howett May 2017

Follows a direct line up the wall into the hanging groove in the rib between 6 & 7. Belay on small twin ledges 5m down right. Follow the groove on the right then step right into a crack and follow it until an overlap in the curving groove of 7. Pull over leftwards on slopers, then direct to a blocky roof. Cross this and up the hanging groove, finishing by the fine groove in the arête.

GUARSAY MOR

NL 5491 8426

THE BOULEVARD

A superb 50m high clean grey wall extending south from the northernmost tip of the headland. Routes described from north-south.

Descents: The base of routes can be gained by climbing down the ridge leading to the tip of Guarsay Mor (Difficult). From the base follow seaweed-covered platforms back south towards the cliff to reach a slabby ramp. Belay at the top of this. This point can also be gained more conveniently by a 50m abseil.

> From large tidal ledge on the north-west tip of the headland, the crack and chimney then direct up the wall is 1 *Soggy Chalk* ★ Severe 4a; the left of twin cracks 2 *Aqualung* ★ Severe 4a. 3 *Man Overboard* ★ HVS 5a – starts as for 4. Traverse left for 3m then direct, trending right to large ledge then up wall to corner left of 4.

4 Port Pillar ★★　　　　　　　　45m HVS 5a
FA Grahame Nicoll, Andy Cunningham & Bob Reid 2 June 1995

1 **25m 5a** Climb into a short crack in the bulge above the belay then go right below the base of an obvious large corner to climb the face of the fine pillar forming the left side of the cliff face. Belay on a ledge at the top of the pillar.

2 **20m** – Climb easily direct to the top.

5 Oh No, Norman's Due Back Tomorrow! ★★★
　　　　　　　　　　　　　　　　　　50m E3 6a
FA Andy Cunningham, Grahame Nicoll & Bob Reid 2 June 1995

1 **30m 6a** Descend a little from the belay and move back right onto a slabby wall. Move up into a layback corner-crack and climb this to a good ledge on the left. Climb up then go right into a diagonal crack under an overlap. After a few moves pull onto the wall above and make hard moves left into another diagonal crack. Follow this into a right-trending corner leading to the right end of a belay ledge.

2 **20m 4a** A corner and easier ground leads to the top.

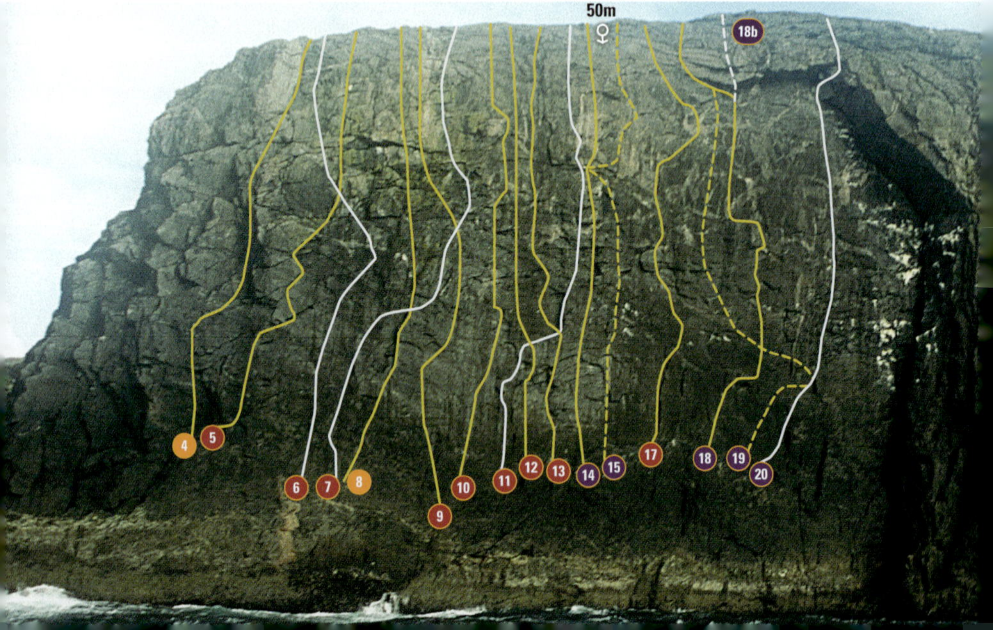

6 Haunt of Seals ★★   50m E2 5c

FA Louise Thomas, Twid Turner & Gary Latter 1 June 1998

Scramble down and left from the left end of the long ledge at the base of most of the routes to belay on a small ledge. Step left off the belay. Climb the wall directly to a niche below the distinctive thin crack in the middle of the wall (right of the right-slanting corner of 5). Climb the crack (good small wires) to a slanting break and follow this rightwards then directly up the wall to a big break. Finish up the black wall just left of a corner.

Descent: There is a long ledge beneath the base of the remaining routes, which can be gained by making a 50m abseil from a point about 50m south of the northernmost point of the headland.

7 Under the Pink ★   50m E1 5b

FA Graham Little & Bob Reid 2 June 1995

Traverse leftwards from the left end of the ledge to a small stance on a black slabby wall.

1. **25m 5b** Move up and left to the base of a smooth scalloped groove. Ascend this (crux) then follow a flaky fault line rightwards to belay at a small ledge at its end (in common with *Okeanos*).
2. **25m 4b** Climb directly upwards to pass a big blotch of pink quartz-feldspar on its left then finish directly.

8 Oh No, Archie's Going Round in Circles! ★★   50m HVS 5a

FA Andy Cunningham & Fraser Fotheringham 26 June 1996

From the small ledge at the start of 7 climb straight up the wall to the right groove. Climb this for a few metres then go left into the middle of the wall, crossing the groove of 7. Climb more or less directly up the middle of the wall through a small quartz recess to easier ground above.

9 Okeanos ★★★   50m E2 5c

FA Grahame Nicoll & Andy Cunningham 2 June 1995

Start at the left end of the big ledge.

1. **25m 5c** Gain a good spike then make hard moves up and left to holds leading back right into a steep crack. Climb the crack then move left along a juggy break to twin diagonal cracks leading to a ledge and belay (in common with *Under the Pink*).
2. **25m 4b** Climb slightly rightwards, passing to the right of a big blotch of pink quartz-feldspar then go up a left-facing corner to finish.

10 A Word With the Bill ★★★   50m E3 5c

FA Andy Cunningham & Grahame Nicoll 2 June 1995

1. **30m 5c** Climb the thin crack just left of *Ossian Boulevard* with a hard pull up into an easier-angled scoop. Step left and climb another crack for a few moves then head right and up to an overlap. Traverse right under the overlap then climb straight up to a ledge.
2. **20m 5a** Follow the right-curving crack above and pull left through a quartz-feldspar bulge to finish directly.

11 Ossian Boulevard ★★   60m E1 5b

FA Andy Cunningham, Grahame Nicoll & Bob Reid 31 May 1995

Start about 5 metres right of the left end of the big ledge at a slightly right-slanting groove.

1. **35m 5b** Climb the groove until moves right above an overhang lead into a series of corners going right across the wall. Belay under a bulge at the top corner (as for *Crystal Daze*).

Mike 'Twid' Turner following on the first ascent of Haunt of Seals.

2 25m 4b Climb left through the bulge then go directly to the top with one move left to cross a patch of quartz-feldspar.

12 Heel Yo Ho ★★ 50m E3 6a
FA Gary Latter, Twid Turner & Louise Thomas 1 June 1998

Start beneath the right-facing groove on the right side of the pillar of *Ossian Boulevard*. Climb the groove, pulling slightly leftwards to large sloping holds on the ledge (crux). Pull right and up the crack to the long ledge on *Ossian Boulevard*. Move slightly leftwards on good flat holds on the wall above then finish directly.

13 The Mushroom of My Fear ★★ 50m E3 6a
FA Robert Durran & Charlie Henderson 21 July 2000

Start beneath the left-facing corner 5m right of *Heel Yo Ho*.

1 15m 6a Climb the corner and small roof at 10m then a short wall with difficulty to belay at the right end of a ledge.

2 35m 5b Go up and slightly leftwards for a few metres then slightly rightwards before continuing directly through some *"entertaining"* bulges to easier ground. A superb sustained pitch.

14 Longships ★★ 25m E4 6a
FA Paul Thorburn & Rick Campbell 29 May 1997

Excellent wall climbing between *Crystal Daze* and *Ossian Boulevard*. Start at a small ramp below a small roof at 5m. Climb to the roof and make hard moves up right to gain better holds at the base of a short flared crack. Move up then right to a deep slot below a bulge. Direct over the bulge and up the wall above to belay on *Ossian Boulevard* or continue boldly following the line of most resistance.

15 Crystal Daze ★★★ 50m E4 6a
FA Kev Howett & Graham Little 2 June 1995

Start below a wide vertical pink band at a thin crack.

1 25m 6a Sustained climbing up the thin crack (bold start) leads to a pull out right to gain a big pocket. Climb the wall above, trending left to belay on a small ledge below a bulge (as for *Ossian Boulevard*).

2 25m 5b Move right under the bulge then climb up to a short dark quartz corner. Ascend this then follow the curving arch continuation until a big pocket over the lip on the left allows a pull out and the wall above to be climbed.

16 Precious Days ★★ 50m E5/6 6a
FA Steve Crowe & Karin Magog (on-sight) May 2003

A bold variation on *Crystal Daze*. Start two metres right and move up to a large pocket and good protection. Continue boldly on adequate holds but with very small (and very poor) wires to eventually reach good holds and better protection. Continue more easily in a direct line to the top of the cliff finishing just left of the capping roofs.

17 Taxing McPhee ★★★ 50m E2 5c
FA Kev Howett & Graham Little 31 May 1995

Start at a dark flake at the right end of the big ledge.

1 25m 5c Climb the flake-crack to its top then pull up and move left across the wall into a slight scoop. Climb up through the cleavage in the roof above to a ledge.

2 25m 5a Follow the right-rising line to a glacis. Move up to a distinctive quartz flake, pull over this then step left and finish directly.

18 Lost Souls ★★★ 55m E4 6a
FA Kev Howett & Graham Little 2 June 1995

Superb bold climbing. Traverse 10 metres right from the right end of the big ledge to a small ledge.

1 30m 6a Climb rightwards off the ledge then move up to a higher ledge. From near its right end make thin moves out right and up to a small flake. Step right and follow small quartz holds up a narrow wall between two small roofs. Step left to the edge of the second roof and climb through the break to better holds. Move up to a small roof, step right under it then climb to a horizontal crack which is followed out left to belay in a small niche.

2 25m 5b Climb the slabby wall above, trending slightly right to reach the right end of a horizontal breach in the capping roof. Gain and follow the hand traverse line out left in a spectacular position.

18a Direct Start *   25m E2 5b
FA Neil & Pete Craig 12 June 2004

The rib and wall directly above the groove on the first pitch of *Save Our Soles*.

18b Swimming to America ***   20m E4 6a
FA Paul Thorburn & Rick Campbell 29 May 1997

Climbs the 4m capping roof of *Lost Souls* directly. Follow the parent route to the roof then pull left onto the weakness and direct to the gargoyles on the lip to finish.

19 Sruth na Fir Gorm **   50m E5 6a
FA Rick Campbell & Pete Craig 13 May 2003

Breaks through the first weakness in the bulge left of *Lost Souls*. Move up and right along a ledge into the quartz recess on *Save our Soles*. Belay. Move left round a rib and climb up the wall to the flake hold on *Lost Souls*. Move up left to a position under the centre of the overlap then move left again before making a hard move up into a groove. Continue steeply to easier ground and finish as for 18.

20 Save Our Soles **   60m E5 6b
FA Twid Turner, Louise Thomas & Gary Latter 1 June 1998

Good climbing up the right side of the wall. Start on ledges on the far right.
1 **40m 5c** Step down right into a groove and follow it and cracks directly to the prominent quartz niche with a crack in the back. Pull out right and head up to a small flake then straight up on perfect juggy rock to belay on a good ledge beneath the roof.
2 **20m 6b** Move easily up right to a break near the right end of the roof. Reach out to a good flat hold halfway out (R #3 in horizontal slot) then make hard moves to reach and pull over the lip. Easily to finish.

NL 5491 8421

THE NORTH PILLAR
The next section of cliff just south of **The Boulevard**. The cliffs start to gain height and the angle eases a fair bit.
Descent: Abseil 80m to small ledges just above the high-tide level.

1 Alzheimer's Groove **   70m HVS 5a
FA Fraser Fotheringham & Andy Cunningham 26 June 1996

Climbs a line starting from the lowest ledge under the start of *No Puke Here*.
1 **40m 5a** Move left into grooves running up to the right end of the roofed recess. Switch from the right to the left groove then trend right and up to belay above the right end of the roof.
2 **30m 4a** Step left and trend left and up above the roof to the top.

2 No Puke Here **   65m VS 4c
FA Chris Bonington & Mick Fowler 30 May 1993

Follow the rib to the immediate right of a recess roofed by a huge overhang to the left of 3.
1 **30m 4c** Climb the slabby rib on excellent rock, moving left from a short crack to gain a good ledge.
2 **35m 4a** Continue straight up on good holds.

3 Grey Rib **   70m Severe 4a
FA Chris Bonington & Mick Fowler 30 May 1993

Start from the highest point of the ledge just above the high-water mark at the foot of the buttress on the north side of the inlet.
1 **35m 4a** Climb 3m leftwards to gain a ramp leading up right onto a short corner. Move up left out of the corner on to the crest of the buttress and continue for 12m to a stance.
2 **35m 4a** Climb steeply straight up on superb holds.

4 Poet's Corner **   50m Severe 4a
FA John Given, Phil Swainson, David Craig & Bill Skidmore May 1997

Start on ledges 10m above the sea approximately 30m right of 2.
1 **25m 4a** Climb up and left from the left end of the ledge into a big left-facing corner. Ascend this, trending right and over an overhang to a belay.
2 **25m 4a** Wander up the superb juggy wall above.

NL 5496 8421

THE GREAT ARCH

Continuing south from **The North Pillar**, the cliffs stretch for around 300m, gradually gaining height at the southern extremity, **The Cobweb Wall**, overlooking the edge of the Stac of Lianamul. **The Great Arch** is the area of rock immediately north (left) of a huge sea cave, adjoining **The North Pillar**. There are also extensive seabird colonies on some sections, though the majority of the routes are on superb clean rock, avoiding most of the birds.

Descent: A broad broken gully runs down to a mini geo at the base. Gain an open recess just over the lip and make a 90m abseil from here (70m to base of *The Arch Deacon* and *Razorbill Roofs*).

❶ McCall of the Wild ★★　　　　　　95m VS 4c
FA Mick Tighe & Kathy Harding 2 May 1997

Start at a sloping ledge just above the high tide line and to the left of the arch.
1. **25m 4c** Step across a wee inlet and climb a short wall to a big 'dance floor' which is a big open cave.
2. **30m 4c** Exit the cave left around a rib onto a tricky wall (crux) and ascend wall to a break in the right end of the overlap, then leftwards to ledges.
3. **40m 4a** Finish directly up the wall.

❷ The Arch Deacon ★★★★　　　　　120m HVS 5a
FA Mick Tighe & Kathy Harding 2 May 1997

A wonderful atmospheric route. Describes an amazing arc across the roof of the arch, initially above the serried ranks of guillemots and then above space! Start at a sloping ledge, beneath the centre of the long overlap at 10m.
1. **30m 4c** Step across the top of the deep slot and climb a shallow groove up the centre of the wall. Traverse right under the overlap until possible to pull leftwards through it on jugs. Continue the obvious line up and right easily to belay in a deep pegmatite recess between overhangs.
2. **45m 5a** Go right again on a grey band of immaculate rock on the very lip of the arch with an overhang above and a yawning abyss below. Take a hanging belay at the end of the band and *"praise the lord"* (?) A stunning pitch – strictly spacewalking!
3. **10m 4c** Traverse the rail right for 3m, then up a small hanging groove to good ledge.
4. **35m 4a** Continue fairly directly to an overhanging finish.

❷ₐ The Five Star Finish ★★★　　　　50m HVS 5a
FA Martin McKenna & Rob Lovell 25 May 2018

A spectacular finish up the headwall above the arch.
2. **5m 5a** Instead of belaying at the end of the overhangs, climb a flake groove to a good ledge.
3. **45m 5a** Climb leftwards to an obvious nose in the hanging corner. Use this to pull over onto the wall and finish direct.

❸ Razorbill Roofs ★★　　　　　　　65m E1 5b
FA Ruaraidh Mackenzie & Tim Sweeney 25 May 2000

Belay at the top of the small inlet at the base of the ramp.
1. **30m 5b** Step across the inlet and climb a groove to the roof above. Traverse on undercuts 2m rightwards and surmount the roof. Trend easily rightwards to a larger roof and take a wonderfully exposed hanging stance under it.
2. **35m 4b** Exciting moves directly over the roof on jugs is followed by an easy but wild-looking wall to the next roof. Tackle this directly, again on jugs, to reach a ledge near the top.

NL 5494 8416

THE ARENA

The area of rock at the back of the bay, immediately south (right) of the huge sea cave. In calm seas and low tides it is possible to traverse sea-level sloping ledges at least as far as the leftmost routes on **The South Pillar**. Otherwise, best to abseil directly to the base of the chosen route.

Descent: Abseil from near an old boundary wall, 100m directly down to the base. For *Arch Angel* abseil 70m to the left end of a guano ledge at one third height (or a little lower in the nesting season).

Photo Steve Crowe

4 Hakkar **** 110m E4 6a

FA Gordon Lennox & Kev Howett 6 May 2004

An amazing line leftwards out across the lip of the cave and the overhanging wall above. Start from a good ledge at the base of the pillar forming the right edge of the cave.

1. **20m 6a** Pull with difficulty directly through the bulge into the base of a pink quartz studded corner. Make a slightly rising traverse along the lip of the cave to a ledge.
2. **55m 5b** Climb directly up a groove to pull right onto ledges (possible kittiwakes!). Head diagonally up right to a guano-covered alcove, then direct up a steep wall and a hanging right-facing corner. Turn the roof on the left, then back right on the lip. Climb the wall and large hanging corner to belay on ledge on left.
3. **35m 4a** Finish direct up the corner and obvious line above.

5 Eye of the Storm *** 110m E1 5b

FA Gordon Lennox & Kev Howett 5 May 2004

The line of stepped left-facing corners up the left edge of the grey wall.

1. **35m 5b** Move up into a left-facing recess, then a short left-slanting green groove. At its top, move left, then diagonally leftwards under roof to gain a small ledge.
2. **40m 5a** From under the left end of the roof, exit left into cracks and climb the corner to pull out right at the top. Continue easily up the wall rightwards into a flake leading to an isolated pink quartz roof. Traverse hard left to belay at the end of the roof.
3. **35m 4a** Move out left into a large right-facing corner. Climb this, finishing up wrinkly quartz rock.

6 Too Young for a Gladiator ★★★★   100m E1 5b
FA Ruaridh MacKenzie, D.Ostler & Robert MacKenzie 6 May 2004

Lovely climbing on good holds, with an immaculate first pitch. One of the best routes of its grade on the islands. Start on the small left ledge.

1. **50m 5b** Climb the left-facing corner to an overlap, cross it on the right, climb diagonally left then up the stunning wall to the perched ledge on *Cuan a' Cheo*.
2. **25m 4c** Climb the wall left of the corner of *Cuan a' Cheo* to ledges. Belay under a roof on the right.
3. **25m 5a** Pull through the roof at its narrowest point and finish up the juggy pink streaked headwall.

7 Cuan a' Cheo ★★★   100m HVS 5a
FA Mick & Kathy Tighe, Janice McClenaghan, Janice Cargill & Graham Leckie 5 May 2000

An outstanding first pitch. Start on the small right ledge.

1. **50m 5a** Start up the short shallow groove, then pull out left and climb diagonally left to the right end of the overlap on *Too Young for a Gladiator*. Head diagonally right and up easier ground on black flakes to a band of roofs. Traverse left and break through these on the left, then direct to a perched ledge, beneath a rib and right-facing corner.
2. **50m 4c** Climb the slabby pale corner to ledges, finishing either up the broken fault on the left, or better (5a), over the roof and up the juggy headwall, close to *Too Young for a Gladiator*.

8 Arch Angel ★★★   110m HVS 5a
FA Mick & Kathy Tighe, John McClenaghan, Janice Cargill & Graham Leckie 6 May 2000

An impressive slightly rising left traverse across the centre of **The Arena**. Start from the guano ledge.

1. **30m 5a** The eye of faith traces a fault line going diagonally left towards the lip of the sea cave. Follow this to belay on the first available ledge.
2. **30m 5a** Continue 'a walk on the wild side' leftwards across the roof of the cave to a fantastic ledge in 'space' beneath a groove/fault line.
3. **50m 4b** Follow the fault line and the pink and black wall above directly.

Karen Latter "above the yawning abyss" on the spectacular airy second pitch of The Arch Deacon.

NL 5496 8406
THE SOUTH PILLAR

A square-shaped stone sits 50m back from the cliff top near a series of tiny weed-filled lochans. A 100m abseil from the cliff top in line with this stone gains a ledge system sloping down into the sea.

9 Pressure Band ★★   100m HVS 5a
FA Chris Bonington & Mick Fowler 31 May 1993

Start down and right of a deep recess, just left of a small cave.

1. **45m 5a** Step left and climb the short left-facing groove for 5m then pull out left round a rib and follow the obvious steep crack-line to a good ledge.
2. **25m 4a** Step up right then continue to the ledge below the twin roofs. Traverse left for 5m to the foot of a steep groove.

3 30m 4c Climb the groove to the top.

⑩ Stugeron ★★   105m HVS 5a
FA Chris Bonington & Mick Fowler 31 May 1993

The groove line to the immediate left of the crest of the buttress. Start as for *Pressure Band*.
1. 30m 5a Step left and climb a subsidiary groove until it is possible after about 10m to move right to gain the main groove. Follow this to pull out at a small roof to a ledge on the right.
2. 45m 4b Up and right through the bulge above and straight up to reach a ledge system below the headwall.
3. 30m 4c Move left to a deep V-groove, pull over a small roof and continue to the top.

⑪ Mayday ★★★   100m E1 5b
FA Mick & Kathy Tighe, John McClenaghan, Janice Cargill & Graham Leckie 1 May 2000

From the sloping belay ledges go left to a fine looking smooth grey wall, north from where the cliff starts to fall into the next bay.

1. 20m 5b Climb the wall via various small flakes to belay in a fine groove in an airy position.
2. 45m 4c Go up and right into a groove for a few metres then move back left slightly to follow a system of grooves and bulges to a large ledge beneath an impressive open corner with a grooved grey left wall.
3. 35m 4c Climb the corner and a wee overhang direct to the top.

⑫ Fisherman's Blues ★★★   95m E1 5b
FA Mick Tighe, Hamish Roberton & M.Horlick 27 April 2000

1. 25m 4c Follow a series of shallow stepped grooves rightwards, then direct to a big ledge. Belay beyond the right end of the isolated roof above.
2. 25m 5b Go steeply up on excellent rock for a few metres before going diagonally right again to pull through an area of pink bulging rock on good jugs. Go diagonally right again to belay on the only guano covered rock hereabouts.
3. 45m 5a A vertical 4m crack leads to an 8m left-facing corner. More cracks in the gently overhanging wall lead to easier ground.

NL 5495 8397
THE UNDERCUT WALL

Between **The South Pillar** and **Cobweb Wall**, just left of the latter, is an impressive undercut wall capped by a band of large roofs at the top with a convenient non-tidal shelf at its base.

Bird Restrictions: Routes at the left side are unaffected by birds, though the centre is heavily birded, avoid from May – August.

Descent: Make a 100m abseil from a good block in a recess about 40m south of the southmost **The South Pillar** abseil point to gain the left end of the shelf at the base. Use a 480cm sling on the block, as a full 100m is required.

① Kelvin and Hobs Direct ★★★   115m E3 5c
FA Helen Hall & Hugh Harris 30 May 2003;
Direct: Gary Latter & Ed Nind 10 June 2014

A great first pitch on lovely rock, up the fine wall left of the corner.

1. 55m 5c From one move up *Rayburnt*, strenuously traverse out leftwards above the roof for 5m, then move up to a projecting flake. Continue slightly left, then direct on beautiful rock to gain ledge in a rightward facing corner (45m - possible belay). Continue direct to large clean ledge.
2. 40m 5b Follow huge holds and cracks through steep guano-covered rock, aiming slightly rightwards to a huge ledge below a groove. Pull into this groove

and follow it for 10m to below a projecting block that forms a small roof. Move out right, then up and then back left to stand on the block. Climb up rightwards to a ledge and then up leftwards to a steep pull onto a big ledge (fulmar shooting gallery!).

- 2a **40m 5c** The many birdy ledges can be avoided by climbing directly up the fine groove right of the triangular roof. Finish by scrambling (15m) up rightwards to regain the abseil block.
- 3 **20m** Step right and climb an easy ramp-line leftwards, finishing up steeper rock.

② Rayburnt ★★★★   **110m E4 6a**

FA Lucy Creamer & Kev Howett 23 May 2001

Excellent climbing, the highlight the stunning right-facing corner system bounding the left side of the wall. Start at the left end of the wall below a narrow corner.

- 1 **50m 6a** A fantastic pitch. Climb through the initial overhang to gain the groove, making use of a helpful large incut pocket on the left wall. Continue steadily up the groove until forced out onto the right wall. Follow a crack just right of the groove, leading to better holds. Pull out leftwards at the top and continue more easily to good belay ledge in corner.
- 2 **40m 5c** Climb direct towards a prominent large triangular roof. Step right into a corner to breach the roof, then traverse right onto small ledges. Continue up a black groove to a steep wall, then follow sharp flakes up and left, then a quartz wall leading into a final steep corner. Ascend this, with a hard final pull onto ledge.
- 3 **20m 4a** Finish up the easy final corner.

③ The Secret's Out ★★★   **95m E5 6a**

FA Greg Boswell & Mike Shorter 11 June 2014

Start off a large step down on the left side of the ledge, just right of a quartz 'smile'.

- 1 **35m 6a** Make a hard pull from a jug to reach a short crack. Step left and make powerful moves to reach then follow the rising rightwards crack. Belay at a ledge.
- 2 **35m 5c** Move up directly from the ledge, weaving through some large roofs to belay at an obvious ledge.
- 3 **25m** Scramble to the top.

④ The Ocean of Time ★★★   **110m E5 6a**

FA Sam Williams & Uisdean Hawthorn (on-sight) 10 June 2014

- 1 **45m 6a** Start 3m left of *Taking the Hump*. Use black jugs and make a long move to a prominent spike (good gear). Move up to obvious corner above. Step left, gain a slopey right-rising hand-rail, then lunge to a big pocket. Continue straight up more steadily. Follow the quartz tongue of rock to belay under the left end of the large roof.
- 2 **45m 5c** Step left, continue straight up, taking a hanging corner with interest.
- 3 **20m** Scramble to glory.

⑤ Taking the Hump ★★★   **135m E5 6a**

FA Trevor Wood & Gary Latter 10 June 2005

A line breaching the centre of the wall, spectacularly breaking through the capping roofs.

- 1 **35m 6a** Climb the prominent right-facing capped groove. Break out right at the roof and continue up to a prominent horizontal break. Move up left through bulges and continue to belay on a good ledge.
- 2 **35m 5c** Continue straight up to the first small roof, move right and follow a rising right-trending line to a commodious belay ledge.
- 3 **30m 5b** Continue right along the ledge until a weakness in the bulging wall. Climb this then move right to a block belay on a ledge below roofs.
- 4 **35m 6a** Pull through the roof using a quartz rail clump then follow crazy runnels to the second roof. A long stretch reaches good holds. Continue to a third roof which is surmounted via a diagonal left-trending crack. Traverse right along an easy break (birdy!) under final large capping roofs past a lichenous yellow hanging corner. Climb a groove right of this on good holds to the top.

6 The Aga Sanction ★★★ 125m E4 6a

FA Henry Tyce, John Crook & Gary Latter 17 August 2011

Superb climbing up the centre of the wall. Start just right of the long narrow pool.

1. **35m 6a** Climb the vertical pegmatite band, with difficult reachy moves to gain good holds beneath the prominent right-slanting flake/groove system. Continue up this, then direct to belay on sloping ledge below a small roof.
2. **25m 5b** Traverse right 4m, then straight up the corner/groove above to a comfy ledge.
3. **30m 5c** From right end of ledge, climb the steep wall on rounded holds, then straight up to belay beneath the roof.
4. **35m 5c** Traverse left, then climb straight up to gain and climb the hanging roof-capped corner. Climb this, then step right onto small slab, pull out rightwards on superb holds in a stunning position and finish directly on good holds.

7 Fine Lines ★★★ 23m E5 6b

FA Gary Latter & Ed Nind 10 June 2014

Start a few metres left of *Hot White Spider*. Climb undercut crack with difficulty to good holds at base of hanging right-facing corner, then up this. Trend leftwards more easily to belay on small bollard (shared with *The Aga Sanction*). Abseil off.

8 Hot White Spider ★★★ 120m E4 6a

FA Henry Tyce, Gary Latter & John Crook 18 August 2011

Another superb varied route up the wall. Start beneath the short hanging right arête, just left of large low roof and the leftmost of two deep caves.

1. **40m 6a** Climb the twin hanging cracks in the arête with difficulty to good jams leading more easily to the large open groove. Continue fairly directly, steeply on big holds to guano-covered ledges. Traverse right and up to belay on perfect clean triangular ledge.
2. **40m 5b** Move out right, then directly up wall on incut holds, trending rightwards on easier ground, heading for prominent leaning pegmatite band breaking through right side of second last roof system. Belay on large guano ledges, just left of large (possibly suspect) spike.
3. **40m 5c** Climb initially gritty rock up to roof, move left then up through overlap on good holds. Continue up the fine sustained overhanging groove with good gear to small roof. Cross this slightly leftwards on surprisingly good holds, then directly, then move out right to follow crack up wall in a superb position to the top.

9 Burning Desire ★★★ 125m E5 6b

FA Kev Howett & Lucy Creamer 26 May 2001

A spectacular line up the right side of wall, through the upper cobweb section and through the right break in the capping roofs. Start on the large pedestal at the right side of the cave.

1. **50m 5c** Climb the easy flake up the green slab to a ledge in a large pink patch under a large hanging flake. Climb the flake to gain a small ledge, then go up and left into a recess with an obvious protruding spike on its left side. Leaving this head up and left to undercuts below a left to right undercut flake. Tricky moves up and right gain a belay ledge under the horizontal roof.
2. **25m 6b** Climb directly to the roof and launch leftwards (slightly harder for the short) to flake holds and an obvious jam in the lip to pull powerfully round onto the wall above. Climb the still steep wall to a big ledge.
3. **30m 5c** Climb sculptured rock features to reach a steepening pink pegmatite soaring arête. Climb it on slightly unnerving rock to bridge the slight groove above to under an overlap. Step steeply left and pull over into a short clean-cut right-facing corner. From its top step right to a black sloping ledge.
4. **20m 6a** Climb to loose looking blocks above. Use these with care to gain height on the left, then make bold moves up to the roof. Undercut leftwards into a wild position at the top of the cliff. Finish into the final groove.

NL 5495 8395

COBWEB WALL

The following routes are on the south-west tip of Guarsay Mor just before it turns 90 degrees back into Sloc Chiasigeo.

Descents: Abseil as for **The Undercut Wall** and scramble round right (south-east) at barnacle level (mid-low tide & calm seas) to a good ledge system running out right. Alternatively from a ledge at the SW tip of the headland opposite a cave on the north side of Lianamul, abseil 50m from twin blocks to the farthest west part of a sloping grass terrace/ledge system. Continue a further 80m to belay at sea level beneath the bulging pink walls.

10 Bikini Dreams ★★★   120m E2 5b
FA Andy Lole & Gary Latter 10 June 2006

Two excellent pitches. Start beneath a short V-slot above the initial roof.

1. **40m 5b** Climb easily up to good flakes and cross the initial roof on these. Continue directly then up a fine right-trending pegmatite ramp to belay in a recess.
2. **30m 5b** Climb directly up the wall then trend right on good flakes to an awkward step right into a shallow groove. Step up right onto an exposed ledge then pull directly through a roof to better holds above. Continue more easily up the right-slanting ramp to belay on a large ledge above.
3. **50m 4a** Continue easily up slightly right then back left and direct to finish.

11 Cuan a' Bochan ★★★   130m E1 5b
FA Mick & Kathy Tighe, Janice Cargill, John McClenaghan & Graham Leckie 2 May 2000

'Sea of Ghosts'. Ascends the pink veined wall and lower right overhangs. Start from a wee ledge below a small overhang.

1. **35m 5a** Go left 8m into a recessed groove and ascend this to gain another shallow groove of wonderful pink rock. Go up and slightly left over gently bulging pink and black rocks on fabulous jugs and pockets to belay below a small overhang 20m below the main line of overhangs.
2. **45m 5b** Go up and right under the wee overhang and slightly bulging rock, making for a break in the centre of the much bigger line of overhangs. Pull through the overhang and climb the pleasant ramp leading to the abseil ledge.
3. **50m 4a** A pleasant ramble leads to the top of the cliff, taking care with the sometimes fragile rock.

12 Itsy Bitsy Spider ★★★   105m HVS 5a
FA Gary Latter & Carl Pulley 15 August 2004

Tackles a rightwards trending groove/ramp system at the right side of the pink veined wall. Start just right of *Cuan a Bochan*.

1. **50m 5a** From a small ledge below a small overhang move up to the small overhang. Tackle it on its right side and follow jugs up to a pink bay. Follow bulging rock and a crack, again via jugs, on the right side of the pink bay to an obvious rightwards-rising grey ramp line. Follow jugs up this to belay at its top. A fantastic pitch.
2. **55m 4b** Follow a series of short corner systems and a broken slab to rejoin the first abseil ledge. From this, pleasant easy climbing on fragile rock leads to the top.

13 Jugs to Blow your Mind ★★   110m E1 5b
FA Shane Ohly & Jon Morgan 29 May 2003

1. **30m 5b** Traverse right into the groove/ramp below a roof, then steeply up over the left side of the lower roof. Move right along the pegmatite band to belay on a ledge beneath another big roof.
2. **50m 5b** Climb through the roof above and slightly right for 10m, then continue more easily to the huge ledge.
3. **30m 4a** Finish up the groove at the top left of the ledges.

14 Pieces of Eight ★★   120m E1 5b
FA Shane Ohly & Jon Morgan 30 May 2003

1. **35m 5b** Traverse right for 15m to gain a good ledge beneath a distinctive groove with a right-slanting

Photo Steve Crowe

hand crack. Follow the crack to a good ledge.
2 **15m 5b** Follow the groove, then up the wall slightly right to an obvious spike hold. Continue up to belay under the lower roof.
3 **20m 5b** Move diagonally right and through the roof at the right edge (crossing *Bill's Yellow Edge*). Continue directly up the wall to a good ledge.
4 **20m 5a** Continue direct on yellow rock to the huge ledge.
5 **30m 4a** Finish up the groove at the top left of the ledges.

15 Bill's Yellow Edge ★★   110m HVS 5b
FA Ruaridh MacKenzie & Tim Sweeney 22 May 2001

Climbs the right edge of the wall, beyond the cobweb section.

1 **35m 5b** Climb rounded jugs heading to the lower roof. Breach the roof on the right and traverse left above it to gain the base of yellow corners.
2 **35m 4c** Ascend corners then trend left to gain a left trending crack. Continue up the shoulder to gain the huge ledge.
3 **40m 5a** Keeping to the fine edge above, follow rounded rock past a yellow scoop to finish.

DUN MINGULAY

NL 543 820 1hr

SRON AN DUIN (FORTRESS PROMONTORY)

The spectacular cliff-girt headland at the south-west of the island. Tidal in rough seas only. From its southernmost tip a 90m high section of cliff extends northwards for over 200m culminating in a wonderful arch crossed by bands of roofs. Beyond the arch the rock continues at a lesser angle, becoming more broken as it bends round towards Arnamul.

Approach: From Mingulay Bay head south-west over the bealach between Hecla and Carnan. Contour round right and head out west (unsightly railings at the neck of the headland).

Descent: For the first 5 routes is by a 90m abseil from a collection of large blocks (small cairn) about 70m north of the most northerly of the twin cairns.

1 Children of Tempest * 95m E1 5c
FA Graham Little & Kev Howett 1 June 1995

The pillar bounding the north side of the clean main wall. Start at the left end of the highest ledge, at a flake.

1 **25m 5a** Trend left up a black slabby wall to enter a short slim groove with a cracked left wall. Climb this to a horizontal break. Pull up the wall above, step left then climb another short groove to reach a small triangular rock ledge. A fine intricate pitch.

2 **40m 5c** Ascend the diagonal crack rightwards with a thin move at its end to gain ledges above. Climb easily to below the base of a deep flake-crack in the steep clean pillar above. Follow this on grand holds to a large ledge.

3 **30m 4a** Trend right up rock steps to belay at the abseil point.

2 The Great Shark Hunt ** 100m E3 5c
FA Grant Farquhar & Noel Craine 12 June 1998

Spectacular line through the big roof at the left side of the roofed arch.

1 **55m 5c** Climb the immaculate wall left of the arch bearing right up an overhanging groove to a rest underneath the roof. Climb spectacularly leftwards through the roof and up the wall above to belay.

2 **45m 5b** Climb up bearing rightwards hastily past vomiting fulmars to the top.

3 Ride the Monster ★★   120m E4 6a
FA Kev Howett & Lucy Creamer 22 May 2001

A line up the headwall above the roof and flying groove of *Perfect Monsters*. Start as for 2 below a slightly left-trending line of flakes and grooves.

  1 **40m 5a** Go up the flakes and discontinuous grooves to a small ledge about 5m below the big roof.
  2 **25m 6a** Continue to follow 2 up to and through the big roof leftwards to below the secondary roof. Instead of continuing to traverse left, make hard moves right along the lip of the big roof to gain an open book corner. Follow this to a small stance on the left arête.
  3 **30m 5c** Continue up the slimmer corner above for 3m until a thin traverse line right can be taken to step onto an obvious small loose block. Step right again into the underclings under the roof. Follow these under the roof into a slight recess then pull directly over to a good flake-crack. Take this and the easy wall to a ledge.
  4 **25m 4c** Go up the wall direct to take a belay on a block back from the edge.

4 Perfect Monsters ★★★★   130m E7 6b
FA Twid Turner, Gary Latter & Louise Thomas (1 rest) 4 & 5 June 1998; FFA Carlos Simes & Nils Guillotine 6 June 2008

An outrageously exposed route following a diagonal line rightwards through the impressive roofed arch at the north end of the cliff, topping out above the apex.

  1 **40m 5c** Follow a line of shallow grooves and cracks to undercut right at a diagonal line of smaller roofs 6m beneath the main roof system. Belay on a flat spike and nuts in the leftmost of two grooves, directly beneath the big roof.
  2 **40m 6b** A spectacular sustained and well protected pitch. Move up to the main roof. Undercut right to a jammed block jug then launch over the roof to a good jug over the lip (the finger points the way!) then step out right (original belay). Continue following the awesome overhanging slanting roof/corner. Undercut, bridge or whatever seems right to a good nut belay at a small foot-ledge where it becomes a vertical corner. Gear good – Fs up to #3 and several PRs.
  3 **50m 6a** Another truly awesome pitch – sustained and pumpy. Climb the short black corner to the roof then undercut this rightwards to pull round into a slim cracked groove. Climb this, pulling leftwards over the bulge on good holds. Traverse right along the obvious juggy handrail for 8m then pull up through the roof to gain a good knee-bar rest on a horizontal spike. Psyche up and launch straight up on 'perfect monsters' (jugs) to finish up an immaculate vertical wall on good holds.

5 Ray of Light ★★★★   125m E4 5c
FA Crispin Waddy & Andy Cave June 1998

An impressively situated route near the centre of the arch, which stays dry in the rain. Start 10m right of *Perfect Monsters*.

  1 **40m 5c** Up a rightwards facing groove for 15m, move horizontally right across the wall then make harder moves to belay in a short leftwards-trending corner below the big roof.
  2 **40m 5c** Swing right round a bulge, go up a few moves then traverse spectacularly right above the arch to a corner. Move right and belay on a small ledge in a great position.
  3 **45m 5c** Climb directly up the wall to a humungous tusk in the roof. Move up onto it, pull right then climb direct more easily to finish.

5a Searching in the Sun ★★   65m E4 6a
FA Donie O'Sullivan, Ross Cowie & Tim Marsh 6 June 2008

An intimidating right start. Belay at the left end of small ledges below the wet offwidth/chimney.

  1 **40m 6a** Traverse easily up and left to the bottom of a short black left-facing corner. Climb this and then traverse horizontally left along the lip of a small overhang for 5m. Now launch up the bulging arête to a good rest. Continue up and left to belay among the birds at the prominent horizontal break.
  2 **25m 5c** Traverse left to gain the upper section of *Ray of Light*, which is followed to belay at the big roof.

John Crook on the second pitch of Voyage of Faith.

2 **30m 5b** Follow the flake-crack to its top to belay on small foot-ledges.

3 **25m 5c** Climb the wall, moving rightwards to a groove. Climb the groove to a small corner under a roof. Traverse right to break through the roofs on huge holds. Follow the big crack back left to belay.

4 **30m 5b** Step left and round some huge flakes to pull out right at 10m onto the wall at prominent spiky flakes. Continue up the wall to beneath a slim smooth groove. Traverse left 5m and climb the wall above on good holds, easing towards the top.

7 The Lobster Men ** 110m E4 6a
FA Andy Cave & Crispin Waddy June 1998

A direct line between up the wall right of the prominent flake-crack of *Les Voyageurs*.

1 **15m 4b** Pitch 1 of *Les Voyageurs*.

2 **45m 6a** Climb the wall direct (right of *Les Voyageurs* crack). Move right and up after a few metres, passing a conspicuous small shield of quartz to make technical moves up to a belay at the base of a crack.

3 **50m 5c** Follow the huge layback flake system leftwards to a good rest in a niche. Break out right on big jugs then continue more easily up to a ledge.

8 Voyage of Faith **** 120m E3 5c
FA Kev Howett & Graham Little 31 May 1993

An outstanding intricate line with much atmosphere and stunning exposure and a bit of a sting in the tail. Start at a groove 10m left of the square cut corner of *Sula*.

1 **25m 5b** Climb the short square-cut corner to a small ledge at the base of an open groove (a more comfortable belay if seas are running). Up the groove then pull out left to belay on a small ledge.

2 **30m 5b** Move out left from the ledge then follow a line of flakes trending left until a vertical flake-crack leads to an obvious horizontal fault. Hand traverse left along the fault then move up to a very exposed belay on a small nose of rock at the base of a slight corner (this whole area is undercut by a large sea cave).

3 **30m 5b** Climb the corner to a small ledge then

Descent: For routes 6–15, two small cairns just back from the cliff top mark the tops of *Voyage of Faith* and *The Silkie* (southmost). Make a 90m abseil from the edge of the cliff just north of the raised clump of thrift (cairn) down the line of *The Silkie*. There is a long ledge along the base, though in rough conditions the precise location of the top of the chosen route may wish to be located if the ledge at the base is awash.

6 Les Voyageurs **** 100m E3 5c
FA Twid Turner, Gary Latter & Louise Thomas 2 June 1998

A fine direct line up the cliff just right of the arch at the north end. Start beneath easy open grooves 5m right of the end of the ledges.

1 **15m 4b** Trend up leftwards to a large ledge at the base of a flake-crack.

traverse 2m left into a parallel groove. Up this then step left and slightly down to a very narrow ledge. Follow this until the overlap above can be bypassed giving access to a traverse line back right, above the overlap, to belay at blunt rock spikes adjacent to an obvious break in the main band of overhangs.

4 **35m 5c** Traverse out right through the overhangs (lower line) then climb directly up on steep rock via a groove to the base of a short, hanging corner. Climb this with difficulty to the top.

8a The Ocean of Air Finish ★★★★ 50m E4 5c
FA Steve Crowe & Karin Magog 21 May 2001

"Phenomenal exposure - unbelievable territory at the grade". Belay on small ledge on pitch 3, at the start of the right traverse.

4a **30m 5c** Step right then climb up to beneath the top roof where a good break leads leftwards through the hanging roofs in a spectacular position to join *Perfect Monsters*.

5 **20m 5a** The upper wall, as for *Perfect Monsters*, or finish up the final pitch of 25 *The Swell*.

9 The Hurried Path ★★★ 115m E3 5c
FA Kev Howett & Hugh Harris 29 May 1998

A fairly direct line up the wall right of *Voyage of Faith*. Start just left of a square bay at the base of the cliff.

1 **45m 5c** Gain and follow the easy left-trending groove until it fades, then follow a crack in a rib to below an overlap. Traverse left under this to enter a quartz niche on its immediate left. Exit right and climb up to gain an obvious fat flake in the steeper wall above and belay on small foot-ledges at its top.

2 **20m 5b** Climb up and slightly right into a small groove leading to horizontal breaks beneath roofs. Follow these rightwards until a step up can be made into a shallow cave beneath the large overhang. Belay at the right side of the cave.

3 **50m 5c** Pull directly through the roof at a prominent quartz flake. Step right and cross the bulge above to easier ground. Climb diagonally left up the steep juggy wall to the top.

10 Sula ★★★★ 100m E2 5b
FA Twid Turner, Gary Latter & Louise Thomas 3 June 1998

A wonderful direct route up the centre of the cliff at a surprisingly reasonable grade for the ground covered. Start 10m left of *The Silkie* at a shallow square-cut groove directly below a triangular roof at 15m.

1 **30m 5b** Climb the slabby wall to the right of the prominent square-cut groove, trending left towards a large flake at 15m (5m right of triangular roof). Move into a shallow groove (spike) and climb to the break. Traverse right a few metres past a bomber hidden runner to a good nut belay over the roof at the apex of a triangular roof.

2 **40m 5b** Climb straight up past good flakes to a delicate section which leads to a small overlap (good wires). Continue straight up, moving slightly right before surmounting a nose of rock below the steep section. Climb the huge flakes in a wild position to pull onto a vertical wall with big holds (8m left of the quartz groove of *The Silkie*). Pull up the wall to a yellow ledge and belay.

3 **30m 4b** Climb the steep juggy wall to the top.

Hugh Jenkins starting up the first pitch of the very amenable Sula.

11 The Silkie ★★★   105m E3 6a
FA Kev Howett & Graham Little 31 May 1993

An impressive direct line with sensational exposure on the third pitch.

1. **15m 4c** From the rock plinth climb a groove to distinctive red bands. Traverse left along these to a small ledge and belay.
2. **30m 6a** Go straight up to below a black diagonal arching overlap and follow it rightwards to below its widest point. Move up then pull through into a small scoop on the left (crux). Step back right across the lip then climb flakes trending left up a wall of compact rock to belay on the right below a square roof. A magnificent pitch.
3. **45m 5b** Turn the square roof on the left then take a quartz corner breaking out right through a second roof. Step left on to its lip then go directly up a juggy wall to another small roof. Cross this to gain a cracked block ledge. Go up slightly right to a better ledge and belay.
4. **15m 4a** Climb steep but easier ground to the top.

12 Call of the Sea ★★★★   100m E3 5c
FA Hugh Harris & Kev Howett 14 May 1999

Surprisingly reasonable climbing between *The Silkie* and *Sirens*.

1. **20m 5a** Climb *Sirens* up to the small roof at the start of the right traverse.
2. **30m 5c** Move right 2m to below a small but obvious flake in the lip of the bulge. Pull over and reach quartz underclings beneath the bulges above. Pull directly over this bulge to gain further underclings beneath the next bulge. Follow these right then up to gain a jug rail beneath a diagonal roof. Follow the hand rail leftwards to where the roof recedes and pull over onto the slab above. Move up into a shallow corner then up and left to belay in a large horizontal break, 3m beneath roofs.
3. **50m 5b** Climb direct through the roofs above via the left end of the block roof of *Sirens* then direct to the top.

13 Sirens ★★★   110m E3 5c
FA Kev Howett & Hugh Harris 28 May 1998

A good line traversing out of the first pitch of *The Silkie* then climbing around the roofs above.

1. **35m 5c** Climb the groove of *The Silkie* until it fades then step right and go up to gain a prominent recess beneath an isolated roof. Traverse right to the distinctive projecting block on *Perfectly Normal Paranoia*. Belay under the roof just above.
2. **25m 5c** Follow the crack leftwards below the roof and pull through the break on good flakes. Continue up and left on flakes to the next roof. Traverse left and climb a small corner to a good ledge beneath another roof.
3. **50m 5b** Pull through the left side of the roof via a spectacular flake then follow a sea of jugs to the top. The roofs on both pitches can be climbed direct at 5c.

> The cliff left of *Sirens* seems possible anywhere at E3. Other routes squeezed in include *The Silk Route* ★★ E3 5b, 5c, 5b left of *Sula*; and *Ribbed for Her Pleasure* ★ E3 4c, 5c, 5b a direct on *The Silkie*.

14 Perfectly Normal Paranoia ★★★   105m E6 6b
FA Paul Thorburn & Rick Campbell 30 May 1997

A committing diagonal line between *The Silkie* and *Rory Rum*. From the plinth at the base of *The Silkie* cross ledges to belay below a left-facing blocky groove. A combination starting up the bottom pitch of *Sirens* would give an excellent E4.

1. **25m 6b** Climb the groove through the square recess in the left side of the lower roof then make increasingly difficult moves right under the final overlap until it is possible to follow a shallow groove to a projecting block ledge. Belay under the roof above.
2. **15m 5c** Traverse right under the roof, rising slightly to a semi-hanging stance at the start of a left to right diagonal line of undercuts.
3. **25m 6a** Follow the undercuts to the obvious fault in the roof. Pull through this and continue to a shake-out. Climb rightwards up the wall then left under the roof to an uncomfortable belay

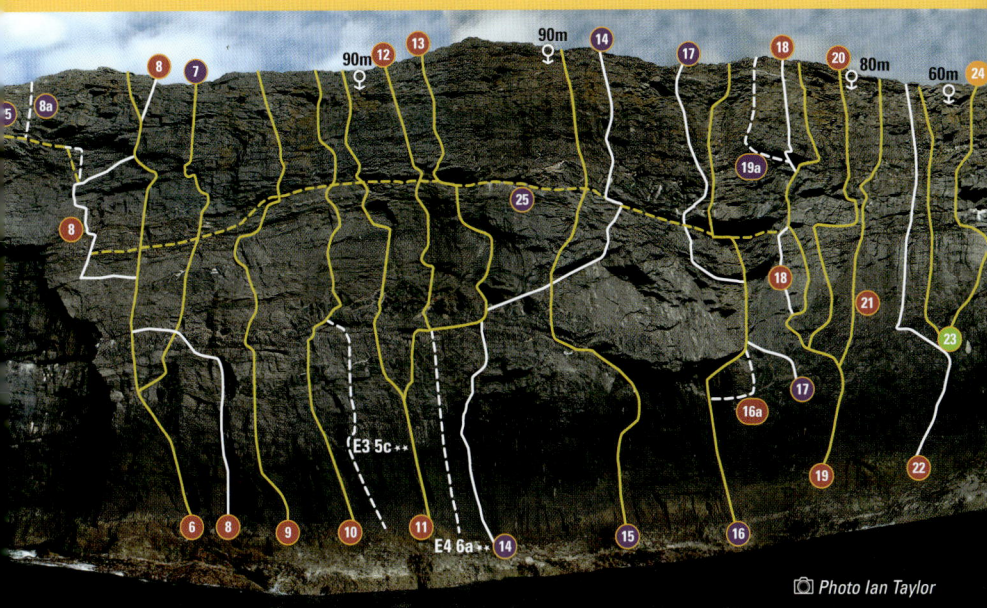

Photo Ian Taylor

in slanting breaks under the main weakness.
4 **40m 5b** Pull through the weakness then direct to the top. Sustained.

14a Where's Paranoia ***   120m E3 5c
FA Andy Watmough & Karin Magog 4 June 2007

An attempt to follow the E4 version of 14.
1 **40m 5c** Follow *Sirens*.
2 **10m 5c** Follow pitch 2 of 14 for 10m until below obvious large undercuts in the roof above. Take an uncomfortable hanging belay below these.
3 **30m 5c** Climb through the roof using the undercuts and continue to belay in the main break under a jutting flake.
4 **40m 5a** Climb direct to the top.

15 Subterranean Exposure **   100m E5 6b
FA Rick Campbell & Gordon Lennox 14 May 1999

Follow the tidal platform south to scramble across to belay at the left side of a slabby pillar, 10m short of a sea cave.
1 **20m 6a** Climb the left side of the pillar to overhang. Undercuts lead right to a groove which is followed to wide break underneath the next roof. Traverse right for 8m and move over roof into hanging flake-crack which leads with interest to belay in Guano Cave.
2 **35m 6b** Tunnel leftwards and continue traversing past a desperate section to a point where the roof can be breached. Blast straight up the bulging wall above (through the *Perfectly Normal Paranoia* belay at a slight rib) to follow a sustained line of side pulls and undercuts bearing rightwards to belay on a flaky block in a break.
3 **45m 5b** Follow jugs direct to the top.

SOUTHERN SECTION

Descents: Go to the southernmost point of the headland and scramble down a short easy chimney to gain a wide ledge running north, about 8m below the cliff top. For routes from *Big Kenneth* to *Done Mingulay*, make an 80m abseil from near the end of the ledge, 10m north of a small cairn marking the top of *Fifteen Fathoms of Fear*. For the rightmost routes, make a 60m abseil from just north of the cairn.

16 Big Kenneth ★★★★ 90m E5 6a
FA Crispin Waddy & Andy Cave June 1998

Another superb route following big features through triple roofs cutting through the main pitch of *Rory Rum...* finishing via the hanging crack in the final roof. From the base of the abseil, traverse down left then back up on seaweed-covered ledges to belay at the base of a rightwards facing corner.

1. **25m 6a** Climb the corner for a few metres to the base of the first roof. Undercut rightwards initially on big holds. At the end, swing out strenuously right to a big jug then trend up and slightly right to belay below the second roof.
2. **20m 6a** Move up right then back left to a horizontal break below a roof. Pull over the roof then make interesting moves left then up to belay below the final crack.
3. **45m 6a** Layback and jam the overhanging crack on big holds until forced out right, making a long reach in a stunning position to a positive pocket. Easier to the top.

Glyn Stanworth nearing the top of the first pitch of Dun Moaning.

16a Little K ★★ 35m E3 6a
FA Steve Crowe & Karin Magog 9 June 2006

A more often dry and splendidly bold variation on the first pitch of *Big Kenneth*. Follow *Big Kenneth* as far as the first roof to check whether it is dry. If not step down and traverse rightwards and continue slightly downwards until it is possible to pull round into a groove that leads back up to the roof (a few metres right of where you left it!) just in time to swing out strenuously right to a big jug. Trend up and right to the belay.

17 Rory Rum the Story Man ★★★ 95m E5 6a
FA Kev Howett & George Ridge (2 rests & hanging belay) 26 June 1996; FFA Rick Campbell & Gordon Lennox May 1999

Follows an impressive line through the big roofs left of *Dun Moaning*. Start from a small quartz ledge just over the lip of the lower water-washed bulge left of *Dun Moaning* (down and left of a large rounded quartz ledge).

1. **25m 6a** Climb the obvious left-slanting diagonal overlap to its end then make hard moves to a small ledge above. Follow the thin flake above to below a bulge. Teeter left under it to gain an obvious block ledge at the base of a small groove.
2. **40m 6a** The 'shorties revenge pitch'. Climb the groove and move up and left to good holds under the big roof. Traverse left under the roof with increasing difficulty past a deep slot then follow sloping holds to a jug. Pull directly through the roof above by a large projecting hold then climb directly through the roof above into a curious hole. Belay on the big ledge above.
3. **30m 5a** Traverse 5 metres right and follow easy ground to the top.

18 Where's Rory? ★★★ 75m E3 5c
FA Paul Thorburn & Rick Campbell May 1997

Start as for *Dun Moaning*. New line climbed in error, thinking they were repeating *Rory Rum the Story Man*.

1. **35m 5b** Follow *Dun Moaning* to its triangular niche then trend up and left to belay on top of a projecting block.
2. **15m 5b** Continue straight up before belaying left

PABBAY & MINGULAY DUN MINGULAY | 439

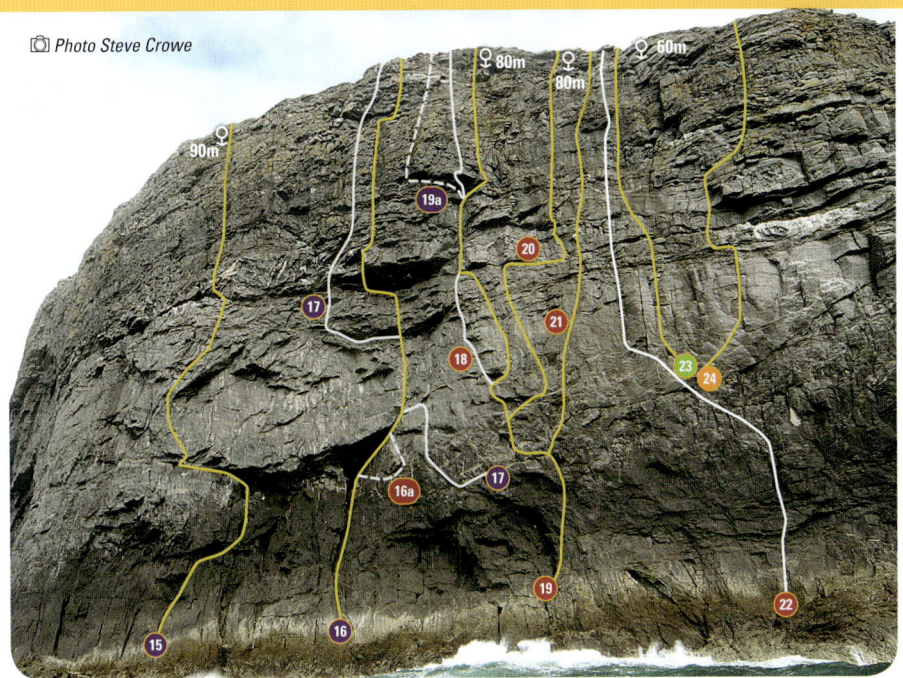

Photo Steve Crowe

of a small triangular roof (just right of a very large roof – same belay as *Dun Moaning*).

3 **25m 5c** Above and left is another huge roof. Pull left into a hanging corner (as for *Dun Moaning*) then climb through the widest part of the roof going slightly left then pulling right on the lip. Easy to the top.

19 Dun Moaning ★★ 75m E2 5b
FA Kev Howett & Graham Little 1 June 1995

Takes a line just to the left of *Done Mingulay*, starting as for that route.

1 **25m 5b** Climb the initial black wall then trend left into a triangular niche. Exit from this and climb to a ledge on the left under a bulge.

2 **25m 5b** Climb the short corner on the left of the bulge with difficulty then step back right above it to gain a groove-line heading up left to the right side of the huge upper roofs. Belay below the roof at a tiny ledge.

3 **25m 5b** Move up to the roof and pull left over it to gain a corner which leads to the upper, larger roof. Traverse right below it to pull over its right edge at an obvious hanging groove. Ascend a black wall on the left to finish at the abseil ledge.

19a Alternative Finish ★★ 30m E4 6a
FA Kev Howett & Graham Little 1997

Follow pitch 3 to the upper roof. Traverse left under the roof and climb the wall to the top.

20 Dunne Slimmin' ★★★ 70m E2 5b
FA Rich Kirby & Paul Tanton 7 June 2000

The best of the trilogy of E2s, with a superb long main pitch. Start as for *Dun Moaning*.

1 **25m 5b** Climb to the triangular niche, then move up and right to a ledge.

2 **45m 5b** Move up left by an obvious right-facing groove to prominent break 5m below roofs. Traverse right 8m until below the right side of the roof. Climb steeply up a crack to a large thread and pull left over the roof, then direct above.

21 Done Mingulay ★★ 70m E2 5b
FA Andy Cunningham & Grahame Nicoll 1 June 1995

Belay on a ledge in an alcove at seaweed level (low tide desirable!)

1. **50m 5b** Climb up and right on the initial black wall then trend left into an obvious groove-line heading for a prominent roof (well right of the larger ones). From the top of the groove climb right into a flake-crack leading to the roof. Pull rightwards through the right end of the roof and into a corner leading to belay ledges.
2. **20m 4a** Climb straight up a right-facing flake-crack to the top.

22 Yob and Yag Go Climbing Part 3 ★★ 60m E1 5b
FA Alan McSherry & Mike Howard August 1998

Start on tidal ledges at the undercut base of the wall (15m below the starting ledge on *Fifteen Fathoms of Fear*).

1. **25m 5a** Climb through the bulging wall by the obvious break to join *Fifteen Fathoms of Fear* belay. Continue to a good flake up left, traverse left 3m and climb a groove to a belay.
2. **35m 5b** Traverse left for 3m to a wide crack in a slim corner, climb this, then direct up the wall above.

23 Fifteen Fathoms of Fear ★★★ 50m Severe 4a
FA Grahame Nicoll & Andy Cunningham 1 June 1995

An impressive intimidating route for the grade. Belay on a small ledge above the undercut base of the wall. Climb up leftwards into a vague corner-crack (the rightmost of several) then continue straight up, passing the left end of a long roof with guano below. A wide depression leads to a steeper finish at the abseil point.

24 A Few Fathoms More ★★ 50m VS 4c
FA Grahame Little & Kath Pyke 27 June 1996

Climbs some very impressive terrain for the grade. Start from the right end of the belay ledge, as for *Fifteen Fathoms of Fear*.

1. **30m 4c** Climb up rightwards to another ledge, then a flake-crack on the right. Continue direct until a few metres below a wide slot above the horizontal break (guillemot colony). Make a short left traverse (crux), then up to belay in horizontal fault, just left of the birds.
2. **20m 4c** Climb a groove immediately left of the wide slot, step right then climb direct through bulges to finish.

25 The Swell ★★★ 235m E4 6a
FA Donie O'Sullivan, Ross Cowie & Tim Marsh 5 June 2008; pitches 6 & 7 Steve Crowe & Karin Magog 21 May 2001

A stupenduous right to left girdle, following for the most part an obvious fault-line which delineates the boundary between the smooth lower wall and the more broken upper wall. Amazing climbing.

1+2. **50m 5b** Climb the first two pitches of *Dun Moaning* to belay at the right end of the upper roof of *Big Kenneth*. In wild seas, this point could be gained by a 30m pitch traversing the break from the belay at the top of pitch one of *A Few Fathoms More*, just left of the guillemot colony.
3. **15m 5c** Traverse left around the arête and continue under the roof to belay at a slot just beyond where *Big Kenneth* breaches the roof.
4. **30m 6a** Follow the fault strenuously left to the arête and then easily for another 20m.
5. **30m 4c** Cruise the juggy fault-line to belay above the plinth of *The Silkie*.
6. **40m 5b** Continue easily left for 20m and then descend a few metres to a lower break. This leads left past an orange shield to a comfortable belay on the edge of the huge arch (as for *Ray of Light*).
7. **40m 5c** Now take a diagonal line up and left to gain the break under the huge roof. Traverse easily left for 7m and belay on *Perfect Monsters*.
8. **30m 5c** An exposed traverse left on the lip of the roof gains a small ledge. Finish direct.

RUBHA LIATH (GREY PROMONTORY) 40min

The headland at the extreme south-west end of the island overlooking the small offshore islands of Geirum Mor and Geirum Beag.

Approach: As for Dun Mingulay to the col then head south-west down the slope to the promontory, overlooking the small rocky islands.

SEAL SONG GEO
The extensive geo just north of the headland of Rubha Liath.

NL 551 816 1hr

NORTH WALL
A good fairly extensive wall set back from easy-angled tidal ledges.

Descent: Scramble down an easy grassy rake then a short rock step (easier descents further west) to a large flat shelf with a prominent large block perched immediately above the top of the crag. For routes 1 to 4, abseil (Ns & Fs at the back of the ledge) down to good ledges at the base; for routes 5 to 7 from a smaller block further west.

① The Girl with Extraordinary Eyes ★★   25m E3 6a
FA Robert Durran & Charlie Henderson 23 July 2000

Down and right of 2 is a clean wall with an undercut on its right side by a low cave. Abseil direct to the slightly tidal platform at the base. Surmount the left edge of the cave and move right to the prominent line of right-trending flakes. Climb these to a rest below the capping roof and surmount this with difficulty in a fine position to finish.

② Delayed Reaction ★★   30m E1 5c
FA Louise Thomas, Twid Turner & Gary Latter 3 June 1998

The prominent hanging crack on the right side of the wall, gained via the lower corner. Climb the corner on good holds to a huge platform on the right. Traverse left on good holds to gain the crack. Follow the crack, the crux being saved for the final moves to gain good holds just short of the top.

Louise Thomas making the first ascent of Delayed Reaction.

③ Fergus Sings the Blues **   35m E4 6a

FA Gary Latter & Fergus Murray 3 June 1998

Excellent sustained climbing breaking through the roof on the right side of the crag. Start at the base of the corner. Move up and leftwards along a good flake handrail. Climb the wall above past some good horizontal slots to the roof. Pull out right to two good undercut flakes then make a long reach to a good break (F #2.5 & #3). Pull up the wall above on jugs then go left and follow slabby twin cracks. Finish quite boldly up the steady impending wall above.

4 *Gneiss Helmet* ★ E3 4b, 5c follows a left-slanting diagonal line under the roofs starting from 2.

⑤ Castlebay Hen Party **   45m E1 5b

FA Carl Pulley & Peter Hemmings 13 August 2006

Start beneath a steep left-facing corner.

1 **30m 5b** Climb up to the corner via blocks and a short chimney then the corner and its continuation to a large ledge. Break through the awkward capping roof on the left (above a birdy ledge) to belay on the pink quartz ramp of 4.

2 **15m 4c** Traverse airily left beneath a triangular roof to finish up the corner of 6.

⑥ Mistaken Identity **   30m VS 4c

FA Peter Hemmings & Carl Pulley 13 August 2006

Start at a chimney cleft near the left end. Climb rightwards to the base of a steep crack at the left end of first steep wall. Climb this and the broken corner to birdy ledges. Break through the roof on the right to finish up the airy corner.

⑦ Dancing with Hens ***   30m VS 4c

FA Peter Hemmings & Carl Pulley 13 August 2006

Start left of sea level niche below a prominent orange band of rock and a corner. Climb the corner to the steep orange wall and pull up on jugs. Continue up the corner, pull though the roof and step out right above the void. Spacewalk rightwards and pull through to a slab leading to easy ground.

NORTH-WEST FACE   NL 551 815   1hr

The heavily grooved face extending from the back of the geo to the tip of the point. The left side of the face is split by a ledge system at two-thirds height – some of the routes climb only the shorter top section.

Descent: Locate the abseil point for most of the routes from the opposite side of the geo. A small cairn lies at the top of the fairly obvious clean-cut corner of *The Power of the Sea*.

UPPER TIER

1 The Extraordinary Relief Map of Iceland ★★
25m E2 5b

FA Robert Durran & H.Lawrenson 13 August 2003

Start at the extreme left end of the ledge beneath an obvious hanging roof-capped groove. Climb very steeply up, move left then up and back right to the base of the groove. Climb the groove, turning the capping roof on the right.

2 The Boat ★   15m HVS 5b
FA Robert Durran & Alan Taylor 9 July 1999

The striking right-slanting groove in the wall left of the top corner of 13. Good jamming and bridging to a steep finish.

3 Flying Hex ★   15m VS 4c
FA Allison Callum & Helen Thorburn 4 June 1998

Climb to a horizontal flake then up into a corner. Climb this to finish up prominent twin cracks.

4 The Girl in the Boat ★★   15m E3 6a
FA Robert Durran & Alan Taylor 4 July 1999

The thin flake/crack in the right wall of the top corner of 1. Climb the wall to a good side pull at the base of the flake then make hard moves with improving protection to a good flake and finish more easily.

5 Solid Dude ★★   18m HVS 5a
FA Allison Callum, Helen Thorburn & John Sanders 4 June 1998

The prominent diagonal crack midway between two corners at the left end. Climb the crack to beneath a daunting overhang (hex #11). Fist jam the roof in a wild position.

6 The Mooring ★★   15m E1 5c
FA Robert Durran & Alan Taylor 4 July 1999

The unappealing corner right of 13 has a steep well-protected crack in its right wall.

7 *The Wake* • E4 6a climbs wall to right.

8 Not Ali's Crack ★   15m E1 5b
FA Fergus Murray & John Sanders 4 June 1998

Climb the wall via ledges then the overhanging right-slanting crack.

9 Pumping Up ★   15m VS 4c
FA John Sanders, Allison Callum & Helen Thorburn 4 June 1998

Start as for the previous route. Move into the corner-crack on the right and climb to exit left.

10 Doppelkratzer   15m HVS 5a
FA Allison Callum, John Sanders & Helen Thorburn 4 June 1998

Start in the centre of the steep bulgy wall at a thin crack. Ascend the crack delicately (poorly protected) with an awkward balancy move up and left to mantelshelf onto a ledge. Step right to finish.

11 The Monster Waves ★   15m HVS 5a
FA Neil Morbey & Piotr Bamberski 27 May 2013

Start 2m right of 10. Climb up to a small overhang, surmount this via small jugs heading for a rightwards diagonal line, which tops out on the arête.

12 The Trusted Scallop ★   15m E2 5c
FA Danny Carden & Eamon Quinn 27 May 2013

Follow a right-facing corner for 5m to a hard but well-protected move off sloping scalloped crimps up a steep wall to the rail beneath the prominent grey roof. Lurch up and left through the overhang in a very exposed position to better holds.

PABBAY & MINGULAY SEAL SONG GEO

LOWER TIER

13 The Power of the Sea ★★ 40m E2 5b
FA Kath Pyke & Graham Little 26 June 1996

Start from a tidal ledge well above the sea.
1 **25m 5b** From the left end of the ledge climb the spectacular overhanging flake-crack. From its top step right to enter a narrow slot breaking through overhanging rock. Climb this to a horizontal fault.
2 **15m 4c** Enter and climb the fine corner above.

The overhanging groove and arête is 14 *It's Not My Fault* ★ E1 5b,4c.

15 Seventh Heaven ★★ 55m E3 6a
FA Kev Howett & Janet Horrocks 15 May 1999

Excellent climbing with a technical crux in a space-walking position. Start on the ledge as for 14.
1 **10m 5b** Climb the left-arching corner to meet the right end of the luminous green ledges.
2 **30m 6a** From the extreme right end of the ledges climb a slim tapering corner to reach a good undercut in an overlap. Swing immediately out right round the arête into another overhanging corner and climb this more easily to the midway ledges to belay beneath the abseil corner. Initial corner climbed direct to the same point is E3 5c.
3 **15m 5b** Climb the left arête of the big corner via a shallow tapering groove in an excellent position to a rounded finish.

16 Far From the Dogging Crowd ★★ 45m E2 5b / S3
FA Crispin Waddy (on-sight solo) June 1998

Start from a small ledge 15m down and right of 14. This

can be gained by abseil or by down climbing a crack in an arête that leads to a groove and hence the lower ledge at about 5a, making a good first pitch to 12. Climb the left groove for 9m to a large break. Traverse right under a steep slim groove to gain an easier-looking one. Climb this for a metre or so then move left onto a flake on an arête that leads to another groove. Climb this to the huge fault line. Finish up another large groove.

17 *Propaganda* • E2 5c,4c S3 takes the arêtes between 16 & 18.

18 Ocean Wrath ★★ 40m E2 5c
FA Tim Rankin & Gordon Lennox 10 May 1999

Start from triangular platform well above sea at the base of the next groove right of 14.

1 **25m 5a** Move up left and climb a crack to a ledge. Climb a groove then move left and climb another groove and ribs to a large ledge.
2 **15m 5c** Move up left and climb cracks in the right wall of the slanting groove to finish out right.

19 Walking on Waves ★★ 40m E1 5b
FA Gordon Lennox & Tim Rankin 10 May 1999

Great climbing up the next groove right of 18 starting from a small triangular plinth 15m above the sea.

1 **25m 5b** Move up left on jugs to a good ledge beneath a bulging rib. Climb the bulging rib between green grooves to a large ledge.
2 **15m 5a** The wildly overhanging groove on equally wild jugs. A sensational pitch

20 Spitting Fury ★★★   45m E6 6b
FA Gordon Lennox & Tim Rankin 10 May 1999

Outstanding climbing finding a way through the guarding overhangs in the centre of the wall. Start from the same plinth as 19.

1. **25m 6b** Traverse round right to an obvious spike. Make committing moves up and right to pull round into a hanging right-facing corner. Further hard moves lead up to the roof. Squirm right round the roof and climb an overhanging groove to pull out left and up an easier-angled arête to a ledge.
2. **20m 5c** Climb the outrageously steep and juggy flying groove right of 19.

> The long corner just left of 22 is 21 *The Wet Look* ★★ E1 5b,4c.

22 Durdle Huxter ★★   45m E2 5b
FA Dave Towse & Glenda Huxter 9 May 1999

1. **15m 5a** Climb direct up the tapering corner, stepping out right to bypass the roof.
2. **30m 5b** Ascend corner with deep crack in right wall to a roof, traverse right to finish up a groove.

23 Mingin' in the Rain ★★★   50m E3 5c
FA Hugh Harris & Kev Howett 9 May 1999

1. **15m 5a** Traverse out right to base of hanging corner. Climb this, exiting left to an airy ledge on the arête.
2. **35m 5c** Follow the slim groove past a small ledge (poorly protected) to easier ground. Trend right then left to finish.

24 Sundew ★★   45m E1 5b
FA Glenda Huxter & Dave Towse 10 May 1999

The right arête of the offwidth chimney. Finish slightly rightwards, then direct.

THE POINT

Abseil from the very tip of the headland to a ledge above the sea. The first two routes are round on the north west face.

1 Rubha Soul ★★   30m E1 5a
FA Graham Little & Kath Pyke 26 June 1996

Move up a little then traverse left on jugs across an overhanging wall to pull up into a groove. Follow this to below a roof, traverse left then pull up into the final groove to finish.

> The short hanging groove in the very edge of the point itself is 2 *Soul Sister* ★ E4 6a, 5a.

3 Eaglesea ★★   35m VS 4c
FA Mick & Kathy Tighe, John McClenaghan, Graham Leckie & Janice Cargill 3 May 2000

Climb the inset chimney and the easier corner of the last route above to the top.

4 Cracknan Euan ★★★   35m VS 4c
FA Mick & Kathy Tighe, John McClenaghan, Graham Leckie & Janice Cargill 3 May 2000

From the big hole traverse right past the chimney and climb into the superb clean crack and corner forming the right side of the pillar, finishing in a wide open easy corner.

5 Flyaway ★★   35m VS 4c
FA Mick & Kathy Tighe, John McClenaghan, Graham Leckie & Janice Cargill 3 May 2000

From a big hole traverse right past the obvious huge chimney along the steeper sea-level rocks to the base of the second more slabby corner. Climb this and easy rocks above to the top.

THE GEIRUM WALLS   NL 5514 8143

Short walls extending from the tip of the headland east to beyond the eastern tip of Geirum Beag. A convenient wide platform dips down eastwards from the tip of the headland, petering out about 60m along before continuing lower down beneath prominent 45 degree roofs forming the left end of **The Main Walls**.

NL 5500 8145
HIDDEN WALL

The pink wall rising from the sea just east of the point.
Descent: From the top of the point take an easy scramble descent eastwards down to a large platform running eastwards. Halfway along the platform descend a series of short corners back westwards to a ledge about 5m above the sea, overlooking the wall. Abseil onto wave-washed ledges and rush across to a small elevated ledge under the wall. Or abseil directly down the wall.

1 The Gull Who Shagged Me ★★★   25m E3 5c
FA Dave Towse, Glenda Huxter & Dave Turnbull 26 May 2000

Take a rising traverse left on flakes until it is possible to climb back right. A short wall provides the crux to gain a down-pointing spike and a ledge. Finish direct above. Excellent position and immaculate rock.

2 Whipsplash ★★★   25m E4 6b
FA Glenda Huxter, Dave Towse & Dave Turnbull 26 May 2000

Climb a gently overhanging crack directly above the small ledge then the corner above it to a ledge. Move leftwards to finish up a final steep wall.

THE PLATFORM WALL

The wall above the large platform at the left end. Beyond the descent for the **Hidden Wall** the platform is topped by an increasingly steep orange wall, which merges with a series of roofs at the far right (east) end. Initially the walls are broken but they start at an obvious hanging corner and arête. **Access:** By an easy descent from the very point itself.

1 Crooked Thumb ★   10m VS 4c
FA Mick Tighe & Hamish Robertson 24 April 2000

Start under an isolated roof at 4m. Climb the fierce roof and the wall above via a crack.

2 Corner and Slab ★   10m VS 5a
FA Kathy Tighe & E.Knudson 24 April 2000

Climb the steep lower wall below and left of the hanging corner to gain the easier slab above.

3 Lunar Pull ★★   10m VS 5a
FA Mark Robson, Finlay Bennet & D.Godfrey 18 September 1998

The excellent loft facing hanging corner climbed direct through the steep lower wall and roof.

4 Pocket Wall ★   10m E1 5b
FA Mick Tighe & E.Knudson 24 April 2000

Start right of 3. Climb the lower wall on big holds to the horizontal break, then pockets up the wall to the top.

5. The Abyss of Numbers *   10m E2 5c
FA D.Godfrey, Mark Robson, Finlay Bennet 18 September 1998

Just right of the arête is an obvious vertical crack. Gain the crack through the guarding roof and follow it to its end. Finish direct on to a sloping ledge.

6. Let Things Go *   10m E2 5b
FA Finlay Bennet,, D.Godfrey & Mark Robson 18 September 1998

Start where the platform narrows. Follow the large flake rightwards to a crack through the overlap. Continue up the crack to the top.

7. Obvious Crack **   15m E3 5c
FA Dave Turnbull & Kev Howett 22 May 2000

Pull over the roof onto the hanging ledge and into a hanging right-facing groove/flake. Up this then traverse left and up to holds leading back right to gain a 'phallic-looking' downward pointing projection. Pass this to gain a big break. Pull out direct into a scoop (hidden jug) to finish.

8. Horizontal Hamish *   10m E1 5b
FA Mick Tighe, Hamish Robertson & Yvonne Colwell 25 April 2000

Climbs a line just left of the 45 degree roof. Take a horizontal flake below and left of the roof to gain an upright position with difficulty into a left-facing groove and finish up this.

9. Hot Enough for ya? **   25m E2 5c
FA Gary Latter & Matt Harding 16 August 2011

Climb direct by grooves and through roof on good holds to gain the left end of the long tapering ledge below the main roofs. Pull through the roof leftwards in a fine position, then direct up wall, pulling out right at horizontal crack to finish up crack on right.

THE MAIN WALLS

These extend from the 45 degree roofs eastwards for about 100m. The platform re-emerges at the roofs and extends the full length of the walls, dipping down eastwards. It is possible to view the 45 degree roofs easily from the top of the crag, above a clean-cut, west-facing corner (*After the Basking Shark*).
Descent: Abseil down to an extensive dark ledge, 5m above sea-washed ledges.

> The roof is breached by 10 *Sunshine's Better* ** E4 6a; 11 *Little Miss Sunshine* ** E3 6a and 12 *Pragmatist's Folly* ** E5 6a.

13. Junior Keel **   15m E4 6b
FA Ed Brown 29 June 2007

The right crack in the 45-degree roofs. Climb the deceptively steep juggy wall to below the crack. Make wild moves out to and over the lip.

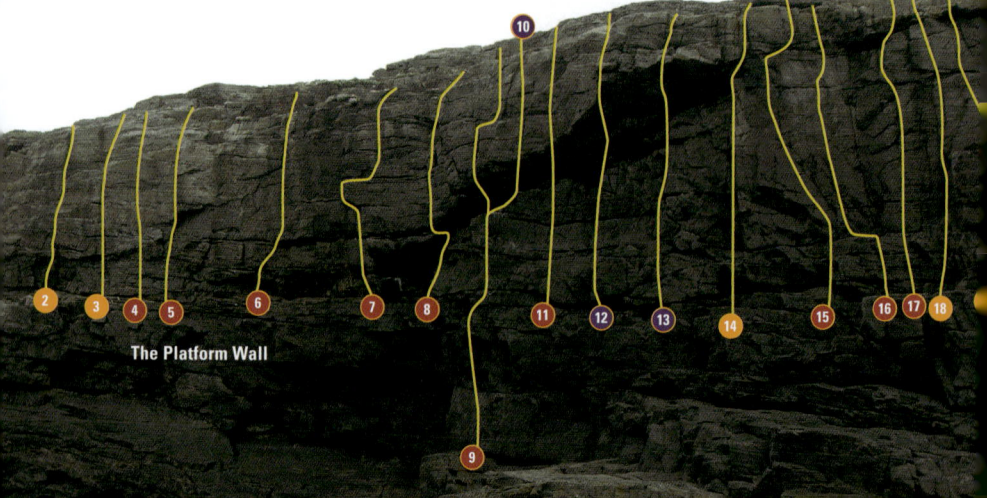

The Platform Wall

14 Seriously Twitching *   10m HVS 4c
FA Janet Horrocks & Claudia Birmelin 13 May 1999

Bounding the right edge of 45 degree overhanging wall is a left-facing corner. Climb the corner, pulling out right in an exciting and strenuous position on big holds.

15 The Crack that Tim Forgot **   10m E2 5c
FA Tim Carruthers & Chris Boulton 31 May 1999

Strenuous. Climb the short tapering slab immediately right of 14 then a thin crack above to the top horizontal break. Step right and finish in a shallow V-groove.

16 The Singing Seal **   10m E2 5b
FA Janet Horrocks & Claudia Birmelin 13 May 1999

Crack emerging from a broken niche. Climb the left side of cracks to a good ledge, traverse left 2m and pull over the steep headwall.

17 Big Sea in My Trousers *   10m E2 5b
FA Tim Catterall 23 May 2000

Crack immediately left of the niche of 18.

18 Screaming Seal *   10m HVS 4c
FA Tim Catterall, Stephen Porteus & Bill Renshaw 22 May 2000

Crack emerging from left-facing niche in the centre of the wall.

19 Try the Shark Fin Soup **   10m HVS 4c
FA Hugh Harris & Lesley Beck 22 May 2000

Start 2m left of 20. Directly up the wall to finish over the capping roof on good holds. Poorly protected.

20 After the Basking Shark *   8m Severe 4a
FA Fergus Murray & Mike Snook 4 June 1998

The large left-facing corner. Start at the bottom of the corner (scramble up from main ledge). Up the corner-crack-line, taking the right corner exit for the last 2m.

21 The Curious Grey *   8m VS 4b
FA Steve Crowe (solo) 21 May 2000

Hard start up wall just R of 20, soon leads to easier climbing.

22 Beagles Above the Shitehouse **   10m VS 4b
FA Tim Carruthers & Chris Boulton 31 May 1999

The arête, climbed from its lowest point.

23 Eagles Above the Lighthouse *   10m VS 4c
FA Fergus Murray & Mike Snook 4 June 1998

Surmount overhangs then follow the crack.

24 First Time for Everyone *   10m HVS 5a
FA Hugh Harris & Lesley Beck 22 May 2000

Wall between the cracks.

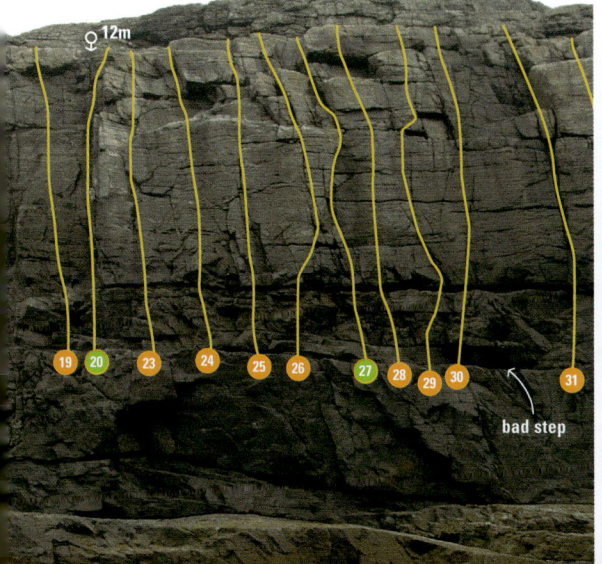

Gary Latter starting up Evening Sun. Photo Karen Latter.

PABBAY & MINGULAY THE GEIRUM WALLS

25 Snooked for a Crack ★　　　　　　**10m VS 4c**
FA Fergus Murray & Mike Snook 4 June 1998
The crack.

26 Confidence Booster ★　　　　　　**10m HS 4b**
Pull over a bulge left of 27 and up to climb a crack just to its left. Moving left from 3m up 27 is ★★ Severe 4a.

27 Crisis of Confidence ★　　　　　**10m Severe 4a**
FA Mike Snook & Fergus Murray 4 June 1998
Climb a groove and overhanging right-facing corner.

28 The Old Man and the Sea ★　　　**10m HVS 5a**
FA Chris Boulton & Tim Carruthers 31 May 1999
The wall immediately right of 27 direct via twin breaks.

29 Sunshine All Day ★★　　　　　　**10m HVS 5a**
FA Fergus Murray & Mike Snook 4 June 1998
Start 3m right of 27. Surmount the overhang and follow a crack with some delicate moves.

30 Karaoke Craik ★　　　　　　　　　**10m VS 4c**
FA Tim Caterall, Stephen Porteous & Bill Renshaw 22 May 2000
Climb onto a pedestal, then right crack and slabby left arête.

31 Bloody Obvious Crack ★★　　　　**10m HVS 5a**
FA Hugh Harris & Lesley Beck 20 May 2001
Up the …

32 Super Crack ★　　　　　　　　　　**10m E1 5b**
FA Dave Turnbull & Kev Howett 22 May 2000
Climb up the lower bulges to a short, fat, left-facing flake. Pull out the top to a good horizontal break. Step slightly left and up a good crack on to a ledge then direct up the final wall.

33 Wise Crack ★　　　　　　　　　　**10m E1 5b**
FA Kev Howett & Dave Turnbull 22 May 2000
Pull up on to an overhung ledge and gain a fat flake in the wall above. Gain a further flake up and right then exit on to the ledge above via a short vertical crack.

34 Black Crack ★　　　　　　　　　　**10m HVS 5a**
FA Bruce Kerr & Alan Smith 5 July 1999
The crack, finishing in a recess.

35 Sealed with a Kiss ★★　　　　　　**10m E3 6a**
FA Robert Durran, Mark Somerville & Bruce Kerr 6 July 1999
Climb the wall to a good break. Make a long reach for an obvious hold on the lip, pull onto the wall with difficulty and finish directly. 35a *Dwarf Variation* E2 5c omits the meat of the route by traversing right to gain the hold on the lip.

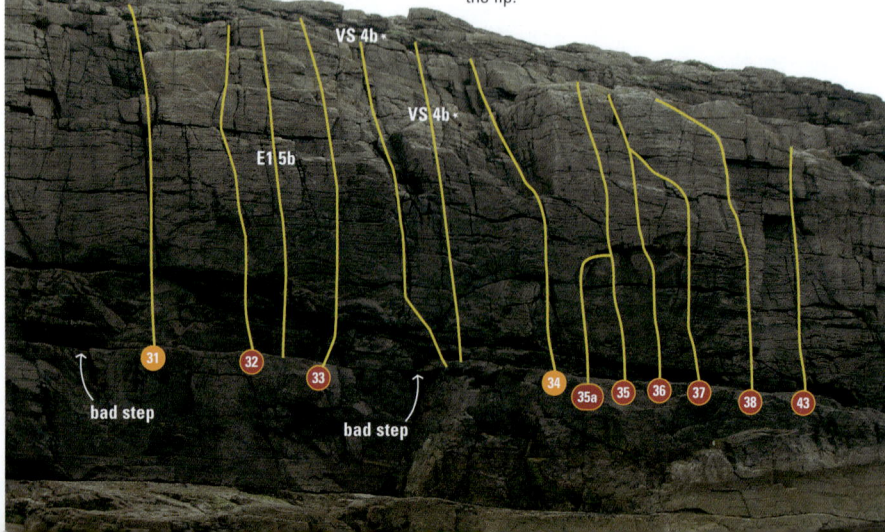

36 Seal Clubbing ★ — 10m E1 5c
FA Gary Latter 19 August 2004

Climb up to the right end of the small overlap then direct up the wall to finish up the final section of the flake-crack.

37 Under the Boardwalk ★ — 10m E2 5c
FA Charlie Fowler & Kathy Tighe 3 May 1997

Initial hard moves lead to good horizontal breaks and a ledge. Finish easily up the left-slanting flake-crack.

38 Evening Sun ★ — 12m E1 5c
FA Gordon Lennox & Tim Rankin 8 May 1999

The arête, easier after a bouldery start.

39 On the Beach ★ — 12m E1 5c
FA Charlie Fowler & Kathy Tighe 3 May 1997

Technical moves up the wall right of the arête lead to a steep crack to finish.

40 Hawaiian Tropic ★★ — 12m VS 4c
FA Charlie Fowler & Kathy Tighe 3 May 1997

Excellent climbing up the big right-facing corner with a thin start.

41 Mesajanier ★ — 12m E3 6a
FA Michael Tweedley & Mark Somerville 6 July 1999

The wall right of the corner. Climb direct with a long reach to the break then a further hard move to stand in the break. Continue more easily to finish up the niche on the left going through the overlap.

42 Water Babies ★★ — 12m E2 5c
FA Charlie Fowler & Kathy Tighe 3 May 1997

Climb the right-facing groove for 3m then move left along the break to gain the crack and follow it over a bulge (crux) to the top.

43 Mary Doune ★★★ — 12m E1 5b
FA Charlie Fowler & Kathy Tighe 3 May 1997

The vertical rounded crack and roof above.

44 Double Walrus ★ — 12m HVS 5a
FA Tim Rankin & Gordon Lennox 8 May 1999

Start at left end of roof. Straight up the wall just left of a short right-facing groove to a ledge and thin cracks.

45 The Sirens of Mingulay ★ — 12m E2 5c
FA Charlie Fowler & Kathy Tighe 3 May 1997

Start just left of the deep cave. Climb over a bulge and up a steep left-facing corner to gain a ledge. Short thin cracks up the face above lead to the top.

46 Underseal ★ — 12m E2 6a
FA Robert Durran & Rob Adie 13 August 2006

Gain and climb a short hanging groove between two overlaps with difficulty, finishing up a short diagonal crack.

47 Calling Seal ★★ — 12m E3 6a
FA Tim Rankin & Gordon Lennox 8 May 1999

Start in the middle of the arch. Use an obvious flat jug to reach a break. Pull out right to good holds on the lip. Continue up and right to a hard finish up a short hanging right-facing groove.

48 Fringe Elements ★★ — 20m VS 4c
FA Mick Tighe, Hamish Robertson & Yvonne Colwell 25 April 2000

A line traversing the lip of the cave. Start off the pillar and climb up the wall then right across the lip of the roof until an easy wall leads to the top.

ORKNEY

The Orkney Islands comprises over 70 islands, about one third of them inhabited. The main town and administrative centre is Kirkwall. Stromness, further west, is the main port for ferries from mainland Scotland.

Access: NorthLink Ferries (☎ 0845 6000 449; www.northlinkferries.co.uk) from Scrabster – Stromness (1½hours) and Aberdeen – Kirkwall (6hours); John O'Groats Ferries (☎ 01955 611353; www.jogferry.co.uk) sailing from John O'Groats – Burwick on South Ronaldsay (40 minutes) with a connecting bus to Kirkwall; Pentland Ferries (☎ 01856 831226; www.pentlandferries.co.uk) from Gills Bay, Caithness – St Margaret's Hope, South Ronaldsay. Loganair operates flights to Kirkwall from Aberdeen, Edinburgh, Glasgow and Inverness.

Accommodation: Youth Hostel: Kirkwall (Apr – Sept; ☎ 01856 872243 ; www.hostellingscotland.org.uk). **Hostels:** Brown's Hostel (☎ 01856 850661; www.brownsorkney.co.uk); Hamnavoe Hostel (☎ 01856 851202; www.hamnavoehostel.co.uk) – both Stromness; Orcades Hostel (☎ 01856 873745; www.orcadeshostel.com); The Peedie Hostel (☎ 01856 877177; www.stayinkirkwall.co.uk) – both Kirkwall. **Campsite:** Point of Ness Campsite (Apr – Sept; ☎ 01856 873535 ext. 2901; www.orkney.gov.uk) on the point at Stromness, though it can be quite noisy with all the boats leaving the harbour early in the morning.

TIC: Kirkwall (☎ 01856 872856; www.visitscotland.com). Local information for Stromness at www.stromnessorkney.com.

Amenities: There are numerous grocers and delicatessens in the delightful main street in Stromness, along with a supermarket on the edge of town and numerous cafés and bars.

HOY

The second largest of the Orkney Islands, the name Hoy comes from the Norse *'ha ey'*, meaning *'tall isle'*. The north-west coastline of the island contains 6km of cliffs, extending northwards from Rora Head past the famous landmark of the Old Man of Hoy to St John's Head and beyond.

Access: The most convenient access is a small passenger ferry (☎ 01856 872044; www.orkneyferries.co.uk) 3 or 4 times daily in summer from Stromness to Moaness Pier (25 minutes), 1km from the tiny village of Hoy, at the north-east end of Hoy. Complete the 5mile/8km journey west to Rackwick by minibus which will meet the ferry if arranged (☎ 01856 791315), or take a bike. A larger vehicle ferry (☎ 01856 872044; www.orkneyferries.co.uk) runs from Houton to Lyness (35 minutes), 9 miles/14km further down the east coast of the island.

Accommodation: Hostels: Two at the north end of the island, both run by Orkney Islands Council (☎ 01856 873535 ext. 2901; online booking at www.orkney.gov.uk), at Hoy and, more conveniently, the wonderfully situated Rackwick (Apr – Sept) from where all the cliffs (except The Needle and The Berry) are approached. There is also an open bothy at Burnmouth in the centre of the bay at Rackwick. Wild camping is permitted on most of Hoy, outwith the RSPB Nature Reserve at the north end – the usual spots are in the vicinity of the ruins near the car park at Rackwick or in the garden of the bothy. There are a couple of small cottages for rent in Rackwick Bay. Self-catering also available in Longhope – details at www.hoyorkney.com or from **TIC** at Kirkwall (see above).

Amenities: Beneth'ill Café (☎ 01856 791119; www.benethillcafe.co.uk) in Moaness does local seafood. Nearest provisions from Lyness or Longhope (also petrol station), though better to bring over from Orkney Mainland.

The island holds the only example of a Neolithic rock cut-tomb in northern Europe, the Dwarfie Stane, on the south side of the road midway between Hoy and Rackwick. Also on Hoy is the most northerly natural wood in Britain at Berriedale – a 20-minute walk east from Rackwick.

HOY

THE NEEDLE ND 243 901  45min

The prominent stack at the south end of the cliffs on the westerly seaboard of the island. A grassy promontory just out from the main cliffs almost level with the top of the stack, forming the south side of a narrow geo biting deeply into the cliffs. An abseil stake is in situ at the end of the promontory.

Approach: Leave the B9047 at Saltness and follow track west for 1km. Continue west up Glen of the Berry for 1.7km then continue contouring west round the south side of The Berry.

Descent: Remove clothes and abseil for 60m directly into the sea in the geo. Swim across to ledges on the far side and traverse round to opposite the stack. Swim across to ledges on the south side.

1 The Needle ★★★   60m XS 5c
FA Mick Fowler, Steve Sustad & Nicki Dugan 27 May 1990

An excellent adventure.

1. **15m** – From the landward corner of the south side trend up leftwards then back right above overhangs to a good ledge.
2. **30m 5c** Climb through the band of overhangs above at the obvious place near the centre of the south face (crux) and trend rightwards to a shallow depression which leads left to another good ledge. Serious.
3. **15m** – Move round onto the seaward face and climb on to the summit. Jumar back to the cliff top or swim off to the south.

THE BERRY ND 242 902

A big impressively steep cliff with a very adventurous approach.   45min

1 Beri-Beri ★★★   220m XS
FA Mick Fowler & Crag Jones (8 PA) 17 July 1996

An adventurous route up the huge red wall which forms the skyline edge of The Berry when viewed from the cliff top above *The Needle*. The approach given is that taken by the first ascentionists and is only possible for a couple of hours either side of low tide. Abseil directly into the sea from a stake (in situ) and swim across the narrow geo to ledges on the far side (as for *The Needle*). Continue traversing at greasy 5b to reach exposed boulders. On the far side more greasy boulders lead to tunnels leading through the next buttress. Continue until an awkward diagonal abseil from a poor P (in situ) is necessary to gain exposed boulders. Walk through the arch/tunnel to gain the next bay. The route is now clearly visible. On the far side of the bay a surprise geo cuts deeply back into the cliff and necessitates a 25m swim to gain ledges which lead easily to beneath the route. Scramble up to the start of a crack just right of the left-bounding arête.

1. **25m** Climb up through an awkward overhang to a ledge beneath large projecting plates of crenellated rock.
2. **25m** Tackle the difficult overhangs above via the right weakness. Move back left and continue up the main fault line to more overhangs. Traverse right 5m to belay.
3. **25m** Move up right from the belay, traverse right and break through a further band of overhangs to gain a grass ledge.
4. **25m** Make a rising traverse rightwards across slabs and climb a short awkward corner forming the left side of a prominent block. Belay on the block.
5. **25m** Steep pulls above the belay lead to ledges. Climb up and left to belay directly beneath a prominent overhanging corner capped by a

bomb-bay chimney (this is about 15m right of an obvious crack-line close to the arête).

6 **10m** Climb up to and aid (about 4 points) a short overhanging red bulge to gain the foot of the corner proper.

7 **25m** Climb the corner to the seriously overhanging upper section (leader used some aid to rest/clean — second climbed free). Use 3–4 points of aid, the last one being a very fortuitously-positioned natural chokestone, to gain the outer edge of the bomb-bay chimney which leads quickly to a stance.

8 **10m** Climb easily up right to the foot of a prominent grey corner.

9 **30m** Up the corner to the roof then traverse left across the unprotected wall to a small ledge. Make a series of strenuous moves to reach a ledge.

10 **20m** Move back right into the grey groove and follow this to the top.

These spectacular old red sandstone cliffs extend for about 1.5km both east and north of the point of Rora Head itself. The rock quality is variable, best on the seaward faces where it is most weathered. At various locations, a deep-red glazed surface gives particularly fine quality rock. On some locations it is best to climb the routes after 2–3 days of dry weather as the rock becomes sandy and greasy after wet weather.

THE GEOS

Approach: Head up the hillside behind Rackwick Hostel to the highest cottage on the hillside, to pick up a well constructed path (signposted 'Old Man') which contours round the side of Moor Fea. Cut down left where the coast pulls away, as the path starts to drop and the top of the **Old Man** comes into view. Four distinctive geos indent this section, numbered from east to west. **Flingi (Number 4) Geo** the furthest west, provides an easy descent to a non-tidal beach. Crags described from east to west, as encountered on the approach.

ND 183 994   30min

LANG (NUMBER 1) GEO – EAST WALL
Walk down the gully to start.

1 Sea an Enemy ★★   **25m E1 5b**
FA Edward Nind & Frazer McCallum 17 April 2019
The obvious corner at the left end of the wall.

2 Fulmar Cavity ★   **30m VS 4b**
FA Al Evans, Catherine Rolfe, Roy Carter & Dave Moss 23 July 1997
The central crack, 3m left of 3.

3 Craa'nest ★★   **30m E1 5b**
FA Kath Pyke & Andy Donson 17 September 1996
The right of three prominent crack-lines on left side of the orange wall.

4 Banana Transfer Theory ★★   **45m E1 5b**
FA Andy Hein, Tom Spreyer & Olly Metherell 7 July 2004
Start at the same place as 3. Traverse right along a ledge for 4m to the base of a steep crack. Climb the crack for 5m to a horizontal break then step right on to a ledge. Go up and right to join 5 at the base of the crack. Traverse right along a small ledge into the corner of 6 and climb this until it is possible to step right onto the arête. Hand traverse right to finish up 7.

5 Hewin's Route ★   **35m E2 5c**
FA Tom Spreyer & Andy Hein 7 July 2004
Climb the initial finger-crack of 6 then step left and climb between horizontal breaks (crux) to the base of a prominent right diagonal crack in the centre of the upper wall. Climb this in its entirety then step right to finish direct.

6 Mater ★★   **35m E2 5b**
FA Andy Donson & Kath Pyke 17 September 1996
The obvious bottomless left-facing groove in the centre of the face. Approach via an indefinite finger-crack.

7 Paneer ★   **38m E2 5b**
FA Andy Donson & Kath Pyke 17 September 1996
The wall right of 6. Attain a jutting ledge at 10m and follow a flake line above to a break. Step right and climb up, trending left to a niche beneath the left end of the roof. Pull over to fine finishing cracks.

8 Paternoster ★   **50m HVS 4c**
FA Al Evans, Catherine Rolfe, Roy Carter & Dave Moss 23 July 1997
A good climb, low in the grade, taking the prominent crack and corner on the right side of the wall.
  1 **25m 4c** Climb the crack on slightly worrying rock to belay ledges with an in situ P and fulmar chick.
  2 **25m 4b** Continue up the crack and corner on superb rock, exiting left below the roof.

GEO 3

1 Rosamund's Birthday ★★   40m E4 6a
FA Mick Carnall & Crag Jones 6 June 1992

This superb route climbs the outer wall. It is best approached by a free abseil down the line of the route to a bog atop the pillar at its base. The difficult first pitch could be avoided via the seaward face of the pillar, thus reducing the grade to E3.

1 **10m 6a** Climb the initial cracks with difficulty to the first ledge.
2 **15m 5c** Climb up until it is possible to traverse above the lip of the roof on the right arête then continue to the next ledge.
3 **15m 5c** Continue directly to the final steepening where the crack closes then finish with hard moves up and left.

2 Slick John ★★   40m E4 6a
FA Dave MacLeod & Andy Turner 20 June 2011

An attractive finger crack in the centre of the wall, left of 1. Abseil to a footledge on 1, about 8m above the grassy start of that route. Climb 1 for a few metres to its normal belay. Traverse left along a ledge to a prominent right-slanting wide crack. Climb this for a few metres, then break out left to gain the striking thin finger crack. Climb this on great rock and protection to the top.

3 Action Replay ★★   55m E3 5c
FA Crag Jones & Mick Fowler (1 PA) 16 July 1996

Climbs the seaward edge of the wall, just round the corner from 1. Approach as for 1 and walk easily round the corner. Start just right of the arête.

1 **20m 4c** Climb sandy corners and breaks to the right of the arête then make an awkward traverse right to the base of a groove which marks the right side of a black bulge.
2 **20m 5c** Climb the groove and its capstone. Move up to flakes on the steep wall above (rest point) then climb diagonally left to reach a ledge at the foot of another groove.
3 **15m 5b** Finish up the groove.

On the West Wall of Geo 3, facing east is:

4 Roarer ★★   40m E1 5b
FA Mick Fowler & Crag Jones 16 July 1996

A good pitch, taking the prominent right crack in the wall, opposite 1. Abseil down the gully to a line of ledges leading out to the base of the crack.

1 **10m** Traverse the ledge system leftwards to belay where it ends.
2 **30m** Step up and hand traverse leftwards for 3m to gain the crack and follow it to the top.

ND 173 998 **Alt:** 20m
MUCKLEHOUSE WALL

The following routes are located on an 80m wall, some 70m north of the obvious high point of the headland.
Approach: As for **The Geos** but continue along the main path towards the **Old Man** for a further 500m then head west across the moor, crossing the burn, heading just north of the obvious high point of the headland.
Descents: To all the routes is via a 70m abseil, utilising long slings for equalizing blocks and cairns(!). It is also possible to gain the base by heading south along the beach from the **Old Man** descent, though possibly not at high tide.

      45min

1 Roring Forties ★★★   80m E3 5c
FA Dave Turnbull & Andy Donson 20 May 1991

An excellent line based on the obvious towering arête and crack system just to its left. Start beneath the seaward arête.

1 **25m 5c** Climb the right corner crack to a small roof. Continue up the crack to a step up left and traverse the higher break to the arête. Continue up 3m to a good ledge.
2 **20m 5b** Make some bold moves up the left edge of the arête, step left and continue up the obvious

crack to a belay ledge where the crack widens. Alternatively, from the belay mantelshelf onto the huge ledge, then step back right into the line.

3 **35m 5b** Climb the wide crack to a ledge beneath a corner/roof. Swing left beneath the roof and continue to the top bearing left and finishing just right of a short corner.

2 Mucklehouse Wall ★★★   100m E5 6a

FA Dave Turnbull & Andy Donson 25 May 1991

The first and easiest way up the wall right of the arête. The wall overhangs some 15m and is therefore somewhat strenuous.

1 **30m 5c** Climb pitch 1 of 1 but continue up the arête, swing out on to the overhanging face and belay just below a small roof.
2 **35m 5c** A tremendous fist jamming pitch up the slanting crack in the centre of the face. From the belay hand traverse a break right to dubious flakes at the base of the crack. Climb the crack before moving left to the arête and up to belay on a large ledge.
3 **10m 5b** Traverse right along the ledge, continuing across the break to belay beside a small stepped groove. Take care with unattached block here.
4 **25m 6a** Climb direct up the dark red streak and pull up into the 'Fairy Grotto' cave (often wet). Slither out of this leftwards via a block to finish easier up the cracked groove on immaculate rock.

3a Rats Stole My Toothbrush ★★   20m E5/6 6a

FA Andy Donson & Dave Turnbull 23 May 1991

A bold and difficult alternative start to 3. Scramble up easy ledges on the right of the face to a ledge right in the corner; this can also be gained from the abseil. Climb the obvious flake above then traverse the red wall on flat holds until moving up to a semi rest in a corner under a roof. Swing out left (6b for the short) and up to belay at the base of pitch 2.

3 Two Little Boys ★★★   85m E6 6b

FA Dave Turnbull & Chris Rees 14 June 1991

A stunning route taking the main challenge of the wall. Very sustained and strenuous. Start as for 1.

1 **30m 6b** Climb 1 and move up to the overhanging twin finger-cracks right of the arête. Fix protection and climb the crack on finger locks past an in situ hex #3. Continue up the overhanging wall and belay just above the roof.
2 **35m 5c** As for pitch 2 of 2. Fist crack to the arête and ledge belay.
3 **20m 6a/b** A photogenic pitch finishing up the dark red headwall. Climb up the obvious right-trending line of white flakes then finish up the headwall.

4 Many a Mickle makes a Muckle ★★★
                                              105m E6/7 6b

FA John Arran & Dave Turnbull (on-sight) 27 May 1997

A stupendous line, overhanging continuously for 75m. The crux pitch consists of two E6 6b sections with a reasonable recovery position in between, essentially connecting 3a and 2.

1 **18m 5b** From a comfy ledge at the foot of the right side of the wall, climb up and left into the obvious corner and follow it to a large ledge.
2 **20m 6a** As for 3a.
3 **40m 6b** Traverse right along sloping breaks for 9m then move up and right to gain a groove with difficulty. Climb twin cracks above then swing left, up and back right, taking care with loose blocks to belay on the highest of three good ledges. #0.5 & #1 cams useful for the belay.
4 **27m 6a** As for 2.

5 The Wise Hoy Hawk ★★★★   50m E5 6a

FA Alex Mason & George Ullrich 28 May 2013

An awesome finger crack on some of the best rock on the island. From the top of **Mucklehouse Wall** head north for 150/200m to a cairn at the top of an arête. Abseil into a mid height ledge to belay on west face. (Good Cam #4). Climb diagonally left across the north face to gain the base of a crack. Follow this past a stepped 'Fern Hill' style section to a technical move back left (potential belay). Ascend trending slightly right to turn a small overlap. Once round this follow intermittent cracks to a good ledge belay just below the top on the right of the arête.

OLD MAN OF HOY

HY 176 008 45min

"... like being on a little satellite out in space, dropping away to nothingness on every side." – Tom Patey, BBC outside broadcast 1967

Although not actually a sea stack as such, since the base is not submerged in the sea, at 137m it is the highest of any Scottish stacks.

Approach: Head up the hillside behind Rackwick Hostel to the highest cottage on the hillside to pick up a well constructed path (signposted 'Old Man') which contours round the side of Moor Fea, leading to a popular viewing promontory opposite the stack.

Descent: Starting from 120m north of the obvious viewing promontory, a small well worn path leads diagonally leftwards down the grass rake and the north side of the ridge then across precarious rubble to the base.

Descent from Old Man: Abseil down the *Original Route* on the **East Face**. Masses of slings are always in situ and often a rope to reverse the traverse on pitch 2. Unless using 60m ropes, an additional rope should be left on ascent, linking the belays on pitch 2, in order to facilitate retreat to the stance.

EAST FACE

1 Original Route ★★★　　　135m E1 5b

FA Rusty Baillie, Tom Patey & Chris Bonington 18 July 1966;
FFA Joe Brown & Pete Crew July 1967

The hugely popular route up the landward face. Start at the end of the neck of rubble.

  1 **25m 4b** Climb a shattered pillar on the South Face to a large ledge, The Gallery.
  2 **35m 5b** Climb down 3m and across easy ledges to the foot of the great crack and up this with interest over two roofs, stepping right at the top to belay in an alcove – take some long slings, plus large hexes/cams.
  3 **20m 4b** Climb the wide crack above to a large ledge.
  4 **35m 4b** Move diagonally right from the right end of the ledge for a few metres then trend back left and up a tiny V-chimney. Continue up the corner above, past a large grass ledge to belay at the base of the final corner.
  5 **20m 4c** Finish up the final corner crack on superb rock – an excellent pitch.

1a Space Station Finish ★★★   25m E1 5b
FA Dan Moore & Shauna Clarke 17 August 2015

5a From the belay at the bottom of the final corner pitch, climb up onto the left wall of the corner and gain an obvious left-trending flake line. Follow this, then move left and up to a wide crack in the bulging wall above. Gain a thin crack on the right and make tricky moves up the wall to gain a good foot ledge below two parallel hand cracks. Climb these, then move right to a wide crack and continue more easily to the top. Very well protected.

SOUTH FACE

2 South Face ★   150m E2 5c
FA Joe Brown & Ian McNaught Davis 8–9 July 1967

A fine sunny route on reasonable rock.

1. **25m 4b** As for *Original Route*.
2. **30m 5b** Climb the corner on the left, then boldly up the steep wall above to a flake on the left. Climb this to a ledge. Walks left 12m to blocks beneath a shallow chimney.
3. **25m 5b** Climb the shallow chimney to a ledge and cave.
4. **40m 5c** Strenuously surmount the roof of the cave and continue up chimney to a ledge. Pull over thuggy green crack in overhang (crux), move right and climb corner and the wall above to steep grass leading to a crack at the top of the grassy Haven.
5. **30m 4c** Climb up and left to a ledge, then a big flake on the left to further vegetation. Continue up a series of ramps and ledges leading to an easy chimney and the south summit.

WEST FACE

3 GMB ★★★   145m E5 6a
FA John Arran & Dave Turnbull 29 August 1997

The centre of the **West Face** and **North-West Arête** rivals *A Few Dollars More* as perhaps the best route on the **Old Man**. Start in the middle of the **West Face**, beneath a short left-facing corner.

1. **18m 5c** Climb a short corner/roof and continue left to a block belay on a ledge.
2. **25m 6a** A flake crack leads up right. At its top traverse left and up to a committing move below a roof just right of the arête then swing right to a belay perch above the Atlantic.
3. **30m 5c** Mantle up to a larger ledge then continue up and left to a belay on the arête.
4. **42m 6a** Climb the arête direct to a belay terrace. Technically sustained and exposed.

📷 *Karen Latter on the crucial second pitch of Original Route.*

ST JOHN'S HEAD

HY 184 034 1hr ½hr

The third highest sea cliff in the British Isles, that particular distinction going to the 430m high Conachair out on St Kilda, climbed only once in 1987. The Kame on Foula in the Shetland Isles falls second on the list, though it does have a football pitch-sized grass ledge splitting the cliff.

Approach: From Rackwick head due north for 1.5km then north-west for just under 3km, skirting round the south side of Sui Fea, the prominent hill.

Descent: Down the grassy slope and short rock step about 350m north of the top of *Longhope Route*.

① Big John ★★★ 430m E5 6a
FA Mick Fowler & John Lincoln 20 June 1988 (1 PA);
FFA Andy Donson & Kath Pyke 15 July 1996

This takes the soaring arête on the left. *"Not many routes compare"*. Start on the left side of the grass slope at the base of the cliff.

1–4 **135m** Climb grass to a tangle of ropes beneath the centre of the upper wall. Belay at the top of a rope hanging down a rock wall.
5 **40m 5b** Climb the slabby wall trending right to a ledge then go back left to grassy ledges level with the base of the 4b chimney on *Longhope Route*.
6 **45m 5c** Traverse horizontally left for 35m and climb up and back slightly right to a stance 20m below the prominent overhanging flake crack leading up left to the arête.
7 **20m 4c** Climb to a ledge at the start of the flake crack.
8 **25m 5c** Layback the overhanging flake and struggle sensationally up the upper flake to a small corner ledge.
9 **15m 5b** Continue in the same line up the corner to a ledge on the arête beneath a prominent overhang.
10 **35m 5b** Trend left round the overhang and follow a vague fault line to a ledge after 25m. Move right along this to the arête, surmount an overhang and gain a ledge.
11 **25m 6a** Climb a difficult but well protected crack on the right side of the arête to a ledge. Traverse this round to the left side of the arête to belay where two large blocks have dropped from the

5 **20m 6a** Climb grooves in the wall just left of the arête passing a cracked roof. Traverse right beneath the upper roof then hand jam a crack to a belay ledge.
6 **10m** Scramble up easier terrain to the top.

NORTH FACE

④ A Few Dollars More ★★★ 130m E3 5c
FA Murray Hamilton, Pete Whillance & Paul Braithwaite Aug 1994

The rock improves with height, but becomes more lichenous. The prominent crack-line in the centre of the face. From platforms below the **South Face** traverse an obvious break across the **West Face** to gain access to the introductory buttress on the **North Face**. Scramble up 10m to belay.

1 **30m 4c** Climb an open groove for 10m then up a chimney in the right wall to its top. Traverse a ledge leftwards to the main groove and up to a belay ledge at the top of the introductory buttress.
2 **40m 5b/c** Move right onto the wall and up a groove/flake to its top. Climb steeply to a break in the overlap and follow the crack-line above to reach a large cave and belay.
3 **30m 5b** Climb the steep crack out of the left side of the cave and follow it for 20m to ledges near the left arête. Up short walls rightwards to a grassy ledge below the middle of the headwall.
4 **30m 5c** Climb thin cracks in the wall leading to a bottomless groove/corner and up this to a ledge on the left. A short crack and wall above leads to the top.

overhang above, about 12m left from the arête.

12 30m 5c Pull over the overhang and climb direct for 6m to a traverse crack. Follow this rightwards to a ledge just left of the arête. Move up via two dubious undercut flakes and gain a ledge (crux).

13 30m 5b Climb a delicate wall on the left to gain a shallow groove leading to a ledge. Climb the short chimney above to a further ledge and belay below an overhang on the left.

14 30m Surmount the overhang in the fault line then continue more easily to the top.

2 Longhope Route ★★★★   493m HXS/E7 6c
FA Ed Drummond & Oliver Hill July 1970;
FFA Dave Turnbull & John Arran 29 – 30 May & 30 – 31 Aug 1997

One of the longest, most demanding undertakings in British rock climbing. Awesome. The route may be possible in a two-day continuous ascent, or less. It should be possible to combine some of the pitches and aiding pitch 21 would reduce the grade to HXS/E6 A1. Start right of the grassy bank at a boulder platform near the right side of the clean red wall.

1 25m 5b Climb up trending left then back up right to belay on a large rounded block.

2 27m 5c A bold start leads to an easier section working up right on good rock then back left and up to a belay beneath the centre of a large roof.

3 25m 6a Hard moves just right of a thin crack in the roof lead to good protection. Climb the right-slanting corner boldly to a good ledge complete with a belay seat boulder. A hard pitch.

4 15m 5b Move up just left of the belay then left along an enormous concave break to a belay at the end of the grass ledge.

5 30m 5a Climb direct to a wide crack in a rock band. Trend left on steep grass to find a belay.

6 20m 4a Climb diagonally left more easily on grass to belay at base of a vegetated slab (P).

7 20m 5a Continue left then find a way up right and belay on good cams and an in situ P directly beneath a prominent short corner. Possible bivi on left.

8 35m 5b A slab, corner and groove lead to good belay ledges beneath the main groove in the upper headwall. Excellent.

9 18m 5a Chimneys on the right lead pleasantly past in situ razorbills to a good ledge.

10 30m 6a The 'Vile Crack' lives up to its name. Traverse left for 5m then climb the slimy offwidth above via two chokestones. Swing 3m left at its top to belay flake. Large cams #4 - #6 essential.

11 25m 5c Up the flake and right around a roof then up to a second roof and traverse right with difficulty (bold) to belay on good ledges. Possible bivi site.

12 30m 5c Drop down (back rope possible for second) and traverse back left for 12m to sandy bulges. Move up a series of steps and climb a green crack to belay on the arête.

13 18m 4a Walk left across the headwall along a wide break and over some massive blocks to belay below a left facing corner/groove.

14 27m 5b Climb the corner, step right and continue direct to some steps leading right to a band of roofs. Traverse left for 11m to belay in a niche.

15 18m 5b The 'Giant Steps/Vice' pitch. Move up and right to a narrow roof then stomach traverse left to belay directly beneath the 'Guillotine' flake.

16 20m 6a The notorious 'Guillotine' flake. Climb direct to the frighteningly detached flake (some old bolts), grapple onto it and belay on top.

17 20m 6a Move up to the horizontal crack (old PR) then traverse left and diagonally up through vertical broccoli to a belay perch on the arête. Bold.

18 12m 6b Move right to the overhanging groove and use layaways to climb past a jammed 1970 stopper. Constricted belay. (The original route traversed right from here to climb the headwall crack/seam on bolts and blade pegs.)

19 20m 6a Traverse right then up into the left slanting groove with difficulty. Continue to another superb belay ledge on the arête. A good pitch. Pitches 18 & 19 may be combined.

20 12m 6a Make a heel hooking traverse along the 30cm wide break running across the severely overhanging headwall in a position of considerable exposure. Hanging belay in the continuation headwall crack.

21 **8m 6c** Climb the crack and short wall with great difficulty or resort to aid.

22 **20m 6a** It's not over yet. Move up and right beneath the tiered roofs to an obvious right traverse line across the hanging slab (ancient PR). Good belay ledges.

23 **18m 5a** Move right then up a series of white layback flakes heading back left to a grass terrace. Scramble up to the much welcomed summit.

2a Variation Finish *   167m E5 6b
FA John Arran & Dave Turnbull 30 May 1997

13 **45m 4a** Cross the entire headwall along a narrowing break to a vice crack and belay on the arête.

14 **20m 5c** Up an obvious line on the left to belay beneath a band of roofs.

15 **12m 6b** From a hand jam on the lip of the roof pull over with difficulty and climb up left to two obvious large boulders (on *Big John*).

16–18 90m As for the last 3 pitches of *Big John*.

2b Longhope Direct ★★★★   65m E9 7a
FFA Dave MacLeod (Andy Turner) 21 June 2011

A free ascent of the original aided crack in the headwall. This straightens out the A2 crack pitch with a more direct entry to the crack and finish through the final roofs.

7 **65m 6c** Traverse left along the break, then climb the overhanging wall boldly to the base of the headwall crack. Climb this past several cruxes to a small ledge below the capping roofs. Move up to these, step right and then climb leftwards through two roofs. Move right to fulmar ledges and climb grassy ledges to the summit. F8b climbing.

Ian Jones getting lost on the spectacularly positioned Roring Forties (page 457), Mucklehouse Wall. The correct line traverses the upper break. Photo Lucy Spark.

YESNABY

HY 218 154   15min

QUI AYRE POINT

These sunny crags reach just over 25m at their highest point, running down at their western end into the sea, making an almost perfect wedge shape. The majority of the routes are tidal and calm seas are required to access the bases of many. The lovely compact Middle Red sandstone is by far the best on Orkney and has been quarried for centuries to make millstones and stone troughs. A number of miniature climbs and **boulder problems** can also be found in and around the very sheltered quarry workings. There are also over a dozen short sport routes here, from F5-F6c+; mainly around F5+ to F6b.

Access: Follow the A967 north from Stromness for 4.8 miles/7.5km then continue straight on along the B9056 for 0.25 miles/0.4km, to take a left for 2 miles/3.2km to the old military buildings at the road end.

Approach: Follow the coastline south for 800m to arrive at the crags, which lie on the north-west side of a large V-shaped bay.

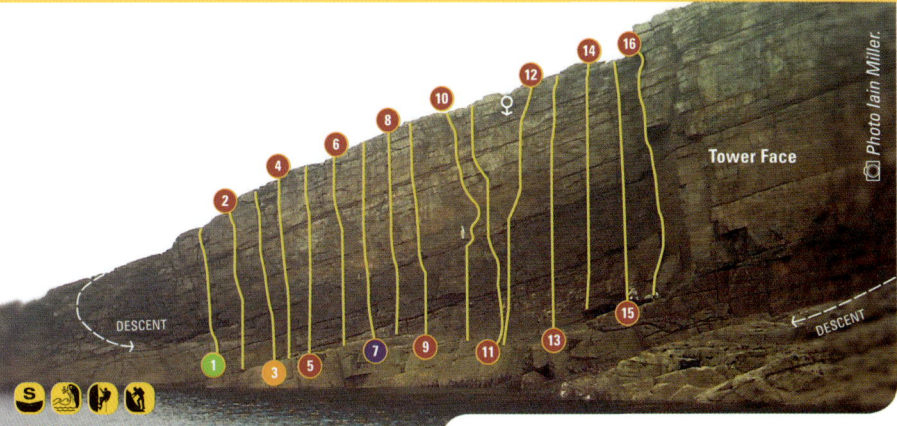

POINT WALL

An excellent wall of superb weathered sandstone packed with lines. Most are strenuous but well protected, particularly with small cams. It is in an exposed position and a calm sea is required for the bulk of the routes here.

Descents: At low tide the base can be accessed by a steep little down climb from the west (left looking in) from 1, or from the east by the 'crevasse' then along the wave cut platform. Quickest by direct abseil. Routes from 9 rightwards can be accessed at higher tides by abseil to belays on tapering ledges below 12.

1 The Half Buoy ★★   6m Severe 4a
FA Mick Tighe, James Armour, Colin Duncan & Howard Clarke 18 June 1997

The first line in from the point. Follow a little honey-combed fault with huge jugs and superb protection.

2 Bullet ★★   8m E2 5c
FA Tim Rankin & Neil Morrison on-sight 25 July 2006

An excellent little pitch up the thin crack-line left of 3. Excellent protection.

3 Route 91 ★★   8m HVS 5a
FA Mick Tighe & Colin Duncan (headpointed) June 1998

So called because *"it overhangs by one degree"*. Take the first vertical crack-line in from the west, up the otherwise blank wall. Perfect rock with excellent protection.

The parallel crack-line 1m right again is 4 *Quoybank Crack* ★ E1 5b; the wall 2m further right is 5 *The Fantastic Mr Fox* ★ E2 6a.

6 Up tae High Doh ★★★   10m E1 5b
FA Tim Rankin & Derren Fox July 2005

5m right of 3 is another fine crack running the full height of the wall. A superb well protected pitch.

The wall on the right is 7 *Peedie Breeks* ★ E4 6b – *'tough with fiddly protection'*; the thin crack and left-facing corner is 8 *The Cog* ★ E2 5c.

9 Deep Blue ★★★   10m E3 5c
FA Neil Morrison & Chris Webb 22 July 2004

Stunning climbing up the superb crack immediately right of 8.

10 Billy Bean's Dream ★★   12m E3 5c
FA Tim Rankin & Derren Fox July 2005

Right of 9 is a white calcite mark at ⅓rd height. Start below this and climb the steep wall to jugs just right of the mark, stand up right then step back left to follow superb breaks direct to the top, always to the left of the stepped corner. Low in the grade.

11 The Bends ★   12m E2 5c
FA Neil Morrison & Derren Fox July 2005

Right again at half-height are two left-facing overlapping

corners. Gain these from below and right (leftmost end of tapering ledge), finishing direct from their top left side.

12 Blue Crush ★★★ 12m E1 5b
FA Neil Morrison & Derren Fox July 2005

Right of 11 corners is a right-slanting crack running between horizontal breaks. Start as for the previous route. Lovely climbing.

13 Birdman ★★ 12m E1 5b
FA Neil Morrison & Derren Fox July 2005

Right again and before the vague black crack of 14 is a thin crack. Climb to then up the crack and the wall above.

TOWER FACE

The cliff juts out a little now to form a sort of *"tower face"* with an excellent groove line at either side.
Descent: Down the *"crevasse"*, a 5m V.Diff scramble down the chimney/groove at the east end.

1 The Quarryman ★★★ 20m E2 5b
FA Mick Tighe, K.Forbes & O.West June 1998

Stupendous climbing up the left groove.

14 Tuttie's Wall ★★ 11m E2 5b
FA Mick Tighe 17 June 1997

This first, wedge-shaped part of the quarry walls runs into an almost perfect plumb vertical corner. Start a couple of metres left of the corner beneath vague black crack. Follow the crack then a series of fabulous horizontal faults. Strenuous.

15 Tuttie's Crack ★★ 11m E2 5b
FA Neil Morrison & Scott Johnstone 16 July 2001

The crack right of 14.

16 Tuttie's Neuk ★★ 12m E1 5b
FA Mick Tighe, Key Proudlock, Kathy Harding, Janice Cargill & Simon Fraser 3 June 1995

The fine open book corner not easily seen except from immediately above or below. An acrobatic start with a slightly easier finish.

2 Standing Stone ★ 20m E3 5c
FA Neil Morrison & Derren Fox July 2005

Climbs the cracks on the edge of the impending wall immediately right of 1. Climb through a niche into the cracks (as for 3) then continue up the edge. This soon leads into 1 for a rest of sorts. Step back right onto the wall and forge on up the cracks to the top.

3 The Big Swall ★★ 20m E5 6b
FA Tim Rankin & Scott Johnstone August 2002

Start just right of 1. Go up through a niche to a break, move right along this then climb the smooth wall just right of twin thin cracks (crucial micro), finishing more easily directly.

4 No Maybes ★★ 18m E3 6a
FA Tim Rankin & Neil Morrison 7 July 2002

The right groove, becoming a crack in its upper reaches. After a stiff start, follow the line with a 'stiff pull' fnarr fnarr! on the upper wall.

Photo Iain Miller.

5 Deceptively Groovy ★★   18m E2 5c
FA Rich Rogers & Dave Turnbull July 1993

The 'deceptively easy-looking' wide right-facing groove, continuing up the gently overhanging fault above.

5a *Definitely Maybe* ★ E2 5c follows the groove for 10m before moving left onto a cracked arête and the top; the thin left groove/crack is 6 *The Forgotten* ★ E1 5b. 7 *Ebb and Flo* ★ VS 4b the wee groove in the centre of the slabby black wall.

ARCH WALL

Around the corner again going east is a lovely wall of almost perfect rock with a small curving arch midway along. A fault line runs horizontally across the wall about 6–8m above the tidal ledge.

1 Crab Crawl ★★   40m HVS 5a
FA Mick Tighe, Iain Lee & Janice Cargill 13 May 1997

Follow the traverse line in either direction on immaculate rock. Sometimes delicate, sometimes strenuous. There is a convenient ledge for a rest and/or belay half way along.

A shallow groove line at the extreme left is 2 *The Lunge* ★ E1 5c, 2a *Velvets* VS 4c avoids the crux by escaping left into the *"crevasse"*. Escapable line 3m right of the left side of the wall is 3 *Taustie Wall* ★ E3 6a with an inordinately hard top move.

4 Bleed it Dry ★★   20m E4 6a
FA Tim Rankin & Neil Morrison August 2007

One of the best lines on the wall, taking the groove and crack-line running directly to and passing the left end of the arching roof. Make a bouldery start up pockets to gain a slab ramp at the base of the groove. Follow the groove and crack to a good hold beneath the roof. Pull over and follow a thin crack direct to the top.

5 Nuckelavee ★★★   20m E4 6a
FA Gary Latter 22 June 1998

Spectacular climbing through the centre of the arching roof. Climb an easy flake to a ledge at 3m then up the wall with a long reach to a good undercut under the roof. Reach straight over for a good hold in the horizontal break, span left and finish on good holds.

6 Long Hard Winter ★★★   20m E2 5b
FA Dave Turnbull & Rich Rogers July 1993

The crescent overhang, or arch, that gives the wall its name has a thin crack coming from its right end. This route climbs the steep wall and open groove directly below the right end of the overhang then takes the crack above to the top.

7 Ronnie the Axe ★★   20m E5 6a
FA Dave Turnbull & Tony Park 24 May 1999

Good steep climbing, easier than it looks, though the gear is hard to arrange. Start 3m right of the groove of 6. Climb up to a small roof then follow holds leading up and right to a small ramp in the centre of the wall. Finish direct on good but hidden holds.

8 Mack the Knife ★★   20m E5 6a
FA Tim Rankin & Iain Miller 2 May 2004

Another excellent sustained pitch. Low in the grade. Climbs through the right end of the roof by an obvious little niche just left of 9. Climb the lower wall to the ledge, cross the roof at the apex of the niche and continue up the sustained wall to finish up a thin crack, as for 7. Could be climbed in a big sea by starting from the ledge.

Tim Rankin on the first ascent of Bleed it Dry. Photo Neil Morrison.

Wall and twin cracks past obvious flaky jug is 9 *Hajj* ★★ E4 6a; 10 *Summer Pilgrim* ★ E3 5c is the rightmost crack; 11 *Nyook Waa* ★ Severe 4a the chimney/cleft, finishing up the right wall. 12 *Sunset Crack* ★ HS 4b takes crack up arête.

13 The Lang Huddauf ★   20m Very Difficult
FA Key Proudlock & Jock Finnan 3 June 1995

Around the corner from 12 is another chimney/groove line with some brownish rock near the top which is a little bit loose.

14 The Langer Huddauf ★   20m Very Difficult
FA Iain Miller (solo) 24 August 2004

Start at the extreme right end of the tidal platform, as for 15 & 16. Climb directly up on perfect rock to gain a sloping ledge, follow the ledge and step up at its highest point to finish up a big hand crack. 14a *Direct Start* is Severe 4a.

15 Vision Quest ★   60m 4c-5c
FA Iain Miller (solo) 12 August 2003

A fine sea-level traverse which can be done for itself or as an approach to all the routes on **Gardyloo Wall**. Start as for 14 and traverse right on good sea-washed rock, (4c at low tide, increasing in difficulty as the tide rises) to finish on a huge ledge in the cave at the far right (east) end.

16 Wee Lum ★★   20m HVS 5a
FA Mick Tighe, Key Proudlock & Ken Sherstone 3 June 1995

Around the corner again from 14 the beautiful clean wall sweeps back into the bay. The first feature encountered is a fierce little bottomless chimney reached by a short sea level traverse from the bottom of 14. Wide bridging saves the day!

17 Lum Crack ★★   20m E2 5c
FA Iain Miller & Howard Clarke 1 October 2004

The perfect steep hand/finger-crack 3m right of 16. At low tide traverse in to gain the start. At high tide, abseil in to the small ledge at the base of 16.

GARDYLOO WALL

The plumb vertical sweep of cliff that now issues eastwards has been so named (Gardez L'Eau) on account of the old quarryman's rubbish tip that is evident part way along. 30m or so along from the top of *Nyook Waa* and *The Lang Hudauf* is a small depression on the cliff top and a diagonal overhanging fault line in the cliff below.

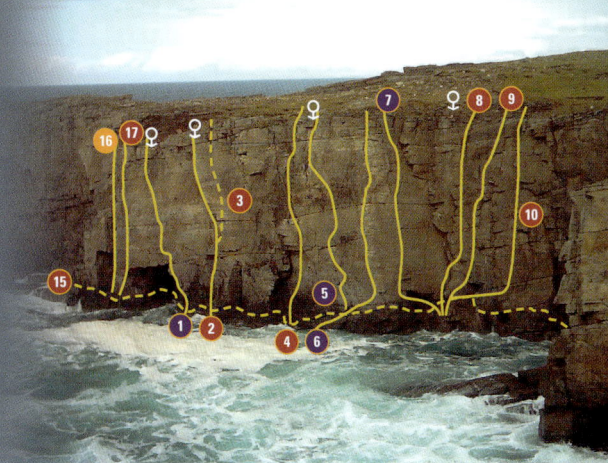

1 Dragonhead ★★★★ 22m E6 6b
FA Tim Rankin & Neil Morrison (practised on abseil) 25 July 2006

"A stunning route, amongst the best of its grade in the country!" Sustained, well protected on superb rock. It links cracks up the wall left of the groove of 2. Abseil into a small triangular ledge down and left of the larger ledge of 2, below an overhanging arête (the right edge of an impressive sea cave – low tide or low swell required). Climb the steep arête to a break, gain the next break, step left and make hard moves up the crack to a good hidden hold on the right. Move hard left to gain the next crack and follow it with sustained interest to the top break. Finish out right into the notch (stake, block belay well back).

2 Skullsplitter ★★★ 22m E2 5c
FA Dave Turnbull & Rich Rogers July 1993

The fault line. Abseil from the depression to a fine little black triangular ledge just above the high water mark. Climb to the left-facing corner/V-groove and climb it, exiting right at the top.

3 Freeloader ★ 22m E1 5b
FA Nick Kekus & Tony Park 7 May 1995

Climb 2 for 10m, before pulling steeply up and right onto the wall with small pockets. A shallow left-facing groove leads to the top. The direct start up the obvious crack is the same grade.

4 Ebb Tide ★ 24m E2 5c
FA Mick Tighe, Simon Fraser, Kathy Harding & Janice Cargill 3 June 1995

About 6m below and right of the triangular ledge another, bigger ledge appears at half tide. From the ledge climb up the wall passing a wee overhang on the right at 6m then follow the wall to the top.

5 The Orkney Sessions ★ 22m E5 6b
FA Tim Rankin & Neil Morrison (on-sight) 22 July 2006

The fine wall. Start off the tidal ledge, as for 6, or if the tide is high abseil to the square niche in the middle of the wall. Traverse breaks right to gain the niche, climb the crack out the top of the niche to a good pocket and move right to a flake. Step up to a good hold and trend left with difficulty to a good break below an overlap. Gain holds above, reach right to two tiny crimps and use these to gain the next break (crux). Boldly gain the slab above and traverse good foot holds left to a crack. Finish up this.

6 Gardyloo Gold ★★ 28m E4 6a
FA Tim Rankin & Colin McLean 10 September 2003

Fantastic climbing up the flake crack on the left side of the arête. Either abseil to the large tidal ledge as for 4 or down the wall to the right to a hanging belay at high tide. Veer right and up slightly to join the crack 3m above its base and follow it with 'sustained interest' throughout.

⑦ Thing of Dreams ★★★   25m E4 6a
FA Tim Rankin 10 September 2003

The excellent thin crack up the right side of the blunt arête. Gain the base by abseiling down the corner just right of the crack to take a hanging belay at its base below a roof. Traverse left below the roof and pull through it on jugs to the base of the crack. Cruise up the stunning crack.

⑧ Sea of Dreams ★★   22m E2 5c
FA Steve Herd & Iain Miller 16 September 2003

From the same hanging belay ascend the first clean-cut corner to beneath the roof. Swing right and follow the right-slanting groove strenuously in a fine position.

⑨ Dreamcatcher ★★   20m E3 5c
FA Tim Rankin & Neil Morrison 8 August 2007

The shallow groove line. From the belay step right and climb the right rib of the groove (crux) to gain better holds in the groove above. Follow the groove with sustained interest to cross a block roof onto a slab; climb the slab to finish up a little groove.

⑩ Dreamweaver ★★   20m E3 5c
FA Tim Rankin & Neil Morrison 28 July 2008

The wall and flake crack just right of 9 gives another fine pitch. Make a move up 9 and span right to a horizontal break, follow this right to below the upper crack line. Climb the wall to below a small roof then gain an obvious jug up and left. Step back right and continue up the crack to the top.

THE FALSE STACK

The pseudo stack with a little slab, or *"drawbridge"* propping it up.

Descent: By abseil from a large recess at the eastern end of the summit.

① Dark Island ★★★   15m E3 6a
FA Neil Morrison & Tim Rankin 25 July 2006

The north-west arête, left of 2. A technical and well protected start leads out left onto the bold arête. Finish carefully using the obvious shaky but secure flake.

② Summer's End ★★★   15m E2 5b
FA Chris Webb, Iain Miller & Don Rigby 10 August 2003

Marvellous sustained climbing with perfect rock and protection, taking the left-slanting crack in the centre of the seaward face.

③ The Crows Nest ★★   20m VS 4c
FA Mick Tighe, James Armour & Colin Duncan 17 June 1997

Take the south-west arête for a few metres by a groove-line or some big steps on the right. Go right at the top of the groove (tricky) on to the beak. Don't go straight up the obvious arête above which is a bit loose. Instead, follow the lovely little slabby wall diagonally rightwards to the top.

④ Storming the Bridge ★★★   12m E5 6a
FA Tim Rankin & Neil Morrison 30 July 2009

The right arête of the south face, finishing onto the left end of the 'drawbridge'.

⑤ Three Wise Idiots ★   15m E1 5b
FA Don Rigby, Iain Miller & Chris Webb 10 August 2003

The fine looking arête behind the false stack. Abseil from the 'drawbridge' to a non-tidal platform at the base. Follow the arête direct, passing a precarious block (crux), traversing left to finish on top of the 'drawbridge'.

⑥ Variety Show ★★★   20m HVS 5a
FA Mick Tighe & Janice Cargill 14 May 1997

30 to 40 metres south of **The False Stack** is a little geo that can only be reached by abseil. At the south end of the geo is a rib split by a perfect crack-line. Climb through the initial overhang on immaculate rock and with perfect protection. Follow the crack until it becomes a browny coloured, slabby depression near the top. Keep going, or go right under a rock beak and finish up a little groove.

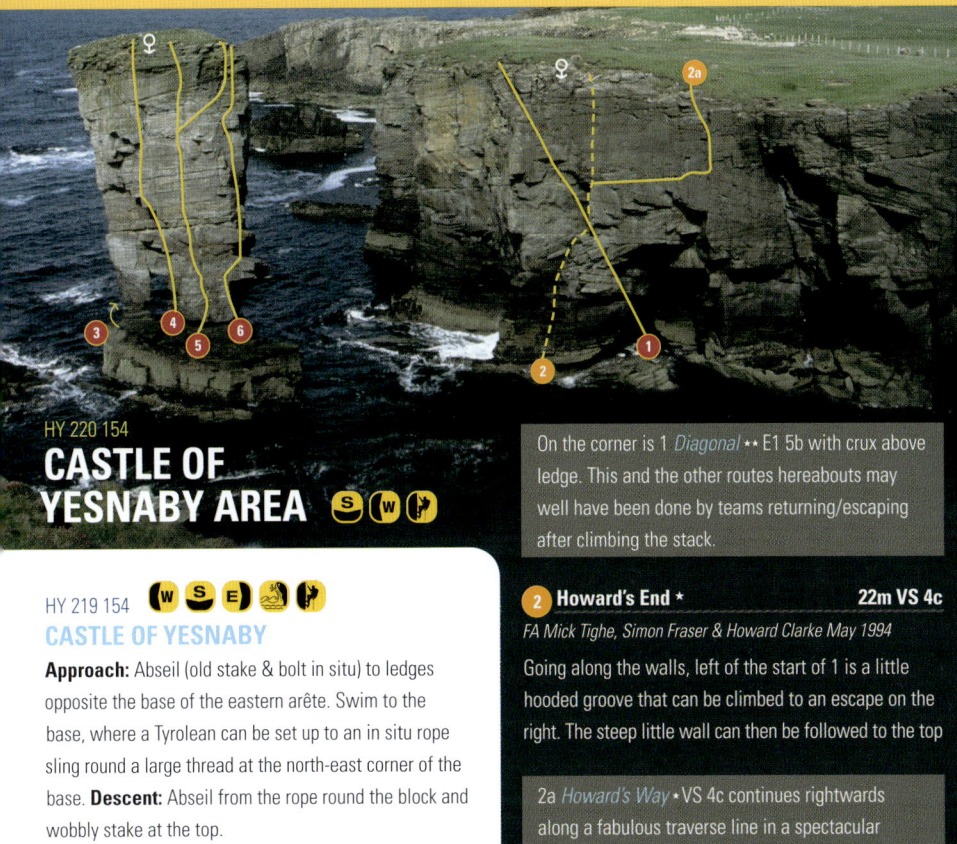

CASTLE OF YESNABY AREA

HY 220 154

HY 219 154
CASTLE OF YESNABY

Approach: Abseil (old stake & bolt in situ) to ledges opposite the base of the eastern arête. Swim to the base, where a Tyrolean can be set up to an in situ rope sling round a large thread at the north-east corner of the base. **Descent:** Abseil from the rope round the block and wobbly stake at the top.

3 Yes Please! ***   25m E3 6a
FA Mick Fowler, Julian Freeman-Attwood & Crag Jones 19 July 1996

Excellent climbing up the flying finger-crack on the seaward (western) edge. Start on the right side. Move up and swing round to the left side on a good hold (poor PR). Climb boldly up right to a resting place on the arête then follow the strenuous finger-crack through an overhang to finish up an overhanging hand crack.

4 Meditation **   25m E2 5c
FA Gary Latter & Tom Pringle 10 July 2002

Good climbing up the left side of the south face with a short well-protected crux. Start in the arch and move easily up right onto a large ledge. Move out left on good holds then climb a difficult wall on sloping holds to better holds leading up to an easy flake-groove. Finish up this.

On the corner is 1 *Diagonal* ** E1 5b with crux above ledge. This and the other routes hereabouts may well have been done by teams returning/escaping after climbing the stack.

2 Howard's End *   22m VS 4c
FA Mick Tighe, Simon Fraser & Howard Clarke May 1994

Going along the walls, left of the start of 1 is a little hooded groove that can be climbed to an escape on the right. The steep little wall can then be followed to the top

2a *Howard's Way* • VS 4c continues rightwards along a fabulous traverse line in a spectacular position, heading for the top as soon as you can. *"This looks about E5!"*

5 Original Route *   25m E2 5b
FA Joe Brown & party (1 PA) July 1967

The crack towards the right side of the south face. Start in the centre of the face and climb up to the thin crack and up this (old PRs), finishing by stepping out right up the final section of 6. (The FA party traversed left into 4, using a sling for aid.)

6 East Arête **   25m E2 5b
FA Joe Brown & party July 1967

Follow the edge to a good ledge then the crack past a PR to ledges just below the top. Finish with care.

SPECTATORS GEO

The bay around the stack forms a natural amphitheatre to view the stack and climbers. At the south east corner of the bay is a small geo at the base of an impressive steep compact wall seamed with cracks, overlooked from the south by a prominent headland popular with tourists. The routes on this wall feel even more impressive as they start 5m above the sea from ledges perched over the geo.
Descent: Abseil to the spacious ledge from either the fence strainer post (spare rope required) or in-situ stakes.

Right-facing corner and thin crack is 1 *Blue Baron* • E2 5b; next thin crack finishing with long reach is 2 *The Loved One* •• E4 5c.

New Sensation ★★★   20m E3 5c
FA Tim Rankin & Derren Fox 19 July 2005

Excellent well protected climbing in a fine position, taking the fine crack with protruding blocks high up. From the right end of the ledge move up to climb the crack and shallow groove to a roof. Cross this, step right and continue up the sustained crack to the top.

④ Guns in the Sky ★★★   22m E5 6a
FA Tim Rankin & Neil Morrison August 2007

The thin left crack, just right of 3 gives a stunning pitch. Follow breaks up and right to climb a shallow groove marking the right side of a roofed alcove. Step up right and follow the superb sustained crack to the top.

⑤ Elegantly Wasted ★★★   25m E5 6a
FA Tim Rankin & Neil Morrison August 2007

The flake and shallow groove line right again gives another superb sustained route. Belay as for 4 or from the large niche out right. Climb diagonally out right to the base of a thin crack below a faint shallow groove. Climb the crack and the delightful shallow groove to gain the left end of the block ledge. Make a hard move up then step right to gain the eroded flake (crucial protection on left) climb this then boldly move out left to a good hold. A further hard move gains the superb crack and groove line which leads to the top.

Tim Rankin on the first ascent of Guns in the Sky. Photo Neil Morrison.

THE LOOSE HEADLAND

Descent: Abseil to platforms at the base, easiest from the large ledge at the top of the 1 *The Castle Escape*.

The open corner in centre, traversing ledges out left to finish is route 1 *The Castle Escape* Difficult.

② Muckle Thrutch Crack ★★   25m E4 6a
FA Tim Rankin (on-sight) 19 July 2005

A good varied pitch. On the right is a shallow cave with a thin crack springing from its lip. Climb the left arête of the cave to get jammed in the roof (stylish knee bar available). A further thrutch gains the crack proper (crux), follow the crack steeply at first up onto the slab. Step right onto a large block on the arête, cross the small overlap above direct and finish leftwards to a belay on the platform below the top (F #1.5 essential for belay).

⑥ Devil Inside ★★   28m E5 6b
FA Tim Rankin & Neil Morrison August 2007

Another excellent route up the next continuous crack to the right.

1 **8m 4c** From the belay ledge traverse horizontally right to belay at the second smaller niche.
2 **20m 6b** Climb breaks direct to the right end of the block ledge. Use the crack on the right to move up and then left to the eroded flake line of 5. Climb the flake with protection in the crack on the right to a good rest at its top. Step back right and place crucial micro wires before climbing the difficult and sustained crack to the top.

⑦ Tiny Daggers ★★   18m E6 6b
FA Tim Rankin & Neil Morrison August 2007

Yet another stunning route up the thin right crack, only let down slightly by a possible escape right below the crux. Abseil down the corner on the right to belay on a ledge 10m above the sea. Step out left and climb breaks then a miniature groove to gain the thin crack proper. Follow the excellent technical crack to a slightly easier finish.

SOUTH FACE

Descent: Abseil down the **North Face**, (or down climb *The Castle Escape* Diff.) then walking round to gain the southern end of the platforms. Drop down to sea level and traverse right to a **non-tidal** platform at the base.

③ Nemesis ★★   25m E3 5c
FA Iain Miller, Steve Herd & Paul Manson 6 September 2003

A corner, overhanging on both walls. This gives a sustained and committing pitch with the crux the strenuous mid-height roof. Unfortunately the rock is a bit suspect and there can be lurking fulmars.

ACKNOWLEDGEMENTS

Special thanks to my wife Karen, who has helped throughout the protracted work on this 3rd edition. In particular, special thanks to Ian Taylor for extensive feedback on a multitude of venues, along with allowing me to use many of his photographs. Others who have helped by providing route descriptions, feedback or photos are: Michael Barnard, Alan Cassidy, Dave Cowan, Steve Crowe, Robert Durran, Dave Fowler, Peter Herd, Lawrence Hughes, Murdoch Jamieson, Martin Kocsis, Jules Lines, Ewan Lyons, James Mchaffie, Andy Moles, Tim Rankin, George Smith, Lucy Spark, James Sutton, Paul Tattersall, Mick Tighe, Graham Tyldesley and Crispin Waddy.

ROUTE INDEX

007 232	Alba/Return to Mecca 201	Another Rude Awakening 267	Astar 155	Banks of Locharron, The 67	Before the Deluge 81
1–800–Ming 266	Alchemist, The 353	An Ros 264	Ataka 183	Bardo Thodol 313	Behaving Badly 157
101 Damnations 406	Alice in Wonderland 156	An Sulaire 261	Athlete's Foot 245	Barnacle Butter 335	Bends, The 465
A Bit on the Side 219	Alien Territory 76	Anthology Arête 405	Atlantic City 341	Barndance 176	Beri-Beri 454
Abomination 169	Ali-Shuffle, The 252	Anthrax Flake 205	Atlantic Crack 253	Barrel of Fun 189	Berie-Berie 337
Above the Blue 296	All Abilities Path, The 274	Anxiety Nervosa 343	Atlantic Crossing 355	Barrel of Laughs 240	Bernera Prow, The 334
Abridged Version, The 405	All Hail King Silly 330	Any Spare Change? 73	Atlantic Pillar 187	Barrier Reef 336	Between the Monsoons 198
A Bridge Too Far 341	All Quiet on the Western Front 82	Aorta 181	Atlantic Wall 304	Barrier Reiff 237	Beyond the Ranges 382
Absent Friends 235	All the Arts 144	A Paddler's Tale 324	At Last 402	B.A.R.T. 391	Big Al 408
Absolution 406	Altar Ego 21	Applecross Jam, The 125	A Touch Too Much 103	Bastinado 32	Big Ballin' 164
Abyss of Numbers, The 448	Alzheimer's Groove 423	Apple Pie 289	Atropos Direct 35	Bat Day 199	Big Banana Feet 324
Ace of Diamonds 263	A Man in Assynt 270	Apprentice Bhoys 116	At the Whelks 73	Batman 241	Big Chief Turning Bull 418
Achevalier 363	Ambassadors, The 272	A Prophet's Doom 370	Auld Nick 240	Batman and Robin 197	Big C, The 185
Acrimonious Acrobat 219	Amber Nectar 395	Aqualung 72, 420	Automaton 231	Bat's Gash 167	Big Flapper 207
Action Replay 457	Am Burach 353	Aquamarine 125	Autumn Rib 191	Battle Axe 140	Big Foot 215
Adalat 181	American Vampire 72	Aqua Rambling 256	Autumn Sonata 253	Batty 206	Big John 461
A Diamond is Forever 288	A Midsummer Night's Dream 69	Aquarium Arête 263	Avoid the Paint 138	Bay-watch 184	Big Kenneth 438
Adventures of Baron Von Midgehousen, The 327	A Million Years BC 112	Archangel 110	Avon Man, The 58	Baywatch 65, 390	Big Knives 157
A Few Dollars More 461	Amphitheatre Arête 30	Arch Angel 426	A Walk Across the Rooftops 235	Beached Whale 18	Big Lick, The 375
A Few Fathoms More 440	Ancient Mariners, The 394	Arch Deacon, The 424	A Walk on the Wild Side 132	Beagles Above the Shitehouse 449	Big Luigi 381
Africaan Problem, The 262	Ancient Mariner, The 134	Archer Thomson's Route 36	Awesome 247	Beach Groove Garden 181	Big Money, The 68
After Dark 302	Anduril 91	Argonaut 347	A Word With the Bill 421	Beach Wall 305	Big Sea in My Trousers 449
After Eight 148, 379	Andy had Fish and Chips for Tea 108	Arial 162	Axe Grinder 141	Beam Me Up Scotty 365	Big Swall, The 466
Afterglow 118	An Faidh 243	Ark of the Covenant 22		Beast in the Undergrowth 217	Bikini Dreams 430
Afterglow Variation 117	An Fiosaiche 243	Armburger 181	Back Stage 290	Beastmaster 172, 217	Bills Yellow Edge 431
Aftershock 333	Angel Face 96	Around the Bend 340	Bad Dream 71	Beast of Bolsover, The 60	Billy Bean's Dream 465
After the Basking Shark 449	Angel of Sharkness 22	Arrow Route 33	Balances of Fate 132	Beast, The 319	Billy Bones 301
After the Storm 207	A Night at the Opera 354	Archer Thomson's Route 36	Balaton 170	Beating Heart 245	Bingo wings 70
Aga Sanction, The 429	Animal 151	Aspen Croft 267	Bald Eagle 136, 402	Beat the Beak 194	Bint There Dun It 413
Ageing Bull 150	Anonymous 350	A Spot of Deception 219	Balding Oldie 149	Beauty's Edge 286	Birdman 466
Age of Confusion, The 108	A.N. Other 350	Asp, The 44	Ball Park Incident 141	Because I'm Black 164	Birdman of Bewaldeth 60
Agfa 78	Another Perspective 281	Assault Slab 148	Bamboozle 197	Beer Bottle Dilemma, The 137	Birdsong 72
A Horizontal Desire 401		As Sound as Mr J.A. 415	Bampot 343		Birthday Boy 326
Airs 290		Assyntialist, The 273	Banana Transfer Theory 456		Bisection Crack 186
			Bank of Scotland 245		Bit-Coiner 70

ROUTE INDEX

Blackadder 247
Black Affronted 350
Blackballed 295
Black Carrot, The 347
Black Chimney 76
Black Chimney, The 252
Black Crack 450
Black Crack, The 354
Blackcurrent 326
Black Donald 240
Black Gold 241, 284, 313
Black Groove 74
Black Guillemot 241
Black Hole, The 365
Blackjack 295
Blacklight Sleaze 195
Black Magic 252
Black Mischief 169
Black Night 299
Black Pig 241
Black Queen, The 110
Black Recess 373
Black Sabbath 343
Black Sox 200
Black Sox Left Finish 200
Black Streak, The 176
Black Wall Special 186
Black Zone 238
Blanco 129
Blasad Den Iar 163
Bleached Whale 110
Bleed it Dry 467
Blessed are the Weak 370
Blind as a Frog 111
Blind Bandit 260
Blind Faith 293
Blind Faith Direct 293
Bling 164
Blitzkrieg Bop 191
Block and Beak 112
Block Chimney 258
Blo' na Gael 402
Blood Feud 136
Bloodlust 297
Bloodlust Direct 298
Blood of Eden 251
Blood Red Roses 138
Bloody Hand 341
Bloody Obvious Crack 450
Blow Out 147
Blue Baron 472
Blue Crush 466
Blues Before Sunrise 191
Bluff, The 302
Blyth Spirit 138
B-Movie 200
Boab's Corner 123
Boat, The 471
Bodhisattva 208
Body and Soul 335
Bodyheat 98
Boggle 99
Bogie 119
Bogie Wonderland 268
Bog Talla 200
Bonus Asylum Seekers 407
Bold as Brass 135

Boldered Out 147
Bolshie Ballerina 219
Bones 365
Bonus, The 260
Bonxie 354
Bonxie, The 394
Boogie Street 164
Boosh 413
Bootless Crow 203
Booty Sweat 165
Born to Run 141
Bostadh Strangler, The 334
Bothy House Crack 359
Bovnahackit 140
Bowmore 213
Bow Wave 260
Boyish Behaviour 145
Brace Yersel Becky 235
Brainbiter 244
Brasso 257
Brave Heart 259
Brave New World 125
Brave New World Left Start 125
Bravura 396
Brazen 51
Break Dance 252
Break In 175
Breath of Life, The 412
Bridge Builder 335
Bridging Interest 68
Bridging Loan 66
Brigitt's Liberation 334
Brimstone 117
Broken Silence 197
Broken Wing 73
Broons' Wall 122
Brother Ray 415
Brow Beaten 270
Brown Streak, The 200
Brutal Reality 339
Bubblyjock 250
Buckets for Breakfast 415
Buena Vista 154
Bug, The 161
Bullet 465
Bumblyone 91
Bumblytwo 91
Bunny Ears 165
Buoy Racers 318
Buried Treasure 221
Burka 331
Burning Desire 221, 429
Burn Out 300
Burnt Offering 135
Burnt Umber 269
Bus Stop 206
Busted Flush 22
Bye Bye to the Widows 403
Bygone Comrades 140
Caberfeidh 199
Cailleach 349
Cairnaholics Anonymous 108
Cairn Terrier 107
Lakewalk 178
Calamoose 164

Caledonian McBrain Justice 376
Calling Seal 451
Call of the Sea 436
Call of the Wild 193
Calum's Rest 266
Campa Crack 351
Caoraich Mhor 257
Capillary Wall 181
Captain Beanheart 268
Captain Oates 338
Captain Patience 59
Captain Planet 25
Captain's Log 365
Carnival of Folly 250
Carnmore Corner 174
Carnmore Corner Direct 174
Carved from Stone 216
Casey Jones 295
Cask Conditioned 189
Cask Strength 318
Cassin's Crack 318
Cast and Shadow 414
Castlebay Castaway 409
Castlebay Hen Party 442
Castle Escape, The 473
Cat Burglar 139
Cat on a Hot Tin Roof 228
Cat, The 134
Cave Wall 235
Celtic Horizons 263
Celtic Ray 183
Cengalo 310
Censor, The 322
Central Route 29
Cereal Killer 404
Chambre Finish, The 41
Champagne Rhubarb 268
Channering Worm 237
Chapel Crack 340
Charleston 143
Charlie Potatoes Direct 70
Charlie's Corner 205
Charlie's Tower 122
Chasing Tails 330
Cheese-grater Slab 136
Chemistry 83
Chew the Route 369
Chiaroscuro 130
Chicken Run 247, 350
Child of the Sea, The 410
Children of Tempest 432
Child's Play 181
Chimney Route 37
Chisel, The 384
Chockarockaholic 399
Chokestone Crack 248
Chokestone Gully 189
Chugger's Elbow 73
Cioch Corner 88
Cioch Corner Superdirect 87
Cioch Crack 349
Cioch Direct 31
Cioch Grooves 31
Cioch Gully 30
Cioch Nose 34, 87
Cioch Nose Direct Start 88

Cioch West 30
Circus, The 165
Clach Glas - Bla Bheinn Traverse 16
Cladonia Dreaming 289
Clam Jam 246
Clandestine 51
Clansman, The 264
Classic Crack 280
Clatterbridge 233
Claustrophobia 208
Claymore 264, 362
Clean Hand Gang 368
Cleopatra's Asp 247
Clingfilm 109
Clinging On 40
Clockwork Rat 109
Closer to the Edge 372
Close to the Bone 219
Cloudburst 199
Cloud Cuckoo Land 158
Clubmoss 281
Clyneleish 213
CMB 140
Cnip-Fit 337
Crippy Sweetie 337
Coalition Chaos 141
Coaster 320
Cocoa Cracks 47
Cog, The 465
Coigach Corner 259
Cold Turkey 79
Collie's Route 33
Colonel Huff 340
Coloured Rain 341
Come around to my way of thinking 75
Comeback, The 252
Comes the Breanish 378
Commando Crack 44
Completely out to Lunge 112
Complete Works, The 405
Conception Corner 335
Conch Corner 405
Con-Con, The 121
Condemned to Happiness 419
Condescending 119
Condome 120
Conflagration 120
Confluent 120
Conglomerati 326
Congruent 119
Conjuror, The 39
Conquistador 149
Con's Cleft 44
Consensus 119
Constipated Miser 145
Contiguous 120
Contumacy 120
Convoluted Contortionist 219
Convolutionist, The 261
Cookie Monster 152
Cook the Shooter 104
Cool Breeze 77

Cool Dudes 252
Coopers Crack 292
Copper Koala 363
Cormorant Corner 350
Corn Choked Corner 404
Corncrake Corner 400
Corncrakes for Breakfast 407
Corner and Slab 447
Corner Cimb 350
Corner, The 238
Corner Wall 253
Cortes 144
Coughed up from Hell 209
Coup du Monde 185
Cowrie 181
Craa'nest 456
Crab Crack 205
Crab Crawl 467
Crackers 175, 367
Crackin' Corner 296
Cracking-up 343
Cracknan Euan 446
Crack of Ages 105
Crack of Dawn 47
Crack of Desire, The 239
Crack of Doom Direct 36
Crack of Double Doom 36
Crack of Zawn 21
Crack Route 204
Crack that Tim Forgot, The 449
Crack, The 200, 286
Craik in Everything, The 140
Craik, The 409
Cramp Crack 286
Crann Tara 250
Creagh Dhu Grooves 39
Credit Zone 295
Creep, The 131
Crembo Cracks 31
Crimebusters of the Sea, The 352
Crimpology 330
Crimson Cruiser 290
Crisis of Confidence 450
Crivvens 123
Crooked Thumb 447
Cross Dressing 112
Cross-Eyed 260
Crossover 260
Crossroads 146
Crows Nest, The 470
Cruel Crack, The 330
Cruel Sea, The 134
Cruiser, The 79
Crusader 203
Crypt Robber 324
Crystal Daze 422
Crystal Maze, The 357
Crystal Shell 268
Cuan a' Bochan 430
Cuan a' Cheo 426
Cuckoo Conundrum, The 200
Cuddane 296
Culach 256
Cullinan, The 270

Culture of Silence 295
Cup Final 402
Curare 175
Curious Bulge, The 403
Curious Grey, The 449
Curry Island 80
Curtains 65
Curving Crack 248
Curving Crack, The 200
C Weed 280
Cyclonic Westerly 102
Cyclops 260
Da Bomb 145
Daddy Longlegs 363
Dalriada 241
Damn Your Eyes! 360
Dancing with Hens 442
Dangerous Dancer 221
Dark Angel 299
Dark Crystal, The 356
Dark Flush, The 298
Dark Island 470
Dauntless 345
Daunt's Arête 231
Dawn Grooves 47
Daylight Robbery 70
Dead Calm 193
Dead Giveaway 82
Dead Mouse Crack 115
Deaf Violinist, The 141
Death Pirate 76
Death Rattle 363
Death-Wolf 171
Decadent Days 159
Deceptively Groovy 467
Deep Blue 465
Deepest Blue 335
Deerstalker, The 105
Definitely Maybe 467
Delayed Reaction 441
Demon Lover 55
Demon Razor 139
Derek the Shaman 419
Descent Corner 236
Desire Direct 239
Desmond the Slapper 81
Destitution Man 162
Devil Inside 473
Devil Music 208
Devil You Know, The 300
Diabaig Corner 114
Diabaig Tiger 125
Diabolic Finish 114
Diagonal 471
Diagonal Crack 235
Dial Card 58
Diamond Back 243
Diamond Face Route 275
Diaper Mention 82
Die Another Day 233
Digitalis 21
Dilemma 40
Dilithium Crystals 365
Direct Nose Route 222
Director's Corner 345
Direct Route 37
Dire Straights 114

ROUTE INDEX

Dire Wall 114
Disco Fever 340
Dishonour 177
Dispossessed 203
Distant Voices 357
Disturbing the Wildlife 78
Diura 40
Divided Fears 341
Divided Loyalty 137
Dividing Line, The 362
Diving Board 340
DIY Arête 22
Djapana 325
Doddle 206, 280
Dogs of Law 390
Dolphin Friendly 110
Dolphins and Whales 299
Dominis Vobiscus 374
Domino 246
Done Mingulay 440
Don't Fool Yourself Girl 407
Don't Leave Your Dad in the Rain 246
Don't Look Now 350
Don't Think Twice 316
Doozer 152
Doppelkratzer 443
Double or Quits 330
Double Walrus 451
Dougie's Ordinary Route 251
Down 83
Down Under 367
Do You Expect Me to Talk? 283
Dragon 171
Dragonfly 289
Dragonhead 469
Dragons of Eden 251
Dreaded Dram, The 346
Dreamcatcher 470
Dreams by the Sea 298
Dreams of Utah 248
Dream the Dhearg Goch 417
Dream Ticket 131
Dreamweaver 470
Driftwood 306
Drip Drip Drip 141
Droppin' Bombs 267
Dubhs Ridge, The 18
Ducks with Attitude 194
Dulux Corner 81
Dump, The 145
Dung Beetle 289
Dun Moaning 439
Dunnard 141
Dunne Slimmin' 439
Dunskiing 245
Durdle Huxter 446
Dwarf Variation 450
Dying Direct 293
Dying in Vein 293
Dynamo Thrum 322

Each Uisge Direct 160
Eag Dubh 253
Eagle Has Landed, The 352
Eagles Above the Lighthouse 449
Eaglesea 446

Earthbound 66
Earth Shaker 236
East Arête 471
East Chimney Crack 60
East Ridge 20
Easy Day for a Shag 419
Eaves, The 253
Ebb and Flo 467
Ebb Tide 469
Echolocation 191
Eclipse 300
Ecstasis 16
Ecstasy 177
Edged Out 192
Edge of Beyond 52
Edge of Distinction 372
Edge of Enlightenment 103
Edge of the Sea 235
Edges and Spaces 257
Edgewood Whymper 115
Edgy 342
Eeyore 248
Eight Below 150
Eighted 150
Eight Sisters 379
Eightsome Reel, The 196
Elastic Collision 243
Elbow Room 104
Electric Bagpipe, The 51
Elegantly Wasted 472
Elephant of Surprise, The 403
Eliminator 105
EliminEight 379
El Passe 149
Elysium 396
Empty on Endorphins 259
Endolphin Rush 400
Endurance 367
Enigma 39
Enigma Grooves 224
Enlightenment 240
Entasis 143
Entropy 140
Epicentre 333
Ergot Kernel 376
Escape from Reality 300
Es Gibt Reis Baby 412
Eureka 381
Evasion 119
Evening Sun 451
Every Cormorant is a Potential Shag 391
Every Which Way But Loose 242
Evil of Spuds, The 263
Evolution of Wings, The 225
Ewephoria 148
Ewereka 148
Ewe Tree Slab 148
Exact Epicentre 333
Exasperated Escapologist Direct 221
Executioner, The 243
Exit Stage Left 412
Exorcist 299
Expecting to Fly 226
Experimental Learning 60

Exterminator 105
Extraction 372
Extraordinary Relief Map of Iceland, The 443
Eye of the Storm 317, 425

Face Off 342
Fade to Grey 191
Failte Gu Inbhirpollaidh 266
Falconer Cracks 268
Fallout 321
False Men, The 339
Fancy Free 263, 316
Fantastic Mr Fox, The 465
Far From the Dogging Crowd 444
Fascist Groove Thang 97
Fat Cats 68
Fat Man's Folly 80
Fatmouth 209
Fatwah, The 203
Fear an Bhata 415
Fear of Flying 227
Fear of the Dark 302
Feathering the Nest 147
Fe Fi Fo Fum 53
Felo de Se 225
Fergus Sings the Blues 442
Fertility Left 22
Fertility Right 23
Fian Grooves 171
Fidgey Muckers 199
Fifteen Fathoms of Fear 440
Fifty Fifty 373
Fight Club 72
Fighting on all Fronts 157
Final Demands 115
Final Fling 243
Fine Lines 429
Fingal 309
Finger in the Dyke 15
Finger Picker 267
Fingers 300
Fionn Buttress 169
Firecracker 175
Fire Walk With Me 60
First and Ten 263
First Born 369
First Fold 373
First Fruits 218
First Time for Everyone 449
Fisherboys 134
Fisherman's Blues 427
Fisherman's Dream 120
Fishnet Necklace 327
Fistfighter 104
Fistful of Dollarite, A 68
Five Minute Crack 187
Five Star Finish, The 424
Flag Iris 154
Flake Chimney 186
Flakeway to the Stairs 382
Flaky Shakes 302
Flaky Wall 187
Flaming June 135
Flaming June Crack 290
Flamingo 302
Flannan Chimneys 351
Flannan Crack 351

Flannan Slab 352
Flannan Slab Direct 352
Flannan Slab Left 352
Flashing Blade, The 139
Flawed by Design 192
Flea de Wean 74
Fleeced 108
Flock Talk 364
Flotsam 294
Flounder 296
Flowsnake 197
Fluid Dynamics 82
Flushed-out 151
Fluted Buttress 46
Flyaway 446
Flying Hex 443
Flying Pig 241
Flying Scotsman 141
Flying Teapot 367
Foamo 269
Focus 332
Foil 119
Fondue Macpac 393
Fool's Gold 73
Footloose 52
Forbidden Fruit 251
Forgotten Corner 316
Forgotten, The 467
Fossil Hunters 140
Fracture Clinic 414
Fraggle Roll 152
Freaker's Crack 317
Freakshow 196
Freakshow Direct 196
Fred West Finish, The 225
Free Base 247
Freedom! 259
Free Fall 319
Freeloader 469
Freeze Dried 77
Friendly Groove, The 220
Friends for Life 245
Friends in the North 61
Friends Retrieval 221
Frieze, The 114
Fringe Elements 451
Frisky After Whisky 53
From Hero to Zero 262
From Riches to Rags 220
From the Hole to Heaven 419
Frozen Smoke 363
Fukushima 140
Fulmar Cavity 456
Fulmar Squaw 418
Fulminate 363
Funky Groove 340
Fun Prow 198
Furious Fifties 261
Future in Computer Hell 267

Gaff 287
Gaffer's Wall 206
Gaia Designs 265
Galactica 282
Game Over 141
Game Over Extension 141
Gamhnachain's Crack Variation 117

Gammy's Purse 68
Gampy's Wallet 69
Gannet Crack 81, 350
Gap-Toothed Gypsy 198
Garden of Eadan 334
Gardyloo Gold 469
Gargantua 309
Gas 351
Gathering, The 34
Gem 270
Genesis 209
Geomancer 399
Geovannie 408
Gerda 190
Geriatrics 298
Gervasutti's Wall 319
Gideon's Wrath 90
Gideon's Wrath Direct
Gift Horse 112
Gift, The 260
Gill 189
Gilt Edge 257
Gimp Route 353
Girl in the Boat, The 443
Girl with Extraordinary Eyes, The 441
Giro Day 73
Gleaning the Bone 367
Gle Mha 318
Gloaming Finish, The 384
Global Warming 111
GLOP 296
Glorious Five Year Plan 59
GMB 460
Gneiss 188
Gneiss and Easy 189
Gneisser 188
Gneissest 188
Gneiss Groove 187
Gneiss Helmet 442
Gneiss is Nice 346
Gneiss Knowing You 284
Gneiss Pump 266
Gneiss Too 284
Gneiss to See You, to See You Gneiss 331
Gneiss Won 292
Gneissy 191
Gneiss Yin 284
Goat of Barten, The 285
G.O.A.T., The 199
Gob 173
Gobling Grooves 419
Gods, The 254
Godzilla 52
Gogmagog 207
Going Spare 343
Golden Eagle 137
Goldeneye 258
Golden Eyes 238
Golden Fleece 258
Golden Mile 77
Golden Plover 258
Golden Road, The 380
Golden Samphire 305
Golden Shower 72
Golgothic 165

Golgothic/Circus 165
Golgothic/Testify 165
Goodbye Donella 373
Goodbye Ruby Tuesday 345
Good, the Bad and the Ugly, The 258
Gorbachev 59
Grampus 68
Grand Central 349
Grand Dièdre 45
Grant's Bad Hair Day 356
Grap 322
Gravity Man 345
Gravity's Rainbow 214
Grazing Beast 334
Great Arch, The 412
Great Brush Robbery, The 112
Great Flake, The 338
Great Gig in the Sky 359
Great Northern 334, 349
Great Prow, The 15
Great Shark Hunt, The 432
Greedy Weeds 141
Greek Exit, The 141
Green Lady, The 71
Green Vote 60
Grey Coast, The 319
Grey Cossack 403
Grey Panther 52
Grey Rib 423
Grime of the Century 376
Groove Armada 324, 341
Grooveless Bodily Harm 79
Grooves, The 240
Groove, The 201
Groovin' High 98
Groovy 280
Groovy Mover 263
Gruinard Corner 207
Grumpy Groper 218
Grunter with Right Finish, The 116
Guanissimo 273
Gudgeon 159
Guga, The 395
Guillemot Crack 321
Gulf Coast Highway 160
Gull Who Shagged Me, The 447
Guns in the Sky 472
Gunslinger 185
Gussetbuster 242

Habit Forming 208
Haddie 295
Hadrian's Wall 109
Hafgufa 165
Hafgufa/Circus 165
Haggis 75
Hairdubh 155
Hairsplitter 244
Hairy Beast 20
Hairy Mary 23
Hajj 468
Hakkar 425
Halcyon Days 184
Halcyon Daze 250
Half Buoy, The 465

ROUTE INDEX

Hamilton's Groove and Arête 158
Hamilton's Route 101
Hand Jive 58
Hand Rail, The 160
Handsome Hog 124
Hand Traverse, The 238
Hanuman for a Day 293
Happily Married 157
Hard to Swallow 367
Harold 257
Harry Hoofter 413
Hashi-Watashi 199
Hate-Mail 182
Hatrick for Patrick 180
Hats off to the Catman 326
Haunt of Seals 421
Have a Nice Day 70
Haven, The 323
Hawaiian Tropic 451
Head and Heart 409
Head-Bred-Ian 389
Headlong 256
Headstrong 233
Heart of Beyond, The 272
Heather Said Sunshine 109
Heave-ho 152
Heavy Duty 317
Hebridean Overtures 411
Heebie-Jeebies, The 356
Heel Yo Ho 422
Helen 37
Helga's First Time 134
Help ma Boab 123
Henry's Hard Times 367
Herbaloner, The 391
Herbrudean, The 391
Here and Now 294
Heresy 161
Heretic, The 161
Hewin's Route 456
Highland Cragsman, The 202
Highlander, The 34
High Noon 55
Hole in the Wall 239
Hollow Be Thy Name 312
Homer 73
Homosuperior 196
Honey Pot 248
Honey Trap 415
Honorary Cathar 390
Hooded Claw, The 354
Hoofer's Route 414
Horizontal Hamish 448
Hornblower 281
Horny Corner 82
Horror Beneath, The 418
Horseshit Direct 289
Hostile Witness 158
Hot Blast 77
Hot Enough for ya? 448
Hot Pants 312
Hot White spider 429
Hourglass Groove 240
Hovis 23
Howard's End 471
Howard's Way 471
How Soon is Now 220

How the West Was Won 82, 186
Huffin' 'n' Puffin 394
Huffin' 'n' Puffin Direct 394
Huffin Puffin 241
Hughie's Cocktail Mixture 359
Hullabaloo 361
Hullabaloo Left-Foot 361
Hull Wall 123
Human Cargo 408
Human Sacrifice 144
Hummer 65
Hump, The 201
Hunter Killer 104
Hunter Killer Left Start 105
Hurricane Hideaway 69
Hurried Path, The 435
Hy Brasil 236
Hydraulic Dogs 257
Hydro Hek 142
Hydrotherapy 198
Hyperballad 401
Hypercentre 333
Hyperlipid 165
Hyperoceanic 261
Hypertension 82
Hypnotise 414
Ian's Easy Times 367
Icarus 231
Ice Box Prose 404
Ice Bulge, The 125
If All Else Fails 361
If You See Kay 232
Illegal Alien 409
Illuminations 318
Ill Wind 54
I'll Try Up Here Again 361
I'm a Tit, I Love Flying 157
I'm going out now (I may be some time) 338
Immaculate Conception 389
Immaculate Crack 349
Immaculate Deception 235
Immaculate Walk 235
Immigrant, The 408
Immiscible 83
Imperial Lather 317
Imposter, The 150
Impure Thoughts 245
Inanimate Objects Fight Back 80
In Between Days 296
Incisor 148
Incognito 108
Incommunicado 408
India 21
Inertia 265
Inner Demons 360
In Profundum Lacu 393
Inside Information 137
Inside Out 67
Insider Dealing 67
Inspired Guest 266
Integrity 35
Interactive 335
Internationale 52
In the Groove 104

In the Pink 151, 295, 409
In the Shop – On the Hill 359
Inverianvie Corner/Spotty Dog 190
Invest Wisely 145
In Woods and Wild Places 312
In Yer Face 245
Iolaire 309
Iridescence 289
Irish Agreement, The 253
Irish Rover 390
Iron-Crow 52
Island Fling 353
Island Life 353
Island of No Return 369
Islivig Direct 377
I Suppose a Cormorant's out of the Question Then? 394
Italian Job 73
It's No Good Captain She's Breaking Up 365
It's Not My Fault 444
It's not the size that matters … 392
It's Raining Rocks! 359
Itsy Bitsy Spider 430
It Wasn't My Fault I Ran Over the Cat 163
Ivory Highway, The 380
Jack o' Diamonds 37
Jack the Ripper 225
Jagged Little Thrill 342
Jamie Jampot 21
Jarldom Reach 163
J.A.'s Maelstrom 415
Jean and Jim 56
Jeemy 121
Jellyfish Roll 80
Jellyfish Slab 235
Jelly Wobbler 248
Jessaya 65
Jessie James 368
Jesus Don't Want me as a Shelf Stacker 391
Jesus Made Me Stumpy 405
Jetsam 294
Jewel in the Crown 286
Jib 15
Jigsaw Wall 262
Jim Nastic 246
Jings 123
Jivaro Crack 174
Joik 51
Joint Account 145
Joker, The 37, 197, 263
Jonny Scuttlehutt 399
Joplin's Wall 374
Joyful Departure 152
Judicial Hanging 245
Jug Abuse 264
Juggernaut 297
Juglust 297
Jugs of Deception 58
Jugs to Blow your Mind 430
Jungelknügen 195
Junior Keel 448

Junior's Groove 235
Juniper Rib 65
Just Add Lib 216
Just a Tease 290
Just for the Crack 367
Just Visiting 323
Jutting Blocks 143
K9 / Easy Tickings 190
Kamikaze 97
Kanga 248
Karaoke Craik 450
Katrin's Cream 360
Keeler 73
Keeping the Bofs Happy 66
Kelvin and Hobs Direct 427
Kenny's Cavity 372
Kermit Direct 151
Kermit's Crack 112
Kew 206
Kick Ass Yoga 145
Killer Fingers 361
Killer Whale 52
Kilt Classic 57
Kind of Gentle 209
King Cobra 48
King Cobra Direct 48
King of the Swingers 157
Kings of Midian, The 91
King Solomon's Marbles 109
Kiska 300
Kismet 383
Kissing the Pink 352
Kling On Corner 365
Klondyker, The 42
Kneel and Pray 208
Knob, The 110
Knowledge/The Scoop, The 62
Knuckle Sandwich 384
Kraken, The 248
Krill, The 236
Kruggerand 36
K & S Special 417
Labrador Chimney 263
Laggavoulin 214
La Mer 235
Land of the Dancing Dead 313
Landward Face 304
Langer Huddauf, The 468
Lang Huddain, The 468
La Petamine 214
Laphroaig 320
Lap Land 110
Lard of the Pies 330
Lassie 189
Last Orders 354
Last Tango 183
Lateral Thinking 58
Lats in Space 59
Lat up a Drainpipe 58
Latvian, The 59
Leac McCac 143
Leaning Meanie 229
Leaning Wall, The 198
Le Cigogne 232

Left Edge 372
Leftie 412
Left in the Lurch 106
Legend of Finlay MacIver, The 337
Leg Over 240
Le Pig Penn 232
Le Slot 373
Less Awkward than The Principle 362
Les Voyageurs 434
Lethe Walk 256
Le Trip 274
Let Sleeping Storks Lie 389
Letterbox Wall 331
Let Things Go 448
Lifeline 389
Lightfoot 49
Lighthouse Arête 356
Lightning Corner 81
Like it Hot? 145
Lilidh 264
Lily of the West 138
Limka 351
Limpet Crack 364
Limpet Olympics 364
Ling Dynasty 97
Lion Rampant 172
Lithium Fry-up 325
Little Gully 32
Little K 438
Little Leaf 157
Little Miss Sitting Pretty 418
Little Miss Sunshine 448
Little Red Rooster 214
Little Star 282
Little Valhalla 135
Llama, The 320
Lobster Men, The 434
Local Hero 115
Lochlann 379
Loctite 159
Lone Triathlete, The 141
Long Hard Winter 467
Longhope Route 462
Long Road Heavy Load 165
Longships 422
Long Way Home 76
Lonmore 142
Look Back In Anger 350
Looking for Atlantis 295
Looks Different 104
Loom of the Land 66
Lord Oliphant's Bicycle 327
Losgaidh 260
Losing It 343
Lost at Sea 262
Lost Souls 422
Lost Supper 90
Lottery Winner 81
Loved One, The 472
Lucid Visions 338
Lucifer's Link 299
Lucky Strike 81, 135
Lucy 143
Luin Crack 468
Lum, The 139
Lunar Pull 447

Lunge, The 467
Luscious 78
Lusting after Glenys Kinnock 60
Ma Broon's Variations 121
Macallan's Choice 318
Macdonald 147
Mackintosh Slab 106
Mack the Knife 468
Macro Crack 254
Mac's Route 236
Mac Talla 198
Mad Dogs and Englishmen 253
Magic 39
Magician, The 353
Major-domo 193
Major's Reserve, The 331
Making Bacon 246
Mallory's Slab and Groove 29
Malpasso 154
Man from Ankle, The 72
Man of Straw 75
Man Overboard 420
Manumission 232
Many a Mickle makes a Muckle 458
Marble Corner 311
March of the 56 141
Margaret Thatcher's Funeral 140
Marie Celeste 263
Market Day 217
Mark of a Skyver 105
Marram 306
Mars Crack 254
Mary Doune 451
Mary Hinge 23
Master of Morgana 62
Mater 456
Maverick Phenomena 389
Maybe Later 293
Mayday 17, 427
May Tripper 298
McCall of the Wild 424
Mechanical Sheep 109
Median 29
Meditation 471
Mega Flake 269
Mega Tsunami 333
Mega Tsunami - Prow Finish 333
Meikle Neuk 241
Melting Pot 137
Melting, The 269
Mercury and Solace 365
Mesajanier 451
Micheal 280
Michelangelo Buanarotti 72
Mickey Mouse 254
Mick's Corner 345
Micro Crack 254
Microlight 218
Midas Touch 67
Middle of the Road 106
Mid Flight Crisis 226
Midgard 381

ROUTE INDEX

- Midget 270
- Midreiff 236
- Mighty Atom, The 198
- Milk-Traigh 337
- Milk Tray 252
- Millennium 310
- Millstone Corner 264
- Minch and Tatties 62
- Minch Crack 254
- Mind the Gap 342
- Mingin' in the Rain 446
- Mini Tsunami 333
- Minjeetah 262
- Minke, The 18
- Misha 256
- Misha Direct 256
- Missing Link, The 193
- Miss Moneypenny 232
- Miss Piggy 151
- Mistaken Identity 377, 442
- Mistral Buttress 38
- Mixed Blessing 330
- Mixmaster Snipe 397
- Moac Wall 362
- Modern Thinking 243
- Mollyhawk 401
- Mongo 183
- Mongoose Direct 48
- Monkey Man 293
- Monkey Tribe, The 208
- Monster Breaker 239
- Monster Waves, The 443
- Moody Blues 243
- Moondance 216
- Moondust 281
- Moon Jelly 237
- Moonman 270
- Moonshine 95
- Mooring, The 443
- Moral Turpentine 284
- More Lads and Molasses 415
- More Noise 317
- More of the Same 235
- More Steam McPhail! 396
- More Wrath Variation 90
- Morning After, The 142
- Morning Tide 319
- Moronic Inferno 250
- Mosaic 263
- Moscow Mule 361
- Moskill Grooves 385
- Mother Goose 302
- Mother's Pride 23
- Mountain Ash 143
- Mr Big Comes Clean 370
- Mr Bridger 257
- Mr Sheen 311
- Mr Smooth 156
- Mucklehouse Wall 458
- Muckle Thrutch Crack 473
- Muc-Sheilch 165
- Muir Wall 299
- Murphy's Law 250
- Murray Mint, The 79
- Murray's Arête 160
- Muscle Hustle 219
- Muses from Afar 404
- Mushroom of My Fear, The 422
- Mussel Meltdown 335
- Mustard Pickle 306
- Mutineers 133
- (My Own) Personal Mingulay 273
- Mystic, The 243
- My Wave 334
- Na Far Clis 334
- Naismith's Route 25
- Naked Saltire, The 27
- Nalaxone 231
- Nasal Abuse 109
- Natural Look 81
- Neart Nan Gaidheal 217
- Neaster's Crack 74
- Necromancer 356
- Necronomicon 251
- Needle, The 454
- Neeps 75
- Neighbourhood Watch 363
- Neisty Beisty 82
- Nemesis 473
- Neptune 365
- Neville the Hedgehog 107
- New Addition 369
- New Sensation 472
- Newton's Law 349
- New World 369
- New World Order 97
- Nice One 322
- Nick the Niche 194
- Ni Dubh 156
- Nightshade 264
- Nisbet's Route 101
- No Beef 136
- Nobody's Crack 320
- No Brats 106
- No Choice 367
- Nocturne 290
- No Maybes 466
- No Mr Tick, I Expect You to Die 283
- Noodle, The 197
- Nook, The 300
- Noose, The 197
- No Porpoise 299
- No Puke Here 423
- Norse Face Route 135
- North Buttress 374
- North by North-West 132
- Northern Alliance 325
- Northern Exposure 63, 265
- Northern Lights 62
- Northern Sky 117
- Northumberland Wall 118
- Northumbrian Rhapsody 410
- North West Arête 205, 360
- North-West Corner 275
- North West Orient 159
- Nosferatu 228
- Not Ali's Crack 443
- Not Bad 188
- Nothing Special 252
- Notorious B.I.G., The 408
- Nought to Sixty 261
- November Groove 225
- Nuckelavee 467
- Nuclear Cop Out 141
- Nuclear Litemare 140
- Nuclear Nightmare 140
- Nuggets 43
- Number 3 373
- Nyook Waa 468
- Oars Aft 281
- Oatcakes for lunch 401
- Oblimov 327
- Obvious Crack 448
- Occam's Razor 323
- Ocean of Air Finish, The 435
- Ocean of Time, The 428
- Ocean View 349
- Ocean Voyeur 417
- Ocean Wrath 445
- Octopod 371
- Officer Jesus 209
- Off the Shelf 356
- Off Wid Emily's Bikini 404
- Off With Her Head 110
- Ogee, The 326
- Ogre 214
- Oh No, Archie's Going Round in Circles! 421
- Oh No, Norman's Due Back Tomorrow! 420
- Oh No, Norman's in Reverse! 400
- Oi Big Nose 109
- Okeanos 421
- Old Dog, New Tricks 219
- Old El Pastis 149
- Olden Glory 201
- Old Goats 203
- Old Hex, The 81
- Old Man and the Sea, The 450
- Old Man's Beard 140
- Old Salt 366
- Old Snapper 155
- Old Warden, The 81
- Old Wounds 90
- Olympus 259
- Omega Link 200
- Omission 264
- One Foot in the Grave 401
- One for Q 232
- One Hundred Years of Solitude 74
- One Last Look 406
- One over the Eight 379
- One Scoop or Two 187
- Only Way is Up, The 292
- On the Beach 451
- On the Western Skyline 217
- On Yer Bike 327
- Oor Wullie 123
- Open Secret 136
- Orange Bow, The 174
- Orange Flake 280
- Orange Wall 241
- Orca 82
- Orchid Hunter, The 325
- Orcrist 91
- Ordinary Route 100
- Orifice, The 228
- Original Master 266
- Original Route 275, 303, 366, 459, 471
- Orkney Sessions, The 469
- Ossian Boulevard 421
- Other Landscape, The 318
- Otto 259
- Outer Space 281
- Outlaw 368
- Out of Reach 320
- Outswinger 109
- Overcharged 77
- Overhanging Crack 243
- Overhanging Crack
- Variation 34
- Overjoyed 342
- Overlord 186
- Over the Rainbow 54
- Over the Top 356
- Pabbarotti 408
- Pabbay Express, The 273
- Pagan Love Song 162
- Painted Wall, The 346
- Palace of Colchis 347
- Palace of Swords Reversed 381
- Pale Dièdre, The 99
- Pale Rider 99
- Paneer 456
- Panting Dog Climb 375
- Pants on Fire 145
- Parabolic Head 245
- Paradise Regained 184, 398
- Paranoid 343
- Paranoid Slippers 359
- Parapente, The 218
- Partial Bastard 403
- Parting Glass, The 189
- Parting Shot 366
- Party Direct 224
- Party Kitchen 409
- Party on the Patio 224
- Passing Out 63
- Paternoster 456
- Path 146
- Path of Righteousness 103
- Pause for Jaws 408
- Peedie Breeks 465
- Peek Practice 152
- Pegboy 66
- Penguin 252
- Penguin, The 197
- Penny Lane 170
- Pennywhistle 76
- Pensioner's Link 198
- Perfect Days 116
- Perfectly Normal Paranoia 436
- Perfect Monsters 433
- Perky 360
- Pesto Macho 155
- Petronella 32
- Peweky 148
- Pickpocket 23
- Pictures of Pluto 141
- Pieces I've Ate 301
- Pieces of Eight 430
- Pie Party, The 350
- Piety 35
- Piggott's Route 100
- Piggy Bank 69
- Pig Monkey Bird 190
- Pilastre 308
- Pillar, The 114, 200
- Pink and Black 345
- Pinky 360
- Pinnacle Face 49
- Pinnacle Ridge 24
- Pinnacle Slab Left Edge 237
- Pipit at the Post
- Pirates of Coigach 257
- Pistachio 320
- Pistolero 185
- Playtime Wall 138
- Pleasure Beach, The 189
- Plonker's Start 280
- Plum McNumb 301
- Plum Prow 198
- Pockets of Resistance 183
- Pocket Wall 447
- Pocks 40
- Poet's Corner 423
- Polar Bear 252
- Polka 246
- Pomarine 354
- Poodle, The 197
- Pooh Corner 248
- Poop 406
- Pope Must Die, The 20
- Pop-out 236
- Port Pillar 420
- Positive Mental Attitude 316
- Poster Boy 197
- Post-it 182
- Posture Jedi, The 401
- Pot Black 241
- Pothole Slab 186
- Poultry in Motion 350
- Power-broker 68
- Power of Tears, The 157
- Power of the Sea, The 444
- Pragmatist's Folly 448
- Prawn Broker 80
- Pray 316
- Precious Days 422
- Prelude 381
- Premonition 382
- Presdigitateur 38
- Presence, The 251
- Presidents Chimney 349
- Pressure Band 426
- Presumption 298
- Pretty in Pink 264
- Price is Right, The 67
- Priest, The 411
- Primary Care 138
- Primary Corner 317
- Primitive Dance 216
- Primo 200
- Pringles 367
- Prog 65
- Prominent Nasty Looking Off-width Groove 402
- Propaganda 445
- Prophecy of Drowning 411
- Proprietor, The 175
- Prosopagnosia 339
- Prow Direct, The 198
- Prow Left Finish, The 198
- Prozac Link, The 358
- Psychopomp 156
- Puckered Wall 236
- Puffin Attack 321
- Puffing Crack 341
- Pullin' on Puddin' 327
- Pumpernickel 155
- Pumping Up 443
- Punky Dory 165
- Pure Splendour Start 21
- Quagga 169
- Quail 186
- Quantum Tunnelling 81
- Quarryman, The 466
- Quartzvein Crack 342
- Quartz Warts 110
- Quavers 367
- Queen of Hearts 110
- Queen's Freebie 352
- Queen's Mute Termination 322
- Quickening, The 259
- Quick on the Draw 185
- Quite Fatigued 81
- Quoybank Crack 465
- Rabid Wanderings 338
- Radical Jewish 183
- Radio Gnome 205
- Raglan Road 183
- Raiders of the Lost Auk 393
- Rainbow Warrior 25, 165
- Rain in the Face 160
- Rainman 49
- Ramadan 203
- Rampant Groove 238
- Rampart 295
- Ramp it Up 271
- Ramp, The 150, 238, 248, 313, 414
- Rapid Learning Curve 22
- Rapture 302
- Rare Breed 107
- Rats Don't Eat Sandwiches 361
- Rats Stole My Toothbrush 458
- Raven's Edge 148
- Raven, The 214, 407
- Rayburnt 428
- Ray of Light 433
- Razorbill Roofs 424
- Razor's Edge 242
- Reach for the Sky 316
- Read My Lips 269
- Reaper, The 96
- Reap the Wild Wind 253
- Rebel without a Porpoise Direct 390
- Rebirth 209
- Recess Ramp 334
- Recovery Day 73
- Red Bull 289
- Red Crack, The 174
- Reddy Ribbed 152